FOR THE
COMMON
GOOD

FOR THE COMMON GOOD

Redirecting the Economy
toward Community,
the Environment, and a
Sustainable Future

Second Edition
Updated and Expanded

Herman E. Daly and
John B. Cobb, Jr.

With contributions by
Clifford W. Cobb

Beacon Press, Boston

Beacon Press
25 Beacon Street
Boston, Massachusetts 02108-2800

Beacon Press books
are published under the auspices of
the Unitarian Universalist Association of Congregations.

Text design by Dennis Anderson

Library of Congress Cataloging-in-Publication Data
Daly, Herman E.
For the common good : redirecting the economy toward community,
the environment, and a sustainable future / Herman E. Daly and
John B. Cobb, Jr. ; with contributions by Clifford W. Cobb.
— 2nd ed., updated and expanded.
p.   cm.
Includes bibliographical references and index.
ISBN 0-8070-4705-8
1. Economic development—Environmental aspects.   2. Environmental
policy.   3. Sustainable development.   4. Common good.   5. United
States—Economic policy—1993–   I. Cobb, John B.
II. Cobb, Clifford W.   III. Title.
HD75.6.D35   1994
338.9—dc20   93-24460

Contents

Part Four: Getting There

Acknowledgments

We gratefully acknowledge both the intellectual and the moral support of many friends and colleagues as well as the material support of several institutions. Jay McDaniel worked together with the Meadowcreek Project to hold two conferences that were invaluable stimuli for the writing of this book. We are indebted to all participants. Iliff School of Theology invited the authors at a late stage in the writing to offer a summer workshop on the manuscript. The critical support of the students enabled us to make improvements in the final version. Louisiana State University and the School of Theology at Claremont have provided the basic assistance necessary for scholarly work.

Some colleagues read the whole manuscript and contributed beyond the call of duty. We are especially appreciative of the help of Daniel Finn, Robert Goodland, Dennis Goulet, David Griffin, and David Orr. Many others read parts of the manuscript at various stages and gave substantial help. These include David Batker, Shelton Davis, Kurt Dopfer, Salah El Serafy, George Foy, Robert Hamrin, Les Muray, Robert Schutz, and Ted Winslow. Carol Johnston contributed extensively, providing detailed notes and quotations on classical economists as well as critical evaluations of portions of the manuscript.

The material on economic measures, including most of Chapter 2, part of Chapter 18, and all of the Appendix, resulted from the work of the Economic Welfare Study Group, made possible by support of the Miller Social Ethics Fund of the School of Theology at Claremont. The group was composed of John B. Cobb, Jr., chair, Sandy Dawson, Dean Freudenberger, Chris Ives, and Carol Johnston, assisted by Tokiyuki Nobuhara. Most of the detailed work and writing was done by Clifford Cobb, whose work is thus extensively represented in this volume.

Marcia Daly not only typed the manuscript in successive versions, but refused to type anything that did not make sense and thereby helped us to clarify many points.

None of the individuals or institutions named above are responsible for any shortcomings in this book, nor do they necessarily agree with everything (or anything!) we have said. In Herman Daly's case this disclaimer should be explicitly extended to his current employer, the World Bank, even though this book was written while he was on the faculty of Louisiana State University.

Introduction

Words ought to be a little wild, for they are the assault of thoughts upon the unthinking.

J. M. Keynes

The Wild Facts

In our time, it is the facts themselves that are more than a little wild and that constitute an assault on unthinking economic dogma. We need little help from wild rhetoric. The wild facts are summarized in calm words in the various *State of the World* reports put out by the Worldwatch Institute, and especially in the first essay of the 1987 volume by Lester Brown and Sandra Postel, entitled "Thresholds of Change." Some of the facts are:

1. There is a hole in the earth's protective shield of ozone. More ultraviolet radiation now reaches the earth and will predictably increase skin cancer, retard crop growth, and impair the human immune system. In an unprecedentedly wise response, representatives from thirty-one nations have agreed to a quantitative limit on the production of chlorofluorocarbons, the probable cause of the ozone depletion.

2. There is evidence that the CO_2-induced greenhouse effect has already caused perceptible warming of the globe. As recently as 1983, noticeable change was not expected for another 50 years. Now the warming is being connected by careful students to the 1988 drought in the Midwest.

3. Biodiversity is declining as rates of species extinction increase due to takeover of habitat, especially of the tropical rainforests, which support half the world's species on only 7% of its land area (Goodland 1987).

In addition, acid rain kills temperate zone forests and raises the acidity of lakes above the tolerance thresholds for many species. Because of

1

industrial accidents, people in Chernobyl, Goiania (Brazil), and Bhopal are dying from air pollution, toxic waste contamination of ground water, and radiation poisoning.

All of these facts appear to us to be related in one way or another to one central underlying fact: the scale of human activity relative to the biosphere has grown too large. In the past 36 years (1950–86), population has doubled (from 2.5 to 5.0 billion). Over the same time period, gross world product and fossil fuel consumption have each roughly quadrupled. Further growth beyond the present scale is overwhelmingly likely to increase costs more rapidly than it increases benefits, thus ushering in a new era of "uneconomic growth" that impoverishes rather than enriches. This is the fundamental wild fact that so far has not found expression in words sufficiently feral to assault successfully the civil stupor of economic discourse. Indeed, contrary to Keynes, it seems that the wildness of either words or facts is nowadays taken as clear evidence of untruth. Moral concern is "unscientific." Statement of fact is "alarmist."

In *An Inquiry into the Human Prospect* (1974), economist Robert Heilbroner reflected about the meaning of this pressure of the human economy on the biosphere. He considered especially the political traumas that will be faced when economic growth is no longer possible. In a 1980 revision of his *Inquiry,* he projected a continuing (but gradually slowing) growth economy until the middle of the first decade of the next century. When that ends, he sees (as in the earlier 1974 edition) the need for highly authoritarian governments to control the transition to economic decline (Heilbroner 1980, p. 167 ff.).

We appreciate Heilbroner's rare willingness as an economist to connect the growth economy and the physical limits of the ecosphere. This is at the heart of our project as well. But we believe that thought, foresight, and imagination can lead to a much less disruptive transition. Whereas Heilbroner assumes there are no realistic alternatives to capitalism and socialism (both growth economies), we do not agree. This book seeks to outline just such a realistic alternative. To conceive of such a radically different economy forces us both to think through the discipline of economics as well as beyond it into biology, history, philosophy, physics, and theology. Part of the assault of the wild facts has been against the very disciplinary boundaries by which knowledge is organized (produced, packaged, and exchanged) in the modern university.

The Ambiguity of the Economic Achievement

The wild facts of today and their conflict with standard economic theory both have a well-known history. During the past two centuries, the economy has transformed the character of the planet and especially of human life. It has done so chiefly by industrialization. Industry has vastly increased the productivity of workers, so vastly that in spite of the great population increases in industrialized nations, the goods and services available to each have increased still more. The standard of living has soared from bare subsistence to affluence for most people in the North Atlantic nations and Japan. Singapore, Hong Kong, Taiwan, and South Korea share in this prosperity. These are immense accomplishments.

During the same period, the study of the economy has matured, approaching the status of a science. Economics alone among the social studies is sometimes accorded that label by natural scientists. A Nobel prize is given in economics as in physics and biology. Other students of human society often envy and emulate the economists, much as economists emulate physicists.

Public policy has been deeply affected by the ideas and proposals of economists. Without this help the economy could not have grown to anything like the extent it has. Economists have reason to believe that if politicians and government bureaucrats would pay closer attention to their arguments, the purposes of government could be more efficiently realized. Again and again they are able to show the waste of resources that follows from regulatory measures that ignore market principles. Even Eastern European economists are now arguing for greater reliance on the market, for reasons similar to those given by their Western counterparts.

But the industrial economy has consequences for the greater economy of life. Psychologists have been disturbed by what is happening to individuals. In 1937, Karen Horney cited the pressures on Americans created by their industrial, competitive, materialistic society. She noted that three basic value conflicts had arisen: "aggressiveness grown so pronounced that it could no longer be reconciled with Christian brotherhood; desire for material goods so vigorously stimulated that it can never be satisfied, and expectations of untrammeled freedom soaring so high that they cannot be squared with the multitudes of restrictions and responsibilities that confine us all" (Henderson 1978, p. 25). Walter Weisskopf (1971) more recently has engaged in an extensive study of what the economy has done to human beings morally and existentially. He sees that it has worked against objective judgments of value and encouraged moral relativism. It has also emphasized a few aspects of human existence at the expense of others, and thus caused alienation.

Other critics have pointed out the negative social effects of economic progress. In moving words, Karl Polanyi, a great economic historian, described the social developments associated with the rise of the market as the "Satanic Mill." The opening sentence of his 1944 work states: "At the heart of the Industrial Revolution of the eighteenth century there was an almost miraculous improvement in the tools of production, which was accomplished by a catastrophic dislocation of the lives of the common people" (Polanyi [1944] 1957, p. 33). Joseph Schumpeter was equally troubled. He sees economic thought as a part of the utilitarian philosophy that dominated the nineteenth century. "This system of ideas, developed in the eighteenth century, recognizes no other regulatory principle than that of individual egoism. . . . The essential fact is that, whether as cause or consequence, this philosophy expresses only too well the spirit of social irresponsibility which characterized the passion, and the secular, or rather secularized, state in the nineteenth century. And in the midst of moral confusion, economic success serves only to render still more serious the social and political situation which is the natural result of a century of economic liberalism" (Schumpeter 1975).

Recently it has been ecologists especially and those whom they have aroused who have turned on the economy as the great villain. They see that the growth of the economy has meant the exponential increase of raw material inputs from the environment and waste outputs into the environment, and they see that little attention has been paid by economists either to the exhaustion of resources or to pollution. They complain that economists have not only ignored the source of inputs and the disposition of outputs, but also that they have encouraged the maximization of both, whereas living lightly in the world requires that throughput should be kept to the minimum sufficient to meet human needs.

Most economists have ignored these criticisms. They are convinced that the great majority of people are far more interested in the economic goods whose production economists have encouraged than in any psychological or environmental losses. They suspect that those who speak of the suffering accompanying industrialization exaggerate. They show that the industrializing nations grew rapidly in wealth, a wealth in which most shared, albeit unevenly. And they are convinced that those who worry about the future of the environment underestimate the capacity of a prosperous economy to take care of that, too. Where there is capital and ingenuity there will be technological breakthroughs. Now that the environment is a concern, inventive genius will be directed to solving these new challenges.

Toward a Paradigm Shift in Economics [1]

When a discipline is both this successful and this severely criticized, one may assume that its assumptions and methods apply well in some spheres and poorly in others. The key assumptions in this case have to do with *Homo economicus,* that is, the understanding of the nature of the human being. Economic theory builds on the propensity of individuals to act so as to optimize their own interests, a propensity clearly operative in market transactions and in many other areas of life. Economists typically identify intelligent pursuit of private gain with rationality, thus implying that other modes of behavior are not rational. These modes include other-regarding behavior and actions directed to the public good.

The assumption that rationality largely excludes other-regarding behavior has deep, although conflicting, roots in the Western theological understanding of human nature. Theologians have held that other-regarding action is an ethical ideal, but many, especially after St. Augustine, have seen self-regarding behavior as dominant in the actual "fallen" condition. This fallenness was strongly accented by the Reformers and their followers, encouraging general suspicion of claims to genuinely other-regarding action in Protestant cultures. It is not surprising that the philanthropist Robert Owen, living in such a culture, rejected Christianity for its individualism (Polanyi [1944] 1957, 128). Catholic theology followed St. Thomas in giving more credence to socially concerned, community-building aspects of human activity.

In Calvinism, the skepticism about human virtue was connected with the suspicion of earthly authority in both church and state. The relation to God was conceived as immediate and decisive. This led to a claim to personal autonomy in both secular and religious affairs and restrictions on government interference. In Roman Catholic cultures, the emphasis

1. The term "paradigm" is difficult to define, and its applicability in the social sciences has been questioned. See Richard J. Bernstein, *The Restructuring of Economic and Political Theory* (1976, 84–106). We believe the term can be useful in relation to economics, but admittedly we use it loosely.

on community was connected with hierarchical organization in both church and society.

Modern economic theory originated and developed in the context of Calvinism. Both were bids for personal freedom against the interference of earthly authority. They based their bids on the conviction that beyond a very narrow sphere, motives of self-interest are overwhelmingly dominant. Economic theory differed from Calvinism only in celebrating as rational what Calvinists confessed as sinful.

Calvinism encourages other-regarding behavior as truly Christian even while warning against believing too readily in its reality. Catholicism encourages other-regarding behavior as a natural virtue. When Christianity was dominant, these forces checked blatantly self-seeking activity, although they certainly did not prevent it. But economists have taught us to think that checks on self-interest are both unnecessary and harmful. It is through rational behavior, which means self-interested behavior, that all benefit the most. Well-meaning attempts by government to oppose or check such behavior actually do more harm than good. As this belief displaces traditional Christian thinking, and as the market in which these principles are applied takes over a larger and larger role in society, the psychological, sociological, and ecological problems noted by critics of the economists have become more acute.

Economics contributed to freeing individuals from hierarchical authority, as well as to providing more abundant goods and services. These have been achievements of such importance that it has seemed wise to most persons of good will to treat the negative effects as secondary, as a necessary price for a crucial advance. For a long time that may have been an appropriate stance. But with each passing year, the positive accomplishments of the economy have become less evident and the destructive consequences larger. There is a growing sense that it is time for a change. The change may well take the form of a paradigm shift. The recognition of the importance of paradigm shifts in physics generated by the work of Thomas Kuhn has opened the way for thinking about paradigm shifts in the social sciences as well.

Shlomo Maital (1982) reports on a poll of professors of economics at fifty major universities. One question asked was, "Is there a sense of lost moorings in economics?" Two-thirds of the respondents answered affirmatively (p. 17). Maital believes the discipline is at a crisis. "Evidence contradictory to the conventional wisdom of economics continues to accumulate." "As dissonant evidence mounts and assails cherished propositions of a discipline, virtuoso acrobatics of that discipline's believers put things right again" (p. 262). To Maital, all this is a sign that a paradigm shift is on its way.

Lester Thurow (1983) concludes *Dangerous Currents* on a similar note. "Economics cannot do without simplifying assumptions, but the trick is to use the right assumptions at the right time. And the judgment has to come from empirical analysis (including those employed by historians, psychologists, sociologists and political scientists) of how the world *is,* not of how our economics textbooks tell us it *ought* to be" (p. 237). Elsewhere in the book, he notes: "Psychology, sociology, and politics all have theories that might produce a set of expectations very different from those ascribed to *Homo economicus.* Patterns of socialization, cultural and ethnic history, political institutions, and old-fashioned human will power all affect our expectations" (p. 226). Thurow points in the direction of a new paradigm when he says: "Societies are not merely statistical aggregations of individuals engaged in voluntary exchange but something much more subtle and complicated. A group or community cannot be understood if the unit of analysis is the individual taken by himself. A society is clearly something greater than the sum of its parts" (pp. 222–223). He distinguishes, following Stephen Marglin, "private-personal preferences" from "individual-social" ones (p. 224), and chides economists for trying to work with the first alone.

Human beings are extremely complex and can be studied from many points of view. Each point of view abstracts from the concrete actuality and focuses on particular aspects of human behavior. *Homo religiosus* is the human being considered as religious; *Homo politicus,* as political; and *Homo economicus,* as economic. Our book focuses on *Homo economicus* while trying not to forget that human beings can also be viewed, among other things, as religious and political. It undertakes to follow Thurow's injunction to avoid viewing *Homo economicus* in terms of private-personal preferences alone. Accordingly, instead of *Homo economicus* as pure individual we propose *Homo economicus* as person-in-community.[2] This is more consonant with the other social sciences and

2. There is nothing original about this term. According to Max L. Stackhouse (1985) the "Christian sociologists" responded to the industrial revolution in the United States "in conversation with the best social theories available to them . . . and equally fully committed to the biblical witness as the source and norm for their efforts," and "articulated a doctrine of 'person in community' that attempted to establish decisive boundaries for Christian thinking about economic life" (p. 132). For current efforts in the Protestant context to find a third way, see Ulrich Duchrow, *Global Economy: A Confessional Issue for the Churches?* (1987, pp. 158–162): "It is

with the evidence that economists are themselves uncovering. It does not deny that in the market the actions of person-in-community approximate to those attributed to *Homo economicus* in the received theory. But normative conclusions about the goal of economic life should not be drawn from this fact alone. Polanyi notes that in capitalist society, "instead of economy being embedded in social relations, social relations are embedded in the economic system" ([1944] 1957, p. 57). It is this reversal that an economics for community cannot tolerate.

We cannot claim that our model fully meets Maital's requirements for a new paradigm. He writes: "No science will agree to junk its tried and true axioms, even when they become trying and untrue, until a new and more powerful set of axioms is available" (1982, p. 262). We are not offering a new set of axioms. Indeed, we will suggest in Chapter 2 that this view of economics as a system of deductions from axioms is part of the problem. But we do believe that economics can rethink its theories from the viewpoint of person-in-community and still include the truth and insight it gained when it thought in individualistic terms. It need not "junk" its axioms. Many of them can continue to function, only with more recognition of their limits. The change will involve correction and expansion, a more empirical and historical attitude, less pretense to be a "science," and the willingness to subordinate the market to purposes that it is not geared to determine. This is part of what we want to show.

The New Paradigm and the Old Options

The first question in many people's minds when confronted with an economic proposal is how to locate it on a scale from left to right. Dudley Seers offers a diagram, which we reproduce in figure I.1, that expresses what many people have at least vaguely in mind (Seers 1983, pp. 46–48).

Leaving out the extremes of anarchism and fascism, there are important issues debated along this line. But Seers is quite correct in arguing that the larger issues are better represented when another axis is introduced. He does this in terms of nationalism and antinationalism (see fig. I.2).

Seers discusses not only national economy but also the European

---

false to say there are no alternatives. There are new economic approaches which make the meeting of the basic needs of concrete human beings and ecological sustainability the starting point for the economic system." Duchrow finds support for this direction in the work of institutional economists, especially Christian Leipert and R. Steppacher.

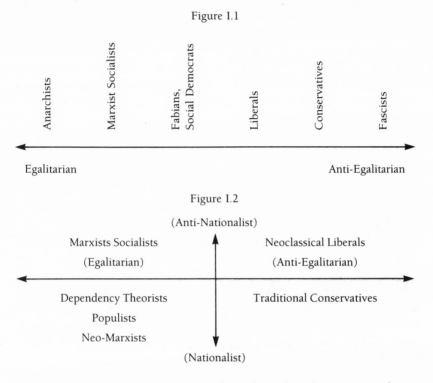

Figure I.1

Figure I.2

economic community. Hence his title, "The Political Economy of Nationalism," is a bit misleading. It associates his ideas more closely with the long tradition of economic nationalism in the nineteenth century than is warranted by his fresh reading of the situation. We would like to carry his qualifications of traditional nationalism much further. Nations are only one of the levels at which community is to be prized and served. In Chapter 9 these various levels will be discussed at some length. Our diagram would replace "nationalist" and "antinationalist" by such words as "communitarian" and "anticommunitarian." Nevertheless, nations are a desirable form of community and in many instances today, the only ones that have the power to assert themselves effectively against anticommunitarian forces. For practical purposes, therefore, the alternatives posed by Seers are important and will play a considerable role in our analyses and proposals. With these caveats, we accept his formulation. Our attention, like his, is focused on the vertical axis.

Viewing matters in this light, Seers writes at length of the close similarities of Marxism and standard Western economics in a chapter startlingly entitled "Marxism and Other Neo-Classical Economics." Among other commonalities, both oppose nationalism in particular and, at least implicitly, attention to community in general. Because we believe that the extent to which an economy supports or destroys healthy communities is more important than where it is to be located from left to right, we, like Seers, refuse to see our proposals as somewhere on the horizontal line of his diagram.[3] The greatest obstacle to gaining a hearing for proposals like Seers's and ours is the continuing widespread assumption that all positions must be located along the line from left to right. It is an idée fixe that every economy must be socialist, capitalist, or a compromise between the two. Unless the reader relaxes this assumption, this book cannot be understood. To pave the way for such relaxation we offer our understanding of how this situation came about and of the limited options remaining when these parameters are assumed to be exhaustive.

This whole way of thinking was brought into being by the problems and promises of the industrial age. It is for an industrial society that capitalism and socialism are supposed to be the only options, and it is their common participation in the methods and structures of industrialism that determines the extensive similarities between the two systems.[4] Some features of industrialism are necessary in any society in which manufacturing plays a large role. Other features are not. Since we intend to offer an alternative to both forms of industrialism, we need to explain how we understand its basic features.

The well-known features of industrialism include the use of new energy sources: coal first, followed by petroleum and natural gas; use of new materials: iron and steel; new inventions: the steam engine, the spinning jenny; advances in transportation and communication: the steamship, the locomotive, telegraph, and radio; new techniques: the factory system of production; and the increasing application of science to technology. Along with this in England went the enclosure of the commons that "freed" rural labor for the urban industrial factories. Later came the increasing mechanization of agriculture.

3. A similar polemic against regarding the alternatives as capitalism and socialism has been made by Benjamin R. Barber in "Against Economics: Capitalism, Socialism, but Whatever Happened to Democracy?" (1986). He calls for democratic control over the economy, which would require community control. He seems to have the national level of community in mind.

4. Others have noted that Marxism and capitalism are but two forms of a modern industrial society that is more determinative of the human and ecological conditions than is any difference between them. See Robert Nisbett, *The Sociological Imagination* (1966). Also Robert Heilbroner (1980) writes that both capitalist and socialist societies have organized work, life, and even thought "in ways that accommodate men to machines rather than the much more difficult alternative" (p. 94).

The invention of the factory system stands out in this list as the one item that was truly an economic rather than a technical invention. The factory is not a new tool but an organization of production that eliminates the periods of idleness in the use of tools, machines, and men that are characteristic of agrarian and artisan production. In the artisan's shop the saw, chisel, file, and so forth are all idle while the hammer is being used. In the factory all tools are simultaneously in use in the hands of specialized workers; production is "in line" rather than "in series." But production in line requires a large scale of total output before it becomes feasible. The division of labor is limited by the extent of the market, as Adam Smith told us. But transportation, urbanization, and international trade provided a market of sufficient scale. In agriculture, of course, harvesting equipment must be idle during seedtime, and planting equipment idle during harvest. Seasonality in agricultural production limits the applicability of factory organization on the farm. We can be sure, for better or for worse, that the economic impetus of modern genetic engineering will be to reduce seasonality, to design plants and animals capable of being fitted into a factory system of production. This is already evident in "chicken farms," which are really chicken factories.

The feature of the industrial revolution whose implications are insufficiently appreciated is the shift to fossil fuel energy and mineral materials. This is a shift from harvesting the surface of the earth to mining the subsurface; or, in Georgescu-Roegen's (1971) terms, it is a shift from dependence on energy currently coming from the sun to stored energy on the earth. This shift is extremely significant because these two ultimate sources of life sustenance differ in their patterns of scarcity. Radiant energy from the sun is practically infinite in total amount (stock), but it is strictly limited in its flow rate—that is, the amount that arrives on earth during any period. Energy stored in fossil fuels and minerals is strictly limited in its total amount (stock), but relatively unlimited in its flow rate—that is, we can use it up at a rate largely of our own choosing. We cannot use tomorrow's sunlight today, but in a sense we can use tomorrow's petroleum, coal, iron, and helium today. The industrial revolution has shifted dependence from the relatively abundant to the relatively scarce source of the ultimate resource: low-entropy matter-energy.

The idea that low-entropy matter-energy is the ultimate natural resource requires some explanation. This can be provided easily by a short exposition of the laws of thermodynamics in terms of an apt image borrowed from Georgescu-Roegen. Consider an hour glass. It is a closed system in that no sand enters the glass and none leaves. The amount of sand in the glass is constant—no sand is created or destroyed within the hour glass. This is the analog of the first law of thermodynamics: there is no creation or destruction of matter-energy. Although the quantity of sand in the hour glass is constant, its qualitative distribution is constantly changing: the bottom chamber is filling up and the top chamber becoming empty. This is the analog of the second law, that entropy (bottom-chamber sand) always increases. Sand in the top chamber (low entropy) is capable of doing work by falling, like water at the top of a waterfall. Sand in the bottom chamber (high entropy) has spent its capacity to do work. This hour glass cannot be turned upside down: waste energy cannot be recycled, except by spending more energy to power the recycle than would be reclaimed in the amount recycled. As explained above, we have two sources of this ultimate natural resource, the solar and the terrestrial, and our dependence has shifted from the former toward the latter.

This shift was not consciously made, but it was certainly no accident. The newly discovered terrestrial resources had advantageous properties. Fossil fuel is a more concentrated energy source than sunlight, or even wood. Iron and steel have properties of strength and durability that, unlike wood and stone, permit construction of the machines and boilers capable of harnessing the more intense energy sources. Technology exploited these new qualities. Furthermore, the new materials and energy came from under the ground. That meant that they did not (until the advent of strip mining) compete for land surface area capable of capturing sunlight. As populations grew, the land previously devoted to growing fodder for draft animals was devoted to growing more food. The new mechanical oxen were fed with fossil fuels from underground and far away. In the enthusiasm for growth and the unlimited faith in technology, the realization that the benefits of industrialism came at a price, namely increasing dependence on the scarcer source of ultimate means, was submerged.

The industrial revolution is still being repeated in traditional societies today and is almost synonymous with "economic development." Its evolution has been toward larger scale and greater specialization, with the consequences of increasing integration and interdependence and of increasing vulnerability to systemic failure. At the same time, industrialization has given a higher standard of consumption to more people than any other mode of production, so its universal dominance is hardly surprising.

Although industrialism grew up historically under capitalist institutions, it has proven to be compatible with socialist institutions as well. The conflict between capitalism and socialism is not about the desirability or possibility of industrialism. That is taken for granted by both sides. The conflict is over which economic system can better produce a growing quantity of goods and services and equitably spread the benefits of the industrial mode of production. Whatever their ideological differences both systems are fully committed to large-scale, factory-style energy and capital-intensive, specialized production units that are hierarchically managed. They also rely heavily on nonrenewable resources and tend to exploit renewable resources and waste absorption capacities at nonsustainable rates.

Capitalism consists of private ownership of the means of production along with allocation and distribution provided by the market. Individual maximization of profit by firms and maximization of satisfaction (utility) by consumers provides the motive force, while competition, the existence of many buyers and sellers in the market, provides the famous invisible hand that leads private interest to serve the public welfare. Collective action by government is limited to (a) providing the institutional precondition of property rights enforced by law, (b) providing certain public goods or natural monopolies and prohibiting the formation of private monopolies, (c) maintaining aggregate demand at a level that gives an "acceptable" combination of inflation and unemployment; (d) providing a minimum social welfare safety net to keep people from destitution; and (e) intervening to correct "externalities" (situations in which voluntary exchange between two individuals, although mutually beneficial to them, has important effects on third parties).

Socialism is defined by government ownership of the means of production with allocation and distribution by central planning, but with some reliance on the market when central planning gets overwhelmed. Motive force comes from a combination of moral and material incentives. Reliance on the market comes in degrees, and Polish economist Jan Drewnowski (1961) has distinguished first-, second-, and third-degree market economies. In a first-degree market economy, quantities of consumer goods are fixed by planners, but households are free to purchase or not. The planned mix of goods may be rationed by queues or by prices, but the planner does not adjust quantities in accordance with this information on shortages and surpluses. In the second-degree market economy, the planner does adjust quantities of consumer goods according to observed shortages and surpluses, or according to changes in price if that is allowed. However, the planner only reallocates current resources among existing plants. No new capital investment takes place as a result of consumer demand signals. In the third-degree market economy, the pattern of new investment also responds to the pattern of consumer demand, but the overall volume of investment, the decision of how much to consume and how much to invest, is still made centrally by the planners.

When household decisions on saving versus consumption are allowed to determine the aggregate social investment, then we would have a "fourth-degree" market economy, which would require capitalist rather than socialist institutions, since households must own the means of production if they are going to invest in them as individuals. But the first-, second-, and third-degree market economies are consistent with socialist institutions. Just as in the capitalist world we have considerable variation in collective influence, extending to indicative planning and extensive social welfare sectors in such countries as France or Sweden, so in the communist countries there exists a wide range of market influence extending to the relatively decentralized economies of Hungary and Yugoslavia.

The issues raised along the spectrum of socialist and capitalist options are real. Therefore once we have made clear that these are for us secondary to the question of community, it behooves us to locate ourselves with respect to them. Our position is that centralized economic planning is inefficient, that allocations are better effected in the market than by bureaucratic planning. The role of government is to set fair conditions within which the market can operate. It is also responsible for setting the overall size (scale) of the market. The market is not the end of society and is not the right instrument through which the ends of society should be set. We favor private ownership of the means of production. We favor the widest possible participation in that ownership, including worker ownership of factories, against its concentration in a few hands.

Nevertheless, our opposition to Marxism is not automatic opposition to all policies and proposals stemming from socialist thinkers. Where those policies and proposals require centralized planning for their implementation, we remain skeptical. But we hope to be open to ideas from every source, and when the thinkers are passionately committed to justice and the relief of suffering, we intend to listen with special care. We find that today many who come from the socialist tradition have shifted attention away from centralized planning, indeed that they share our suspicion of centralization and our concern for community. Some explicitly support, as we do, decentralization of political and economic power, worker ownership of factories or participation in their management, and the subordination of the economy to social goals, democratically defined. Socialism of this sort is not what we have described above.[5] Instead it is a partner in fresh thinking about the possibilities of humane life in community.[6]

5. As an example of radical social thinking with congenial views, see Samuel Bowles and Herbert Gintis, *Democracy and Capitalism: Property, Community, and the Contradictions of Modern Social Thought* (1986). The democratic control of the economy they advocate involves decentralization rather than centralized planning. The recent work of Michael Harrington hardly focuses on socialism as we have treated it. His ideas about a shorter work week, empowering citizens, and worker participation in industrial decisions are highly congenial to us. See Michael Harrington, *The Next Left* (1986). He himself comments on the similarities between the programs of the sophisticated Right and Left (p. 15). Their difference, he says, is that the Right wants to move from the top down, and the Left from the bottom up. By this definition we are on the Left. This is quite different from centralized planning. But we find the Left as well as the Right to be lacking in appreciation of ecological limits to economic expansion.

6. Our hope is to move forward to a new type of economy different from either capitalism or socialism as they have been understood in the past. But for those who still find it difficult to think of an economy that does not fit on this spectrum, we suggest that they consider feudalism. Feudalism, surely, is neither capitalist nor socialist, yet it endured longer in Europe than either of these is likely to do. Feudalism is the bête noir of both, and that will help to indicate how one can be opposed to both. The feudal system was more communitarian than either socialism or capitalism in both theory and practice. It has been badly maligned since the Enlightenment by those whose interest required the extirpation of the continuing power of community in human life. Even economically the mature medieval society was far more successful and affluent, as well as more just and humane, than moderns have been willing to acknowledge. John Stuart Mill noted that the widespread proprietorship of the late Middle Ages gave England a "yeomanry who were vaunted as the glory of England while they existed, and have been so much mourned ever since they disappeared" (1973, p. 256). It was of course the application of capitalism to agriculture that destroyed these products of feudal society. Marshall also writes favorably of features of the feudal society: "In the Middle Ages . . . the great body of the inhabitants frequently had the full rights of citizens, deciding for themselves the foreign and domestic policy of the city, and at the same time working with their hands and taking pride in their work. They organized themselves into Guilds, thus increasing their cohesion and educating themselves in self-government" (1925, p. 735).

We do not recite these points in order to call for a return to feudalism. It had many faults, and in any case it is not directly applicable to an industrial society. But we do believe that surveying a wider range of economic systems can open our eyes to new possibilities. Of these, feudalism is worthy of careful consideration.

The Third Model

This interest in a third model based on concern for human community is not new. It was vigorously pursued by the Roman Catholic Church in the nineteenth century. The Catholic critique of both capitalism and socialism is quite similar to our own. Richard E. Mulcahey summarizes this criticism:

Individualism sees in society no real unity. What it calls "society" is a mere mechanism, the interplay of the actions of individuals seeking their own ends; or it is a mere sum of economic relations. It postulates a natural order based on unrestrained freedom, on whose unhindered effect the welfare of all depends. The national economy is viewed as a sum of isolated units, which are bound together only by mere exchange relationships. . . . In socialism the concept of the unity of society is distorted. The collective society which it requires presents the unity of "oneness" rather than a union of the many. The individual is only an "associate," not an autonomous personality. [Mulcahey 1952, p. 161]

Mulcahey is describing and affirming the economic theory of Heinrich Pesch, a Roman Catholic economist whose work both informed and was informed by papal encyclicals. Pesch understood economics as "the science of the economic life (the process of providing material goods) of a people, considered as a social unit, bound together by the politico-social community life" (Mulcahey 1952, pp. 13–14). Mulcahey states, "Pesch's solidaristic system rejects the one-sidedness of a mere aggregate concept of the economy and of a single economy controlled by society, and proposes an economic order and a moral-organic unity and community of many independent private economic units" (p. 27). Pesch thus aims at "the full carrying out of the idea of community" (p. 161).

The most careful comparison of English life at the end of the feudal era with modern life has been made by Peter Laslet in *The World We Have Lost* (1965). Those interested in a sustained argument for the superiority of the medieval system should see Hilaire Belloc (1913). Belloc contrasts the medieval system of ownership of the means of production with the capitalist and Marxist systems. In the medieval system, it is owned by the many; in capitalism, by the few; in Marxism, by the state. Leopold Kohr (1957) argues that mature medieval economies did better than ours. Nicholas Georgescu-Roegen (1950) has shown that feudalism, under conditions of overpopulation and low productivity, will allow more people to live than would capitalist institutions—in other words, in poor countries feudalism allows fewer people to starve than does capitalism. Our own hope is to recover some of the communal advantages of premodern society in a postmodern form, that is, without sacrificing the gains in individual freedom, human rights, and political equality achieved in the modern period (see Gould 1978, chap. 1).

It would be easy to suspect that Catholic teaching is simply calling for a return to more authoritarian and hierarchical patterns. But this is not true. Central to Catholic teaching is the "principle of subsidiarity." According to Pius XI, "It is an injustice, a grave evil and a disturbance of right order for a larger and higher organization to arrogate to itself functions which can be performed efficiently by smaller and lower bodies" (1931, p. 80). Commenting on this, Bernard W. Dempsey writes: "Each higher society is *subsidiary,* that is, designed to be of help to the lesser societies beneath it. It is not the other way around: the *persons* who comprise the more fundamental societies are not means to serve the *societies.* Nor are the closely knit natural communities such as the municipality to be used as means by the larger but more remote organizations like the regional or provincial government (our 'states') or the national state" (1958, p. 281).

These Roman Catholic doctrines are remarkably similar to those of Thomas Jefferson, who wrote: "The article nearest to my heart is the division of counties into wards. These will be pure and elementary republics, the aim of all of which taken together composes the State, and will make of the whole a true democracy as to the business of the wards, which is that nearest and daily concern. The affairs of the larger sections, of counties, of States, and of the Union, not admitting personal transactions by the people, will be delegated to agents elected by themselves, and representation will be substituted where personal action becomes impracticable" (Dumbauld 1955, pp. 97–98).

Alexis de Tocqueville also emphasized the importance of community in American life. In the explanation of why American democracy worked, he noted, "too much importance is attributed to legislation, too little to customs." These customs were nurtured in local communities, and it was "the influence of customs that produces the different degrees of order and prosperity which may be distinguished in the several Anglo-American democracies" (1945, p. 334).

After noting these views of Jefferson and de Tocqueville, Edward Schwarz comments: "Unfortunately, most political leaders and writers today have forgotten these communitarian concerns of Jefferson, de Tocqueville, and early Americans in general. The irony is that a wide range of evidence is now affirming empirically what these traditional theorists could assert only instinctively. It now appears certain that a strong, local community is essential to psychological well-being, personal growth, social order, and a sense of political efficacy. These conclusions are now emerging at the center of every social science discipline" (1982, p. 264).

Schwarz exaggerates at one point. John C. Raines is more careful: "That the social is primary in regard to the human has become by now less a claim than a taken-for-granted starting point in most American sociology and anthropology. But it is a starting point that has little penetrated American political and economic thought" (1982, p. 295).

The emphasis on community was important when Pesch was writing sixty years ago. Today it has become urgent. Amitai Etzioni devoted the first half of *An Immodest Agenda* to analyzing the critical situation in the United States resulting from the dissolution of community into individuals. He rightly notes that "the individual and the community make each other and require each other" (1983, p. 25). Further, he writes, "A society and its members require mutual civility for sheer survival. Unless the retreat to ego is overcome and community institutions reconstituted, the level of conflict and frustrations will rise, and the limited energy channeled to shared concerns will make for an ineffectual 'can't do' society, continued deterioration, and even, ultimately, the possibility of destruction" (p. 185). Unfortunately, when he turns to economics in the second half of the book, he seems to ignore its role in the undercutting of community through its own individualistic ideology and practice.

There is one major respect in which our approach is markedly different from that of Pesch and the papal encyclicals. Certain issues have become critical today that were little anticipated during Pesch's lifetime. Today it is important to think of the community served by the economy as enduring indefinitely through time. It is also important to see that the human communities Pesch envisioned are part of a larger community that includes the other creatures with whom human beings share the world. The industrial economy is only a part of what Wendell Berry has called the Great Economy—the economy that sustains the total web of life and everything that depends on the land. It is the Great Economy that is of ultimate importance.

The Program for This Book

Like Pesch, we are approaching economics for community from the side of the market economy, discussing the revisions required in neoclassical theory and in actual capitalist practice in order that the destruction of community be ended. Precisely for this reason, it is inevitable that our book should appear to be an attack on the current discipline. In one sense it is. We do emphatically believe that humanity is in need of an approach to its economic problems that differs markedly from that supported by most of the practitioners of the present discipline, and since we think these practitioners are sensitively and honorably expressing the implications of current theory, it is this theory we criticize. We believe the failures of the discipline of economics as now practiced have to be shown before there is much chance of reconstructing economics on a different basis.

But while the book *is* a severe critique of the contemporary discipline of economics, our purpose is not to reject the core of its teaching. On the contrary, we are convinced of the general soundness of the account of markets and of the affirmation of their excellence for certain purposes that is at the heart of classical and neoclassical theory alike. We believe many public purposes could be better served by the application of market principles than by the patchwork of government regulations now so prevalent. Our intention is not that economic theory begin over again, but that it be reconstructed on the basis of a paradigm that both clarifies the excellence of its past work and sets it in a larger context. Newtonian science continues to play an extremely important role in the context of the Einsteinian worldview. The analysis of the market can continue to play an extremely important role within a context that sees the purpose of the economy as the service of community.

Of the authors of this book, one is an economist, one a theologian. Both of us have strong ecological concerns. We have come to our economic views through disturbance about what standard development is doing in the Third World. Both of us are Protestants. Both have been influenced by the philosophy of Alfred North Whitehead.

We recognize that much of this book falls outside the boundaries of what is regarded as the discipline of economics, but we feel that the economy, the Great Economy, is far larger than what that discipline studies. We think that our collaborative work is a type of reflection in which citizens from many backgrounds need to share. Decisions that will be made soon in this country will shape the world of our children and grandchildren, probably irreversibly. They should not be made within the restricted context that now governs the academic discipline of economics.

The book is divided into four parts. Part One views economics as it is. The great achievement of economics is to have become a "science." That involves two major elements: it has the characteristics of an academic discipline and it has chosen the deductive model. Immersion in the science makes it very difficult to remember the degree of abstractness involved and to discount one's scientific results with that in mind. After explaining that problem in Chapter 1, we illustrate the consequences for economics with respect to selected basic concepts: the market, measures of success, *Homo economicus,* and land.

Part Two presents an alternative approach to the economy. Instead of shaping the study to the requirements of a science, this approach proposes that reflection be ordered to the needs of the real world. This will not put an end to abstraction, since all thought abstracts, but it will provide a basis for selecting better abstractions and for keeping the elements abstracted from constantly in view. The topics treated in Part One are reconsidered from this point of view in the same sequence, although the chapters do not correspond directly.

Part Three proposes policies that would follow from this different perspective. At an abstract level, the policy implications everywhere would have certain similarities, and at some points the formulations are quite general. But policies mediate between overall perspective and particular situation. In order to avoid too high a level of abstraction, we have focused on one country—the United States. Obviously, if the United States actually decided to move in the directions proposed, much more exact and detailed analysis would be required.

Part Four discusses how changes in the required direction might come about. Even less than elsewhere is there an effort to be exhaustive. We have seen our chief task to provide an image or vision of an economic order that, in the language of the World Council of Churches, would be just, participatory, and sustainable. We need help from many points of view in thinking through how it could be attained. Nevertheless, we do want to broach the subject and initiate some lines of discussion. We do so in two ways. First, we propose a variety of reforms toward which we can now work, and we recommend ways of raising public consciousness so as to make deeper changes possible. One of our proposals is to use a more appropriate measure of how well the national economy is doing, and the Appendix is devoted to spelling this out in some detail. Second, we discuss some of the emerging worldviews that offer hope for change at a deep religious level. It is our judgment that without changes at this level responses to crises will be ad hoc and insufficient. Accordingly, clarification of the needed religious worldview is urgent. Our own convictions, adumbrated at many places in the volume, are spelled out here in comparison with others.

A final word. We have tried to follow the academic conventions of fair description and dispassionate analysis and argument. We believe in them. We want, above all, *not* to disparage the lifelong efforts of many who have advanced the discipline of economics and shaped policies to reflect it. We respect their integrity, their commitment to human welfare, and the keenness of their insights.

But at a deep level of our being we find it hard to suppress the cry of anguish, the scream of horror—the wild words required to express wild realities. We human beings are being led to a *dead* end—all too literally. We are living by an ideology of death and accordingly we are destroying our own humanity and killing the planet. Even the one great success of the program that has governed us, the attainment of material affluence, is now giving way to poverty. The United States is just now gaining a foretaste of the suffering that global economic policies, so enthusiastically embraced, have inflicted on hundreds of millions of others. If we continue on our present paths, future generations, if there are to be any, are condemned to misery. The fact that many people of good will do not see this dead end is undeniably true, very regrettable, and it is our main reason for writing this book.

Victor Furkiss describes our situation graphically: "Present-day society is locked into four positive feedback loops which need to be broken: economic growth which feeds on itself, population growth which feeds on itself, technological change which feeds on itself, and a pattern of income inequality which seems to be self sustaining and which tends to spur growth in the other three areas. Ecological humanism must create an economy in which economic and population growth is halted, technology is controlled, and gross inequalities of income are done away with" (1974, p. 235). We would add also an arms race that feeds on itself. We believe that an economics for the common good is what ecological humanism calls for, and even more what stewardship of creation calls for.

The global system will change during the next forty years, because it will be physically forced to change. But if humanity waits until it is physically compelled to change, its options will be few indeed. None of them will be attractive. If it changes before it *has* to change, while it can still choose to change, it will not avoid suffering and crises, but it can be drawn through them by a realistic hope for a better world.

For this reason we do not want our proposals to be viewed academically, at least not *only* academically. Before this generation are set two ways, the way of life and the way of death. May humanity choose life!

1

ECONOMICS AS AN ACADEMIC DISCIPLINE

1

The Fallacy of Misplaced Concreteness in Economics and Other Disciplines

In the modern university, knowledge is organized into academic disciplines. There are clear norms establishing what such disciplines must be. These provide criteria that divide subject matter among the disciplines and establish goals for the internal structure of each one. This organization of knowledge has been brilliantly productive, but it also has built-in limitations and dangers, especially the danger of committing what Alfred North Whitehead called "the fallacy of misplaced concreteness." This fallacy flourishes because the disciplinary organization of knowledge requires a high level of abstraction; and the more successfully a discipline fulfills the criteria established for it, the higher is the level of abstraction involved. Inevitably, many practitioners of successful disciplines, socialized to think in these abstractions, apply their conclusions to the real world without recognizing the degree of abstraction involved.

Outside the physical sciences no field of study has more fully achieved the ideal form of academic discipline than economics. Precisely because of its success, it has been particularly liable to commission of the fallacy of misplaced concreteness. This chapter emphasizes both the success of economics in realizing the ideal form of the academic discipline and the inevitable limitations that accompany this achievement. It gives some egregious examples of the fallacy of misplaced concreteness in prestigious economic writing. The following chapters illustrate the pervasive effects of the fallacy in more fundamental ways.

Much of the thought of the modern world has been shaped by admiration of the brilliant success of physics in the seventeenth and eighteenth centuries. Physicists developed a conceptual model of nature from which a vast range of predictions followed. These were tested and some were found to be correct. Other empirical results required that

25

concepts and theories be altered. Large bodies of mathematics that had been developed for purely theoretical purposes in earlier centuries turned out to be applicable to the working out of the explanatory and predictive power of the world model.

Physics was empirical in two very important senses. First, the hypotheses that contributed to the world model were suggested by observation and experiment. Second, the validity of the model was tested by drawing forth its implications and examining their correspondence to what could be observed. What distinguished this science from other investigations of nature, however, was not its empirical element but its formal and deductive aspect. Aristotle had encouraged the assemblage of empirical data and its classification. But he had not anticipated the possibility of elaborate deductive systems. The study of living organisms long continued to follow Aristotelian lines more than Newtonian ones, but the ideal of science was established as the discovery of laws from which facts could be deduced.

Of course, in a strictly empirical sense, the observed facts do not directly correspond with the laws. For example, Galileo's famous proof that the speed with which bodies fall to the earth is not affected by their weight does not correspond with experience. Everyone knows that a rock falls faster than a leaf. What is shown is that in a vacuum, the speed would be the same. Even here further qualifications are needed. The moon does not fall to the earth at all in an empirical sense. The law applies empirically only to objects that are stationary with respect to the earth, or in the same relative motion. Further, the law applies only to objects that are within the gravitational field of the earth and that are unaffected by other gravitational fields.

All of this was well understood by the early physicists. To explain empirical phenomena, it was necessary to develop models that simplified reality in order to bring out fundamental features. The right abstractions embodied in simplified models made possible far more powerful analyses and predictions.

The difference between the predictions of the simplified model and the actual behavior of objects allows for the study of other forces. For example, consideration of the fact that the moon does not fall to the earth despite the gravitational force of the earth upon it calls attention to the tendency of any moving object to continue in a straight line. The actual movement of the moon results from the joint operation of two principles—the gravitational pull of the earth and the moon's own momentum. Any deviation of the movement of the moon from what is predicted by these two principles, however tiny, will require search for whatever additional forces are operative.

Admiration for the success of physics has led to two somewhat divergent ideals for the organization of knowledge. One ideal is to attain a unified science in which it would be shown that every aspect of nature can ultimately be explained from the laws of physics. This would mean that chemistry would become a subdivision of physics, and biology a subdivision of chemistry. Some would aim to display human social phenomena and psychology as a branch of biology, thus ultimately as a part of the world machine.

Although this vision continues to play an important role in the Western psyche, it has thus far proved impossible to make much progress in the study of living things by deducing their behavior from the laws of physics. Even chemistry exhibits far too much novelty by combination to be reduced to physics. For practical purposes it must be studied in its own terms. This applies a fortiori to biological and social phenomena. Accordingly, the way in which the norm of science informed by physics has actually functioned is by establishing the several sciences in relative autonomy, with each aiming in its own field to achieve a form resembling that of physics, one in which laws or models are found from which facts can be predicted. Yet this aim remains unrealized even in the other natural sciences. Even in chemistry, there are numerous brute facts that are underivable from any small set of premises. Nevertheless the deductive ideal guides theoretical work.

Despite the prestige of physics there has been resistance to this model in some areas, especially in the study of human beings. For the most part, at least until recently, history was held to be fundamentally different from nature. The question for historians was what in fact took place. No attempt should be made to deduce what occurred from laws of history or unchanging models. Other students of history have stressed that the essential task is to understand rather than explain or predict. They have concentrated on hermeneutics as their special method.

In the nineteenth century, the organization of knowledge that took place was shaped by the second type of influence of physics—that is, the division into autonomous sciences—combined with the power and prestige of the different methods used to study human phenomena. German universities provided the leadership in organizing knowledge into *Wissenschaften. Wissenschaft* is often translated as "science," but because "science" in English strongly favors the model of physics against that of history, it is better to translate it as "discipline." Thus knowledge in Germany was organized into two types of disciplines, the disciplines of nature, modeled on physics, and the disciplines of the human mind or spirit.

The study of human social phenomena never fit comfortably into either type of discipline, so that social studies have displayed the tension between them. They have humanistic elements and also elements that relate them to the natural sciences. In the United States, however, there has been a strong tendency for them to think of themselves as social "sciences."

One way of stating the underlying difference of the scientific and humanistic disciplines is that the former focus on what is universal and necessary, the latter on what is particular and contingent. Of course, the universality of the sciences cannot be absolute in most cases. Classical physics could view the structures of nature as absolute, but biology could study only what was universal to living things, and the social sciences could attend at most to what was universal to human beings. More often, the social sciences studied what is universal to particular types of society. Nevertheless, the quest for models or laws of general applicability rather than the effort to identify and understand the contingent features of reality shaped the methods of those social studies that most emphasized their status as social sciences.

The Place of Economics

The work of Adam Smith and the other early British economists had a strong historical and humanistic component, but the movement of economics initiated by them and especially accented by David Ricardo has been toward being a science. In part it has sought to find models and laws applicable to all human beings, but primarily it has focused on the laws governing modern industrial economy. It is sometimes not as careful as one would wish in clarifying the limits of the type of society to which these laws are applicable.

The choice of economists to focus on the scientific rather than the historical study of the economy was fateful. On the one side, it has made possible the development of powerful analytical tools and predictive devices. On the other side, it has led to serious distortions. These were inevitable once the choice was made.

When physics arose, it assumed that what it studied had not changed from its creation. The specific configurations of matter had of course changed, but the laws governing them were assumed to be immutable.

This assumption was quite appropriate to the data and paved the way for enormous progress. Today, physicists know that this assumption is not entirely true. It is now generally held that the laws of physics came into being with the structures of nature that evolved in the Big Bang. The crucial determinations may have taken place in a fraction of a second. But though this means that the laws of nature are not eternal, that at some point they may come to an end, there is every indication that they are very stable throughout the whole intermediate course of events. For physicists, in most of their work, to abstract from evolutionary change in their subject matter does very little harm.

Nevertheless, the fact that physical reality and the laws that describe it are not immutable, does call attention to the subtle error that has too often entered the notion of "law." It shows that laws are correlative to the things whose behavior they describe. There could be no laws of electricity until there were electromagnetic fields. In this sense all laws are contingent. The necessity that lies in the law is grounded in the fact that certain patterns necessarily characterize entities of a particular sort. Entities that did not "obey" the laws of electromagnetism would not be electromagnetic fields.

This recognition that law and subject matter are correlative is not practically important when what is studied is for practical purposes unchanging. A biologist interested only in how members of a species now behave can ignore it. But when biologists became interested in how species arise, and how they change, then the limits of the laws became clear. Those who want to find more fundamental laws seek the laws of evolution—that is, the universal characteristics of evolutionary change. But even the laws of evolutionary change themselves change with the types of organisms that are evolving.

In the United States, those who established the several branches of the study of human society as sciences modeled their understanding of science more on physics than on evolutionary biology. That is to say, they concentrated on the laws exemplified by the societies they studied rather than on the way the behavior expressed in these laws came into being or changed through time into other forms. This means that the laws that are discovered are laws "governing" specific types of society and become unapplicable as those types of society give way to others. But there is danger that the habit of attending to laws will lead the practitioners of the disciplines to attempt to apply them beyond their limited sphere of relevance.

Economists know that the structures they study are not eternal and that most of them are not coterminous with human existence in general. Adam Smith begins by contrasting the system he studies, that in which the division of labor is far advanced, with earlier forms of human society in which there was little division of labor. He knew that the industrial developments that interested him in England were virtually absent in Poland. Obviously what he studied were historically contingent phenomena. Furthermore, he was no mean historian.

The early economists theorized both as to how the industrial system arose and as to where it was heading. The classical economists saw a temporary phase of growth that must culminate in a new steady state economy. Hence, even when they discerned models and laws that were operative in the economic events of their time, they recognized that at some point in the future different models and laws would function. In short, they knew that the laws "governing" the economic system change as the system changes.

The evolutionary or historical character of the economy has never been denied or wholly ignored. Hegel and Marx gave it rich attention in the nineteenth century. Alfred Marshall, the founder of neoclassical economics, was highly sensitive to the historical character of the actual economy. Nevertheless, economists on the whole wanted economics to become increasingly scientific, and their idea of science was based on physics rather than on evolutionary biology. That meant that economics had to focus on formulating models and finding laws "governing" present economic behavior rather than seeking laws "governing" the changes of economic systems or asking about contingent historical matters. As a result, when useful models have been found and when hypotheses have proved successful, they are treated as analogous to the models and hypotheses of the physicist. Their limitation to particular historical conditions is neglected. Leon Walras, in his *Elements of Pure Economics,* undertook "to do for economics what Newton had done two centuries earlier for celestial mechanics" (1954; Maital 1982, p. 15). In the twentieth century, economics has followed Walras. Milton Friedman notes of economists that "we curtsy to Marshall, but we walk with Walras" (1949, p. 489).

The choice to follow physics in this way has proved partially successful. It has made economics by far the most theoretical and rigorous of the social sciences. It has allowed economics to guide and predict as no other social science has been able to do, at least during certain historical periods. But it has exacted its price by accentuating the problems that follow from having elected to be a science that abstracts from the deep changes in that which it studies. If it had followed Marshall (1925, p. 14), who claimed that "the Mecca of the economist lies in economic biology rather than in economic dynamics," it would have observed these changes and adapted to them. Having followed Walras, the observation of facts has been subordinated to the concerns of theories. Those facts not correlated to the theories have been largely ignored.

The decision to follow physics was the decision to mathematize. Mathematics can work only with what can be formalized. In economics, this has meant, in practice, what can be measured. Hence the aim of mathematization biases economics toward aspects of its subject matter that can be measured. In *The Economics of Education*, John Vaizey recognizes this with unusual candor: "I must confess to an instinctive conviction that what cannot be measured may not exist" (1962, p. 14). The "instinctive conviction" is more likely to be the result of socialization in the discipline, but in any case Vaizey's awareness of his bias led him to deal with nonquantifiable aspects of education. There have been others who have declined to do so. Prestige increasingly is associated with mathematical sophistication and less with what light may be thrown on what is actually going on.

Not all mathematicians have welcomed the mathematization of economics. Witness Norbert Weiner's biting comment: "Just as primitive peoples adopt the Western mode of denationalized clothing and of parliamentarism out of a vague feeling that these magic rites and vestments will at once put them abreast of modern culture and technique, so the economists have developed the habit of dressing up their rather imprecise ideas in the language of the infinitesimal calculus. . . . Any pretense of applying precise formulae is a sham and a waste of time" (Weiner 1964, p. 89).

Nor did earlier economists unanimously accept the mathematization of their discipline. Witness the challenge of J. E. Cairnes to the new mathematical methods championed by his friend Jevons: "So far as I can see, economic truths are not discoverable through the instrumentality of mathematics. If this view be unsound, there is at hand an easy means of refutation—the production of an economic truth, not before known, which has been thus arrived at; but I am not aware that up to the present any such evidence has been furnished of the efficacy of the mathematical method" (Cairnes 1875, p. vi).

A century later there are certainly some economic insights arrived at with the help of mathematics. For the most part, however, mathematics has simply been used to restate more rigorously economic truths arrived at by other more intuitive modes of thinking. Rigor is not to be despised, but neither should it become a fetish, as it in fact has become in academic economics. There are probably no important theoretical or policy debates that have been resolved by econometrics, which was supposed to provide the empirical test for resolving all disagreements. What happened, however, was that each side of any debate developed its own econometricians (or "economeretricians" as some critics have called them). Historically the attempt to use mathematics to further economic discovery was certainly justified. But disappointing results must be admitted. Even mathematical economists such as Nicholas Georgescu-Roegen and Wassily Leontieff believe that further effort toward mathematization is counterproductive.

Leontieff, a Nobel Laureate in economics, has been sufficiently distressed by this tendency to write an open letter to *Science*. In this letter he declares that the king is naked, but that few in academic economics recognize this, and that those who do recognize it do not dare to speak up: "Page after page of professional economic journals are filled with mathematics formulas leading the reader from sets of more or less plausible but entirely arbitrary assumptions to precisely stated but irrelevant theoretical conclusions . . . econometricians fit algebraic functions of all possible shapes to essentially the same sets of data without being able to advance, in any perceptible way, a systematic understanding of the structure and operations of a real economic system" (Leontieff 1982, pp. 104–105).

The Limitations of Academic Disciplines

Some of the limitations and failures of economics result from its modeling itself on the discipline of physics rather than on that of biology or of history. But for economics to have defined itself as a subdivision of biology or history would have had other limitations. The problem lies with the disciplinary organization of knowledge that so dominates the modern university and through it the thinking of the contemporary world. It is this organization of knowledge that forces economists to choose between scientific and historical understanding of what they are doing.

Adam Smith lived and thought before the effort had been made to organize all knowledge into disciplines. He saw the economy as part of the whole of human activity, and he investigated it historically and empirically. Out of these investigations he formulated generalizations that have proved extraordinarily illuminating, and he drew conclusions from them.

As a *discipline* economics must differ from the work of Adam Smith in two ways. First it must identify its subject matter in more separation from the rest of reality. Second, it must articulate the method that it finds most appropriate to the subject matter, the method that will then define it as a discipline. These needs are not dictated by advantages in understanding the actual economy. They are dictated by the disciplinary organization of knowledge.

This organization requires that each discipline have a subject matter clearly distinguished from the others. That necessitates a drawing of boundaries not present for the early economists. The definition of a discipline also requires methodological self-consciousness, and the method must be one that not only illumines the separated subject matter, but further selects the features of the subject matter that will be noticed and treated. In addition, it limits the number of people who may call themselves economists and who receive a salary as an economist.

The early economists studied the economy as an aspect of the whole of social life. Its interconnections with other aspects of that life were as important as its own inner principles. For example, many of the debates among economists were shaped by concern for the relation of economic developments to population. But from economics as a discipline this concern and others like it must be expunged. The study of population belongs to demography. The debates of the early economists can occur now only in interdisciplinary contexts, and the disciplinary organization of knowledge makes these peripheral. Within economics as an academic discipline the complexities of the impact of economic growth on population, and of population growth on the economy, are largely ignored. Again, this is not because it has been shown that these relationships are not important. It is because the disciplinary organization of knowledge requires a separate subject matter for economics, for demography, for sociology, and so on.

This whole process of replacing the concrete with the abstract is encouraged in one further way. This organization leads to the social organization of the university into departments. In addition, the most important relations of the members of a department with persons outside it are not with members of other departments within the university, but with other practitioners of the same discipline in other universities. The primary loyalty of university professors is likely to be to the guilds and to the promotion of their discipline rather than to their particular university or to their students. Indeed, there are many for whom the advance of their discipline is the major source of meaning, the organizing center of their lives, their deepest commitment. The discipline becomes their god. We call this "disciplinolatry." That disciplinolatry is far advanced in economics was implicitly acknowledged by Paul Samuelson in his presidential address to the American Economic Association: "In the long run, the economic scholar works for the only coin worth having—our own applause" (1962, p. 18).

Commitment to the discipline and its future leads to keen interest in recruiting students who will major in it. The tendency is that courses taught for the general student body function more to attract majors and start them on their way than to facilitate the understanding of the subject matter by outsiders. In any case, concentrated attention is paid to socializing students into the discipline and to preparing leaders for the future through graduate programs.

Once socialized into the guild, relations with other members of the guild are far more comfortable and satisfying than those with outsiders. There is a wide range of common assumptions that express themselves also in shared values. In this way the external threat to these assumptions and values is minimized. The result is, of course, that what has come to be assumed within the discipline appears self-evident and in no need of critical analysis. New generations build on the work of earlier ones without asking whether these earlier achievements are truly relevant to the new situation. Indeed, the study of the *newness* of the new situation is not encouraged.

A recent study of graduate education in economics concludes that "graduate economics education is succeeding in narrowing students' interests." According to the study's survey of the perceived relevance of other fields to economics, physics scored the lowest, and ecology or any other biological science was not even listed among the fields to be ranked (Colander and Klamer 1987). Small wonder that economic models sometimes conflict with biophysical realities.

Those students of the discipline who do raise radical questions about it are rarely appreciated. Indeed, they find jobs scarce and encounter difficulties in getting their work published. They are likely to be denied a place on the program of guild meetings and to be made to feel unwelcome there. In short, they are ostracized. The discipline can proceed in a cumulative fashion increasingly canalized by what has been accepted in the past, currently referred to as "the mainstream." The abstractions that are universally accepted are taken as the reality.

This procedure is far advanced in economics. Leontieff's letter to *Science* protests about this, too. He expects the sterile scholasticism to which he objects to persist as long as the tenured members of leading economics departments continue to exercise, largely through journal editorships, tight control over training, promotion, tenure, and research grants. The methods employed to maintain intellectual "discipline" within the academic descipline of economics can, he says, "occasionally remind one of the those employed by the Marines to maintain discipline on Parris Island" (Leontieff 1982). What Leontieff does not seem to recognize is that the problem is not so much an abuse of power by biased senior faculty as an outgrowth of the disciplinary organization of knowledge itself. The likelihood that the successors of the present generation of leaders will have a broader view of economics and of its responsibility to society is slight, unless there is a conscious criticism of the forces that have pressed the discipline of economics to focus on these abstractions.[1]

The Fallacy of Misplaced Concreteness

The problem with economics is that it has succeeded all too well by the standards of the academic world. It is a successful discipline, and it has succeeded much better than any other social study in becoming a deductive science. These successes have involved a high level of abstraction, yet the whole ethos of the university in general, and of the department of economics in particular, discourages the full realization of the extent of the abstracting that has gone on. The result is that conclusions are drawn about the real world by deduction from abstractions with little awareness of the danger involved.

Alfred North Whitehead noted that this tendency began early with economics.

It is very arguable that the science of political economy, as studied in its first period after the death of Adam Smith (1790), did more harm than good. It destroyed many economic fallacies, and taught how to think about the economic

1. Since one of the authors of this book is a theologian, it may be well to make explicit that the problem with theology as an academic discipline is similar to that with economics. Cornel West contrasts a theological effort of which he approves with academic theology, as follows. "Shunning the narrow confines of the intellectual division of labor in academic institutions, DEI [Departmento Ecumenico de Investigaciones, in San Jose, Costa Rica] rejects the compartmentalized disciplines of our bureaucratized seminaries and divinity schools. Instead DEI promotes and encourages theological reflection that traverses the field of political economy, biblical studies, social theory, church history, and social ethics. In this way, DEI reveals the intellectual impoverishment of academic theologies that enact ostrichlike exercises in highly specialized sand—with little view to the pressing problems confronting ordinary people in our present period of crisis" (Hinkelammert 1986, p. v).

revolution then in progress. But it riveted on men a certain set of abstractions which were disastrous in their effect on modern mentality. It dehumanized industry. This is only one example of a general danger inherent in modern science. Its methodological procedure is exclusive and intolerant, and rightly so. It fixes attention on a definite group of abstractions, neglects everything else, and elicits every scrap of information and theory which is relevant to what it has retained. The method is triumphant provided the abstractions are judicious. But, however triumphant, the triumph is within limits. The neglect of these limits leads to disastrous oversights . . . [Whitehead 1925, p. 200]

These tendencies in economics were recognized at the time. The great Swiss economist, Sismondi, observed the error in the early nineteenth century.

The new English economists are quite obscure and can be understood only with great effort because our mind is opposed to making the abstractions demanded on us. This repugnance is in itself a warning that we are turning away from the truth when, in moral science where everything is connected, we endeavor to isolate a principle and to see nothing but that principle. . . . Humanity should be on guard against all generalization of ideas that causes us to lose sight of the facts, and above all against the error of identifying the public good with wealth, abstracted from the sufferings of the human beings who create it. [Sismondi 1827]

Walter Bagehot, in his *Economic Studies,* wrote of Ricardo: "He thought he was considering actual human nature in its actual circumstances, when he was really considering a fictitious nature in fictitious circumstances" (1953, p. 157). Whitehead called this "the fallacy of misplaced concreteness." He defined it as "neglecting the degree of abstraction involved when an actual entity is considered merely so far as it exemplifies certain categories of thought" (1929b, p. 11). More generally it is the fallacy involved whenever thinkers forget the degree of abstraction involved in thought and draw unwarranted conclusions about concrete actuality. Nicholas Georgescu-Roegen wrote: "It is beyond dispute that the sin of standard economics is the fallacy of misplaced concreteness" (1971, p. 320).

Sismondi, Bagehot, and Whitehead did not oppose all use of abstractions. The problem lies in neglecting the extent to which our concepts are abstract, and therefore also neglecting the rest of the reality from which they have been abstracted. In Whitehead's words, "The methodology of reasoning requires the limitations involved in the abstract. Accordingly, the true rationalism must always transcend itself by recurrence to the concrete in search of inspiration. A self-satisfied rationalism is in effect a form of anti-rationalism. It means an arbitrary halt at a particular set of abstractions" (Whitehead 1925, p. 200).

What is the set of abstractions that political economy has riveted on economic thought and at which it has come to a self-satisfied halt? One of the most important is the abstraction of a circular flow of national product and income regulated by a perfectly competitive market. This is conceived as a mechanical analog, with motive force provided by individualistic maximization of utility and profit, in abstraction from social community and biophysical interdependence. What is emphasized is the optimal allocation of resources that can be shown to result from the mechanical interplay of individual self-interests. What is neglected is the effect of one person's welfare on that of others through bonds of sympathy and human community, and the physical effects of one person's production and consumption activities on others through bonds of biophysical community. Whenever the abstracted-from elements of reality become too insistently evident in our experience, their existence is admitted by the category "externality." Externalities are ad hoc corrections introduced as needed to save appearances, like the epicycles of Ptolemaic astronomy. Externalities do represent a recognition of neglected aspects of concrete experience, but in such a way as to minimize restructuring of the basic theory. As long as externalities involve minor details, this is perhaps a reasonable procedure. But when vital issues (e.g., the capacity of the earth to support life) have to be classed as externalities, it is time to restructure basic concepts and start with a different set of abstractions that can embrace what was previously external. (The distinction in Chapter 3 between localized and pervasive externalities is a step in this direction.) The frequency of appeal to externalities is a good index of the overall problem of misplaced concreteness in economic theory. But there are more particular examples as well.

Perhaps the classic instance of the fallacy of misplaced concreteness in economics is "money fetishism." It consists in taking the characteristics of the abstract symbol and measure of exchange value, money, and applying them to the concrete use value, the commodity itself. Thus, if money flows in an isolated circle, then so do commodities; if money balances can grow forever at compound interest, then so can real GNP, and so can pigs and cars and haircuts.

No less an intellect than John Locke committed this fallacy in his theory of private property. He at first argued that one's legitimate accumulation of property was limited to what one could use before it spoiled. Thus the physical tendency to spoil, rust, rot, and decay set a kind of natural limit to accumulation of real wealth. But, Locke argued, with the advent of a money economy, that natural limit disappears because money does not spoil, and wealth can be accumulated in the form of money. Note that the characteristic of the abstract symbol (nonspoilage) comes to dominate the characteristic (spoilage) of the concrete reality being symbolized. Locke's limitation on wealth disappears even though wealth still spoils. One might as well argue that butter accumulation is not limited by spoilage because the quantity of butter is measured in pounds, and pounds can be summed indefinitely in a ledger without spoiling.

Clearly, the existence of millionaires does not necessarily imply rotting stockpiles of goods. Indeed, money balances do not imply the existence of any real goods at all. The willingness of the community to hold money derives from the inconvenience of barter, and the fact that money is an indent or lien against *future* production, which cannot spoil because it does not yet exist. But the real wealth of a community, even in a money economy, consists of goods to which the principle of spoilage still applies. So accumulating money balances cannot indefinitely be matched by accumulating real wealth. Therefore at some point accumulated money becomes a lien against future production rather than a claim check to simultaneously existing goods. The willingness of future producers to honor those past claims on their current production will at some point become an issue. In practice, such an excess of money claims over real wealth will likely result in debt repudiation by inflation. Current producers would charge more and pay themselves more money for their product and thus bid that product away from those whose claims do not result from current production but derive from past claims stated in fixed money amounts. The concentration on money and the market rather than on physical goods, with the concomitant decision to model itself on the methods (but not the content!) of physics, has been characteristic of the whole of modern economics. This paved the way for the primacy of deduction and the focus on mathematical models and computer simulations that are the hallmark of current practice in the discipline. Such elaborate and beautiful logical structures heighten the tendency to prize theory over fact and to reinterpret fact to fit theory.

An extreme example of this tendency is provided by Gary Becker and Nigel Tomes (1979) in their model of intergenerational distribution of income. They attempt in rigorous fashion to extend the model of individualistic utility maximization over intergenerational time periods and use it to explain long-run changes in the distribution of wealth and income. The model requires a self-identical, well-defined decision-making unit over intergenerational time. Individuals die off, so they won't do. Families won't do either because although they endure they are neither self-identical nor independent. Families endure only by merging and mixing their identities through sexual reproduction, and thus are not independent or well defined over intergenerational time.

Your great-great grandchild will also be the great-great grandchild of fifteen other people in the current generation, many of their identities now unknown. Presumably your great-great grandchild's well being will be as much an inheritance from each of these fifteen others as from yourself. Therefore it does not make sense for you to worry too much about your particular descendant, or to take any particular action on his or her behalf. The farther in the future is the hypothetical descendant, the greater the number of co-progenitors in the present generation, and consequently the more in the nature of a public good is any provision made for the distant future. To the extent that you are concerned about the welfare of your descendant, you should also be concerned about the welfare of all those in the present generation from whom, for good or ill, your descendant will inherit. Thus a concern for future generations should reinforce rather than weaken the concern for present justice—contrary to what is often supposed. Although we are not all brothers and sisters in the literal sense, we are quite literally co-progenitors of each others' distant descendants.

The thrust of these evident consequences of sexual reproduction is toward community and away from individualism—a thrust generally resisted by standard economics, especially the Chicago school, of which Becker is a prominent member. To avoid this thrust and keep the world safe for individualistic maximization, Becker and Tomes adopt the obvious if extreme expedient of assuming asexual reproduction! It is one thing to abstract from the incidental in order to highlight the fundamental. It is something else to abstract from the fundamental to save a model. When the concrete fact of sexual reproduction conflicts with the abstractions of individualistic maximization, the authors hang on to their abstractions as somehow more real. Becker and Tomes try to convince the reader, quite unsuccessfully in our opinion, that this absurd assumption is for expository convenience only and that nothing important hangs on it (Daly 1982).

The focus on mathematics in place of empirical attention to physical reality takes its toll also in a crucial argument of Julian Simon in *The*

Ultimate Resource. He wishes to show that we need not be concerned about absolute shortages of natural resources. He writes: "The length of a one-inch line is finite in the sense that it is bounded at both ends. But the line within the endpoints contains an infinite number of points; these points cannot be counted, because they have no defined size. Therefore the number of points in that one-inch segment is not finite. Similarly, the quantity of copper that will ever be available to us is not finite, because there is no method (even in principle) of making an appropriate count of it" (Simon 1981, p. 47).

Note that Simon switches from the concept of infinite *divisibility* to infinite *amount,* from the infinity of points on a line to the infinity of copper in the ground, with nothing but the word "similarly" to bridge the gap. No doubt the abstract properties of numbers can be used to describe many facts about copper, but not every property of abstract numbers is obliged to convey a concrete truth about copper.

A final example also has to do with resource availability. Lester Thurow argues:

> In the context of zero economic growth and other countries, a fallacious "impossibility argument" is often made to demonstrate the need for zero economic growth. The argument starts with a question. How many tons of this or that non-renewable resource would the world need if everyone in the world now had the consumption standards enjoyed by those in the US? The answer is designed to be a mind-boggling number in comparison with current supplies of such resources. The problem with both the question and the answer is that it assumes that the rest of the world is going to achieve the consumption standards of the average American without at the same time achieving the productivity standards of the average American. This is, of course, algebraically impossible. The world can consume only what it can produce. When the rest of the world has consumption standards equal to those of the US, it will be producing at the same rate and providing as much of an increment to the world-wide supplies of goods and services as it does to the demand for goods and services. [Thurow 1976, p. 40]

Professor Thurow thought well enough of this argument that he reproduced it verbatim five years later in Chapter 5 of his otherwise admirable book, *The Zero-Sum Society* (1981, p. 118). Thurow appeals to the abstract accounting conventions of the circular flow of exchange value in order to "prove" that the physical flow of resources can never be a constraint on economic growth. He tells us that it is not only possible for the U.S. standard of resource consumption to be generalized to the entire world, it is "algebraically impossible" that it should be otherwise! Never mind about tons of nonrenewable resources and all those numbers that are "designed" to be mind-boggling. Aggregate production equals aggregate income, and that is all there is to it! Unfortunately for Thurow's argument, the algebra of circular-flow accounting identities tell us absolutely nothing about the adequacy of biophysical resources to sustain worldwide a per capita resource use rate equal to that of the United States (Daly 1985).

Enough examples have been presented to lend credence to Georgescu-Roegen's claim, cited above, that misplaced concreteness is the cardinal sin of standard economics. Nor can these examples be dismissed as straw men. We have quoted only from deservedly respected economists of diverse ideological bent, professors from such prestigious universities as Chicago, MIT, Maryland, and Yale. Our purpose is not to impugn their professional status, but merely to argue that when the best economists fall so easily into the trap, we should have greater respect for the trap and guard more against it.

Avoiding the Fallacy

How can we guard against misplaced concreteness in economics? For one thing, we could warn students about it in the early chapters of economic principles texts, as we already do for the fallacy of composition, *post hoc ergo propter hoc, petitio principii,* and other Latin crimes against reason. As far as we have been able to ascertain, no text mentions the fallacy of misplaced concreteness. They do talk about abstraction, but mainly in order to emphasize its powers, not its dangers.

One must admit that avoiding misplaced concreteness is not easy. We simply cannot think without abstraction. "To abstract" means literally "to draw away from." We can draw away from concrete experience in different directions and by different distances. To expect perfect judgment in choosing the direction and distance of abstraction proper to each argument, and never to mix up levels in the middle of an argument, is to expect too much. It seems we must always commit this fallacy to some degree, and we must think of minimizing it rather than eliminating it entirely. For this reason it is a very subtle fallacy—more a general limitation of conceptual thought than an error in logic.

There are nevertheless two rules of thumb that will help us to minimize misplaced concreteness. One is, in Whitehead's words, "recurrence to the concrete in search of inspiration." One technique for getting back to the concrete is to look at all four of Aristotle's notions of cause. These four causes (material, efficient, formal, and final) can be explained with reference to a house. The material cause is the lumber, bricks, and so forth from which the house is made. The efficient cause is the carpenter and his tools, which effect a change of form in the material. The formal cause is the blueprint that the carpenter is following. The final cause is the purpose for building the house—for example, shelter and privacy. In economics our attention is overwhelmingly focused on efficient and formal causes. If we remember material and final causes as well, we will be less likely to commit the fallacy of misplaced concreteness. Whitehead said, "A satisfactory cosmology must explain the interweaving of efficient and final causation" (1929a, p. 28). Likewise for a satisfactory political economy.

One could hardly accuse Whitehead, the coauthor of *Principia Mathematica,* of harboring a vulgar prejudice against abstract thought. He just insists, like a good economist, that we constantly weigh the costs of our particular abstractions against the benefits, and that we be willing to recur to the concrete now and again.

Whitehead describes the costs and benefits of abstraction as follows.

The advantage of confining attention to a definite group of abstractions, is that you confine your thoughts to clear-cut, definite relations. . . . We all know those clear-cut, trenchant intellects, immovably encased in a hard shell of abstractions. They hold you to their abstractions by the sheer grip of personality.

The disadvantage of exclusive attention to a group of abstractions, however well-founded, is that, by the nature of the case, you have abstracted from the remainder of things. Insofar as the excluded things are important in your experience, your modes of thought are not fitted to deal with them. [Whitehead 1925, p. 200]

The second and related rule of thumb is to avoid excessive professional specialization.

The dangers arising from this aspect of professionalism are great, particularly in our democratic societies. The directive force of reason is weakened. The leading intellects lack balance. They see this set of circumstances, or that set; but not both sets together. The task of coordination is left to those who lack either the force or the character to succeed in some definite career. In short, the specialized functions of the community are performed better and more progressively, but the generalized direction lacks vision. The progressiveness in detail only adds to the danger produced by the feebleness of coordination. [1925, p. 200]

That this danger is an aspect of the fallacy of misplaced concreteness is indicated in the following paragraph where Whitehead adds, "There is development of particular abstractions, and a contraction of concrete appreciation. The whole is lost in one of its aspects" (1925, p. 200).

Those fields of economics that deal more with the whole and the concrete, such as economic history, comparative systems, history of economic thought, and economic development ought to be more emphasized, not only for their own sakes, but also as an antidote to the near toxic levels of rarefied abstraction encountered in the "core courses."

Recognizing the fallacy of misplaced concreteness is particularly important to establishing economics for community, because community is precisely the feature of reality that has been most consistently abstracted from in modern economics. The need is not for one more theorem squeezed out of the premises of methodological individualism by a more powerful mathematical press, but for a new premise that reinstates the critical aspect of reality that has been abstracted from—namely, community.

2

Misplaced Concreteness: The Market

The Strength of the Market

The most important insight that economists have to convey about the market is how independent, decentralized decisions give rise, not to chaos, but to a spontaneous order. This is a truth that is not immediately grasped by common sense. Even after careful explanation it remains a bit mysterious, as Adam Smith's metaphor of the "invisible hand" suggests. But market societies are not chaotic. Certainly they are generally less chaotic than centrally planned societies.

The apparent paradox of individual freedom leading to social order also occurs with language. Individuals are free to try to communicate in whatever ways they wish. But to succeed they have to conform to certain community conventions. The result is not a Tower of Babel, but an amazingly well-ordered structure, as is evident in the grammar of any language. No one designed a language, not even the French Academy. Yet language has an order and logic that would appear to have been the product of rational planning. In addition, language is the most basic foundation of community. The market also has its grammar, the rules that govern its particular mode of communication. It is not as rich and sophisticated as a language, but it is quite marvelous in its ability to collect, communicate, and use masses of scattered, piecemeal information that, like the millions of tons of gold dissolved in the ocean, would be quite useless without some means of collecting it.

This ability of the market to make use of scattered, fragmentary knowledge is its most remarkable feature, as emphasized by F. A. Hayek:

What is the problem we wish to solve when we try to construct a rational economic order?

On certain familiar assumptions the answer is simple enough. *If* we possess all the relevant information, and *if* we can start out from a given system of preferences and *if* we command complete knowledge of the available means, the problem which remains is purely one of logic. That is, the answer to the question of what is the best use of available means is implicit in our assumptions. The conditions which the solution of this optimum problem must satisfy have been fully worked out and can be stated best in mathematical form: put at their briefest, they are that the marginal rates of substitution between any two commodities or factors must be the same in all their different uses.

This, however, is emphatically *not* the economic problem which society faces. And the economic calculus which we have developed to solve this logical problem, though an important step toward the solution of the economic problem of society, does not yet provide an answer to it. The reason for this is that the "data" from which the economic calculus starts are never for the whole society "given" to a single mind which could work out the implications, and can never be so given.

The peculiar character of the problem of a rational economic order is determined precisely by the fact that the knowledge of the circumstances of which we must make use never exists in concentrated or integrated form, but solely as the dispersed bits of incomplete and frequently contradictory knowledge which all the separate individuals possess. The economic problem of society is thus not merely a problem of how to allocate "given" resources—if "given" is taken to mean given to a single mind which deliberately solves the problem set by these "data."

It is rather a problem of how to secure the best use of resources known to any of the members of society for ends whose relative importance only these individuals know. Or, to put it briefly, it is the problem of the utilization of knowledge not given to anyone in its totality.

This character of the problem has, I am afraid, been rather obscured than illuminated by many of the recent refinements of economic theory, particularly by many of the uses made of mathematics. [Hayek 1945, p. 520]

Individual consumers know their preferences better than anyone else and act directly to satisfy them in the marketplace. Individual producers know their own capacities and options better than anyone else and they too act on this information in the market. This essential feature of *decentralized* decision making is what permits all this knowledge to be used. If decision making were centralized, as in a planned economy, then all this information about particular ends and means would have to be collected and summarized to an amount manageable by a single intellect, albeit amplified these days by computers.

To get some concrete appreciation of the information problem consider two common commodities. First look at wool. This homogeneous white stuff from sheep would seem to present no great information problems. Yet there are some five thousand categories of wool recognized by traders in the world wool market. Wool differs by length of

fiber, tensile strength, electrostatic properties, elasticity, and susceptibility to various dyes, not to mention spatial and temporal patterns of
availability. Combinations of the various grades in each category with
those in other categories can easily exceed five thousand. If one thinks
that these differences must be too insignificant to worry about, that
thought is belied by the fact that people do worry about these differences enough to pay a premium to get the combination of qualities they
most want. In a centrally planned economy, this vast amount of qualitative information is suppressed. Wool is just homogeneous stuff. Indeed,
for many decisions the applicable category is probably not even wool,
but "animal fibers," or this category is perhaps even aggregated with
cotton to give "natural fibers," or further aggregated with nylon and
other synthetics to give simply "fibers."

The humble wood screw provides an even better example. How
many different kinds are there? Screws differ along the continuum of
length, and of diameter, measured in inches or centimeters, or in some
other special metric. The helical pitch of the threads can differ. The materials differ: steel, aluminum, brass, Monel. Screws of one metal can be
plated with another: chromium, nickel, cadmium, copper, zinc. The
heads of screws differ greatly: flat or oval countersunk; round, square,
hexagon; slotted, Phillips or Allen heads; pan head. Clearly there are
infinitely many types of wood screw, each designed for particular uses.
The same holds for machine screws and hundreds of other items of
common use.

A market system can handle all the information about these qualitative differences. Central planning cannot. To have only, say, a dozen
types of wood screw and four grades of wool is like playing the piano
with your fists rather than your fingers. For allocating resources among
commodity uses, the market is the most efficient institution we have
come up with thanks to its ability to use information. It is also more
responsive to changing circumstances, and it is much more participatory
in that thousands of users and producers are deciding the mix of wood
screws to be produced, not some remote bureaucrat—or even a committee of bureaucrats—who might not know which end of a screwdriver to hold.

What is it that leads private producers to be so responsive to user needs
that they concern themselves with the differences between chromium-
and cadmium-plated wood screws? The competitive quest for profit.
Economists see profit as both a signal of misallocation and an inducement to correct the very misallocation signaled. If profits earned on

chromium-plated wood screws are higher than on cadmium-plated ones, then resources will shift to supply more of the former and less of the latter until profits are equal at the margin. Profit provides information as well as incentive. In an efficient economy, all abnormal profits will have been competed down to the normal level. Entrepreneurs' profit will be no greater than the income they could earn in their best alternative employment.

Some Market Grammar: The Equi-Marginal Principle of Maximization

The notion in the preceding paragraph that resources are reallocated until profits are "equal at the margin" is an example of an important general principle in economics—the "equi-marginal principle of maximization." Whenever any resource (time, money, energy, etc.) is to be allocated between alternative uses so as to maximize the attainment of some goal (profit, welfare), the rule is that the marginal or incremental contribution to the goal of the last small unit of the resource applied should be equal in each alternative use. For example, a consumer is allocating his leisure hours between reading and hiking. Suppose that at the existing allocation he finds that the last hour spent hiking is tiring, while the last hour spent reading is enjoyable. This consumer, a representative of the species *Homo economicus,* reallocates his time so as to increase overall satisfaction or utility. He takes away one hour from hiking and sacrifices a small marginal utility. That hour is then added to reading, and by it he gains a relatively large marginal utility. Since utility lost is less than utility gained by the reallocation, total utility must have increased. As long as the marginal utility of hiking (the increment to total utility of one more hour spent hiking) is not equal to the marginal utility of reading, then total utility can be increased by taking time away from the lower marginal utility use and devoting it to the higher marginal utility use. Only when the marginal utilities are equal is it no longer possible to increase total utility by reallocation. What cannot be further increased must be at a maximum. The same logic holds, of course, for allocating income among commodities, or investment funds among projects. The sacrificed alternative (hiking) is referred to as the "opportunity cost." It is defined as the *best* alternative sacrificed in making a choice. Since our example has only one alternative to reading, it is naturally the best alternative and is thus the opportunity cost.

A related reason for economists' focus on the margin is that the margin is the locus of economic choice. As margins become large or irreversible (to marry or stay single, to emigrate or stay in your own country, to go to war or be a pacifist), the corresponding choice becomes less economic and more "heroic." Economic choices have small, reversible margins.

Margins are also closely related to prices (exchange value). Consider the famous example of Carl Menger (1950): a farmer has just harvested five sacks of corn. The first sack is withheld as seed corn for next year, the second he eats directly for energy, the third he feeds to chickens so as to improve his diet with eggs and meat, the fourth he ferments to make whiskey, the fifth he feeds to a parrot whose antics amuse him. Anyone who wants to trade with the farmer for a sack of corn must give the farmer something that the farmer values more than—what? More than the parrot, of course, which is the marginal use of a sack of corn. It is the marginal or least important use value that determines exchange value. Price—exchange value—measures marginal utility. Note that the sum of the utilities of the five sacks of corn would be much greater than the product of the marginal utility (price) times five. That difference is known as "consumer's surplus." It makes it very difficult to estimate total welfare by values based on prices. This story also illustrates the "law of diminishing marginal utility"—the commonsense idea that sensible people satisfy their most pressing wants first, so that each additional unit of income added is used to satisfy a less pressing want.

There are some important qualifications and limitations to the virtues of the market, but before considering them let us put aside a confused objection. Some people have simultaneously condemned both the market, with its reliance on profit, and the concentrated power of centralized bureaucracy. This involves an inconsistency. If one rejects the very concept of profit then everyone must be a salaried employee—no independent artisans, professionals, small farmers, merchants, and so on. If all are employees, then who is left over to be the employer? Presumably the state—a single massive, centralized bureaucracy. If one favors independence, participation, decentralized decision making, and small- or human-scale enterprises, then one has to accept the category of profit as a legitimate and necessary source of income. There is plenty of room to complain about monopoly profits, but that is a complaint against monopoly, not against profit per se. People who want to abolish the category of profit and at the same time foster decentralized decision making and participation in economic life have not thought very clearly about their proposal. If one dislikes centralized bureaucratic decision making then one must accept the market and the profit motive, if not as a positive good then as the lesser of two evils. A third alternative (as opposed to varying mixes of the two basic ones) has not been identified. We have no hesitation in opting for the market as the basic institution of resource allocation. The alternative to capitalism and socialism that we will propose later in this book is not intended as an alternative method of allocating resources, for on this issue we side unequivocally with capitalism.

Economists do not spend all of their time celebrating the virtues of the market. Much effort has gone into specifying both the conditions under which markets work as advertised and the conditions that give rise to "market failure." If we focus on market limitations and failures throughout this book, it is not because we are antimarket. Much to the contrary, we are eager to identify and correct those conditions that lead to market failure as a way of enhancing the market as our basic institution for allocating scarce resources among alternative uses. Three broad categories of problems with the market have been identified by economists: (1) the tendency for competition to be self-eliminating, (2) the corrosiveness of self-interest on the moral context of community that is presupposed by the market, and (3) the existence of public goods and externalities. Of these types of problems, the first two are cases of the market eroding its own requirements, which we treat in the following section. The third is considered under "Public Goods and Externalities" below.

The Market's Tendency to Erode Its Own Requirements

Competition means not rivalry, but the existence of many alternatives for both buyer and seller. How many buyers and sellers are required for a market to be competitive? Enough so that no one can alone appreciably influence price. Competition is what keeps profit at the normal level and resources properly allocated. But competition involves winning and losing, both of which have a tendency to be cumulative. Last year's winners find it easier to be this year's winners. Winners tend to grow and losers disappear. Over time many firms become few firms, competition is eroded, and monopoly power increases. To the extent that competition is self-eliminating we must constantly reestablish it by trustbusting. This is practically a forgotten word in the current age of mergers, takeovers, and misguided efforts to reestablish international competitiveness by allowing gargantuan expansion in the vain hope that economies of scale have not yet given way to diseconomies of scale—as if General Motors were not already much bigger than Toyota.

Monopoly is by definition anticompetitive, but even bigness that falls short of monopoly presents a problem. A firm has been characterized as an island of planning in a sea of market relationships (Coase 1937). Within a firm, centralized decision making, or central planning, is the organizing principle. Between firms it is the market, or decentralized decision making, that rules. As firms become larger and fewer the consequence is that more and more of economic life is coordinated by planning (at the within-firm level), and less and less by the market (at the between-firm level). At the limit lies one giant conglomerate that would be indistinguishable from a centrally planned economy.

The proper size of firms must in part be determined by a balance between the conflicting principles of planning versus market. Decisions can be too decentralized as well as too centralized. If the boss had to negotiate a market contract for every memo to be typed, it would be very inefficient. The same would be true if practically nothing were contracted out and the boss had to be concerned with every detail of production of every intermediate product used by the firm. But mere bigness, even when it becomes technically and managerially inefficient, can confer the advantages of political and financial power.

There is a conflict between favoring markets and favoring complete laissez-faire. Maintenance of competitive markets requires the abandonment of laissez-faire at least to the extent that government must assume the role of limiting monopoly and excessive bigness. The Reagan administration tended to favor big business over competitive markets. It is quite amazing how economists have neglected their trustbusting heritage as guardians of competitive market structures. All the more credit therefore is due Walter Adams and James Brock (1987) for their recent effort to revive this tradition.

Somewhat analogous to the tendency of the market to erode its own competitive foundations is the corrosive effect of individualistic self-interest on the containing moral context of the community. However much driven by self-interest, the market still depends absolutely on a community that shares such values as honesty, freedom, initiative, thrift, and other virtues whose authority will not long withstand the reduction to the level of personal tastes that is explicit in the positivistic, individualistic philosophy of value on which modern economic theory is based. If all value derives only from satisfaction of individual wants, then there is nothing left over on the basis of which self-interested, individualistic want satisfaction can be restrained. Depletion of moral capital may be more costly than depletion of physical capital, as Fred Hirsch has argued in *The Social Limits to Growth* (1976). The market does not accumulate moral capital; it depletes it. Consequently, the market depends on the community to regenerate moral capital, just as it depends on the biosphere to regenerate natural capital.

Unfortunately, the market as a category of economic thought abstracts from the community and the biosphere. As a result these issues do not gain attention within the discipline of economics. Yet in the real world, failure to respect the limits of both social and biophysical community is the greatest threat to a market society. How to draw the attention of economists to these massive problems and how to deal with them in the real world will be a major theme of subsequent chapters.

Public Goods and Externalities

The first two problems of market societies just discussed have to do with the market's tendency to destroy its own necessary social context. The third problem is the more technical one of market failure proper, and it receives much more attention from economists than do the first two. Even if the competitive structure and the community of basic values are intact, the market still cannot effectively deal with externalities and public goods.

Public goods have the property that their use by one person does not exclude use by others. Many goods have this property: information, scientific knowledge, highways, lighthouses, national defense, parks. Whenever use by one person is at no cost to others, the marginal opportunity cost is zero and therefore the price should be zero. But the cost of production of knowledge, parks, highways, and so forth is greater than zero. There is no market incentive for any firm to supply costly goods for a zero price, and so they would never be supplied by the market alone. And yet such goods are clearly beneficial and wanted by individuals. They are also the physical infrastructure of community.

If a firm is able to charge a positive price for a public good by virtue of being permitted to exclude nonpayers from its use—for example, a private toll road—that will permit the good to be produced, but it would still not result in its efficient use. The marginal opportunity cost would still be zero—nothing is sacrificed by allowing one more car on the toll road—yet the price would be positive. Consequently the road would be underused. Benefits to some citizens that cost nothing to other citizens are in this case being forgone, violating the principle of Pareto efficiency. Normally, competitive markets in private goods achieve a Pareto optimum (after Vilfredo Pareto) in which no individual can be made better off without making some other individual worse off. The rule then is always to do whatever is good for someone and harms no one, as judged by the parties themselves. When no such actions are any longer possible then social welfare can no longer be unambiguously improved—that is, we are at an optimum. Note that any action that redistributes income is ruled out, because someone would have been made worse off. Consequently there is a different Pareto optimum for each possible distribution of income, of which there are infinitely many.

Markets need the help of governments to provide public goods efficiently. Much effort has gone into estimating the demand or willingness of individuals to pay for public goods. The sum of all individuals' willingness to pay (assuming honest answers to questionnaires) is taken as the total value of the public good, to be compared against the total cost, which is usually more objectively known. The fundamental individualism of economics is evident in its insistence on reducing all value to individuals' willingness to pay, rather than to any organic notion of commonwealth or public interest. And this continues in spite of Kenneth Arrow's impossibility theorem, in which he proved that a social welfare function having certain basic, reasonable properties could not be derived from individual welfare functions (Arrow 1966). We will not have much more to say about public goods, but we will have a great deal more to say about externalities, the most general and intractable instance of market failure.

The economists' image of a market is a system of voluntary exchanges made by the parties concerned only because all consider it to their advantage to engage in these transactions. What has so impressed economists is the fact that all participants in the market gain. But this vision abstracts from the real world in which everything that happens has much wider effects. In fact, market transactions have consequences that are not limited to those who choose to engage in them.

Unlike the communal and natural contexts of the market, which remain outside the discipline of economics, this "spillover effect" of market transactions has been noticed and named within the discipline. The name given them is significant. They are called "externalities." The term suggests both that the phenomena are external to the market and also that they are external to the main body of theory built on the market as an economic concept.

What is "internal" and what is "external" to a "market" as conceived by the discipline is not determined by the real world but by the abstractions made from it. After the abstractions are made, there is a strong tendency not to notice what has been abstracted from. Economists did not notice the spillover effects in general until the 1920s. When something is noticed that does not fit the system built on the abstractions, then either the abstractions will be changed or the new phenomenon will be viewed as an "externality" deserving only of separate and peripheral attention. Ptolemaic astronomy is famous for having maintained its central model of circular motion in the face of contrary evidence by adding epicycles. The treatment of externalities in contemporary economics is like that, witnessing to the power of the original abstraction over the minds of economists. We believe that a model that would internalize "spillover effects"—that is, the interconnections among things—into the basic economic theory would be a better response. We also believe, as previously noted, that the frequency of appeal to externalities is a good index of the overall problem of misplaced concreteness in economic theory.

An externality occurs when production or consumption by one firm or consumer directly affects the welfare of another firm or consumer, where "directly" means that the effect is not mediated through any market and is consequently unpriced. "Nonmarket interdependence" is a close synonym for externality. In the common synonym we have used, "spillover effects," the image is that the effects of one person's acts on another's welfare are generally channeled through markets, but occasionally spill over the levee of the market channel so that third parties "get wet."

Such nonmarket interdependence can have positive or negative effects on welfare. As a positive effect, consider that if some people are vaccinated against polio, even those who are not vaccinated benefit since their probability of catching the disease is also reduced. People who pay for their own vaccinations are thus providing an external benefit, a positive externality, to others without receiving any compensation from them. We might hope that people would be glad of this external benefit to their neighbors, but economists assume that there will be a sufficient number of "free riders" (those who decline vaccination but are still effectively protected as long as most others are vaccinated) to cause resentment and a breakdown of the system. Fairness requires that the external benefit should be credited to the person who pays to be vaccinated and debited to the person who refuses to pay but also benefits. A subsidy to the vaccinated persons financed by general taxes would accomplish this result. This solution, however, is a collective action, not a free market outcome, and requires sufficient moral consensus to agree to tax free riders and subsidize the vaccinated in the public interest. It goes beyond pure individualism. To the extent that individuals' self-identity is constituted by relations of community, then free riding would be rare. But economists view individual identity as independent of community relations, and they expect free riding to be the rule rather than the exception. Nevertheless they do assume a degree of social cohesion and consensus sufficient to enact laws to diminish the opportunity to take a free ride.

Negative externalities are more prevalent. A standard example is a factory whose effluent into a river spoils fishing downstream. The factory does not have to pay the fishermen for the loss directly inflicted on them by the factory's actions. The standard solution is an effluent tax on the factory equal in value to the external costs imposed. This assumes that the use of the river for fishing dominates the use of the river as a waste receptacle. If the opposite were the case, then the fishermen would have to pay a tax sufficient to compensate the factory for the cost of having to dispose of its waste in a manner that did less harm to the fish. In either case the external cost is accounted for and reflected in the price of the product. In one case the river is held to belong to the fishermen, in the other case to the factory. Who should in effect "own" the river is an important question, but in either case the external cost is internalized, whether in the accounts of the factory or the fishermen.

If the upstream factory and the downstream fishermen were merged into a single conglomerate, then the external costs would become internal to the new firm. This does not mean that pollution would cease—only that it would be held to an "optimal" level. That would be the level at which the marginal cost of fish lost just equals the marginal benefit of cheaper waste disposal. The optimal level is thus the profit-maximizing level of pollution, where pollution counts as a cost.

Of course, this account, like most treatments of externalities in economics, greatly simplifies the real issues. In fact, the freedom of the river from pollution is ordinarily of interest for many diverse reasons to many people beside the fishermen, so that the full social cost would certainly not be internalized in the new firm. Chapter 10 will suggest that effects on fish cannot be fully measured by the costs to human beings alone. On the other side, the economic costs to the factory of reducing pollution may lead to its moving away or closing part of its operation. The result may be loss of livelihood for workers and weakening of the human community. As the circle of effects is pursued, the realization dawns that conforming reflections to what the discipline requires necessitates a simplification so drastic as to be erroneous and likely to mislead policymakers.

"Externality" is such an all-encompassing term that some distinctions have to be drawn. We distinguish between *localized* and *pervasive* externalities. The former can be dealt with, at least to some reasonable extent, by adjusting prices, or by other nonradical changes. Pervasive externalities, on the other hand, are general in scope, and cannot be effectively dealt with by tinkering with relative prices. They require quantitative limits or major institutional changes. There are also intermediate cases. The coal industry provides good examples of each category. Black lung disease is a localized externality: it is clearly associated with coal mining and nothing else. Only coal miners and their families are directly affected. Pervasive externalities associated with coal include CO_2 buildup (greenhouse effect) and acid rain. In these cases the costs do not fall only on a clearly defined group, nor is the cause traceable to a single localized activity. In this chapter we will consider mainly localized externalities, because that is all standard economic theory knows how to deal with. The more challenging and realistic issue of pervasive externalities will be treated in Chapter 7.

All conclusions in economic theory about the social efficiency of pure competition and the free market are explicitly premised on the absence of externalities. The undeniable importance of externalities in today's world is therefore a serious challenge to the relevance of these conclusions. The challenge has been met very forthrightly by declaring that all external costs and benefits must be "internalized" in the money price paid by whoever buys the good or service the production of which gave rise to the external cost. Usually the adjustment is assumed to be made by a tax which would be calculated to measure the external cost of the commodity. Adding this per unit Pigovian tax (after A. C. Pigou [1920], who first suggested such an adjustment) to the market would in effect represent the addition of external cost to internal or private cost, giving the full social cost. Decisions by consumers and producers would then be made in the light of full-cost prices. In the case of an external benefit or positive externality, the proper Pigovian tax would be negative; that is, a subsidy. In theory, the solution is neat and simple—if prices to the consumer do not measure full cost, then adjust those prices by means of adding a tax in the amount that results in full cost, and the market's efficiency is restored.

Coal mining companies could be required to pay the full cost of black lung disease among coal miners. To do this they would charge a higher price for coal in order fully to cover all medical expenses of miners with black lung disease. To the naive citizen who asks, "But can our society afford to pay those costs?"—the answer is that society is already paying them. It is not a question of choosing whether to pay or not pay external costs. The costs are there and will be paid by someone: either the miner, the general public through socialized medical care, or the producers and users of coal who pay a sufficiently high price for coal to cover these costs. If the miner gets no medical attention then he pays the cost in terms of suffering and lost years of life. The principle of internalization argues that the producers of coal should bear the cost, since it is they who undertake the activity that gives rise to the cost. All or part of the increased cost is passed on to consumers in the form of a higher price for coal. That is as it should be. Economizing on the use of more costly coal means that less will be produced, and the incidence of black lung will decline. Internalization creates an incentive to reduce the activity that produces the external cost. If the external costs were not internalized in the price of coal but were paid through the tax system, they would still be paid, but not by the people who use the product the production of which gives rise to the cost. This mode of payment gives no incentive to reduce the cost-generating activity. On the contrary, if the general public rather than the producers and consumers of coal pay for black lung, then the coal industry will find it unprofitable to take any measures at all to reduce black lung disease, since the cost is being paid by others. The principle of internalization is not only equitable (whoever causes the cost should pay for it) but also socially efficient (the one who pays the cost is also the one who is in a position to reduce the activity that causes the cost and will benefit from doing so).

To some it appears that in this case equity and community conflict with efficiency. They would argue that since everyone needs coal and benefits from its use, then everyone should share in paying the social costs of pneumoconiosis, and that it should be done in a community manner through the tax system. This is certainly better than leaving the coal miner uncompensated. However, requiring the users of coal to pay the added cost is a person-in-community solution. It rejects the collectivism of totally socializing costs, and the individualism of letting the coal miner bear his own misfortune. It says, let us as a community abide by the rule that the prices we pay for commodities should reflect the full value of all the sacrifices required for the production of that commodity. We do not want cheap coal at the expense of coal miners' diseased lungs. The least that we, the users of coal, can do is to pay the cost of medical treatment, or preferably the cost of prevention. By paying the external cost in the price rather than through the tax system, we give consumers the incentive to economize not only on the depletion of coal, but also on depletion of the coal miner's health. We give coal producers an incentive to reduce black lung disease just as they have an incentive to reduce any other cost. As for the argument that since everyone benefits from coal, all should share the external cost collectively as taxpayers, we can reply that internalization means that all will indeed not only pay, but will pay in exact proportion to the use they make of coal. If coal use is truly universal, then payment will automatically be universal also. Internalization accomplishes everything that socialization accomplishes plus a great deal more by way of avoiding perverse incentives and establishing cost-reducing incentives.

The individualistic free marketeer would argue in reply that the miner's wages, in a perfectly competitive market, would already include a premium for risk of black lung. Therefore there is no external cost in the first place. This is, of course, true, but simply another way of saying that if the miners had alternative employment without the risk of black lung, to which they could move without cost, then they would do it in order to escape the mine. To get them to return as miners the employer would have to pay them a premium to make it worth their while. The availability of such alternatives, along with costless mobility, is what perfect competition means—but perfect competition is unrealistically abstract, in this case, since the miners are not free to move at will.

Another example comes from four fertilizer producing companies along the Mississippi River in Louisiana. The companies want to dump into the river 10 to 12 million tons per year of gypsum, which contains cadmium and low-level radioactivity. Negative consequences for New Orleans' water supply and the oyster, shrimp, and fishing industries along the Louisiana Gulf coast are probable. The companies have been piling up mountains of gypsum and are running out of space. If they have to pay for transporting the gypsum to the deep ocean for dumping, they claim they will not be competitive and will have to close, eliminating jobs from Louisiana's already depressed economy. It is a familiar story. It would appear that these companies have been keeping fertilizer prices lower than full cost, in the expectation that they would at some time be able to externalize their deferred waste disposal costs—literally throw them on to fishermen and residents of New Orleans, and indeed all eaters of seafood and drinkers of water. Already we are moving away from the localized externality toward the pervasive. Even so, internalization of waste disposal costs into the price of fertilizer remains a reasonable solution. If that means that less fertilizer is produced, then so be it. We should never sacrifice more value to produce an extra amount of product that is of less value than what was sacrificed. Of course it is still possible to accept internalization of costs in principle while arguing that as a matter of fact the external costs of dumping are negligible. One may claim that concentrations of cadmium and radio-activity are small, they won't hurt the oysters, nothing bad has happened so far, and so on. And of course in dealing with a novel event there is always a legitimate range of uncertainty, and expert witnesses can be found on both sides—though seldom on the side contrary to their employer's interests.

Sometimes internalization of costs can be effected without Pigovian taxes. One example of internalizing costs of water pollution along a river is to require that a plant's intake pipe be located downstream from its outflow pipe. The same internalizing effect occurs, as already mentioned, if an upstream firm merges with a downstream firm. The new firm will now count the cost of its upstream plant polluting its down-stream plant. Another somewhat trivial but instructive example occurred in the student union of a university. The presence of a juke box created the external cost of noise, which disrupted conversation. Conversationalists petitioned for removal of the offending machine. Music lovers petitioned to keep it, arguing that it was a very democratic machine—if you do not like what you hear you can vote with your quarters to hear something else. But the conversationalists replied that what they wanted to hear, silence, was not among the options offered. The ingenious resolution was to include a three-minute silent disk among the records. While not precisely a case of internalizing external costs, this comes close in that it restores an excluded alternative value (silence) among the market options.

Allocation, Distribution, and Scale

In addition to these three limitations of the market—maintaining competition, restraining self-interest, and externalities—there are two further incapacities of the market. One is well recognized and has already been mentioned in connection with our brief discussion of Pareto optimality. This is simply the observation that efficient allocation does not imply just distribution. The other is less well recognized but quite analogous: efficient allocation does not imply an optimal scale of the economy relative to the ecosystem. It does not even imply a scale that is ecologically sustainable.

The market does only one thing: it solves the allocation problem by providing the necessary information and incentive. It does that one thing very well, when supplemented by enough community or collective action to maintain competition, restrain self-interest, and deal with public goods and externalities. But these two additional limitations are of a different kind: they are not allocation problems at all, but are independent questions of distribution and scale.

In pricing factors and distributing profits, the market does of course influence the distribution of income. Providing incentive requires some ability to alter the distribution of income in the interests of efficiency. The point is that the market's criterion for distributing income is efficient allocation, not justice. In any case, historical conditions of property ownership are major determinants of income distribution and have little to do with either efficiency or justice. These two values can conflict, and the market does not automatically resolve this conflict. This is recognized by economists today, but there still exists a residual feeling from the heyday of marginal productivity theory under the influence of John Bates Clark that the market rewards everyone in close proportion to his or her contribution to the total product. It is simply incorrect, however, to think of marginal product as measuring an *individual's* contribution to the economy, since the marginal product of one factor is determined by the availability of all other factors as well as by the state of technology.

The market has no built-in tendency to grow only up to the scale of aggregate resource use that is optimal (or even merely sustainable) in its demands on the biosphere. Internalization of externalities is a good policy for improving allocation, but it provides no answer to the issue of optimum scale.

If one starts from the vision of the economic process as an open subsystem of a closed finite total system, then the question of how big the subsystem should be relative to the total system is hard to avoid. How then have we managed to avoid it? In two ways: first by viewing the economic subsystem as infinitesimally small relative to the total system, so that scale becomes irrelevant because negligible; second, by viewing the economy as coextensive with the total system—if the economy includes everything then the issue of scale relative to a total system simply does not arise. These alternatives correspond to Boulding's colorful distinction between the "cowboy economy" and the "spaceman economy" (1968). The cowboy of the infinite plains lives off linear throughput from source to sink, with no need to recycle anything. The spaceman in a small capsule lives off of tight material cycles and immediate feedbacks, all under total control subservient to his needs. For the cowboy, scale of his economy is negligible; for the spaceman, scale is total. There is no separate ecosystem relative to which the scale of the spaceman economy must be determined; there is no ecosystem, only economy. In each of these polar cases the only problem is allocation—scale is irrelevant. It is only in the middle ground between the cowboy and the spaceman that the issue of scale does not get conflated with allocation. But the middle ground happens to be where we are. Between the cowboy and the spaceman economies is a whole range of larger and smaller "bull-in-the-china-shop economies" where scale is a major concern. We are not cowboys because the existing scale of the economy is far from negligible compared to the environment. But neither are we spacemen, because the vast number of matter-energy transformations of the ecosystem are not subject to human control either by prices or by central planning. In a finite system subject to the conservation of mass, the more that is brought under our economic control, the less remains under the spontaneous control of nature. As our exactions from and insertions back to the ecosystem increase in scale, the qualitative change induced in the ecosystem must also increase. The feedbacks from these accelerating modifications of the ecosystem are characterized by surprise, uncertainty, and novelty (Perrings 1987). This leads us to the theme of pervasive externalities, which will be discussed in Chapter 7.

Those who want to rely on the market for allocation will only weaken their case if they expect the market also to solve the independent problems of distribution and scale. These are a part of the community context that a market society must both presuppose and nurture. Scale and distribution are data required by the market to solve the allocation problem and are not themselves variables to be solved for by the market. We will return to the issues of scale and distribution in Chapter 7.

Polanyi's Distinction between "Market" and "market"

The exchange of commodities during fairs and market days is a practice of ancient origin. The market in this sense existed in feudalism, and continues to exist even in communism. This exchange of products Polanyi refers to as market with a little "m." It is not the basic organizing principle of the economy. The Market as the basic organizing principle of society had its historical origin in the transition from feudalism to capitalism. It is what today's economists blandly refer to as the "factors market." Its creation required the transformation of nature into land, life into labor, and patrimony into capital. This was for Polanyi "the great transformation"—the conversion of the means of production (not just their products) into commodities to be allocated by the market—or in this case, the Market. Land was abstracted from the totality of the natural world and treated as an exchangeable commodity. Work time or labor was abstracted out of life and treated as a commodity to be valued and exchanged according to supply and demand. Capital was abstracted out of the social inheritance, no longer to be treated as a collective patrimony or heirloom, but as an exchangeable source of unearned income to individuals (Polanyi [1944] 1957).

But labor is not just a commodity like any other, to be priced by supply and demand. The price of other commodities can approach or become zero if necessary to clear the market. The wage of labor cannot fall below a subsistence minimum, which may be defined biologically in poor countries or by custom and social standards in wealthy countries. Welfare depends on conditions of work perhaps even more than on commodities purchased with the wage. These points are obvious and have given rise to a subdiscipline of labor economics, which, thirty years ago, emphasized these differences but which now seems more devoted to celebrating the commodity aspect of labor.

Land too is a very peculiar commodity. The biosphere exists in the land, but does not separate its functions along lines drawn by surveyors and according to plots bought and sold in the real estate market. We will have much to say in future chapters about land as the basis of biophysical and social community. We do not, however, give equal treatment to the problems arising from the commodification of labor, much less from the conversion of patrimony into capital. This is a limitation of our work. However, the commodification of labor and capital has been widely discussed for many years. We recognize the importance of these topics, but have little to add to the discussion. We do feel that we have something to add on the issue of land—hence our focus.

3

Misplaced Concreteness:
Measuring Economic Success

The GNP: Its Political Importance

Economists want the market to perform well. They are deeply convinced that when the market performs well, people in general benefit. Most of their research is geared accordingly in one way or another to understanding what makes the market function well.

Although many of their theories about healthy market functioning are deductive, economists are also interested in measurements of market success, both in particular sectors of the market and for the market as a whole. The single most important measure in this country is the gross national product. Almost all economists view growth in GNP, or GNP per capita, as a sign of a healthy market, which means for them a healthy economy.

With respect to some aspects of economic teaching, such as opposition to government intervention in the labor market, the economists are regularly overruled by the public, acting through its elected representatives. But with respect to growth as measured by GNP, there has been no major public dissent. Both political parties are committed to economic progress, and for both that means an increased GNP. When alarm is expressed about the difficulty of stimulating adequate growth today, the meaning is that the policies adopted have not sufficiently increased the GNP. The general public also accepts this view of economic health and is more likely to keep a party in power when it believes the economy—and that means chiefly the GNP—is growing.

Other countries also measure their national products. Although complete standardization has not been attained and difficulties in intercountry comparisons are recognized, the GNP measurements are also used by international financial agencies to measure the comparative success of development programs. Both the World Bank and the International Monetary Fund shape their policies by this indicator. Successful economic development *means* that the rate of increase of per capita GNP is satisfactory.

Humanitarians also often cite GNP figures. Their object is to arouse our sympathy for people whose income is very low. They usually imply that the countries with high per capita GNP should find means of transferring some of their wealth to countries with low per capita GNP. In short, GNP as the standard measure of economic success is accepted by economists, politicians, financiers, humanitarians, and the general public. It is enormously important. This makes its closer examination worthwhile.

All groups assume that GNP measures something of importance to the economy and most assume that this is closely bound up with human welfare. It is recognized, of course, that human welfare has dimensions other than the economic one. But it is rightly held that the economic element in welfare is *very* important, and that the stronger the economy the greater the contribution to human welfare. It is also often thought that the economy is the major area of welfare subject to political influence. In any case, there is little consensus on any other measurement, so that none of the others that have been proposed exert a remotely comparable influence on public policy.

The tendency to forget that the GNP measures only some aspects of welfare and to treat it as a general index of national well-being is, of course, a typical instance of the fallacy of misplaced concreteness. It is obvious and need not detain us. It can be countered by giving increasing visibility to social indicators, such as the Physical Quality of Life Index, which measures literacy, infant mortality, and life expectancy at age one. Indicators of ecological health should also be developed and publicized. Although not stated in the form of statistical indexes, Lester Brown's annual *State of the World* volumes help in this regard.

The assumption that economic welfare as measured by GNP can simply be added to other elements of welfare reflects the view of reality that underlies the academic world generally. The whole is found, supposedly, by putting together the parts into which it is divided for study. That assumes that the parts are in fact unchanged by their abstraction from the whole. That is clearly not true. Hence the first question to ask is whether growth in the economy as measured by GNP actually contributes to the total well-being of people.

Until recently this question was hardly raised, and even today it is not taken seriously in most economic and political circles. Nevertheless, the question is now before the world. There is a mounting chorus of critics who point out how high the cost of growth of GNP has been in psychological, sociological, and ecological terms (Wachtel 1983). The relation of GNP to total human welfare requires further discussion.

But there is also a question about the relation of GNP to economic welfare itself. This question is familiar to economists. Indeed, no knowledgeable economist supposes that the GNP is a perfect measure of welfare. Most recognize both that the market activity that GNP measures has social costs that it ignores, and that it counts positively market activity devoted to countering these same social costs. Obviously GNP overstates welfare! There are other weaknesses that make it vulnerable to ridicule. But there is a widespread assumption that these are minor weaknesses and that what the GNP measures comes close enough to economic welfare that it can be used without further ado in a whole range of practical contexts. When economists or political leaders forget that what is measured by GNP is quite distinct from economic welfare, and when they then draw conclusions from the GNP about economic welfare, the fallacy of misplaced concreteness appears again. Although economists quickly acknowledge this, they as quickly deny its importance. Our task will be to examine more closely the discussion of GNP and economic welfare to determine whether this wide consensus among economists is justified or whether the fallacy, in this instance, is more important than they suppose. We will discuss two moves away from GNP. First we consider a move toward a conceptually more correct concept of income (Hicksian income). The issue here is not to measure welfare at all, but simply to do a better job of measuring income. Of course there is a relation between income and welfare, and a better measure of income is likely to be a better index of welfare also, but Hicksian income does not directly address the relation to economic welfare in general. The second move away from GNP is toward a measure of economic welfare. Examining this move does involve us in the relation of income to welfare, component by component, both in this chapter in our review of the attempts of others, and in the Appendix, where we offer our own attempt at designing an index of welfare.

GNP: Concepts and Measurement

For a standard textbook account of GNP, we are using Howard J. Sherman's *Elementary Aggregate Economics* (1966). So far as we can tell it differs little from other standard treatments:

The gross national product (GNP) may be calculated in two different ways, corresponding to the money flow from households to business or the equal money flow from business to households. In the first way, we examine the aggregate money demand for all products. This is the flow of money spending on consumer goods, investment goods, government expenditure, and net export spending. . . .

The second way is to add up the money paid out by businesses for all of its costs of production. Most of these costs of production constitute flows of money income to households. These incomes include wages paid for services of labor, rent for the use of land, interest for the use of borrowed capital, and profit for capital invested. [pp. 30–31]

The text notes that depreciation and excise taxes must be added to the second way. When this is done, the first and second ways must attain identical results. Equality between the spending and income streams is guaranteed by the residual nature of profit. Any difference between the two streams appears as either profit or loss, which when added to the income stream guarantees the equality of the two flows.

Sherman goes on to show that by subtracting depreciation from GNP one arrives at *net national product;* by subtracting indirect business taxes also, one arrives at *national income;* by subtracting retained corporate profits, corporate income taxes, and contributions for social insurance and adding government transfer payments and net interest paid by government, one arrives at *personal income;* and by subtracting personal income taxes from this, one arrives at *disposable personal income.*

If Sherman were asked directly whether GNP is a measure of economic welfare, we are not sure what he would answer. But that he regards it as such for practical purposes and communicates this regard to his readers there can be no doubt. After having cautioned that each industry's contribution to the national product is only the value added rather than the total value of its output, he writes:

A second qualification is necessary if we wish to measure accurately the year-to-year improvement *in national welfare.* . . . We must always deflate the changes in the money value of the national product by the price changes to find the real amount of change in the national product.

Lastly, we may not be interested in the total national product but in the national product per person of the population. . . . Therefore, if we wish to measure the improvement in *individual welfare,* we must always deflate the increase in our total national product by the increase in our population. [emphasis added; pp. 52–53]

One would expect from this textbook account that the actual measure of the GNP in the National Income Accounts was a straight measure of market activity only. There are those who would find this limitation beneficial in their work (Eckstein 1983). However, this has never been the case.

The reason that GNP has never been based on market activity alone is that this would distort the actual economic situation drastically. From the beginning of the accounts, two major additions to market activity have been the food and fuel produced and consumed by farm families and the rental value of owner-occupied dwellings. The reason for including these is obvious. Consider a scenario. Suppose one lives in a home one rents from someone else while owning a house elsewhere that one rents out to another party. Both rentals constitute market activity. If, then, one moves into one's own home, market activity is reduced, and if only market activity is counted then the GNP is reduced. Yet intuitively, no one feels that the economy has been damaged. (Also imputed have been the value of food and clothing provided to the military, and banking services rendered to depositors without payment [Ruggles 1983, p. 40].

Our point is that from the beginning there has been a tension in the consideration of what it is that GNP measures. The tension is visible in the textbook accounts. On the one hand, the emphasis is on market activity. On the other hand, there is a concern to make judgments about improvement in welfare. The GNP has emphasized the market but has made modest adjustments in the direction of welfare by imputing a value to farm-family production of household consumed goods and to owner-occupied housing. But the same logic that justifies the inclusion of these items would justify the inclusion of many others. Accordingly, many proposals have been advanced to impute additional values in computing the GNP. Thus far, none have been adopted. As Otto Eckstein comments, "NIPA [national income and product accounts] has many purposes: to gauge economic performance, compare economic welfare over time and across countries, measure the mix of resource use between private and public sectors and between consumption and investment, and to identify the functional distribution of income and of the tax burden. Inevitably, these purposes clash and the accounts must be a compromise" (Eckstein 1983, p. 316).

A compromise cannot be completely satisfactory to anyone. Our concern, however, is not whether as a result of the compromise comparisons of "economic welfare over time and across countries" are slightly warped, but whether the GNP, which remains primarily a measure of market activity, is in general a useful measure of economic welfare at all. Might it not be better to have a measure of market activity that would work well for the more technical purposes to which the GNP is put, and which made no adjustments whatever in the direction of measuring welfare? Then the question of how much correlation there is between increasing market activity and the economic welfare of the people could be asked more clearly and neutrally.

There is a second respect in which the GNP fails to be a pure measure of market activity. At some points it also concerns itself with wealth; specifically, capital. This is apparent where depreciation is included as a part of the cost of doing business. This operates in a rather odd way. The greater the depreciation of capital assets of business in a given year, the greater the GNP (all other things being equal). The decline in the value of a factory and its equipment increases the GNP. That this decline is not a contribution to economic welfare is recognized by the deletion of this figure in calculating the net national product and the national income. But we must remember that it is GNP rather than these other figures that functions in most comparative studies of economic welfare.

These comments indicate that although depreciation of capital assets does enter into GNP figures, it does so in a way that is opposite to its relation to national wealth. Some of the figures in the GNP do indicate a positive relation to the increase of national wealth; others are neutral in this respect and some, as we have seen, are negative. It is possible to ask whether measures of national wealth might not correlate more highly with national economic welfare than does either market activity or GNP. In fact, one great economist, Irving Fisher, argued strongly that this is the case (Fisher 1906). In Fisher's view nearly all consumer goods are classed as capital or as wealth, and their consumption represents depreciation. For Fisher, welfare is the service (the psychic sense of want satisfaction) rendered by this wealth, and for the most part would have to be imputed—for example, the value of the annual service of your overcoat is what it would cost you to rent it, which is the same imputation as with owner-occupied houses, only more difficult since we have no rental markets for overcoats. But the logic is the same. It is at least essential that no one suppose that GNP measures national wealth or has any necessary correlation with its increase or decrease.

None of these comments are intended to imply that the National Income and Product Accounts of the United States government or similar accounts in other countries are of no use. Our concern here is with one particular use—namely, use as a measure of economic welfare. Until we understand exactly what GNP does and does not measure, we cannot make reasonable judgments on this question.

Like most of what happens in the world, the explanation of why the GNP measures what it does is historical rather than systematic. The Commerce Department began reporting statistics on the net product of the national economy in 1934. But it has been noted that "it was the mobilization for World War II and the consequent demand for data relating to the economy as a whole that was primarily responsible for shaping the accounts. The central questions posed by the war were how much defense output could be produced and what impact defense production would have upon the economy as a whole" (Ruggles 1983, p. 17).

Similar developments were occurring in other countries, and the United States compared its approach with those of the British and Canadians during 1944. The next year the League of Nations convened a meeting on national income accounting. So, by 1947, the United States was ready to publish its newly developed national accounting system. Although this was supplemented in various ways in later years and revised in 1958 and 1965, with respect to our concerns it has remained basically unchanged.

There have, however, been critical discussions of the National Income Accounts that raised questions relevant to our concerns. This was especially true of the 1971 Conference on Income and Wealth, which did concern itself with welfare questions. It became clear that: "Many users considered that the present emphasis of the national income and product accounts on market transactions led to a perspective that was too narrow for the measurement of economic and social performance. It was cogently argued that additional information was required on nonmarket activity, on the services of consumer and government durables and intangible investment, and on environmental costs and benefits" (Ruggles 1983, p. 332).

There was some discussion of the evaluation of leisure. But such considerations involved large imputations that would render the accounts less useful to "those who used the national accounts for the analysis of economic activity in the short run, with a focus on inflation, the business cycle, and fiscal policy" (Ruggles 1983, p. 332). For this reason the concerns of those interested in measuring long-term economic and social performance have not been dealt with in the accounts. On the other hand:

> BEA has established a new program to develop measures of nonmarket activity within the framework of GNP accounts. In part this work is a response to

the emphasis put on this topic at the 1971 Conference on Income and Wealth, but it also reflects the strong interest in environmental studies within the Department of Commerce. The federal government's concern with the measurement of the costs of pollution control and environmental damage has stimulated work in this area. BEA's current program, however, includes not only environmental questions but also (1) time spent in nonmarket work and leisure, (2) the services of consumer durables, and (3) the services of government capital. The close relationship to the national income accounting system in this work is stressed, but as yet it has not been formally integrated. [Ruggles 1983, p. 35]

The tension we have noted between a measure of market activity and a measure of economic welfare is clearly being felt by those responsible for National Income Accounts. The problem seems to be insoluble as long as the effort is to have a single summary figure, such as GNP.

Richard Ruggles, whose historical account we have been following, concludes:

There is no well-defined universe of nonmarket activities and imputations to be covered. The set of all possible imputations is unbounded. The only criterion that can be employed is whether the imputations are considered to be useful and necessary for the particular purpose at hand. . . .

For all these reasons, an explicit separation of market transactions from imputations in the national accounts would seem highly desirable. . . . It would be recognized, however, that imputations alone cannot meet the information needs for measuring economic and social performance. . . . No amount of imputation can convert a one-dimensional summary measure such as the GNP into an adequate or appropriate measure of social welfare. [pp. 41–43]

From GNP to Hicksian Income and Sustainable Development

Not only is GNP a poor measure of welfare, it is also a poor measure of income. In this chapter, as well as in Chapter 7 and in the Appendix, the effort is to move from GNP toward a measure of welfare. This is a very difficult task involving many controversial issues. In this section, the focus is on the less controversial issue of converting GNP into a better measure of income. Unlike welfare the concept of income has a fairly clear theoretical definition, although there are big problems in making that definition operational. In measuring welfare one cannot avoid to a large extent implicitly defining the concept by one's very measure of it. With income we have an explicit independent definition to which our measurements may to a greater or lesser degree correspond. With welfare we have no such independent theoretical definition. It is therefore useful to keep these two departures from GNP quite separate.

The central criterion for defining the concept of income has been well stated by Sir John Hicks in *Value and Capital*:

> The purpose of income calculations in practical affairs is to give people an indication of the amount which they can consume without impoverishing themselves. Following out this idea, it would seem that we ought to define a man's income as the maximum value which he can consume during a week, and still expect to be as well off at the end of the week as he was at the beginning. Thus when a person saves he plans to be better off in the future; when he lives beyond his income he plans to be worse off. Remembering that the practical purpose of income is to serve as a guide for prudent conduct, I think it is fairly clear that this is what the central meaning must be. [1948, p. 172]

The same basic idea of income holds at the national level and for annual time periods. Income is not a precise theoretical concept but rather a practical rule-of-thumb guide to the maximum amount that can be consumed by a nation without eventual impoverishment. We all know that we cannot consume the entire GNP without eventually impoverishing ourselves, so we subtract depreciation to get net national product (NNP), which is usually taken as income in Hicks's sense. Note that the central defining characteristic of income is *sustainability*. The term "sustainable income" ought therefore to be considered a redundancy. The fact that it is not is a measure of how far we have strayed from the central meaning of income, and consequently of the need for correction.

But could we really consume even NNP year after year without impoverishing ourselves? No, we could not, for two reasons: first, because the production of NNP at the present scale requires supporting biophysical transformations (environmental extractions and insertions) that are not ecologically sustainable; second, because NNP overestimates net product available for consumption by counting many defensive expenditures (expenditures necessary to defend ourselves from the unwanted side-effects of production) as final products rather than as intermediate costs of production. Consequently, NNP increasingly fails as a guide to prudent conduct by nations.

For example, a developing country may obtain 6% of its GNP from timber exports. Perhaps 2% of that is based on sustained yield exploitation and the remaining 4% is based on deforestation. The maximum sustainable consumption has been overestimated by 4%, not even counting the loss of unpriced natural services of the forest. That may sound small, but in an economy whose conventional GNP was growing at 3%, a 4% reduction is the difference between growth and decline, which makes a very big qualitative difference in a nation's perception of itself and its policies, and, indeed, of its leaders. The last difference is one reason for resistance to this change in income accounting. No politician wants to be known as the minister under whom the country went from growth to decline in one year! Yet there is an opportunity for someone to be known as the leader who finally introduced the income accounting system that saved the nation from eventual impoverishment (Repetto 1987, pp. 94–99).

Two adjustments to NNP are necessary to arrive at a good approximation to Hicksian income and a better guide to prudent behavior. One adjustment is a straightforward extension of the principle of depreciation to cover consumption of natural capital stocks depleted as a consequence of production. The other is to subtract defensive (regrettably necessary) expenditures made to defend ourselves from the unwanted side effects of growing aggregate production and consumption. Defensive expenditures are of the nature of intermediate goods; that is, they are costs of production rather than final products available for consumption. To correct for having counted defensive expenditures in NNP, their magnitude must be estimated and subtracted in order to arrive at an estimate of sustainable consumption or true income.

To summarize, let us define our corrected income concept, Hicksian income (HI), as net national product (NNP) minus both defensive expenditures (DE) and depreciation of natural capital (DNC). Thus,

$$HI = NNP - DE - DNC$$

No interference whatsoever with the current national accounts (or loss of historical continuity or comparability) is entailed in this suggestion. Two additional adjustment accounts are introduced, not for frivolous or trendy reasons, but simply to gain a better approximation to the central and well-established meaning of income. Since these two adjustment accounts are also relevant to our attempt to measure welfare, they will be discussed in that context and are not further considered here.

What does deserve some mention in this context is the recent surge of interest in "sustainable growth" or "sustainable development" within development agencies and Third World countries, following the publication of the Brundtland Report (1987). Although the two terms are used synonymously we suggest a distinction. "Growth" should refer to quantitative expansion in the scale of the physical dimensions of the economic system, while "development" should refer to the qualitative change of a physically nongrowing economic system in dynamic equilibrium with the environment. By this definition the earth is not growing, but it is developing. Any physical subsystem of a finite and nongrowing earth must itself also eventually become nongrowing. Therefore growth will become unsustainable eventually and the term "sustainable growth" would then be self-contradictory. But sustainable development does not become self-contradictory. Now that these terms have become buzzwords among the development agencies it is important to make this distinction, and even more important to define sustainable development in operational terms. If we had defined development operationally as an increase in Hicksian income rather than as an increase in GNP, then sustainability would have been guaranteed, as we have seen.

The main operational implication of Hicksian income is to keep capital intact. Our problem is that the capital we have endeavored to maintain intact is humanly created capital only. The category "natural capital" is left out. Indeed it is left out by definition as long as one defines capital as "(humanly) produced means of production." We suggest a functional definition of capital as a stock that yields a flow of goods or services. There are then two categories of capital, natural and humanly created. Natural capital is the nonproduced means of producing a flow of natural resources and services. Only humanly created capital has been maintained intact, along with some natural capital stocks that are privately owned (herds of cattle, plantation forests).

Why has natural capital been ignored? Aside from the past nonscarcity of natural capital due to the relatively small scale of the human economy, neoclassical economic theory has taught that humanly created capital is a near-perfect substitute for natural resources, and consequently for the stock of natural capital that yields the flow of these natural resources. Even if this assumed near-perfect substitutability were true, it would still be necessary to maintain intact total capital (humanly created plus natural) in arriving at Hicksian income. That is, the running down of natural capital would have to be offset by the accumulation of an equivalent amount of humanly created capital. Maintaining the total capital intact in this way might be referred to as "weak sustainability" in that it is based on generous assumptions about the substitutability of humanly created and natural capital (which imply high substitutability between capital and natural resources in production functions). By contrast, "strong sustainability" would require maintaining both humanly created and natural capital intact separately, on the assumption that they are complements rather than substitutes in most production functions (our reasons for believing that this is the case are given in Chapter 10). We advocate the strong sustainability approach to operationalizing sustainable development. But even weak sustainability would be an improvement over present practice.

Another approach that is relevant both to making GNP a better measure of income and to operationalizing the definition of sustainable development has been advanced by Salah El Serafy (1988). El Serafy tackles the difficult issue of how to treat receipts from nonrenewable resources in defining income (or, what comes to the same thing, how can a community avoid the absurdity of leaving its nonrenewable resources forever in the ground doing no one any good, yet not allow their exploitation to deflect the community from the path of sustainable development?). He argues that receipts from a nonrenewable resource can be divided into an income and a capital component. The income component is that portion of the receipts that could be consumed annually in perpetuity on the assumption that the remainder of the receipts were invested in renewable assets. The return on the renewable assets and the amount invested each year are such that when the nonrenewable resource is exhausted the new renewable assets will be yielding an amount equal to the income component of the receipts.

The basic logic underlying El Serafy's method is that "the finite series of earnings from the resource, say a 10-year series of annual extraction leading to the extinction of the resource, has to be converted to an infinite series of true income such that the capitalized value of the two series be equal. From the annual earnings from sale, an income portion has to be identified, capable of being spent on consumption, the remainder, the capital element, being set aside year after year to be invested in order to create a perpetual stream of income that would sustain the same level of *'true'* income, both during the life of the resource as well as after the resource had been exhausted."

To make the separation into income and capital components, it turns out that one need know only the rate of discount (which must ultimately be related to the rate of growth of renewable resources and the rate of growth of factor productivity, although this relation is not discussed by El Serafy), and the life expectancy of the nonrenewable resource (total reserve stock divided by the annual extraction rate). Social choices or assumptions about these magnitudes will allow the calculation of the percentage of the nonrenewable resource receipts that should be counted as income. For example, if the life expectancy of a nonrenewable resource is 10 years and the discount rate is 5%, then it can be shown that 42% of current receipts is income and the remaining 52% is the capital content that must be reinvested. Alternatively, if the discount rate were 10% and the life expectancy remained at 10 years, the income component would be 65%. A discount rate of 10% and a life expectancy of 50 years would result in a 99% income component.

El Serafy's method is elegant and parsimonious in terms of its information requirements. The effect of rising costs of extraction can be taken into account as a reduction of reserves. The whole calculation can be redone on the assumption of rising relative price of resources, rather than the assumption of constant prices used for simplicity. As a correction of GNP, El Serafy's method is more radical than the subtraction of depletion of natural capital from NNP, because it would change the very calculation of GNP itself. Instead of keeping the present overestimate of Hicksian income and then subtracting an adjustment figure, El Serafy's method would avoid the overestimate from the beginning by calculating GNP differently. While this is logically neater, it is politically more difficult to convince national income accountants to do this because it sacrifices historical continuity in the way accounts are kept. But even if the estimation of a natural capital depreciation adjustment account were favored for this reason, El Serafy's method would still be useful in calculating natural resource depreciation, which would still be receipts in excess of the income component, assuming this amount was being consumed rather than invested. In the Appendix we seek to employ El Serafy's method in this way, and in that context we will point out some technical difficulties with it.

If a development bank or agency takes sustainable development as its guiding principle, then, ideally, each of the projects it finances should be sustainable. Whenever this is not possible, as with the exploitation of a nonrenewable resource, there should be a complementary project that would insure sustainability for the two taken together. The receipts from the nonrenewable extraction should be divided into an income and capital component as discussed above, with the capital component invested each year in the renewable complement (long-run replacement). Furthermore if projects or combinations of projects must be sustainable, then it is inappropriate to calculate the net benefits of a project or policy alternative by comparing it with an unsustainable option— that is, by using a discount rate that reflects rates of return on alternative uses of capital that are themselves unsustainable. For example, if a sustainably managed forest can yield 4% and is judged an uneconomic use of land on the basis of a 6% discount rate, which on closer inspection turns out to be based on unsustainable uses of resources, including perhaps the unsustainable clearing of that same forest, then clearly the decision simply boils down to sustainable versus unsustainable use. If we have already adopted a policy of sustainable development, then of course we choose the sustainable alternative, and the fact that it has a negative present value when calculated at a nonsustainable discount rate is simply irrelevant. The present value criterion itself is not irrelevant because we are still interested in efficiency—in choosing the best sustainable alternative. But the discount rate must then reflect only *sustainable* alternative uses of capital. The allocation rule for attaining a goal efficiently (maximize present value) cannot be allowed to subvert the very goal of sustainable development that it is supposed to be serving! Use of an unsustainable discount rate would do just that. We suspect that discount rates in excess of 5% often reflect unsustainable alternatives. At least one should be required to give, say, five concrete examples of sustainable projects that yield 10% before one uses that figure as a discount rate.

Given acceptance of the goal of sustainable development, there still remains the question of the level of community at which to seek this goal. International trade allows one country to draw on the ecological carrying capacity of another country and thus be unsustainable in isolation, even though sustainable as part of a larger trading bloc. The trade issue raises again the question of complementarity versus substitutibility of natural and humanly created capital. If we follow the path of strong sustainability then this complementarity must be respected either at the national or international level. A single country may substitute humanly created for natural capital to a high degree if it can import the products of natural capital (the flow of natural resources and services) from other countries that have retained their natural capital to a greater degree. In other words, the demands of complementarity can be evaded at the national level, but only if they are respected at the international level. One country's ability to substitute humanly created for natural capital to a high degree depends on some other country's making the opposite (complementary) choice. For reasons elaborated in Chapter 11, we advocate seeking this complementary balance of humanly created and natural capital mainly within each nation rather than between nations.

One reason for the unanimity of support given to the phrase "sustainable development" is precisely that it has been left rather vague—development is not distinguished from growth in the Brundtland Report, nor is there any distinction between strong and weak sustainability. Politically this was wise on the part of the author. They managed to put high on the international agenda a concept whose unstated implications were too radical for consensus at that time. But in so doing they have guaranteed eventual discussion of these radical implications. Consider, for example, two questions immediately raised by any attempt to operationalize their definition of sustainable development as development that "meets the needs of the present without compromising the ability of future generations to meet their own needs." First there is the question of distinguishing "needs" from extravagant luxuries or impossible desires. If "needs" includes an automobile for each of a billion Chinese, then sustainable development is impossible. The whole issue of *sufficiency* can no longer be avoided. Second, the question of not compromising "the ability of future generations to meet their own needs" requires an estimate of that ability. It may be estimated on the basis of either strong or weak sustainability, depending on assumptions about substitutability between natural and humanly created capital. This will force deeper discussion of the substitutability issue, which lies near the heart of present economic theory.

We are very grateful to the Brundtland Commission for their fine work on this critical issue and suspect that they were not unaware of the difficulties we have raised, but rather chose wisely not to try to go too far too fast. In legitimating the concept of sustainable development they have made it easier for others to press the issue further. We hope that the international development banks and agencies will not abandon the ideal of sustainable development as its radical implications are realized. However, we hope they will abandon the oxymoron "sustainable growth," which is beginning to function as a thought-stopping slogan.

From GNP to a Measure of Economic Welfare

Without claiming to devise a comprehensive measure of social welfare, it may still be possible to develop a convincing measure of the positive contribution of the economy to social welfare. This is the goal of Nordhaus and Tobin in the construction of a Measure of Economic Welfare (MEW). However, this goal was for them a means to another goal, namely, the demonstration that the consensus among economists is correct, and that the existing GNP correlates sufficiently well with economic welfare to make it unnecessary to use the instrument they devise! This is their clear conclusion despite their early statement that "maximization of GNP is not a proper objective of policy" (Nordhaus and Tobin 1972, p. 4). We will ignore this puzzling contradiction and describe their careful work on a new indicator, the MEW—in which they "attempt to allow for the more obvious discrepancies between GNP and economic welfare" (p. 6).

Nordhaus and Tobin begin with the GNP and make three types of adjustments: "Reclassification of GNP expenditures as consumption, investment, and intermediate; imputation for the services of consumer capital, for leisure, and for the product of household work; correction for some of the disamenities of urbanization" (p. 5). With the exception of environmental costs and benefits they covered all the questions raised in the 1971 Conference on Income and Wealth mentioned above. We will follow their argument in summary.

GNP is a measure of production, not consumption, whereas economic welfare is a matter of consumption. Hence, the first task is to separate consumption from investment and intermediate expenditures. This entails the deletion of depreciation, as is already accomplished in the NNP. Beyond this, Nordhaus and Tobin consider the effects of treating all durables as capital goods but find that this has little effect. More important is the result of allowing for government capital and reclassifying education and health expenditures as capital investments.

An especially interesting adjustment follows from the recognition that welfare correlates with per capita consumption rather than with gross consumption. To sustain per capita consumption for a rising population, some portion of the NNP must be reinvested. Nordhaus and Tobin accordingly subtract from NNP for this purpose to gain a "sustainable" per capita consumption figure. We will quote only these sustainable MEW figures.

The authors also note that some expenditures are regrettable necessities rather than contributions to welfare. In this category they place the costs of commuting to work, police services, sanitation services, road maintenance, and national defense. The assumption is that when more people spend longer periods driving to work, the increase in the GNP does not mean that more human wants are being satisfied. And so with the others. These figures are, accordingly, subtracted.

The second task is to make appropriate imputations for capital services, leisure, and nonmarket work. The latter two have a very large effect on the statistics, and there is no one indisputable method for valuing them. Nordhaus and Tobin propose three methods. The question is whether leisure and nonmarket activity are affected by technological progress. The authors prefer the measure that leaves the value of leisure unaffected by technical progress even though nonmarket productive activity is so affected. We will report only the statistics generated by this choice.

The third task is to consider urban disamenities. Nordhaus and Tobin recognize that there are negative "externalities" connected with economic growth and suggest that these are most apparent in urban life. "Some portion of the higher earnings of urban residents may be simply compensation for the disamenities of urban life and work. If so we should not count as a gain of welfare the full increments of NNP that result from moving a man from farm or small town to city" (p. 13).

We now have before us the full range of adjustments made by Nordhaus and Tobin. One or another may appear inappropriate to some. For example, it may be argued that police protection is a contribution to welfare, and that it should not be deleted. The counterargument, however, is convincing if our purpose is to compare welfare over time. The increasing cost of police protection does not imply that we are less vulnerable to crime than we were in the past. Should the social situation change so that much less protection were needed, this should not be regarded as a reduction of economic welfare.

The real question is whether the list of regrettable necessities is sufficiently inclusive. As Nordhaus and Tobin recognize, "the line between final and instrumental outlays is very hard to draw. For example, the philosophical problems raised by the malleability of consumer wants are too deep to be resolved in economic accounting. Consumers are susceptible to efforts of producers. Maybe all our wants are just regrettable necessities; maybe productive activity does no better than to satisfy the wants which it generates; maybe our net welfare product is tautologically zero" (pp. 8–9).

Having said this, they ignore the problem. The same problem has been briefly considered and dismissed by Denison and Jaszi, who believe that regrettables or defensive expenditures *should* be counted as final consumption, as is currently the case (Jaszi 1973). All expenditures, they argue, are basically defensive: thus food expenditures are a defense against hunger, clothing and housing expenditures defend against the cold and rain, and so forth—and even expenditures on churches defend against the devil! Clever though this riposte may be, it misses the point—namely that "defensive" means a defense against the *unwanted side effects of other* production, not a defense against normal baseline environmental conditions of cold, rain, and so on. It is not the case that "our net welfare product is tautologically zero." Defensive expenditures are only those that were "regrettably made necessary" by other acts of production, and consequently should be counted as costs of that other production; that is to say, counted as intermediate rather than final goods.

We are now ready to consider the results of Nordhaus and Tobin's new MEW. What is of special interest to us is how it correlates with GNP, since the question of whether growth of GNP indicates improved economic welfare motivated the whole study. First, we will quote the conclusion of Nordhaus and Tobin, and then we will examine the figures on the basis of which they make their judgment: "Although the numbers presented here are very tentative, they do suggest the following observations. First, MEW is quite different from conventional output measures. Some consumption items omitted from GNP are of substantial quantitative importance. Second, our preferred variant of per capita MEW has been growing more slowly than per capita NNP (1.1% for MEW as against 1.7% for NNP, at annual rates over the period (1929–65). Yet MEW has been growing. The progress indicated by conventional national accounts is not just a myth that evaporates when a welfare-oriented measure is substituted"[1] (p. 17).

When their findings are more carefully examined for time frames other than the full period from 1929–65, the relatively close association between growth of per capita GNP and MEW disappears.[2] For example, between 1945 and 1947, per capita GNP fell about 15% (from $2,528 to $2,142) while per capita sustainable MEW rose by over 16% (from $5,098 to $5,934). Of course, this is the period of demobilization after World War II, so no conclusions should be drawn from this short-term negative relationship. Yet the presumption that the growth of GNP could be used as a reasonable proxy for MEW growth does not find confirmation in other periods either. From 1935 to 1945, per capita GNP rose almost 90% (from $1,332 to $2,528), while per capita sustainable MEW rose only about 13% (from $4,504 to $5,098). More significantly, during the postwar period, 1947–65, when neither depression nor war nor

1. In fact the growth rate of per capita MEW from 1929 to 1965 was only 1.0% per year, as opposed to 1.1%. The correct evaluation can be found in table 18 on p. 56 of Nordhaus and Tobin's study.

2. We have chosen to compare per capita MEW with per capita GNP rather than with per capita NNP as Nordhaus and Tobin have done. We do this for the sake of consistency with other studies (especially the one by Zolotas, discussed below). The differences in annual growth rates are not large, though the growth of per capita NNP is slightly slower than for per capita GNP.

recovery had a major impact on growth rates, per capita GNP rose about 6 times as fast as per capita sustainable MEW.[3] (Per capita GNP grew by 48% or about 2.2% per year, while per capita sustainable MEW grew by 7.5% or about 0.4% per year.) Moreover, if we assume, as Nordhaus and Tobin did in one of their options, that the productivity of housework has not increased at the same rate as the productivity of market activities, then per capita sustainable MEW actually registers a decline of 2% during the period 1947–65. Alternatively, we might consider the growth of per capita sustainable MEW in the absence of any imputation for leisure or household production because, as Nordhaus and Tobin admit, "Imputation of the consumption value of leisure and nonmarket work presents severe conceptual and statistical problems. Since the magnitudes are large, differences in resolution of these problems make big differences in overall MEW estimates" (Nordhaus and Tobin 1972, p. 39).

If that imputation is omitted, per capita sustainable MEW grows by 2% from 1947 to 1965. In any case, whether the appropriate figure for the change during that period in per capita sustainable MEW is 7.5%, 2%, or −2%, each of these results suggest that in fact "the progress indicated by conventional national accounts is . . . just a myth that evaporates when a welfare-oriented measure is substituted" (1972, p. 13). With their own figures, Nordhaus and Tobin have shed doubt on the thesis that national income accounts serve as a good proxy measure of economic welfare.

Nordhaus reflected again on the significance of his work with Tobin five years later. His interpretation of the results was unchanged: "Although GNP and other national income aggregates are imperfect measures of the economic standard of living, the broad picture of secular progress that they convey remains after correction for their most obvious deficiencies" (Nordhaus 1977, p. 197).

He had still failed to remark upon the lack of similarity between the growth of MEW and GNP during the last 18 years of the period that he and Tobin had reviewed.

Net National Welfare: Japan

Although Nordhaus and Tobin decided that the similarity between MEW and GNP sufficed to drop pursuit of the former as an independent mea-

3. Interestingly, though Nordhaus and Tobin calculate the growth rate of per capita NNP and per capita sustainable MEW for the period 1929–47 and 1947–65 (see table 18 on p. 56 of their text), they never refer to the remarkable difference

sure, others have taken up where they left off. Their work attracted interest in Japan, and a team of leading economists developed a measure of Net National Welfare (NNW). Although based on the work of Nordhaus and Tobin, this measure differs in several respects. The Japanese study does not dismiss considerations of environmental damage, and it includes an item for the cost of highway accidents. On the other hand, it makes no imputation for housework or leisure.

The Japanese team presented figures for the period 1955–70. This was a period of extremely rapid growth in the Japanese economy, and, by any measure, the economic welfare of the Japanese people rose. Indeed, the correspondence between the growth rates of per capita NNW and per capita Net Domestic Product (NDP) was high from the beginning and increased over time. Per capita NNW grew at 6.3% per year from 1955 to 1960, while per capita NDP grew at 8.9% per year during the same period. During the last five years of their study period, 1965–70, the gap closed. Per capita NNW grew at 13.5% per year, and per capita NDP grew at 14.9%. The contrast between this close association between NNW and NDP in Japan and the lack of one between MEW and GNP in the United States may be due either to real differences in national experience or to the differing methodologies used in the studies. Since we have only summary figures for the Japanese study, we were unable to determine the relative importance of those two possibilities.

Economic Aspects of Welfare: Zolotas

The most recent proposal for a measure of economic welfare is the Index of the Economic Aspects of Welfare (EAW index) proposed by Xenophon Zolotas in his book, *Economic Growth and Declining Social Welfare* (1981). Zolotas differs from Nordhaus and Tobin by more sharply focusing on the current flow of goods and services and by largely ignoring capital accumulation and the issue of sustainability. Also, he considers only changes in aggregate national welfare rather than in per capita welfare.

Despite these major conceptual differences, the largest items in his EAW are much like those in MEW: personal consumption and imputa-

---

between those two periods in their discussion. To do so would have required them to explain why the growth rate for per capita sustainable MEW had flattened out, even as per capita NNP kept rising.

tions for leisure and household services. EAW resembles MEW in a number of other ways as well. Like the MEW, EAW subtracts the cost of commuting to work as a regrettable necessity. It deducts expenditures on consumer durables and public buildings and adds the imputed annual services derived from them. EAW treats most educational expenditures as investment rather than consumption, but unlike MEW, it does not reintroduce investments under the category of sustainability. Zolotas merely omits consideration of investment as a factor in welfare altogether. Another difference, minor by comparison, is the deduction in EAW of half the cost of advertising, on the assumption that only half of it provides a valuable information service to consumers.

Environmental damages enter only very obliquely into MEW as an imputation for urban disamenities. Zolotas, by contrast, directly addresses the issue by deducting half the pollution control costs for air and water pollution and all of them for solid waste. (His aim is to subtract only those antipollution expenditures that are paid for by private parties rather than by the government, since the former are classed as intermediate and the latter as final expenditures). He also subtracts the estimated damage cost of air pollution. Finally, because he believes that much of the increase in medical expenses has been necessitated as a response to greater environmental stresses, he subtracts half of the per capita growth in real health care costs both public and private.

EAW is the first index to include a figure for resource depletion. Zolotas recognizes that this is particularly controversial, so he regularly gives his summary conclusions with and without this figure. Nevertheless, his procedure is based on the standard economic view that nonrenewable resources should rise in price at a rate equal to "the long-term interest rate plus a premium for risk and user cost." Since resource prices have not in fact risen at that rate, Zolotas reasons that the market does not function properly at setting prices for the optimal depletion of resources. Thus, as part of EAW, he deducts the difference between actual resource prices and imputed prices derived from the long-term interest rate and an estimated risk premium.

In order to compare EAW with MEW, we have calculated the former on a per capita basis. Given the significant difference in the elements included and excluded in the respective calculations, the results are surprisingly close. From 1950 to 1965, per capita growth of EAW was around 9% for the full period, or .57% per year. During the closest comparable period for MEW, 1947–65, per capita sustainable MEW grew by approximately 7.5%. That amounted to .4% per year. In other words, both increased less than one-third as rapidly as the 2.2% per year growth of per capita GNP from 1947 to 1965. Furthermore, Zolotas carried his statistics down to 1977. From 1965 to 1977, the approximately one-to-three ratio of the growth of per capita EAW and GNP remained the same as during the earlier period. Per capita EAW grew at .71% per year while per capita GNP continued to increase by 2.2% per year. Thus the gap in the growth rates of EAW and GNP continued, although it remained less than the gap between the growth rates of MEW and GNP in the earlier postwar period.

Conclusions

In this chapter we have shown that the national product, whether gross or net, is not identical with true national income and that subtracting indirect business taxes from NNP, as is done in the National Income Accounts to arrive at "national income," still does not give us a true measure of national income. True income is sustainable, and to calculate this Hicksian income would require a quite different approach.

This chapter has also shown that there is a marked difference between what the GNP measures and economic welfare, and that the latter has been growing much more slowly than the former as measured by the two proposals that have been made for judging the U.S. economy. A defender of the continuing use of GNP as a guide to policy could argue that, even so, economic welfare *has* advanced along with GNP. If *any* advance in the welfare measure is truly a gain, and if increase of GNP tends to promote that gain, it is still desirable to increase GNP. The recognition that it takes a great deal of increase in GNP to achieve a small improvement in real economic welfare could be used to argue that ever greater efforts are neeeded for the increase of GNP.

To counter such a claim two points need to be made. First, there are social and ecological indicators that seem to be adversely affected by growth of GNP. Not all of these are dealt with in any of the welfare measures. This is especially true of many of the pervasive externalities.

Second, the major reason that the welfare measures show some growth as GNP grows is that they incorporate the largest element of the GNP as a part of their own statistics. That is private consumption. These welfare measures assume that the more goods and services that are consumed by the public, the better. For example, excessive consumption of tobacco, alcohol, and fatty foods are all counted positively. Few suppose that these actually add to welfare, but the task of sorting out approved and disapproved expenses would be formidable indeed. Furthermore, economists generally regard any effort to make such distinctions as elitism of a sort they reject. However a person spends money in the market is assumed to be in the interest of satisfying that person's wants, and no further consideration of value is possible. We are not arguing against the necessity of assuming for these statistical purposes that consumption in general must be positively appraised. But we do think it well to point out that it is this inability or unwillingness to make judgments of this sort that allows welfare measures to advance even a little as GNP advances a lot. The small advance in welfare held to accompany the larger advance in GNP might well disappear if the most questionable items were deleted from the private consumption column.

This survey does not suffice to establish a way of measuring economic welfare. Closer examination of decisions that must be made in any such index shows how large the arbitrary element is. Any measure would abstract from many features of actual economic welfare and its use would lead to ignoring the degree of abstraction involved. The very existence of a measure *invites* the fallacy of misplaced concreteness. But whether a new measure should be devised and used, or whether measured welfare is a will-o'-the-wisp that should be abandoned, the results make clear that GNP does not come close enough to measuring economic welfare to warrant its continued use for that purpose. To use it as if it were a significant indicator of economic well-being—much worse of well-being in general—is an egregious instance of the fallacy of misplaced concreteness. The movement from GNP to Hicksian income faces many similar problems, but since the goal is more modest the difficulties are correspondingly less. Hicksian income (maximum sustainable consumption) is inherently more measurable than economic welfare. Although the aim of Hicksian income is not a measure of welfare, but rather a practical guide to avoid impoverishment by overconsumption, the component of sustainable consumption looms large in most welfare indexes. One would therefore expect a significant positive correlation between Hicksian income and most welfare indexes. Also since natural capital depletion and defensive expenditures are among the most difficult categories to measure, the operational advantages of Hicksian income over our Index of Sustainable Economic Welfare (Appendix) should not be overstated.

4

Misplaced Concreteness: *Homo Economicus*

Homo economicus as the Basis of Price Theory

The most important abstraction basic to contemporary economic theory is that of *Homo economicus* from real flesh and blood human beings. No one doubts that considerable abstraction is involved. But most economists believe that for the purposes of their discipline no harm is done. They are confident that they know enough about human behavior from their model without examining actual human behavior in detail. In this chapter we will examine this abstraction as it functions in economic theory in order to determine to what extent it leads to the fallacy of misplaced concreteness.

Homo economicus attains its sharpest delineation in the theory of exchange value or price. Here there are two assumptions. First, it is assumed that the individual's total wants are insatiable. But second, as individuals acquire particular goods, their desire for additional consumption of that good, called the utility function of that good, diminishes. Marginal analysis, the cornerstone of neoclassical economics, is based on this latter insight combined with the recognition that price is determined by marginal utility. This means that the price one will pay for a commodity is what an additional unit of that commodity is worth to us, given the amount we already have. One is likely to be less interested in a third dish of ice cream than in the first, or the tenth pair of shoes than the second. If one already has five neckties but only one shirt, one will pay considerably more to acquire a second shirt than a sixth necktie. At some point, one will have all one wants of some commodity and will lose interest in acquiring more at any price.

This is a sound basis for economic theory, and we affirm the value and validity of marginal analysis. But price theory takes a second step that is more questionable. The need to be a deductive science capable of quantification leads it to declare that only commodities consumed by an

individual contribute to that individual's satisfaction or "utility function." "Consumption" as conceived here does not exclude gifts. One can
buy gifts for friends, and the pleasure one takes in their happiness is
included in the utility function. Thus one's enjoyment of the enjoyment
of others counts as long as one has paid for it. As long as this condition
is met, *Homo economicus* may act generously.

What is excluded from *Homo economicus* are concerns for other
people's satisfactions or sufferings that do not express themselves as
one's market activity. For example, *Homo economicus* takes no pleasure
when a neighbor receives a gift from someone else or a promotion, or
when a philanthropist endows a park for underprivileged children. This
adds to the utility function of the philanthropist, but not to other members of the community. Similarly, *Homo economicus* is not envious of the
neighbor's new car or pained by defeat in competition for an honor.
Homo economicus knows neither benevolence nor malevolence in any of
these instances, only indifference.

When *Homo economicus* is compared in these respects with flesh and
blood people, the contrast is striking. *Homo economicus* is indifferent to
relative position in society, but in the real world much of the satisfaction in life felt by individuals is a function of how they stand in relation
to other individuals; in other words, their relative status in their community. On the whole those who are relatively better off report that they
are happier than do other members of their society who are relatively
worse off. This is what most of us would expect. But when comparisons
are made over time or between societies, there is little difference in self-
reported happiness from one society to another. That is, the fact that at
a later date most people are consuming much more absolutely does not
have much effect on happiness. And people in affluent societies do not
on the whole report that they are happier than those in poorer ones. In
short, the absolute level of economic well-being contributes little to personal satisfaction, whereas the relative level within a given society contributes considerably. An abstraction that neglects this point entirely
cannot provide adequate guidance for policy.

Contemporary economic theory cannot easily adjust for these dis-
continuities between *Homo economicus* and real people. Much in the
theory requires the model and cannot be formulated without it. It requires the assumption of independent utility functions, which means
that the satisfaction of each individual is derived from goods acquired
by that individual in the market. Without this assumption it would become a tangle of mathematical intractability, and in particular it could

not be shown that pure competition leads to an optimal allocation of resources. General equilibrium would become an even more impossible attainment, and the invisible hand would become invisible to reason as well as to the naked eye.

The chief feature of *Homo economicus* that appears in this picture is extreme individualism. What happens to others does not affect *Homo economicus* unless he or she has caused it through a gift. Even external relations to others, such as relative standing in the community, make no difference. In addition, only scarce commodities, those that are exchanged in the market, are of interest. The gifts of nature are of no importance, nor is the morale of the community of which *Homo economicus* is a part. When economists draw conclusions about the real world from this model, there can be no question but that the fallacy of misplaced concreteness has been committed.

Whereas we affirm the principle of marginal utility, disputing only that utility is derived in such limited ways, we are much more dubious of the other fundamental characteristic of *Homo economicus* posited by price theory: insatiable desire for commodities. The law of diminishing marginal utility applies to income, and therefore to goods in general. If the marginal utility of income diminishes, then beyond some amount, for all practical purposes, one would have enough. The nonsatiety postulate denies this by appealing to new goods and new wants, and to leisure as a good that we also want more of. But again, does not leisure also have a declining marginal utility and can we not get enough of it? And doesn't a stream of new goods become a bore if we have not yet learned to deal with the old ones? The nonsatiety postulate seems poorly founded and in considerable tension, if not contradiction, with the much better-founded law of diminishing marginal utility. Even the commonsense argument for nonsatiety, that the very rich seem to enjoy their high consumption, fails to be a generalizable proposition because the rich hire others to do the maintenance work associated with consumption. They reserve their time just for riding their horses, letting the hired help wash and comb them and clean out the stable. One might counter that this is just an aspect of leisure scarcity. With more leisure the rich could ride more horses and clean out their own stables. But then the irksomeness of stable cleaning would set a limit to horse riding. Without the poor to help them, the rich would consume a lot less. And if all were rich, then where would the hired help come from?

If nonsatiety were the natural state of human nature then aggressive want-stimulating advertising would not be necessary, nor would the barrage of novelty aimed at promoting dissatisfaction with last year's model. The system attempts to remake people to fit its own presuppositions. If people's wants are not naturally insatiable we must make them so, in order to keep the system going. Already in the 1940s this was evident to John Steinbeck, whose character in *The Wayward Bus,* Pimples Carson, spent half his income on doctors and salves whose advertisements promised to cure his acne, and the other half on candy bars and sugary pies whose advertisements told him that a working man needs quick food energy. Thus Pimples Carson becomes the insatiable consumer, much to the benefit of the makers of candy bars and acne ointments but to his own personal detriment.

Advocates of the principle of insatiability can point to the evidence that even the very rich—or some of them—work hard for the acquisition of more. It does seem that their desire is insatiable. But these are often people who spend comparatively little on personal consumption—that is, on the goods that economic theory expects them to have an insatiable desire for. Their drive seems to be for power or for relative standing with other wealthy people, factors in which *Homo economicus* takes no interest.

Perhaps a better case for insatiability could be made if philanthropy were emphasized. Perhaps the enjoyment of the pleasure of those one benefits by gifts is insatiable. Since unlimited giving is easier to conceive than unlimited consuming, it is surprising that this argument is not more prominent.

The explanation is probably that the utility function of *Homo economicus* has been understood overwhelmingly in terms of consumption in an ordinary sense. Allowing the purchase of a gift for another to count as consumption has been a concession from which nothing has followed. If one emphasized the pleasure *Homo economicus* takes in the pleasure of gift recipients, the inconsistency of not allowing him or her to take pleasure in any other enjoyment by others would be too striking to be tolerable. The concession to this enjoyment of generosity is made so that purchase of gifts for others need not be subtracted from utility function. It is not taken as a significant feature of the psychology of *Homo economicus*. The theory requires that *Homo economicus* is acquisitive without limit, and that is the way it is argued.

Sometimes the limitation of the interest of *Homo economicus* to personal gain receives explicit formulation. F. Y. Edgeworth wrote, "The first principle of economics is that every agent is actuated by self-interest" (*Mathematical Psychics* 1881). Edgeworth believed this applied well to war and contract but not to other fields. The literal apotheosis of the doctrine of self-interest was reached by a German economist, Herrmann Heinrich Gossen, whose book, *The Laws of Human Relations* (1854), has been resurrected from obscurity because it anticipated the marginalist theory of Jevons (1924) and Menger (1950). Gossen's golden rule was, "Organize your actions for your own benefit." God implanted self-interest in the human breast as the motive force of progress. By following self-interest we follow God's will. Going against self-interest only inhibits God's plan. Indignantly, Gossen asks, "How can a creature be so arrogant as to want to frustrate totally or partially the purpose of his Creator?" ([1854] 1983, p. 4). But God's purposes will not be thwarted by arrogant moralists because the divinely implanted force of egoism is too strong to be overcome.

Social Consequences of the Model

Whatever conclusion one reaches about the possibility of some generosity on the part of *Homo economicus,* there can be no doubt that the economic theory built on this anthropology has encouraged a less inhibited quest for personal gain in the business world. That does not mean that personal gain failed to play a large role in earlier generations, but only that there was a pervasive disapproval of making that one goal determinative of how one lived and acted. Monks who took seriously their vows of poverty were usually admired more than successful merchants. Honor competed with wealth as a personal goal.

Modern economic theory has taught that these inhibitions of the quest for wealth are not needed for the sake of the general good and that, indeed, they impede its realization. Where each individual seeks to maximize economic gain, the total product of society increases and hence all people benefit. If government was once expected to influence economic activity for the sake of justice to all, now its interventions are seen as preventing that increase of total product which alone can bring widespread prosperity. *Homo economicus* has little incentive to moderate the quest for wealth by other concerns.

In the past the unlimited quest for personal gain was mitigated by the concern for justice, fairness, or the well-being of the community as a whole. This is a dimension of real human beings that is lacking to *Homo economicus.* There is a strong tendency for economists to identify the right or correct distribution of goods with whatever distribution results from unrestricted market transactions. For example, Milton Friedman asserts that "the right percentage (of home ownership) emerges in a free market in which housing is neither subsidized nor penalized" (1981). In a similar vein, Robert Samuelson states, "Efforts to help small businesses as a class are no more virtuous than aiding large businesses as a class" (1982). They may both be correct, but the determination of morality by market behavior is not.

The tension in the economists' view of *Homo economicus* appears when they are confronted with behavior that does not correspond to maximization mathematics. Steven E. Rhoads has studied recent literature and shown how strong is the tendency of economists to suppose that such behavior expresses either a subtler self-interested motive or ignorance. Again it seems that the dominance of maximization mathematics has tilted the meaning of the rationality attributed to *Homo economicus* toward narrow self-interest. Rhoads summarizes some particularly interesting experiments. In these experiments, large groups of people are given tokens they can invest either in an individual exchange that returns 1 cent per token to the individual investing, or in a group exchange that returns 2.2 cents per token but divides these earnings among everyone in the group regardless of who invests. In other words, in the group exchange, the subject receives a share of the return on his own investment (if any), and the same share of the return on the investment in the group exchange made by the other group members. Most economists would predict that a self-interested individual would put nothing in the group exchange, because the group exchange would not maximize individual benefits. (Most of the greater total benefits from investing in the group exchange would go to other members of the group. Moreover, those who do not invest in the group exchange nonetheless share in the proceeds from investments made in that exchange by others, i.e., they get a "free ride.") But, in fact, in a number of experiments people have voluntarily contributed substantial resources—usually between 40% and 60%—to the group exchange (i.e., the public good). Many in the experiments have also said that a "fair" person would contribute even more than they did (Rhoads 1985, p. 161). The power of models is particularly revealed when this experiment is tried on a group of entering graduate students in economics. "They contributed only 20% to the group exchange, found the concept of fairness alien, and were only half as likely to indicate that they were concerned with fairness in making their decision" (Rhoads 1985, p. 162).

That a concern for fairness is difficult for economists to deal with is indicated by their comments on the experiment. A. Rapaport and A. M. Chammah, for example, as quoted by Rhoads, state (without irony): "Evidently the run-of-the-mill players are not strategically sophisticated enough to have figured out that strategy DD [the selfish strategy] is the only rationally defensible strategy" (p. 162).

A similar appeal to lack of sophistication on the part of the public has been resorted to by resource economists who have encountered considerable lack of cooperation in the public's response to contingent evaluation questionnaires, in which the respondents must stipulate amounts at which they are willing to buy or sell environmental goods. Sagoff considers these refusals the most noteworthy result of the experiment, "because the famous Milgram experiments have demonstrated that in social science research settings people are so cowed by authority that they will do anything, even torture and murder, when asked to do so. It seems that the only kinds of experiments that respondents reject in large numbers are contingent valuation surveys conducted by resource economists. Why is this?" Sagoff's answer to his own question is that "respondents believe that environmental policy—for example, the degree of pollution permitted in national parks—involves ethical, cultural, and aesthetic questions over which society must deliberate on the merits, and that this has nothing to do with pricing the satisfaction of preferences at the margin" (p. 62).

When economists attempt to extend their concepts to the analysis of other fields, such as voting, their tendency to view the human being as narrowly selfish is clear. Yet the evidence does not support them. Rhoads points out that those who now pay for social security for the elderly are benefited by the elderly's early demise, and that some economists believe it is rational for them to oppose expenditures of public funds designed to prolong the lives of social security recipients. He notes that in fact most people support such expenditures. He also cites economic literature on criminal behavior that equally abstracts from any ethical considerations. He does not assert that economists in general subscribe to these strictly amoral views, but he notes that articles expressing them are published in respected journals without adverse response from other economists.

We conclude that real human beings are not well imaged by the model of *Homo economicus*. In the major recent study of economic psychology, this judgment is supported. After careful examination of the evidence, the authors conclude that "the axiom of greed must be re-

jected because real people, unlike *Homo economicus,* are not insatiable"
(Lea, Tarpy, and Webley 1987, p. 111). The point here is not that
the fit is slightly imperfect but rather that the effort to draw conclusions about human behavior from the model leads to systematic distortions outside of narrowly defined fields. Furthermore, and even more
important, the use of the model influences actual behavior away from
community-regarding patterns toward selfish ones. We noted in the experiment cited above that the students of economics deviated significantly from the usual pattern in this direction. The descriptive abstraction has unwittingly become normative for these students. But society
as a whole has been affected too. John Kenneth Galbraith has pointed
out that the apparently unlimited desire for wealth results from the fact
that contemporary society "evaluates people by the products they possess. . . . The urge to consume is furthered by the value system" (1958,
p. 126).

Economics and Value Judgments

Homo economicus has unlimited wants but no gradation of values distinct from the strength of those wants. For this reason economists generally accept whatever people desire as normative. The task of the
economy is to meet as many of these desires as possible, whatever they
may be.

The refusal to judge among alternative types of value is often a subject of controversy between economists and critics of economics. Critics
argue that there are higher and lower values and that society should encourage the higher and discourage the lower. They complain that when
left to itself the market encourages the lower by constant advertisement
of consumption goods. The implication is that government may need to
intervene or to counter the pressure toward inferior values with direct
support of superior ones.

Economists in general oppose this form of government intervention.
They insist that the distinction of higher and lower values is elitist.
Some enjoy Shakespeare; others, pornographic movies. Economists do
not want government introducing normative judgments in favor of one
or the other.

In opposing governmental intervention in the form of subsidies or
censorship, economists are clearly expressing their own values. Beginning with its origins in Adam Smith, economics has prized personal
freedom from governmental intervention. It can be argued, of course,

that this is merely the objective claim that the market is the most efficient distributor of goods and that it works best when participants are completely free from governmental restriction. But in the present context it goes beyond that to the insistence that there are no objective criteria of better and worse by which a society can guide its policies. Why adherents to this view continue to take part in policy debates is a puzzle.

We may ask why economists are so nearly unanimous on a topic on which elsewhere there is continuing debate? The answer is that their mechanical, mathematical models abstract from final causation. The policies consistently recommended are designed to increase the total quantity of goods available to those able to buy them. To introduce into this picture judgments about relative values or purposes not correlated with price would disrupt the entire discipline.

Steven Rhoads has ably demonstrated that judgments of relative value are made by most people in criticism of their own behavior. Those addicted to smoking rarely claim that their desire for tobacco should have equal status with food for the hungry or even the enjoyment of good literature. Instead of denying these facts, economists should acknowledge that they neglect them because their science cannot cope with them. But the temptation to deny the facts in favor of theory is great.

Economists do wish to make judgments as to whether a proposed policy will improve the welfare of the people to be affected by it. But they eschew a utilitarian calculus that would add the pleasures and subtract the pains. The satisfactions (economists speak of utility functions) of differing individuals are incommensurable because there is no unit of measure. Hence economists refuse to add different persons' utility functions together to determine the total good to be gained.

According to economists we really cannot say that food for the hungry yields more utility than a third TV set in a rich family's second house. Nor that a leg amputation hurts Jones more than a pin prick hurts Smith. All we can say is that if no one is made worse off while at least one person is made better off, then social welfare (aggregate welfare) has increased. This is the famous Pareto-efficiency criterion. Notice that the existence of malevolence would spoil the criterion. If I feel worse off *because* someone else has become better off, then by the Pareto criterion we would never observe an improvement in social welfare. For the criterion to be operational we must rule out malevolence or spite. Either economists are making the positive statement that people are in fact neither spiteful nor malevolent, or else they are making the normative judgment that people should not be malevolent and spiteful, and satisfactions based on such motives simply will not be counted. As a positive statement the proposition is clearly false. Only as a normative statement does it command widespread assent. This is ironic because it was to escape normative judgment that interpersonal comparisons of utility were ruled out in the first place, leading to the supposedly "value-free" Pareto criterion, which we see now is itself a normative statement. The criterion by which even an efficient allocation is defined rests squarely on a normative judgment. We think it rests on a sound normative judgment, as far as it goes, and that this is preferable to basing it on an erroneous positive statement. But we also believe it ironic that anyone could claim that the theoretical structure built on this foundation is a value-free "positive" science.

The ultimate reductio ad absurdum of the view that the goal is to meet people's desires as they are without imposing critical value judgments has recently become more evident thanks to science's gaining direct access to the pleasure center in the hypothalamus by electrical or chemical means. Previously the pleasure center of the brain was not directly accessible to the individual. Its stimulation was the by-product of other activities done in proper balance and moderation. Eating is pleasurable when you are hungry, sleep is a pleasure when tired, and sex requires an interval between satisfactions as well as a context of trust, love, and playfulness for maximum pleasure. Pleasure is normally a by-product of some combination of activities that are in harmony with the biological good of the individual or the species. Direct access to the pleasure center dispenses with these balanced intermediate activities. Thus cocaine or "crack" gives a direct chemical stimulus to the pleasure center, but is deadly in its effect on the welfare of both individual and society. In any case even the amount of crack desired is finite. And the individual who is directly maximizing subjective satisfaction in this way has reduced interest in other goods and services.

In one of the most symbolic and frightening experiments ever performed, electrodes were implanted in the pleasure centers of some rats.[1] The rats had three levers they could press. One gave a pellet of food, another a drink of water, and the third directly stimulated their wired-up pleasure centers. After learning which lever was which, the rats simply stimulated their pleasure centers until they euphorically died of

1. From a personal communication from Paul Brand (1986); see also *Washington Post,* July 31, 1988, p. 16.

starvation, even though food and drink were easily accessible. We do not yet have neurosurgeons offering to wire-up the pleasure center for us, but that is the logical consequence of a theory of value based only on individualistic maximization of subjective satisfaction. Likewise the current epidemic of cocaine use is probably not just an unfortunate fad, but a logical consequence of a philosophy that places the source of all value in individual pleasure that is as self-contained as possible, independent of all relationships and reduced to activating one substance with another. But the self-centered focus on subjective individual pleasure is literally deadly.

Conclusions

We have argued that *Homo economicus* abstracts from human feelings about what happens to others and about one's relative standing in the community. It abstracts from the sense of fairness and from judgments of relative value. We have shown that this abstraction leads to differences between the behavior posited of *Homo economicus* and that of real people.

It would in principle be possible for contemporary economists to avoid neglecting the degree of abstraction involved in their models and therefore in the theories based on them. They might recognize that their theories are like the physical theory that in a vacuum, objects of differing density fall at the same speed. Physicists do not conclude from this that a stone and a feather dropped from the top of a cliff on a windy day will reach the bottom simultaneously. Physicists know that the real world is not a vacuum, and economists should remember that a real human being is not *Homo economicus*. But in general they forget the abstracted from dimensions of real people.

Our point is not that a science of "pure" economics is impossible or undesirable. Our point is that economics as a discipline does not present itself in that light with sufficient care. It enters the arena of explanation of aspects of what transpires in the real world and offers recommendations for policymakers and businessmen. We are glad that it does. But too often, in the process of doing so, it neglects the degree of abstraction involved in its concepts and arguments, and the results of its reasoning can be dangerous to public well-being when applied directly to the actual world.

Too often economics has shaped its anthropology and its theories with an eye to "analytical convenience" rather than empirical warrant. As a result, policy decisions are determined by mathematical theorems whose virtue is their deductive fruitfulness rather than their connection to the real world. The abstraction has gone too far, and the practitioners of the discipline are too little aware of it. The fallacy of misplaced concreteness is too pervasive.

5

Misplaced Concreteness: Land

Land Economics

The preceding chapters have shown how the aim of economics to be a deductive science has led it to highly abstract treatments of exchange, of success indicators, and of the human being—and then to draw conclusions from these abstractions as if they corresponded to concrete facts. This chapter adds land to the list. There is, however, a difference. Whereas the market, GNP, and *Homo economicus* are abstractions that powerfully shape thinking about the economy, the abstractions by which land has been represented as a distinctive aspect of the economy have faded to the periphery or disappeared altogether.

This chapter, accordingly, has a double project. First, it needs to determine how land has been viewed by economists, and, second, it needs to show why their abstractions have proved unimportant or uninteresting. This negligibility of "land" for economists does not mean that its neglect is unimportant. The consequences that follow from ignoring land altogether are at least as extensive as those that follow directly from the particular abstractions that have represented it.

It is important to note at the outset that "land" as used by economists is the inclusive term for the natural environment. There is no separate discussion of the oceans or of the atmosphere or of solar energy. What is treated under this heading of land might have been called nature, creation, the world, the environment, or earth. That it was called land is due to the use of "land" in relation to agriculture, and the fact that agriculture was primarily in view in the discussions among economists. Once the abstractions functioning in economic theory were formed on this basis, there has been almost no point of contact for consideration of other aspects of nature. The extreme difficulty in drawing the attention of economists to the wild facts is due to such factors as these.

Land has not disappeared entirely from economics. There is a subdiscipline called "land economics" of which Richard T. Ely (first president of the American Economic Association) may be regarded as the founder. In 1922 he published a preliminary version of this thinking, entitled *Outline of Land Economics*. At the outset he expressed his puzzlement about the neglect of land by economists. "It is peculiar and not altogether easy to explain the fact that land as an economic concept, that is, as a requisite of production, sharing in the income of society—has received comparatively little attention" (p. 3). He notes the large literature on labor and capital, the other traditional factors of production, and then comments that his own work seems to be the first sustained analogous treatment of the land.

Some clue to the lack of attention to land as a factor of production can be found in Ely's treatment, especially the process of abstraction that goes on as he defines his task. He notes, first, that "*land,* as used by economists, means the forces of nature so far as they have economic significance." He then points out that land is studied by many disciplines so that the question for land economics is the distinctiveness of the economic approach. "What is it that marks out a field for land economics? It is the concept of property" (p. 3). In a footnote he comments that his original intention was to entitle the work, "Landed Property and the Rent of Land."

Although a considerable abstraction, not to say shift, has occurred in the move from "the forces of nature" to "landed property," the term "property" could still direct attention to the physical reality of what is owned. Ely makes it clear that this is not intended. "Economics in general is a science of human relationships and so is land economics as one of the major divisions of economics" (p. 4). The "property-idea" is that of "property-relations." The topics to be dealt with under the heading of "land economics" are "tenancy in city and country, price of land, single tax, public ownership, community ownership, the open range, large landholdings, conservation, the congestion of urban populations" (p. 4).

It seems that Ely has answered his own question as to why land is not given the same attention as the other factors of production. If "land" were really viewed by economists as "the forces of nature so far as they have economic significance," then considerable attention to "land" as a quite distinct element of great importance would be warranted. It would be not only a factor of production but also a precondition of the whole of economic life, as of life in general. The wild facts would be self-evidently important to economics. But when land has become a property-relation, distinct from other property relations in rather minor respects, then it is merely one commodity among others. The "forces of nature," and therefore nature in general, have disappeared from view. Economics as a discipline floats free from the physical world.

Nevertheless, it is quite significant that even when "land" is abstracted to this extent, attention to the topic can sensitize one to issues normally ignored by economists. Conservation was included in the topics of 1922, and when Ely joined with George S. Wehrwein to publish *Land Economics* in 1940, they showed remarkable sensitivity to issues most Americans did not appreciate until much later. Although the bulk of the book deals with land as property and focuses on the property-relation, the authors are clear that the physical reality can be distinguished from this relation, and they demand attention to it in its own right. For this reason "land policies must be based upon the operation of nature's laws as well as upon the economic drives of man" (p. 25). This reference to the laws of nature contrasts with the near indifference to such laws common among economists. This concern for the physical world leads Ely and Wehrwein to notice an interaction between economic activity and nature that lies outside of economics as a whole. "Too often the 'conquest of nature' benefiting immediate generations has resulted in the 'conquest of man' by those natural forces operating into eternity." Since "man has become a geographical factor along with wind, water, and climate, changing the character of his environment and sometimes with more destructive speed than nature itself," land economics therefore "has to concern itself with the 'private' economic factors in land utilization but even more with the 'political economy' of the conservation, restoration, and augmentation of natural resources" (p. 27). Attention to the land seems to work for long-term views and to work against discounting effects on future generations.

It is disappointing to find, side by side with such statements, a much greater number of others to the effect that in the production of economic goods and services, "the earth is the inert and man the active factor" (p. 25), and "land in itself is not productive" (p. 50). These standard economic views rather than an awareness of the ecological destructiveness of the human economy govern the content of the book as a whole. Hence the economics put forth does not go far to encourage the restoration and augmentation of the land for which the authors call. Nevertheless, we could wish that contemporary economists as a whole would pay even as much attention to land as physical environment as Ely and Wehrwein did. Unfortunately, a glance through current issues of the journal that bears the same name as their book, *Land Economics,* shows that even in this subdiscipline there are few traces of this side of Ely's legacy. Concern for physical reality and for nature has become ever more peripheral to land economics, and land economics has remained peripheral to economics in general.

Just as policies derived from a discipline that knows nothing of human community are destructive of that community, so policies derived from a discipline that knows nothing of the physical world are destructive of that world. The wild facts are in large part the consequence of that destructiveness. Economics needs to be rethought in terms of a more adequate model of land, just as much as it needs to be rethought in terms of a more adequate model of *Homo economicus*.

For "land" to represent the forces of nature in their economic significance is not new. Indeed, it is very old. What is new is for the forces of nature to be subsumed under the property-relation. The entire view of land changes when this subsumption occurs. In order to appreciate the richer alternatives that are available for thinking of land in economics, we propose to review briefly the primal vision of the land, especially as transmitted through the Jewish Scriptures. They have not lost their resonance or their relevance, and they bring the level of abstraction involved in modern economics into high relief.

Ancient Views of the Land

In typical instances of hunting and gathering peoples, the land is the giver of life and the source of all good. In modern terminology, it is *the* factor of production. But it is much more than that. The people belong to the land and reverence it and gratefully receive its bounty. The land includes all the plants and animals that share it with the people.

The land is also the place of the people. The reference is not to the continents but to that particular land that the people know. They are related through it to their ancestors and descendants. There is no concept of ownership of land. The land belongs to them as it belongs to all the animals who share it with them. More properly, they all belong together. Again, in modern terms, they constitute an ecosystem.

In this vision, the spirits or deities are local. They are related to features of the landscape or ancestral graves or special animals. The land itself may be worshiped as all-giving, and perhaps also as all-consuming, Mother.

Some of these themes are expressed in the poetry of New Mexico author Nancy Wood. Her deep concern with the cultural dilemma of the

Taos Indians is reflected in poems about their displacement from much
of the land by Spanish, Mexican, and American settlers.

> All as it was in this place timeless.
> All as it was between the human soul and the earth.
> This land was the land
> Of our great waters
> The beating heart of nature flowing through time
> That we could not remember.
> This was our land.
> The land that provided everything good for my people.
>
> . . . .
>
> Then the land was taken from us.
> It is your land.
> Do you know how to speak to the land, my brother?
> Do you listen to what it tells you?
> Can you take from it no more than what you need?
> Can you keep its secrets to yourself?
> Sell the land, my brother?
> You might as well sell
> The sun, the moon, the stars.
>
> For there is no difference between
> The life of a man and the life
> Of all growing things.
> Who is to say if a man
> Shall not be a tree instead?
> We pray to all nature and do it no harm.
> These are our brothers
> All men and all trees.
> Some part of ourselves
> Is in earth and sky and everywhere.
>
> [from Wood, ed., 1972, *Hollering Sun*]

With the domestication of animals, other tendencies appeared. Pas-
toral nomads can experience the land as a place of wandering rather
than dwelling. It remains important, but they are not part of the land in
the same way as hunting and gathering people. The principle of action
in nature may be associated with sun and rain. The land receives more
than it gives. Human action assumes a larger role, and it may be understood more in relation to the heavenly deities than to the land.

With the domestication of plants and the agricultural revolution,
people are more firmly tied to smaller units of land. As with hunters and
gatherers the land assumes primacy, although sun and rain are also of
great importance. Above all, attention is focused on fertility. The increase

that nature provides, transforming a seed into a plant that produces many seeds or bringing into being more and more domestic animals, is seen as the great miracle. Sexuality in general and human sexuality in particular take on religious importance as a symbol of fecundity.

Ancient views of land have been mediated most influentially to European civilization through the Jewish Scriptures. For the ancient Jews as for other ancient peoples land was a central category. Indeed, one may say that Jewish life and thought centered around the people (Israel), their God (Yahweh), and the land.[1] These are their three factors of production! They are relatively separate actors but have their meaning and full reality only in their interconnectedness. The people remember a mixed history of nomadic wandering and agricultural settlement in Egypt. The land, therefore, is not simply their self-evident place apart from which they have no collective existence. It was given them by Yahweh, and if they did not live rightly in the land, they could be exiled from it. Separation from the land was the supreme threat, and being able to dwell in the land forever was the supreme promise. Thus their dwelling in the land, the fulfillment of their hopes, was contingent on their relations both to the land and to their God.

The land was not an inert member of the triad. It bore fruits and gave good gifts. It was to be treated with respect and allowed to cease from work on the Sabbath. It could be described as mourning, or rejoicing, and even as vomiting the people as a result of their numerous sins. The land could be polluted by human sin and require cleansing.

The land was seen in general as the "inheritance" of Israel. This did not mean property in the modern sense. The land was entrusted to Israel as long as Israel kept the covenant with Yahweh and with the land. Further, the inheritance was personalized. Each family received its inheritance. It was responsible to keep this inheritance, and Yahweh held the community as a whole responsible for maintaining an order in which each family preserved and transmitted its inheritance. Stewardship comes closer than ownership to express this relation. But the maintenance of this widely distributed system of land rights proved extremely difficult, for some extended their holdings by buying up their neighbors' "inheritance," especially in times of crisis. Climaxing in the eighth century B.C.E., the urban elite turned agriculture from village

---

1. For much of this account we are indebted to Walter Brueggemann, *The Land* (Philadelphia: Fortress, 1977). The relation to economics is brought out more explicitly in Archer Torrey, *The Land and Biblical Economics* (New York: Henry George Institute, 1985).

subsistence to mono-cropping for export, forcing peasants to become day laborers on large estates instead of independent farmers. Much of the prophetic denunciation is directed against this violation of the covenant. The norm of a Jubilee year was asserted in which all land would revert to its original inheritors.[2]

The people understood themselves as "planted" in the land. Above all they "dwelt" there. They belonged to, or at least with, the land. They were the people of that land. It was home, beloved when they were there, longed for when they were away. Existence separated from the land was incomplete. To dwell in their inheritance forever, faithful to the covenant with Yahweh, was for them salvation.

But despite the depth of this relatedness to the land, this relation was penultimate, not ultimate. The people could exist apart from the land, and in such existence they were not separated from Yahweh. Yahweh took up abode in the land, but Yahweh was not bound to it. Yahweh could leave or even be driven out. There was also a more sophisticated tradition that held that Yahweh could not be, in this sense, localized at all.

The distinctive features of this Jewish view of the land arose out of the peculiar history of a people who had both nomadic and agricultural experience. Their view of Yahweh is more closely related to the nomadic experience; their view of the land was more closely related to the agricultural experience. Both views were modified in their mutual relations. The result was a rich literature that has provided the germ of most Western thought on the land, at least prior to the modern period.

The peculiar sense of intimate relation to a particular land combined with separability from it has been preserved by the Jews themselves. It is an important factor in world politics today. In Christendom the unity tended to fall apart. Beginning with the New Testament itself, and especially in the Gentile church, the intimacy of the relation to the particular land faded. Themes stating or at least implying separability from the land have dominated. The true home of the Christian is not any particular land but the coming realm of God or an otherworldly heaven itself. Christians are wanderers and pilgrims on the earth. Thus the aspects of the Jewish vision derived from their nomadic memories and their exilic experience were appropriated more than the agriculturalist love of the land. Yet Christians were generally (in premodern times) agriculturalists,

2. Martin L. Chaney has developed these points in detail. See his "Systematic Study of the Israelite Monarchy," in *Social Scientific Criticism of the Hebrew Bible and Its Social World,* ed. N. K. Gottwald, *Semeia* 37, pp. 53–76.

so that the love of the land remained a prominent Christian experience. Occasionally the two came into combination again as in the Puritan identification of the New World as the promised land. But the main themes of Christian sensibility expressed independence from the land.

One can trace in this movement from the Jewish to the Christian Scriptures, and within some lines of Christian thought, a tendency to accent the transcendence and objectification of land. The separability of human life from the land, in conjunction with the emphasis on the relation of the human being to God, have tended to deemphasize the importance of the land. These trends pave the way for the further objectifications and abstractions of modern philosophy and economics. But before we turn to this topic we should consider one aspect of the relation to the land not emphasized thus far, the relation to the living creatures with whom the land is shared by people. The Jewish view can best be seen in the first Creation story.

In this story, after the land is separated from the water, the earth brings forth vegetation, and water brings forth sea creatures, and God creates the birds and animals. At each stage God sees that what is created is good. Then, on the sixth day, God creates a man and a woman; only they are created in God's own image. Then God views the whole creation together and sees that it is "very good."

Translated into philosophical terms this means that all creatures have intrinsic value, and that the addition of the human species gives to the whole a special excellence. Existence in general, and especially life, are to be affirmed in themselves, not merely in relation to ends that transcend them. The goodness of the world in general cannot be understood simply as its value for human beings.

On the other hand, human beings are not merely one species among others. They are specifically authorized to have dominion over the earth and its plant and animal life. This means that all of these also function as means to human ends. Other living things thus function as both ends and means. But the fact that human beings may use other living things as means, especially as food, does not warrant their extermination, for they too are authorized to be fruitful and multiply. The right of human beings to use them does not supersede their right to a place in the world.

This double message of human fellow creaturehood with other living things, all of which are to flourish, and human dominance over them has been better preserved in Judaism than in Christianity. Both have tended to emphasize the latter point of dominance more than the sense of joint participation in making up the excellence of creation. But Christianity has focused on the creation of humanity in the image of God as a basis for a more spiritualized understanding of salvation that applies only to human beings and hence reduces the remainder of creation to background for the story of Redemption. Until quite recently, only such eccentrics as St. Francis and Albert Schweitzer have stressed the intrinsic value of all created things and the community that human beings share with them.

Christian teaching did continue the biblical view that the land is ultimately God's and is to serve the common good. This was not an argument against private property, but only against its misuse. All economic decisions should serve the common good. Unfortunately, the Catholic church so allied itself with landed interests that its definitions of the common good lost credibility with the rising industrial classes, and this tradition has grown weak. Nevertheless, it is interesting to find it recurring occasionally in secular discussions, including those among economists. A particularly fine example can be found in John Stuart Mill's *Principles of Political Economy*. After describing the heartless treatment of tenants by landlords he states: "When landed property has placed itself upon this footing it ceases to be defensible, and the time has come for making some new arrangement of the matter. No man made the land. It is the original inheritance of the whole species. Its appropriation is wholly a question of general expediency. When private property in land is not expedient it is unjust. . . . The claim of the landowners to the land is altogether subordinate to the general policy of the state" (1973, pp. 232–33).

Land in Modern Philosophy and Economic Theory

Economics is often criticized for being materialistic. It is in fact materialistic in the sense that it sees human beings as intent on possession and consumption of goods, and it supports the satisfaction of these wants. But in a deeper, philosophical sense, it is much more allied to idealism. It neglects the land, and that means in general the physical basis of human existence. In this section we explore the movement of economic thought in this idealistic direction in tandem with that of modern philosophy.

Although "land" is not a technical term in philosophy, which has taken its categories more from the Greeks than from the Bible, modern philosophy's discussion of matter, or nature, and of the nonhuman world generally has immediate and obvious implications for the view of the land.

In philosophy modernity began with Descartes. Although most philosophers disagree with Descartes in important respects, nevertheless, he has set the agenda for much of philosophy in the present day. Prior to Descartes, philosophy generally assumed as its starting point that the thinker is part of a larger world. The question of how people know this world was worked out in a context that assumed the existence of both the knower and the known. Descartes refounded philosophy on the basis of radical doubt. This meant that the question of whether anyone knows anything, and if so, how, became the starting point of philosophical inquiry.

Descartes' universal doubt quickly gave way to confidence in his own existence. He saw that if he doubted, then he existed. There could be no doubting without the doubter. What remained questionable is how one can get from the sheer fact of subjective existence to an objective world, remembering that the objective world includes the human body.

Descartes himself solved this problem through a form of the ontological argument for the existence of God. Having proved to his own satisfaction that his idea of perfection entailed a perfect being, he could argue that a perfect being would not allow him to be fundamentally deceived in his interpretation of sensory experience. Hence, in addition to the knowing subject or mental substance, he could be confident that there also exist objects, or material substances. As a result Descartes divided the world into two metaphysically distinct orders: mind and matter.

Few philosophers have followed Descartes in bringing in God to insure the reality of the material world, but his dualistic way of thinking has remained deeply influential in two respects. First, for much of the common sense of the modern world, the sharp distinction of subjects and objects has seemed evident and necessary, and there has been a strong tendency to identify them with mental and material substances. Second, with the exception of certain materialists, the primacy of the subject has remained the philosophical starting point.

When Descartes divided the world into mental subjects and material objects, he put animals entirely on the side of the latter. This implied that they were complex machines without subjective experience. Descartes argued as follows: "It seems reasonable since art copies Nature, and men can make various automata which move without thought, that Nature should produce its own automata, much more splendid than artificial ones. These natural automata are the animals" (Macey 1980, p. 76). Although many modern philosophers did not fully commit themselves to that position, the line of division that has remained for modern thought is between human beings—specifically, human beings as mental subjects—and everything else. This division has been treated as very fundamental, and in Descartes' case, as a metaphysical dualism. For ethical reflection this has meant that human enjoyment or virtue constitutes what is valuable in itself. Everything else is a means to that end.

It is evident that this Cartesian worldview has provided the context and assumptional matrix for economic thought. For economic theory, value is to be found solely in the satisfaction of human desires. The subjective theory of value has totally replaced earlier "real" theories of value that took land or labor as the locus of value. Since, following Descartes, only humans possess subjectivity, it follows that only humans can be the locus of value. The rest of nature is viewed as land or improvement or product. Land represents all natural resources and includes all the living things supported by the land, except for the labor expended in raising them. Labor would include the labor expended by human beings in raising the food the horse eats. Labor would not include any value attributable to the contribution of the horse's labor. For purposes of economics, the horse is treated, as with Descartes, as a machine. Its value is its value to human beings, determined finally by the market.

In short, the typical modern dualism reappears in economic theory from Adam Smith to the present. On the one side there are human beings, the satisfaction of whose wants is the single end of economic activity. On the other side there is everything else, all of which comes into consideration only as means to the end of satisfying human wants.

Although it is correct to characterize this as dualism in both Descartes and economic theory, it is important to see that the two types of beings are not given analogous roles. One exists for the other. The "other" is, of course, the human being. Accordingly, even more illuminating of modern thought than the label "dualism" is the label "anthropocentrism." Modern thought is anthropocentric through and through.

Despite his anthropocentrism, Descartes overcame his doubt about the fully objective reality of the material world. Similarly Adam Smith takes seriously the physical reality of "land" as one of the factors of production, but like matter it remains passive, its produce depending entirely on human labor. Since the time of Descartes and Smith there has been a strong tendency in Western thought to move further still with anthropocentrism. The result is called idealism.

The difficulty in affirming dualism when one begins with the human subject is that it is difficult to justify the move from the reality of the undoubted subject to the reality of the object. It has seemed that the world of the subject is limited to the contents of the subject's experience. Nevertheless common sense strongly affirms that these contents are given to the subject from without, even forced on the subject's experience. As long as this sense of being passive in sensory experience was not challenged, dualism reigned supreme in the modern sensibility, even though philosophers had difficulty in justifying it.

If Descartes originated modern philosophy, the greatest revolution within modern philosophy was effected by Immanuel Kant. At the beginning of the nineteenth century he captured the attention of the intellectual world by arguing that the human mind is far from passive in its experience. The mind is active in building up its world. In fact, anything we can speak of as a world at all is in some sense a product of the human mind. Although Kant posited an unknowable reality as the source of sensory experience, many subsequent philosophers dropped this in favor of a consistent idealism.

There is little direct connection between the abandonment of physical reality in the dominant philosophical tradition and the elimination of land from consideration in economics. But the parallelism deserves note. The intellectual climate of the nineteenth and twentieth centuries has been congenial to the shift of economic thought from attention to natural and empirical facts given to us in experience, to the products of the economist's mind. Thus a preoccupation with economic theory, models, and mathematical formulas expresses the direction encouraged by the shift of the modern mind from dualism to post-Kantian idealism. The shift of attention from land, labor, and capital to landlords, laborers, and capitalists, and then to rents, wages, and profits also coheres with the loss of interest in the physical world.

Economists are not to be criticized for having participated in the best thought of their time. They are, however, to be asked to share in the growing recognition of the limitations of the modern worldview in both its dualistic and idealistic versions. There are practical reasons today to take the reality of the physical world very seriously. For example, the threat of a nuclear war and accompanying destruction of most of the human race cannot well be understood in idealistic terms. We all know that such a war would make real changes in a real physical world independently of how people thought about it. Similarly, pollution of the air and rising sea levels appear to be quite independent of how people think about them. Also, at a theoretical level, the evolutionary kinship of the human species with other species makes nonsense of metaphysical dualism and renders suspect all the conclusions drawn by ethicists from that dualism. There seems no way to take the evidence of science and of universal experience seriously without affirming the reality of the natural world and the place of the human being as a part of it. At a political level few would deny these points altogether. Yet idealistic theories underlie many of the academic disciplines and direct attention away from natural events in their own integrity. At times these theories lead scholars, including economists, to extreme statements.

For example, George Gilder writes: "The United States must overcome the materialistic fallacy: the illusion that resources and capital are essentially things, which can run out, rather than products of the human will and imagination which in freedom are inexhaustible." And then to make the point as clear as possible, he adds: "Because economies are governed by thoughts, they reflect not the laws of matter but the laws of mind" (Gilder 1981, p. 232). And Julian Simon has said, "You see, in the end copper and oil come out of our minds. That's really where they are" (1982, p. 207). These statements illustrate in hyperbolic fashion the fallacy of misplaced concreteness. Yet the views of these two economists are very influential in Washington. They are rarely criticized for their angelistic idealism by other economists.

The Disappearance of Land as a Factor of Production

Let us look now more closely at the virtual disappearance of land from its once prominent place in thinking about the economy. In agricultural societies the two factors of production universally evident are land and labor. The question was not whether both were necessary but how to conceive their relation. Sir William Petty (1623–87) is noted for his view that labor is the active principle of wealth and land is the passive principle. This emphasis continued in John Locke (1632–1704), who held that value is a function of the labor expended, and that it is this expenditure of labor that justifies private property. Indeed, whereas Petty did assign the role of "mother" to the land, Locke treats it as negligible as far as the economic order is concerned. Nature's gifts are equally there for all until labor has been applied to them.

The French physiocrats, on the other hand, saw land as the active source of wealth. Land works along with the laborer in production. Indeed, the surplus product is considered to result solely from the contribution of land. Adam Smith, in a similar way, interpreted the landlord's rent as the result of the land's contribution to production. And the active contribution of land was taken up again by John Stuart Mill: "Nature, however, does more than supply materials; she also supplies powers. The matter of the globe is not an inert recipient of forms and properties impressed by human hands; it has active energies by which it co-operates with, and may even be used as a substitute for, labour" (1973, p. 23). "Labour, then, in the physical world is always and solely employed in putting objects in motion; the properties of matter, the laws of nature, do the rest" (1973, p. 25).

Later Alfred Marshall also spoke up for the positive contribution of nature. "In a sense there are only two agents of production, nature and man. But on the other hand man is himself largely formed by his surroundings, in which nature plays a great part" (1925, p. 139). Despite these occasional flashes of recognition that nature or land is a productive agent of fundamental importance, the actual course of economic thought followed Locke. Ricardo developed Locke's labor theory of value, denying a contribution by land to the determination of exchange value or price even in the case of agricultural commodities.

Karl Marx followed him in this regard. Thus the passivity of land was followed by its exclusion from any contribution to value. In reaction to Marx's use of the labor theory of value non-Marxist economists ceased to employ it. But they did not return to an analysis of the contribution of nature to production. On the contrary they sought to find the way in which subjective individual preferences, aggregated through the market, autonomously establish prices. In either case, land no longer contributes to value, and, seen as passive, it ceased to be significant in the analysis of production.

The American school that began with Alexander Hamilton drew the conclusion that land is a form of capital rather than a distinct factor in production. Henry C. Carey, in his *Principles of Political Economy* (1965, reprint), argued that the earth is only the material for machines. It represents the farmer's capital. This position was also held by Wilhelm von Hermann, who defined capital as a good that endures and yields an income. Land fits his definition. If land is just one form of capital alongside others, then a theory of the role of capital suffices, and no separate treatment of land is required. This theory reflects the widespread modern view that capital can substitute for land, and that consequently the goal of increasing capital can proceed without attention to what is physically happening to the land.

Some economists protested this trend. Marshall, with his view of land's active contribution to the economy, is one. He argued that "there is this difference between land and other agents of production, that from a social point of view land yields a permanent surplus, while perishable things made by man do not" (1925, p. 823).

The issue here is not merely theoretical, since theory is related to practice. When land is viewed as Marshall sees it, it is likely to be treated so that it does in fact yield an enduring increase. When land is treated as capital, its fertility can be depreciated as other forms of capital are depreciated. Marshall's view contains remnants of the ancient and biblical views of land. When land is subsumed under capital, the connection disappears. In today's world, however, it is frequently a gain to get land treated with the same respect as capital, rather than as inert, passive, indestructible building blocks.

Ricardo had also spoken of the indestructible features of land in distinguishing it from capital, and like Marshall he included its fertility. Subsequent economists, treating that fertility as capital, retained the point that there is still something indestructible about land—its extension. They came to call space "Ricardian land."

The end result of this story is that, despite many dissident voices, the discipline of economics has come to treat land as a mixture of space and expendable, or easily substitutable, capital. Both are treated as commodities, that is, as subject to exchange in the marketplace and as having their value determined exclusively in this exchange. Land is no longer a factor of production in any important sense. It is relegated to the level of a "residual" in econometric models that estimate the relative roles of capital and labor in production.

Even when it is regarded as space and expendable capital one might expect some attention to be paid to the land's physical properties. But in general, economics abstracts from the physical characteristics of the commodities, attending only to their price. Insofar as different locations or other characteristics affect price, the characteristic is briefly noted. But economists want as far as possible to abstract from the physically differentiated character of the commodities they treat. The preferred idea has been that, while fertility of the soil varies and mines vary in the richness of their ores, all matter and energy is potentially useful, given the right technology. Witness the view of Barnett and Morse: "Advances in fundamental science have made it possible to take advantage of the uniformity of matter/energy—a uniformity that makes it feasible, without preassignable limit, to escape the quantitative constraints imposed by the character of the earth's crust. . . . Science, by making the resource base more homogeneous, erases the restrictions once thought to reside in the lack of homogeneity. In a neo-Ricardian world, it seems, the particular resources with which one starts increasingly become a matter of indifference. The reservation of particular resources for later use, therefore, may contribute little to the welfare of future generations" (Barnett and Morse 1963, p. 11).

Although such an explicit statement is rare, the assumptions it articulates play a central role in economic theory. This is visible in the standard analytical representation of production in terms of a Cobb-Douglas type of production function. Even when it includes resources (i.e., "land") it permits these to approach zero while output remains constant, as long as capital or labor increases by a compensatory amount. The fact that resources may only approach zero, but cannot actually reach zero, is taken in some quarters as a great concession to their importance (Stiglitz 1979).

There is a further contradiction that results from applying marginal analysis too single-mindedly to a confused definition of land. This is that the notion of marginal product does not really make sense for capital or even labor once land is understood to include the flow of resources from nature. Marginal product only makes sense for resources. To calculate the marginal product of one factor requires holding the other factors constant. If labor and capital are held constant and the resource flow is increased, then it is possible to produce more output by working harder or more efficiently or for longer hours. But if the flow of resource inputs is held constant, then there is nothing from which more output could be made, not even by working harder, more efficiently, or for longer hours. The law of conservation of matter-energy forbids increasing material output when material input (resources) is held constant. And to calculate marginal productivity of capital or labor requires holding the resource flow constant. Of course, the fixed flow of resources may include some waste that could be salvaged for use by additional labor or capital, but, once that bit of slack is tightened up, the marginal products of capital and labor must be zero as long as resource inputs are held constant. The way economists have avoided this contradiction is to drop resources out of the analysis completely and substitute "Ricardian land," by which they simply mean space. Only then can one increase total product by increasing labor or capital while land is held constant. Even though space is constant the flow of resources through that constant space into production remains variable and outside the analysis. But after having defined marginal product of capital (or labor) on the assumption of constant Ricardian land, economists frequently slip back to the resource definition of land without realizing that they are contradicting the first law of thermodynamics by assuming that constant resource inputs will permit an increasing physical output. Marginal products for capital and labor must be zero if resource flows are held constant. It is devastating for the marginalist theory of production and distribution if the marginal products of labor and capital are zero, as that would imply a zero wage rate and a zero interest rate! Therefore the theory requires that resources be left out of the picture, or remain a part of the invisible, passive background, like air, and that land be reduced to space. (For a historical analysis of this point see Christensen, 1989.)

In these examples the passivity of land is taken to its extreme limit. Even its differentiated character that makes some materials better adapted to some purposes loses significance. Land is matter in the strict philosophical sense, pure potential to be formed by labor and capital, or in Cartesian terms, it is extended substance. Since all space on the earth's surface is occupied by some matter, Ricardian space alone requires consideration.

There can be little doubt that land is characterized by space and by exploitable resources such as soil and minerals. There is little doubt that economic practice increasingly treats land in this way. But there can also be little doubt that this model of land is highly abstract in comparison with the full reality of land in the way it was understood in the premodern period. The question is whether the abstractions are helpful and whether they direct attention and energy in the best ways as they shape policy and practice. Clearly no one concerned with the wild facts can think so.

Rent

Long before land had been transformed into Ricardian space and usable capital, the attention of economists had been directed away from land as a factor of production to rents paid for the use of land as a factor in price and profits. This was analogous to the shift of attention from labor to wages. Money is the common denominator for land and labor as well as capital. It is the commodity of money that makes possible the quantification of economics as an exact, deductive science. Features of this world that cannot be assigned a monetary price finally disappear from the present forms of economic science. For economics as a whole the question is not the disappearance of land as a physical reality—that is inevitable once basic decisions have been made about the nature of economics—it is the role and interpretation of rent.

The focus of attention on the rent of land, rather than on the land itself, is present already in Adam Smith. He distinguished the "produce of the land" into two types according to whether it always or only sometimes affords rent. Still, in his presentation, the land functions as a contributor to this production.

It is with Ricardo's systematic development of the labor theory of value that rent is explained entirely in terms of labor. Smith had held that before land came to be privately owned, the relative exchange value of things depended entirely on the labor involved in procuring or making them, but that once land became scarce rents derived from it added to exchange value. Ricardo held, in contrast, that rent is an effect and not a cause of relative values, these still being determined by labor. Ricardo saw capital as congealed or stored-up labor (Haney 1949, pp. 294–95). Rent, according to Ricardo, is "that portion of the produce of the earth which is paid to the landlord for the use of the original and indestructible powers of the soil." It "invariably proceeds from the employment of an additional quantity of labour with a proportionally less return" (p. 55) (1951, pp. 47, 55).

After quoting these passages Lewis H. Haney proceeds to summarize the argument:

"Accordingly, the position of landlord may be discovered by considering the successive steps by which the land of a country is brought under cultivation. So long as the best land is abundant and every one can have it by taking possession, it is manifest that there can be no such thing as rent. As population grows and the needs of the people become greater, however, the best land is gradually taken up until none remains. It is now necessary to have recourse to land of an inferior quality, which may be called land of the second class. Now those who have already taken possession of land of the first class have a manifest advantage over those who are obliged to take up land of the second class. Land of the second class must pay the wages of labor and the ordinary profits of capital, or it would not be cultivated. But land of the first class does this and something more. The something more constitutes the rent of the landlord; the farmer can give him so much and still receive the usual rate of profits and pay the wages of labor. [p. 295]

The implication of this analysis is clear. The price of agricultural products, like those of industrial products, is determined by labor. But that did not render rent unimportant. Rent constituted the income of the landlord class which was, in Ricardo's day, a major segment of society. Economics written from its point of view would not neglect rent!

But economics was not written from the point of view of landlords. The discipline of economics was oriented to industry. The interest was in capital and wages. If wages determine the value of the produce of the land as well as of industry, then rent, and therefore the income of the landlords as a class, was placed in an anomalous role. It was "unearned income." This analysis itself was an ideological weapon in the power struggle between the rising capitalist and the entrenched landlord. The importance of rent in economics was tied to the importance of the landlord class in society, with the economists themselves contributing ideologically to the weakening of that class.

This means that the decline in importance of land and resources, now abstracted from as rent, has much to do with the political demise of the landlord class. In any agrarian economy the landlord is very powerful. It is natural to see biological growth as the source of net product, and to attribute that net product to the productivity of land, as did the physiocrats. But land is productive regardless of who owns it. Ricardo's theoretical analysis made clear that the rent of land differs from all other income as "unearned." This view gave theoretical basis for the resentment always likely to be felt toward the landlord by those who work for a living. With the rise of industrialism competition arose between landlord and capitalist to hire labor. Also capitalists favored cheap food (low wages), whereas landlords wanted high prices for food and other products of the land, including natural resources. Capitalists, of course, preferred cheap resources. With the further development of industrialism capitalists became dominant and industrial labor began to organize in unions for protection. Thus capital became the dominant class, followed by organized industrial labor, with landlords, the formerly dominant class, a distant third.

Capital and labor are in direct conflict regarding wages, but in agreement in favoring low prices for food and resources. The major social conflict of the industrial era, capital versus labor, was softened by sacrificing the interests of the landlords. Of course, if food and resource prices fell too low, then land would be taken out of production, supply would fall, and prices would go back up. This result was prevented by the capitalization of agriculture, which increased land productivity and kept supply high and prices low without at the same time creating a competing demand for labor. In fact, labor was pushed out of agriculture, exerting a downward pressure on industrial wages.

In sum, the class that had an interest in high resource prices lost power relative to the two classes that had an interest in low resource prices. The fact that capital and labor were in basic conflict with each other only worked to the further disadvantage of the landlord class. The socially dangerous labor-capital conflict was eased by a policy of lower resource and food prices at the expense of landlords. Governments are frequently the largest landowners by far, but have not performed the landlord's function of keeping resource prices high. On the contrary, governments have usually followed a low price policy for resources precisely in the interests of fostering growth and buying peace between labor and capital, at the expense not only of landlords, but also of future generations.

To see the immense long-run economic significance of this realignment of class power, it is necessary to remember an elementary economic principle: efficiency requires that we maximize the productivity of the scarcest factor. Which is the scarcest factor over the long run, land (resources), labor, or capital? Labor is reproducible, given resources and food; capital is reproducible, given resources and labor; but resources are a different matter. Some, especially the minerals and fossil fuels most needed by industry, are not reproducible on human time scales. And even renewable resources can be depleted if exploited beyond reproductive limits. It would seem, therefore, that in the long run resources are the scarcest factor. It is not for nothing that the classical economists called land the primary factor of production. Even in the Ricardian sense of space, land is bound to increase in scarcity as population grows. We are forced to economize on the scarcest factor by its high price. Whatever the injustices entailed by the unearned nature of landlord's rent, the efforts of that class to keep resource prices high did have the effect of leading society to maximize returns to the scarcest factor. The demise of the landlord and the ascendancy of the capitalist led to pursuit of low resource prices and to technologies and policies that maximized the use and minimized the marginal productivity of resources in order to raise the productivity and incomes of labor and capital, especially capital. From a long-run perspective, minimizing the productivity of the scarcest factor is exactly the opposite of what should be done.

Our argument is not that Ricardo's analysis of rent is an error or that a decline of power of the landlord class should have been avoided. Easing labor-capital conflict by sacrificing landlord interests may have been the best solution, given the concrete situation at various times and places. We are not advocating reinstituting the dominance of a class of landlords. We too think it undesirable for unearned income to play so large a role in the economy. But for us this raises anew the question of whether the shift of attention from land to rent has not left out of account much that is of importance. And to abandon interest in land because one wants to reduce the role of rent in the economy shows how widespread the fallacy of misplaced concreteness has been.

2

NEW BEGINNINGS

6

From Academic Discipline to Thought in Service of Community

Beyond Discipline

Part One began with a discussion of the general nature of the discipline of economics. Two basic points were made. First, it is an "academic discipline" and a very successful one. Second, it chose to be a deductive discipline. From these decisions follow the necessary abstractness of its ideas. Three levels of such abstraction were noted. First, a discipline abstracts a discrete subject matter from the totality, treating it as if its connections with the remainder of the world were not important. Second, it develops a method suitable to the study of this subject matter that abstracts from it those features accessible to the method. In addition, because economics elected to be a deductive science, it abstracts from the historical character of what it studies and indeed from everything that cannot be quantified. This means it abstracts from everything to which a monetary value cannot be assigned. In the remainder of Part One major topics of the discipline of economics were examined to see how they were affected by this abstractive process. On every topic we found, in addition to strengths and insights, major weaknesses resulting from the failure to recognize sufficiently the abstract character of underlying assumptions. Economists are no more guilty of the fallacy of misplaced concreteness than other scholars, and economists as a group are not less intelligent, less dedicated, or less thoughtful than others. The problem does not arise from personal weakness; it arises from the nature of academic disciplines in general and from the nature of deductive sciences in particular, especially when the formalizations are applied to a subject matter that changes relatively rapidly. It was the success of economics in becoming what it set out to be, what academia so admires, that had the negative consequences described in Part One.

121

If this is so, then there is something wrong with the disciplinary organization of knowledge in general and with the idealization of the deductive method in particular. Accordingly, the economics proposed in this book is not a deductive discipline, although much deduction can be used in its development. This is why in the Introduction we did not claim to be providing the paradigm shift called for by Maital. He wanted a new paradigm that would enlarge the deductive power of economics. The shift proposed here is more radical. It is, first, away from the ideal of a deductive science.

Chapter 1 showed that not all academic disciplines are deductive. Hence the abandonment of commitment to the deductive form does not in itself reject the contemporary organization of knowledge in the university. Economics could relax its commitment to the deductive model and give a much larger place to historical investigation of the actual course of economic development in various cultures and times. Especially since the choice to be a deductive science rather than a discipline that takes history seriously is a relatively recent one, it is clear that it is not built into the basic theories themselves. The founder of neoclassical economics, Alfred Marshall, supported and practiced a historically sensitive approach. To ask economists to rethink their choice of Walras over Marshall is not to challenge the integrity of their discipline.

Further, deduction can still be important in this context. The difference is that if economics followed Marshall the deductive elements would be formulated hypothetically and the conclusions would be applied to the actual world only after careful determination that the requisite conditions are met. If conditions $A, B,$ and C prevail, then $D, E,$ and F also occur. If a society is composed largely of subsistence farmers with a small merchant class and no industry, then . . . If the primary goal of a society is to increase its GNP, then . . . If the great majority of a people have no independent access to the means of production, then . . . If energy is abundant and its use has no negative side effects, then . . . If the size of the economy is large in relation to the capacity of the environment to absorb wastes, then . . .

If a discipline is formulated in this way, then there are several tasks. One is to develop the implications that follow from the premises. This can be a deductive system, sometimes quite elaborate. A second task is to examine a society to see whether the premise is an accurate representation of an important feature of it. If so, then one will expect the outcome of the deductions to be illustrated there too. A third task will be an empirical check to see whether this is really so, and if not, where the error in the theory is to be located.

But a discipline of this sort will not focus exclusively on these hypothetical deductive systems and their testing. It will also direct energies to more purely empirical-historical studies of the course of events in the process of economic change. It will seek generalizations about changes as well as about patterns illustrated in the successive states. For example, if a free market can only function well in a society that holds certain values, and if the increasing role of the market erodes those values, this poses a problem worthy of sustained investigation by economists. Yet it is rarely noted when development of a deductive system is of primary interest. Our judgment is that in general *if* economics had been understood in this way, *then* the changing global situation would have led to development of new deductive systems instead of the further elaboration of an existing system more properly applicable to an earlier epoch. In that case some of the wild facts might have been avoided.

Beyond Disciplinolatry

Although part of the negative relation between economics and the wild facts is due to economics having chosen the deductive rather than the historical approach in its self-formation, not all of the problems would disappear if it became a different kind of discipline. Part of the problem lies in the nature of disciplines as such. We are proposing the dethroning of the disciplinary organization of knowledge. We are proposing in particular a nondisciplinary economics.

The connection in the educated mind between disciplined thinking in general and academic disciplines in particular is so close that the proposal to subordinate the academic disciplines to other modes of thought is likely to be greeted with horror. It is well to point out that there was disciplined thinking in Athens in the days of Socrates, Plato, and Aristotle. There was disciplined thinking in Paris during the High Middle Ages. There was disciplined thinking among the early modern mathematician-physicists before there was any formalization of their methods and separation of their subject matters from other topics. In none of these cases did the disciplined thinking take the form of academic disciplines. The academic disciplines came into being and then into dominance only in the past two centuries.

Furthermore, the hegemony of the academic disciplines in higher education in this country is quite recent. Prior to World War II, higher education was not dominated by disciplines. Instead, liberal arts colleges provided the major image. They encouraged disciplined thinking, but the education in these colleges was ordered to humanistic ends.

Some of them have succeeded in maintaining a liberal education to this day, but they do so against great odds, because the doctoral programs whose graduates they must hire are disciplinary through and through. Our polemic, therefore, is not against disciplined thinking but against its canalization into departments and its idealization of methods that encourage excessive abstraction. In this section we will discuss the limitations of the disciplines as such, especially of economics, even when economics is practiced in a historically sensitive way.

Since Marshall is a fine example of this historically sensitive economics, he can be used to illustrate the problems that inhere in the disciplinary organization of knowledge itself. Marshall stated, sincerely no doubt, that the dominant aim of economics was "to contribute to a solution of social problems" (Marshall [1920] 1961, p. 42). Yet the relation of his work to that end was quite indirect. This is because he allowed his task to be determined for him by the discipline itself and not by the social problems. Although he wanted to contribute to meeting human needs, his work was not ordered by an analysis of these needs. It was ordered instead by the problems of the discipline and the need to solve these.

If one assumes that the advance of the academic discipline automatically assists in meeting human needs, then the tension is greatly eased, and at some level this assumption does seem to be made by the university, by the practitioners of the several disciplines, and by the public at large. But only the sketchiest arguments are suggested in support of this assumption. One argument is that there is an inherent desire on the part of people to gain knowledge, so that the expansion of available knowledge in itself meets a human need. The disciplines are excellent ways of adding to the existing stock of information—so if information is equated with knowledge, and if the premises are true, the argument holds. The second argument is that the solution of human problems requires the kind of knowledge the university generates, so that the expansion of this knowledge through the disciplines provides what is required.

The validity of both arguments is open to question, but this questioning falls outside of any discipline. It would once have been thought to be a responsibility of theology or philosophy, but insofar as these have become academic disciplines they have abandoned this task. The task of the university, its relation to society, its structural organization, and the concomitant organization of knowledge are not a proper topic of study once the decision has been made to accept the disciplinary organization of knowledge. Hence the confidence that human needs are being met in the ways proposed can be no more than an unexamined faith. Since that faith orders the lives of so many sincere, thoughtful, and committed people individually and collectively, it is religious in character. Because its object is unworthy of such full devotion, we call it "disciplinolatry" and identify it as the overwhelmingly dominant religion of the university. To challenge it within the university is a "sacrilege." From our point of view it is one of the most potent and destructive idolatries of our time.

The argument that the expansion of knowledge is inherently desirable or meets an inherent need could be given an interpretation with which we would agree. People need and will always profit from a better understanding of themselves, of one another, of their lives together, and of their relationship to the wider context in which they live. There is inherent satisfaction in such understanding. Not everyone seems deeply motivated to gain it, but there is widespread appreciation for those who are thought to understand, even among those with other priorities. Hence, to whatever extent the knowledge gained in the university contributes to this understanding, the university is at least partly vindicated. And there can be no doubt that the university does provide such knowledge.

What then is the objection? It is that the *organization* of knowledge in the university is such as to work against its contribution to the broad human need for understanding. This does not prevent bits and pieces of the information it supplies in one form to enter into another organization of knowledge that does promote understanding. It does not prevent members of the university faculties from themselves using knowledge in ways that promote understanding. But it does work toward minimizing rather than maximizing these contributions. The more successful and exclusive are disciplinary goals, the less the contribution of the discipline to true understanding. The result is an "information age" but little comprehension of our real condition.

Some of the reasons for this were noted in Chapter 1. The most fundamental is that what is to be understood is concrete and concretely interconnected. The self that is to be understood is not a bundle of separate aspects, and it has no existence at all apart from its relations to its human and nonhuman environment. To understand it is first and foremost to understand this. But an academic discipline abstracts from this concreteness some aspect for study in separation from the rest. It treats this aspect as if it were self-contained and related only externally to all that from which it is abstracted. In itself this is methodologically justified for some purposes, and it is acceptable if the degree of abstraction is never forgotten. But that it *is* often forgotten, indeed that is sometimes not even recognized in the first place, is attested again and again in the university. The resultant knowledge often works against genuine understanding.

Those shaped by the disciplinary organization of knowledge usually speak and act as if the disciplines additively covered the whole range of what is to be known. This assumes that the real world is made up additively of the elements and aspects into which it has been divided by the disciplines. But since each has been abstracted from its relations to all the others, what are here added together are not the elements and aspects themselves but only those features that for some particular purpose were abstracted from those relationships. The addition of these abstractions provides a great deal of information. It does not provide understanding. Furthermore, the presentation of the information by those who have been shaped by the disciplinary organization neglects and even denies its abstractness, so that it works more against understanding than in its favor.

The deep-seated assumptions of the disciplinary organization of knowledge appear most clearly when those who participate in it recognize its limitations. That each discipline is involved in abstracting a subject matter from the whole is intended and affirmed. Accordingly it is recognized that there are topics not adequately treated in any one discipline. This leads to interest in interdisciplinary work despite the difficulty of pursuing this effectively where the departmental organization of the university is determinative and where status depends on one's contributions to a particular discipline. Unfortunately, even interdisciplinary work does not solve the problems generated by the disciplinary organization of knowledge.

In Part One we repeatedly noted the way that viewing reality entirely in terms of one discipline, in this case the abstractions of modern economic theory, has led to distortions. Some of those who are committed to Third World economic development have recognized this. They have sent teams of scholars to study the countries or regions to be developed. These teams usually include sociologists and political theorists along with engineers and economists. No doubt more of the reality appears in their joint studies than in those done from only one point of view. But the result of adding together the accounts of the several disciplines is still remote from the actuality.[1]

The idea that interdisciplinary work would solve the problem caused by disciplinary fragmentation shows that the nature of the abstractions made in each discipline is not recognized. This expectation reflects the pervasiveness of the fallacy of misplaced concreteness. If in the real world the subject matter studied by political theorists, sociologists, economists, and humanists had separate or separable existence, then the fragments could be put back together by the joint efforts of political theorists, sociologists, economists, and humanists. The problem of fragmentation would be solvable within the system. But this is not the real situation. In reality political, social, economic, and cultural aspects of human existence are indissolubly interconnected. Political behavior studied in its abstraction from social, economic, and cultural aspects of life is not the actual political behavior of real people in real societies. Information *can* of course be gained through this abstraction, and this information *can* contribute to understanding. When real people who are students of diverse disciplines meet and talk, there is often a growth of understanding as well as an exchange of information generated by the separate disciplines. But this growth of understanding is more in spite of than because of the disciplinary organization of the knowledge that is presented. It is often because people become aware of the abstractness of the ideas with which they have been working. For this reason interdisciplinary work is to be encouraged. But it cannot put Humpty Dumpty back together again.

The problem of disciplinary abstractness is exacerbated by the centrality of *method* to the self-understanding of disciplines. Every method entails further abstractions, and the prominence of mathematization as an ideal accentuates this. There is nothing wrong in using methods; indeed all disciplined thinking is methodical in one way or another. Self-consciousness about method is a gain. On the other hand, there is no one right method. To whatever extent any discipline commits itself to one method or one set of methods it thereby limits the aspects of its original subject matter that it will allow to come to view. To whatever extent it redefines the subject matter in terms of what yields to the

1. The inclusion of cultural anthropologists or geographers could reduce the abstractness and fragmentation, because these fields have succumbed less to the dominant disciplinary ideals. Just for this reason their status in the university is usually low.

method, the abstraction is reinforced and made invisible. If the only tool one has is a hammer, then everything begins to look like a nail.

Furthermore, there are many methods of understanding that no academic discipline affirms. Some of these are designed to open oneself to what is in its full concreteness. Buddhists have developed methods to this end. Some forms of modern Western phenomenology also have this purpose. This family of methods tends to undercut or relativize acceptance of the conceptualities basic to any academic discipline. It is not surprising that these methods remain peripheral to the pursuit of knowledge in the university.

Similarly, the method of critical examination of premises is largely absent from the repertory of the disciplines although elements of it sometimes appear in special courses on "critical thinking." The examination of assumptive elements in economic theory in Part One of this book, for example, is not likely to be regarded as a contribution to the academic discipline of economics. But similarly it has no place in the academic disciplines of philosophy and theology. The method employed lies outside of all the disciplines and therefore of the university itself. Yet, we believe it contributes to understanding.

The second argument for the disciplinary organization of knowledge is that it contributes to the solution of human problems. There is no doubt that people are attracted to the study of psychology by the desire to help with psychological problems; to sociology, so as to help with sociological problems; to economics, so as to help with economic problems. We also have no doubt that some of the students of these disciplines who are thus motivated have addressed human problems effectively or that some knowledge gained in the pursuit of the disciplines has proved useful. The question is whether the disciplinary organization of knowledge aided or inhibited them. The evidence is in favor of the latter conclusion.[2]

2. A less generous interpretation of the motives of students majoring in economics is offered by Alan Bloom: "The specific effect of the MBA has been an explosion of enrollments in economics, the prebusiness major. In serious universities something like 20% of the undergraduates are now economics majors. Economics overwhelms the rest of the social sciences and skews the students' perception of them— their purpose and their relative weight with regard to the knowledge of human things. A premed who takes much biology, does not, by contrast, lose sight of the status of physics, for the latter's influence on biology is clear, its position agreed upon, and it is respected by the biologists. None of this is so for the prebusiness economics major, who not only does not take an interest in sociology, anthropology, or political science, but is also persuaded that what he is learning can handle all that

To return to Alfred Marshall, who was no doubt eager to help with the economic problems of his day, there is little doubt that he had the learning, breadth of interest, humanity, and personal commitment to fulfill his purpose. But he directed these gifts to that end *through* the discipline of economics. Measured by his contribution to the discipline, his success has been great. But measured by his contribution to the solution of the problems he had in mind, it was minor.

One might claim that in the long run the development of marginal analysis or some other disciplinary achievement has contributed to the solution of human problems, and no doubt a case can be made. But a case can also be made that the dominance of neoclassical economic theory, the great achievement of the discipline, has had a deleterious effect, working against true understanding of the human situation and misdirecting human efforts. If the growth of the disciplines inevitably contributed to the growth of understanding, then it could well be argued that it promoted wisdom in responding to human problems as well. But if, as argued above, this particular organization of knowledge does not contribute to understanding but only to the increase of information, then it cannot be held to promote wisdom either.

The point is certainly not that the disciplined study of the human economy is incapable of promoting understanding and wisdom. It has done so. But much of this study preceded the development of economics into an academic discipline, and much that has occurred more recently has been in spite of the directive influence of the disciplines. Gunnar Myrdal was one scholar who successfully ordered his reflection on the economy to urgent problems of his day. He may not have made much of a contribution to the discipline of economics, but the contributions he did make to understanding and wisdom may be of much greater importance.

The alternatives of ordering economic thought to the service of human problems and to the advance of the discipline need not be sharply

---

belongs to those studies. Moreover, he is not motivated by the love of the science of economics but by love of what it is concerned with—money. Economists' concern with wealth, an undeniably real and solid thing, gives them a certain intellectual solidity not provided by, say, culture. One can be sure that they are not talking about nothing. But wealth, as opposed to the science of wealth, is not the noblest of motivations, and there is nothing else quite like this perfect coincidence between science and cupidity elsewhere in the university. The only parallel would be if there were a science of sexology, with earnest and truly scholarly professors, which would ensure its students with lavish sexual satisfactions" (1987, p. 371).

separated. John Maynard Keynes is one who used the study of economics to deal with the critical problems of the Great Depression. In the process he achieved formulations that have been integrated into the discipline of economics. This example suggests that there is no need to abolish disciplines altogether. The discipline of economics has its place within the study of economics. But the study as a whole should be ordered more to dealing with the human problems manifest in the economy than to advancing the discipline as such. That task should be the subordinate one. The discipline should exist for its potential contribution to understanding and wisdom. It should not replace understanding and wisdom as the goal of economic reflection.

The kind of thinking appropriate to enlarging understanding and wisdom differs from disciplinary thinking in another way. Just as the disciplinary organization of knowledge posits a world of self-contained subject matters, so also it views the disciplines that treat these subject matters as self-contained. Further, they are conducted with concepts that have the same mutually excluding character. But there are other ways of thinking, most fully reflected in polar and dialectical thought.

Georgescu-Roegen has emphasized the importance of the distinction between dialectical and analytical concepts in economic thought (1971). Analytical or "arithmomorphic" concepts are those which, like numbers, are discretely distinct, having no overlap with their "other." Dialectical concepts are not discretely distinct, but have a penumbra of overlap with their other. In Georgescu-Roegen's definition, dialectical concepts only partially overlap. Land is not sea and sea is not land. But a tidal salt marsh belongs to both. A dollar bill is money, a shirt is not money, but a credit card is in some ways money and in some ways not. In order to use logic and the law of contradiction to build a theoretical science, economists have favored the analytical concept and tried to exorcise dialectical overlap. But well-defined, self-identical, analytical concepts cannot capture evolutionary change. Nothing can evolve into its other if it at no stage overlaps with its other. Without admitting dialectical concepts, and a certain amount of contradiction, we cannot deal with change. This inability to deal with change is a cost of the increasing commitment to analytical concepts and the mathematical orientation of economics. Georgescu-Roegen reminds us that there is a limit to what we can do with numbers, just as there is a limit to what we can do without them.

One of the central limitations of the academic disciplines in contributing to wisdom is their professed aim of value neutrality. That there is here a large element of self-deception has been pointed out frequently and convincingly. The ideal of value neutrality is itself a value that is generally highly favorable to the status quo. Which economic questions are taken up and in what terms, even within the range allowed by the discipline, often depends on the interests of the economist or even of someone who has commissioned the study. More objectivity is in fact obtained by bringing values out into the open and discussing them than by denying their formative presence in the disciplines. We recognize that it is frequently possible to distinguish "is" from "ought," and that the effort to do so is an elementary rule of clear thinking. But to believe that some disciplines should specialize in "is," while others specialize in "ought," is at best a delusion and at worst an escape from ever facing up to "ought" at all. As we have seen, even academic philosophy now prides itself on its positivistic methodology.

As long as the disciplines discourage any interest in values on the part of their practitioners, they inevitably discourage the ordering of study to the solution of human problems. Economics is an interesting case in this respect. When pressed, economists will often say that they simply describe options and the consequences likely to follow from them. It is for politicians to make the decision based on their own values. In fact, economists constitute a lobby for some types of policies and against others. Their shared values are easy to identify. They are, above all, for economic growth. To challenge that as a goal is to place oneself outside the community. (One of us has felt this ostracism personally.) The insistence on value neutrality functions more to suppress dissent about basic values than to support actual neutrality.

Another shared value of the discipline is individual freedom. This value is argued for precisely in terms of value neutrality. Value neutrality of the discipline suggests that policies should not be adopted that impose the values of some, even the majority, upon others.

It would be a healthy development among students of the economy if there were open discussion of how their work supports the interests of some members of the society against others, of their personal commitments in this respect, and of the general values they affirm. Such discussion would make clear the need to work with sociologists, philosophers, and theologians in reflecting on the whole enterprise of study of the economy and of recommending economic policies. The resultant discussions would not be intended as interdisciplinary. They would not consist in sharing the findings of several value-neutral and autonomous disciplines. They would be human discussion of shared human prob-

lems among people whose socialization and special information have
been diverse. In the context of such discussion the real needs of human
beings can become clearer and paths of specialized inquiry ordered to
meeting those needs can be defined.

The proposal here is not to abandon specialization. That would be a
counsel of despair. There is far too much to be thought about for anyone to deal with all of it. The point is rather that the disciplinary organization of knowledge is not the best way to specialize.

Although specialization is needed, it need not go as far as it has or
take on the form it has within the disciplines. Here specialization is defined by some combination of subject matter and method. As more and
more knowledge is gained about any bit of subject matter, the less is the
possibility of any one person being informed of all of it. Similarly, the
more methods are applied, the less likely it is that any person can practice them all or keep up with results attained by those who do. The
adage about knowing more and more about less and less is thereby built
into the disciplinary organization of knowledge.

Since the ideal is value neutrality, every bit of information is supposed to have the same value as every other bit. To speak of a core of
knowledge in the discipline becomes more and more difficult. Hence,
even within a discipline there is less and less unity among the sub-
disciplines. The question as to which bits of information to transmit to
the next generation can have no rational answer. When it becomes impossible for the university to fund all the disciplines and all their sub-
disciplines, the decision as to which to retain and which to drop has no
rational answer from the side of value. It is likely to be answered by
market principles according to student demand or by political principles of faculty power. Since rational arguments must appeal to principles not allowed to be explicit in any of the disciplines, they sound
like rationalization of particular interests.

Within the disciplinary organization of knowledge there is only one
alternative to this sheer fragmentation. This alternative is based on the
view that there is a deductive or quasi-deductive relation among the disciplines. Physics may be held to underlie chemistry; chemistry, biology;
and biology, the social sciences. Within the individual disciplines similar relationships may be affirmed. There is some point to this. What is
studied in physics applies to everything. What is studied in biology applies only to physical entities organized in living forms. Chemistry lies
between these. This pattern of relations could provide a basis for ordering the curriculum (Turner 1986).

Overcoming Disciplinolatry: Some Examples

Several recent examples of serious disciplined thought on real problems have come to our attention, and we briefly discuss them here in order to give concrete examples of rigorous scholarship that avoids disciplinolatry. The most relevant to our book is a study by Thomas Michael Power, *The Economic Pursuit of Quality* (1988), which reexamines the basis of the economic development of local communities in the United States. The other two are studies of the problem of economic development in the Amazon, one by a social scientist who makes use of biology and history (Stephen G. Bunker, *Underdeveloping the Amazon* [1985]), and the other by a biologist who adapts the concept of carrying capacity to human occupation of the Amazon (Phillip M. Fearnside, *Human Carrying Capacity of the Brazilian Rainforest,* [1986]). Both Amazonian studies owe a large debt to the pioneering work on rainforest devastation by Robert J. A. Goodland and Howard S. Irwin (*Amazon Jungle: Green Hell to Red Desert?* [1975]). Focusing on the real problems of real people in specific geographical regions tends to force one out of the disciplinary rut.

Professor Power argues that even in the commercial sector of the economy, what we really purchase is quality, not quantity. Beyond a rather low level of income we do not spend our money mainly for pounds or calories of food, but for taste, nourishment, variety, and so forth. Likewise our clothing budget is not spent on homogeneous body covering, but for qualitatively distinctive and stylish clothes. Many important qualities are supplied outside the commercial economy, such as clean air, scenic beauty, safety, and a sense of community. It is the sum of commercial and noncommercial qualities that accounts for total economic welfare. Of course these qualities are not independent of physical dimensions, but neither can they be reduced to physical dimensions alone. Economic development is the increase in the sum of marketed and nonmarketed qualities available to individuals in the local community, as summarized in the following formula:

$$\text{Total real income to individual} = \frac{\text{Locally available wages}}{\text{Local cost of living}} + \text{Value of nonmarketed locally available qualities of environment}$$

As a result of free migration these three factors interact in such a way that total real income tends to be constant across the country. People in New York City have high wages and a wide variety of marketable qualities. But they also have a high cost of living and lack many nonmarket-able qualities such as safety, quiet, and easy access to open space. If wages were much better in A than in B, people would migrate to A until the resulting increase in the supply of labor in A, and the reduction in B, lowered the wage differential and/or altered the relative availability of nonmarketed qualities and the cost of living difference to the point where the net advantage from moving disappears at the margin. Conversely areas that are crowded and have few nonmarketed amenities have to raise wages in order to keep people from moving away. There is therefore a limit to how much better off one community can be than another in a country with no regional restrictions on migration and trade. This tendency to equality holds at the margin and does not imply equal willingness to move. Some people strongly prefer New York City, and others strongly prefer Missoula, Montana, even though for the marginal migrant the advantages and disadvantages between the two are evenly matched. Because of this limit imposed by free migration, Power suggests that local development policies be targeted to committed permanent members of the community. In other words, projects that seek to expand employment by attracting new workers into the community do not really develop the community, while projects that improve the range and efficiency of the economic activities of local people do develop the local community, and indirectly the larger national community. U.S. citizens have a constitutional right to move to another community, and Power does not oppose that. But he does insist that there is no need to encourage such migration, and that serving the quantitative indices of development does tend to encourage it, usually to the detriment of true development of quality.

Power criticizes the "economic base" models that treat production for export as the "base" or driving force of economic development, and production for the local market as derivative and dependent on export production. However, the only reason to export is to be able to pay for imports. If imported goods and services can be produced locally then the reason for exports disappears, and the variety of local activities increases as well. This is not an argument against all trade and specialization, but rather an argument in favor of short supply lines and local self-reliance, except in those cases where the cost in terms of loss of real technical efficiency may be prohibitive. Logically the economic base model could equally well be used to defend a policy of import substitution, because the increase in income to the region is the product of export receipts times a multiplier, which is larger the more self-sufficient the community is. Import substitution increases the multiplier, and exports increase that which the multiplier multiplies. The effect on the product of a given percentage change in either factor will be the same. For some reason, however, the economic base model is nearly always used to support an export-based development policy. The real economic base of a community is not exports, but rather, "consists of all those things that make it an attractive place to live, work, or to do business. That means the economic base includes the quality of the natural environment, the richness of the local culture, the security and stability of the community, the quality of the public services and the public works infrastructure, and the quality of the workforce. None of these things are produced by the commercial economy or produced for export" (Power 1988, p. 127).

Power criticizes a number of self-defeating strategies of quantitative economic growth, such as increasing the volume of business activity (sales volume); increasing income; increasing the number of jobs; or increasing the total population. None of these quantitative indices measures real development. Development policy should concentrate on things people really want rather than on some abstract description of the economic process. What do people really want? Power offers the following list of goals for local development policy: (1) the availability of satisfying and useful work for members of the community; (2) security for members of the community in access to biological and social necessities; (3) stability in the community; (4) access to the qualities that make life varied, stimulating, and satisfying; and (5) a thriving, vital community.

The sorry spectacle of state and local governments competing in the zero-sum game of attracting footloose industries by offering tax breaks and lax environmental regulations only serves to weaken the true basis of community development, both locally and nationally. Power by no means rejects the economic way of thinking. But he calls for a better balance between the commercial and noncommercial qualities that determine the welfare of individuals in local communities. His book is a fine contribution toward an economics for community.

The sustainable, nonpredatory development of the Amazon Basin is a problem that at first sight may appear unrelated to our theme of economics for community. But ecologist Phillip Fearnside has shown that the key to developing the Amazon is in fact the concept of ecological community, or more precisely the concept of the carrying capacity of the natural community or ecosystem, in this case the tropical rainforest.

By masterfully combining ecology, agronomy, systems analysis, economics, and computer modeling with many years of living in the Amazon, Fearnside has demonstrated the usefulness of the concept of carrying capacity to the formulation of development policy, even though he stopped short of coming up with a specific number. He has also explained historical and present failures of Amazonian development in terms of lack of respect for carrying capacity.

Many resist the application of the concept of carrying capacity to human beings. Certainly the concept is easier to apply to animals than to humans. For animals carrying capacity can be considered almost entirely in terms of population. This is because per capita resource consumption for animals is both constant over time (animals do not experience economic development), and constant across individual members of the species (animals do not have rich and poor social classes). The latter is not to say that animals are egalitarian. Clearly there exist dominance hierarchies and territoriality. But these inequalities are mainly related to reproduction, not to large differences in per capita consumption. Also, for animals technology is a genetic constant, while for humans it is a cultural variable. For human beings we cannot speak of carrying capacity in terms of population alone, but we must specify some average level of per capita consumption ("standard of living"), and some degree of inequality in the distribution of individual consumption levels around that average, and some given level or range of technology. Fearnside not only takes these complications into account but also factors in the stochastic or random factor of variation in yields from year to year. A great deal of human and nonhuman suffering could be avoided by respecting the carrying capacity of the rainforest and by paying attention to Fearnside's disciplined and careful (but nondisciplinary!) scholarship and research. The extraordinary utility of the concept of carrying capacity will be illustrated further in a simple calculation of the human carrying capacity of the Paraguayan Chaco in Chapter 19, in the section on "optimal scale."

Stephen Bunker turned from development theories to a combination of social, economic, and environmental history to explain why development policy to date has resulted in underdeveloping the Amazon. In addition to the history of the boom and bust extractive cycles, he explains the sociology and politics of regional development bureaucracies, the relation of commodity extraction and environmental destruction, and the structure of unequal trade relations in the Amazon. He analyzes the Amazon as an example of an extractive economy, which is an extreme case of the export-oriented regional development model criticized by Power. The value exported from the Amazon reflects not only the labor of the people, but the value of the depleted ecological infrastructure. "Extractive economies such as the pre-Columbian indigenous societies maintained may function well for societies bounded by their own eco-systems, but extractive economies geared to world trade tend to impoverish themselves" (Bunker 1984, p. 1055). Bunker gives the following example:

The reduction of 2,000 turtle eggs in the Amazon to a gallon of oil for luxury consumption in Europe involves greater inequalities in exchange than a calculation of labor incorporated in different commodities would reveal. At rates which exceeded 48 million eggs per year . . . and finally led to the near extinction of the species, the exploitation of turtles resulted in a direct reduction of human carrying capacity of the Amazon. The decimation of the faunal or floral species—manatees, caimans, fish, trees, and so forth—may reduce other species which feed on them. Simultaneously, population reduction of various animals essential to the dissemination of seeds and pollens limits plant reproduction. . . . To the extent that the extraction of resources reduces the use values in the environment itself, the values lost must also be incorporated into calculations of unequal exchange. [p. 1054]

The export-extractive orientation has persisted from the days of rubber to the present-day extraction of minerals both from mines and from the soil through nonsustainable agricultural and ranching practices. Bunker shows that although products change, and although the destination of exports is now more to the south of Brazil than abroad, the dependent character of the extractive economy has remained, and carrying capacity has declined since precolonial times. The recent fiscal incentives to invest in the Amazon have favored large scale enterprises with an export-extractive orientation, and the free trade zone in Manaus has stimulated imports to the detriment of local production.

These brief summaries do not do justice to the books. Our purpose was mainly to point to some concrete examples of the kind of disciplined, but nondisciplinary, scholarship we are advocating. That they also lend support to some of our arguments on the nature and importance of community is lagniappe.

7

From Chrematistics to Oikonomia

The Discipline of Economics as Chrematistics

Aristotle made a very important distinction between "oikonomia" and "chrematistics." The former, of course, is the root from which our word "economics" derives. Chrematistics is a word that these days is found mainly in unabridged dictionaries. It can be defined as the branch of political economy relating to the manipulation of property and wealth so as to maximize short-term monetary exchange value to the owner. Oikonomia, by contrast, is the management of the household so as to increase its use value to all members of the household over the long run. If we expand the scope of household to include the larger community of the land, of shared values, resources, biomes, institutions, language, and history, then we have a good definition of "economics for community."

It appears that in modern usage the academic discipline of economics is much closer to chrematistics than to oikonomia. Wall Street is dedicated to chrematistics of the purest kind. The modern world is full of chrematists. The ancient world had its chrematists also, but perhaps they did not overestimate so badly the importance of their activity. For example, Thales of Miletus was a part-time chrematist. According to Aristotle, the citizens of Miletus reproached Thales with his personal poverty as decisive evidence that his philosophy was of no use, saying, in effect, "Thales, if you're so smart, how come you ain't rich?" To silence these morons Thales decided to get rich. By his knowledge of astronomy he was able to foresee an early bumper crop of olives. While it was still winter he leased all the olive presses in the area at a low price and at harvest time made large monopoly profits. Many other teachers have since tried to emulate Thales' pedagogical method, but with less apparent success.

But neither Aristotle nor Thales took this little trick very seriously. After all, Thales had planted no olive trees, built no olive presses, discovered no new uses for olive oil, and made no one but himself better off. In fact, he enriched himself at other people's expense. Thales enriched the world with his ideas vastly more than he bilked it with his olive press monopoly. But that is not true for most modern chrematists: litigious lawyers, tax-gimmicky accountants, merger manipulators, greenmailers, junk-bond dealers, and unproductive rent-seekers of all kinds.

Oikonomia differs from chrematistics in three ways. First, it takes the long-run rather than the short-run view. Second, it considers costs and benefits to the whole community, not just to the parties to the transaction. Third, it focuses on concrete use value and the limited accumulation thereof, rather than on abstract exchange value and its impetus toward unlimited accumulation. Use value is concrete: it has a physical dimension and a need that can be objectively satisfied. Together, these features limit both the desirability and the possibility of accumulating use values beyond limit. By contrast, exchange value is totally abstract: it has no physical dimension or any naturally satiable need to limit its accumulation. Unlimited accumulation is the goal of the chrematist and is evidence for Aristotle of the unnaturalness of the activity. True wealth is limited by the satisfaction of the concrete need for which it was designed. For oikonomia, there is such a thing as enough. For chrematistics, more is always better.

None of this means much to the modern economist who is convinced that the great discovery of modern economics is that chrematistics *is* oikonomia, thanks to the invisible hand. The academic discipline of economics is at once the study of the manipulation of property and wealth so as to maximize short-term monetary exchange and the study of how the people as a whole gain from this manipulation. Chrematistics thereby intends to assimilate oikonomia. There is then no need to cultivate concern for the wider community or any of the virtues associated with that. Rational self-interest suffices. Witness the statement of Charles L. Schultze, former economic advisor to the president and now senior fellow at the Brookings Institution: "Market-like arrangements . . . reduce the need for compassion, patriotism, brotherly love, and cultural solidarity as motivating forces behind social improvement. . . . Harnessing the 'base' motive of material self-interest to promote the common good is perhaps the most important social invention mankind has achieved" (Schwartz 1987, p. 247).

In fairness to Schultze, he did say "reduce" rather than "eliminate," and he does conceive of the common good as something promoted by, rather than identical to, self-interest. That is perhaps the difference between the Brookings Institution and the Heritage Foundation. We certainly agree that institutions built on the assumption that people are selfless altruists are likely to fail. Our advocacy of internalizing rather than socializing external costs is based on just such an argument. Schultze's statement is a more acceptable modification of a view common among earlier economists. D. H. Robertson, for example, asked the illuminating question, "What is it that economists economize?" His answer was, "love, the scarcest and most precious of all resources" (1956, p. 154). Paul Samuelson quotes Robertson approvingly in his influential textbook. Earlier the view had been expressed by Gossen, noted in Chapter 4, that economizing on love should be absolute in that God made the world to run on egoism, and any attempt to substitute love for egoism, even partially, represented arrogant rebellion against the divine plan.

Economics has progressed since Gossen, but it still tends to overemphasize egoism. While not denying the force of self-interest we are nevertheless unwilling to characterize compassion, brotherly love, patriotism and cultural solidarity as depletable resources that are so scarce that they should rarely be used. We rather view them as analogous to weak muscles that have atrophied from lack of use. Because they are weak it would not be prudent to depend too much on them too soon. But rehabilitation requires exercise, not tranquilized bed rest. While we generally advocate market-like arrangements, we certainly do not view the market as, in T. S. Eliot's words, "a system so perfect that no one needs to be good."

Many economists have noted that matters are not quite that simple. Adam Smith himself emphasized in his *Theory of Moral Sentiments* that the market is a system so dangerous that it presupposes the moral force of shared community values as its necessary restraining context. The market does not economize on moral capital; it depletes it. The moral capital must be renewed by the community. Also there are spillover effects of market transactions on third parties. Chapter 2 discussed these relations of the market to the community as they have been recognized and treated by economists. The key term here is "externalities." Chapter 3 discussed the problem of measuring economic success. The GNP is essentially a chrematistic model with the additional assumption that individual economic welfare is correlative with the growth in the market as a whole. Economists have recognized that this is not true, especially because market activity includes many intermediate costs. Chapters 2 and 3 discussed how economists propose to deal with these questions without altering the basic chrematistic approach.

One main reason that modern economics has been chrematistic is that it has chosen to be a deductive academic discipline. Oikonomia does not lend itself to that; chrematistics does. In the preceding chapter we proposed both that it shift from the deductive to the historical model and that it break out of the straitjacket imposed by the requirements of the academic discipline. If it does so, it could study the management of the community so as to increase use value to all members. This leads to two important contrasts. Whereas those chrematists who recognize externalities try to internalize them into the market and thus into the chrematistic system, oikonomia studies the community as a whole and locates market activity within it. While chrematists, when they recognize that much market activity does not contribute to economic welfare and that some nonmarket activity does, propose to subtract the former and to add the latter, oikonomia, by contrast, suggests that no quantifiable features of the community can measure its actual health. In this chapter we clarify these two points.

Oikonomia and the Market

In Chapter 2 we distinguished between localized and pervasive externalities and discussed the standard policy of internalization as a reasonable solution for localized externalities. Here we must consider the more difficult question of pervasive externalities. To appreciate better the operational difficulty of internalizing pervasive externalities by Pigovian taxes or something similarly piecemeal, consider the problem of calculating the proper tax for internalizing the external costs of the greenhouse effect. Assume the main physical effects would be a rise in sea level and a shift in climate that would alter rainfall and growing seasons in a predictable way. In reality alterations would be unpredictable beyond broad generalization, and this fact alone would make internalization impossible. But for the sake of discussion, assume predictable changes. Even when the physical consequences are not in dispute the evaluation of the economic loss is subject to wide disagreement and uncertainty. Should cost be evaluated at how much the public would be willing to pay to avoid the change? Or at how much it would cost to actually undo the change and put things back the way they were? Since the changes involved in pervasive externalities are by definition not the kind of things that can be purchased piecemeal on markets and valued at any meaningful margin, citizens will have to express their valuations in terms of answers to hypothetical questions, rather than by the actual behavior of buying and selling. Will their answers reflect their honest preferences, or will they engage in "strategic voting"? Or will they, as mentioned earlier, simply refuse to answer such stupid questions?

For discussion assume this problem is somehow solved. Let's go for a number. Add up the value of everything lost to the sea as a result of its higher level. Include the real estate value of all beaches, all low-lying cities such as Cairo, Venice, and New Orleans, plus the cost of relocating people and possessions. To that add the loss in value of farmland due to changes in rainfall patterns and temperatures, plus the cost of relocating farmers, plus the cost of disruption of food supplies. Against those losses there must be balanced certain gains, such as the appreciation in value of new beachfront property and new farmland. Of course the salt marshes and estuaries would be totally disrupted by the infusion of extra salt water, and would take a long time to reestablish themselves in new areas. So we must deduct for loss of shrimp, oysters, redfish, speckled trout, and other estuarine-dependent species. Add the relocation costs of fishermen, the capital loss on shrimp boats, and so on. Let us call an arbitrary halt to tracing out the further consequences. Now we must take this tenuously estimated, nonmarginal, arbitrarily truncated chain of future costs and discount them by some arbitrary rate to get their "equivalent" present value. Then we must take that tenuously estimated, arbitrarily truncated, temporally discounted external cost and allocate it proportionally among all the interdependent activities that gave rise to the greenhouse effect. Allocation of joint costs, as economists are well aware, is arbitrary.

We submit that, while perhaps barely conceivable to a Laplacian demon, such a calculation involves so many guesstimates, uncertainties, and arbitrary assumptions that it is a will-o'-the-wisp, an ignis fatuus, a red herring. The change is too nonmarginal, too systemic and pervasive for prices to mean anything. Yet that is what the logic of internalization strictly requires. Is there not a more operational and less arbitrary procedure for approximating the Pigovian ideal of full-cost prices, and for recognizing at the same time that a change like the greenhouse effect is not really something to be paid for, but something to be avoided?

Fortunately there is. Instead of beginning with the impossible task of calculating full-cost prices and then letting the market determine the right quantities on the basis of these prices, we could begin with the "right" quantities and let the market calculate the corresponding prices. But what do we mean by the "right" quantities? Only that the economy is constrained to operate with volumes of resource flows that are within the renewable biospheric capacities of regeneration and waste absorption. Environmental carrying capacity and sustainable exploitation rates of natural sources and sinks are roughly definable in physical terms. We say "roughly" because we recognize that the concept of carrying capacity has its ambiguities. But these are small compared to the truly impossible calculations required to internalize a pervasive externality by the same method used to deal with localized externalities. Imposing sustainable biophysical limits as a boundary on the market economy will lead to changes in market prices that reflect these newly imposed limits. These new prices would have "internalized" the value of sustainability, the sacrifice of which had previously been an external cost. The market performs the complex price readjustments needed to reflect the newly counted value of sustainability, or better, of optimal scale, as will be argued below.

What we are really arguing is that the economy has a proper scale relative to the ecosystem. By "scale" here we mean physical size, in other words, population times per capita resource use rates. As the economy grows it gets bigger! Sometimes the most obvious things are the ones we overlook. The ecosystem, of which the economy is a subsystem, does not grow. Obviously the world is not static. But equally obviously the diameter of the earth is not expanding. The solar flux and the turnover rates of biogeochemical cycles stay roughly constant, regardless of the interest rate or the rate of growth in GNP. Consequently the economy (subsystem) becomes larger relative to the ecosystem and stresses the parent system to an ever greater degree. This generalized stress is what gives rise to the pervasive and nonmarginal character of some externalities and renders the expedient of piecemeal Pigovian taxes inadequate to deal with them.

Probably the best index of the scale of the human economy as a part of the biosphere is the percentage of human appropriation of the total world product of photosynthesis. Net primary production (NPP) is the amount of energy captured in photosynthesis by primary producers, less the energy used in their own growth and reproduction. NPP is thus the basic food resource for everything on earth not capable of photosynthesis. Vitousek et al. calculate that 25% of potential global (terrestrial and aquatic) NPP is now appropriated by human beings (1986, pp. 368–73). If only terrestrial NPP is considered, the amount rises to 40%. The definition of human appropriation underlying the figures quoted includes direct use by human beings (food, fuel, fiber, timber) plus the reduction from potential NPP due to alteration of ecosystems caused by humans. The latter reflects deforestation, desertification, paving over, and human conversion to less productive systems (such as agriculture). Taking the 25% figure for the entire world, it is apparent that two more doublings of the human scale will give 100%. Since this would mean zero energy left for all nonhuman and nondomesticated species, and since humans cannot survive without the services of ecosystems, which are made up of other species, it is clear that two more doublings of the human scale would be an ecological impossibility, even if it were arithmetically possible. Assuming a constant level of per capita resource consumption, the doubling time of the human scale would be equal to the doubling time of population, which is on the order of 40 years. Of course economic development currently aims to increase the average per capita resource consumption and consequently to reduce the doubling time of the scale of the human presence below that implicit in the demographic rate of growth. Furthermore the terrestrial figure of 40% human appropriation is really the more relevant one since we are unlikely to increase our take from the oceans very much. Unless we awaken to the existence and nearness of scale limits, then the greenhouse effect, ozone layer depletion, and acid rain will be just a preview of disasters to come, not in the vague distant future but in the next generation.

We should think in terms of two optima: an optimal allocation and an optimal scale. The price system, with marginal Pigovian adjustments, leads to an optimal allocation of a given resource flow, whatever its scale happens to be. But the price system does not lead to the optimal scale. Double the present scale or cut it in half and the price system will still give us an optimal allocation in the sense of Pareto. Are we indifferent to the scale of total resource throughput? As long as we are well below carrying capacity, perhaps so. Additional stress on the ecosystem would provoke only negligible feedbacks. But at some point a growing scale converts too many previously free goods into scarce goods. Marginal costs of growth in scale eventually become greater than marginal benefits. But the market does not measure marginal costs and benefits of changes in scale, only marginal costs and benefits of exchanges and reallocations. Imposed boundary conditions deal with the optimal (or at least sustainable) scale issue. The resulting market prices achieve the optimal allocation of particular resources among competing uses, within the selected scale of total resource throughput. The values recognized in selecting the scale are in a sense internalized in the price changes resulting from the scale constraint.

In one sense our emphasis on the optimal scale issue is a profound modification of standard theory. The modification arises because existing theory calls for impossible calculations in order to internalize pervasive externalities. No wonder economic theorists have not followed through on the logical implications of applying Pigovian taxes in today's world and have preferred to pretend that we still live in Pigou's world, where externalities were localized and nonpervasive! And yet in another sense the points just made are totally within the logic of orthodox economics. To say that there is such a thing as optimal scale is hardly news to the economist. All of microeconomics is nothing other than defining the optimal scale of some activity, be it production of shoes, consumption of ice cream, hours worked per week, and so forth. Economists define a cost function and a benefit function for the activity. The optimizing rule is to increase the scale of the activity only up to the point where increasing marginal cost equals declining marginal benefit. But, surprisingly, when economists switch from micro- to macroeconomics we hear no more about optimal scale. Each micro activity has an optimal scale, but the aggregate of all micro activities, the macroeconomy, is supposed to grow forever and never exceed an optimal scale! How can this be? One may be tempted to answer that the limit to the expansion of any one micro activity is simply the fixity or slowness of expansion of other complementary micro activities, and that when all complementary activities expand together in macroeconomic growth these constraints cancel out. But precisely this reasoning should lead us to recognize that when the complementary activity is the hydrologic cycle, or the rate of absorbtion of carbon dioxide, it is absurd to think of it as growing in proportion to economic sectors. Continuous growth in the scale of the aggregate economy could only make sense in the context of an unlimited environment.

Nevertheless, in suggesting that the optimal scale of the macroeconomy relative to the ecosystem is a critical issue (and independent of optimal allocation), we are not so much stepping outside the current paradigm of economics as we are urging greater coherence between the two major divisions within the existing paradigm. Yet another way to get at the issue is to remind ourselves that economic theorists have long recognized the distinction between optimal allocation and optimal distribution. The distinction we have been urging, between optimal allocation and optimal scale, is entirely analogous. Just as the concept of optimal distribution is based on ethical criteria of justice and is not definable in terms of efficiency, so the notion of optimal scale is defined in terms other than efficiency, namely ecological sustainability. The market sees only efficiency—it has no organs for hearing, feeling, or smelling either justice or sustainability. If we consider that sustainability is really justice extended to the future then the parallel is even closer.

It does appear, therefore, that something of a paradigm shift is required in order to admit the Trojan Horse of "carrying capacity" into the citadel of economic theory. Once that concept is taken seriously a shift in prospect from chrematistics to oikonomia will have begun. Little by little, simple growth in scale of product would no longer be regarded as the combined summum bonum and panacea. That indeed would be a radical shift in outlook.

Oikonomia and the Measurement of Welfare

Before leaving the issue of the coherence between micro and macro theory we should note that certain issues in macroeconomics point to the same shift from chrematistics to oikonomia. These have to do with national income accounting, and particularly with the use of GNP or NNP as an index of welfare or even sustainable consumption. Economists have never imagined that all welfare comes from national product. A large part of welfare is recognized to have origins other than production. Thus the equation:

Total Welfare = Economic Welfare + Noneconomic Welfare

As noted in Chapter 3, the working assumption of economists, however, is that total welfare and economic welfare always move in the same direction (Abramovitz 1979). In other words, the possibility that an increase in economic welfare would necessitate a larger decrease in noneconomic welfare and thus a net reduction in total welfare has not been taken seriously. Yet this is exactly the difference between chrematistics and oikonomia. The explosion of the populations of human bodies, artifacts of all kinds, animals and plants exploited for human use, and so on that has occurred in the last 50 years might better be called an "implosion" since it has taken place in a finite environment. The term implosion suggests a compressing together rather than an expanding apart, a process of increasing congestion, mutual interference, and self-cancelling collision. An increasing share of national product will thus reflect defensive expenditures made to protect ourselves against the unwanted side effects (collisions, spillovers, external costs) of imploding production. These extra expenditures, duly registered in NNP, are in the nature of intermediate goods (costs of production of final goods), and their inclusion bloats NNP. Add to that the rapid depletion of natural resource capital that is currently counted as income, and we must conclude that NNP no longer serves its original purpose as a guide to prudent behavior. As discussed in Chapter 3 the purpose of income calculations in practical affairs is to give people an indication of the amount they can consume without impoverishing themselves. A person's or a nation's income is defined as the maximum value that can be consumed during some time period, with the expectation of still being as well-off at the end of the period as at the beginning (Hicks 1946, p. 172). Clearly we cannot consume the value of intermediate expenditures or the depletion of natural capital without eventual impoverishment. NNP, as currently measured, is an overestimate of true income and hence is no longer a guide to prudent behavior.

Note that the central defining characteristic of the very concept of "income" is nothing other than sustainability. The term "sustainable income" ought therefore to be considered a redundancy. The fact that this pleonasm is frequently found in the economics literature is a measure of how far we have strayed from the central meaning of income, and consequently of the need for correction. In an empty world NNP as currently measured would be sustainable for a long future. In a full world it is not. The numbers reflect a different reality, even though accounting procedures remain unchanged. Thus the pervasive externalities of microeconomics are also visible in the macroeconomic perspective. The explanation is the same: the growing scale of the economy relative to the supporting ecosystem.

The classical economist Lauderdale (1819) clarified these issues long before they became politically important (Foy 1987). Lauderdale made a critical distinction between "public wealth" and "private riches." Public wealth "consists of all that man desires, as useful or delightful to him." Private riches "consist of all that man desires that is useful or delightful to him; which exists in a degree of scarcity" (Lauderdale 1819, p. 57). Scarcity is necessary for an item to have exchange value. Use value is a sufficient condition for something to be classed as public wealth, but not as private riches. The latter requires exchange value as well. Lauderdale called attention to the paradox that private riches could expand while public wealth declined simply because formerly abundant objects with great use value but no exchange value became scarce, and thereby acquired exchange value and were henceforth counted as riches. Although scarcity is a necessary condition of exchange value, "the common sense of mankind would revolt at a proposal for augmenting wealth by creating a scarcity of any good generally useful and necessary to man" (p. 57). In the Garden of Eden private riches would be zero but public wealth would be very great. As the Garden gets crowded and previously free goods become scarce, we witness an increase in riches and perversely celebrate, while not noticing the decline in public wealth. Other classical economists rejected Lauderdale's concept of public wealth as too broad to be useful. And indeed it probably was in a world in which the carrying capacity was large relative to the economy. But as our economy puts increasing stress on the environment, Lauderdale's view has the advantage. It obliges us to distinguish between the effect of finding new resources and turning formerly free goods into scarce resources. Only the former increases our welfare. The latter actually diminishes it. Both raise NNP. The Lauderdale Paradox, as Foy has ably demonstrated, is still very much with us. It seems to be the price we pay for defining wealth and income in terms of exchange value. In Lauderdale's time the paradox was simply a vexing anomaly of little practical impact. With the enormous growth in scale the paradox has assumed great significance.

To some degree the distinction between oikonomia and chrematistics lives on in our time in the modern distinction between the profit and not-for-profit sectors of the economy. In the not-for-profit sector we expect oikonomia to prevail over chrematistics. The not-for-profit sector includes government services, charity, public education, public research and information agencies, the military, and the university—and in the limit the socialist state where nearly everything is in the not-for-profit sector. Not-for-profit entities do not escape the discipline of living within a budget. They must make some profit, or at least limit their chrematistic losses to the amount society is willing to subsidize. But their "goodness function," their true bottom line, is something other than profit. The not-for-profit entity maximizes something other than profit, but has to accept some level of minimum profit (or maximum loss) as a constraint on the pursuit of its true goal.

Naturally, not-for-profit entities value success and efficiency as much as do profit entities, but they have no obvious measure of that success analogous to profit. Attempts to employ such a substitute are often unfortunate in their consequences, as illustrated in the following examples which, although admittedly somewhat anecdotal, nevertheless ring true.

The director of a public tuberculosis hospital was instructed to improve efficiency by following a plan of management by quantitative objectives. The director was instructed to define the hospital's objective, develop a measurable index of success in attaining that objective, and to evaluate all activities and personnel in terms of their measured contribution to that goal. A clearer expression of the bottom-line philosophy would be hard to find. Stating the goal was easy: restoring TB patients to health. A measurable index of success was more difficult, but not impossible. TB victims cough a lot. As they get better they cough less. Little microphones were placed by each pillow to record the coughs of each patient. Soon the staff and even the patients realized the significance of those tiny microphones. The frequency of coughing fell dramatically as prescriptions of valium and codeine increased. Relaxed patients cough less. Patients who cough less must be getting healthier, right? Wrong. They were getting worse, precisely because they were not coughing and spitting out the congestion. The cough index was abandoned.

The U.S. Navy reportedly experimented with "number of teeth pulled per month" as an index of how well their dentists were doing their job, with predictably unfortunate results. Number of teeth saved would be a more reasonable index, but too easy to exaggerate. A still better index would be teeth pulled that should have been pulled plus teeth saved that should have been saved. But now our clear quantitative index disappears in a fog of qualitative judgment, and we are back to trusting the judgment and integrity of the dentist—the very thing the objective index was designed to avoid in its implicit quest for a "system so perfect that no one need be good."

Like the dentist evaluated on number of teeth pulled, the university professor is evaluated by articles published. Miraculously the number of publications has soared. Is it because professors now work harder? Certainly they work harder at publishing, but less hard at teaching in many cases. They also work harder at creative adaptations: ways to serve the index directly while totally bypassing the reality which the index was supposed to reflect. One obvious adaptation is to write shorter papers, aiming at the minimal publishable unit (MPU). In this way you get three short, unintelligible papers instead of one longer, integrated and easier-to-understand article. Also expanding the number of coauthors allows the same article to feed more professors, reminiscent of the miracle of the multiplication of the loaves and the fishes. We do not oppose coauthorship (obviously), but it can be carried to absurd and abusive lengths. New journals can be started in each sub-sub discipline, further splintering the wholeness of knowledge. Since the advent of computers, number crunching has become cheaper relative to thinking, so another adaptation is to think less and crunch more—to correlate anything with everything and publish the results as an empirical test of whatever hypothesis seems to have been confirmed after the fact.

We are old enough to remember the time before publish or perish, and confess that university professors probably did not work quite as hard then. But books and articles did get published. Since there was no big extrinsic reward for publication, the intrinsic reward was dominant. Articles and books got published because someone thought it intrinsically worth their effort. From the readers' point of view, that is a good filter and probably contributed greatly to the coherence, unity, and relevance of knowledge.

A similar social filter against ill-conceived contributions to humanity was suggested by the great Swiss economist Sismondi in the eighteenth century. Sismondi argued against granting patents to inventors on the grounds that this would give an incentive for inventions whose only purpose would be to enrich the inventor. By relying on intrinsic motivation we are more likely to get inventions that benefit humanity rather than just enrich the inventor. Likewise an article published only because its author had something to say and took the pains to write it is probably more worth reading than an article motivated mainly by the desire for promotion.

We will come back to university bottom lines in a minute, but first let's look briefly at the ultimate in not-for-profit organizations, the socialist state. It too has a bottom line, an ultimate goodness function—emergence of the new socialist man in the classless society. But that, according to Marxist materialism, requires the material precondition of overwhelming abundance, which in turn requires rapid growth, which in turn requires meeting the quota in the 5-year plan. That quota is expressed in physical units. If the socialist nail factory's quota is set in pounds, then it tends to produce too many heavy spikes and not enough finishing nails and tacks. If the quota is set in number of nails, we get too many tacks and not enough spikes. If the plan tries to specify the quantity of every size and quality of nail, then it is overwhelmed with detailed information requirements and never gets out of the planning office, for reasons discussed in Chapter 1. Similar examples can be multiplied and have led the Soviets to experiment with profit as a bottom line in some sectors, because it seems a better quantitative reflection of the quality of usefulness—as judged by the person with the most information, who is, namely, the user who buys the item. Physical units provide too coarse a quantitative mesh for capturing quality—the quality of usefulness or of being wanted for whatever reason. Monetary exchange value is a far from perfect index of value, but at least it means that someone is willing to pay that amount for the item. That information should not be despised.

But the lure of a monetary index can also be treacherous if it leads a not-for-profit entity to get confused about its basic purpose. This can happen—even in a university.

What is the university's bottom line? On the diploma of one of us it says that the granting alma mater was "founded *ad maiorem Dei gloriam,* in freedom for research to sober fearless pursuit of truth, beauty, righteousness, and to all high emprise consecrated." One can see why it is in the not-for-profit sector! Its purpose is not to serve existing individual preferences, but to inform and improve those preferences by pursuit of objective value. Note the absence of any reference to a winning football team, or to turning out an employable work force. The latter is probably a likely by-product of having spent 4 years in the sober pursuit of truth, beauty, and righteousness (or even in mere sobriety), but is not itself the bottom line.

The lure of the monetary bottom line is so strong that sometimes universities seem to think of themselves as profit-maximizing entities— as when Professor X is lauded for having brought in grant monies in excess of his salary—as if "grants minus salary equals profit" and as if profit were the bottom line. Grant money is an index of success to the chrematist, but to the true economist (*oikonomist*), it has the fatal defect of measuring input rather than output. If the grant results in greater output of published research into truth, beauty, and righteousness then its benefit is already counted in the publication index, which, for all its faults, is at least an index of output. If no extra publications result from the grant then we would hardly want to reward Professor X for having unproductively absorbed public funds. Actually the input of grant dollars is a social cost, and should be counted in the denominator, not the numerator, of the efficiency ratio. The proper efficiency measure is research output of Professor X *per dollar invested in him.* The fact that grant money customarily gets put in the numerator, and the fact that our suggestion to put it in the denominator would be considered totally outrageous, do not alter the self-evident logic on which the proposal is based. If one can view this suggestion with equanimity one is a true economist. If it induces panic then one is still a chrematist.

Discounting the Future

Chrematistics deals with exchange value in the short run. Oikonomia deals with use value in the long run. External costs in today's world are not only pervasive, they are also long run. Twenty-five years from now people will still be developing cancer as a result of the Chernobyl nuclear plant accident. Indeed, with probable genetic effects taken into consideration, the consequences will continue for centuries. The costs of toxic waste dumps, acid rain, and the greenhouse effect will occur long into the future. Pigovian taxes must be levied in the present. How to compare present with future values? Economists, following the actual practice of markets, discount future value by a rate of interest to arrive at an equivalent present value. The present value of a future sum is the amount of money that if invested today at today's interest rate would grow to equal that future sum at that specified date. Thus full-cost prices, reflecting costs that are largely in the future, involve us in discounting. This means choosing a discount rate and assuming it will remain stable.

Even localized externalities can have long-run effects, so the problem of discounting is by no means confined to the case of pervasive externalities. Discounting is a messy and disputed business about which economists themselves disagree (Page 1977). Is the market temporally myopic, as many have charged? We are persuaded that it is, and that it is therefore worthwhile to try to build in sustainability independently of the market, as was suggested in our discussions of scale versus allocation and of the Hicksian meaning of income. Nevertheless many continue to believe that discounting is a rational solution to the social problem of making intertemporal comparisons of welfare, and the practice is universal not only in the marketplace where competition enforces it, but also in cost-benefit analysis where it is not forced but freely chosen. It is worth the effort, therefore, to look at the issue of discounting closely to see why it is not a reliable method of reflecting the needs of the future into the present, and why we prefer the more direct approach of guaranteeing sustainability by means of quantitative limits and safe minimum standards.

Everyone recognizes that individuals acting on their own behalf in markets do in fact discount future values. If for no other reason, mortality and uncertainty make this prudent at the individual level. But the community, unlike the individual, is quasi-immortal. Social decisions therefore should be discounted at zero insofar as mortality is concerned. Social decisions are also less risky than private decisions in the marketplace because the social project does not fail or succeed according to the vagaries of consumer demand.

The operational basis of discounting is that there exists a concrete process of depositing money in the bank where it grows at a given rate of interest, and this process is viewed as an alternative to investing one's money in any particular project. In their models economists seem to consider all good things as equivalent to a sum of money in the bank, and therefore to expect that good thing, whatever it is, to grow like money in the bank. But when in their models economists discount future utility or happiness, then we are already getting into misplaced concreteness, because there is no real world operation by which satisfaction today can be stored in a fund and even if there were, there is no reason to expect such a fund to grow to give greater satisfaction tomorrow. Money grows in a bank account, fish populations grow in a pond, trees grow in a forest, and so on, which may justify short-term discounting of future amounts of money, fish, and wood to their equivalent present value. But to extrapolate this procedure to discounting future satisfaction itself is problematic, and to extend it into the long run leads to unrealistic infinitesimal numbers because of the exponential nature of compound interest. There is, after all, a limit to how many fish there can be in a pond and how many trees in a forest; but there is no limit to how much money there can be in a bank account. Even money in the bank is relatively concrete compared to "utility." Many economic models are based on the maximization of the present value of future utility. Indeed, the "magnitude" to be maximized is not even "utility" (undefined). It is future, discounted, aggregated utility. There is hardly any concreteness here to be misplaced!

The prize for nonsensical discounting must go to those who discount future fatalities to their "equivalent" present value, as described in the following discussion of radiation-induced deaths associated with a nuclear power plant: "If all the predicted deaths over all future years were to be added up, the totals would be very large, 100 to 800 per plant. Some analysts propose discounting these effects to yield their present-day equivalents, just as future incomes are discounted to represent the smaller value of future events in present-day calculations. If these effects are discounted at reasonable rates, such as 5%, contributions for each plant-year would be between 0.07 and 0.3 fatality. Such a treatment of the problem is necessarily controversial; however, this expedient is adopted here as a reasonable compromise solution" (Schurr et al. 1979, p. 355).

No attempt is made to identify any operation in the real world whereby a number of fatalities today are transformed into a greater number tomorrow. Yet we must conceive of fatalities in some sense growing like money in the bank or trees in the forest if the inverse compound interest calculation (discounting) is to make any operational sense at all. The language is revealingly universal. The authors purport to discount future "effects" and "events" which would seem to exclude nothing. The growth of fungible money in the bank thus becomes the archetypal, paradigmatic norm against which all conceivable future events must be measured. This is a rather narrow metaphysics to say the least. As for the ontologically correct discount rate, we are told only that it should be a "reasonable" one, such as 5%. Would 10% also be reasonable? What criterion does reason appeal to in selecting a discount rate? The authors recognize that their whole approach is controversial, but justify it as a "reasonable compromise solution." If it is a compromise, then what are the conflicting approaches that it reconciles? If it is "reasonable" then give some reasons in its favor. Since no reasons are offered one is left with the suspicion that the motivation underlying the whole ludicrous calculation is simply to convert a "very large number" into a very small number under the cover of numerologial darkness.

If we were comparing earlier with later fatalities for the same group of individuals, then there would be a basis for saying that future fatalities are not as bad as present fatalities, since we all value longevity. Something like this is attempted by William Ramsay and Milton Russell (1978). Even here, however, it is far from clear that the inverse exponential function is a reasonable way of taking into account the value of longevity. Years of life are nonfungible and there is no reason to believe that all years of one's expected lifetime are not equally valuable at the time when they are lived. Having recognized these very fundamental objections, the authors brush them aside in order to get on with the calculation.

Even more problematic than the absence of a concrete process by which satisfaction (or fatalities) may grow is the fact that the future satisfactions (and fatalities) are experienced by different people, and the farther in the future the less is the overlap between the population cohort that made the decision and the cohorts that suffer or enjoy the consequences. Discounted present value represents the value to present people derived from contemplating the welfare of future people. It does not reflect the welfare of future people themselves, or even our estimate of their welfare. Rather it reflects how much we care about future people compared to ourselves. Because of the general expectation of growth in productivity it is thought that the future will automatically be better off, and consequently even an egalitarian treatment of the future would require discounting future consumption by the "natural" rate of increase in productivity. Such an expectation of continual increase in productivity into the distant future is little more than a wish, one whose empirical support from the last 100 years seems already to be coming to an end. As high-quality resources are depleted, and environmental services are weakened by pollution and habitat destruction, and as ever more powerful technologies seek to compensate for these losses, we witness greater technological risks (radiation, toxic waste, accidents), the costs of which, if included in the productivity calculation, would probably reveal a decline rather than an increase. If chemical companies were required to pay the full cost of cleaning up toxic wastes would their productivity increase over the last decade not be negative? If productivity growth is expected to be negative then we should discount the future by a negative growth rate, which in effect means that equal consumption for the future requires that we in the present should "appreciate" rather than discount future values—that is, a future dollar would be worth more than a present dollar.

We do not wish to press this point too strongly. Our intention is merely to show that discounting is not a law of nature, but is based on a number of questionable judgments of both value and fact. Consequently we should not hesitate to reject the principle of discounting when it leads to results that do not promote welfare. Directing the market to serve total welfare may well involve rejection of discounting in certain social decisions where community with the future or with other species is threatened. So far we have dealt with the future. Let us consider now the consequences of discounting on other species.

It is well known that discounting can lead to the "economically rational" extinction of species, even in the absence of other market failures (Clark 1976). It is even more well known that common-property externalities can lead to extinction, but this is considered a market failure and no one advocates it. Extinction by discounting, however, is often viewed as the rational consequence of well-functioning markets rather than as a market failure.

The problem can be phrased as, "When is it economically rational to kill the goose that lays golden eggs?" Any exploited species (fish, timber, etc.) managed on a sustained-yield basis is like a goose that lays golden eggs in perpetuity. Folk wisdom says never kill it. Present-value maximization says to kill it under certain circumstances, namely when the rate of growth of money in the bank is greater than the reproduction rate of the exploited species (and the cost of capture relative to the price is not prohibitive). The owner of the goose has two alternatives: keep the goose and sell the golden eggs in perpetuity; kill the goose, sell it, and put the money in the bank and earn interest in perpetuity. If the interest income stream is higher than the golden egg income stream, then kill the goose. Alternatively, the equivalent calculation in terms of present value would be to discount the income stream of the golden eggs at the rate of interest, and if that discounted sum is less than the price you could get for the cooked goose today, then you kill the goose.

The fact that individual capitalists are made better off by killing the goose and putting their money in a faster growing asset does not alter the fact that society has lost a perpetual stream of golden eggs. Of course society has gained another larger perpetual stream of value from the capitalist's new investments. Therefore, economists argue, present-value maximization is socially beneficial, since value gained is greater than value lost, other things equal. The problem is that other things are not equal. The mix of species that corresponds to effective demand (human preferences weighted by an arbitrary distribution of income and an arbitrary discount rate) will not likely coincide with the mix of species that is sustainable ecologically over the long run. Furthermore, the increased value stream from the new investment may reflect the short-term unsustainable depletion of nonrenewable resources, or it may have no real basis at all in a world where mergers, takeovers, greenmail, tax subsidies, litigation, and other forms of rent-seeking represent profitable alternatives to the individual chrematist without increasing social product one iota.

From the point of view of the individual capitalist or resource owner bent on maximizing his private gain the calculation is correct. But it clearly exposes the individualistic presuppositions of modern economics. From the point of view of person-in-community, things look rather different. What are the long-run consequences of everyone behaving in this way? Any commercially valuable species that is not too expensive to capture, and whose rate of reproduction for all population sizes remains below the interest rate, will be exploited to extinction. If the interest rate represents a kind of average of the biological growth rates of all exploited species then we have a truly destructive process. As slower growing species are eliminated the average growth rate of the remaining species (and the interest rate) will increase. Some species will always be below average, and thus candidates for extinction, until there is only one remaining species! Of course there are other factors that influence the interest rate and will likely stop this process short of absurdity. The pure time preference rate may be low enough so that the rise in the rate of interest is stopped. Also the price of capture may become exorbitant as the species becomes depleted. This is especially so if capture is highly capital intensive, so that a rise in the interest rate itself increases cost of capture. But all of this is rather fortuitous and one can imagine opposite contingencies. Technological inventions may reduce cost of capture. Exploitation of *nonrenewable* resources at very rapid rates may offer higher rates of return on investment and drive up the interest rate, putting more pressure on slow-growing species. And of course the interest rate is a target variable for such things as monetary policy and balance of payments policy. Do the Feds worry about the effect of interest rate changes on species extinction when setting monetary policy? When higher interest rates require more exports from Brazil to meet payments on its debt, we can be sure that the rate of devastation of the Amazon Basin will accelerate. If we know anything at all about interest rates we know that they are variable and uncertain—far more so than the biological reproduction rates which are forced into losing competition with interest rates over extended time horizons.

Following present-value maximization as a general rule appears to be a case of micro rationality adding up to macro irrationality. Such situations are well known in economics. For example, at the family level it may be rational for Chinese or Indian peasants to have many children, but from the macro or community perspective it is irrational. Similarly, it may be rational on individualistic premises to kill the goose that lays golden eggs more slowly than the average, but such a policy is irrational from the viewpoint of person-in-community. It is obviously questionable if community extends in some degree to the exploited species, but also irrational from the point of view of human community for reasons just given.

Here the market must be limited by quantitative boundaries in the interest of community. It is difficult to see how Pigovian taxes could correct this anomaly since it arises not from market imperfections, but from the proper functioning of markets within the logic of present-value maximization. It is a further reason for attempting to achieve sustainability by setting quantitative boundaries directly, and letting the prices be determined by the market, rather than by trying to calculate the proper prices with discounted Pigovian taxes and letting the market determine sustainable quantities. Externalities are too pervasive and nonmarginal, and present-value maximization does not sufficiently respect community even in the absence of market failures.

Another way of viewing species extinction is to see it as involving a change in the scale of the economy relative to the ecosystem. Usually scale changes result from growth in the economy with ecosystem constant. Here the relative scale change comes from reduction in the effective "size" of the ecosystem, a reduction in its number of species. We have already seen that optimal scale is different from optimal allocation. Discounting in order to solve the allocation problem leads to a change in relative scale when it calls for extinction. So an optimal scale may be incompatible with an optimal allocation that is based on discounting. Consequently another way of viewing the issue is to say that once optimal scale is determined, no allocative procedures should be allowed to push us off that optimum. Optimal allocation is defined only for a given scale, and therefore allocative procedures that imply a change in scale exceed the confines of the allocation problem and involve us in the customary conflation of optimal scale with optimal allocation, and it is of the utmost importance to keep these separate.

Chrematistics abstracts the market from the community and seeks its unlimited growth. When it is forced to acknowledge that market growth does not always contribute to community welfare, it makes ad hoc adjustments but continues to work for the growth of the market. This is measured in terms of exchange value.

Oikonomia views the market from the perspective of the total needs of the community. It finds the market an excellent instrument for certain functions, especially the allocation of resources. It also finds it dangerous. The management of the community so as to increase use value to all members over the long run requires that the market be of the right size to make its positive contributions while minimizing its harmful effects. For economics for community, the question of optimal scale is central.

Allocation = any distribution of resources

8

From Individualism
to Person-in-Community

The Individualism of *Homo economicus*

The concept of the human being that underlies price theory was described in Chapter 4 as the concept of a person bent on optimizing utility or satisfaction through procuring unlimited commodities. Chapter 7 showed that this way of thinking leads to chrematistics rather than to true oikonomia. True economics concerns itself with the long-term welfare of the whole community. It requires a different understanding of *Homo economicus*.

Kenneth Boulding wrote: "Economics sprang at least half-grown from the head of Adam Smith, who may very properly be regarded as the founder of economics as a unified abstract realm of discourse, and it still, almost without knowing it, breathes a good deal of the air of the eighteenth-century rationalism and Deism" (1968, p. 187). We believe this to be true. And however much one admires the achievements of the eighteenth century, we do not believe that its anthropology suffices for us today. The view of *Homo economicus* derived from that anthropology and still underlying the existing discipline is radically individualistic. Society as a whole is viewed as an aggregate of such individuals. We want to replace this with an image of *Homo economicus* as person-in-community.

The individualism of current economic theory is manifest in the purely self-interested behavior it generally assumes. It has no real place for fairness, malevolence, and benevolence, nor for the preservation of human life or any other moral concern. The world that economic theory normally pictures is one in which individuals all seek their own good and are indifferent to the success or failure of other individuals engaged in the same activity. There is no way to conceive of a collective good—

only of the possibility that there can be improvement for some without costs to others. Even this theory of social gain is possible only by neglecting relative status along with feelings of good will and ill will. It would be difficult to imagine a more consistent abstraction from the social or communal character of actual human existence!

Not all of these characteristics of current theory can be attributed to Adam Smith's view of human beings. It would be absurd to suggest that he was insensitive to the sentiments that bind people together in community. He wrote an important treatise on ethics (*The Theory of Moral Sentiments,* 1759) in which sympathy is the central theme. In *The Wealth of Nations* (1776), however, he begins by setting aside relationships based on benevolence in order to focus on those based on self-love. Benevolence can affect only a small number of our relationships, whereas we are all dependent on myriads of people for our survival. This dependence will work only as long as each person finds that performing services for others follows from self-love. This is accomplished through instruments of exchange, or, finally, the market.

Thus what appears in Smith's writings is an awareness of the bonds of sympathy in intimate personal relationship, but a denial that they have effects beyond that. Where sympathy or benevolence is not reliably operative, only self-love can function as a motive. In standard economic theory this sharp duality is expressed by taking the household as the unit of economic activity. Within the household, presumably, benevolence is decisive; between households, it is self-love.

It is clear that underlying the whole discussion is a profoundly individualistic understanding of the human being. In Smith's vision, individuals are viewed as capable of relating themselves to others in diverse ways, basically either in benevolence or in self-love, but they are not constituted by these relationships or by any others. They exist in fundamental separation from one another, and from this position of separateness they relate. Their relations are external to their own identities. What is true for Smithian economics, however, is not strictly true for Smith himself. As will be discussed more fully in Chapter 11, Smith viewed capitalists' self-interest as reflecting the internal relations to culture, language, traditions, and other connections with the country of their birth. An English capitalist invests in England, even if profits abroad are higher. As will be explained in Chapter 11, this aberration was necessary for the doctrine of comparative advantage that requires capital immobility between nations. But once comparative advantage was firmly in place, the appeal to community was abandoned as if it were a mere scaffold.

Human Beings as Social

This picture of human beings is profoundly erroneous. People are constituted by their relationships. We come into being in and through relationships and have no identity apart from them. Our dependence on others is not simply for goods and services. How we think and feel, what we want and dislike, our aspirations and fears—in short, who we are— all come into being socially. To say this does not deny that every person is something more than simply a social product. People also have some freedom to constitute themselves. Personal responsibility is based on that freedom. But this transcending of relationships does not introduce something separable from the social relationships. It can be only a partial transcending of just those relationships, and it is the quality of those relationships that makes real freedom possible. We are not only members of societies, but what more we are also depends on the character of these societies. The social character of human existence is primary. The classical *Homo economicus* is a radical abstraction from social reality.

In the real world the self-contained individual does not exist. In order to survive, an infant needs not only the goods and services of which economists are very much aware, but also love. The amount, quality, and character of that love, and all that goes with it, affects all that person will become. But among adults we find that some manage to exist with minimal social involvement. And when literature is surveyed for the example that most fully expresses this possibility of separated existence, there appears Robinson Crusoe. He is the self-sufficient individual par excellence. Accordingly he has become the favorite illustration of economic theory. This choice of the limiting case as normative model makes evident how drastically economics abstracts from normal social reality.

Economists may complain that they are misunderstood. What they have shown, they say, is that society as a whole gains as the role of the market grows. In the market, members of the community freely exchange, and the result is that more of the total wants of the society are met.

But just this reply shows the individualism underlying economic theory. The gain of the society as a whole is viewed as identical with the summation of the increase of goods and services acquired by the individual members. The society as such does not appear. There is no reason to suppose that the quality of relationships constituting the society has been improved by the increase of commodities. On the contrary, there is extensive evidence that the means used to increase production often lead to a decline in the quality of social relationships. Society becomes more like the aggregate of individuals that economic theory pictures it as being. The "positive" model inevitably begins to function as a norm to which reality is made to conform by the very policies derived from the model.

This same view of reality governs the influential measures of welfare employed by economists. Per capita gross national product is the total production of the nation divided by the number of people in the country. It ignores the human relationships that make up so much of what is prized in life. Similarly per capita gross world product is the total world product divided by the population of the world. It ignores the diversity of cultural and national societies.

The measure of economic welfare (MEW) proposed by Nordhaus and Tobin, discussed in Chapter 3, is only marginally better in this respect. By considering some of the social costs of increased production it does express an indirect awareness of relations that are ignored in the usual measures.

Again, "productivity" is defined as total production divided by the number of hours of labor required. The persons whose labor is counted are conceived quite atomistically. As "productivity" increases, some workers are displaced. Inefficient plants are closed with massive unemployment resulting. If all goes well, according to the theory, these workers will go to whatever place capital has found it profitable to invest in new plants or other businesses. This is the nature of economic "progress" according to the dominant theory. Here, too, the total lack of attention to social relationships is apparent. As long as wages do not decline it is assumed that nothing important is lost when workers move from place to place. The break-up of existing societies is without significance.

The individualism of economic theory shows up even more dramatically in many Third World countries. Where traditional society still survives, "productivity" is very low. Few goods and services are produced for exchange in comparison with the hours of labor expended. To improve productivity, greater efficiency is needed. This means that subsistence farming is replaced by commercial farming where more fossil fuels can be used instead of so much human labor. The workers no longer needed for agricultural production must move to cities in order to survive. There they can be employed in factories built by income from agricultural products sold abroad. The workers both in agriculture and in industry are now more productive, so the national product rises. This is the fundamental pattern of "development."

We will not belabor the many things that typically go wrong with this scenario but will simply point out its cost to the society when everything goes right. Existing social relationships among subsistence farmers are systematically disrupted. They are replaced by new groupings of farm laborers on commercial farming estates. In ideal circumstances these workers are paid well enough to be able to consume more than when they were relatively self-sufficient. But even in these rare instances, something very precious has been lost. Indeed, their traditional culture is largely destroyed, and they must content themselves with less personal types of relationships. Other members of the former community must leave, often without even their immediate families, for an urban industrial center. Even supposing that they find employment there that pays wages sufficient for them to meet their needs, the quality of social relationships and therefore also the quality of personal existence declines sharply.

The point of these scenarios is simply to show, if it needs showing, that the individualistic model of economic theory leads to advocating policies that weaken existing patterns of social relationships. Since relationships among human beings are not part of the model with which the theory begins, the damaging of these relationships is not signaled by the theory. The destruction of existing societies does not count against the success of policies designed to increase aggregate goods and services.

Jeremy Seabrook interviewed hundreds of older people from the working class in England. He has written of what he found in an impassioned book, *What Went Wrong? Why Hasn't Having More Made People Happier?* (1978). For the most part the people he interviewed were better off, by the norms of economic theory, than their parents had been. Yet they were far from pleased with their new situation. They felt a sense of isolation from others, including their children. Seabrook sees the situation of the children as worst of all. In his words:

The child tends to be stripped of all social influences but those of the market place, all sense of place, function and class is weakened, the characteristics of region and clan, neighborhood or kindred are attenuated. The individual is denuded of everything but appetites, desires and tastes, wrenched from any context of human obligation or commitment. It is a process of mutilation; and once this has been achieved, we are offered the consolation of reconstituting the abbreviated humanity out of the things and the goods around us, and the fantasies and vapours which they emit. A culture becomes the main determinant upon morality, beliefs and purposes, usurping more and more territory that formerly belonged to parents, teachers, community, priests and politics alike. [pp. 95–96]

Even if some believe this is exaggerated, few can challenge the basic point.

Economics based on *Homo economicus* as self-interested individual commends policies that inevitably disrupt existing social relationships. These social costs can be considered only as externalities and are actually little considered even under that heading. For the most part they are hardly noticed. We believe these social costs are of enormous importance, that the increase of gross global product at the expense of human well-being should cease. We believe human beings are fundamentally social and that economics should be refounded on the recognition of this reality. We call for rethinking economics on the basis of a new concept of *Homo economicus* as person-in-community.

The urgency of emphasizing and renewing community has been highlighted recently by Michael Walzer. He points out that "the idea of distributive justice presupposes a bounded world within which distribution takes place: a group committed to dividing, exchanging, and sharing social goods, first of all among themselves. That world . . . is the political community" (1983, p. 31). An economic system that refuses to admit the importance of this political community undercuts the basis on which distributive justice can be sought.

If *Homo economicus* is person-in-community, this fact does not preclude an element of individualism. The persons in question *are* individuals, and in some dimensions of their behavior this individuality and relative separability from others is prominent. Market transactions are generally well characterized in individualist terms. Further, these individuals are without doubt interested in acquiring commodities, and much of their behavior expresses just the rational self-interest attributed to *Homo economicus* in the dominant economics. Hence, many principles of classical and neoclassical economics, with proper historical qualifications, will function in an economics based on the different model of *Homo economicus* as person-in-community.

But what is equally important for the new model—and absent in the traditional one—is the recognition that the well-being of a community as a whole is constitutive of each person's welfare. This is because each human being is constituted by relationships to others, and this pattern of relationships is at least as important as the possession of commodities. These relationships cannot be exchanged in a market. They can, nevertheless, be affected by the market, and when the market grows out of the control of a community, the effects are almost always destructive. Hence this model of person-in-community calls not only for provision of goods and services to individuals, but also for an economic order that supports the pattern of personal relationships that make up the community.

Homo economicus as self-contained individual is the modern economist's model of the human being as consumer. Human beings as workers are those who sell their labor to the highest bidder. Since workers cannot be separated from their labor, they themselves function as commodities. The sale of labor is for the sake of gaining the income with which one can be a consumer. Hence there is a close connection between the two roles, both of which involve the element of seeking one's own maximum gain.

Homo economicus as person-in-community is equally relevant to people in their roles as consumers and as workers. Both are constituted by their relations to others. Although some may have to work at meaningless or socially destructive jobs, suffering discomfort and boredom, this is a sign of the failure of the economy, as is the poverty that precludes the ability to benefit from the market. The goal of an economics for community is as much to provide meaningful and personally satisfying work as to provide adequate goods and services.

Community Development

Almost by definition economics for community supports what is called in development circles "community development." The most impressive effort in this direction today is the Sarvodaya movement in Sri Lanka led by A. T. Ariyaratne. This movement involves a holistic approach to the village: moral, religious, educational, and political, as well as economic. It is inspired in part by Gandhi's vision for India (Ariyaratne 1985).

Community development as applied to village development in general involves taking the village rather than the individual or the nation as the unit of development. One then asks how the village can better meet its needs. The villagers themselves make the decision and thus determine their own fate. The result usually involves increasing their productive capacities. They may increase their water supply by introducing a pump, or their food production by replacing wooden ploughs with metal ones. Whatever the decision, the community is usually made more productive in doing what it wants to do as a community. Its community character and its productive capabilities are strengthened together.

The communities to be served, such as existing Indian or Sri Lankan villages, should not be idealized or romanticized, but on the other hand they are not to be despised. They are real units, social, political, and economic, with recognizable strengths as well as weaknesses. They have the capacity to identify their own needs and goals and to participate in realizing them. Sometimes what is needed for them to advance economically as communities is chiefly to remove obstacles imposed from above. Sometimes progress requires technical help from outside. (Among agencies engaged in offering such help, one of the best is World Neighbors [Bunch 1982].)

There is no guarantee that when a peasant village defines its own goals it will do so wisely. Yet the number and seriousness of mistakes that arise out of this kind of community development are far fewer than those that arise when individualistic theories determine what is to be done. The latter may introduce changes in agriculture (such as the Green Revolution) that destroy traditional village life or dictate the building of a large dam that floods the village lands. It can be argued that the nation as a whole profits through increased GNP, but we are skeptical. Certainly the villagers involved lose. On the other hand, the normal result of community development is genuine economic progress (even if small) from which most of the members of the village derive some benefit. The social and environmental costs are rarely large.

Economics for community supports this essentially Gandhian approach to development, but we recognize that India did not follow Gandhi. If India had adopted Gandhian economics, there would be far less heavy industry there, but there would also be far fewer urban slums and far healthier rural life. The prosperous middle class would be smaller, but the desperately poor would also be far less numerous. Today it seems that Sri Lanka has chosen not to follow Ariyaratne. The results will be similar.

The dominant patterns of economic development throughout the world have been quite the reverse of community development. They have consistently and systematically destroyed existing traditional communities, especially in the rural areas where most people in the Third World still live. Urban industrial "development" has been purchased at the expense of rural communities. Arturo Warman makes this point vividly: "The principal agent of the exploitation of the peasants is the State, which imposes the general conditions for the distribution of resources, their circulation and valuation, for the dominance of capitalism and its preservation. . . . The principal agents in the exploitation of the peasant, those who confront him in an acute and unadorned contradiction,

are the good and the patriotic, the promoters of dependent industrialism, or 'modernization' at any price, of the establishment of growth
as an objective in itself, at the expense of the people who produce the
wealth" (Warman 1980, pp. 5–6). Michael Lipton makes a similar
point: "Resource allocations, within the city and the village as well as
between them, reflect urban priorities rather than equity or efficiency.
The damage has been increased by misguided ideological imports, liberal and Marxian, and by the town's success in buying off part of the
rural elite, thus transferring most of the costs of the process to the rural
poor" (Lipton 1976, p. 13).

Although dominant pressures in development strategy continue in
this direction, some leading Western thinkers on development have realized that Lipton is correct that the urban bias, based on indifference to
existing communities, has "made the development process needlessly
slow and unfair" (Lipton 1976, p. 13). One such theorist, Denis Goulet,
has undertaken to make concrete proposals for overall national development strategy that takes account of the real needs of real people. In
his proposal for Mexico he embodies "a concern for aggregate economic
growth, a high priority assigned to redistributing the economic and social fruits of growth, an allocation of resources aimed primarily at meeting the Basic Human Needs of a country's poorest people, and a planning policy that actively promotes cultural diversity by building on the
foundations of tradition" (Goulet 1983, p. 156). This recommendation
clearly moves toward an economics for community. Goulet's summary
of the two basic options facing Mexico states the options in sharp relief.

The neoliberal model favors (1) a high degree of centralization in decision
making, thus perpetuating the extant mode; (2) elitist control over information,
power, and resources accompanied by a ritualistic homage paid to the 'masses'
and their organizations; and (3) a cultural priority assigned to industry and to
the industrialization of agriculture, with a strong orientation toward making
Mexico competitive (and a strong earner of foreign currencies) in global markets.

Conversely, a 'nationalistic' strategy favors (1) greater decentralization at all
levels—in government, the distribution of funds, the assignment of responsibility, and the diffusion of information; (2) widespread popular participation in
decisions from below, in the case of formal organizations, and from outside the
system, in the case of dealings with the government or the economic power
structure (banks, government agencies, etc.) and (3) a high priority given to
making small agricultural production (of ejidal cultivators, either singly or in
collective organizations, family farmers, etc.) more productive thanks to a clus-

ter of supports enabling it to compete financially and technically with larger commercial farms principally oriented to exports. The smaller farm sector will aim, at first, at satisfying the basic needs of those working in it and, later, at creating an expanded base for economic well-being. [Goulet 1983, pp. 70–71]

The issue of what constitutes the community to be developed is often quite complex, involving as it does groups of individuals who are not necessarily homogeneous ethnically, culturally, or religiously. Gandhi, whose thought is clearly community-oriented, faced such complexities. His most difficult problem was the resolution of Hindu-Muslim tensions in the transition to independence. Gandhi's response to this problem can serve as a reminder of the complexities involved in applying a formal model to the real world.

Before partition India had strong Muslim as well as Hindu communities. Segments of these communities could be found in thousands of peasant villages. Gandhi sought to strengthen the villages as villages, emphasizing the shared community of Hindus and Muslims. Jinnah appealed to the Muslim community to separate itself from the Hindu one. Jinnah was successful, and there was an enormous exchange of populations between what became Pakistan and India. Both the suffering of the dislocated and the deaths from the slaughter on both sides, as feelings rose to fever pitch, constituted a horrendous price. The legacy of bitterness still poisons international relations.

We join Gandhi both in favoring the maintenance of pluralistic communities including Hindus and Muslims and in believing that would have been possible, had Muslim leadership been supportive. History could have taken another course. The villages that included both Hindus and Muslims had greater difficulty in maintaining community than did homogeneous ones. But many had succeeded moderately well for long periods. In the long run, the communities were the richer for the variety within them. We mourn the destruction of those communities.

Definition of Community

Although what we mean by "community" may be conveyed as well in such examples as in abstract formulation, and although some of it can become clear only as we spell out policies for community in Part Three, there is a range of issues that can be didactically discussed at this point to sharpen our meaning and explain our policies.

Like all important terms, "community" has been used in many ways. There is no fixed meaning. Hence we are free within fairly wide parameters to give it that meaning that seems important to our project. Still we hope in doing so not to be simply generating a technical term the meaning of which a reader can only memorize. We hope our use makes contact with wide segments of existing usage and connotation.

Our basic conviction is that persons are internally related to one another (i.e., their relationships define their identities as persons) so that any view of people that treats them as self-contained individuals falsifies the real situation. This view is often called the social view. It is a commonplace of social psychology. It is presupposed in the sociology of knowledge. To express this view we could have offered as our paradigm the social person or person-in-society. We could have made our point in that way, but we have chosen instead to speak of person-in-community. There is no significant denotative difference. The College Edition of *Webster's New World Dictionary of the American Language* gives as its first meaning of "community," "the people living in the same district, city, etc., under the same laws." The first definition of "society" is "a group of animals or plants living together under the same environment and regarded as constituting a homogeneous unit or entity: especially a group of persons regarded as forming a single community." Clearly the process of explaining our meaning could begin with either term. Nevertheless, the choice does have some importance.

This importance stems especially from the influence on the sociological discussion of the German scholar Ferdinand Toennies. He gave to the German words "Gemeinschaft" and "Gesellschaft" quite distinct meanings; and since these are translated "community" and "society," the distinction has had importance also in the United States. In Toennies's usage, "community" is the natural grouping of people based on kinship and neighborhood, shared culture and folkways. The clearest examples would be tribes and peasant villages. Society is based on impersonal contractual and legal relationships that are independent of other commonalities. A modern city or state is necessarily a society rather than a community (Toennies 1965).

If we were forced to adopt this polarized usage of the terms, we would have to write person-in-community-and-society. We are concerned for small, intimate, interpersonal communities and would like to see an economy that enabled these to flourish. But we are also interested in nation-states and even larger groupings such as the European Economic Community, and these certainly cannot be communities in Toennies's sense.

The history of the use of "community" after Toennies raises questions about his definition. It is clear that the commonality and intimacy of relations he associated with this term is most often tied to homogeneity—cultural, religious, and ethnic. To call for community, then, can be to work against pluralism in all these forms. It functioned in just this way in Germany during the Nazi period, so that Gemeinschaft is a word that sensitive Germans can use today only with special precautions.

Although we are not committed to the destruction of all homogeneous communities around the world, and although we think that national aspirations based on language and culture and opposition to arbitrarily drawn boundaries should be taken with great seriousness, the promotion of homogeneity in our pluralistic society is certainly *not* our interest. Diversity may make positive relationships more difficult, but it adds greatly to the richness of the whole. In the United States we have a unique opportunity and challenge to continue to make "out of many one" at the national level, in every larger region, and in most smaller ones as well. If the word "society" avoids the danger of celebrating homogeneity, it might be a better one to use.

Yet it is precisely in this instance that we want to retain the word community. The unity we want in our towns, states, and nations is not merely a legal and contractual one. Such arrangements belong to the pattern of external relations that allows people to keep one another at a distance, indifferent to one another's fate. We want a term that suggests that people are bound up with one another, sharing, despite differences, a common identity. We want to emphasize that people participate together in shaping the larger grouping of which all are members. The word community seems to carry these connotations better than "society."

Another problem with affirming community arises from the connotations the term has for many American readers. They remember the rural communities, small towns, or suburbs of their youth with their oppressive legalism, narrow interests, pressures for conformity, prejudices, and watchfulness. For them the anonymity of the city or the university was a great relief. They want no part in reinstituting the oppression from which they escaped. To avoid these negative connotations of "community," society might be a safer, more neutral, word.

But again we prefer to remain with "community." Communities can certainly be oppressive, and we do not doubt the need of many to escape them in the process of growing up. We hope that the pluralistic communities we envision would be less restrictive and enable their members to grow further. But even if some of the communities are highly parochial, we should not exaggerate the negative character of their life. Most of those who outgrew them were able to do so because of basic securities engendered in that social matrix. And others—many others actually—never needed to leave. If they left it was often because of economic pressures engendered by anticommunity forces rather than from any need for the anonymity of city life.

When the negative features of rural, small-town, and suburban life are contrasted with those of the inner city, the advantages of community are manifest. In the city, gangs express the otherwise unfilled need for group identification. They are far more oppressive of their members than are the pressures of a normal community. The drug culture is widespread indeed, but the problem is most intractable where community is at the lowest ebb. We believe the problems of community life, and they are real even in the best of communities, are to be worked at and solved. The solution is not individualistic cosmopolitanism or anonymity.

The hostility to geographically defined community is certainly in part reaction to real personal problems with real communities. But the tenacity of this hostility in the face of overwhelming evidence of the catastrophes that follow its destruction leads one to sympathize with Baker Bownell's outburst against "the educated" forty years ago: "It is the persistent assumption of those who are most influential in the modern world that large-scale organization and contemporary urban culture can somehow provide suitable substitutes for the values of the human community that they destroy. For lack of a better word I call these persons the 'educated.' . . . They may be capitalist or they may be Communist in their affiliation. . . . But below these relatively superficial variations . . . there is a deeper affiliation. They are affiliated in the abstract, anonymous, vastly extensive culture of the modern city" (Brownell 1950, pp. 19–20).

In any case communities come in all sizes and types. Those who prefer cities can live in them. New types of communities can be welcomed. Our point is only that the personal or interpersonal note, sounded more clearly in "community" than in "society," is part of our intention.

Rather than using "community" and "society" to juxtapose two types of human grouping, as Toennies does, one intimate and the other impersonal, we prefer to view community as one form of society. In this use every community is a society, but a society can be so impersonal as to lack communal character. This is similar to though not identical with René Koenig's usage. He says that "the community is a basic form of society" including cities as well as small towns and rural villages. But he excludes such larger groupings as the nation-state. Nevertheless, his explicit definition is open to the still wider application we make: "The community appears as a 'social system'; that is to say a relationship which is characterized, among other things, by the fact that the people concerned are conscious of the relationship, conscious of its limits, and conscious of its differences from other similar relationships" (Koenig 1968, p. 28).

To have a communal character in this usage does not entail intimacy among all the participants. It does entail that membership in the society contributes to self-identification. We accept this requirement and add three others. A society should not be called a community unless (1) there is extensive participation by its members in the decisions by which its life is governed, (2) the society as a whole takes responsibility for the members, and (3) this responsibility includes respect for the diverse individuality of these members. By these definitions there can be a totalitarian society, but there can be no totalitarian community. To illustrate in another way, for the alienated youth in large cities, those cities remain the societies of which they are members, but they do not constitute, for them, communities.

Clearly, "community" so defined, is a matter of degree. The extent to which a society contributes to the identity of its members, the extent to which they participate in its governance, the extent to which it takes responsibility for its members and the extent to which it affirms them in their self-determined diversity all vary. "Community" in our usage, in distinction from Koenig's, is a normative term. We favor societies at many levels becoming more communal by all four of the criteria listed. Economics for community is economics that encourages these developments.

If community is a normative term, should we not go on to describe the ideal community? As this book proceeds, our preferences for the shape of community will become clearer. But there is a tension between stressing participation and spelling out forms and practices of government. In the United States we can hardly imagine forms of participation other than democratic ones. We favor participatory democracy. But in some cultures what we mean by democracy is an alien imposition that inhibits participation rather than evoking it. Hence, we are disinclined to add to the normative elements mentioned above. We want to be open to many different ways in which societies can function as healthy communities.

At what level or in how large a region do or should the primary communities exist? In the Introduction we wrote approvingly of Dudley Seers's call for national economies. Nation-states are today extremely important societies. They are in many instances the only loci of power capable of asserting themselves effectively against those forces that erode all community. They do, in many instances, contribute strongly to the self-identification of their citizens, and at least some of them allow for considerable participation in governance. Most of them have concern for the well-being of their citizens, and some affirm the diversity among them. Hence nations can be communities, and some are quite good communities. At the present time we join Seers in calling for economics to serve national communities.

It is important to see what difference this would make. The current economic ideal is that national boundaries not impede the global economy. Increasingly this means that economic decisions of determinative importance to the people of a nation are made by persons who are not responsible to them in any way. In short, whatever form of government the state may have, its people cannot participate in the most important decisions governing their daily lives. This weakens the possibility for a nation-state to be a community. With a national economy, on the contrary, there is some possibility for the people through their government to share in decisions. A healthy national community is possible.

There can be no effective national economy if a people cannot feed themselves and otherwise meet their essential needs. Hence a national economy for community will be a relatively self-sufficient economy. This does not preclude trade, but it does preclude *dependence* on trade, especially where the nation cannot participate in determining the terms of trade.

There is, of course, no assurance that a national economy will serve the interests of its people. It may serve the interests of a small ruling class and exploit the people. We do not believe that any system will guarantee justice and righteousness. Nevertheless, there is more possibility for people to participate in the decisions of their own national government than those of another one or of a transnational corporation.

In some instances the nation-state may be too small a level at which to seek relative self-sufficiency. The European Common Market may provide a positive example of a grouping of nations into a larger community. Present trends toward European centralization, however, may threaten national community. Paradoxically, some regional communities (e.g., Catalonia) welcome the weakening of the national state in the expectation of having more regional autonomy under the more remote rule of the Common Market. A common market is probably needed in Central America. Only specialized knowledge of the endlessly varied situations in all parts of the world would indicate when the grouping of nations in this way is desirable.

We believe that the opposite problem is more prevalent. In many instances the nation-state is already too large and too remote from ordinary people for effective participation to be possible. Decentralization of the economy within the nation should accompany nationalization in relation to the global economy. Many regions within the United States could become relatively self-sufficient. With economic decentralization there could come political decentralization as well. The main formal point is that a political community cannot be healthy if it cannot exercise a significant measure of control over its economic life. The second formal point is that of the Catholic teaching of "subsidiarity": power should be located as close to the people as possible, that is, in the smallest units that are feasible. Our special emphasis is that except for a few functions, political power that cannot affect the economic order is ineffective. Hence we tie political decentralization to economic decentralization.

Since economic self-sufficiency is not an absolute, it is possible to think of rather small communities having considerable economic self-determination without supposing that they could supply all their needs. In this country at the level of the states a large degree of self-determination would be possible with a decentralized economy. If the economy moves in this direction, states could become much more the units of self-governance envisioned by the founding fathers. The national government would again become a federal government as intended. Since one of the main reasons for concentrating power at the national level was to promote a national economy, the move toward decentralization of the economy would naturally be accompanied by a reversal of this trend toward political centralization.

There has been, however, a second factor in the nationalization of power that should not be simply reversed. States rights have sometimes been asserted for good causes, such as environmental protection, but they have been asserted too often as a cloak for the oppression of one segment of the state's population by another. The call for states rights has been particularly associated with the disenfranchisement and exploitation of blacks by Southern whites.

Although it should not be the task of the federal government to specify in detail the forms of government employed by states, it should be its responsibility to insure that they have at least the minimal trappings of community: allowing participation by all their citizens, accepting responsibility for all, and respecting them all in their diversity. This means that there are human rights that the federal government can rightly insist the states respect. The majority of the citizens can decide much, but they cannot decide to disenfranchise the minority or force on it a conformity that denies respect to its distinctiveness. Our present legal system should become more decentralized in dealing with economic issues, but it should maintain its present degree of centralization with respect to civil and human rights.

9

From Cosmopolitanism to Communities of Communities

Communities of Regional Communities

People in the United States are citizens both of their states and of the nation. At present, self-identification is generally much stronger with the nation than with the state. This is partly because of high mobility within the nation, which is required by the nationally and now globally integrated economy. It is also because power is concentrated at the national level, so that the most important and interesting decisions are made there. But despite a high level of self-identification as Americans, political participation is low. For example, although the franchise is widely extended, the percentage who bother to vote is small and declining. The low level to which the citizens inform themselves on issues and about candidates is troubling. The United States is not now a healthy community.

But would the situation not deteriorate further if power and decision making were decentralized and self-identification were more affected by state citizenship? Our judgment is that the states would become healthier communities, but that the problem of participation in national affairs would continue. Here, too, a return to the original intentions of the Founding Fathers might help. In the selection of president there could be a shift from the national party system and direct voting to selection of electors by state legislators. The electoral college could become the important institution originally envisioned.

Decentralization of economic and political power to the state level need not be the end of that process. In later chapters we will argue that even much smaller communities can produce most of their basic needs. More political power can then be exercised at the local level. Writing at a time when relative economic self-sufficiency was the rule, Thomas

Jefferson did not need to concern himself about economic decentralization. With that given, he proposed dividing counties into wards of five or six square miles and "to impart to these wards those portions of self-government for which they are best qualified, by confiding to them the care of their poor, their roads, police, elections, the nominations of jurors, administration of justice in small cases, elementary exercises of militia" (see Gevetz 1967, p. 115). Literal following of Jefferson's proposals today would be absurd, but the empowering of people in small regions to run their own affairs is not—if these small regions have viable economies.

Although our emphasis is on the coordination of political and economic power, some political functions can be exercised even in the absence of economic power. An urban neighborhood with no separate economic viability can still hold town meetings to elect representatives to act in their behalf at levels which exercise more significant power. Within the state as well as at the national level a shift can take place from direct popular voting to genuine participation at local levels combined with representative processes for selecting public officials at higher levels.

This political proposal reflects a preference with respect to how smaller communities should be related to larger ones. At present the general pattern is direct participation in the governance of communities at various levels. There is a negative correlation between the likelihood of personal knowledge of those for whom one votes and the importance of the decisions they will make. There is little interest in participation in national affairs because one's participation is uninformed and meaningless. The lack of participation is connected with the view of the individual as a member of communities at many levels.

The alternative is to think of the larger community normatively as a community of communities. One's local community would then become a primary basis for self-identification, and participation in its affairs would take on greater importance for two reasons. First, there would be some increase in the significance of local decisions. Second, the representatives chosen locally would participate in important decisions at higher levels and in the selection of representatives to still higher levels. Personal identification would continue to operate at several levels to varying degrees.

This model could be advantageously applied in other parts of the world. India, China, and the Soviet Union, the world's three largest nations, all already have national economies. At present they are under pressure to join the global system. This proposal would move them in the other direction. They would aim to become both economically and politically communities of communities.

This process of decentralization does not exclude another process of being in community with other nations. There must be, if the human race is to survive, a "family of nations." Even if economic decentralization frees the United Nations from responsibility to oversee the global economy, a task for which its power is now wholly insufficient, more and more other problems are becoming global. This is especially true of environmental problems. Such matters as changes of weather from CO_2, depletion of the ozone layer, acid rain, extinction of species, and the use of the oceans cannot be dealt with at local or even national levels alone. Nations must give to the inclusive community of human communities sufficient power to address the immensely difficult task of mitigating the coming horrors. Similarly, the World Court needs to be strengthened so that in the future nations such as the United States cannot ignore its judgments with impunity.

This is not a call for World Government in any ordinary sense. There must be sufficient power at the world level to deal with urgent problems that can be dealt with nowhere else. If the economy becomes more and more global, with economic decisions not controlled by any political body, then World Government in a strong sense will be needed. It is intolerable that the most important issues about human livelihood will be decided solely on the basis of profit for transnational corporations. The economy *must* be under some supervision. If the economy is global, global government must be instituted sooner or later. But the proposals made in this book are geared precisely to avoid a concentration of political power at the global level following a concentration of economic power there. Decentralization of the economy will allow decentralization of political power. Nevertheless changes on the planet made during the era of unrestrained exploitation of natural resources and sinks for waste have gone so far that global action by the whole community of nations is the only hope for mitigating disaster.

The proposal of conceiving the world normatively as a community of communities is an attenuation of the idea of sovereignty. There should be no sovereign states, nations, or global government. The presently sovereign nation-states would retain important roles but devolve others on smaller units and surrender still others to the United Nations. All communities would exercise some "sovereignty," but none would be sovereign in the sense of modern political theory. The myths of social contract on which these modern theories of political sovereignty were based are obviously false historically. They also distort both theory and practice.

The European Economic Community provides an interesting model. It is clearly not a sovereign supergovernment. Yet the nations that make it up have also restricted their own ability to make autonomous decisions. If these nations would in addition move toward decentralization of economic and political power internally, the model would be excellent.

Thus far "nation" and "nation-state" have been used synonymously. This obscures an important problem. In many places present national boundaries do not correspond with the national identification of the people. In places such as the Soviet Union, where many nations are found within the borders of a nation-state, decentralization of economic and political power can go far toward easing the tension. But where present political boundaries divide people who share a common identity, the solution is more doubtful. There is danger that the vicious cycles of oppression and deepening alienation leading to violence will continue. Nevertheless, decentralization and abandonment of sovereignty would help in these instances as well.

The Kurds are a good example of the problem, being divided between Turkey, Iraq, and Iran. The possibility of carving out a new nation-state from these countries is remote indeed. But it would be possible for each national government to give more regional autonomy to the Kurds as a part of general policy of decentralization. The increased autonomy of the Kurds in the three nation-states would reduce the level of hostility and violence. It would also be possible for the newly autonomous regions to enter into cultural and economic relations with one another that could express much of their sense of identity as a nation. Even some political arrangements could be made across the lines of the present nation-states. Once the ideology of the nation-state was generally weakened and less power was exercised at that level, the Kurds might be satisfied with this type of expression of national identity.

Decentralization is not a magic wand to solve all political problems. The task for the Hindus and Muslims in the villages of India was to constitute communities together despite their deep differences. We believe that they could have succeeded. But there may be other instances in which there is little hope. There are long histories of people living so intermixed with one another that they cannot constitute separate economic communities but so bitter toward one another that they cannot participate together politically and culturally in a single community. A new economic arrangement will not go far to solve such problems. Those situations call for levels of mutual forgiveness that are unprecedented in human history.

Nongeographical Communities

The first dictionary definition of community speaks of people living in the same district. The discussion this far has been guided by that requirement. Geographical regions are important for both political and economic community. Such communities necessarily have a certain primacy. But communities are not all defined geographically. One speaks, for example, of the scientific community or the Jewish community, affirming that there are mutually supportive relations among scientists and among Jews, regardless of geographical location. Much of the self-identification of many scientists and of many Jews comes from being a scientist or a Jew. Many have participated in shaping their respective communities, have a special sense of responsibility for its members, and affirm them in their diversity. They are *good* communities. Both cross national boundaries, and this has advantages in working against the excessive identification in national terms of recent centuries.

An important and precious characteristic of our time is that many people are members of several communities including ones that are not geographically defined. This fact can enrich the geographical communities that many have found stifling for their provincialism. Nonlocal communities can promote many needed activities to which geographical communities are either unable or unwilling to give sufficient support.

In contrast to the international communities of scientists and Jews, there are nongeographical communities that operate within relatively small areas. They provide much of the warp and woof of local community life in those areas. These include local churches and fraternal clubs, and civic, labor, and business organizations. It is important that economics for community be supportive of community in these many dimensions. They can in turn thereby serve the geographical community. Similarly the promotion of community within a particular trade, and between it and those it serves, is an important way of serving a geographically defined community. Edward J. O'Boyle provides a good example of this last point.

In 1972, the construction industry in St. Louis . . . beset by serious problems that were damaging to the interests of many in the industry, formed an organization called PRIDE. . . .

Before PRIDE came on the scene, construction projects commonly were completed behind schedule and above original cost estimates. A major reason for these problems was that work would stop whenever a jurisdictional dispute arose. Further the industry was handcuffed by work rules that had become outdated due to technical change. Since PRIDE, and partly because of a memorandum of agreement that was signed (by contractors, trade unions, designers, suppliers, and customers) in 1977, jurisdictional disputes are handled without a work stoppage and work rules are updated as a changing technology demands. As a consequence, projects are completed on a timely basis and without cost overruns. [O'Boyle 1985, p. 12]

This example shows that an economics for community can enhance productivity. The productivity in question is primarily that of the whole industry. Because the industry works more efficiently, "productivity" as conventionally measured would also increase. But in this case the increased productivity accompanied enhanced and enlarged community.

PRIDE is cited as expressive of Catholic social teaching, which stresses community. We, along with Heinrich Pesch and the papal encyclicals, emphasize the economic and political role of nongeographical communities within geographical ones, whether cities, states, or nations, and we would welcome strong organizations representing workers, management, and the professions. These should constitute specialized communities that develop standards of performance and responsibility to the community as a whole and police themselves so as to reduce the need of government involvement. There should also be a recognized community of interest among these associations so that they can work together for the larger good. In any economics for community there should indeed be a role for these communities, too. Then religious communities, and those organized around other shared concerns, can also play a large role.

Martin Buber was also aware of the important role played by multiple communities in maintaining a healthy geographical one. In *Paths in Utopia* he wrote: "The era of advanced Capitalism has broken down the structure of society. The society which preceded it was composed of different societies; it was complex, and pluralistic in structure. This is what gave it its peculiar social vitality and enabled it to resist totalitarian tendencies inherent in the pre-revolutionary state. . . . This resistance was broken by the policy of the French Revolution, which was directed against the special rights of free associations. Thereafter centralism in its new capitalist form succeeded where the old had failed: in atomizing society" (Buber 1949, p. 139). Buber's book is a study of efforts to reverse the atomization by establishing new communities and a celebration of the success of the Jewish communes in Israel.

Some Political Factors

We have spelled out a vision of a world of communities of communities and the place of the economy in it to indicate that the model of *Homo economicus* we propose calls for policies quite different from those that stemmed from the Enlightenment and its individualistic cosmopolitan model. But it can be objected that this model, too, is an abstraction from the concrete reality. To follow policies derived from the person-in-community model without full awareness of the reality from which this model is abstracted would simply add instances of the fallacy of misplaced concreteness. Some of them could be just as dangerous as those criticized in Part One.

This objection is correct. There is nothing to protect us from this danger except repeated recourse to the fuller reality from which the abstraction is made and seeking to discern features of that reality relevant to whatever the present topic of discussion may be. We have moved into the realm of politics using our model without asking this question. If we go on to propose policies without checking against other aspects of the concrete reality, we will be guilty as charged.

Since this book is about economics and not politics, we cannot go far toward developing a political theory. But since we have protested vigorously against the segregation of disciplines one from another, and since economic and political issues are indissolubly bound up together in the world and also in this account of the world, we must say something more about what has been abstracted from that will affect the way in which our proposals impinge upon the world.

Probably the single most important feature of the political animal that has been neglected in the image of person-in-community is the will to power. The will to belong and participate can be derived from the model of person-in-community, but much of what has been understood by the will to power cannot. Yet it deeply affects all political and economic activity. We have said nothing about the will to control others at an individual level, or the will that the political entity has to impose its rule on other communities. Yet in the actual affairs of political and economic life these are major phenomena. A person in the community may seek to dominate other persons in the community, thus weakening the community, or may seek to have the community dominate other communities, thus weakening the community of communities.

Clearly this reality requires that communities and communities of communities at every level have power to defend themselves and their members against such expressions of the will to power. Yet what is to prevent the power they possess for keeping a just peace from being used for oppression and war instead? The answer is that there can be no final safeguards, but proposals will be made in Chapter 18 relevant to this question.

Since the will to power as the will to dominate has been part of political reality for at least 10,000 years, any political order must take it into account. At the same time, it is appropriate to ask to what extent this is truly natural and inevitable and to what extent social changes can reduce it to more manageable proportions.

Since persons are constituted by their relationships to others, the concrete nature of these relationships is of utmost importance. If there are features of human behavior that are not inherent in human nature as such but are sufficiently widespread to cause major problems for community, then it is natural to ask how the community functions to elicit those patterns. To whatever extent they can be understood, changes can be proposed. Although people are products of community, they also transcend the way the community shapes them. People make decisions that are not made for them by others. Hope lies in the belief that much of what is destructive in social nature is a social product combined with the belief that through the free decisions of many members of society the patterns that generate that destructive behavior can be changed. If people are persons-in-community then genetic determinism cannot be complete. If it were, then we would be like the social insects—neither individuals nor communities, but a single social organism genetically determined to act as a unit. The fact of heredity is itself a major dimension of community. Our inheritance from the past and our bequest to the future each consist of two parts: the genetic and the cultural. Both the gene pool and the cultural patrimony are common property resources. In insisting on freedom and the reality of choice we are far from denying the limiting conditions of either genetics or culture. For reasons to be developed in Chapter 20, we find determinism to be untenable and believe that reduction of aggression is within the range of possibilities among which we can choose. The form taken by the will to power is influenced by socially held ideas about power. A change of ideas does affect behavior.

The ideas that have influenced expressions of the will to power in recent centuries are closely related to the image of human beings expressed by economists in the traditional *Homo economicus*: the self-enclosed individual whose relations to others are external. Control or domination is the external relation that appears as the clearest expression of power. Yet even domination is not solely an external relation. Hegel analyzed the master-slave relation to show how profoundly and adversely the master is affected by it. This has been confirmed again and again. Domination at a deep level disempowers the dominator as well as the one dominated.

If the individualist way of thinking were to give way to a communitarian one, the understanding of power would change. There is, of course, no question but that relations of domination exist, and there is no possibility that a change of ideas by itself would bring them to an end. But a widespread social recognition that the domination sought does not yield the power that is desired could open the way to redirecting the will to power in enough instances to make a public difference. Are there not other relations that express power better and more satisfyingly and toward which more of the will to power could be directed? Four distinctions will contribute to answering this question affirmatively.

The first such distinction is that between persuasive and coercive power. When we understand that the most important relations are internal, then we want to participate in constituting others at a deeper level than overt behavior. We want to influence them. One important way this is done is by communicating to them ideas we want them to hold. The other side of this coin, of course, is being willing to listen to the ideas they want us to hold, and being genuinely open to the persuasive power of ideas. In this way we act on the faith that it is ideas, not persons, that ultimately have persuasive power, and that faith leads us to expect that the ideas that have the power to convince us will also have the power to convince others. To believe in persuasion is to believe in the existence of truth, however cloudily we may perceive it. If there is no such thing as truth, as many seem to believe, then there is nothing to point to in an effort to persuade, and we are left with only coercion or deception. In any case persuasion is never likely to be effective with everyone. There are people who cannot be persuaded to refrain from robbing banks, selling drugs, and murdering. Legal coercion of such people remains a social necessity.

A second distinction is needed. This will to influence can express itself in attempting to control the thought of the other. Behavior can then
be manipulated. The results, while different from direct efforts to control behavior, may not be better for community. Propaganda, advertising, indoctrination, and brainwashing are names for this exercise of
power. Their function is to enlarge the sphere of determination of the
thought and behavior of others and to reduce their freedom. In short, it
is a form of coercion that violates the basic principles of community.

The other way of influencing people is by making new proposals as to
how they might think, suggesting new possibilities that expand the options among which they can choose. This expression of power frees and
empowers others and enhances their personhood. This is the higher
form of power as influence on another. It is illustrated in good teaching
and good communication in general. We hope this book is an example.
It proposes ways to look at the economic order that differ from the ways
most people have viewed it. This does not force a change on anyone, but
an area of thought, feeling, and subsequent behavior that was formerly
determined should now be opened up for choice. Freedom is expanded.
This builds up community.

A third distinction is between receptive power and active power. Receptive power is the power to incorporate into oneself the feelings and
thought of others. Such incorporation is an enlargement of one's very
selfhood. One's ability to understand, to feel, and to think are all increased. In short, one becomes more powerful through the exercise of
receptive power.

At the same time receptive power also empowers others. Nelle Morton
taught us to think in terms of "hearing into speech" (Morton 1983).
When people truly feel that they are heard, they are able to articulate
depths that they hardly knew existed. This is the secret of much of good
psychotherapy, but also of friendship. In this process, community grows.

A fourth distinction is between shared power and individual power.
As community is deepened people can do together what they cannot do
separately. The power one experiences as part of a community effort is
far greater than the power one experiences individually. Of course, this
could be just the kind of power that is most destructive since it can be
the power over other communities. But community action can be directed in many other ways that are not expressions of power over
others. Again, at an elementary level, neither of us could have written
this book alone. Nor is the book the addition of our ideas. By thinking
and working together we are able to achieve something quite different

from any summation of our separate activities. Similarly, by collective action through environmental organizations or labor unions, goals can be attained that are quite different from the sum of individual actions.

These forms of power are characterized by the fact that the more they are exercised the more all are empowered. They all build up community. To the one who thinks of power in terms of external relations, this phenomenon is hardly understandable. That view implies that the more power one has the less others have. But from the point of view of person-in-community, the power that renders powerless those over whom it is exercised is a poor form of power. Removing the power of the other means that there is no longer any power over which one is exercising control. Very little power is involved in controlling the disempowered!

Although it is naive to suppose that new ways of thinking of power will bring an end to the will to dominate and disempower others, nevertheless it is not foolish to unmask the weakness expressed in that power. The habits of thought current in a society do affect behavior. On a matter as important as this, every avenue of hope should be pursued. If the will to dominate others has flourished especially in connection with the individualistic model, then perhaps a basic image of person-in-community can encourage the will to power to take other forms—forms that will build up community.

A second aspect of real human beings important to political life and abstracted from in person-in-community is the will to sacrifice. This is a feature of human beings that is encouraged in most communities. Often communities require of their members a willingness to subordinate personal interests in those of the community as a whole. It can appeal to concern for fairness. That this plays a significant role in political life cannot be doubted. But often still more is wanted: the risking of life for little or no personal gain—except perhaps the respect of others and one's own self-esteem.

It would be easy to glorify this feature of human beings and to view it as simply an asset for community life. But it is in fact highly ambiguous. The impression one receives from ancient history is that small Greek armies were sometimes able to defeat huge Persian ones partly because many of the Persian troops fought unwillingly. They risked their lives in fighting the Greeks only because the danger of not doing so was greater. Their behavior conformed to the classical model of *Homo economicus*. The Greeks, on the other hand, were prepared to go to certain death for the sake of their cities.

Modern wars between nations would be unthinkable without the willingness of millions to die for their countries. Of course, some fight only out of fear of their officers, or more generally fear of disgrace and humiliation. But this is far from the whole story. Most so internalize the belief that they should be ready to sacrifice themselves that many in fact voluntarily do give their lives for their countries.

This self-sacrifice is so extolled that adolescent boys and young men often desire a cause in which they can risk themselves. Hence they are often enthusiastic supporters of national jingoism. Some of this energy can be channeled into sports where great sacrifices are made for the sake of the team and the community it represents. But whether this reduces or intensifies the desire for political self-sacrifice is not clear.

To understand the importance of this phenomenon, suppose for a moment that the classical *Homo economicus* doctrine were adequate to explain political behavior. Then every German and every Frenchman who received a call to arms in World War I would have considered the personal advantages of responding or not. Even if they judged it to be to their interest that their nations win, it is unlikely that many would judge it to be in their personal interest to engage in the fighting. They would fight only if the dangers of not doing so were greater than the dangers of doing so.

Of course, there could be penalties. Public opinion, one might suppose, would shame one who refused his country's call. But if all are rational optimizers, then there can be no public contempt for simply following this norm. Where there is no admiration for self-sacrifice, there will be no disgrace in behaving rationally. Still it may be rational for the government to punish, and probably to imprison. Whether that would be viewed as worse than the dangers of fighting is doubtful. But in any case, our rational calculator knows that others will be calculating rationally too. The prisons cannot hold all the conscripts. The government will gain nothing by taking them out of the system of normal production and consumption. It would not be rational to build the prisons to house them. This would mean that the government, knowing that its people will respond in this fashion, would not use the threat of war as an instrument of policy because the threat would not be credible. There is no point in giving a war if no one is going to come!

Of course, this scenario is absurd. It only highlights how misleading is the economist's standard model of *Homo economicus*. Frenchmen and Germans were both ready to sacrifice themselves for their respective nations, and they did so in large numbers. Governments employ the threat of war credibly because everyone knows that their people are willing to sacrifice themselves. Because of the enormous power this vests in national governments, the temptation to exercise it is always strong.

This is another indication of the fact that the model of person-in-community more nearly expresses reality than that of the rational atomistic individual. But does this mean that stress on community is likely to strengthen this willingness and thus the danger of war? This could happen. Whereas being a Frenchman or a German appears incidental to classical economics, it is constitutive of person-in-community. And bringing this to the foreground could increase its strength.

That would be unfortunate, and it should not follow from a deep appreciation of how we are bound up with one another in community. Communal relations are mutual relations in which the norm is not that one loses when another gains, but that each loses in the other's losses and gains in the other's gains. Of course, that is not the whole story, since people are also competitive individuals. But it is the feature of the story that our model highlights. The proper service of community in this case is not sacrificing one's life but enriching the community through means that enrich oneself as well.

The problem arises when commitment to community is combined with another very deep-seated feature of human character from which person-in-community abstracts. This is the overwhelming human tendency to divide the world into "us" and "them." The "them" is at least "other," and the "other" is viewed with suspicion if not with rivalry. Rivalry passes over easily into enmity. Given this deep-seated tendency, feeling for one community becomes enmity toward others. People begin with the desire for their own community to outshine the others. This often becomes a desire to damage the others and rejoice in their difficulties.

Accompanied by this intense competitiveness, the will to sacrifice can rise to great heights. It is no longer enough to contribute in mutuality to one's own community. It is necessary to punish the other who claims superiority, and to ward off a real or fancied threat. Death itself is acceptable for the greater glory of one's community.

This is a psychosocial reality that will not go away, but it can be mitigated by the vision of a community of communities. The relations of mutuality so important within individual communities are important to the interrelation of communities as well. The communal relation among communities themselves accents those respects in which the gain of one enhances the well-being of all. For example, if one gets atmospheric pollution under control, all benefit. If one fails, all suffer. The competitive elements central to any model that treats social groupings as self-contained entities is secondary to relations of mutuality.

The will to power, the will to sacrifice, and other characteristics of human beings abstracted from by the model of person-in-community are of utmost importance. They may lead to the final holocaust. They will not go away. Proposals for the future must take them into account. But this book is not primarily about politics. It is an inquiry into the contribution of economic life to our collective problems the way the economy can be changed from an enemy of life to a friend. We, like the standard economists, need critics to help us guard against treating our model as if it were more concrete than it is.

10

From Matter and Rent
to Energy and Biosphere

Natural Resources as Energy

The conclusion of Chapter 5 was that the course of modern economic thought reduced nature to land and land to space and matter. These it has dropped from its calculations or left as a vanishing residue. From an early point it shifted its attention from land to the rent of land, held rent to be price determined rather than price determining, and then successfully supported efforts to reduce its role in the economy. Thus land, which is the only element in economic theory pointing to the physical environment, does not function significantly within the contemporary discipline of economics. The dominance of anthropocentric dualism and idealism in philosophy has supported these trends.

Just as the absence of acknowledgment of community in economic theory has led to the destruction of human community in economic practice, so also the neglect of the physical world in economic theory has led to its degradation in economic practice. We do not believe that the reduction of nature to matter as formless passivity or to a construct of the human mind can be justified, and we doubt that anyone can live and think consistently in those terms. Hence we urge a basic reconsideration of nature in light of the best information we have. For purposes of economic or any other reflection, abstraction from the full richness of the natural world is necessary but abstractions need not be as misleading as those that have operated in economics during the past two centuries. We propose in lieu of "land" to refer to "nature."

There is a sense in which nature is matter. Yet the connotations of "matter" have proved profoundly misleading. Chapter 5 showed how nature as "land" came to be thought of as passive and as formless in its relation to human labor and capital. This movement of thought follows from the Aristotelian tradition's most influential philosophical discussion of "matter." In this tradition any entity has a form, or formal cause, but if it exists at all, it is not simply form. It is something with that form. That which distinguishes it from a pure form is material cause or matter. That is, one can entertain the idea of sphericity separate from the existence of a thing of spherical shape, and from this idea much follows in the science of solid geometry. But if there is an actual sphere, then there is matter as well as form.

Ordinarily in the Aristotelian tradition, "matter" is a relative term. The spherical object may be made of rubber. Thus rubber is its matter. But rubber also has a form by which it can be distinguished from steel or wood. Hence the form of rubber (rubberness, if you will) can be distinguished from the matter of rubber. This process of reflection leads the analysis into chemical and physical explanations of the material cause.

For a long time it was thought that this analytical process came to an end with atoms. Indeed, etymologically and philosophically, the "atom" cannot be further analyzed. An atom has form—for example, some kind of shape—but the matter that is formed in an atom has no form. It is formless. Hence it is pure matter, or matter as such.

Aristotle combined this hylomorphic (matter-form) analysis with the view that form or the formal cause is the formative element, and matter the potentiality for form, the passive recipient of form. The understanding of the matter that receives the form of atom was therefore of something purely passive, or potential but not actual. It receives actuality only by being formed. Only form is active.

For Aristotle nature is always both form and matter. Hence the passivity of matter did not mean for him the passivity of nature. Nevertheless, in the act of making, the human being imposes form. For example, the carver shapes the wood. Thus, relative to humanity, the natural resources human beings use function as material—hence as passive.

Through much of human history the male imagination has associated nature with the female. The passivity of nature relative to human action has been associated with the passivity of woman in relation to man. Note for example the *way* in which Petty formulated the respective contributions of labor and land in the production of wealth mentioned in Chapter 5: "Labor is the Father and active principle of wealth, as Lands are the Mother" (1988, p. 68). The importance of this imagery in progressively denying a role to land can hardly be overestimated, and land, woman, and passivity mean matter, or potentiality for form. What is potential for form cannot form itself; it is dependent on the formative principle to be actualized. Land as matter, progressively denied differentiating form in the course of the discussion, requires labor for its significant actualization. Above all, land is conceived as inert. It has no principle of life within itself.[1]

How anyone who has seen wilderness could think of land in this way is hard to imagine. But a priori modes of thought exercise immense control. Land is matter and matter is passive, ergo only human labor can give form to land. Land not formed by human beings is "undeveloped," passively awaiting the actualization of its potentialities. It is "raw material." Thus, relative to human interest it is formless. What is formless is "empty."

Our forebears meant, "empty of European settlement." To them the teeming vegetation and animal life did not "fill" the American continents. Even the human inhabitants left most of the land "empty" because they did not sufficiently dominate the land and reorder it to human use. Even today we describe land that is in its natural state as "undeveloped." And as the world looks at Amazonia, once again the same response is evoked. It appears "empty" and "undeveloped," and at any price to its present inhabitants modern people are determined to "fill" and "develop" it. Indeed in Amazonia, land in its natural forested state is classed as "unproductive" and therefore more subject to redistribution under the land reform. The consequence is that the forest is burned in order to strengthen ownership claims by "improving" it—by giving it a form more suitable to agriculture or cattle ranching. No value is attributed to the forest in its natural, "empty," "passive" state.

We think rather that it is far better to think of the world as always "full" in the sense that its life-support capacity is fully shared among existing populations of many species. The question then becomes, what is the proper mix, how should the limited places in the sun be shared among human groups and with other species? Wilderness with or without its human population is, in fact, already active and formed. The "raw material" it offers for industrial use is not truly "matter" in the Aristotelian sense. It is, as Aristotle knew, formed matter, and its form is of great importance. The form of coal is quite different from the form of diamonds (and even more so from the form of ashes), and according to these different forms different uses become possible or impossible.

1. Compare Carolyn Merchant 1980. Merchant shows how the connection of women with nature and nature with matter adversely affected their status.

No one questions this, but the view of nature as "matter" leads to discounting the importance of form and emphasizing the substitutability of one form of matter for another. Thus coal can be transformed into diamonds, and for this reason there is no need to worry about the scarcity of diamonds. At one level, this is true, and also, as Barnett and Morse note, there is no preassignable limit to this substitutability (pp. 111–12). But what they do not notice is that a great deal of energy is required for this transformation. The form in which nature is found determines its capacity to contribute to the meeting of human needs. This is one reason for not imaging nature as "matter."

There is a second reason. Physics has shown that there is an error in Aristotle's formulation. If we continue to distinguish "matter" and "form," and this is quite useful, and if we press the analysis to the end, we find that at the base of things there is not passivity but activity. Both an act of human thinking and a quark are forms of energy, not of inert matter. The "material cause" in Aristotle's sense turns out not to have the properties (or absence of properties) he attributed to "matter." If the "material cause" is still called "matter," this point must be stressed.

Einstein recognized that the older view of matter does not work, and he proposed "matter-energy" instead. What had been called matter, that is, the substance of physical objects, and what had been called energy are convertible into each other: $E = mc^2$. But the term "energy" is less misleading than "matter" as a way of speaking of "matter-energy."

A practical advantage of emphasizing energy instead of matter as the material cause of natural things is that it more directly challenges the habit of mind that denies the reality of general shortages of natural resources. When natural resources are understood as embodied energy it is harder to suppose that there can be costless infinite substitution of one for another. Consider the standard treatment of specific local shortages by economists with this perspective in mind.

Economists recognize, of course, that there are local scarcities of resources. For example, there are millions of people who cannot procure the firewood they need to cook their meals. But according to standard economic theory this is because they lack the money (earning power) to buy it, not because it does not exist. Whereas once it was available free for the taking on nearby hillsides, now it must be brought from great distances. This requires labor, and labor must be paid. What is immediately scarce, therefore, is money income, not firewood. Economists point out that with sufficient capital, firewood could be made plentiful locally.

Further, in the standard economic view, if firewood should become scarce globally relative to present demand, this would not be economically important. Coal could be readily substituted for wood for the purposes of heating and cooking. Again the difficulties encountered would be from lack of money to buy, not from an absolute shortage. If capital is sufficient, there are no shortages. This is the central dogma of neoclassical economics. Forceful reaffirmation of the dogma occurred in discussions within the World Bank regarding its environmental policy. The magazine *Science* reported, "Economists at the meeting rejected the idea that resources could be finite. Said one: 'The notion that there are limits that can't be taken care of by capital has to be rejected'" (15 May 1987, p. 769). Where capital is lacking, the abundant presence of oil or coal in the ground does not prevent shortages of material for use. But with sufficient capital, these shortages disappear. Hence economists feel justified in continuing to attend only to capital and labor and to ignore land.

The underlying assumption is that all physical things ultimately consist of the same indestructible matter that is arranged in production, disarranged in consumption, rearranged in production, and so forth. The economy is a closed flow from production to consumption to production again. Nothing is used up, only disarranged. If instead, economists thought of physical things, such as trees and coal, as embodiments of energy, they would have to reflect on how useful energy is used up in all those processes.

Entropy

Reflection on the use of energy leads immediately to the second law of thermodynamics. The law asserts that entropy is increased when work is done. The notion of entropy is often misunderstood, so it requires a brief explanation.

The first law of thermodynamics declares that energy (or matter-energy) can neither be created nor destroyed. This seems to suggest that the use of energy will not reduce the amount of energy available to be used again. But this is not the case. The second law declares that whenever work is done, whenever energy is used, the amount of usable energy declines. The decline of usable energy is the increase of entropy (the increase of sand in the bottom chamber of the hour glass, to recall the analogy in the Introduction). For example, when a piece of coal is burned, the energy in the coal is transformed into heat and ash. This, too, is energy, and the amount of energy in the heat and ashes equals that previously in the coal. But now it is dispersed. The dispersed heat cannot be used again in the way it was originally used. Furthermore, any procedure for reconcentrating this energy would use more energy than it could regenerate. In other words, the dispersal of previously concentrated energy would increase. There is no way of reversing this process. Burning a piece of coal changes the low-entropy natural resource into high-entropy forms capable of much less work. In spite of the circular flow celebrated by economists there is something that is irrevocably used up, namely *capacity for rearrangement.* The economic process (production followed by consumption) is entropic. Raw materials from nature are equal in quantity to the waste materials ultimately returned to nature. But there is a qualitative difference between the equal quantities of raw and waste material. Entropy is the physical measure of that qualitative difference. It is the quality of low entropy that makes matter-energy receptive to the imprint of human knowledge and purpose. High-entropy matter-energy displays resistance and implasticity. We cannot with any currently imaginable technology power a steamship with the heat contained in the ocean, immense though that amount of heat is. Nor can windmills be made of sand or ashes.

When nature and its resources for human use are viewed as concentrations of usable energy instead of as passive matter, it will no longer be possible to ignore the fund-flow model of Nicholas Georgescu-Roegen, to whom we owe the path-breaking analysis of *The Entropy Law and the Economic Process* (1971), which we have freely drawn from.

Georgescu-Roegen's fund-flow model begins with the recognition that nature's contribution is a flow of low-entropy natural resources. These raw materials are transformed by a fund of agents (laborers and capital equipment), which do not themselves become physically embodied in the product. Labor and capital funds constitute the efficient cause of wealth, and natural resources are the material cause. Labor and capital funds are "worn out" and replaced over long periods of time. Resource flows are "used up" or rather transformed into products over short periods of time. While there may be significant substitutability between the two funds, labor and capital, or among various resource flows, for example aluminum for copper or coal for natural gas, there is very little substitutability between funds and flows. You can build the same house with fewer carpenters and more power saws, but no amount of carpenters and power saws will allow you to reduce very much the amount of lumber and nails. Of course one can use brick rather than wood, but that is the substitution of one resource flow for another rather than the substitution of a fund for a flow. Funds and flows, efficient and material causes, are complements, not substitutes, in the process of production.

From this commonsense perspective it is very difficult to understand the current neoclassical models of production which (*a*) often do not include resources at all, depicting production as a function of labor and capital only; (*b*) if they do include resources, assume that "capital is a near perfect substitute for land and other natural resources"; and (*c*) fail to recognize any physical balance constraint, that is, do not rule out cases where output constitutes a greater mass than the sum of the masses of all inputs (which would be a violation of the First Law of Thermodynamics). Some recognition of the last problem exists and some efforts have been made to limit substitution by a mass balance constraint on production functions. Economists are occasionally embarrassed by their infractions of the first law, but their more egregious violations of the second law have induced very little shame so far.

Georgescu-Roegen argues that all resources, and indeed all items of value, are characterized by low entropy; but not all items characterized by low entropy have economic value. Value cannot be explained in only physical terms, but neither can it be explained purely in psychic terms of utility without reference to entropy, as neoclassical economics attempts to do. Since we neither create nor destroy matter-energy it is clear that what we live on is the qualitative difference between natural resources and waste, that is, the increase in entropy. We can do a better or worse job of sifting this low entropy through our technological sieves so as to extract more or less want satisfaction from it, but without that entropic flow from nature there is no possibility of production. Low-entropy matter-energy is a necessary but not sufficient condition for value. It is critically important, therefore, to analyze the sources of low entropy (the physical common denominator of usefulness), and their patterns of scarcity.

As noted in the Introduction we basically have two sources of low entropy: the solar and the terrestrial. They differ significantly in their patterns of scarcity. The solar source is practically unlimited in its stock dimension, but is strictly limited in its flow rate of arrival to earth. The terrestrial source (minerals and fossil fuels) is strictly limited in its stock dimension, but can be used at a flow rate of our own choosing, within wide limits. Industrialism represents a shift away from major dependence on the stock-abundant solar source toward major dependence on the stock-scarce terrestrial source in order to take advantage of the variable (expandable) rate of flow at which we can use it. On the basis of this elementary consideration alone, it was possible for Georgescu-Roegen to predict, back in the 1960s when most economists were talking about feeding the world with petroleum, that exactly the opposite substitution would happen: we would be fueling our cars with alcohol from food crops that gather current sunshine. In Brazil this has already happened. *Homo sapiens brasiliensis* has entered into direct competition with *Mechanistra automobilica* for a place in the sun. Sugar cane for fuel is displacing rice and beans for food.

Returning to the issue of the substitutability of capital for resources, our approach is to consider the amount of capital needed in two scenarios: a world of extensive resource depletion and high capital accumulation versus a world of conserved resources and reduced capital accumulation. It is evident that more is needed in a world in which renewable resources have become scarce. Food may be produced hydroponically, but this requires far more capital than producing the same amount of food in naturally fertile soil. Note that here we are speaking of substitution of humanly created capital stock for natural capital stock (soil), and not the substitution of capital for a resource flow. A carrot produced hydroponically embodies just as much matter and energy as one grown in the garden. The extra humanly created capital in hydroponics is not merely a matter of direct costs of equipment, chemicals, and water. It also involves supplying water that will be more expensive than at present. Deforestation will reduce stream flow, increase flooding, hasten the silting of dams, and speed up aquifer depletion. Capital will then be needed for flood control, new dams, diversion of distant rivers, and desalinization of ocean water.

Let us suppose, now, that capital can be accumulated faster as renewable natural resources are exploited unsustainably. Will the extra accumulation of humanly created capital be sufficient to offset the extra loss of natural capital? We believe it will be far easier to accumulate enough capital with sustainable use of resources to enable such use to continue than to accumulate enough capital with unsustainable use of resources to meet human needs in the resulting wasteland. We think this would be true even if we limit consideration to the needs for food, fuel, shelter, and clothing. If we include the need for beauty and a living environment there can be no question.

We think, therefore, that the relative substitutability of capital for land, of which economists legitimately speak, breaks down in the face of the massive environmental crises now faced on the planet. To put it crudely, what good is the capital represented by a refinery if there is no petroleum? The fungibility of money capital does not mean that a refinery can be converted into a solar collector. Substitutability is a principle that has its partial truth, and during much of the past that partial truth was a sufficient guide to practice for many purposes. But there is great danger when, having accustomed oneself to work with a partial truth for practical purposes, one fails to notice that the situation has changed and that the element of error in the partial truth has come to outweigh in practice the element of truth.

If refusal to make such changes in economic practice is something more than ignorance and inertia, then it requires either the factual denial of the finitude of resources and sinks or a substitute assumption that has the same effect on the theory. The latter strategy has been common and consists in "discovery" of an "ultimate resource" which is unlimited, and therefore has the same limits-abolishing effect as the original assumption of infinite sources and sinks. This unlimited ultimate resource is variously referred to as technology, information, knowledge, or the human mind. Anyone who asserts the existence of limits is then accused of wanting to place limits on knowledge and is presented with a whole litany of things that someone once said could never be done but which subsequently were done. Certainly it is a dangerous business to specify limits to knowledge. But it is even more dangerous to presuppose that new knowledge will contain not the discovery of new limits, but only the discovery that old limits are not really binding. It is one thing to say that knowledge will grow (no one rejects that), but it is something else to presuppose that the content of new knowledge will abolish old limits faster than it discovers new ones. The discovery of uranium was new knowledge that increased our resource base. The further discovery of the dangers of radioactivity did not further expand the usefulness of uranium; it contracted it. The new knowledge that asbestos fibers cause cancer limits rather than augments the utility of asbestos reserves.

Furthermore, the most basic laws of science are nearly all statements of impossibility: it is impossible to travel faster than the speed of light, or to create or destroy matter-energy, or to have perpetual motion, or spontaneous generation of living things, and so on. If past progress in knowledge has consisted so much in discovering impossibilities and limits, what reason is there to believe that the future will reverse that pattern? Is it not conceivable, even likely, that the most important new knowledge we acquire will involve new impossibility statements? Also, before getting carried away with the idea that the human mind is an ultimate resource that can guarantee endless economic growth, let us remember that, while certainly not reducible to physical or mechanical terms, the mind is not independent of the body, and the body is physical. "No phosphorous, no thought," Frederick Soddy reminds us. Or as Loren Eisley put it, "The human mind, so frail, so perishable, so full of inexhaustible dreams and hungers, burns by the power of a leaf." Minds capable of such insight ought to be capable of showing more restraint toward leaves and phosphorous than is usually exhibited by our growth-bound economy. Also let us remember that mere knowledge means little to the economic system unless it is embodied in physical structures. As Kenneth Boulding reminds us, capital is knowledge imposed on the physical world in the form of improbable arrangements. But knowledge cannot be imprinted on any kind of matter by any kind of energy. Otherwise we could imprint the improbable structure of a windmill on the material base of sand using the energy of the waves, and then capture the gentle sea breeze to extract gold from the ocean. The constricted entry point of knowledge into the physical economy is through the availability of low-entropy resources. No low entropy, no capital—regardless of knowledge, unless the second law of thermodynamics is overthrown. Maybe someday it will be, in spite of Einstein's and Eddington's firm opinions to the contrary. If so we will have to recur to new concrete experience in search of new inspiration. Until that happens, however, it would be irresponsible in the extreme to base economic theory and policy on the assumption that the second law will not hold. It would be like designing an airplane on the assumption that the law of gravity will be suspended.

In sum, all the talk about knowledge and the mind as an ultimate resource that will offset limits imposed by finitude, entropy, and ecological dependence seems to us to reflect incompetent use of the very organ alleged to have such unlimited powers. Surely knowledge can help us define limits and adjust to them in the most reasonable way. We can even learn to squeeze more welfare from the same resource flow, perhaps without limit. But that does not remove limits on the physical scale of the economy resulting from finitude, entropy, and ecological dependence.

The Biosphere

The category of energy points to what is most important about nature when the question in view is "natural resources." Also, there is nothing that cannot be treated as a form of energy. A bird or a whale is a form of energy just as much as is coal or copper. So is a human being. Aldo Leopold characterized the economy of nature as "a fountain of energy flowing through a circuit of soils, plants, and animals" (Leopold 1966, p. 253). But in dealing with human beings, energy is far too remote an abstraction to be acceptable. Economic theory has come too close to doing this in its discussion of people as workers when it speaks of "labor power." The results have been dehumanizing and alienating. We are treating human beings as persons-in-community both in their role as consumers and in their role as workers, not as units of energy. "Energy" can appropriately name the things that people use and use up, not the people who are using them.

This dualism continues the one that has been basic to the modern period between human beings as ends and nature as means for satisfying human wants. With respect to coal and copper, this seems unobjectionable. The problem is that these are being used at rates and in ways that sacrifice the interests of future people, not that they are used for human ends without regard to their own interests. To attribute interests to coal and copper would be pointless and unjustified.

But is this equally true of birds and whales? Do they exist only to satisfy human wants? Is their value adequately measured by what they are worth to human beings? Or are they also ends to be included in the total health or well-being of the world?

These questions could not arise in the context of idealism, for in its pure form idealism holds that everything except the human mind exists only as it is posited by the human mind. Nothing other than the human mind could have value in and for itself. For dualism, these questions can arise. In its Cartesian form dualism was wholly anthropocentric, identifying everything other than the human mind as matter or extended substance. Since matter can have no value in and for itself, the result was much like that in idealism. Most ethics and all economic theory have followed anthropocentric dualism in this respect.

But the questions, once raised, can be answered in other ways within the dualist context. The line between what is valuable in and for itself and what is mere means at the service of these values can be drawn at a different place. The mentalities of other vertebrates can be grouped with the human mind, with everything else juxtaposed to these as mere means. The problem with any such extension of the mind side of the dualism is that at some point in what appears to be a continuum a line must be drawn, a line that does not represent simply a distinction but a chasm. What lies on the two sides of the line must be viewed as *metaphysically* different. Hans Jonas recognizes this and has proposed to extend the mind side of the dualism to include all life. He is willing to accept a metaphysical dualism between the living and the inanimate (Jonas 1966). But in fact that line, too, is blurred by ambiguous cases, such as viruses, whose classification depends on rather arbitrary definitions. The evidence is, instead, that dualistic thinking itself is the problem. Metaphysically there is only one kind of reality. Everything that is, is an instance of energy. But these instances vary enormously in complexity and richness, in degree and character of subjectivity and value as well as in their modes of relating to one another.

There is no unbridgable metaphysical gulf. Nevertheless, there are very important distinctions, and of these the one to which Jonas points is the most important, at least for our present purposes. For example, the wild facts are not threats to the inanimate world. If they include exhaustion of resources and increasing entropy, these are not calamities in themselves. They are disturbing because of their effects on the living system, the biosphere. Rising temperatures and spreading deserts are not a problem for sand or stones. They are a problem for plants, animals, and especially for the human species. Hence, a second abstract category to place alongside energy for economic consideration of the natural world would be the biosphere.

The old dualism held that only human beings are ends in themselves. They should never be treated merely as means. But everything else *is* merely means. The present proposal is that for practical purposes the inanimate world may be viewed as mere means, so that the category of natural resources is relatively useful and adequate in reference to that part of the environment, once these "resources" are understood in terms of energy rather than matter. But the biosphere, like human beings, is both ends and means. Living things, individually and collectively, deserve consideration in their own right and should not be viewed merely as instrumental to human purposes. They are, certainly, "resources" for one another and especially for human beings (who are also resources for one another). But their intrinsic value as well as their instrumental value must be considered.

Of course, among living things there are vast differences as well. Many further distinctions within the continuum are needed for both theoretical and practical reasons. In some cases a great deal of concern for the welfare of individual organisms would be a foolish sentimentality. In other cases it would not. Sometimes concern should be primarily for species or ecosystems rather than for individuals. A vast range of ethical issues arises that is just beginning to be discussed by philosophers and theologians. These issues go far beyond the scope of this book, although a few will be treated in Chapter 20. (Our position on some of these issues as well as on the distinction between the animate and the inanimate is worked out in *The Liberation of Life* by Charles Birch and John B. Cobb, Jr.) The point here is to say that when economists deal with living things, and especially with large systems of living things, they cannot think of these *only* as resources for fueling the human economy. Instead, the human economy needs to be shaped with the health of the biosphere in view.

How should the biosphere be conceived? The internal relatedness of all its parts forbids thinking of it as composed of self-contained individuals as if the whole were the addition of separable units. Each of its members is social. The biosphere is a society, or rather a society of societies. The dictionary would allow it to be called a community of communities as well, but the criteria for "community" formulated in Chapter 8 cannot be met. These criteria were (1) that membership in the society contribute to the personal identification of its members, (2) that its members participate in the societies' decisions, (3) that those who act for the society have concern for the well-being of the members, and (4) that these members be respected in their individual distinctiveness and diversity. To meet these requirements is possible only with a level of subjectivity rarely found outside human societies. Hence, by the definition adopted above, these societies of societies cannot be communities of communities.

Yet there are approximations to community participation that can and should characterize human involvement in the biosphere. Human beings can derive part of their identity from membership in the biosphere. They can participate in decisions it makes, and they can care for the whole, as well as for its individual members in their diversity. In this qualified sense, *for its human members,* the whole biosphere can and should be a community of communities.

Some sense of kinship and a community of concerns with other species who share the land has been widespread. It was common among hunting and gathering peoples. They usually emphasized their relations to some other species more than their relations to alien human groups. In the Indian subcontinent there has been a strong tendency to think of human beings as only one species among sentient beings, with religion and ethics oriented to a concern for all sentient beings. The humane societies of the West have shown that this sensibility is not alien here. The radical formulation of reverence for life by Albert Schweitzer found widespread resonance. The modern mind regards all this as sentimentality, but it has not been able to eradicate it.

Ironically, Jeremy Bentham, from whom economists got their utilitarian philosophy, was more than willing to extend his philosophy to include "inferior animals." Although the point is relegated to a footnote, Bentham is emphatic: "The question is not, 'Can they reason?' Nor, 'Can they talk?', but, Can they suffer?" (Bentham [1879] 1970, p. 282). Like anyone with common sense Bentham had no real doubt about the capacity of animals to suffer, and argued that their interests had been improperly neglected in legislation.

To view human relations with other living things in the context of a community of communities is to move into a biocentric vision. Its implications for how humanity should order its economy are markedly different from those following from the economists' model of the land as space and matter. We see signs of a rising biospheric consciousness in many segments of contemporary society. We hope it will soon begin to shape economic theory and practice.

Implications for Economics

The implications for economic theory and practice are extensive. Some have been adumbrated in previous chapters. Although concern for the wider environment *can* be purely anthropocentric, most of those who have given leadership in cultivating this concern show sensitivity to the biosphere for its own sake. Although the reasons given for preserving biodiversity, for example, are often purely anthropocentric, one senses that those most concerned to do so are motivated in part by a deep caring for a rich biosphere as an end in itself. If economists are asked to calculate the value of preserving bits of wilderness from an anthropocentric point of view, and if they discount the future, the policies they recommend will not preserve much. If the health of the biosphere becomes an end in itself, the change in practical policies will be important.

The determination of the optimal size of the human economy will also be affected. Of course, this will in any case take account of the biosphere as part of the necessary and desirable environment. But if that reflection is guided by concern for the well-being of other species as well, decisions as to the optimum size of the economy will be affected. This point is illustrated in Chapter 13 on land use. Also, if human beings experience themselves as in community with other animals, their agricultural practices will be affected.

Another relevant topic is genetic engineering, and since this is not treated elsewhere in the volume, it can be used to illustrate the practical change resulting from a changed perspective on the biosphere.

Barring some major breakthrough in fusion or fission energy, we will in the future have to live largely on the current flow of solar energy rather than on the accumulated sunshine of paleolithic summers. In other words, we will shift from major dependence on nonrenewable terrestrial stocks back to renewable solar flow resources. Ricardian land will be one stock resource that gains in importance because space (area) is required to capture solar energy. The natural technology that plants have evolved for capturing solar energy will become more important, and plant genetics will no doubt be pressed into service to increase the amount of solar income captured and stored for human purposes. If our ultimate natural resource is the solar flow of low entropy, then our ultimate capital is the gene pool in which evolution has evolved and stored technologies for tapping this basic flow for life generation.

With the advent of genetic engineering there is a growth-oriented technical thrust toward redesigning the gene pool to serve economic criteria. Without doubt the major goal will be to speed up growth rates of crops and livestock. Bovine growth hormone is an example of this thrust, and was developed in the face of agricultural overproduction. Mass adoption of the fastest growing genotype leads to monoculture and increased vulnerability to disease, pests, and climate shifts. Again we find a conflict between maximizing the productivity of labor and capital in the short run, on the one hand, and concern for long-run efficiency, resilience and sustainability on the other.

In the future the industrial capitalist may go the way of the landlord and may be replaced by a new privileged class that has managed to patent life itself and, through ownership of seed and breeding stock, to monopolize access to solar energy. This development is not inevitable, but it is a troubling possibility. To imagine the common heritage of all life, the gene pool, being taken over as private property is the culmination of individualistic economics, and the ultimate negation of community.

Natural selection is giving way more and more to economic selection as the directive force of evolution. Should we worry about this? After all, it has been going on for a long time in the practice of selective breeding. Genetic engineering merely speeds up the process. Will not economic selection simply make evolution more rational and progressive, as well as a lot faster? Who knows better than the market what the composition of the gene pool should be? The mechanical interplay of individual preferences and competitive profit-seeking will lead, as if by an invisible hand, to a gene pool whose mix of characteristics is optimal in the sense that no individual could be made better off by any rearrangement, without making another individual worse off—a Pareto-optimal gene pool! One can already hear the Chicago economists defending market directed evolution.

What gives pause is the following consideration: that the short-run, individually experienced, subjective pleasure or pain, occasioned by the satisfaction of the present generation's uninstructed whims, addictive personal cravings, and unrealistic expectations of the future—all weighted by their unjustly distributed wealth and income—will replace the collective biophysical wisdom accumulated in the gene pool over millions of years of experience. What used to be the free marketeers' saving grace, their faith in providential laissez-faire and skepticism regarding mankind's ability to improve things by rational collective planning, has now deserted them completely. Economically directed evolution is biological and ecological central planning! It is a sin against free competition, and an arrogant presumption that we possess knowledge that we do not have.

Economic theorists will notice a logical circularity in this not-too-whimsical fantasy of the Chicago economists proclaiming a Pareto-optimal gene pool. After all, they do not shrink from assuming asexual reproduction. The next step in individualism is to advocate reproduction by cloning, so that the genotype can reproduce itself without diluting its individual self-identity. Genes also determine needs and preferences to a large degree. Preferences would no longer be given exogenously, as required by theory, but would themselves be endogenously determined, and would change as the gene pool changes. But this same circularity has been pointed out in connection with advertising's ability to alter preferences psychologically, and economists have been deaf to that argument, so it is unlikely that a new source of the same circularity will be able to crack the hard shell of abstractions in which so many are hermetically encased.

Genetic engineering may appear to be remote from land use, but it is really not. The ultimate use of land is to capture solar energy to support life, human and nonhuman. The technology for capturing solar energy is overwhelmingly natural, or as the energy economists say, "indirect." It is embodied in the plant gene pool. Direct collection of solar energy by humanly made devices does not involve genetic engineering, but it does require space. It seems that Wall Street is betting that it will be easier to "soup-up" existing plant genes than to develop direct methods of solar collection. The central issue in land use is, how do we use the land to capture solar energy? And that inevitably must bring us quickly to the issue of genetic engineering. How far are we justified in rearranging the foundations of creation to better serve our own purposes? That depends on how closely our purposes mirror the creation's purposes. What are these purposes? Until we reflect more deeply and seriously on this question (and we reflect on the question of a divine purpose in Chapter 20), it seems that right action in the world is best approximated by some commonsense rules: if it ain't broke, don't fix it; if you must tinker, save all the pieces; and, if you don't know where you're going, slow down.

3

POLICIES FOR COMMUNITY IN THE UNITED STATES

Free Trade ⎰ Comparative Advantage

Stronger sense of community

11

Free Trade versus Community

*I sympathize, therefore, with those who would minimize, rather than
with those who would maximize, economic entanglement between
nations. Ideas, knowledge, art, hospitality, travel—these are the
things which should of their nature be international. But let goods be
homespun whenever it is reasonably and conveniently possible; and,
above all, let finance be primarily national.*

J. M. Keynes

The Principle of Comparative Advantage

No economic doctrine is more widely accepted among economists than
that of free trade based on comparative advantage. According to MIT
economist Paul Krugman, "If there were an Economist's Creed it would
surely contain the affirmations, 'I believe in the Principle of Comparative Advantage,' and 'I believe in free trade'" (1987, p. 131). The pure
logic of comparative advantage, within the world of its assumptions, is
unassailable. Nine times out of ten the arguments of those who favor
tariffs, quotas, or other trade restrictions can be exposed as self-serving
and against the public interest.[1] Nevertheless, there is a legitimate case

1. Several questions have nevertheless been raised recently by economists, casting doubt on this article of faith. For one thing, nations with identical economies
would not trade in a world governed by comparative advantage. Yet similar economies in the real world do not seem to trade less with each other than do very different economies. Also, the principle of comparative advantage as the rule governing all specialization has come under attack by Glenn M. McDonald and James R.
Markusen. They point out that in theory the workers in a firm should be assigned to
specialized tasks according to their comparative advantage. Yet, as they point out, "It
is not persuasive that the employee with the highest comparative advantage in management should become president. It is plausible that the presidency assignment
will have something to do with absolute advantage . . . a person with poor management skills will not be chosen even if he is relatively worse at every other task in the

against free trade that we find compelling and that we believe Adam Smith and David Ricardo would have found compelling also had they lived in a world of free capital mobility, demographic explosion, ecological stress, and nation-states unwilling to cede any sovereignty to a world government. We will begin with a review of the Smith-Ricardo (classical) position, which, with a few minor neoclassical wrinkles regarding imperfect competition and increasing returns to scale, remains the dominant view today. The theme of individualism versus community emerges nowhere more clearly than in the issue of free trade.

Adam Smith saw that prosperity was dependent on specialization. It was this specialization that made workers more productive. By each one efficiently producing one thing there were more total goods to go around. But this could not happen unless there was a market for the goods. The more specialized the production, the larger the market needed to assimilate it. The division of labor is limited by the extent of the market, to use Smith's famous phrase. Thus there is a high correlation between the size of markets and the extent to which specialization can occur, and between both and prosperity.

The argument for high specialization and large markets does not stop with national boundaries. The same advantages that are gained by trade among free citizens within the nation apply without change to exchanges between citizens and firms in different nations. The ideal is a completely open global market in which goods and services pass freely over all national boundaries.

---

firm" (McDonald and Markusen 1985). We find these anomalies highly interesting, but our argument is much simpler: the basic assumption underlying comparative advantage in international trade, namely international immobility of capital, is obviously false as a description of today's world. We have found support for our argument in a paper by Anthony Brewer. Brewer says of his model that "apart from its theoretical interest . . . it provides a possible justification for the common complaint that foreign competition causes domestic unemployment. It may, for example, provide useful insights into the effect on advanced countries of multinational company investment in low wage countries (mobile capital) if workers in advanced countries resist wage reductions (fixed wages)." In such a case a country may have an absolute advantage in both goods, which means that all capital will flow to it and all labor in the other country will be unemployed. Brewer believes that the two assumptions "are relatively innocuous taken singly," but cause problems when taken together (Brewer 1985). On this point we disagree. The critical assumption is mobile capital—that is what inflicts a cost on the national community. Whether that cost is borne as low wages for all or unemployment for some is determined by whether wages are fixed or flexible. We do, however, find Brewer's analysis very helpful.

This theory, of course, does not take account of limits imposed by finite resources and sinks on the aggregate physical scale of the economy. In Adam Smith's day it would have been foolish to consider such remote limits. Today it is foolish not to consider them, and we have examined these limits in earlier chapters. Here we will consider other problems with this widely supported ideal of free trade.

The claim in favor of completely free trade is that it is advantageous not only to both participants but also to the communities as a whole. The argument requires close attention. Often it is explained in terms of Robinson Crusoe. Crusoe is able to support himself on his own island. But suppose that there are other Crusoes on neighboring islands. They find that they produce different goods because they have either different preferences or different endowments of natural resources. None of them will trade with one another unless they have greater need or desire for the goods they receive than for the goods they give in exchange. On the basis of the exchange all will be better off. Hence the more exchanges among them the better. Further, if one finds that he can produce something desired by the others in greater quantity by concentrating on it, he will do so and receive in exchange more goods from the others than he loses by concentrating only on that one. The process of specialization begins with total production increasing and all Crusoes benefiting.

The Crusoe model is designed to show that trade is always beneficial to the individuals who engage in it and it increases the total amount of goods to be distributed among them all. Of course, they might not all benefit equally. One might prosper greatly while another did not. But none would suffer, since, unless the trading were to one's benefit, one would desist.

Consider now what happens at the national level. The Crusoe model in itself does not tell us whether all nations will benefit by trade. It tells us only that the traders will benefit and that the total product of the region included in the unified market will grow. It does not guarantee that the product of each of the countries will grow, for the regionally increased gross product might be very unevenly distributed. Nor does it guarantee that Crusoe A and Crusoe B might not make a mutually beneficial trade at the expense of Crusoes C, D, and E. This is the case of "externalities" already discussed.

To sharpen the issue as to the desirability to individual nations of free international trade it will be well to state clearly what is *not* at issue. Returning to the Crusoe example and allowing Crusoe and his island to represent a nation, the question is not about the first stage of the trade.

If one nation lying in the tropics produces an abundance of bananas and mangoes but no apples and pears, and another in the temperate zone produces apples and pears but no bananas and mangoes, then there are obvious advantages to both in exchange. Economists have never needed to prove this.

What economists want to show is that even when both nations can produce all the goods under consideration, it is nevertheless to their advantage to specialize and exchange. Again, the case is easily made if one nation can grow a crop cheaply in the field whereas another must go to great expense to raise it in a hothouse. The difficult issue arises when one nation can produce both the commodities in question more cheaply than the other. There seems, then, to be no incentive to trade.

Economists have undertaken to analyze this situation more closely and to demonstrate that despite superficial appearances, both nations benefit in free trade. To do so they introduce the principle of "comparative advantage." The argument, if not the name, goes back to Ricardo. His example is trade between England and Portugal. Portugal is presented as the most advanced economy, capable of producing both wine and cloth with less labor (therefore less cost) than England. His argument is that, nevertheless, it is to the advantage of both Portugal and England that Portugal specialize in wine and England in cloth and that they exchange the products. His reasoning is as follows.

England may be so circumstanced, that to produce the cloth may require the labor of 100 men for one year; and if she attempted to make the wine, it might require the labor of 120 men for the same time. England would therefore find it in her interest to import wine, and to purchase it by the exportation of cloth.

To produce the wine in Portugal, might require the labor of only 80 men for one year, and to produce the cloth in the same country might require the labor of 90 men for the same time. It would therefore be advantageous for her to export wine in exchange for cloth. This exchange might even take place, notwithstanding that the commodity imported by Portugal could be produced there with less labor than in England. Though she could make the cloth with the labor of 90 men, she would import it from a country where it required the labor of 100 men to produce it, because it would be advantageous to her rather to employ her capital in the production of wine, for which she would obtain more cloth from England, than she could produce by diverting a portion of her capital from the cultivation of vines to the manufacture of cloth. [Ricardo 1951, p. 135]

What is illustrated here is called "comparative advantage." Portugal has an absolute advantage in the production of both wine and cloth, and

Portugal has a comparative advantage in the production of wine. The comparative advantage justifies Portugal's importing cloth from England, and England's importing wine from Portugal. If the cost ratios had been equal between the two countries, no trade would occur, regardless of the differences in absolute labor costs. It is the difference between the two countries' internal cost ratios that defines comparative advantage and limits the range of the terms on which wine and cloth will be exchanged. Portugal will not trade wine for cloth on terms less favorable than its own internal cost ratio (1 wine = 80/90 or .88 cloth). Nor will England trade on terms less favorable than its internal cost ratio (1 wine = 120/100 or 1.2 cloth). Bargaining will determine where between these limits the terms of trade will lie. Portugal will push toward England's internal cost ratio, and England will push toward Portugal's internal cost ratio. The terms of trade determines who gains most, but both countries gain something, or at the very least, are no worse off.

The argument is ingenious and, given the conditions it presupposes, no doubt true. In the real world, however, these conditions are not always met. For example, suppose that Portuguese capital continued to flow to wine. Eventually the market would be satiated. The price of Portuguese wine on the world market would fall, so that, however efficiently it is produced, profits would decline. The Portuguese capitalists would look for new areas of investment. Since they have an absolute advantage in cloth as well, capital would flow to cloth and the English cloth makers would be put out of business. In actual fact this quest of capital for additional investment opportunities has come to characterize the real world more than the picture presented by Ricardo.

The Dependence of Comparative Advantage on Capital Immobility

The second qualification is noted already by Ricardo. He emphasizes that the principle of comparative advantage cannot work within a single country, and he asks why it can, then, work internationally. "The difference in this respect between a single country and many, is easily accounted for, by considering the difficulty with which capital moves from one country to another, to seek a more profitable employment, and the activity with which it invariably passes from one province to another in the same country" (Ricardo 1951, p. 136). Obviously if capital flowed freely across national boundaries, the situation internationally would be the same as that within a single country. English capital would flow to Portugal to supplement Portuguese capital, and both wine and cloth would be produced there. If labor also flowed freely across national boundaries, English labor would also go to Portugal, since there would be no employment in England.

In today's world, national boundaries do not inhibit the flow of capital investment, but they do inhibit the flow of labor, though less so than in Ricardo's time. Ricardo did not discuss the effects of this situation. The free flow of capital and goods (instead of goods only) means that investment is governed by absolute profitability and not by comparative advantage. The absence of a free flow of labor means that opportunities for employment decline for workers in the country in which investments are not being made. This represents a more nearly accurate account of the world in which we live than does the principle of comparative advantage, however applicable that may have been in Ricardo's day.

Ricardo points out that if capital were as freely mobile between England and Portugal as between London and Yorkshire, then trade between the two countries would be governed by the labor theory of value (absolute advantage in terms of labor costs) rather than by comparative advantage. Everything that differentiates domestic from international trade depends, for Ricardo, explicitly on the international immobility of capital (labor immobility between nations was taken for granted). Moreover, Ricardo's explanation of capital immobility invokes the theme of community: "Experience, however, shews, that the fancied or real insecurity of capital, when not under the immediate control of its owner, together with the natural disinclination which every man has to quit the country of his birth and connexions, and intrust himself with all his habits fixed, to a strange government and new laws, check the emigration of capital. These feelings, which I should be sorry to see weakened, induce most men of property to be satisfied with a low rate of profits in their own country, rather than seek a more advantageous employment for their wealth in foreign nations" (Ricardo 1951, pp. 136–37).

For Ricardo it is the force of community that keeps capital at home even in the face of higher profits abroad. Furthermore he affirms that he would be sorry to see these feelings of community weakened. Perhaps he already suspected that they would be weakened by the individualistic postulates of classical economics and its faith in the invisible hand's ability to transform private vice into public virtue.

Interestingly, the famous invisible hand passage in Adam Smith also occurs in the context of a defense of free trade. Smith takes it for granted that it is in the public interest for national capital to be employed at home, and then goes on to show that, by and large, because of the same community attachments to the home market mentioned by Ricardo, the capitalist will find it in his own personal interest to invest at home. As Smith put it: "By preferring the support of domestic to that of foreign industry, he intends only his own security; and by directing that industry in such a manner as its produce may be of the greatest value, he intends only his own gain, and he is in this, as in many other cases, led by an invisible hand to promote an end which was no part of his intention" (Smith 1776, p. 423).

Smith presupposes that the capitalist is first and foremost a member of the national community. Smith's capitalist is so thoroughly British, that his very personal identity is defined by internal relations of community with "the country of his birth and connexions." It is not the competitive external relations of the cash nexus that generate the invisible hand in this case, but rather the internal relations of community that constitute this capitalist's very identity. Of course he acts in his self-interest, but when the self is constituted by internal relations of community it is not surprising that private interest should promote community welfare. The invisible hand, in this classic statement at least, presupposes the force of community operating within the personal identity of the individual capitalist. By his very self-identity the capitalist feels a "natural disinclination" to invest abroad, and therefore invests at home for his own satisfaction and security, and incidentally promotes the general welfare even though that was not his direct intention.

It is clear that Smith and Ricardo were considering a world in which capitalists were fundamentally good Englishmen, Frenchmen, and so on—not a world of cosmopolitan money managers and transnational corporations which, in addition to having limited liability and immortality conferred on them by national governments, have now transcended those very governments and no longer see the national community as their context. They may speak grandly of the "world community" as their residence, but in fact, since no world community exists, they have escaped from community into the gap between communities where individualism has a free reign. They have no "natural disinclination" to move their capital abroad with the speed of light at the stimulus of a tenth of a percent difference in rate of return. If Smith or Ricardo were alive today we suspect that they would not be preaching free trade. The whole basis for their case, factor immobility, has been eroded by time and change. They were above all else realists who paid close attention to actual conditions. Their intellectual progeny, however, are idealists, ideologues, and logicians. Academic economists have become so enamored of the logical argument for comparative advantage (a beloved *pons asinorum* in the standard pedagogy) and find it so ideologically in tune with their unrelenting celebration of the free market, that they are loath to reexamine it. They have suppressed recognition of the fact that the empirical cornerstone of the whole classical free trade argument, capital immobility, has crumbled into loose gravel.

We can give personal testimony to the difficulty of freeing the mind from the free trade/comparative advantage dogma, but more impressive is the testimony of Keynes, who tells us that in 1923 he regarded free trade "not only as an economic doctrine which a rational and instructed person could not doubt, but almost as a part of the moral law." Ten years later Keynes was writing in support of national self-sufficiency:

> It does not now seem obvious that a great concentration of national effort on the capture of foreign trade, that the penetration of a country's economic structure by the resources and the influence of foreign capitalists, that a close dependence of our own economic life on the fluctuating economic policies of foreign countries, are safeguards and assurances of international peace. It is easier in the light of experience and foresight, to argue quite the contrary. . . . Advisable domestic policies might be easier to compass, if, for example, the phenomenon known as "flight of capital" could be ruled out. The divorce between ownership and the real responsibility of management is serious within a country when, as a result of joint-stock enterprise, ownership is broken up between innumerable individuals who buy their interest today and sell it tomorrow and lack altogether both knowledge and responsibility towards what they momentarily own. But when this same principle is applied internationally, it is, in times of stress, intolerable—I am irresponsible towards what I own and those who operate what I own are irresponsible towards me. [Keynes 1933, pp. 235–36]

By 1933, Keynes had clearly come to recognize the conflict between community and free trade, and had become "doubtful whether the economic cost of self-sufficiency is great enough to outweigh the other advantages of gradually bringing the producer and consumer within the ambit of the same national, economic and financial organization" (Keynes 1933, p. 238). Keynes was clearly articulating the viewpoint of economics for community.

But since then we have retrogressed on this front. The modern textbook explanations of free trade and comparative advantage make no mention of the assumption of factor immobility. Perhaps one reason this central assumption is overlooked is that frequently the principle is explained in terms of specialization between individuals. A classic example is a lawyer who is a better typist than her secretary. Even though the lawyer has an absolute advantage over the secretary both in knowledge of the law and in typing, she nevertheless finds it advantageous to specialize in law (her comparative advantage) and employ the secretary to do the typing. Since there is no possibility for labor power or any other productive capacity to flow out of the secretary and into the lawyer in response to absolute advantage, the assumption of factor immobility is guaranteed, and the principle of comparative advantage works. But the argument cannot be generalized to nations without the explicit requirement that their productive capacities (factors) not flow across national boundaries.

Consider, for example, the dismissal of the "low-wage foreign labor fallacy" found in one of the best and most widely-used texts: "Stop and think what the argument would imply if taken out of the international context and put into a local one, where the same principles govern the gains from trade. Is it really impossible for a rich person to gain from trading with a poor person? Would the local millionaire be better off if she did all her own typing, gardening, and cooking?" (Lipsey, Steiner, and Purvis 1987, p. 795). In the next paragraph we are assured that "gains from trade depend on comparative, not absolute advantages," which is all very well if capital is immobile. But there is not a word in the discussion about international mobility of factors. Moreover, the shift of context from nations to individuals, far from illuminating the situation, obscures it by abstracting from the very possibility of transfer of productive capacity between the exchanging entities. The fallacy of misplaced concreteness once again!

Another factor greatly complicates the picture. In Ricardo's day, it could be assumed that basic labor costs everywhere represented subsistence wages. Thus the real cost of producing goods could be measured in hours of work. Ricardo's labor theory of value, later taken over by Marx, was both intuitively plausible and also fairly simple to use.

But as a result of growing prosperity, labor unions, and government intervention, the wages for labor in some countries rose far above subsistence. When capitalists today seek the most profitable use of their money, they will not ask primarily how many workers are required to make the product, but what the *cost* of labor will be in each alternative capital investment. Ricardo could ignore comparative wage scales in Portugal and England. The logic of comparative advantage can ignore the units in which cost is measured (since they cancel out in calculating the internal cost ratios in each country). But in moving from labor units to money wage costs, we break the connection between efficiency and cheapness. A country's absolute advantage may now depend simply on low wages (low standard of living) rather than on more efficient use of labor.

Given the great importance of trade to the nations involved and the rapidly changing global situation, economists would have done well to check the assumptions underlying the principle of comparative advantage against the facts. This is particularly true since the policies they have recommended have worked against the conditions under which "comparative advantage" functions. Most of these policies are based on considering the gains of extending as broadly as possible the area of free trade so as to realize the advantages of specialization. National boundaries are to be reduced in importance for economic activity, as far as possible. On the other hand, as Ricardo recognized, it is only when national boundaries play an important role (limiting capital and labor mobility) that the principle of comparative advantage replaces absolute advantage. It will not do to advocate every move toward setting aside national boundaries in the economic order in the name of a principle (comparative advantage) that itself depends on the functioning of these very boundaries. That principle depends not only on free trade of goods, but also on national limits on the movement of both capital and labor. We now have free trade of goods and free movement of capital. It is disappointing that economists have provided so little guidance for rethinking what happens to nations involved in free trade in this quite different situation. An exception is John M. Culbertson, whose writings we have found highly instructive (1984). Unfortunately Professor Culbertson's forceful and cogent challenge to the free trade dogma has been so aggressively ignored by his fellow economists that he had to publish his book himself. We draw freely upon his work in this chapter. For reasons elaborated in Chapter 1, we are not surprised by the treatment Professor Culbertson's work has received from academic economists.

Free Trade's Effects

The effect of free trade is to equalize prices of traded commodities within the free trade area, allowance being made for transport costs. Tariffs have the same effect as an increase in transport costs, driving a wedge between prices in different countries and preventing complete equalization. The same tendency to equalize prices also holds for factors of production, even when the latter do not cross national boundaries. This is recognized in the so-called factor price equalization theorem, which was not a part of classical economics, but was added to neoclassical theory by Bertil Ohlin (1933). That free trade in goods and services should tend to equalize prices of immobile factors is not so surprising if one remembers that trade in goods and services is ultimately trade in the factors of production they embody. Countries tend to export products embodying relatively large amounts of their most abundant factors of production. This means that the demand for those abundant factors derived from exports to foreigners is added to domestic demand, thus diminishing their initial cheapness. Likewise the importation of products whose home production would have required relatively large amounts of the scarce factors tends to reduce the initial relative scarcity and expensiveness of those factors.[2]

When free mobility of one factor of production, say capital, is added to the free flow of goods, however, then the tendency to equalize prices of factors of production becomes very strong. The highly mobile factor is capital. Labor is less mobile but by no means immobile, as anyone can tell by casual observation of the number of Mexicans, Vietnamese, Iranians, and other foreigners working in the United States, not to mention "guest workers" in northern Europe.

Free mobility of either capital or labor has the same consequence: equalization of both wages and returns to capital. Labor can move to where the capital is and compete for the high-paying jobs, bidding down the high wages, or capital can move to where the cheap labor is and bid up the low-wage rate. The tendency toward equalization of wages is completely obvious in the case of free labor migration and only slightly less obvious in the case of free capital mobility. Those who advocate free trade and free capital mobility are simultaneously advocating equalization of wages.

What is wrong with equalizing wages? Of course wages in high-wage countries will fall, but wages in low-wage countries will rise. Is that not

2. For the equalization of factor prices to be complete, many conditions must hold. Some are obvious, such as zero transport cost for goods and services, and pure competition. Others are not so obvious, such as internationally identical constant-returns-to-scale production functions, incomplete specialization, and a whole list of other stringent conditions, all of which add up to the conclusion that factor price equalization by free trade, while theoretically sound as a general tendency, is not likely to be observed as a strong empirical force in the real world. Yet it is important to recognize that free trade, even with factor immobility, pushes us, however incompletely, in the direction of international equalization of factor prices—and factor prices include wage rates.

a good way of sharing—"production sharing," as some business consultants call it? It is indeed a form of sharing, but "wage sharing" would be a better name. The laboring class in the high-wage country shares its wages and standard of living with the masses of Third World workers. The capitalists in the high-wage country benefit from cheaper labor, first abroad, and then at home as well. They are not sharing with cheap foreign labor, and are able to reduce their previous level of sharing with the laboring class of their own national community. Some few U.S. laborers may own enough capital so that what they lose as laborers will be compensated by what they gain as capitalists. But that is a rare case.

Keynes made an interesting parallel argument in terms of the interest rate, rather than wages (1933). Capital shortage in poor countries would, in a free trade regime, exert upward pressure on interest rates in wealthy countries that need a very low interest rate to maintain full employment. This may indeed be part of the explanation for today's unemployment in wealthy countries.

To appreciate the enormous breach of community implicit in modern free trade, consider what the U.S. capitalists are, in effect, telling the U.S. laborers. They are saying that labor has to compete in the world market against the poor masses in the overpopulated Third World countries such as Mexico, Brazil, Hong Kong, and so on. No longer will U.S. labor have the advantage of superior technology or management, because those attributes move with capital. Furthermore, an enormous reservoir of cheap labor in India and China, almost half the world's population, has previously not competed in the world labor market, and is about to enter. India, under British colonialism, was not allowed to compete in world trade. China, under Mao, followed a policy of isolation from the world market. Both countries now appear to be entering the world market, with the competitive advantage of very low wages. In addition, the already large populations of Third World countries are for the most part still growing rapidly, providing a virtually unlimited supply of cheap labor. Equalization of wages means that U.S. and European and Japanese wages fall to the Third World level, and that the Third World level rises hardly at all. By making the world of separate national communities into a single, common, overpopulated labor pool in the name of free trade, the United States would compete away the high standard of living of its working class—the majority of its citizens.

A high standard of living is not the only good thing that depends on community. Once community is devalued in the name of free trade, there will be a generalized competing away of community standards.

Social security, medicare, and unemployment benefits all raise the cost of production just like high wages, and they too will not survive a general standards-lowering competition. Likewise, the environmental protection and conservation standards of the community also raise costs of production and will be competed down to the level that rules in over-populated Third World countries. Free trade, as a way of erasing the effect of national boundaries, is simultaneously an invitation to the tragedy of the commons. Few people would advocate free migration because they can intuitively see the tragic consequences. Free trade and free capital mobility have exactly the same consequences for wages and community standards, but are widely advocated in the false belief that comparative advantage guarantees mutual benefit.

International trade, despite the name, is not trade between nations, but trade between individuals that crosses national boundaries. The individual, not the nation, is the decision-making unit. Mutual advantage between individuals in different countries does not guarantee mutual advantage for the two countries. Trading between General Motors and General Electric takes place between two corporate entities, two communities. Individual employees of the two corporations do not freely make deals in their own interests across corporate boundaries. Each corporation's officers review all deals to make sure they are in the overall interest of the organization. Nations also need such an overall control, a measure that free trade would prohibit. International trade should be an activity carried out between national communities, just as intercorporation trade is between corporations, not between individuals acting in their own behalf across corporate or national boundaries often at the expense of other members of their communities.

Consider, for example, a U.S. firm that moves its production across the Rio Grande into Mexico. It lays off U.S. workers earning 10 to 12 dollars per hour and hires Mexican workers at less than two dollars per hour. The U.S. capitalist-owner is much better off, the Mexican workers are slightly better off, and the U.S. worker is much worse off. Does this firm want to integrate itself into the community of Mexico, and sell in the Mexican product market as well as buy in the Mexican factors market? By no means. The firm does not want to be an integral member of either community. It wants to buy labor in the low-income country, and sell its product in the high-income country. It wants to take advantage of high incomes in the U.S. product market while failing to contribute to the maintenance of that high-income market by buying labor in the U.S. factors market. Nor does it wish to provide a product suitable for raising the standard of living in the low-income Mexican market. The community nature of the issue is made obvious by asking what would happen if all U.S. firms bought labor in low-income Mexico and sold their product in the high-income United States? Clearly the United States would cease to be a high-income country. Would Mexico then become the high-income country? Its wages would tend to equality with the now lower U.S. wages. Both countries' common wage level would then depend on whether Mexico controlled its population growth, and on whether a demoralized U.S. population would maintain its low fertility, or, in the face of growing insecurity and loss of social insurance, would revert to high fertility patterns as wages declined toward subsistence.

Before we address the question of proper trade policy, let us consider another realistic scenario of the likely future consequence of free trade. The United States' trade with Japan can provide the example. Electronics and automobiles can function as illustrations. Let us consider the actual situation in light of the limitations of the principle of comparative advantage as formulated by Ricardo.

First, in Japan and the United States, there is plenty of productive capacity to meet needs for automobiles and electronics. To invest more capital in either automobile or electronic production in Japan will not be to meet needs for increased production, since there is already surplus capacity; it will be to insure a stable or growing share of the international market at the expense of other producers. Suppose that Japan has an absolute advantage in both electronic and automobile production, but that the United States has a comparative advantage in automobile production. Will that provide any incentive for Japanese investors to produce only electronics and import their cars from the United States? Obviously it does not function in that way. There is enough Japanese capital to invest everywhere that Japan has an absolute advantage. Should there be a shortage, international capital, including that from the United States, is happy to flow in to make up the difference.

In obtaining absolute advantage over the United States in so many fields, Japan benefited at one time from lower labor costs. This meant lower wages as measured by the exchange rate of the currencies of the two nations. Japan did not initially enjoy greater productivity of labor in most fields. However, as Japanese income from exports rose, more capital was invested in Japanese industry, and productivity improved. It now exceeds that of the United States in most industries. Hence wages could rise, and have risen considerably, while Japan has maintained and increased its absolute advantage. (An additional factor in productivity is superior management and worker participation, but we will omit this in order to simplify the presentation.)

In the context of unrestricted imports into the United States (punctuated, of course, by protectionist moves), the result has been that the balance of trade between the two nations is extremely favorable to Japan and extremely unfavorable to the United States. Such a bilateral pattern of trade could be sustained indefinitely only if it were balanced out multilaterally in the wider market. But in fact Japan maintains a favorable balance with most of its trading partners, and the United States an unfavorable one. The pattern can be continued for some time because of the great accumulated wealth of the United States and its ability to borrow money on the international markets, especially from Japan itself, which finances some 25% of the U.S. federal deficit. Also the fact that the dollar functions as an international currency means that most nations hold dollar balances for transaction purposes. These balances constitute an interest-free loan to the United States, which further eases balance of payments pressure. Foreigners acquired these dollars by giving the United States real goods and services in exchange. So long as they hold these green bits of paper rather than buying U.S. goods and services with them, they are, in real terms, extending us interest-free credit. But no economist believes that an unfavorable balance of trade can continue indefinitely.

The nation's trade can be brought into balance either by increasing exports, by reducing imports, or by some combination of the two. Within the context of free trade this will happen only as United States goods become more attractive on the world market in comparison with those of other producers. That means that their relative price must decline.

There are three ways in which this decline can be effected. One would be that productivity of American labor increase relatively to that of others. That could happen if investment flowed into American industry in unprecedented amounts. But investment will not flow into American industry if the same investment is more profitable elsewhere. Hence this part of the solution must await changes in other respects.

The second possible change is a decline in dollar wages of U.S. workers. This change is in fact occurring. Labor negotiations today are more often over wage reductions than over wage increases. Nevertheless, these reductions have not cut the cost of labor sufficiently to make American goods competitive.

The third possible change is in the comparative value of the dollar. This change is also occurring. The dollar has fallen quite drastically in comparison with the yen. This forces up the dollar cost of Japanese goods in the United States and reduces the cost of imports from the United States in Japan.

Thus far the combined effects of lower wages and the fall of the dollar have hardly begun to rectify the trade imbalance. Partly, this is a matter of time. Japan is absorbing much of the change in lowered profits. But it also indicates that greater reductions of wages and greater reduction of the value of the dollar in relation to the yen will be needed.

Assuming that the balance is achieved, as economists generally hope, more as a result of increasing exports than as a result of decreasing imports, the inflationary effect of the rising cost of imports will be considerable. Lester Thurow notes: "If the econometricians are right, a 38% fall in the value of the dollar would have been necessary to restore balance in the balance of trade in early 1985. Since America imports 12% of GNP, a 38% fall in the value of the dollar means a 38% increase in the price of 12% of those things purchased by Americans and as a consequence a 4.6% ($38 \times .12$) decline in the standard of living of the average American" (Thurow 1985, p. 93). Thurow points out that this is only the direct effect of the falling dollar on prices. He anticipates that the indirect effect through higher prices of U.S.-made goods would be "apt to be bigger than the direct effect" (1985, p. 40).

This solution to the problem will cost all Americans something like 10% in their standard of living. Since labor is also suffering a decline in dollar wages and relative position in distribution, its decline in living standards will be considerably greater. Further, Thurow notes that this will not be a one-time adjustment. Unless the U.S. rate of increase in productivity matches that of its trading partners, further relative decline will be required each year. Thurow concludes that rapid improvement in the rate of growth of productivity is urgently needed, and he offers many valuable suggestions as to how that can be attained. Naturally, other nations will redouble their efforts to grow faster than we do.

Thurow is probably correct that this exponential growth of GNP would succeed in avoiding a massive further reduction of the standard of living of American workers after the first inevitable adjustment if we consider only the current major trading partners. Their wages, too, are far above subsistence levels. But Thurow does not consider that the area of free trade encompasses many Third World nations as well, where wages are very low indeed, and where environmental protection and social security standards are also very low. Nor does he consider that nearly half of the world's low-wage labor in India and China has been kept out of the free trade arena by British colonialism and the policies of Chairman Mao, neither of which remain in effect today. American productivity can increase only with massive infusions of capital. The question is, where will that capital find it most profitable to invest?

Increasingly, the answer is free trade zones in Third World countries. The hunger for capital investment in those countries is such that they compete for it with offers that are as favorable as possible to the investors. Thus factories can be built that have no financial obligations to their host countries. They pay no taxes and often no rent. They are assured of cheap and docile labor. For the rest, they may purchase their raw materials and export their products where they will. They are unhindered by any community obligations. The productivity of such factories, as measured by product per *hour* of labor, may be similar to that which obtains in the United States. But if production is divided by the *cost* of labor, the figure will be much higher. This figure is in fact more important in determining investment. Production in the United States and in the First World generally will have to compete for capital against these investment opportunities. Such competition will be difficult to win. The decline in the standard of living of labor in the United States will continue, followed by similar declines in other First World countries. The prospect is for a return to the classical conditions in which the basic wage is determined by the cost of subsistence.

This does not mean that the standard of living of all Americans will decline. One segment of American society lives from capital rather than labor. The freedom of such capital to move internationally offers unparalleled opportunities for profit. The growth of the gap between rich and poor will continue. Community will be further sacrificed.

It is important to see that the decline of labor in this scenario cannot be stemmed by bargaining for higher dollar wages. The rise of wages will necessarily be compensated by the fall of the dollar. If demands for higher dollar wages further discourage investment, the net results will be negative.

Before proceeding in this vein it will be well to review the traditional economic opinion on these matters. The truth is that, at least until recently, the concerns we have raised were not taken seriously. The reason, apart from complacency over the principle of comparative advantage, was that until recently trade worked to the advantage of countries like the United States. The low wages paid in other countries did not undercut high wages here. Even Thurow, who sees that free trade threatens high wages in the United States, puts matters entirely in terms of productivity rather than actual labor costs. The concern about competition with low-wage countries has been treated as a phobia. An example is instructive to show the level of argument deemed sufficient to dispose of this question:

There is . . . a widespread phobia about trading with countries whose wage levels are lower than ours, about buying products produced with "cheap foreign labor." This same phobia is never logically extended into domestic commerce, because if it were, trade and its underlying pattern of specialization would be wiped out. Well-paid steel workers frequently do take their dirty clothes to be done by laundry workers whose wages are far below their own; important executives of General Motors and Bethlehem Steel, despite their six figure salaries, often ride in taxicabs, and in fact are served by public officials, including the President, whose incomes are but a fraction of their own. . . . Much of the time of the economist concerned with international transactions is taken up with attempting to dissolve the mythology that makes sound economic activity seem unsound when national boundaries are crossed. [Eggers and Tussing 1965, pp. 274–75]

Unfortunately, the analogies provided are wide of the mark. A better analogy would be a laundry paying high wages in competition with a nearby one paying low wages. Concern about what would happen to the well-paid workers and their employer in this case would not be passed off as a phobia.

The reason why trade between high-wage societies and low-wage societies has not threatened high wages until recently is that the high wages were based on heavy capitalization and advanced technology not available in the low-wage countries. Hence the goods of low-wage countries were not as cheap as one might expect and, in any case, did not include major industrial products. What has happened is twofold. First, a few countries, especially Japan, have generated sufficient capital internally to enter international competition with brilliant success. Second, investment capital has become international. It is this latter point that, as we have repeatedly emphasized, has the widest ramifications for the future of the American economy.

Consider again how the system is supposed to work. When enhanced productivity displaces workers in one area, the profits generated thereby are invested in something else. New jobs are created. The workers move to this new industry. The economy as a whole advances.

But when investment capital becomes supranational, there is no assurance that the new investment will be in the country where the jobs are lost. Indeed, acting on individualistic economic principles unencumbered by community, investors seek the best return on their money. A factory employing docile and cheap labor that can export its products to the American market from abroad will be more profitable than one built in the United States. Labor-intensive industry will naturally move to countries where labor is cheaper. Wages will decline in countries where capital investment is reduced.

It may be argued that this downward pressure on wages toward subsistence will eventually turn around, and that the rapid industrialization made possible by free trade will involve the vast labor force of the world in productive work. The expectation is that the Gross World Product will be enormous, and all will enjoy together a hitherto undreamed of prosperity.

But even granting this cornucopian dream, at what point can labor in the First World expect relief? One possibility would be that global minimum wages would be set well above subsistence. But in the absence of world government, how this would be done and enforced is difficult to imagine. A second possibility would be that labor would organize on a global scale to secure higher wages for all. But the national barriers that capital can so easily ignore still remain high with respect to labor. The probability of success against the perceived national interest of many countries is remote indeed. The third possibility is that the growth of the global economy would reduce unemployment to the point that labor would become scarce relative to demand. This would then raise wages. But this is equally improbable, even though it seems to be the expectation of many economists.

There are hundreds of millions of unemployed people today and many more who are underemployed. The size of the work force is growing very rapidly in most Third World countries as a part of the population explosion. The method of capitalist economic growth requires ever fewer workers in relation to production. It is hard to share the expectation that this increasingly automated industry will absorb this vast work force.

The likelihood that the problem will be solved by growth seems even more remote when the process of industrialization is placed in the context of what is known of the environment. The quantity of resources required and the quantity of waste produced in this scenario stagger the imagination. Certainly the global warming and melting of the icecaps will be accelerated, so that the societies undergoing this transformation will also have to cope with massive physical dislocations. In reality there is no prospect at all of maintaining or reachieving good wages by eliminating global unemployment through global industrial growth.

There is a further problem with free trade that deserves consideration. In what sense is it free? The Crusoe model will be useful for considering this question, too.

At the outset of the story there is no question but that Robinson Crusoe trades freely and that, unless he is tricked, he trades to his advantage. But as the scenario unfolds, he decides to specialize. That is as it should be, according to economic theory. By specializing he increases his total produce and gains more in exchange than he could have produced if he continued his diversified efforts. He continues to trade successfully with the other Crusoes. But now his situation has changed in one respect. He trades freely, but he is no longer free not to trade. His survival depends on his imports from the other islands.

This is to say nothing more than that, economically speaking, he is now in the same position as everyone else. All are dependent on a host of others for survival from day to day. Adam Smith already emphasized that. The new Robinson Crusoe differs only in that he voluntarily chose a state of dependence whereas others have never known any other state.

Politically speaking, on the other hand, there is a difference. Most of those who are mutually dependent participate in a common political unit, a community. The government of this community has the responsibility to maintain an order that protects its citizens, to some extent at least, from exploitation by others. The Crusoes have no such government. Hence, a couple of Crusoes, on whom Robinson is wholly dependent for survival, may devise a plan. One year they acquire a sufficient supply of the commodity Robinson supplies so that they do not need it in the following year. That year they refuse to provide Robinson with the commodities he needs unless he gives them his island in exchange. They allow him to remain on the island, but his produce is now theirs to distribute as they see fit.

Economists would say that Robinson still participates in the free market. He freely chooses to exchange his island for the food he needs for survival. What he sells now is his labor. If he is dissatisfied with the terms offered him by the new owners of the island, he can seek better terms from some other Crusoe. So he is still a participant in the free market and a beneficiary thereof. At every point he has traded only to his benefit. Yet surely he is far less free than when all the trading began!

The Crusoe traders, without a government checking their actions, are a fair model for international free trade. What happened to Robinson has happened to many Third World countries. Following the pressures of the market and the advice of the economists, they have given up their relative self-sufficiency, have specialized, and have entrusted themselves to the magic of the market. Their economies are based on the export of one or two commodities. They must export to survive, for they can no longer feed themselves, and they cannot pay for food imports without exporting. Nor can they produce domestic commodities without imported inputs such as machinery and fertilizer. Their dependence on the market is complete. Meanwhile the terms of trade progressively deteriorate. They have little influence over the prices of their exports, which seem to them to be manipulated by international corporations with an interest in low prices. Frequently Third World governments act in the interest of the international corporations. Again we confront the fact that free trade leads to global economic power of corporations that are controlled by no government. To whatever extent individual nations follow the prescriptions of economists, they become dependent on a system of trade influenced, if not controlled, by this supranational economic power. Increasingly they must conform national policies to the desires of this economic power, for their economic survival depends on doing so.

Restoring Comparative Advantage by Balancing Trade and Reducing International Finance

The scenarios offered in this chapter are quite different from those proposed in standard economics texts. Nevertheless, they follow from well-known economic principles. Much depends on which economic principles one adopts. Our judgment is that the empirical test is important. We see no evidence that the principle of comparative advantage determines international trade relations in the real world. We think economists should not continue to propound it without empirical evidence of its truth.

By what principles, then, should international trade be governed, if not by comparative advantage? Following Culbertson (1986), our strategy is to consider policies that would, if adopted, restore the conditions presupposed by comparative advantage. Basically this means that, as in the textbook examples of comparative advantage, we have *balanced* trade between *national* entities. This means that trade is between En-

gland and Portugal as two communities, not between individual Englishmen and Portuguese each seeking only their own advantage. Of
course it will still be individuals who ultimately exchange goods, but
subject to rules designed to protect community interest. The first of
these rules is that trade should be balanced. In the textbook explanations of comparative advantage this condition is implicit in the use of
barter examples: English cloth is traded directly for Portuguese wine.
Money is a "veil" that only obscures the real transaction. But barter
trade is always in balance, while in a monetary economy trade need not
balance, the difference being made up with money and with transfer of
liquid capital assets. Barter too is a "veil" that obscures the possibility of
unbalanced trade.

Under barter there is no tendency for trade to give rise to net capital
flows from the surplus to the deficit country, since there is no surplus or
deficit. More importantly there is no possibility for the Portuguese capitalist to undersell the English in both wine and cloth, thereby transferring jobs from England to Portugal. Within this context of imposed balance, trade between individuals takes place freely. Must this balance be
bilateral (between each pair of nations) or could it be multilateral (between each nation and the rest of the world)? Multilateral balance is all
that is really required to prevent a net loss of jobs. Perhaps the simplest
way to balance trade is to limit imports to rough equality with expected
exports by issuing import quota licenses, and auctioning them to competing import firms. Resale of the quota license could be permitted during the time period for which it is valid. The subsequent time period
would begin with another auction.

We have spoken only of balanced trade—but do we mean to seek
balance only in the trade account, or in the capital account as well? And
should we seek a separate balance in each account, or an overall balance
of both together? Capital transfers (borrowing and repayment) would
be impossible in real terms without a compensating trade account imbalance. But again, the whole logic of comparative advantage and free
trade was premised on capital immobility. Balanced trade and capital
immobility are two sides of the same coin. The way a country borrows
in real terms is to import more than it exports. If that is forbidden, then
so is international lending and borrowing. The latter are also deals made
by individuals or entities in different countries for the sake of private
interests. The absence of safeguards to protect the national community
from the effects of excessive international debt are very obvious in today's world. The debtor countries (not just the individual debtor) are

being squeezed to cut home consumption (expand exports, contract imports) in order to earn foreign exchange to service the external debt. And in the event of default it is the community in the creditor country (the FDIC and the U.S. taxpayer, for example) that suffers the consequence, not just the private lender.

Balanced trade and capital immobility imply each other. If we have balanced trade there is no need for, or possibility of, international capital flows. By insisting on balanced trade we automatically heed Keynes's admonition, cited at the beginning of this chapter: "Above all, let finance be primarily national." The consequence of free international finance (a necessary complement to free trade) has been the running up of unrepayable debts. Large surplus accumulations of money resulting from trade imbalances sought ways to grow exponentially and to recycle back to the deficit country to finance further trade deficits. Banks pumped money (the surpluses of petroleum-exporting countries) into Third World countries at a rate much greater than the ability of those governments to build wisely or to administer honestly. Government officials and associated elites wasted or stole large amounts of the borrowed funds, which consequently generated no increase in wealth. Yet these loans must be paid back at interest—not by those few who benefited, but by the general public, who received none of the benefits. The benefits were privatized, and the costs socialized.

In Brazil, for example, the general public has benefited little from the unproductive megaprojects of the government and highly subsidized enterprises. To repay the debt requires a large surplus of exports over imports. Consumption by the Brazilian people is being cut to release goods for export. This is done by lowering real wages (keeping money wage increases below inflation) and by taxing away middle-class purchasing power. Shoes made in Brazil, to take one example, cost less in the United States than in Brazil because exported shoes are exempt from many Brazilian taxes that raise their price in Brazil.

The ecological consequences of debt repayment are often severe. The Amazonian rainforest is being rapidly burned and converted into rangeland and cropland, the productivity of which is exhausted in 3 or 4 years. But that provides exports to meet debt payments for 3 or 4 years. The effect on income distribution is also bad because the big enterprises carrying out these "investments" (if the consumption of ecological capital can, even with quotation marks, be called an investment) are given large tax subsidies as an incentive to undertake an activity that otherwise would not likely be profitable. The revenue loss to the government is made up by increasing taxes on the middle class, or by allowing a larger fiscal deficit to result in more inflation.

These consequences are the result not only of free trade but also of growthmania, the belief that unfettered economic growth is always both possible and desirable. The "solution" to the debt crisis offered by the orthodox economist has been a further dose of growth. The way to grow is to invest, and the way to invest is to borrow. The solution to the debt is to increase the debt! Just why it is believed that this new debt will be used so much more productively than the older debt is never explained. The main motivation for pushing the new loans seems in some cases to be to supply the foreign exchange to enable the debtor country to meet its current payments on the old loans. This means that the old loans do not have to be written off as losses to the creditor banks. But borrowing to meet interest payments leads to a snowballing of the debt and is little more than a Ponzi scheme. This is recognized in secondary markets, where the sovereign debt of many countries is traded at discounts of greater than 50%.

International debt is a topic for a book in itself (see George 1988). Our purpose has been to show that the current debt crisis is part and parcel of the free trade regime that permits large trade imbalances and compensating financial transfers that can easily exceed the repayment capacity of deficit countries. Large trade surpluses actively seek ways to grow exponentially, and banks eager to grow turn a blind eye to corruption and incompetence in many debtor governments. Or perhaps they are not quite so blind—some of their biggest depositors are the very officials and elites of the debtor countries. The foreign exchange provided in the loan may be used to finance capital flight rather than capital investment (Henry 1986).

The consequences of debt generated by unbalanced trade are more visible in poor countries, but, as we have emphasized, they are now becoming visible in the United States, which has with astonishing rapidity transformed itself from the world's largest creditor to its largest debtor. The debt crisis is not likely to be solved in a world committed to the free trade dogma. Solution will require a commitment to balanced trade.

Does this mean that developing countries can no longer import needed capital equipment from the United States? By no means. Brazil can still import tractors and computers and pay for them with coffee and shoes. Brazil simply cannot borrow in order to import tractors and computers *faster* than they can export coffee and shoes. Nor of course can the United States borrow by importing shoes and coffee faster than it can pay for them with tractors and computers. But elimination of all international lending and borrowing seems extreme even to us who believe it should be greatly curtailed. Is there not room for permitting some international transfer on capital account along with the compensatory imbalance on trade account? We believe there could be a reasonable extension of the principle of balance from short-term balanced trade to long-term balanced borrowing and repayment, if the latter were limited to clearly beneficial and productive projects as judged from the perspective of both communities. Like international trade, international borrowing and lending should be between nations as communities, not between subnational entities seeking only their private interests. This is an area for further reflection and research.

Meanwhile there seems to be an actual evolution toward balanced trade in the increasing practice of "countertrade," whereby the exporter agrees to import goods up to a certain amount as partial payment. These are sometimes simple barter arrangements but are usually separate parallel transactions, obviously linked at the stage of making a deal, but independently carried out or enforced. Estimates are that countertrade arrangements governed between 10% to 20% of world trade in 1981, and some 50% of trade between Western and Communist bloc countries. Perhaps the biggest countertrade deal yet involves investment and repayment—the construction by European firms of a natural gas pipeline from the Soviet Union to Western Europe, the loan to be repaid with natural gas delivered to Western Europe up to an agreed upon amount (Welt 1984).

Clearly there is a wide middle ground between free trade and autarky. Neither extreme has ever been practiced and we advocate neither. We cannot settle the question of exactly what trade policies are best, but we believe that policies currently err on the side of too much free trade because of misplaced concreteness in the argument from comparative advantage. We have argued that free trade is a case of individualism riding roughshod over community interests. Free traders will certainly reply that it is they who are serving the community, the larger world community, and it is we who are disrupting that community. They will invite us to overcome our parochial, individualistic nationalism and rejoice with them in the goal of a cosmopolitan world without borders. Trade between England and Portugal will be no different than trade between Yorkshire and London.

But what is really entailed by this cosmopolitan vision? For one thing, as already noted, in a world without borders the whole logic of comparative advantage loses its basis, and the rule of absolute advantage along with world equalization of wages is the consequence. If world traders are to be analogous to Londoners trading with Yorkshiremen, then we need something analogous to English law courts and police to define property rights and enforce contracts. We have no such world authority and have failed repeatedly at even modest attempts to institute one.

Free traders, having freed themselves from the restraints of community at the national level and having moved into the cosmopolitan world, *which is not a community,* have effectively freed themselves of all community obligations. World community at least at present is an abstract vision. It is by no means a concrete reality that would be undercut by a policy of balanced trade. Real community now exists only at national and subnational levels. The goal of building up a community of communities, a community of nations at the world level, is one we share. But we are sure it will not be achieved by sacrificing the real bonds of community at the national level. For a nation that has attained a high standard of living for most of its people to have its capitalists say to its working class, "You must now compete in the world labor market against the hungry of other nations, and in the interest of efficiency your wages must fall to the world level," is the destruction of existing community in the interests not of a broader world community that does not yet exist, but in the interests of a much smaller "community," a class of wealth and privilege, which does exist.

The free trade position today is, ironically, reminiscent of the mercantilists, against whom Adam Smith's arguments were aimed. To export and maintain a favorable balance of trade the mercantilists were quite explicitly prepared to follow a low-wage policy to keep their exports competitive. The surest way to keep wages low was to have an oversupply of labor. Rapid proliferation of laborers plus the absence of unions and social insurance keep wages low. A country is efficient and productive when the vast majority of its citizens are living at subsistence! Of course this absurdity was masked by the fact that the laboring class was not really considered part of the community. They were closer to slaves than citizens. Centuries later we believe that the welfare of the community includes the standard of living of the working class. But the "free-trade mercantilists" of today urge the same exclusion of the working class from the national community. U.S. workers are invited by U.S. capitalists to share their wages with the hungry of the world in the name of "world community." The majority of the nation is invited to lower its standard of living so "we" can be more "efficient." But who is "we," and efficient at what? Certainly not efficient at providing a decent living standard for the majority of our citizens! And while we are about the business of lowering wages in the interest of efficiency, let us not forget to lengthen the working day, lower the minimum legal age to work, cut back retirement and sick leave, and so on. Equilibrium with the world labor market will not permit such benefits.

In sum, we believe it is folly to sacrifice existing institutions of community at the national level in the supposed service of nonexistent institutions of community at the world level. Better to build and strengthen the weakening bonds of national community first, and then expand community by federation into larger trading blocs among national communities that have similar community standards regarding wages, welfare, population control, environmental protection, and conservation. True efficiency lies in the protection of these hard-won community standards from the degenerative competition of individualistic free trade, which comes to rest only at the lowest common denominator.

12

Population

Population Policy in a Community

The conflict between individualism and person-in-community emerges nowhere more clearly than in the issue of population. As individualists we value reproductive freedom, but as persons-in-community we recognize that such freedom can have unacceptable social consequences. Even in *On Liberty,* John Stuart Mill's classic defense of individual freedom, a limitation on reproductive freedom is explicitly urged:

"The fact itself, of causing the existence of a human being, is one of the most responsible actions in the range of human life. . . . And in a country either over-peopled or threatened with being so, to produce children, beyond a very small number, with the effect of reducing the reward of labor by their competition, is a serious offense against all who live by the remuneration of their labor. The laws which, in many countries on the Continent, forbid marriage unless the parties can show that they have the means of supporting a family, do not exceed the legitimate powers of the State" (Mill [1859] 1952, p. 3191).

In some other species the instinct of territoriality automatically limits reproduction to those with a territory sufficient to support progeny. Nature's way is not always best, but in this instance it seems more responsible than our current practice of allowing new human beings to be unintended by-products of the sexual fumblings of teenagers whose natural urges have been stimulated by drugs, alcohol, TV, and ill-constructed welfare incentives. The nineteenth century's pure individualist solution was like nature's: let the unfortunate offspring starve. Few take that position nowadays. Certainly we do not. But if the benefits of community are to be extended to all new members as a matter of right or duty, then the community must also accept the correlative responsibility of limiting the flow of new entrants to a rate such that each can have a reasonable chance of a decent existence. This principle applies to

236

new entrants by net immigration as well as by net natural increase. Curiously the United States is much more willing to limit immigration than to limit natural increase. A close corollary of this principle was considered in Chapter 11, where it was argued that free trade, which has the same wage-equalizing effects as free migration, might also have "the effect of reducing the reward of labor by their competition," at least for the receiving country. One could reply that wages in the sending country would tend to rise. But when new entry is by natural increase there is no "sending country" and this offsetting feature is absent. All the more curious, then, is our unwillingness to restrict natural increase while we vigorously restrict immigration. Immigration cannot be free, for the same reasons that trade cannot be free. And by extension neither can natural increase be entirely free of community control, once full-world economics has replaced empty-world economics.

Actually the effusive welcoming of unlimited births is often the upper class welcoming the replenishment of the lower class, which supplies useful citizens who are willing to work hard for low wages. What would we do without them! The upper and middle classes limit their numbers. The poor are more prolific (indeed the world "proletarian" derives from the same root as "prolific") either because of the incomplete democratization of birth control, or because of structural incentives to high fertility as a substitute for old-age insurance or for other economic advantages at the family level. The class consequences of population growth are especially evident in Brazil, which has historically always followed a cheap labor policy. First African slaves were the source of cheap labor. After abolition of slavery the government subsidized the immigration of poor southern Europeans to provide cheap labor. Now the natural rate of increase of the working class is more than enough to guarantee an unlimited supply of labor at subsistence wages. A more passive policy of going slow on birth control is now all that is needed to preserve cheap labor to fuel Brazil's economic growth. In northeast Brazil the lower class reproduces twice as rapidly as the upper class, a fact that by itself dooms even the most sincere conventional efforts to narrow the gap in per capita incomes. The adoption of capital-intensive, labor-saving technology in the modern sector also contributes to unemployment and cheap labor.

Countries that have not followed a cheap labor policy but have sought high wages in the interest of the welfare of the majority of the national community (the United States and Australia, for example) are now, in the name of either free trade, free migration, or free capital mobility asked to throw away those welfare gains and let capital enjoy the competitive advantage of cheap labor. Foxes have always advocated high fertility and free immigration for rabbits, without thereby gaining a reputation for generosity.

Population issues bring out not only the conflict between individualism and person-in-community, but also the conflict between the latter and collectivism. The collectivists have generally been even more pronatalist than the individualists. Producing citizens for the Fatherland has long been thought of as a contribution to the power of the nation. Societies that are more collectivist in orientation will seek the population size that maximizes surplus above subsistence rather than average per capita income available for individual consumption. Alfred Sauvy has shown that the collectivist optimum occurs at a larger population than the individualist optimum (1948). But sometimes there are collectivist forces even in basically individualistic societies that push in the direction of larger population. A case in point is the military, which has traditionally favored a larger population. This line of reasoning has recently been revived by Ben Wattenberg and Hans Zinsmeister:

"Even in an atomic age, it is sometimes forgotten, only large populations have tax bases broad enough to support the defense systems that are the basis of national power and security. Perhaps the clearest example of a national security system that could not possibly be built by other than large nations is the Strategic Defense Initiative, popularly known as 'Star Wars.' At an estimated $300 billion, it could be put together only by amortizing it over a large population" (Wattenberg and Zinsmeister 1986).

We think that this is an argument against Star Wars rather than in favor of a larger population. But if the driving motive is the building of pharaonic collective projects, be they pyramids or orbiting laser-reflecting mirrors, then the tendency will be to maximize the social surplus rather than per capita consumption. And the former requires a larger population than the latter.

Corresponding to the population boosters' unmerited reputation for generosity is the neo-Malthusian's equally unmerited reputation for stinginess and misanthropy. It is not that neo-Malthusians do not want to share nature's bounty with others. It is precisely because they do wish to share with the working class, with future generations, and with other forms of life that they advocate limiting the population of human bodies and their mechanical extensions. The only way to maximize the cumulative number of lives over time is to avoid having so many alive simultaneously that carrying capacity is eroded. The only way to preserve a diversity of species is to forgo the option of turning their habitat into farms and factories to support more people or higher-consuming people. Ten billion human lives are better than five billion, as long as the ten billion are not all alive at the same time.

The neo-Malthusian's goal of maximizing cumulative lives ever lived is, however, subject to certain constraints. First is the constraint of an acceptable standard of per capita consumption. As Malthus put it, "There should be no more people in a country than could enjoy a glass of wine or a piece of beef with their dinner." This is not a precise definition of "optimum population," but it is far from meaningless. There is no call for meat at every meal, with plenty of alcohol, tobacco, and sweets. All that is bad for us anyway. But the level of surplus and comfort represented by a piece of meat and a glass of wine once a day is desirable (even if one is a vegetarian or a teetotaler). If additions to the present population cannot be given these comforts then better to postpone the additions until later. As far as we know God is not impatient for all lives to be lived soon. We believe the divine discount rate is zero. And as for the people who say, where would I be if my parents had practiced birth control?—all we can do is answer with the question, why were you born to your parents instead of to some other couple in some other time and place? The pairing of a particular self-conscious identity with a particular birth is such a total mystery that it can hardly be appealed to as a criterion for population policy.

The Chinese advocated a laissez-faire population policy in the Bucharest World Population Conference in 1974, where the United States was urging birth control measures. At the 1984 Mexico City World Population Conference the positions were reversed: China had the most stringent population control policy in modern times, and the United States under the Reagan Administration was pushing the laissez-faire, no-limits doctrine. On the one hand, it pointed to the demographic transition thesis (which will be explained below) as the sufficient cure for population growth, but on the other hand even the need for that thesis was undercut by some Reagan advisors, who argued that population growth is a general economic benefit and will remain so (Simon 1981; Wattenberg 1986). It looks as if the United States now favors an international cheap labor policy; let foreign labor be cheap, let capital be mobile, let trade be free. The consequence is that U.S. wages will also fall as jobs move abroad with capital. And immobile domestic capital will benefit from cheap domestic labor. The U.S. consumers, that is, those professionals and public officials who still have high-paying jobs, will of course benefit from lower prices. We are glad that China's leaders saw the error of laissez-faire individualism, and we hope for a reversal of recent trends in the United States.

The Issue of Scale

The official Washington trend toward laissez-faire and pro-natalist population policies is reflected in a report by the National Academy of Sciences, entitled *Population Growth and Economic Development: Policy Questions* (1987). Many interesting questions were discussed, but most interesting was the question that was never asked, namely: Does the physical scale of the economy (population times per capita resource use) make any difference? The question does not occur within the neo-classical mind set, which sees only allocation of resources. The entire focus is on allocation of any given flow of resources among alternative uses. If the allocation is optimal in the sense of Pareto, then that is all there is to consider. If we double the scale of resource use or cut it in half the market will still grind out a (different) Pareto-optimal alloca-tion. The question of optimal allocation is one thing, that of optimal scale is something else entirely, as discussed in Chapter 7. Under pure com-petition (many small buyers and sellers, perfect knowledge, no exter-nalities), market individualism leads to an optimal allocation. But, as Chapter 7 showed in some detail, there is no analogous tendency toward optimal scale. The very concept of an optimal scale for the entire econ-omy, relative to the supporting ecosystem, just does not exist in current economic theory. Since the physical dimensions of the ecosystem are fixed, growth in the scale of the economy (population times per capita resource use) must result in an increase in the scale of the economy *relative* to the ecosystem. The question of what relative scale is best is an obvious one and is totally independent of what is the best allocation of a given scale of resource flow (throughput) among alternative uses. Neo-classical economics manages to conflate these separate issues, assuming, evidently, that scale issues can all be transformed into allocation issues through proper definition of property rights. But this is incorrect.

Suppose that at a certain scale we have an optimal allocation. Eco-nomic and demographic growth are occurring, so some years later we have a larger scale. At the larger scale, clean air is no longer a super-abundant free good. Very well, says the neoclassical economist; that simply means that the old zero price for air is too low, so we somehow grant property rights in clean air to individuals or public bodies, and the result will be some positive price for clean air and a resulting reallocation to a new optimal allocation. Problem solved. But only the allocation problem has been solved. Once air has become a scarce good then of course it is poor economics to try to maintain its price at zero. But there remains the question of whether we were better off at the smaller scale when the correct price of air was zero, or at the larger scale, which correctly requires that air have a positive price? That is an issue of scale, not of allocation. To deal with the optimal scale issue we must implicitly be willing to control or influence scale, once we know the direction in which the optimum lies. But control of scale cannot be left to individualistic measures. There is no invisible hand leading individuals motivated by self-interest toward the social good of an optimum scale. The invisible hand, to the extent that it works, leads us to an optimal allocation. An optimal allocation, in a growth regime that has already overshot the optimal scale, is just a way of always making the best possible adjustment to an ever-worsening situation.

Economics for person-in-community must face the question of scale: how many persons simultaneously living at what level of per capita resource use is best for community, where community includes concern for the future and nonhuman species as well as presently living humans? The next question is what are the best means of controlling the scale of population and per capita resource use?

The first question is a reformulation of the notoriously difficult issue of optimum population. We do not need a precise answer. A sufficient definition is a population size that is sustainable for a very long time at levels of per capita resource use that permit a good life for all. There is plenty of evidence that in rich countries the scale of throughput (population times per capita resource use) is ecologically unsustainable. Therefore it is clear that we must reduce one or both of these factors. Currently both are growing globally. Our first goal therefore should be to stabilize at existing or nearby levels as soon as we reasonably can. Once we have learned to be stable at some level, then we can worry about moving to the optimum level. Note that this argument for learning to be stable holds even if, contrary to our opinion, one believes that we have not yet reached the optimum scale. Continuing growth would eventually bring us to this larger scale at which point we would then want to be stable. If we do not know how to be stable, then identification of an optimum scale will only allow us to recognize and wave goodbye to it as we grow beyond it. So, operationally speaking, those who argue that there is no point in talking about stability unless you can first specify the optimum scale at which to remain stable, have got it backwards. Unless we are willing and able to be stable, there is no point in knowing the optimum. Therefore policies aimed at stability need not wait for precise clarification of the optimum scale, which will require much collaboration among economists, ecologists, philosophers, climatologists, and so on and will never be precisely defined. But precise definition has never been a prerequisite for existence, and since there is overwhelming evidence that the present scale of throughput is much too large, policies must be adopted to reduce it. Throughput can be reduced by lowering one or both of its two factors, population and per capita resource use. In general the first alternative is relevant to poor countries, while the second is more relevant to rich countries. We will consider both cases in the following sections.

Where Population As Such Is the Problem

Per capita resource use in poor countries is very low, so low that we share the general concern that it be increased. This increase cannot be achieved while population doubles every 30 years. Globally, nothing is more urgent than slowing and then stopping this rapid growth by reducing the birthrate rather than by increasing the deathrate.

The recognition of this need is now widespread. Forty-five heads of states (including many of the most populous, such as China, India, Indonesia, Bangladesh, Nigeria, and Egypt) signed a "Statement on Population Stabilization by World Leaders" and presented it to the Congress of the United States on April 24, 1987. It includes the following statement:

At present there are 76 million more births than deaths on our planet each year. If present rates continue, by the year 2,000, there will be 100 million more births than deaths. A billion people have been added in the last 13 years and the next billion will be added in 12 years.

Degradation of the world environment, income inequality, and the potential for conflict exist today because of over-consumption and overpopulation. If this unprecedented population growth continues, future generations of children will not have adequate food, housing, medical care, education, earth resources, and employment opportunities.

We believe that the time has come now to recognize the world-wide necessity to stop population growth within the near future and for each country to adopt the necessary policies and programs to do so, consistent with its own culture and aspirations. [Fornos 1987, pp. 110–11]

The real question is not whether population should be stabilized, but how. One view has been that economic growth itself is the answer. By 1983, twelve European countries had attained the desired balance of births and deaths, at low levels of both. Lester Brown explains what happened. "Declines in fertility flowed from economic gains and social improvements. As incomes rose and as employment opportunities for women expanded, couples chose to have fewer children. The improved availability of family planning services and the liberalization of abortion laws gave couples the means to achieve this. Population stabilization in these countries has been the result, therefore, of individual preferences, the product of converging economic, social, and demographic forces" (Brown et al. 1984, p. 2).

These twelve countries embody what was identified in 1945 by Frank Notestein as the "demographic transition." This transition was from a period of high birth and death rates (low life expectancy), through a period of high birth rates and low death rates, to a new balance of birth and death rates where both are low (high life expectancy). The second period is, of course, one of rapid population growth accompanying industrialization. The third period occurs when the social and economic changes described above cause couples to choose small families. The presentation of this demographic transition as a general theory of what development brings about led to considerable complacency about rapid population growth around the world. The message was that the economic development that made rapid population growth possible would also bring it to an end.

Lester Brown sadly shows that for many of the world's poorest countries this scenario is not working. "The theorists did not say what happens when developing countries get trapped in the second stage, unable to achieve the economic and social gains that are counted upon to reduce births. Nor does the theory explain what happens when the second-stage population growth rates of 3% per year—which means a twentyfold increase per century—continue indefinitely and begin to overwhelm life-support systems" (Brown et al. 1987, p. 20). What happens, of course, is that famine and pestilence return and the nation slips back into the first stage of high birth and death rates with low life expectancy. Brown sees this fate threatening a number of countries already.

There is a further difficulty even if one accepts the demographic transition hypothesis. The hypothesis says in effect that parents substitute consumer durables and other goods for extra children. The policy is to "buy" fewer births with more refrigerators, cars, TVs, and so forth. India tried to buy reduced births cheaply with transistor radios, but that did not work. Nothing is said in the demographic transition thesis about the "terms of trade" at which babies and consumer goods are "traded off," and whether they are ecologically feasible. Could the Chinese give every family a car and a refrigerator in exchange for having only one child? Not at an ecologically acceptable cost. Would the per capita consumption level of the average Indian have to rise to that of the average Swede for Indian fertility to fall to the Swedish level? What would the required levels of throughput imply for the Indian ecosystem? Even worse for the demographic transition thesis is the fact that before it comes into play in Third World countries, a per capita income increase must be experienced by the poorest two-thirds of the population since they are the ones having most of the children. This presupposes a massive redistribution as part of economic development, or aggregate growth rates so high that even the trickle-down is substantial. We doubt that either event is likely. It is encouraging to note a substantial fall in fertility in Brazil. Superficially this seems to support the automatic demographic transition thesis. But in fact the fall in fertility has occurred in the lower social classes, which experienced no increase in income and in some cases even a decrease. This is more of a contradiction to the demographic transition, but it offers hope that democratization of birth control can reduce the birth rate independently of increases in consumption of consumer durables.

Fortunately, many Third World countries have not depended on the demographic transition to take care of their population problems. The most dramatic instance is China, where pressures of a variety of kinds are now exerted in favor of one-child families. In one decade China lowered its birth rate from 34 per thousand to 20. Systematic efforts to educate the people, to give ready access to contraceptives and to abortion, to provide opportunities for women to participate in the community outside the home, and to assure that the aged will be cared for whether or not they have children have achieved improvements elsewhere. Nevertheless, the problem in most of the world remains acute.

We believe that the application of market principles to this problem holds a still unappreciated promise. The market can allocate goods well with far less coercion than the Chinese have been compelled to employ. Its weakness is that it cannot rightly determine its own scale or assure just distribution. The transferable birth quota plan (Boulding 1964; Daly 1974; Heer 1975) proposes that scale and distribution of the rights to bear children be determined by the community at large, but that these rights then be traded in the free market.

This plan is based on the perception that the right to reproduce can no longer be treated as a free good. It must be seen as a scarce good in a full world. As with other scarce goods, reproduction rights must be subject to distribution and allocation. The quota plan is based on equal distribution of a total amount of reproduction rights that would guarantee replacement fertility. But the rights are transferable, in recognition of the obvious fact that not everyone can or desires to reproduce, while others are very anxious to have more than the replacement number, which under U.S. mortality conditions is about 2.1 per couple. Since children only come in integral units the decimal presents a problem. This is solved by issuing rights in one-tenth of a child units (deci-child certificates), ten of which are required for a legitimate birth. Certificates are freely transferable by sale or gift. Thus initial distribution is on the principle of strict equality, but reallocation is permitted in the interests of allocative efficiency—in other words, providing a better match-up of rights to reproduce with desire to reproduce and ability to pay. It is the latter to which many people object—ability to pay should have nothing to do with reproduction, they think. This attitude is not supported in nature by territorial species, nor by human history where financial viability is often a precondition for marriage, a practice which even Mill, as we have seen, thought entirely proper. Indeed Mill might object to this scheme for being too lenient in that it gives everyone, including the indigent, equal right to reproduce and only permits but does not require reallocation. In addition the effect of this scheme on distribution of per capita income is clearly toward equality. A further and most important effect would be to raise the probability of a child's being born to a couple that wants and can afford the responsibility of nurturing a new human being. From the point of view of the child, this is certainly an advantage. So many arguments focus only on the individualistic "freedom of choice" of the parents that we find it necessary to emphasize the obvious fact that the child's welfare is also at issue.

Although much of the outrage with which this plan is often met is based on unexamined sentimentality, there are some real difficulties with it. Foremost is the problem of appropriate punishment for those who have children without the certificate. The alternatives range from ex post acquisition of certificate, perhaps on easy credit terms, to forced surrender of the child for adoption. Adopting parents would of course be required to have the necessary certificates. Any scheme of population control faces a similar difficulty. This plan is far less harsh than the Chinese plan, and in our opinion respects individual freedom to the highest degree compatible with demographic control. The divisibility of certificates into tenths permits a gradual change in growth rates and offers a further advantage over the Chinese plan. In order to stop population growth the Chinese had to adopt the drastic measure of the one-child family. Just how drastic a social change the one-child family represents can be appreciated by noting that it implies the absence of brothers, sisters, cousins, uncles, and aunts. This is not entailed by the certificate plan. This scheme could be calibrated to the demographic situation more precisely and could permit more gradual change.

We find it odd that this plan arouses so much opposition from people who accept such realities as rent-a-womb services and Nobel Laureate sperm banks for single mothers, practices about which we have serious reservations. Also this scheme does *not* involve buying and selling babies, but only legal rights to reproduce.

Our proposal is offered as an alternative to the Chinese approach for countries that are both in need of drastic action and capable of implementing it. There are countries whose needs are peculiarly desperate but which lack the national infrastructure through which such a plan could be implemented. There are others in which more moderate and focused steps will suffice. The United States is probably one of these.

Where Per Capita Resource Consumption Is the Problem

The U.S. population is growing at about 1% annually. This places the United States among those countries where the primary problem of excessive scale derives not from population growth as such but from per capita consumption. Subsequent chapters in this book propose a variety of policies the effect of which would be to reduce per capita resource consumption by Americans without reducing their genuine economic welfare. In view of the wild facts and the particularly large role of the U.S. economy in causing them, this reduction is of great importance for all humanity.

But even a relatively slow population growth will greatly reduce the benefits of these policies for the planet and increase the likelihood of real economic hardship within the nation. This country needs to join Europe in the attainment of a stationary population. If it can go beyond that for a period to a gradually declining population, the contribution to dealing with the global problem of the scale of throughput will be still greater.

Population growth in the United States is caused about equally by net immigration and the excess of births over deaths. Stopping population growth requires changes in both areas. Immigration can further be divided between legal and illegal. We favor continuing legal immigration close to its present volume of 600,000, although a gradual reduction may be necessary. But we also favor current efforts to gain control of our borders and to bring an end to illegal immigration.

Many economists vigorously dissent from this policy of restricting immigration. They urge free population growth and free migration along with free trade. These three policies are logically consistent among themselves and are also consistent with the underlying assumptions of empty-world economics. Naturally they are inconsistent with the assumptions of full-world economics. If there are no limits to resource substitution or to human knowledge, and if resources are therefore "not meaningfully finite," and if the goal of human existence is to satisfy more and more wants of more and more people, then of course the whole system is a perpetual growth machine and that is all there is to it.

One great political advantage the empty-world partisans have is that they can appear to be so generous. Don't limit the number of guests at nature's banquet, there is room for more! Let the wretched masses into our country; how can children of immigrants say "no" to new immigrants? It all sounds so big-hearted. But is it? It is easy to be generous if resources are infinite. But it is also easy to be generous at someone else's expense even when you know that resources are not infinite. Consider the interests served by "generous" immigration or tolerance of illegal aliens. The supply of cheap, docile labor is increased. Unions are weakened. Wages decline and profits rise. Capital benefits from free migration just as it does from free trade. It is our laboring class that pays the bill for the generosity of the capitalists who want to let poor immigrants in.

One reason for maintaining a generous quota for legal immigration is that the United States has a responsibility to refugees, especially if U.S. actions helped to create the situation from which people are fleeing. Compared to other countries the United States has traditionally been quite generous in acceptance of refugees. There are limits to the number of refugees we can absorb, but we do not think those limits have been surpassed.

Unfortunately these humanitarian policies have been radically politicized, as can be seen in any comparison of our treatment of refugees from El Salvador and Nicaragua. In Nicaragua our national policy has been to take all possible actions to destabilize the Sandinista government. To this end the United States has done what it can to disrupt the economy so as to cause hardship and dissatisfaction with the government. It also recruits and finances armed rebels against the government. Any Nicaraguan who chooses to flee from the ensuing poverty and danger is welcomed by the United States Immigration Service. These individuals are supposed to be testimonials to the oppressiveness and ineffectiveness of the Sandinista regime.

In El Salvador the United States has long supported the government's efforts to suppress a popular rebellion that needs no outside support to survive. The prolonged warfare exacerbated by extreme brutality and terrorism on the part of the dominant families has caused many to seek sanctuary in the United States. However, United States government policy is to deny sanctuary except in extraordinary cases. These refugees are not "illegal" according to international law but only according to politically dictated Immigration Service policies.

The adoption of the policies to be recommended in subsequent chapters would reduce frictions in other parts of the world or, at the very least, United States involvement in them. It would create a situation in which the United States would have fewer obligations to receive refugees as well as fewer pressures toward politicizing the decisions about whom to admit.

Although there are, of course, no accurate figures on illegal immigration, estimates indicate that its cessation could reduce population growth by as much as one million a year. We suggest that this is an appropriate goal of policy.

Consider now how the United States can reduce the annual surplus of births over deaths that also contributes to its population growth. Before instituting any across-the-board reductions, we favor reductions that are personally and socially beneficial for reasons other than population stabilization. We offer three proposals.

First, too many babies are born to adolescent mothers. The rate of adolescent pregnancy is higher in the United States than in any other developed country. Only in the United States is the rate still rising. The number is around half a million. We believe it should be a matter of public policy to reduce this number drastically.

There is nothing inherently wrong with teenage girls becoming mothers, and there have been societies in which this was normal and

healthy. Even today in this country there are instances of happy adolescent marriages producing physically and psychologically healthy
children. We affirm these. But this is not the character of teenage
motherhood in general. Half of the girls who give birth do not complete
high school. Their ability to compete for jobs is severely impaired. Many
of them lock themselves into lives of poverty. Many of the fathers take
no responsibility for the children.

Children of adolescent mothers are likely to be psychologically,
sociologically, and economically deprived. Many of the girls themselves
become mothers at an early age, perpetuating the cycle of dependency,
poverty, and hopelessness. The public also pays a high price. "Taxpayers
spent nearly $18 billion in 1986 on foodstamps, medical care and in-
come supports for all families begun by teenage mothers" (Weber, ed.,
1987, p. 70).

This whole phenomenon is a symptom of the breakdown of community. It is our belief that the inherited economic order bears a large responsibility for this breakdown and that the changes we recommend
would provide a context in which healthy local communities would not
perpetuate the destructive sort of youth culture now prevalent in many
places. But the problem of too many teenage mothers is too urgent to
await drastic social changes. The crisis must be addressed also in the
present social context.

The question is, "How?" We have no answers other than those generally discussed. Sex education is badly needed, and it may be that the
greater willingness of society to accept explicit sex education in face of
the threat of AIDS will also reduce the ignorance and irresponsibility on
the part of both boys and girls that is one cause of teenage pregnancy.
Also as society offers better education for all and greater opportunities
for women, and as hope for a brighter future becomes a part of the life
of more adolescent girls, we can expect that they will be more concerned to postpone pregnancy until they have completed their educa-
tions. We should work for a situation in which education, opportunity,
and hope lead to a sufficient reduction of teenage pregnancy. In the
meantime, for those who become pregnant, abortion is sometimes the
least evil of the remaining options.

The following summary of a study of what is happening in various
states supports the general direction of our suggestions. "Low birth
rates (and, generally, high abortion rates) were found in politically liberal states where women's status is relatively high, where a high propor-

tion of women are served by family planning clinics, where Medicaid funding is available for abortions and where public education expenditures and teacher-student ratios are high. Contrary to popular myth, states with high maximum welfare payments had relatively low birth rates" (Weber, ed. 1987, p. 71).

A second focus of efforts to reduce the excess of births over deaths should be on unwanted babies of mothers of any age. In earlier times when more children were an asset to the community as a whole, a woman had an obligation to have children, and, on the whole, more rather than fewer of them. All the great traditional religions arose during that period, and their teachings are deeply affected by that social need. Today, however, a different basic attitude is required. Having children is a privilege rather than a duty. The community may not have to deny that privilege to any couple who truly desires to exercise it. But by the same token, those who choose not to exercise that privilege deserve the respect and appreciation of all. They should be aided and morally encouraged to act on their choice and not to allow themselves to be caught in the trap of an unwanted pregnancy or birth.

A third focus may be even more controversial than those discussed thus far, but we feel the need to raise an issue that grows more important as the population ages. Older people should have the right to die on their own terms. A major dread of the elderly is that they will be kept alive at great expense to society and with much trouble to their children long after their lives have ceased to have any meaning for themselves and for others. This is, on any large scale, a new problem brought about by the triumphs of modern medicine. The proper response cannot be found in ancient religious texts that came out of a very different social and demographic situation. Society is beginning to take a few tentative steps toward releasing doctors from the need to take extreme measures in preserving the life of one who wants to die. We hope that with due caution it will go considerably further. Quite apart from any general demographic considerations, a proper respect for human freedom and the needs of the elderly should grant them the right to die and aid them in implementing their decision. In a world in which population presses upon ecological limits, there are additional reasons to take these humane steps.

These policies relating to the surplus of births over deaths are designed to maximize the chance that babies will be born into families that want them and are able to care for them, and that people will live as long as they desire and no longer. They are, therefore, as noncoercive as it is possible for them to be. But we stress that we do not rule out elements of restriction of individual preference by the community as a whole in the interests of the well-being of all.

Accordingly, we would hold in reserve the transferable birth quota plan described above, should present demographic trends reverse themselves. Such a reversal in the United States appears unlikely to us, but then the baby boom of the 1940s appeared an unlikely prospect to the demographers of the 1930s. It is worth considering all possibilities.

13

Land Use

Sharing the Land with Other Species

In economics "land" is the one term that points to the natural world. In Chapter 10 we suggested that instead of treating land as matter and space, as modern economics has largely done, we should think of it primarily as energy and biosphere. Of course, space is very much bound up with both. When land is thought of as biosphere, and when the biosphere is understood as a community of communities among which humanity is but one of the communities, then the most inclusive question about the use of the land is how we share it with the other creatures. In view here is primarily wildlife. What portions of the planet do human beings, who now have undisputed dominion, leave to wilderness? What portion should be left to wilderness?

The question has arisen even from the dominant anthropocentric point of view. Human beings gain satisfaction from the existence of other creatures in their native habitat, and there are scientific, aesthetic, and recreational needs for wilderness. As a result, wildlife refuges, national parks, and wilderness areas have been set aside. But they constitute a very small portion of the land, they are under constant pressure from human beings, and most of them are too small to support major predators. More and more the talk is of "wildlife management." Meanwhile the extinction of species proceeds unabated.

From the biospheric perspective the situation is bad. Humanity is not showing a real willingness to share the planet with other creatures. They are not allowed to be what they are and to continue to evolve according to natural principles. Domestication proceeds everywhere, and with it degradation of the gene pool. The richness contributed to the biosphere by the vast multiplicity of creatures declines.

Collective human attitudes and habits were shaped through time, and, for most of human history, when the wilderness was vast in relation to the settled world. Civilization existed around the Mediterranean surrounded by unmeasured wilderness to the north and south. To extend the cultivated and settled area seemed, and probably was, a gain. In the United States these attitudes were renewed and intensified. For a long period the western frontier seemed vast in relation to human presence.

There was another human perspective. There were those who dwelt within the wilderness in symbiotic relationship with the other creatures. From the point of view of the civilized, that is, the citified, their place was anomalous. Because they did not conquer and dominate the land, they were not felt to have truly inhabited it. The wilderness remained empty and open for conquest to those who would settle it and tame it. The earlier inhabitants were an obstacle but did not really count. This attitude prevails even today as Brazil sets out to settle and tame the Amazon Basin. Fortunately, some change is occurring. For example, the World Bank now refuses to finance development projects that require the removal of peasants and indigenous peoples unless adequate resettlement is included as a cost of the project. But that is not sufficient protection.

Wilderness is compatible with a sparse human habitation and use by hunters and gatherers, but not with settlement by agriculturalists or exploitation by city dwellers. It is the attitude of the latter groups that has prevailed. Only as wilderness has become manifestly in short supply around the world have attitudes begun to change. Now agriculturalists and city dwellers, without giving up their earlier views, have also developed an interest in preserving something of the older world. But as long as the anthropocentric perspective prevails, there will be little willingness to preserve enough land for genuine wilderness to survive. That would require a certain renunciation on the part of human beings in behalf of other species—a renunciation that hunters and gatherers might understand, but that is still outside the experience of most of the citified.

Nevertheless, a new appreciation of land is emerging and with it a new possibility that the economy might be geared to the needs of this wider community. If that happened, what policies would be appropriate in the United States?

Some important steps could be taken relatively easily. The government owns vast tracts, especially in the West. Small portions of these were declared wilderness on the ground that their pristine condition has survived. That is progress. But these areas are far too small. For-

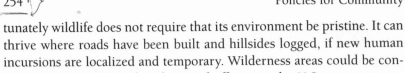

tunately wildlife does not require that its environment be pristine. It can thrive where roads have been built and hillsides logged, if new human incursions are localized and temporary. Wilderness areas could be considerably expanded with only trivial effects on the U.S. economy as a whole. The protections built into present wilderness classification would apply to these expanded areas.

Another step would be to withdraw cattle from the national forest. This would allow the wildlife population to recover even in areas that have long been used by human beings. Wildlife could use the meadows now grazed by cattle, and cattlemen would cease to press for the killing of predators. A lessened human presence would follow.

The economic cost of this withdrawal of grazing rights from cattlemen would be greater than that resulting from the expansion of wilderness areas. But it would still be small. It is not as if these cattle were important to the American economy or to the diet of the public. Beef is not in short supply, and if a reduction in beef-eating did follow, this would help the health of the American people. Unwillingness to adopt such policies can only reflect the anthropocentrism that rates the most tenuous economic gain to human beings more highly than any enrichment of the life of other animals. Although much could be accomplished by these initial steps, much more should be done to rectify the balance between humanity and other species. Another step would be to buy back from its owners much of the rangeland of the West that has been badly overgrazed. With the removal of domesticated animals, this land will gradually recover its ability to support a considerable population of wildlife. Wild animals are far less likely to damage the ecosystem than are domesticated animals.

In partial compensation to cattlemen for the withdrawal of rangeland in favor of wildlife, some land now used for crops could be turned over to cattle. Just as cattlemen have overgrazed pasture, so lands that would serve better as rangeland have been planted in crops. Many of these require irrigation, and much of this irrigation comes from aquifers that are being rapidly exhausted. Charging realistically for the cost of this water would lead to greatly reduced use and the abandonment of irrigation in many areas. These lands would then cease to be useful for farming but would be highly appropriate for cattle. There would be some reduction of crops now, but recharging depleted aquifers would make water available for crops in the future when they will be needed more. Today there is no shortage of food. A balanced reduction of both rangeland and cropland would hardly be noticeable in the supermarket, nor would it reduce food availability in other parts of the world. The current problems of surplus production would be eased.

When individuals and businesses sustain losses as a result of such public policies, some compensation is in order. But if the full cost of present production were included in the price of the products, most of those affected by these policies would have difficulty staying in business anyway. The cost of overgrazing rangeland and exhausting aquifers should not all be paid by the future! Once costs are internalized, it will be seen that there is a positive net value to be gained by desisting from exploitative practices.

These illustrations are given to describe the beginning of a process of withdrawal of human pressure on wildlife. They have dealt only with the American West. Similar possibilities, if on a smaller scale, exist in northern New England, the upper Midwest, and the South. In Alaska a majority of the land already enjoys some protection.

Half or more of the land area of the United States could be freed from human settlement, agriculture, and the grazing of domesticated animals. Interspersed with these primarily natural lands would be not only existing settlements but also places for recreation: ski resorts, summer resorts, dude ranches, hunting and fishing lodges. The greatly expanded natural areas should contribute to human enjoyment as well as to the well-being of other species.

Commercial use would also continue. Logging should be more ecologically managed and cutting should be less than growth, but logging would continue, except in the expanded areas designated for wilderness. Mining would be permitted in most areas.

In many places new settlement would be forbidden and some existing roads and settlements would be gradually closed. But none of this need involve drastic or disruptive changes. The major requirement is removal of domestic animals and prevention of further encroachment on wildlife habitat. A second requirement would be the understanding that in large areas human beings should adjust to the presence of wild animals rather than adjusting the environment to human convenience. Instead of wildlife management there would be management of human activity in primarily natural areas. The human species would share the land with others.

These considerations about sharing the earth's life-support capacity with other species bring into focus once again, albeit from a different angle, the issue of scale that we have repeatedly emphasized. The optimal scale of the human economy relative to the total biosphere might be defined in a totally anthropocentric way as the scale best for humans (even that would be a great advance over present practice). Or optimal scale may be defined biocentrically as that scale of the human economy that is best for all forms of life. The former views other species only instrumentally; the latter recognizes both their intrinsic and instrumental value. The biocentric optimum is likely to be smaller than the anthropocentric optimum. How much smaller we cannot say.

From Commodity to Trust

When land is viewed as matter and space, it is easy to treat it as something to be bought and sold. Chapter 5 showed how it had changed from being viewed as the human home and source of the means of life to a commodity valued only by its price in the marketplace, a value determined chiefly by location and size. Chapter 10 argued that this is a mistake, that nature is not a human possession but is that of which human beings are a part. In the biblical view human beings are that part of the creation which has a special responsibility with respect to the whole. We accept that view. It can be called the stewardship doctrine.

What economic policies with respect to the land would express a view of stewardship rather than ownership? One famous, if rather eccentric economist, Henry George, gave extensive consideration to this question. His "concept of the land is ecological in character; he views it as the natural milieu in which communities exist in relation with the surrounding environment, animate and inanimate. The atmosphere, sunlight, and water alike the gifts of nature—are contributing elements" (Wasserman 1979, p. 35). For this reason, "the natural land ought everywhere to be regarded as a community rather than as a private resource" (p. 30).

George believed that all the ills of the economy followed from the commodification of land and could be eliminated by its abolition. It is not our concern here to debate that larger thesis. But his specific proposal about taxation can be supported on the basis of a shared rejection of the idea of land as only a commodity. George proposed that all land be taxed near its rental value. In determining rental value, he followed Ricardo: "The rent of land is determined by the excess of its produce over that which the same application [of labor and/or capital] can secure from the least productive land in use" (Wasserman 1979, pp. 34–35). Thereby the land loses virtually all value as a private commodity. Essentially it becomes community property that is rented or leased to private parties.

Such a tax may be accused of being confiscatory, but it is important to see what George wanted to "confiscate." He certainly did not want to confiscate the products of human toil, or the capital these efforts generated. Indeed, he opposed all taxation on these. He believed "that there is a fundamental and irreconcilable difference between property in things which are the product of labor and property in land; that the one has a natural basis and sanction while the other has none, and that the recognition of exclusive property in land is necessarily the denial of the right of property in the products of labor" (George 1879, p. xv). George wanted to "confiscate" only gains that resulted from no human effort, or what tax accountants so frankly call "unearned income." These gains, he thought, appear *uniquely* with land. In this he exaggerated. Rent is not unique to land. Any factor can earn a return over and above its minimum supply price. But since the minimum supply price of land is zero, rent is much more identifiable in the case of land. Rent on land arises because of social changes, such as the extension of a city that makes nearby land rise many-fold in price. This phenomenon inspires speculation, which absorbs capital that should be productively invested and keeps from use land that should be contributing to the community. It is the unearned profits on land, resulting from social changes, that George would appropriate for the community as a whole.

Shifting to a Georgian tax would have extensive consequences. At present a vast amount of capital investment is in land. This is partly for present use of land but partly also for expectation of appreciation. Often this speculative element is the dominant factor. If land were taxed at or near its full rental value, its price would be very low. Most of the cost of holding land would be the tax placed on it. Since this tax would rise as the value of the land rose, or would fall as it fell, there would be no basis for speculation in land. Land would be acquired for its use value only, not for speculation on its increasing scarcity value.

At present the major tax is on improvements. This is a factor in deciding on construction. Today apartment owners and homeowners who improve their property—thus benefiting the community—must subsequently pay higher taxes. Under a Georgian system their taxes would not be affected.

At present a large capital investment is required to purchase land for a farm. Under a Georgian system this would not be required. What *would* be required is a large annual payment comparable to that on a lease. This would be calculated in such a way that the farmers' own toil and improvements on the land would redound entirely to their own benefit. Hence the amount of the tax should not discourage would-be farmers from acquiring the land. It *would* discourage speculators from doing so.

Many urban communities want to establish agricultural zones interspersed with residential areas. The Georgian tax in itself would not lead to that. This is a matter of zoning rather than taxing. Nevertheless, the Georgian tax would remove much of the pressure against this zoning. Farmers near cities today can sell their farms to developers at huge profits; they therefore resist zoning that forbids them to do so. On the other hand, in a situation in which private profits on land sales would tend to zero, farmers would have no reason to oppose zoning that kept taxes on agricultural lands appropriate to the profits that can be realized from farming.

Although the logic of taxing away unearned income on land is often acknowledged, its practicability is doubted. But in fact it can be done without massive social disruption. Once the wider community determines the desirability of this shift, it can be implemented gradually by raising taxes on land and lowering taxes in improvements. As we will point out in Chapter 17, this has already been done in some cities, with good results.

If even this is felt to be unfair to those who have invested speculatively in land under the present system, another approach is possible that would eventually achieve many of the same ends. Harvey Bottelson has suggested that governments could purchase all land at current market value.[1] (As an alternative to current market value we might suggest using value assessed for current tax purposes, especially if that value is self-assessed.) Payment would not be made in cash but would be extended over a long period so as to be paid from rents. This method would reward present landholders for the appreciation of their property and gain less immediate income for the community. On this basis it would be financially more difficult to begin to withhold large tracts from profitable use. Future rises in land values, however, would be fully captured by the community by this plan also. Meanwhile community ownership would give maximum freedom for planning patterns of healthy development. Capital would be invested in productive enterprises.

When land has been de-commodified by a Georgian tax or a Bottel-

1. Harvey Bottelson made the suggestion in a personal communication, 1987.

sonian purchase or by some combination of the two, it becomes a public trust. Then the community's interest in the health of the land can also be expressed in tax policies or in a system of grants and penalties. In the former instance, if farmers lose topsoil and poison the land, they can be taxed additionally for the damage they have done. If they build up the soil and increase its fertility this contribution to the social good can be deducted from their tax, while they could continue to benefit from improved agricultural profits.

This same policy could be applied to rangeland. In many instances degraded Western rangelands would not support sufficient cattle on a truly sustainable basis to be financially practical. If owners were taxed for the further degradation inflicted each year, much of the present rangeland would be abandoned. This would make public acquisition of this land inexpensive and its return to wilderness financially practical. Similarly, some farmers in arid regions would find it unprofitable to continue growing crops when taxed in terms of the damage to the land and the exhaustion of aquifers. Some of this land would be suitable for raising cattle and would be made inexpensively available to ranchers. In general this system would encourage employment of land for its most profitable *sustainable* use.

Land as Energy

The focus above has been on the biosphere. This is the part of our world that is most clearly sustainable if its processes are not distorted by human intervention. It is itself an embodiment of solar energy, and transforms that energy into the vast multiplicity of living things that make it up. Also land as Ricardian space is the primary recipient of renewable solar energy. But much of the energy human beings use comes in the form of nonrenewable low-entropy resources, or matter-energy. Metals and fossil fuels are particularly important here.

With respect to nonrenewable resources the goal is to approach sustainable use in an area in which strictly sustainable use makes no sense. To reduce the consumption of oil to the rate at which oil is produced by natural processes would remove it from commercial use. This would be utterly and unnecessarily disruptive of the economy of the whole world. Instead, the nation would decide what percentage of its own proven reserves of each nonrenewable resource would be used each year. It could then auction rights to extract that amount. Whether the extraction were on government or private land would not matter. The cost of these rights would be added to other costs of production, so they would be reflected in price.

The calculation of proven reserves is a complex matter for technicians to work out. It cannot mean, with respect to oil, all that is known to be in the ground. Much of that oil could be extracted only by using more energy in its extraction than will be realized by burning it. Proven reserves are by definition limited to the amount that, by present technology, can be profitably extracted.

Suppose the extraction of 2% of proven reserves were allowed each year. This would be more than was wanted of some minerals, such as coal. In this case the new policy will have little or no effect. In some other cases, such as oil and copper, this limit would be below present extraction rates and would drive up the price of the right to extract. This would add to market price and encourage frugal use, the development of substitutes, and, in the case of copper, recycling.

This system would also stimulate the development of more energy-efficient technologies of extraction. Success along these lines would increase proven reserves and hence allowable extraction. Search for new sources would also be encouraged, with similar effect.

When no technological advances are made and no new resources found, the amount of allowable extraction will decline slightly. The 2% will be figured on just 98% of the previous year's base. Also it must be expected that the best quality and most accessible resources will be extracted first. As time passes there will be less, and what there is will be more costly. Nevertheless, the transition to other sources of energy and substitutes for minerals will be gradual. Crises occasioned by relatively abrupt exhaustion can be avoided.

These policies would be meaningless without control over imports. They imply a system of tariffs or quotas. In this case controls cannot be used to prevent imports, since the nation's economy cannot function well without certain imports. But for reasons given in Chapter 11, domestic production should be favored in most cases. The ideal is eventually to adjust the national economy to domestic resources for all essential needs.

If other nations institute similar policies the availability of raw materials will decline and their prices will rise. On the other hand, their availability will last much longer, and the abrupt interruption of world supplies will be avoided.

Closely related to the use of nonrenewable resources is the use of nature's capacity to deal with our wastes. The goal, of course, is to keep pollution within the capacity of the environment to cope. Factories cannot altogether avoid polluting, and streams can purify some of their waste. The use of this scarce renewable resource by the factory should be paid for, and this payment should be in the form of a tax. The tax should be set at a level that would encourage the factory to keep its wastes within the capacity of the stream to purify. Of course the tax will be passed on as far as possible to the consumer, as it should be.

Similarly the quantity of solid waste must be reduced. One instrument should be taxation of goods to cover costs of their disposal. Producers will then have an interest in making goods that can be recycled or are biodegradable. If a tax is placed on nonreturnable containers, producers will be more interested in reusable ones. In general, packaging, if taxed to cover the costs of disposal, will become more conservative and more biodegradable. Also the increase in price of materials resulting from slowing depletion will by itself increase the incentive for materials recycling. Of course the reduction in depletion along with the extra incentive to recycling will reduce the volume of waste even without a pollution tax. However, as an instrument of fine tuning, we feel a pollution tax is needed.

But when we come to the wild facts, we noted in Chapter 7 that internalizing costs is hardly an adequate response. This does not mean that factories should not be taxed for their contribution to damaging the ozone layer, building up carbon dioxide in the atmosphere, and adding to the quantity of long-lasting nuclear poisons in the earth. But it does mean that other policies must be adopted that go far beyond what individual factories can do.

We require a massive national effort to envision and implement an energy policy. Since the whole economy is based today on very large use of nonrenewable energy, especially oil, and since supplies of oil will be giving out within forty years, one of the most critical issues of land use is energy policy in this narrow and direct sense. The most careful recent study of our energy options is *Beyond Oil* (1987) by Gever, Kaufmann, Skole, and Vorosmarty of the University of New Hampshire's Complex Systems Research Center. The authors do all they can to avoid being alarmist, and they project as positive a picture as they can. But it is not encouraging.

They describe two paths into the future, following Amory Lovins in calling them the hard and soft paths. The hard path uses nonrenewables, nuclear power, and highly centralized energy production. The soft path shifts to the use of renewable forms of energy in decentralized ways. What is striking is that the differences between these two paths take a long time to show up significantly in their graphs. It turns out that in the 40-year period they have chosen to consider, both paths depend increasingly and predominantly on coal to maintain the current level of energy. Neither path offers an increase of total energy available.

The authors worry that coal is polluting the atmosphere and that its mining scars the earth's surface. They note in passing the problems of the greenhouse effect (p. 71). But they can propose no other options than to stop increasing our use of energy and to double and triple our use of coal as gas and oil are exhausted.

The authors clearly prefer the soft path despite their view that it will leave the country dependent on coal for a long time. In an afterword they point in directions that we also favor: "Gain control of population growth, raise fuel taxes and/or impose import duties; develop cogeneration capacity; conserve through efficiency; encourage the federal government to set an example; promote new farming methods; and invest in renewable fuels" (pp. 251–255). But they do not hold out a great deal of hope that such steps will change the general picture.

Indeed, reflection on their conclusions leaves the reader distressed. They have not drawn the full negative implications of the heavy use of coal to which they see no alternative. If they factored in the greenhouse effect, their projections would have to be much worse. Within the 40-year period the continued heavy use of fossil fuels will lead to a measurable rise in ocean levels, resulting in extensive damage to delta areas and coastal cities, and it will also lead to major changes in the weather, disruptive of agriculture and human settlement. The energy cost of responding to these changes will reduce net energy available for other purposes or worsen the causes of the problem by using more coal. Can such a vicious circle be avoided?

Amory Lovins is far more optimistic than they about the possibility of continuing present levels of end use with much less energy. To demonstrate this possibility he has built the Rocky Mountain Institute at Snowmass, Colorado. This building uses no fossil fuels, about one-tenth of the amount of electricity used in comparable buildings, and about one-half the water. There is no sacrifice of comfort or convenience. All savings are achieved by the use of passive solar energy, excellent insulation, and efficient electrical devices and toilets. "The net additional cost of the energy-saving features (after subtracting the savings from not needing a furnace) is on the order of $6,000. Compared with normal local building practice and with the cheapest conventional fuels (wood and propane), the building saves more than $7,100 worth of energy per year. This saving repays its own cost in about ten months and should pay off the entire building in 40-odd years" (Lovins and Lovins 1985, p. 5).

Even apparently slight changes in energy efficiency can have a large effect on plans for supply. According to Richard Munson: "Achieving a 2% annual reduction in energy use worldwide would cost $5–10 billion a year; yet it would save an estimated $20 billion annually. One percentage point difference in the annual growth rate of electricity demand equals the equivalent of 100 large nuclear power plants by the century's end, costing about $400 billion" (Munson 1987, p. 55). Munson sees prospects for cogeneration to produce about 45,000 megawatts of electricity by the year 2000, perhaps more if state regulatory inhibitions are removed.

Munson also calls attention to gains that would be possible if more competition were allowed. The Public Utilities Regulatory Policies Act of 1978 has opened the door to competition in production of electricity. This has led to rapid development of cogeneration technologies as well as solar ones by requiring utilities to purchase electricity produced by independents at the cost that the utility saves by not increasing its own production. Nevertheless, more could be done. At present utilities can buy from their own facilities at much higher rates. Munson notes that "if utilities had been able to pay themselves only the avoided cost rate for new units, many of today's reactors would not have been completed. Ironically, a utility can add a reactor that generates electricity costing 16 cents per kilowatt-hour, but it can reject 4 cent per kilowatt-hour electricity from a cogenerator by manipulating the avoided cost calculation" (p. 57).

If building habits across the country were to change drastically, and if fair competition were allowed in the production of electricity, reliance on both coal and nuclear plants would be reduced. Much more electricity would be produced in small-scale local units that would fit well with a decentralizing economy (see Lovins 1977). Similar savings can be effected in automobiles. *Beyond Oil* refers to cars on the drawing board capable of getting 100 miles per gallon. Superconductors might greatly reduce the loss of energy in transmission. In short, if national energy policy concentrated on efficiency use rather than increased production, the use of fossil fuels could be reduced during the 40-year period of the *Beyond Oil* study.

Nevertheless, we think that other changes are also needed. *Beyond*

Oil points to new methods of farming that are not so dependent on fossil fuels. In the next chapter we will discuss these and how a change in agriculture in this country could enable them to be implemented. A changed view of national security, to be discussed in Chapter 18, could lead to greatly reduced use of fossil fuel by the military. Decentralization of industry, discussed in Chapter 14, and greater regional and national economic self-sufficiency would lead to greatly shortened supply lines with much less fuel needed for transportation.

Urban Habitat

Another area of change that has great potential for reducing demand on nonrenewable resources and sinks for wasters is habitat. As Barbara Ward and René Dubos stated: "There is no single policy that deals more adequately with full resource use, an abatement of pollution, and even the search for more labor-intensive activities than a planned and purposive strategy for human settlements" (Ward and Dubos 1972, p. 180). Today more and more of the American people live in several megalopolises sprawling over once productive land and requiring enormous expenditures for utilities and commuting. The effort to take advantage of the city while still having a bit of land of one's own, the ideal of suburbia, is losing its charm.

There are two directions that hold promise. One direction is the dispersal of population into the countryside and into small towns across the land. This would accompany the resettling of America described in the next chapter. The possibility for such rural communities and towns to be significant economic units is discussed in Chapter 15. There are millions of people for whom return to such towns would meet deeply felt social and psychological needs. The nation as a whole will be far healthier if a high portion of its population finds habitat in such places. Many have been driven from them by economic necessity and will gladly return when the economy decentralizes.

The other direction that seems promising is a change in the nature of larger cities. These, too, have their place and are able to meet deep-seated social and psychological needs. Those who have found life in rural areas and small towns oppressive need to have the option of urban life. Cities can also be, or contain, communities in the terms of this book. This does not require, however, the continued growth of megalopolis. On the contrary, megalopolis cannot be a community and rarely nurtures community in its parts. In Europe cities are often surrounded by countryside within which there are scattered towns connected to the urban center by excellent public transportation. This provides a much better model. The endless building and rebuilding that characterizes the American city today should be channeled into this pattern at the same time that the total population to be housed in urban centers would decline. These changes would lead to reduced use of private transportation and hence a reduced demand on rapidly dwindling energy supplies. They would also encourage community.

But by careful planning, the energy savings can be greatly increased. Amory Lovins has already demonstrated the possibility that individual buildings could be so well insulated and so well planned to take advantage of solar energy that dependence on fuel for heating could be virtually eliminated. He has also shown that lighting and other electrical needs can be met with far less electricity. These are major loci of energy use, and the reductions thus effected could be enormous. We have also seen that cars can be designed to transport people from one part of the city to another, or from outlying villages into the city, with much less use of gas, and very efficient use of energy can also be made in public transportation systems. Can still more be done?

Clearly it can. For example, one of the great inefficiencies of energy use in this country is the failure to capture waste heat from power plants and factories and channel it into useful ends. Europe does much better. One main limitation here is that the sources of the waste heat are often at some distance from the places where this heat could function usefully as energy. New towns could be planned so that this would no longer be the case. In the rebuilding of cities maximum use of cogeneration could be a major consideration.

Paolo Soleri (1969) proposes a further step that would integrate and maximize all these gains. He envisions an architectural ecology, or "arcology," that would build a town or a city as a single unit. It would attain greater compactness than existing towns and cities by abolishing all motor transportation. There would then be no need for the freeways, streets, parking lots, and filling stations that occupy so much of the land in modern towns and cities. This would at the same time bring everything much closer together, so that the abolition of motor transportation also does away with much of the need for it!

Of course, in a large city distances would still be uncomfortably great if it were spread out over the land. This problem is solved, as in great cities today, by rising upward. Already in the center of existing cities there are complex structures in which shops, businesses, restaurants, hotels, offices, and recreational areas are all under one roof. Within the complex one often finds large open spaces with trees, ponds, and works of art. One moves from one part of these buildings to another on escalators and in elevators. The feel is much less crowded than on sidewalks and when crossing streets as automobiles allow. The absence of motor vehicles makes for quiet and relaxation. Soleri's buildings would expand these beginnings. They would include schools, hospitals, government offices, factories, and even parks and football fields. Most important of all, they would include homes.

Soleri's expansion is needed in order to accomplish the exclusion of the automobile. Under one roof there must be available to citizens all the usual amenities of a town or a city, whether one of five thousand or of five hundred thousand people. Even in the larger city, the three-dimensional structure would allow the inhabitants access to all sections in a fraction of the time now required (and without the use of any transportation except escalators, elevators, and perhaps moving sidewalks).

Citizens could also get outside of the arcology in a few minutes. This would be a very different experience from going outside one of the urban structures described above. In that case, when one is outside, one is on a sidewalk in the heart of a city. But when one steps out of Soleri's arcology, one would be in the countryside. To go further into the countryside to a satellite town or to another city, one would, of course, need transportation, and there motor vehicles might still be required. But that very large portion of our energy budget that goes for commuting and making one's way around the city would be greatly reduced.

The abolition of motor transport within the town or city carries to its limit the reductions in motor transportation sought above by the reduced population of megalopolis and its transformation into discrete communities. The potentials for cogeneration are also fully realized. Industries are located in the lowest levels of an arcology so that their waste heat is easily captured for use elsewhere in the building. Obviously there is no difficulty in making use of all those energy-saving devices that Lovins employs and recommends. And finally, Soleri proposes that the entire arcology can derive all its energy needs from receiving directly and indirectly the energy from the sun.

The indirect receipt is connected with food production for the arcology. Soleri envisions an arcology surrounded by greenhouses that would both grow all kinds of crops and channel heat into the arcology for use as energy. Whether in these ways the arcology could be wholly self-sufficient in energy no one knows. But there is little doubt that it would require but a tiny fraction of the nonrenewable energy used in present towns and cities.

Locating a city on a small fraction of the land now covered by urban sprawl would also release most of the land for more productive uses. Cities are often built on the best agricultural land. Some of this could be returned to agricultural production, replacing the marginal land that would be returned to wilderness.

Those interested in living close to nature are often as repelled by the idea of arcologies as they are by large areas of existing cities. Not everyone is attracted to the sharply discontinuous division of the total environment into the "indoor" and "outdoor," or the totally artificial and totally natural. Since no prototype exists, as in the case of the Rocky Mountain Institute, there are many unanswered questions about what life in an arcology would be like. Nevertheless, as we begin to attend to the wild facts and imagine urban habitat in the world to which they point, we will do well to take seriously what has thus far appeared to most as purely visionary. Soleri enables us to imagine a livable future with minimal dependence on fossil fuels and without giving up the cultural excitement that living in a city involves. Others are invited to do better.

Although the idea might be to experiment with a city of this kind at some distance from existing cities, the basic idea could be tried out within an existing city. Consider an area of New York or Chicago virtually uninhabited because of the decay of old tenements or housing projects. An arcology could be built in the center of such an area, while converting the rest to parks and garden plots. The structure would both house and employ the people as well as provide schools, shopping, and so forth. A full life could be lived in such a structure without the expense of owning an automobile and with minimal utility bills. Public transportation would, of course, be needed when citizens of this minicity wished to visit other parts of the metropolitan area. If such an experiment succeeded, more and more deteriorating sections of old cities could be rebuilt in this way. This city as a whole could become a community of such communities, interspersed with parks and small farms.

14

Agriculture

Agricultural Self-Sufficiency

Modern economic theory grew up with industrialization and has focused attention on industrial production. Its thoroughgoing application to agriculture has been late. But now that it has occurred the effects of this application on rural community have been disastrous.

Policies following from present theory work in three interrelated ways. The commitment to productivity reduces the need for farmers and depopulates the rural area. The commitment to profit maximization, with prices not including social and ecological costs, leads to unsustainable use of the land. The commitment to free trade leads to specialized production for export and, especially in the tropics, to inability of rural peoples to feed themselves.

If economics is reconceived in the service of community, it will begin with a concern for agriculture and specifically for the production of food. This is because a healthy community will be a relatively self-sufficient one. A community's complete dependency on outsiders for its mere survival weakens it. It is often unable to develop the policies it desires for the sake of its own members, since its survival depends on terms dictated by others. The most fundamental requirement for survival is food. Hence, how and where food is grown is foundational to an economics for community.

The conceptual question that must be further clarified is how much self-sufficiency is to be sought at what levels of community. The ultimate end of the now operative policies would be a self-sufficient world in which all less-than-global units would be dependent for their survival on the functioning of the global trading system. The opposite extreme would be a world made up entirely of subsistence farmers and hunters and gatherers. Their community can hardly extend beyond the tribe or the village. Between these extremes is an image of a world made up of communities of communities. The smallest community is the family, the next is the face-to-face community, and beyond that are towns and cities, larger regions, nations, continents, and the world. Obviously, the degrees of self-sufficiency to be sought at each level vary. What guidelines can help determine what is appropriate?

The Robinson Crusoe illustration in Chapter 11 showed that the more self-sufficient the trading units are, the more they are free to participate in setting the terms of trade, and the more certain it is that all will benefit in trade. On the other side, there is the point underscored so strongly by Adam Smith that the quantity of goods available for consumption is a function of specialization. Where there is a healthy community—that is, where there is mutual concern among the members of a political system—a great deal of household self-sufficiency can be safely sacrificed for the sake of increased total production in a larger community. Hence, the levels at which self-sufficiency is to be sought are the levels where personal humanity or political responsibility can be counted on to care for the members. The national level is the highest one at which this kind of mutual concern can be expected to be effective. Hence basic self-sufficiency in agricultural production should normally be a goal of national policy.

Although the aim at self-sufficiency is particularly needed at the national level, it should not be ignored at lower levels. Although a responsible national government can be expected to show some concern for the basic needs of all its citizens, it cannot always be counted on to respond sensitively to these needs in all its regions. Meanwhile a region that is economically dependent on centers of power outside it, even if these centers are within the nation, often takes on characteristics of a colony. It cannot control its internal economic life, and sometimes it cannot take care of its residents. Presently dominant economic theory encourages such regions to intensify specializations for export. But even if in this way more profits are earned, the region accentuates its dependence on external centers.

The economic policy here proposed encourages a different approach to development. The region, like the nation, should aim at relative self-sufficiency. If it can meet its own most basic needs, then it can trade to its own advantage with other regions. It can maintain itself as a viable community.

This general picture of economic decentralization does not require specification of what these "regions" should be. The most practical answer is to point to existing political divisions. For administrative purposes the federal government has divided the country into ten regions. A first step toward decentralization would be to examine the possibilities for self-sufficiency in each of these.

The bioregional movement points to the existence of different types of ecosystems within the nation. Before the coming of Europeans the Native American settlement corresponded roughly to these. Each provided the basis for a distinct economy and culture. If the federal administrative regional boundaries were redrawn to correspond more closely to the bioregions and if more functions were transferred to them from both Washington and the state capitals, bioregions would take on growing significance in American economic, political, and cultural life (Love 1977).

These regions in turn are already divided into states, and states, for the most part, into counties and cities as well as several types of districts. These are also regions. To seek relative self-sufficiency at regional levels refers to any and all of them. Of course, the degree of self-sufficiency possible or desirable at the city level will be different from that at the state or federal level.

If we were now free to start over in the drawing of boundaries, they would not correspond to existing states or other units. Nevertheless, in the remainder of Part Three we take these existing divisions as given. With so many changes to make, it is important to build on existing resources of structure, experience, and sentiment.

The fullest extension of self-sufficiency would lead to a nation of subsistence farmers, each farm sufficient to itself. This is neither a realistic nor a desirable goal. An economics of community aims at self-sufficient communities at a level beyond the family. Nevertheless, it is desirable that individual farm families produce much of their own food and fuel. As farmers in this country ceased to produce their own food, seed, fertilizer, and fuel and became increasingly dependent on complex economic systems they could not influence, their fortunes declined. The great majority have had to give up agriculture altogether. Rural America has been devastated. Agricultural communities are much healthier and have a greater capacity to survive if they too, even at quite small levels, are relatively self-sufficient. That means reduced dependence on the market price of commodities as well as on the interest rates of loans. A rural community based on such family farms together with the towns they support and rely on can survive changes in the national and global economy that destroy other types of communities. The total economy will be more stable if its units are more independent, if its supply lines are shorter.

If a nation seeks not only its own agricultural self-sufficiency but also relative self-sufficiency in its regions and agricultural units, what policies should it adopt to move in this direction? First, in the case of the United States, it should give up most of the policies that have operated in recent decades. These are the policies that have led to the displacement of relatively self-sufficient family farms and rural communities by monocultural agribusiness, despite occasional rhetoric to the contrary.

Walter Goldschmidt states clearly what has given the advantage to agribusiness: "Governmental and other institutional policies have favored the large grower and given impetus to the constant process of industrialization and corporate control. The most important of these special advantages are (1) the agricultural support programs, (2) tax policies, (3) agricultural labor policies, and (4) the research orientation of the USDA and of the land grant colleges" (Goldschmidt 1978, p. xxxii). In the depth of the Depression, the New Deal programs directed to the farms differed from other programs in that they "did not require a 'means test.' Instead, the amount of the subsidy payments were directly proportional to the total productivity of the farm enterprise, so that the more a person (or corporation) owned, the more relief he (or it) received" (p. xxxiii). Kirkpatrick Sale writes in a similar vein:

Price supports, soil-bank arrangements, direct payments, export controls, research-and-development funds, disaster-assistance payments, marketing agreements, tax write offs—all have been designed to work chiefly to the benefit of the largest, usually corporate, farmers, and have done so for more than forty years. . . . The Farmers Home Administration underwrites loans every year overwhelmingly for chemical-based, machine-intensive, monocultural, and large-scale farms, thus setting the pattern for local banks and credit institutions and also for equipment and chemical suppliers. And because federal funds have accounted one way or another for *between 20 and 40 percent* of all farm income since 1955—easily the largest single source—what the Federal government does is the single greatest element determining the character of American agriculture. [Sale 1986, p. 232]

These policies have been based on the belief that there are economies of scale in bigness, and the collapse of so many smaller farms is taken as evidence that this is true. But on closer examination it turns out that it is government policy that has given the advantage to the larger farmers.[1] Study after study has shown that small family operations are in fact

1. According to Wendell Berry, "Throughout this period of drastic attrition on the farms, we supposedly have been 'subsidizing agriculture,' but as Wes Jackson has pointed out, this is a misstatement. What we have actually been doing is using farmers to launder money for the agribusiness corporations, which have controlled

more productive per acre. Though cash income may be small, they can support a family. It is when they are drawn into increasing their size or into excessive borrowing for "modernization" that they are sucked into the downward currents that lead to bankruptcy.

The only measure by which the large farms are better is that of productivity of labor.[2] On these large farms enormous quantities of energy are substituted for labor. But if productivity is measured in other ways, such as production per acre or per unit of energy or amount of capital input, it is the small farm that always excels. It is federal policy that has destroyed family farms in so much of the country, not any inherent weakness in the family farm system. The cessation of federal interference is the first requirement for the recovery of healthy rural life.

Of course, helpful governmental policies are possible. The most important would be taxing oil to include all externalities. The true price of oil-based agriculture would then become apparent, and monocultural production on huge acreages oriented to supplying distant markets would be at a disadvantage in relation to small farms raising a variety of foods for nearby consumers. Almost all regions of the country can produce most of the food they need close to population centers (Sale 1986, pp. 237–38). Growing food locally is a practical goal, though it will have to struggle against well-entrenched interests in the present complex global system of production, processing, and distribution.

Sustainable Agriculture

A second aim of an economics for community is that the self-sufficiency of agricultural production should be indefinitely sustainable. That means that land should be as productive a century from now as it is at present. This runs counter to current practice just as drastically as the aim of regional self-sufficiency.

The recent study *Beyond Oil* makes clear how thoroughly unsustainable current agricultural practice is. The United States is already becoming increasingly dependent on imported oil. Within the next forty years the nation must "make the transition away from oil and gas, which to-

---

both their supplies and their markets, while the farmers have overproduced and been at the mercy of the markets" (Berry 1987, p. 170).

2. Walter Goldschmidt suggests that even this may be illusory. "When a tractor draws a combine to harvest wheat, the farmer is employing hundreds of hours of urban manpower expended in steel mills and the oil refineries (Goldschmidt 1978, p. xxxi).

day make up 75% of the U.S. energy budget, to some yet-to-be determined alternative model." Meanwhile:

The production of food has become almost totally dependent on oil and gas, not only to provide chemicals and machinery now used on our farms, but also to process and distribute farm products. At the same time, and partly as a result of industrial farming methods, the land base has been degraded by soil erosion, chemical pollution, and water depletion. For the last few decades, the impact of this degradation on crop production has been more than offset by the intensification and refinement of industrial agriculture, including (but not limited to) the development of hybrid crop varieties. But over the last few decades, the amount of energy needed to produce a unit of food in the United States has risen steadily. Moreover, yearly increases in agricultural productivity attributable to improved technology have become smaller in the last fifteen years, and some agronomists are warning that the well of agricultural technology may be running dry." [Gever et al. 1987, p. 14]

Sometime during the next 40 years the cost of oil will necessarily rise to the point where the present agricultural system will collapse. The transition to an older, much less energy-intensive style of farming can occur less disruptively if the real costs to the future are charged to the current users of fossil fuels. The more labor-intensive methods of traditional family farming will then prove most cost effective.

Even based on highly mechanized farming it has been shown that a one- or two-person operation is optimal. A 1972 study indicates that in California, a farm of 440 acres could take advantage of all economies of scale of mechanized farming. In any case, as Michael Perelman notes, "all other things being equal, mechanization tends to decrease yields" (Sale 1986, p. 234). Smaller, less mechanized farms are competetive even under present circumstances. Wes Jackson (1987) has pointed out that the Amish, with their traditional methods, have been surviving the farm crisis quite well, while the modern agribusiness farmers who listened to the experts at the land-grant colleges have been going bankrupt.

Further, although smaller farms can be energy intensive, they are able to shift away from oil both by substituting human and animal labor and by introducing solar energy. Sale points out: "A series of tests by the Small Farm Energy Project in Nebraska has shown that retro-fitting and insulation, wind and biogas systems, and solar heat and hot water collectors can be installed cheaply in single-family farms and that the savings they produce are almost immediate. At least a dozen farms in the U.S. get their full energy needs from methane systems powered by the manure of their animals" (Sale 1986, p. 235).

The Resettling of America

A third aim of economics for community is to preserve and rebuild rural community in the United States. Once again the small family farm is key. To say this is only to reaffirm what has been recognized since the founding of the nation. In his foreword to Goldschmidt's *As You Sow,* Gaylord Nelson makes the point well:

> The family farm provides a social environment in which the central virtues of American life are fostered. It is at once a business, a job and a set of family relationships. At best, it does not provide an easy life and in bad times there are often harsh difficulties. But it provides a good life, and one in which independence, industry, hard work, foresight, cooperation and other qualities central to America's needs are fostered. For most of our history, the family farm has been the seedbed of our culture.
>
> This relationship was well understood by the founders of our nation, and support for it was written into our constitution and reaffirmed in legislation, particularly the homestead laws and the Reclamation Act of 1902. The independent family farm is therefore an institution created by the foresight and planning of the makers of America. [Goldschmidt 1978]

As You Sow is a book that carefully describes what has been happening in rural America as family farms have been replaced by agribusiness. In 1954–56 Walter R. Goldschmidt conducted studies of the towns of Dinuba and Arvin in the central valley of California. The two towns were chosen for their similarity in size and land resources, and their difference in the size and number of farms surrounding them. Arvin had 133 farms averaging 497 acres. Dinuba had 722 farms averaging 57 acres. The gross farm income of the two towns was approximately equal. On the other hand, Dinuba had 141 business enterprises compared to 62 in Arvin, and Dinuba's gross volume of retail sales was nearly twice that of Arvin. Clearly Dinuba was economically speaking a much healthier community! This contrast was even more marked when examining the quality of human community in the two towns.

Sale cites a recent study by George Goldman that makes the point by modeling (Sale 1986, p. 241). He shows that by breaking up large farms of 1,280 acres into smaller ones of 320 acres, the economy of the region is improved, generating more jobs, more income, and more retail sales. Clearly rural American community has not gained by the increased "productivity" of agriculture.

Since the attainment of regional and local self-sufficiency, sustainable food production, and rural community life all depend on the family farm, it is important to be clear about what that is. By a family farm we do not simply mean any farm owned by a single family. Under pressure from the U.S. government many families have enlarged their holdings repeatedly. Most of these have ultimately failed, but some have survived. They differ from corporate farms only in that the owners still live on the land.[3]

On the other hand, by a family farm we do not mean subsistence agriculture. Subsistence farming is attractive to some as a life-style, and that is not to be opposed, but it is a different model from what is properly meant by a family farm. The family farm produces much of the food for its own consumption, but it produces mainly for the market and supplies the needs of townspeople and city dwellers. It is farms of this sort that can be the mainstay of rural community. To achieve the three aims identified above the goal must be to resettle rural America with family farmers.

But can this be done? The trend of replacing people with machines has dominated for so long that it may prove irreversible. But every effort should be made to reverse it—and soon. There are two basic requirements: the availability of land at an affordable price, and the willingness of people to resettle it.

To assure the availability of land at reasonable prices four policies can be instituted. First, federal subsidies and other supports of agribusiness should end. This infusion of federal money not only favors the large farms over the small, but it also raises the price of land. Second, the price of oil should be raised by selling extraction rights and imposing tariffs on imports. It should also be taxed for its polluting effects. If left to the market the price will rise in any case, but adjustment will be better if it begins sooner and there is a longer period of time in which some oil is available. Oil-based agriculture will immediately be placed at a disadvantage by these prices, and much corporately held land will be sold. Third, farmers should be taxed for the deterioration of their land as well as for pollution of air and streams. This will make agribusiness noncompetitive with farms practicing careful husbandry. Fourth, as proposed in Chapters 11 and 17, unimproved land should be taxed at much higher rates than now current, but taxes would not be raised because of the improved quality of the farm based on good agricultural practices. Indeed this improvement would be credited against taxes. The value gained from the regeneration of the land would be earned income of the farmer.

Policies of this sort would insure the availability of land at low cost,

3. For a far richer account of the family farm, see Wendell Berry, "A Defense of the Family Farm," in his *Home Economics* (1987, pp. 162–78).

so that the capital investment required to begin farming would be small. In some cases the government could buy the land and make it available for homesteading. If regenerative farming practices were followed, taxes would be low.

Although we are confident that land for resettlement can be made available quite rapidly, we are not as confident of the availability of people who are willing and able to reestablish rural community. Certainly there are some; so we have no doubt about a successful beginning to the project.[4] And certainly there are millions who would be better off in healthy rural communities than in the tenements of great cities where they now reside. Many of these were themselves driven from the land, but more are the children and grandchildren of those who were. Those who are unemployed or underemployed in the city should be given every inducement and every help to return where their labor is needed and can be properly rewarded. But can they become farmers again?

Wendell Berry has made us aware that farming is not merely a series of techniques that can be easily taught, but it is also a culture. He shows how this can be lost even while people are still raising crops:

> The concentration of the farmland into larger and larger holdings and fewer and fewer hands—with the consequent increase of overhead, debt, and dependence on machines—is thus a matter of complex significance, and its agricultural significance cannot be disentangled from its cultural significance. It *forces* a profound revolution in the farmer's mind: once his investment in land and machines is large enough, he must forsake the values of husbandry and assume those of finance and technology. Thenceforth his thinking is not determined by agricultural responsibility, but by financial accountability and the capacities of his machines. Where his money comes from becomes less important to him than where it is going. He is caught up in the drift of energy and interest away from the land. Production begins to override maintenance. The economy of money has infiltrated and subverted the economies of nature, energy, and the human spirit. The man himself has become a consumptive machine [Berry 1977, pp. 45–46]

Berry worries that the culture of agriculture is being rapidly lost and that once lost it will be almost impossible to recover.

More recently Berry has written in a slightly less pessimistic vein: "I have seen enough good farmers and good farms, and a sufficient variety of both, to convince me beyond doubt that an ecologically and cultur-

---

4. Hundreds were ready to buy family farms in federally irrigated parts of California if the law restricting holdings had been enforced. (See Davis 1979, pp. 208–9. Davis sees the changes recommended here as inevitable consequences of the rising costs of oil.)

ally responsible agriculture is possible" (1981, p. ix). He goes on to note the two obstacles to the widespread renewal of such farming. "First, the discipline of farming has a low public standing." Second, "After a half-century of industrial agriculture, farmers of any kind have become a tiny minority, and good farmers rare" (Berry 1981, p. x).

Clearly the task of reversing national attitudes and especially of educating a new generation of family farmers is intimidating. But it is not hopeless. When the government abandons the policies that have ruined so many farmers, when agricultural produce and land are priced in appropriate relationships, and when new attitudes of respect for farming and for rural culture replace the low esteem of the recent past, the context will be prepared. At that point a massive program of education can be successful, when education is understood not as the mere teaching of skills, though that is important, but as a fresh encounter with nature and human relationships in a rural setting. A major part of the nation's educational budget should be devoted to reorienting millions of its citizens to rural life. The popularity of a publication such as the *Mother Earth News* means that there are a lot of people who want to get back to the land. We confront a major opportunity to deal at once with our urban and our rural problems.

Answers to Objections

Four objections are typically raised to proposals that reverse the trend toward the industrialization of agriculture. First is the argument that it would reimpose back-breaking labor on those who are blessedly free from it. This is thought to be entailed in the fact that it would be less capital- and energy-intensive and more labor-intensive. It is a proper warning against sentimentalizing earlier epochs of farm life.

Only detailed analysis of where economic incentives would lead farming could answer this objection. If energy became expensive enough and labor became cheap enough the fear could be realized! If we simply let present trends continue, that will happen eventually. However, nothing in this proposal anticipates such an extreme. No elimination of machinery has been suggested, although draft animals often prove more efficient. A shift of scale would reduce the use and size of machinery, not eliminate it. Also, life on a family farm entails far more varied chores than does manual harvesting on agribusiness monoculture farms. There would be a reduction of the worst forms of hard labor, although there would certainly be some increase at other points.

When a family decides what machinery to buy, narrowly economic considerations loom large, but the family is also motivated by the desire to reduce those chores its members find most unpleasant. On the whole, investments will be designed to enrich life. This is much less true when relations between decision makers and workers are remote.

A second objection is that a return to family farms would reduce the food supply at a time when the world is running short of food. This objection is less well-founded than the first. The improved "productivity" of agribusiness does not mean that more is raised per acre, only that fewer human beings are involved in raising it. On a per acre basis the evidence is that more labor-intensive methods can at least match, and usually surpass, those of agribusiness. If all costs are included, this is quite certainly the case.

It is true that in some countries the breaking up of large estates into peasant farms has reduced production for the market. This has occurred especially in cultures where the peasant ideal is subsistence farming. Peru and Chile are often cited in this respect. After the peasants did the work they needed in order to subsist, they did no more, for they had never been introduced to a standard of living that made them want or need goods they could receive only in exchange for cash crops. They were insufficiently motivated to raise enough crops to feed the people of the towns and cities.

But in other cultures the results have been very different. In Japan, the land reform instituted under General MacArthur provided the basis for an increase of food production as well as for general economic success. Taiwan and South Korea are similar success stories. Every indication is that families in this country would be motivated to produce for the market as well as for themselves. Hence, these examples are more relevant. Nevertheless, it should be acknowledged that during the transition there will be many failures, and these will entail losses in production.[5]

5. In the much more limited transition from conventional to organic farming a temporary decline in production has been noted. "Farmers who had previously farmed conventionally reported crop yields were often markedly reduced during the first several years following the shift from chemical to organic farming. During this transition, severe weed infestations occurred and crops were sometimes difficult to establish. Occasionally the crops showed symptoms of nutrient deficiency. Farmers said that after the third or fourth year, as the rotations became established, yields began to increase and eventually equaled the yields they had obtained chemically" (U.S. Department of Agriculture 1980). Is that a serious objection? It seems not to be. At a time of overproduction and excessive storage it is worth trading off current production for future fertility and current surpluses for community.

It is objected that global needs and deficits are increasing, that our resources are required in order to meet needs everywhere. This argument has initial plausibility since world hunger is a very serious problem. However, the cause of hunger is not now, and will not be in the near future, a global shortage of food. Food is now available to all who can pay, and we know that there are huge surpluses rotting away. The problem is that so many cannot pay. The problem is also that those who have no money now have no access to land on which they could raise their own food. This land has been taken to raise crops or cattle for export, sometimes to the United States.

Even today most countries could feed themselves if they were not using their land for purposes of international trade. Most "world" hunger could be ended by national food policies that made feeding one's own people the highest priority. This is the single most important step toward alleviating hunger. Hence the greatest contribution toward reducing world hunger that the United States can make will be to become self-sufficient in basic food and to encourage, by precept and example, others to do likewise. Of course there are exceptional cases in which this is not possible, and there are times when surplus should be moved across national boundaries to alleviate hunger. But there is no reason to fear that the quantities needed for such purposes will exceed capacities.

The third objection is that the price of food will rise. This is probably true. If present trends continue mindlessly, the rising cost of oil combined with the declining productivity of the soil will drive prices up. Careful husbandry of the land will require more labor, and for that, the consumer should pay. But if that food is produced near at hand and sold through local farmers markets, the many savings involved may counterbalance that added cost.

The fourth objection is that the quality and variety of food available to the consumer will decline. There is some truth here, but less than most would suppose. With respect to quality, the decline will be mainly in appearance—often a misleading appearance. With reduced use of pesticides consumers will need to accustom themselves to occasional imperfections. Many chemical additives now used for appearance would be omitted. With regard to taste and food value, there will be marked improvement.

With respect to variety, it is true that most locally grown food will be seasonal. Nevertheless, this limitation can be largely mitigated. As Sam Passmore has written: "Farmers can grow different varieties—hardy crops in the cooler months, heat-tolerant ones in the summer. . . .

Through capital investment, farmers and food purchasers can make an end-run around seasonality. The farmer can use inexpensive technologies like mulch and cold frames to extend the seasons of many crops. Food providers can buy local produce in season and store, freeze or can it" (Passmore 1987). In any case, the idea of localization of food production is not absolute. At a price food can still be brought from around the country and the world.

Those who are still skeptical of the possibility of a successful agriculture in this country based on family farms are invited to remember the Amish communities mentioned earlier. By avoiding entanglement in the policies of the United States government, they have survived and prospered. Their produce has competed successfully with that of subsidized agribusiness even in present market conditions and with government policies geared against them. If both agribusiness and the Amish farmers were forced to pay the full social and environmental costs of their produce, the price of agribusiness produce would soar while that of the Amish would be little affected.

We are not proposing that Amish-style farming would be the national norm. Although it has much to teach us, it requires a style of life that many find unattractive. Even if they tried, most Americans would not be able to live as the Amish do. A much less extreme style of agricultural life will do.

The point of this reference to the Amish is that they prove the *economic* feasibility of the proposal. They show that family farms can produce cheaply and sustainably. They show that rural community can be stable. They do not prove that with different cultures and customs others will be equally successful. But if the Amish could succeed in spite of hostile national policies, others should be able to succeed when national policies give full support. The venture is not hopeless.

Energy Use

Chapter 13 showed the urgency of re-envisioning society so as to reduce the use of energy and make more of the energy used benign. The proposals made in this chapter move in the same direction. The family farm can be far less energy-intensive than agribusiness. The move to family farming, with emphasis on organic methods, is fundamental to any solution of the energy problem. We are calling for relative agricultural self-sufficiency in fairly small regions. This can help resolve the energy crisis in two ways. First, it reduces transportation. Second, it can lead to a much reduced role for the processing and packaging that characterizes the supermarket.

These are not minor considerations. "When the agricultural system is understood to include the transportation, processing, packaging, and distribution of food, it is even more inefficient in terms of edible food energy produced per unit of fuel input and even more dependent on fuel. About three times as much energy is consumed in these off-farm activities as is used in the nation's farms" (Gever et al. 1987, p. 28). If the regionalization and localization of food production could reduce this dependence by two-thirds over the 40-year period, that, too, would make a significant contribution.

There is another needed change related to agriculture not yet mentioned. That is in habits of consumption. Here the culprit is animal products: 35% of our calorie intake is made up of these products; 60% of these animals are fed on crops; and these animals consume 80% of all the crops grown in the United States. It is common knowledge that our health would be improved by reducing consumption of animal products.

Such reduction of consumption could have a very considerable effect on the amount of land needed for crops. Accurate calculations would be very complex since many variables would have to be considered. But simply to show the importance for land use of a reduced dependence on animal products, consider the following calculations based on the hypothesis, obviously false, that everything else remained the same.

Suppose that over a period of 40 years people reduce their consumption of animal products by 30%. That would be a reduction of calories attributable to animal products from 35% to 24.5%. This would mean an increase of fruits, vegetables, and grains in the average diet, while the need for livestock would be reduced by 30%. Remember that 80% of all crops are now fed to livestock. If 30% fewer animals were needed, then clearly cropland could be reduced considerably. Specifically, if we suppose that the amount of livestock production now not dependent on grains (40% of the present total) remained the same, then the production dependent on grain could be reduced by half, that is, the whole 30% reduction could be from this 60%. Since 80% of agricultural land is now used to feed this 60% of the livestock, only 40% of the land now farmed would be needed to feed the 30% remaining. That would release 40% of present farmland. Of course, some of this would be needed to raise food for direct consumption, but even when this is considered, a reduction of at least 35% of cropland would be effected.

Now let us suppose that this 35% of present cropland no longer needed to produce grains for animals were turned into pasture. Most of the livestock left dependent on grain could be grazed on this land. Dependence on grain for animal feed would be drastically reduced. Only 25% of the land now used to grow crops would be needed for that purpose. Thus a fairly moderate shift in eating habits would allow most of our cropland to be transformed into pasture.[6]

Shifting much of our cropland to pasture would be a regenerative process that would prepare the way for growing more crops if and when they are truly needed some time in the future. Livestock could again be part of the typical farm rather than a specialized large-scale industry. Since pasturing animals is less labor-intensive than raising row crops, the temptation to use nonorganic energy-intensive methods would decline. Animals would provide excellent organic fertilizer, and methane from manure could also contribute to meeting farm energy needs.

We have acknowledged that the figures used in this scenario are exceedingly crude, and that accurate calculations would be far more complex. Nevertheless, these calculations do indicate that a relatively minor change in eating habits, one that would be beneficial to human health, could make the transition to benign food production much easier. They also suggest that, if accompanied by a change in eating habits, taking marginal lands out of production need not lead to food shortages.

If a simple and healthful change in eating habits along with localization of most food production and a major shift toward organic farming were to take place over the next generation, food production and distribution could be weaned from their current heavy dependence on fossil fuels. In the process, the enormous suffering now inflicted on livestock would be greatly reduced. The question is not whether this is possible— it is whether we will do it.

6. If the policy of greatly increasing wilderness advocated in Chapter 13 were adopted, the supplementary supply of meat from hunting would not be insignificant.

15

Industry

Tariffs

If a nation accepts sustainable self-sufficiency as its primary economic goal, it will give first attention to agriculture. Food is a more basic need than industrial products. In some Third World countries the decision for self-sufficiency may virtually preclude anything beyond quite elementary industries for some time.

In the United States, on the other hand, the crisis is not one of food production. The United States is, or can easily be, quite self-sufficient in food. It is an industrial nation, and for it self-sufficiency must include the production of the industrial products it needs. This self-sufficiency has recently been lost as labor-intensive industries have either given up the effort to compete internationally or have moved to other countries where labor is cheaper.

It used to be thought that productivity was much lower in Third World countries where labor was less well educated. This made it worthwhile for industry to pay high wages in the United States rather than to take advantage of low wages elsewhere. But that situation has now changed. Previously uneducated workers can be trained while their wages remain low. According to Peter Drucker, "The most telling examples are the 'maquiladoras,' the plants on the Mexican side of the U.S. Mexican border, where unskilled and often illiterate people produce labor-intensive parts and goods for the U.S. market. It takes three years at most for a maquiladora to attain the labor productivity of a well-run American or Japanese plant even in turning out highly sophisticated products—and it pays workers less than $2 an hour" (Drucker 1987, p. 32).

As long as there are no tariffs on industrial imports into the United States it is evidently more profitable to invest capital elsewhere, use cheap labor, and ship the products back into the U.S. market. Many like to describe the new situation of numerous factory closures as post-industrial, but it is in fact more aptly called deindustrial. In this de-industrialized economy, real wages will be much lower. While capital prospers from investments where labor is cheap, American labor will continue to experience a rapid drop in standard of living. The United States will become more and more of a class society.

Yet the opposition to economic nationalism expressed in tariffs is almost unanimous. It is an article of faith that there should be no restriction on trade. In Lester Thurow's words, "Tariff protection and subsidies imprison us in a low productivity area. If we cannot learn to disinvest, we cannot compete in the modern growth race" (1981, p. 77).

Thurow is correct. If the United States is committed to compete in the great international growth race, then it should impose no tariffs. It should cease producing whatever can be produced more efficiently (that is, cheaply) elsewhere and produce only what it can produce competitively. It will, of course, cease to be even remotely self-sufficient, since the growth race encourages specialization. Wages will fall toward Third World levels, and competition for capital will keep pollution standards low. Still, the nation can be sure that its capital will be used efficiently. It will be competing in the modern growth race. That race, meanwhile, will speed the exhaustion of oil and hasten the greenhouse effect.

Setting aside environmental concerns that would question the desirability of any growth race, we note that there is one implicit assumption made by Thurow and not by us. According to the standard models of economists, the capital would be reinvested where the same labor that was thrown out of work by disinvestment could move (i.e., within the country). If that were the case, wages would not fall toward Third World levels. But in Chapter 11 we showed that the transnational mobility of capital has changed that situation drastically. While capital flows across national boundaries, labor, on the whole, does not. The new investment employs a different work force. It does not create new jobs to replace the old ones. Average wages decline and must continue to do so.

We see no reason to hold competition in the modern growth race as sacrosanct. There are other means of meeting human needs that induce less suffering and are far less costly to the planet. We are exploring an alternative in this book. That alternative is an economics for community. The nation is a community; so in the first instance our interest corresponds with that of Dudley Seers in a "political economy of nationalism." We would opt out of the international growth race and all the disinvestment that entails in order to rebuild a self-sufficient national economy. The simplest, most effective policy instrument for doing that is the tariff.

Tariffs would protect now-endangered industries from further erosion and allow them to begin to recover lost ground. Tariffs would also encourage new enterprise in areas where the United States has become dependent on imports. With the assurance that these industries could be profitable while paying suitable wages, capital would flow to these opportunities. The operation of the free market, within national boundaries reinforced by tariffs, would lead to the industrial self-sufficiency that would make possible truly free trade, that is, trade in which the nation is free to engage or not.

A system of tariffs is not without its economic costs, as any economist will quickly point out. It is designed to raise the price of goods. Raising the price of many of the goods we consume will have a negative effect on the purchasing power of consumers. Of this there can be no question.

But there is also no question that in one way or another the American standard of living, and especially that of workers, will be reduced. Chapter 11 considered the various scenarios within the context of free trade. All of them include a major setback for the American worker. To point out that this one does also is correct. A correction for America's vast international debt and profligate spending these past years cannot be avoided. The question is whether the United States should continue with the system that has forced this cut upon the masses of its people and will continue to force further cuts, or whether it should try another system. We do not argue that this other system will work better in terms of the increase of GNP. By that standard it may well be worse. We argue that it will work better in terms of a true index of economic welfare and much better in terms of what are considered noneconomic goals. It is madness for a nation to make more and more desperate efforts to preserve community while its economic system works ever more strongly against it.

Obviously, change on the part of the world's greatest trading nation from commitment to a global system of free trade to the goal of national self-sufficiency will have enormous effects on its trading partners. To introduce such policies abruptly could cause untold hardship. They should be phased in gradually, perhaps over a 10-year period. This would allow time for needed adjustments. But however gradually such changes are instituted they will be painful for producers abroad. Hence the effects of our proposals should be compared with the suffering to be expected from continuation of present policies.

Currently the United States has an extremely unfavorable balance of trade, which is supported largely by borrowing from abroad. This can continue only through the rapid sale of the nation's assets. To avoid de-capitalization the nation must either export more or import less. The solution built into present policy is to allow the dollar to fall so far that the imbalance will be rectified. The policy is slow to take effect, but sooner or later it will do so. The price of imported goods will rise so high that Americans will not be able to afford to buy many of them. This will lead to a smaller rise in price of homemade products as well. In short, there will be a decrease in real purchasing power.

If the response to this decrease is to raise wages, the cycle will con-tinue. The dollar will fall until the new wages do not allow workers to buy so many imported goods. Prices must go up faster than wages in order to reduce imports. Real wages must decline. Chapter 11 played out this scenario to show that in the context of free trade, wages must fall very far.

We have not taken very seriously the scenario toward which most economists gear their recommendations. It is that United States indus-try would again become competitive through the rising productivity of its work force. For most economists the rise in productivity is the key to prosperity. It enables industry both to pay high wages and to sell goods at competitive prices. For this reason most economists focus their atten-tion on how to attain this improvement. They see the key in capital in-vestment, both in the training of labor and in improved or expanded plant. If this investment were sufficient, their models show, productivity would rise and exports increase.

The question is how to get this investment capital. The possible sources for generating more within industry are reduced business taxes, reduced dividends, or reduced wages. The possible source for generat-ing it outside is increased savings. This could be achieved by reduced consumption, reduced taxation, and reduced government borrowing. In all these matters government taxation and borrowing appear to econo-mists as the greatest competitors for the money that should be invested so as to attain higher productivity. Hence, bloated budgets, especially federal budgets, are the primary target of criticism. These are held to be the culprits in the decline of American industry.

Many economists imply that budget reduction should come from social spending. They believe that only by growth are the poor truly benefited and that funds now being distributed to them should be invested to insure that growth. Ironically it is not the differential in social spending but in the military budget that distinguishes the United States from its most successful competitors. We agree with these economists that improvements and savings are possible in government social programs. But simply to cut without proposing new ways of dealing with urgent human needs is unacceptable and is unlikely to improve productivity.

It is not at all certain that lack of capital is the reason for failure to invest in productive enterprises in the United States. In 1978, *Business Week* found that the nation's biggest corporations had eight billion dollars in savings available for investment. They did not invest because "of inadequate demand for the goods and services that could be produced if investment in new plant and equipment were made" (Bluestone and Harrison 1982, p. 198). We conjecture that much of this inadequate demand was due to the greater interest of consumers in imported goods. In any case simply adding to this large kitty will not in itself do much to improve the situation.

For these reasons we have neglected the dominant proposal that calls for going further in the direction the Reagan administration led. Thus far there has been little real gain from these initiatives. There is no reason to think that going farther will solve the problem as long as nothing is done to direct American consumption to goods produced in the United States, within a context of balanced trade. If Americans buy goods produced elsewhere, U.S. capital will go elsewhere to invest until the cost of producing at home—the wage—drops drastically. Continuation of unsuccessful policies is not the answer.

It is important not only to consider the suffering of the American worker but also to consider effects on America's trading partners of the imposition of tariffs. Japan is the partner with which the United States runs the largest deficits. A tariff on imports from Japan will have an important negative effect on the Japanese economy. This must count as an argument against the imposition of tariffs.

But what is the alternative? The United States *cannot* continue indefinitely to import huge quantities of Japanese goods while exporting much less. This is not the alternative against which to measure tariffs. The question is only in what way will the trade balance be attained? According to the free trade scenario this will be done by automatic devaluation of the dollar and lower real wages for American workers. That will cut imports from Japan and raise exports. Will that be less disruptive to Japan than reducing imports by tariffs?

Or consider the scenario that is the economists' hope. Suppose that U.S. productivity so improved that American cars crowded Japanese ones out of first the American market and then elsewhere. This would indeed do much to solve the problems of the American economy, at least the more obvious ones. But would it be less disruptive of the Japanese economy?

In one way or another the Japanese economy *must* adjust. This will be difficult, but it need not destroy Japan's prosperity. It may move Japan toward producing for its own markets and becoming less dependent on global trade.

Effects on Third World Nations

The moral concern arises much more with respect to Third World countries. They will suffer like Japan in having tariffs imposed on their exports to us. In some cases the possibility of balanced trade is greater with these nations, so that more options may exist. Some adjustments are possible. But the basic policy of national self-sufficiency for the United States will dash the hopes of Third World countries for emulating Japan's export-led growth, which in the aggregate is an unrealistic hope in any case, since it is impossible for all countries to be net exporters.

Equally threatening to these countries would be the reduction of international capital that would be invested in their industrialization. If industries in the Third World do not have ready access to the United States market, there would be less incentive for American investors to build plants there. A moral argument can be made that the United States should do nothing to slow down the industrialization of the poorer nations. This argument has force only to the extent that industrialization actually benefits poor people in poor countries and not just the elite. This is frequently not the case.

It is well, therefore, to consider just how this industrialization is occurring. Many of the factories are built in free trade zones sealed off from the rest of the country. Much of their raw material is imported from elsewhere, and often all of their produce is exported. The only connection to the economy of the host nation is the employment at subsistence wages of the labor force. No doubt the host country is better off by gaining foreign exchange from its supplying of labor to the factories.

With this it can import goods from abroad. But if the same workers were so employed as to reduce the need for imports, the country would gain more from their labor. At best the benefit to the host country is small and ambiguous.

There are other investments more integral to the economies of the host countries. Modern plants are built inside these countries both to serve their citizens and to export. They build up a modern sector within these countries where standards of living rise.

Typically these advances for the elite are accompanied by a widening gap with the majority of the citizens. Sometimes the majority become progressively worse off as the elite grow more prosperous. The only "development" that would help the masses would be based on an "appropriate" technology, one that enhances the ability of ordinary people to deal with their problems. But this is not what is of interest to foreign investors. International capital introduces techniques and methods that render Third World countries more dependent on the First World sources of the technology (Stewart 1977, pp. 274 ff). Only fundamental social and political changes can render "development" beneficial to the majority of the people (Kurien 1978, pp. 126 ff). Increasing U.S. investment does not facilitate these changes.

The United States has two basic choices. It can remain in the free trade system, paying a high price in the standard of living of its workers and its future economic power. In this way, it can for some time export capital and scatter industry around the world. This would help Third World elites. Alternately, the United States can seek self-sufficiency and control over its own economic life. If it does that, it will have a strong moral responsibility to assist many Third World nations in becoming self-sufficient again. Since the United States bears major responsibility for having persuaded or forced them to abandon relative self-sufficiency for the international trade system, if it then abandons that system it must be prepared to pay some price to help others do so as well. The price would be much smaller than that entailed in the present rush toward poverty.

The question of the effects of our proposals on Third World countries is of very great importance to us. We do not want to save the economy of the United States at the expense of the Third World. But we have come, as have many others, to the painful conclusion that very little of First World development effort in the Third World, and even less of business investment, has been actually beneficial to the majority of the Third World's people. On the whole, just as government policy in the

United States has driven most farmers off the land while enriching a few, so development policies in the Third World have made many landless, filled the vast slums surrounding Third World cities, and added to the problem of hunger. In *How the Other Half Dies* (1976), Susan George reports on her studies of case after case of business investment. She finds only one or two out of scores that are truly beneficial to the people who are "being developed." Samuel L. Parmar (1974) argues that the result of bringing western technology into India has been catastrophic. The results of other studies are less harsh. But David C. Pitt is typical in his moderate assessment: "Development from above at the centre was not a great success. . . . The failure of external aid in itself is an important reason for underdevelopment in the countryside and slums of Afro-Asia" (1976, p. 266). Pitt quotes Leo Strauss as saying that it is only our own society that we can change without destroying (p. 14).

Assessments such as these have led us to the painful conclusion that for the most part the Third World would have been better off without international investment and aid. This investment and aid have destroyed the self-sufficiency of nations and rendered masses of their formerly self-reliant people unable to care for themselves. Even if there are complaints from the elite in Third World countries (who alone have benefited from our aid), and even if we could find no way to help these countries renew self-sufficiency (which we do not believe), we think in the long run it is better in most cases that we de-link their economy from ours.

Approaching matters from Third World and European perspectives, Dudley Seers (1983) comes to the same conclusion. He sees nationalism as the healthiest basis for nations, including Third World nations, to deal with their problems. He sees the bond to the superpowers as a major obstacle to the adoption of the needed policies. The adoption of a nationalist economic policy by the United States would greatly facilitate the achievement of these goals.

Competition within the Nation

Assuming now that the nation chooses the path of balanced trade through tariffs for the sake of self-sufficiency, the problem that will arise would be that of retaining incentives for efficiency in production. Even if tariffs were kept low enough for foreign products to exercise some competitive pressure on American markets, this would not suffice. The whole purpose of the tariff is to reduce that competition. Yet healthy competition is essential to the market system.

To insure healthy competition in the national market would require renewal of past policies that were designed to prevent consolidation of economic power in a few hands. These policies were allowed to lapse in order to support competition with Japanese and European giants. But a policy that handicaps imports must be accompanied by others that would intensify competition at home.

Every effort should be made to reverse the trend toward mergers and takeovers, friendly and unfriendly, and to increase the number of smaller businessmen and manufacturers. National policies should encourage the challenging of industrial giants on the part of small-scale businesses and entrepreneurs. But what would those policies be?

The most effective approach is to order the economy so that the market itself encourages the attainment of the ends of policy. The adoption of the pricing system frequently discussed above would help. For example, conventional energy production and, even more, nuclear energy, are extremely capital-intensive. That means that small businesses cannot enter these fields. On the other hand, entrepreneurs have much to contribute to the development of small-scale renewable energy production and energy conservation. Their efforts have been restricted chiefly by the fact that the energy produced is typically more costly than that of conventional sources.

The question is whether the market prices energy fairly in the two instances. One step in determining this would be to remove all subsidies, direct and indirect, from all forms of energy production. For example, the nuclear industry would cease getting help from the government and would have to pay the full costs of insurance, waste disposal, uranium enrichment, and decommissioning of old reactors. If these steps were taken small-scale renewable energy plants would become very attractive, from a strictly market point of view, in comparison with nuclear energy. Taxes to internalize the environmental costs of fossil fuels would have the same effect in that comparison. Numerous small businesses could enter the field.

Since taxes play so large a role in mergers and spin-offs, tax laws can be written to discourage mergers and to encourage spin-offs. Taxes can favor spin-offs to become independent rather than being taken over by other large corporations. If corporate income taxes were abolished (as will be advocated in Chapter 17), we believe that the decentralization and breakup of conglomerates would be encouraged. Government can also use economic incentives to encourage this development. All of this can be supplemented by enforcing antitrust laws already on the books and passing new ones as needed. In one way or another the nation must insure adequate competition. The United States is of sufficient size that this should not be difficult.

The usual argument against decentralization is the importance of economies of scale. These, however, are often misunderstood. In most industries economy does not grow with the size of the plant beyond a certain point. According to Barry Stein, economies of scale are "generally achieved in individual plants of modest size" (Sale 1986, p. 310). According to Sale, "In the United States the number of production workers per unit was only 49.5 in 1947 and declined steadily to 44.9 in 1967 and 1972" (1986, p. 310). Indications are that the decline continues. Roger Schuemmer has found that "scale economies either [no longer] exist or are comparatively modest" (Bluestone and Harrison 1982, p. 224).

It might still be argued that by central management of many plants each becomes more efficient. However, according to Sale, a House subcommittee report, "Investigations of Conglomerate Corporations" (1971), states that "of the twenty-eight conglomerates it studied, only seven showed a profit after acquisitions, three remained unchanged, and eighteen companies had ratios lower in the years after acquisition [and] it would be reasonable to conclude that these ratios reflect ineffective management" (Sale 1986, p. 312).

Amory and Hunter Lovins conclude a thorough study of the relation of economy to scale in the production of energy with these words: "By now, in short, the evidence of compensatory diseconomies of large scale which favor smaller technologies is so overwhelming that no rational decision-maker can ignore it. However these many competing effects are balanced, it is difficult to imagine a way—save in the most centralized applications, such as operation of giant smelter—that they can yield lower net costs of delivered energy services at very large scale than at moderate, and often quite small, scale" (Lovins and Lovins 1982, p. 353).

Regional Decentralization

The single greatest factor leading to the deindustrialization of America has been capital mobility across national lines. Tariffs would greatly reduce the incentive to produce goods for the American market outside the country. But a second problem, almost as serious, is capital mobility within the country. John C. Raines writes: "The rapid mobility of capital investment that does not include within its calculation of costs the social cost to community is undermining our nation's communal foundations" (Raines 1982, p. 298).

Capital mobility is responsible for making the struggle of management against labor a very unequal one. When dissatisfied with labor's demands, plants are closed in areas of strong unions and opened where they are weak. Labor is thus "disciplined." It is also demoralized. The hard-won gains of the union movement are quickly dissipated. "More than 30 million jobs lost to plant closings and permanent physical contractions in a single decade, the virtual abandonment of older industrial cities, and the helter-skelter development of Sunbelt boomtowns" point to a serious problem, much of it due to capital mobility within the country (Bluestone and Harrison 1982, p. 193).

Capital mobility also gives industry the upper hand in relation to the states. States and local communities bargain shamelessly to attract new plants or keep old ones. Social considerations other than jobs are set aside, and legitimate tax income is forgone. States and regions cannot manage their own economies as long as the industrial economy is national. Unable to manage their economies, their political autonomy is also necessarily quite limited.

An economics for community holds that political power must be vested at the level at which economic power is located. As long as capital moves freely through the nation, political power must be national. That is why so much of our discussion throughout Part Three is of national policy even while we call for decentralization of power to smaller communities.

The nation is a community very remote to most citizens. It is better to conceive it as a community of communities. Citizens can participate better in less remote communities. The goal of an economics for community is to restore to communities at lower levels the power to determine their own affairs. That requires a regionalization of economic power and activity that would attach capital to regions. A variety of industries would be needed in each locale, and these would identify their well-being with that of states and cities, working with them for the well-being of the community rather than playing states or cities off against each other to extract maximum concessions. This would be a deep reversal of recent trends. What policies will encourage such a reversal? Some suggestions can be made.

First, the breakup of conglomerates and decentralization of industry recommended for purposes of assuring competition is a first step toward their regionalization as well.

Second, before plants are closed, efforts should be made to buy them locally. Sales to workers are an ideal solution. Federal law already facilitates such sales. Local and state governments could help with their financing instead of spending money to attract new plants that may not put down roots in the community. Worker-owned plants will be strongly bound to the communities in which they are located.

Third, whenever a plant is about to change hands, workers or other local interests should be given an option to bid against the proposed purchaser. This could accelerate the move to regionalization.

Fourth, programs of education about how the community gains from buying community-made products can begin to counter national advertising with the resulting attachment to name brands. A growing demand for locally made products will stimulate new business.

Fifth, a city might involve leaders of the business community more formally in its decision-making process. Such involvement could be through a council to which such groups as business, labor, the professions, and religious institutions elected representatives. Although the council would have no formal power, it would be understood that no important policies would be adopted by the mayor and council without consultation. The mayor could then bring any problem to this group not only for advice but also for help. Members of the group could air their grievances as well as interject their ideas. Participation in such councils would tend to build community and deepen roots in such a way as to reduce mobility. It would increase their interest in encouraging local business. Most new jobs now come from these businesses (Jacobs 1960, p. 49).

Thus far we have thought in terms of states and cities as the communities that might gain economic self-determination. Kirkpatrick Sale shows that this can also be done even at still smaller levels. A community of ten thousand people could economically produce all it really needs. Of course, to establish such a thesis, everything depends on the definition of needs. A community of this size cannot manufacture tanks and planes or even automobiles. Nevertheless, Sale is not proposing the abandonment of most modern comforts:

A community of 5,000 or 10,000 takes on the stature necessary for real economic independence—as indeed, if we needed reassurance, the greater part of human history has demonstrated. At that size . . . agricultural self-sufficiency and community energy systems are most economical and efficient, and at that level the labor force available for the rest of the economy (if it approximated current American percentages) would amount to between 2,000 and 4,000, divided about evenly between manufacturing and services. Now if we take the figures for current American manufacturing, we can see how many people it might take (both front office and production) to operate a plant in the sort of basic industries an independent community might require:

Industry	Workers per plant
Textiles	132
Apparel	56
Lumber and wood products	29
Furniture and fixtures	50
Paper and allied products	104
Soap, cleansers, toilet goods	43
Stone, clay, and glass products	39
Primary metal industries	163
Fabricated metal products	50
Machinery (except electrical)	45
Electrical and electronic equipment	135
Motorcycles, bicycles, parts	81
Instruments and related products	75
Total manufacturing employment	1002

In other words, using current standards, a thousand people could operate one plant in each of the thirteen basic manufacturing categories—and as we know, those current standards are far bigger than the optimum for either efficiency or humanity and they include some truly behemothian places. In a rational economy it would no doubt be possible to reduce those sizes by half, but even if it were by no more than a quarter, that would still mean a community of 10,000, with 2,000 factory workers, would be able to staff *three plants* in each of these basic categories—enough to supply a small population with practically all of its manufacturing needs and allow it considerable diversity as well. [Sale 1986, pp. 398–99]

The goal is not that all communities of ten thousand follow just this pattern. But it is important to be rid of the notion that an industrial society requires the surrender of authority to distant centers of economic power. Even steel can be produced locally. Small communities can exercise far more control over their economic lives than has been generally realized, and as they do so their political lives will also take on importance. Relatively self-sufficient towns can join together in still more self-sufficient states. The national government would lose the importance it necessarily has when the economy of even small towns is dependent on the global trading system.

Energy Use

In this chapter we have stressed the need to gain control of the economy at both national and local levels. Since the nation is to become as self-sufficient as is practicable, it must regain much of the industry it has lost. But the goal is not a return to past levels of production. A huge and growing industry imposed severe strains on resources and sinks. Being concentrated in a few regions, it needed a massive transportation system to dispense its products. That required more energy and more industrial production to maintain. To increase production required construction of more factories and more machinery. In short, growth fed on growth with little benefit to consumers.

Suppose that reindustrialization is in relatively self-sufficient regions, most of them quite small. The distribution of products will not require massive expenditures on trucks, highways, and rail. Since fewer trucks and trains will be used, fewer factories will be needed to build them as well as fewer machine tool factories to support expansion. Reductions in both transportation and manufacturing will lessen the use of energy. Since production of energy also takes energy, there is a multiplier effect.

But if with no reduction of the quantity of goods provided to the consumer, there can be a considerable reduction of economic activity, then what about employment? If there are fewer jobs, will not unemployment programs have to become massive? With a smaller industrial base and fewer workers, where will the taxes come from to support such programs?

There are simple answers to these questions. The means of producing more with fewer people has been the substitution of fossil fuel energy for human labor. If energy were abundant and labor scarce, that would make sense. But energy is not abundant, and the concern underlying these questions is that there is a great surplus of labor. If this is so, then labor should be substituted for fossil fuel.

That will not involve a return to backbreaking labor. The substitution of energy for that has been one of the real gains during the past century. But much energy has been used to replace interesting human work with boring assembly lines. That switch can be reversed. Crafts, now pursued chiefly as hobbies, could expand into major centers of production while energy-intensive mass production declines. The high cost of energy relative to labor will make that reversal economical.

These changes will probably leave the quantity of goods produced and consumed unchanged. But a reduction in that total quantity is also possible without lowering the economic quality of life. That quality does not depend on the quantity of goods but on the quantity and quality of service they provide. Fewer goods better constructed and longer-lasting can serve as well. Well-made goods are worth repairing. If the need for style changes is reduced, many goods can be made to last much longer. The legitimate desire for novelty (not everyone wants to wear the same long-lasting shoes for ten years) can be met by exchange in second-hand markets and ever popular "garage sales." The quantity of waste will decline. Comfortable houses can be built to last and to require little energy for heating and cooling.

There can also be changes in the ordering of the life of the city that will remove the need for some present consumption. Living close to work, to shops, and to all services, together with good public transportation, reduces the use of private cars without lowering the quality of life. When some streets are closed to cars they become more attractive for walking and bicycle riding, further reducing the use of cars. Arcologies would carry these changes still further.

If the desire of individuals for goods is less and the needs of industry for labor also declines, then leisure increases. With increased leisure households will do more for themselves. Gourmet cooking can become an art and a joy. The preference for pre-processed and expensively packaged food declines as its price rises.

None of these changes reduces the quality of life, but all of them reduce the need for industrial activity and for motor transportation. They thus reduce the demand for scarce resources including energy. In the past, growth has fed on growth with little gain in the quality of life; now reduction can feed on reduction with little loss in the quality of life. Indeed, we believe that the quality of life will be improved!

Changes of this sort can occur along with the decentralization and deindustrialization of food production, a shift from animal products to whole grains and vegetables. The reduction that can be effected in the use of fossil fuels is enormous. The transition to a solar-powered world can be eased and speeded. The nation can be genuinely self-sufficient. The worst of the projected ecological disasters can be avoided. Life will be better.

Perhaps this scenario is too optimistic. Perhaps there will have to be some reduction in the material quality of life as well. Even that would be quite tolerable. The majority of affluent Americans have more goods than they need for a comfortable and satisfying life.

But if people do not choose a transition that enables them to live comfortably through it, if they struggle to maintain the growth system in the face of the exhaustion of the resources that have made it possible, if they wait until they are physically forced to change, then the quality of life will fall drastically. Today we still have the choice. The next generation may not.

16

Labor

Worker Participation in Management and Ownership

A major feature of the rise of the industrial system was the transformation of labor (like land) into a commodity. As a commodity, labor is bought and sold in the market at a price determined by supply and demand. In the productive enterprise it functions simply as a means to ends established by owners.

Karl Polanyi's *The Great Transformation* (1944) is a massive expression of horror at what is implied in this and the actual consequences that resulted. "To separate labor from other activities of life and to subject it to the laws of the market was to annihilate all organic forms of existence and to replace them by a different type of organization, an atomistic and individualistic one" (p. 163). The system that required this "could not exist for any length of time without annihilating the human and natural substance of society" (p. 3). "The economic advantages of a free labor market could not make up for the social destruction wrought by it" (p. 77). Robert McIver takes up the theme in his preface to the book: "The satanic mills were heedless of all human needs but one; relentlessly they began to grind society itself into atoms." "Man failed to realize what the cohesion of society meant. The inner temple of human life was despoiled and violated" (p. x).

Polanyi points out that the vaunted laissez-faire attitude was quite selective in its operation. The government was told not to interfere in the way industry treated land and labor. But government was needed to help reduce labor to a commodity. Non-interference was in fact interference to "destroy noncontractual relations between individuals and prevent their spontaneous reformation" (Polanyi [1944] 1957, p. 163).

Of course, in the end no society can tolerate the consequences of this system when left to itself. The worker is, after all, a human being who is a member of the community and whose personal interests must concern other human beings. Hence all industrial societies have legislated some restrictions on the pure commodification of labor.

Further, workers themselves have energetically protested. Through unions they have established collective bargaining that has raised wages, at least in some parts of the industrial system, above the level set by supply and demand alone. They have demanded and obtained working conditions that recognize their humanity.

An economics for community supports this resistance to the commodification of labor. But it sees the need for more basic changes in the relations of labor, management, and capital if the gains thus far achieved are even to be preserved, and much more if they are to be extended. Today's broad economic trends are forcing labor back toward subsistence levels and will eventually weaken the safeguards established over a century of struggle. Labor unions will be powerless to stop this trend if the nation remains committed to "free trade." Efforts to resist the trend in particular industries where labor is strong will only speed up the closing of those factories with capital moving freely across national boundaries to places where labor is more docile and much cheaper.

Even if a system of tariffs changes the situation and increases the incentive of management to bargain with labor unions, a return to the dominant situation of the past will not be healthy. That situation was one of opposition. It was supposed that the interests of labor and management were in conflict more than they were in harmony. This was true when capital treated labor as a commodity, and when apart from unions, management could submit labor to almost any working conditions with impunity. It is much less true today. In general labor and management share a common interest in the healthy functioning of industry. Both benefit when this is improved. Both lose when this is damaged. That management and labor constitute a single community of interests has been much more clearly realized in Germany and Japan than in the United States, but its recognition is coming here, too.[1]

This does not mean that labor should passively leave all decisions to management, trusting that its interests would thereby be cared for. Far from it. But the goal should be to increase communications between labor and management so that the situation would be improved for both. Decisions should be made only in a context where concerns and suggestions from labor have been effectively heard and considered. The Japa-

---

1. See Michael Harrington's account of the GM-UAW contract in *The New Left* (1986, p. 14).

nese have developed structures for insuring this active participation of workers in decisions that affect them. The results have been beneficial for business at large. Much management theory now calls for this collaboration. Labor should demand it and government should support it. The Japanese have also provided workers with a considerable measure of job security. This, too, is appropriate. One cannot expect high morale and cooperation from workers who know that the first adjustment to a business slowdown will be to lay them off—and without any "golden parachutes." In theory risk and uncertainty are supposed to be borne by the capitalist-entrepreneur. This is the major justification for high rates of return to capital. Yet in the United States it is the laborer's income that is most subject to the risk and uncertainty of the business cycle.

Businesses function better when workers are satisfied with the conditions of work and are able to contribute their insights and suggestions. This is now a commonplace of management thinking in the United States. Progressive enterprises of all sorts are currently engaged in experimental programs designed to improve the "quality of work life" (QWL). According to Robert Zagen and Michael P. Rosow, "more than 850 articles and books have been written on the subject, and at least four national and international study and research centers focus on quality of life as such" (1982, pp. 88–89).

The lesson that there is a community of interests between management and labor has now been learned. The transformation of practice to conform to the new appreciation of community is slow and beset by many pitfalls. But the direction is set.

A step beyond QWL and participation in decisions is employee codetermination in the management of an enterprise. This may be through a union structure or by direct election by the workers. In Germany, where codetermination has deep roots in the nineteenth century and has been official national policy since World War II, as many as half of the members of a supervisory board of an enterprise may be chosen by the workers. This supervisory board then elects a management board, which also has worker representation. The effect is to give workers a major voice in, and in some cases veto power over, management decisions. It also provides a channel of communication from management to labor, such that workers have management decisions interpreted to them by their own representatives. (For a detailed account of the history and practice of codetermination in Germany, see Alfred L. Thimm, *The False Promise of Codetermination* [1980]. Despite the negative title, the overall impression is of a remarkably positive development.)

Worker Ownership

In the United States codetermination has not been seriously considered, but since 1974 the government has encouraged worker participation in ownership through the employee stock ownership plan, ESOP, developed by the economist Louis Kelso and promoted through the legislation of tax incentives by Senator Russell Long. The idea "has been endorsed by everyone from Ronald Reagan to Ted Kennedy, from the New York Stock Exchange to the Teamsters Union, from Paul Volcker to Pope John Paul II" (Quarry, Blasi, and Rosen 1986, p. 23). The primary purpose is to expand participation in capitalism. "Over 8,000 firms with more than 11 million workers now have employee ownership plans" (p. viii). In the vast majority of cases, the workers own less than 15% of the whole and have little participation in decision-making. But a million workers are in plants where ownership is significant. Especially when companies need wage concessions from employees, they sometimes offer in exchange substantial participation in ownership. With this much development in a single decade, promise for the future is considerable.

We do not wish to deny the positive features of the Kelso Plan, but one must recognize that it is not the panacea its authors have claimed. This claim is explicit in the subtitle of their book: *Two Factor Theory: How to Turn Eighty Million Workers into Capitalists on Borrowed Money* (Kelso and Hetter 1967). Giving everyone a second income from capital is a fine idea, but doing it on borrowed money with no redistribution of income, with everyone just getting richer and richer, assumes extremely high growth rates that doom the plan on ecological grounds alone. But in addition to that, one must ask why capitalists would lend to workers at a rate of interest less than the rate of return the workers will be getting on the borrowed money. The worker, who is not an entrepreneur, appears as a middleman who could easily be cut out of the deal. What induces the capitalist to keep the worker in are the tax breaks extended to the capitalists who participate. The capitalist's rate of return from the worker and the government combined is greater than what the capitalist could make by investing directly in whatever it is the worker is investing in. But the government's subsidy to the capitalist has to be paid for through the tax system. A subsidy rate to the capitalist means a higher tax rate for everyone else or reduced government services for all. There is, as economists are fond of saying, no free lunch. Employee ownership will have to be financed largely out of savings, not borrowed money.

Employee ownership without participation in making decisions has not been shown to make a great difference in employee attitudes or productivity. The need is to combine ownership with something like codetermination. No one pattern will work everywhere, but the combination of these two programs is promising.

A final step beyond the integration of worker ownership of stock and codetermination is outright ownership. There are already about a thousand firms with half a million workers in which employees own 50% to 100% of the stock. Some of these companies have been outstandingly successful. Existing federal legislation facilitates the process of workers taking over their companies in some instances. Much further support could be given. Dramatic cases have occurred when workers purchased plants or stores that were otherwise to be closed. In several cases they have restored profitability.

Decentralized control of American industry would make worker ownership more practical. Government policies favoring spin-offs could offer opportunities for purchase by employees. With active public support the portion of American business owned by employees could grow rapidly. Such companies would embody community and support wider regional community as well.

Of course, there are many problems still unresolved. One of them is worker mobility. Consider an example. In successful, fully worker-owned enterprises, the value of the share owned by a single worker may become tens of thousands of dollars. When that worker wants to retire or move, she or he will either become an absentee owner or else sell the share to a new worker/owner. It is often impossible to find someone who wants to work in the enterprise who has sufficient capital to buy the share. Some successful worker-owned businesses have sold out as a result of this dilemma.

A solution to this problem is proposed by Ota Sik in *For a Humane Economic Democracy,* (1985). He proposes the "neutralization" of capital, by which he means that the share of the capital belonging to the workers would be owned by them collectively rather than individually (pp. 92 ff). All workers would be members of an "assets management association" and an "enterprise management association," which would elect representatives to share in decision making. Part of the profits would be distributed to the workers.[2]

2. For a remarkable success story of this kind of worker ownership, see E. F. Schumacher's account of Scott Bader in *Good Work* (1979, pp. 76–83).

Although unions in Europe have given leadership in moves to work-place democracy along lines such as those discussed here, especially co-determination, labor unions in the United States have resisted. Their history and reason for existence have been bound up with adversarial relations with management. Since most of the changes thus far insti-tuted have been initiated by management for the sake of improving pro-ductivity, labor leaders are understandably suspicious. They note that "one team of management consultants has promoted executive seminars on humanization of work called 'Making Unions Unnecessary'" (Zwerd-ling 1980, p. 171). They complain that "whatever benefits workers do gain from humanization of work reforms, they are never guaranteed. Just as management bestows the benefits on the employees, so manage-ment can take them away" (Zwerdling 1980, pp. 171–72). They are es-pecially disturbed when hard-won pension programs are forfeited in ex-change for stock (Bluestone and Harrison 1982, p. 261). They object that "putting workers or union officials on the board will blur the sharp distinction between employees and employers—the distinction which gives unions and union officials their identities" (Zwerdling 1980, p. 172). Union officials also note that as workers identify their interests with a particular firm, their solidarity with other workers in other firms gives way to competition between firms. The fears of the effect of work-place democracy on traditional unions are justified. These have been built on adversarial relations assuming that companies could make prof-its and that the struggle is over dividing the profits between workers and owners. Management interest in accenting a community of concerns with workers is based partly on the realization that unless the adversarial re-lationship is overcome, there will be no profits and plants will be closed. Labor leaders are coming to recognize this new reality as well.

Workplace democracy is in tension with traditional trade unions, but it is certainly not in opposition to organized labor in general. It calls for the evolution of unions to perform new functions in a new context. In-creasingly, "union leaders genuinely see the struggle for more democ-racy in the workplace as the desirable and logical outgrowth of the union struggle during the past 50 years" (Zwerdling 1980, p. 175).

It is our conviction that for the sake both of workers and the whole national community, worker ownership in combination with participa-tion in the making of decisions should become the basic form of busi-ness in the future. According to *Employee Ownership in America*, it is the alternative to present trends that are leading to an economy "made up of a small number of very wealthy owners, a larger number of highly paid workers, and a much larger group of poorly paid service workers, the underemployed, and the unemployed" (Rosen, Klein, and Young 1986, p. 189). The book argues, "We need a system that encourages growth while fostering equity, not one that insists that one side's gain is the other's loss. We need a system that provides a workable structure for labor-management cooperation, one that provides incentives for employees to assume more responsibility and initiative. If new industrial technologies eventually reduce the amount of labor needed in society (much as the industrial revolution did), we will also need a system in which people can earn from owning, not just working" (Rosen, Klein, and Young 1986, p. 188). The case that employee ownership is the answer to these needs is impressive.

It may be thought that worker ownership can play a significant role only in small companies. However, plans can be devised where it will gradually function in large companies as well. Brian Burkitt has reviewed this possibility as a part of a comprehensive proposal for economic democratization of society. He summarizes his recommendations on the basis of

. . . the Swedish proposals whereby companies with more than a hundred employees transfer a portion of their total profits (currently suggested at 20%) in the form of newly issued shares to employee investment funds administered by the relevant trade unions. This transferred profit remains within the firm for reinvestment. The voting rights of the stock belong to the unions, which elect directors in proportion to the relative size of their equity stake for a four-year period, half retiring or standing for re-election every two years. On present rates of growth, the most profitable Swedish firms would become worker-controlled in approximately thirty years while trade unions are more immediately able to supervise, and where necessary, check management. After fifty to sixty years the majority of equity capital would be collectively owned. [Burkitt 1984, p. 180]

The Rehumanization of Work

Even if workers begin to participate in management and ownership of the businesses in which they are employed, a deeper problem in the industrial system will remain. This is the alienating and dehumanizing character of much of the labor required in modern business and industry. This problem is addressed only superficially by those interested in the Quality of Work Life. Their contributions are in the areas dealt with by personnel departments whose task is to improve worker morale in doing work the fundamental character of which is determined by others. Peter Drucker makes this point clearly:

> Personnel Administration and Human Relations are the things talked about and written about whenever the management of worker and work is being discussed. They are the things the Personnel Department concerns itself with. But they are not the concepts that underlie the actual management of worker and work in American industry. This concept is Scientific Management. Scientific Management focuses on the work. Its core is organized study of work, the analysis of work into its simplest elements and the systematic improvement of the worker's performance of each of these elements. Scientific Management has both basic concepts and easily applicable tools and techniques. And it has no difficulty proving the contribution it makes. Its results in the form of higher output are visible and readily measurable. [Braverman 1974, p. 88]

The profoundly dehumanizing character of so much work is a function of the inherent drive of the system toward productivity through specialization. There seems to be an inherent tension between humanly satisfying work and the quantity of production per worker. Economic theory has focused on satisfying the human being qua consumer, its *Homo economicus,* and it has viewed the human being as worker only in terms of wages and productivity. But when *Homo economicus* is viewed as person-in-community, satisfaction derived from work is of equal importance with satisfaction derived from consumption. The one-sided approach that has dominated consideration of the aims of the economy must end. As Paul Wachtel says: "Any gains in available consumer goods must be weighed against the extra pressure and deprivations undergone during the heart of the day when we are at work" (Wachtel 1983, p. 156).

Jeremy Seabrook is more impassioned. For him the gains in consumption do not compensate for the losses. "We are doubly deluded: on the one hand the market-place cannot provide the happiness it promises; and on the other, our creative skills, which could provide something more modest but more real—a sense of worth—have been taken from us, and locked in the machines that have displaced us" (Seabrook 1978, p. 282). Even if one thinks Seabrook exaggerates, the phenomenon to which he points is one of great importance. It is bound up with the whole history of industrialization in both its capitalist and its Soviet forms, and it profoundly shapes the character of mass, consumer-oriented society. Although we do not profess to have any fundamental or utopian solutions, we do believe that vivid consciousness of the dehumanizing nature of so much work in the modern world is a good starting point for policy reflection.

The division of labor has been a part of human economy from the hunting and gathering period to the present. As society became more complex, more distinct tasks were distinguished. Some of them were demeaning and back-breaking; others were humanly satisfying and fulfilling.

The origins of the industrial system came when particular tasks were analyzed and subdivided. Adam Smith's account of the making of pins is classic. Instead of one specialization of pin-making, there were now eleven subspecialties. No one person made a pin; each performed, instead, repetitively, a single act that contributed its part to the process. Production was vastly increased, but workers no longer were persons who could develop complex skills and take pride in their product.

In 1832 Charles Babbage called attention to another advantage of the subdivision of production into simple acts. "The master manufacturer, by dividing the work to be executed into different processes, each requiring different degrees of skill or of force, can purchase exactly that precise quantity of both which is necessary for each process; whereas, if the whole work were executed by one workman, that person must possess sufficient skill to perform the most difficult, and sufficient strength to execute the most laborious, of the operations into which the art is divided" (Babbage [1832] 1963, pp. 175–76). How far this could go is illustrated in a table of jobs and wages he offers for the making of a type of pin. The table shows (reproduced here as table 16.1) how a truly "free" market in labor functioned, as well as the extent to which work became mechanical.[3]

Precisely because so many of the functions of workers had become mechanical, a further step in the industrial process was possible. Machines could be invented that replaced the mechanical actions of workers. Human beings became primarily observers of the working of machines. Skill was less and less required, and intelligence became more of an obstacle to efficient performance than an aid.

Andrew Ure celebrated this development with clarity and enthusiasm in his remarkable book, *The Philosophy of Manufacturers* ([1835] 1967). He saw the problem with the mode of production described by Smith: "It was indeed a subject of regret to observe how frequently the workman's eminence, in any craft, had to be purchased by the sacrifice of his health and comfort. To one unvaried operation, which required un-

3. This table appears in Babbage, p. 184, and is reproduced in Braverman 1974, p. 80.

Table 16.1

Drawing wire	Man	3s. 3d. per day
Straightening wire	Woman	1s. 0d.
	Girl	0s. 6d.
Pointing	Man	5s. 3d.
Twisting and cutting heads	Boy	0s. 4 1/2 d.
	Man	5s. 4 1/2 d.
Reading	Woman	1s. 3d.
Tinning or whitening	Man	6s. 0d.
	Woman	3s. 0d.
Papering	Woman	1s. 6d.

remitting dexterity and diligence, his hand and eye were constantly on the strain" (p. 22).

Yet Ure seems oblivious to the ambiguities of the new system. "It is, in fact, the constant aim and tendency of every improvement in machinery to supersede human labor altogether, or to diminish its cost, by substituting the industry of women and children for that of men; or that of ordinary labourers, for trained artisans. In most of the water-twist, or throstle, cotton mills, the spinning is entirely managed by females of sixteen years and upwards. The effect of substituting the self-acting mule for the common mule, is to discharge the greater part of the men spinners, and to retain adolescents and children" (Ure [1835] 1967, p. 23).

Society finally disrupted the "free" market in labor that made it possible to replace adults with children, but in other respects the principles governing Babbage's thought were carried further. Frederick Taylor gave them the most thorough and consistent expression and in doing so established "scientific management" as supreme. Harry Braverman summarizes his position as follows: "Workers who are controlled only by general orders and discipline are not adequately controlled, because they retain their grip on the actual processes of labor. So long as they control the labor process itself, they will thwart efforts to realize to the full the potential inherent in their labor power. To change this situation, control over the labor process must pass into the hands of management, not only in a formal sense but the control and dictation of each step of the process, including its mode of performance" (Braverman 1974, p. 100).

The process involves three principles: "The first principle is the gathering and development of knowledge of labor processes, and the second is the concentration of this knowledge as the exclusive province of management—together with its essential converse, the absence of such knowledge among the workers—. . . the third is the *use of this monop-*

oly over knowledge to control each step of the labor process and its mode of execution" (Braverman 1974, p. 119). The application of this system not only increases production but reduces the skills needed by workers and hence also the wages paid to them. In his *Shop Management,* Taylor wrote that the advantages of his methods "will not have been realized until almost all of the machines in the shop are run by men who are of smaller calibre and attainments, and who are therefore cheaper than those required under the old system" (Braverman 1974, p. 118).

Although recently there have been many reports that contemporary industry needs greater education and skill on the part of its workers than was true in the past, Braverman disputes this claim, showing that the basic principle of simplifying and routinizing work has not changed. What industry needs are persons willing and able to work diligently at narrowly defined tasks for which they can be trained rather easily. Although he wrote before the full impact of the computer, it is doubtful that the situation has greatly changed. The rules to be learned may be more complex but once they are learned the operations are still repetitive, requiring a minimum of creative imagination or decision on the part of the worker. For example, some fast-food chains have computerized cash registers with pictures of their products and pictures of all currency notes on the register keys, so that the cashier need not even be able to recognize numbers, much less subtract.

These same fast-food companies employ teenagers at the minimum wage, which is fine, but the youngsters are frequently sent home when business is unexpectedly slack, and are required to be available to be called back during an unexpectedly busy time. Even the length of their working day becomes an unpredictable variable to fit the convenience of their employer. Temporary and part-time workers are filling more and more secretarial and construction jobs. They receive no insurance or retirement benefits, and can be laid off the minute business falls off and hired back the minute it picks up. Surely this is cheap chrematistics, not efficient oikonomia. Only our obsession with competing in the international growth race makes us willing to tolerate such poor treatment of the work force.

That the dehumanization of work in this system is far from incidental is apparent. Since in general, if not in detail, "scientific management" is the basis of business and industry, the problem is pervasive and fundamental. The question is whether anything can be done beyond the superficial changes of the Quality of Work Life movement.

The answer is that the free market works against any fundamental improvement, and the larger the size of the market the more difficult it will be to redirect economic activity so as to provide more satisfying and fulfilling work. Nevertheless, some existing trends and some of the proposals made in this book could jointly lead to a new situation in which new decisions could be made.

Among existing trends, two may be noted. First, there seems to be increasing willingness to take lower-paid work if it is more satisfying. This suggests that at some point there could be upward pressure on wages for routine work that would make other options more attractive to business. Second, there is increasing interest in handicrafts. These have a growing popularity despite their greater cost and often less perfected appearance, in comparison with their manufactured rivals. They are produced both as hobbies and commercially, so that artisan skills are kept alive and appreciated.

Among proposals in this book, decentralization of the economy is of particular importance combined with the expected rising of the cost of energy. In a decentralized economy with high energy costs, artisans will be able to compete with factories better than at present. But more important, when decentralization and high energy costs are combined with worker management and ownership, decisions about changed procedures can be made with an eye to restoring thought, skill, and initiative to the workplace. It is not impossible that machines can be brought into the service of workers instead of dictating their activities.[4]

Full Employment

Even if work could be rehumanized and through worker ownership the threatening class divisions of American society reduced, there would remain a massive and invidious distinction between the employed and the unemployed. No labor policy that fails to deal with the issue of unemployment is acceptable.

In a genuine community, all who can will participate in generating the wealth in which all share. Of course, child care and housework and many roles in volunteer organizations are forms of such participation just as much as paid work. But in the great majority of families at least one member will take part in the paid arena. That means that the only

4. This was a project close to the heart of E. F. Schumacher. His book, *Good Work* (1979), is a discussion of what may be possible. He finds no clearcut solutions.

possible goal of a community in this respect is full employment. But while the aim at "full employment" is almost universal, quite different strategies can be proposed for realizing it.

The dominant neoclassical strategy warns against policies that would artificially attain full employment now at the expense of curtailing growth. Instead, it favors technological changes that reduce the need for workers because in this way productivity—output per hour of labor—is increased. In classical and neoclassical theory this is the heart of economic progress. The workers displaced by improved productivity will be employed when the capital engendered by this improvement is invested. Full employment is to be attained by a rapid growth in the economy as a whole with a mobile labor force going where the growth is occurring.

The theory has allowed for cyclical slowdowns in growth accompanied by temporary unemployment. But these are part of a long-term trend that should keep the great majority of workers employed most of the time. Efforts to reduce the suffering caused by the business cycle have been somewhat successful, but the long-term trend, contrary to the theory, is toward increasing chronic unemployment. True believers insist that the problem is that growth is too slow, and they call for less government intervention as the way to fulfill the model.

In part the true believer is correct. If workers had no choice but to work or starve, more would take available jobs at substantially lower wages than those to which they have been accustomed. Unemployment is often a matter of lack of jobs of the sort people want or expect rather than absolute lack of employment opportunities. If labor again became a pure commodity, the system might generate full employment except for cyclical changes.

We have already seen how "free trade" is closing higher paid jobs and substituting low paid service jobs. If this were not occurring the economists' model might be more realistic. New capital investment within the nation might in fact generate new jobs at the same wage as those lost. Hence, if the policy of establishing a national economy is adopted, this type of unemployment could be eased by these standard policies.

Still there is reason to be doubtful. What works in the economists' models has not in fact worked in the real world. Increased productivity has in fact led to less need for work. This has been expressed in more part-time jobs and growing unemployment. David Orr describes the economist's typical prescription cynically: "The emphasis on production leads to the ever greater use of ever more scarce resources in order to conserve labor that has become abundant" (1979, p. 80).

Beyond Oil warns that this policy cannot proceed. It can be projected into the future only on the basis of invalid assumptions about the ability of technology to replace diminishing resources. During the next 40 years fossil-fuel energy will be in increasingly short supply. Improved productivity of individual workers has correlated very closely with energy use and cannot be further increased without the application of more energy per worker. That increase will not be possible for the growing number of people seeking employment. "It will not be possible to provide all these workers with rising amounts of fuel per worker-hour, unless the number of worker-hours is reduced" (Gever et al. 1987, p. 241). Reduction of the number of worker-hours means either employing fewer people or employing more people for fewer hours. The alternative will be to employ more people for more hours by settling for less energy per worker and, therefore, lower productivity. Without abundant cheap energy, solving unemployment by growth is impossible, and this will soon become apparent.

The authors of *Beyond Oil* rightly insist that we must look at net yields gained from energy rather than from gross output. Exploring for oil ends when the amount of energy expended in the exploration equals the amount that can be expected from the oil found. "By 2005 it will be pointless to continue exploring for oil and gas as energy sources in the United States: after that more energy would be used to look for these fuels than the oil and gas we found would contain" (Gever et al. 1987, p. 20). Technology enables us physically to reach other deposits of energy, but in our century it has not appreciably reduced the amount of energy required to do this. Our romance with nuclear energy is not encouraging. "It now appears that the United States will be lucky if the nuclear industry eventually produces as much energy as it has consumed" (Gever et al. 1987, p. 223). The assumption that new technologies will solve the problem, an assumption common among economists, does not hold up.

Fortunately, when the prejudice against policies that inhibit growth is removed, it is not difficult to see how progress can be made to achieve full employment. First, one set of such policies is continuous with those already discussed. The resettlement of rural America would draw millions back into useful work that would greatly add to the health of the nation. The shift from capital- and energy-intensive to more labor-intensive technologies in some industries will also help. In general the preservation of existing industry and the gradual reindustrialization of the nation will help. These are our primary policy proposals.

However, they may not meet all the needs. Consider the situation in which improved means of production in a factory reduce the need for human labor. The usual procedure is to release some of the employees. The alternative is for all to work fewer hours. This procedure would be easiest to adopt in the case of the employee-owned business. In that case it would be clear that the new procedures would not be adopted if they did not improve the condition of the business as a whole. If this condition is improved, then each worker should be able to receive as much income as before. If less labor is needed, then all should labor less.

This idea played a major role in U.S. economic policy down to the Great Depression. It led to the reduction of the work week from 60 to 40 hours. In the early days of the Depression, there was a move to reduce it to 30 hours in order to reemploy many of the unemployed. This was opposed by the Roosevelt administration, which favored other responses to unemployment. It saw that in a time of Depression, if the work is shared, the result will be that each will have a smaller piece of a diminished pie. It thought that enlarging the pie was more important. This commitment to enlarging the pie has dominated economic thinking about unemployment ever since (McGaughey 1981, pp. 2–3). But the pie has grown much larger while unemployment has at times risen to Depression levels.

When growth ceases to be the central goal or means to effect the goal, the standard objections to a shorter work week evaporate. However, the shortened work week should be viewed as one form of a larger proposal, namely, reducing the total hours of labor per year. It is this larger idea to which attention should be directed first. If it is affirmed, a second question should be: how is it best effected?

Reducing hours of labor per worker is not supported by management at all, and it is only a secondary goal of labor. Management generally prefers to employ fewer workers for more hours, even if labor costs are the same or higher. Labor on the whole is more interested in increasing wages than reducing work. It is the unemployed and society as a whole who suffer from this arrangement.

Opposition is not, however, monolithic on the part of either management or labor. There are indications that productivity declines with long hours, so that management has something to gain from spreading the work. On the side of labor, there has been interest in paid holidays and vacations as well as increased pay. Indeed, there are many workers seeking part-time employment because the pressures of full-time employment are too great. Reducing the time of work and hiring more people across the spectrum of positions would tend to alleviate this problem.

Assuming that reduced hours of work per year are a desirable element in the struggle against unemployment, what pattern of reduction is best? Longer vacations and shorter workdays both have their advantages. A four-day work week is also worth considering. If 36 hours are worked in four days, persons who commute an hour a day will save an additional hour for leisure each week. Experience has already shown the popularity of the three-day weekend, and this could become the norm.

We expect that the pattern of changes here proposed would reduce unemployment substantially. But we must suppose that it would not eliminate it. Some unemployment is entailed in the fact that no society can provide to all those who want to work the types of jobs they desire, and some will choose not to work at all rather than to take jobs of certain sorts or at too low a wage. In the next chapter we will propose a program that will guarantee subsistence for such people without removing incentives to work. We would substitute this program for unemployment compensation, leaving the latter to private insurance or arrangements between workers and employers.

A community should not force on its members work they consider demeaning or acutely unpleasant. On the other hand, a community should offer to all its members who desire it an opportunity for some kind of useful work at *some* wage. In this sense, the government should be the employer of last resort. No one who is willing and physically able to work should be refused the opportunity.

Our proposals here assume the income policies that we describe in the next chapter, so that no one is faced with homelessness and starvation as the alternative to work, so that no one is dependent on work simply to subsist. The work provided by the government can then be considered as a source of supplementary income rather than livelihood.

When a government employment center is unable to place a would-be worker in a regular job, it should offer three alternatives—a job training program that would likely lead to long-term employment, help in homesteading in the countryside, or an immediate, low-paying government job either full- or part-time, as desired by the worker. Some of these jobs could be like those of CETA, designed to support overworked public servants. But others would be manual labor, such as cleaning up trash along the highways or beautifying public parks. Still others should be such that they could be done in the home and by handicapped persons.

It would also be possible to invite the would-be worker to suggest constructive work she or he would like to do if modest pay were provided. Some might be aware of unmet community needs they are qualified to work on. Motivation is likely to be higher when the selection is by the worker.

Pay should be very low, perhaps $3 an hour (by 1989 standards) or in some cases an equivalent amount on a piecework basis. There would be little possibility of advancement, but good work would lead to strong recommendations for proper jobs. The goal would not be to compete with the regular job market but to supplement it by hiring those not wanted for existing jobs. The intention would be to feed them back into the regular market.

It can be objected that such a program draws off resources that could otherwise be used to expand regular employment opportunities. Our goal would be to draw off as few resources as possible and to focus the government efforts here on hard-core unemployment. It is truly a matter of "last resort." Success would depend on the effectiveness of the other policies in greatly reducing the number of unemployed to be dealt with in this way.

Such a program should replace the minimum wage. If people want to work in the private sector at even lower rates than government would pay, that should be allowed. But the fact that a government job is guaranteed would serve as inducement to the private sector to pay more.

17

Income Policies and Taxes

The Negative Income Tax

Neoclassical economic theory is focused on the marketplace and prefers as little government interference in the economy as possible. The strength of the market is seen as its encouragement of overall growth and efficient allocation. No one claims that the distribution of income by the market will be fair or that none will fall below subsistence if left alone. During the epoch of social Darwinism, this was interpreted as a desirable expression of the survival of the fittest. The early death of the unfit was accepted as beneficial to the gene pool. The market's distribution of income was accepted as normative.

Today few profess such ideas. Nevertheless, market enthusiasts continue to be reluctant to allow for any but the most limited involvement of government in helping the poor. Consider the following passage by Alvin Rabushka, one that expresses a widespread tone among neoclassical economists: "No one would quarrel with the desire to help others who, through no fault of their own, cannot take care of themselves. Compassion is indeed a virtue. Helping the disabled, the handicapped, the blind, the frail, or abandoned children has a place in public life. But these needy people differ from able-bodied men and women who choose the dole over work. They are not the same as widows whose husbands chose not to buy insurance. They are not in the same class with alcoholics, drug addicts, or criminals. Where private charity fails to help these truly needy people in our society, few would totally oppose that we give them public help" (Rabushka 1985, p. 213).

We agree with the preference for employment over the dole when this is possible. If economics is to be for community, then work should be available for all who want it, and there should be clear incentives for at least one member of each household to seek employment. If millions who want work are denied jobs and forced on the dole, this is a sign of profound failure. But we do not agree with the implications of Rabush-ka's statement that most of those who are now unemployed have chosen that status out of preference for the public dole. Indolence is a problem, but surely not the main one.

Furthermore, an economics for community cannot agree that "wid-ows whose husbands chose not to buy insurance," "alcoholics," and "drug addicts" are simply to be left to starve. In a true community, the basic needs of all are met so far as the community can do so. This is the aim of all developed nations now, and it has been characteristic of tradi-tional village life as well. Whereas Rabushka would sacrifice this con-cern for the sake of growth as measured by GNP, we would measure true growth largely by the success of the economy in meeting the basic needs of all on a sustainable basis. The question is not whether, but how, to accomplish this.

The present pattern in the United States is a crazy quilt of social leg-islation. As presently administered it is a net through which increasing numbers are falling into destitution. Homelessness is growing into a major social problem and malnutrition is extensive, some of it based on sheer lack of money for the purchase of food. In an affluent nation this is intolerable.

The present system is inequitable. While some of the poor can no longer house themselves, others benefit from multiple programs and be-come affluent on the dole. It is inefficient. It requires an expensive bu-reaucracy for its administration. It is demeaning. Many benefits can be received only by detailed demonstration of one's poverty and helpless-ness. It is destructive of family. Aid to dependent children often requires that there be no male parent in the household. It induces a culture of dependency. There are now second and third generations of persons on welfare. And it fails to provide an incentive to work. Benefits are abruptly lost when one earns even a small wage, so that the working poor are often no better off than those who live by welfare alone.

That the system is unsatisfactory is universally recognized, but major changes are politically difficult to make. Here, however, we are not focusing on how to effect reform, but on the direction reform should take. A preferred system should: (1) require that the truly basic needs of all be met, (2) be simple and inexpensive to implement, (3) require a minimum of information from recipients and impose a minimum of special conditions upon them, and (4) provide strong incentive to work.

One approach that meets all these requirements is the negative in-come tax first advocated by George Stigler (1946). It was supported by

Milton Friedman in *Capitalism and Freedom* (1962). Although details can be complex, the basic idea is that the government would send checks to those whose reported income was below a certain amount. The checks would become smaller as the income increases, but not to the full extent of the increase, so that there would always be a positive incentive to earn more.

In 1962 Friedman's proposal was that the existing income tax exemptions and standard exemptions be used as a basis for the calculation. For a family of four, these amounted to about $3,000. Exemptions and deductions have not kept up with inflation, but we can estimate that today the equivalent figure would be around $12,000. Friedman's proposal would work out somewhat as shown in table 17.1 (adapted from Wogaman [1968, p. 29]):

Table 17.1

Family's gross income	Grant to family	Total net income
0	6,000	6,000
2,000	5,000	7,000
4,000	4,000	8,000
8,000	2,000	10,000
12,000	0	12,000

Since it is doubtful that a family of four can subsist on $6,000 today, we propose that Friedman's purposes could be better fulfilled with a 50% increase to $9,000 as minimal, with descending payments as shown in table 17.2.

Table 17.2

0	9,000	9,000
2,000	8,000	10,000
4,000	7,000	11,000
8,000	5,000	13,000
12,000	3,000	15,000
15,000	1,500	16,500
18,000	0	18,000

Because even these larger sums cannot suffice to deal with unpredictable medical expenses, we propose a system of national health insurance covering everyone. To reduce its costs and discourage frivolous use, we recommend something like a 20% deductible on the first $500 and a 10% deductible on the next $1,000 as well as a charge of $5 per patient-initiated visit thereafter.

A more market-oriented alternative supplement to the above measures would be to increase the supply of medical services by removing the restrictions to entry exercised by the medical schools, which turn away thousands of capable students each year. Increasing the supply of doctors by subsidizing the expansion of medical schools would be the next step, if necessary. This approach would avoid the difficulties of trying to control fees, leaving that to supply and demand. But supply would have been increased and effective demand exercised by the poor would have been increased as well.

The Positive Income Tax

Friedman estimated in 1962 that his proposal would reduce government spending. It would substitute for aid to dependent children, old-age assistance, social security benefit payments, farm price supports, public housing, and all other subsidies (see Wogaman 1968, p. 28). We would add food stamps and Medicare to the list. Apart from the medical insurance program, we think our proposal should not add to current costs. It would simply require that social security and other taxes now levied separately be covered by other taxes. The medical insurance would add to costs because it is a new program which, unlike Medicare, would cover everyone. We believe that most, if not all, of the funds needed could be recovered by continuing the 50% tax rate inherent in the tables above. But we hasten to add that the 50% figure was chosen mainly for numerical convenience in our example, and that the issue of the best income tax rate is a complex one that requires much further study.

For the income tax to be effective it should, as Adam Smith noted of all taxes, be equitable, simple, economical, and certain (Davies 1986, p. 17). Taxes should not distort economic decisions unless there is a clear public decision that supports the distortion in question. For example, there might be a decision to discourage the smoking of tobacco by taxing cigarettes. In its present form the personal income tax does not measure up well, by Smith's criteria.

The present system exempts various types of income from taxation or treats them in special ways, as with social security. We propose to count it all and to add the rental value of one's home as well as all benefits with which salaries and wages are now supplemented, and to include capital gains as well. These proposals are similar to those of the early Chicago economist Henry C. Simons, set forth in his *Federal Income Tax Reform* (1950). A variety of deductions are now allowed: for interest payments on homes, housing allowances for ministers, and state and local taxes, to cite only a few. We would retain or adopt only four: (1) taxes and costs of repairs and improvements on the home whose rental value is added to income; (2) expenses necessary for earning a living, such as child care when it is needed to enable a parent to work; (3) gifts to private institutions and charitable activities (needed to counterbalance the dominance of the state); and (4) small gifts to politicians, since these at least somewhat decrease their dependence on large donors. At present many taxes are postponed through retirement programs. We suggest that this not be allowed.

A special problem surrounds capital gains. The substitution of capital gains for other income is a major method of tax avoidance. Capital gains should be treated just like any other income. But huge gains accumulated over long periods, partly because of inflation, can lead to an overwhelming and unfair tax burden. For example, in constant dollars one's home may not have appreciated in thirty years of ownership, but in current dollars it may be sold for a great profit. To pay taxes on that profit would make it impossible to buy another comparable home. There is merit in the special consideration now given to this matter, but the inflationary element in many other profits is not thereby relieved.

We propose that income for each year include the increased value of assets during that year. This increase will be calculated in constant dollars using a deflator provided by the government so as to avoid taxing inflationary increments. Costs of doing business will be deducted. But real gains will be taxed as income whether the property is kept or sold. On this system the problems now surrounding capital gains will end. Also the buying and selling of property will no longer be significantly affected by taxes. One more element of distortion will be removed from the system.

Including capital gains in annual taxes will add complications for those who own property. Hence the total simplification will not be as great as might be wished. However, if homes are appraised annually, and if investors are provided annually with a statement of the value of their investments, the difficulties will be modest, and they will be largely counterbalanced by obviating the present calculation of capital gains. For those who do not own property, the new tax structure will be quite simple.

What objections might be raised to these proposals? We are aware of seven, and consider each one below.

1. *Revenue will not suffice to cover costs of the Negative Income Tax and other government programs now dependent on income tax receipts.* This

may be true. Our rough estimates indicate that taxes would be less than current ones on families with incomes of up to about $60,000 when social security taxes are factored in. The somewhat higher taxes beyond that point would certainly not compensate. However, our proposal makes much more income taxable; so this is a misleading comparison. In any case, any shortfall here can be made up in other taxes to be discussed in the following section of this chapter. Indeed, a case could be made for lowering income taxes and raising a larger proportion of federal needs from other sources, especially severance taxes.

2. *$9,000 is too little for a family of four to live on.* Under many circumstances this is no doubt true. However, we think very few would be forced to do so. Given a government guarantee of work, full time or part time, almost all families of four have at least one member who can do some work. This work can be in the home if necessary. Hence almost all will be able to supplement the social benefit by at least a few thousand dollars. On the other hand, we should point out that the way we proposed to deal with government employment of last resort was contingent on the social dividend. Given that basic security, these government jobs can be conceived as supplementary income rather than living wages. Furthermore, since this benefit will not be tied to where one lives, families unable to work can move to rural areas where rent is cheaper and there is more opportunity to grow some of one's own food.

3. *Any system of guaranteed income combined with a high tax on earned income will lead to some deciding to live off the dole without seeking work.* No doubt this is true. Our expectation is that this tendency would be measurably reduced among those now receiving assistance by the reduced disincentive to earn more and the guarantee that such earning is possible. But there are persons who might otherwise be middle class who will also now have this opportunity. Some students who now have part-time jobs might go to school full-time. A few with artistic inclinations may be freed from the necessity of earning money to devote themselves to their true vocation, in the proverbial garret. A few idealists may give their time to causes as full-time volunteers. And some may simply live indolent, if frugal, lives. Our judgment is that society has little to fear—and something to gain—from these decisions. At present there are not enough jobs for all who want them. The withdrawal of a few from competition for these will not damage society. For students to be relieved of some financial pressure while attending college will be to society's benefit in the long run. Artistic and idealistic endeavors will, on

the whole, benefit everyone. And even the loafers will at least consume less of society's scarce resources.

4. *The high marginal rate of taxes—50% of all earned income—discourages additional work.* Referring to a situation in which the marginal tax rate is only 45%, Davies writes: "Under these conditions, opportunities for overtime or moonlighting are foregone, retirement may come at an earlier age, more sick leaves and absenteeism occur, vacation and time between jobs become longer" (Davies 1986, p. 7). We do not understand about sick leaves and absenteeism, but the rest is plausible. Is it damaging?[1] Davies' objection, like that of many economists, is that it reduces economic growth. But if less work by some who choose to work less makes room for work by some who are otherwise unemployed, the total product is not reduced and the crucial problem of unemployment is alleviated.

Indeed, there are ironies in the current economic literature on taxes, incentives, and unemployment. In the discussion on taxes, as above, the emphasis is often on the disincentive they involve for working overtime or for a second member of a family taking a job. In the literature on unemployment the issue is the lack of jobs and the importance of business generating more of them. One way to create more jobs, of course, is for those who have them to work fewer hours. But that would require cutting the pie into smaller pieces and workers, it is objected, do not want to sacrifice income for shorter hours.

5. *The new program would fall short of the present social security program for some of those whom it covers.* This is the most serious problem we can see with these proposals. It means that the present pattern cannot be simply abandoned overnight without breaking commitments. We do not advocate that. No retiree's current income should be reduced.

This does not warrant continuing the present program indefinitely. There are notorious problems. There is an inherent confusion in this program between its welfare aspects and its role as a retirement plan. The social dividends (negative income tax payments) are directed to deal only with the former of these two roles. We have advocated private retirement programs. But if one believes that there should be a community interest in retirement the dual function of social security could be

1. The most thorough study of the extent to which various systems of guaranteed income and tax on earnings would affect the incentives to work is in Philip K. Robins, Robert G. Speigelman, Samuel Wiener, and Joseph G. Bell, *A Guaranteed Annual Income* (1980).

served by the social dividend. Dividends were kept low to avoid reducing the incentive to earn additional money. But there is no reason to maintain that incentive beyond a certain age, say 65. Since possibilities of working and reasons to encourage work are severely diminished by then in most cases, a higher social dividend payment is feasible.[2] Payments could rise at retirement from $3,000 to $4,500. At this rate the social dividend would cover more of the benefits of the old. During a transition period adjustments could be made to fulfill moral obligations to those who would lose.

6. *Our proposals are insufficiently paternalistic. Many people are unable to manage money responsibly, so giving them money does not help. They need assistance in kind: food stamps, housing, and so on.*

Undoubtedly this too is true for some people, but we think they are not "many." We would also err on the side of expecting too much from people than on the side of underestimating their ability to care for themselves. The judgment of incompetence would be made only in the courts, which would then, in cooperation with state or local government, provide alternate means of insuring that the social benefit be used to meet basic needs.

7. *Major reliance on income tax both for welfare and for tax purposes leaves unsolved the problems of tax evasion and avoidance.* Although this problem would not be new, we acknowledge its importance. Taxes need to be certain as well as equitable, simple, and economical. We believe that the system we propose will make tax evasion much more difficult. The remaining loopholes would be in the complex interconnection between individual income and corporate income. In the next section we offer our proposals for dealing with that. But tax avoidance is a more difficult matter. The underground economy is estimated by the Congressional Research Service to have grown in current dollars from 13.4 billion dollars in 1950 to 264.5 billion dollars in 1978 (Rabushka 1985, p. 191). This was less than 5% of the GNP in 1950 but around 12% in 1978. If it continues to grow it can undermine the integrity of the entire system whether in its present form or in the one we propose. We regard it as a matter of high priority to contain and reduce this side of the economy. We believe that a major reason for opting out of the formal economy and living "off the books" is precisely the breakdown of community

2. The same logic would apply to younger persons who are mentally or physically incapable of work, although the first effort should be to find work they are capable of performing.

experienced in the formal economy. All of our community-enhancing proposals should diminish the retreat to the informal economy.[3]

We are not utopian and do not expect a perfect tax system. There will always be some inequity and some cheating. There will always be cases of hardship that are not fairly addressed. No system written for general application can avoid these limitations. We believe, nevertheless, that the income tax system proposed here would do better than the present system in meeting most basic human needs, retaining the incentive to work, and reducing the exaggerated spread of income between the rich and the poor.

Other National Taxes

We do not believe that it would be healthy or wise to rely on only one type of tax at the national level. To raise sufficient revenue to meet all needs by the income tax alone would force tax rates much too high. The objections raised to our proposed 50% rate would have increasing force. The underground economy might get out of hand. There needs to be flexibility to adjust the income tax downward to reduce these tendencies while raising other taxes to cover the income lost.

Traditionally one of the taxes that has been balanced against personal income taxes has been the corporate income tax. But we believe this to have been a mistake. Its distortion of rational market decisions is critical, as well as its provision of opportunities to evade personal income taxes. Drastic simplification and standardization would help. But there is another, much better, solution. The corporate income tax should be abolished. In this we agree with Irving Kristol (1980, p. 28), Norman Ture (1981, p. 28), Martin Feldstein (1981, p. 24), and Lester Thurow (1981, pp. 97–101). They are correct, and their recommendations should be followed. Many distortions in present business decision making would be reduced or ended.

We would accompany the cessation of this tax with the requirement that corporate profits be distributed to stockholders as income. There would be no double taxation here, but these profits would be taxed as part of the income of the stockholders. This addition to the individual

3. Martha N. Ozawa proposes a program of income maintenance somewhat more complex than ours and relying less on income testing. It is an example of a legitimate option for meeting the need. See chapter 8 in *Income Maintenance and Work Incentives* (1982).

income tax revenue would probably more than compensate for losses from the corporate income tax. In any case, it would shift away from internal financing of new investment out of retained earning of corporations to competition in the capital market for investment funds. This is a more arms-length transaction in which harder questions are likely to be asked about the viability of the proposed expansion.

While abolishing the corporate income tax, we would continue gift and inheritance taxes. Since it is our policy that no one type of tax be used at more than one governmental level, the national tax on gifts and inheritance should be increased to cover what has in the past been taken by states. As a matter of social policy, for redistributive effect, it should be increased more than that.

Tariffs are currently a minor source of federal income. Our proposal in Chapters 11 and 15 to use tariffs as a major means of encouraging a more self-sufficient national economy would make them a much larger factor in the total situation. This would also make them a larger source of revenue. However, there is a conflict between the protective and revenue-raising functions of the tariff. A prohibitive tariff, one so high that it stops all imports of a good, will raise no revenue. But most tariffs will be set at nonprohibitive levels in the interest of maintaining competitive pressures on domestic firms, as well as in the interest of gaining revenue for the government.

We have proposed two new sources of revenue for the federal government: the pollution tax and the auctioning of depletion quotas (or its close substitute, a severance tax). These have been discussed in earlier chapters as means of encouraging efficient reduction of pollution and controlling the scale of the economy. The sale of depletion quotas functions in terms of revenue as a severance tax, and for simplicity we will speak of it in that way in this chapter.

In Chapter 12 the severance tax was discussed as a means of limiting the use of nonrenewable resources. Our proposal here is that it should apply to such renewable resources as timber as well, so that it can help to determine the total scale of the economy. Land, including all natural resources, is the scarce factor of production in the long run. With the historical demise of the landlord class, the tendency has been to sacrifice resource prices and productivity. By taxing resources, the government performs the landlord's historical role of protecting resources, only now the unearned income—rent—will be public revenue. The incentive will be toward more resource-saving, labor-using patterns of production and consumption. Holding down the scale of the throughput reduces pollution as well as depletion. We would be taxing what we want less of.

Although we urge the severance tax first and foremost because it will help to limit the physical scale of the economy relative to the ecosystem, we believe it can also be an important source of revenue. As a source of revenue it has definite advantages. Unlike the income tax, the severance tax is very hard to avoid. Like a sales tax, it will automatically be included in the price of all commodities using the resource. Since the tax will be levied on all basic resources, and since all commodities require some resources, that means all commodity prices will embody the tax. The only point at which the tax could be avoided is at the point at which it is levied, namely at the wellhead or mine-mouth for nonrenewable resources. These are very restricted points of entry and would be easy to monitor. Renewable resources from forests and farms would not be as easy to monitor, but the difficulty would still be less than with a general sales tax.

It has been argued by some that not much revenue can be gained from a severance tax because resources account for only about 5% of GNP, while wages account for 80%. This means that to raise the same amount of revenue a much higher tax rate would have to be applied to resources than to income. This is obviously true, but it could still be done. Nevertheless our proposal is to rely on both severance and income taxes. By gradual trial and error we could move toward a system that relied mainly on the income tax (negative portion) to achieve equity, and on the severance tax to raise revenue and keep the physical scale of the economy within ecological carrying capacity.

Alongside the severance tax should be the pollution tax. We have repeatedly discussed the importance of internalizing social and environmental costs, as well as the limitations of this approach to dealing with pollution. It must be supplemented by direct action to limit the scale of the economy in relation to the ecosphere. But as a complement to such action, internalization promotes equity in that consumers will then pay the real costs of what they buy rather than passing on much of it to society at large. It can also lead to adoption of the most efficient means of reducing pollution within the given scale of the economy. Hence we propose that economists work out as full and fair a system of pollution taxes as possible, internalizing in the price of goods the cost of their ultimate disposal as well as the social and environmental cost of their use.

Each tax has its problems. The income tax encourages growth of the underground economy. The severance tax, like a sales tax, is regressive in that it falls most heavily on those who must spend most of their income. The pollution tax is complex, and pollution is difficult to monitor accurately. We recognize this and regret that on balance our proposals do not greatly simplify the existing tax structure. Justice and efficiency demand something like the system we have advocated. But since administrative capacity is in itself a scarce resource we are eager to find simplifications.

We would like to reduce federal taxes considerably, and believe that the policies proposed in this book can lead to that end. But we do not favor continuing the astronomical build-up of the national debt that has so far been the most obvious result of tax reductions! The budget must be balanced, including debt servicing, and this balancing should not be at the expense of the poor. Beyond balancing the budget a second priority should be debt reduction. If we are in community with our children and grandchildren we have no right to bequeath to them a heavy burden that will be more difficult for them to handle than for us. This will require sacrifice. The sacrifice is not due to the policies advocated in this book but to the profligate borrowing and spending of the past decade. Once the national debt is substantially reduced, taxes should be lowered.

State and Local Taxes

This book recommends decentralizing the economy and shifting economic as well as political power to the states. Yet in discussing how to meet the basic needs of all citizens and how to finance this, only a national program has been proposed. There is a tension here. We are proposing tax policies that could be implemented now, whereas we are envisioning other policies that would lead to gradual decentralization of the economy. At some point in that process, we would shift primary responsibility for welfare to the states along with the income tax itself. Also at some point severance and pollution taxes might be shifted to the states. But as long as labor and capital are highly mobile, only a national program can be effective. The first step now is to gain control of the economy at the national level.

But even now there can be some increase of responsibility at the state level. We suggest that responsibility for education, health, safety, agriculture, and highways all be located fully at the state level. The same would be true of all welfare programs beyond the social dividend (negative income tax). These might include aid to those not able to work, and to those with disabilities requiring special expenses not covered by health insurance. Child care programs may be needed to enable single mothers to work. There should be special programs for alcoholics and drug addicts. We propose that states implement these matters.

As part of our aim to make the tax structure equitable, simple, and economical, we propose to avoid duplication between federal and state taxes. That means that states should not tax income, gifts, estates, severances, or pollution. That could reduce state revenues severely; so we must consider how that reduction can be avoided.

At present the single greatest source of state income is the sales tax. That should continue to be the sole prerogative of the state. Closely related to the sales tax is the excise tax, which we eliminated at the federal level. States could considerably increase their excise taxes so as to capture what formerly was federal revenue. Unlike sales taxes, whose only justification is income, excise taxes can play a socially beneficial role as well by reducing the use of harmful commodities such as tobacco. Wherever possible revenues should be tied to such positive social functions, even though success in reducing tobacco consumption will beyond some point also reduce revenue from the tax on tobacco.

A special tax of considerable importance to both states and the federal government at this time is the gasoline tax. The federal tax on gasoline at the pump would be discontinued, but there would be a severance tax and pollution taxes that would raise the price of petroleum. It might seem double jeopardy to tax gasoline again when it is sold. However, the purpose of the gasoline tax is to make users pay for the transportation system that is built and operated for them. If the states take over the full responsibility for highways, they will certainly need to tax gasoline to capture both what they have been collecting and what the federal government has taken.

In addition there are social and economic reasons to discourage the use of private transportation as it competes with other uses of the diminishing supply of oil. Most countries recognize this and place a much higher tax on gasoline than is done in the United States. We recommend that state taxes on gasoline rise to at least $1 a gallon. This would enable states to recover much of the revenue lost by the abandonment of income, gift, and estate taxes.

We believe a combination of sales taxes, excise taxes, and gasoline taxes would suffice. If not, we recommend as a last resort a value-added tax (VAT). This is a tax on the value added to commodities by labor as they are processed at each step of their production. This tax is virtually universal in Europe. As long as it is not complicated by exemptions and differentials, it is equitable and hard to avoid. Rates in Europe range from 6% to 20%, indicating that, according to the amount needed, it can be adjusted. The reason for treating VAT as a last resort is that we prefer to tax things we want less of, other things equal, such as depletion and pollution. Value added (labor, jobs) is something we generally want more of. Since labor is such a large part of the value of total product it is hard not to tax it, and indeed we have advocated an income tax system that taxes labor rather heavily. Taxing labor income tends to reduce the supply of labor; taxing labor as a factor of production tends to reduce demand for labor (supply of jobs). The latter incentive works against full employment, and we would like to avoid it.

This division between federal and state taxes leaves the property tax to cities, counties, and other local taxing authorities. This is their present mainstay, but limits on property taxes have encouraged duplication of other tax sources such as sales and even income taxes. The property tax should be virtually the only tax levied at the local level.

The problem is that taxing buildings as property discourages construction and improvements. The owner pays first for the construction and improvement and then again for having made this socially beneficial investment (Rybeck and Pasguariello 1987, pp. 470–72). Hence the taxation to maintain services and for education inhibits the development and maintenance of the city. Many areas in the older cities are in decay or are virtually abandoned at least in part because of the tax structure.

Several economists, including especially Henry George and his followers, have called for differentiated treatment of land and buildings in property taxation. Whereas a higher tax on buildings encourages holding land unused or allowing buildings to deteriorate, a higher tax on land encourages efficient use of the property. Although the point has often been made, and in other parts of the world such as Australia and New Zealand it has influenced the tax structure, little application has been made of this principle in the United States. Recently, however, the idea has again come into serious discussion. A model law encouraging this tax reform has been drawn up by the American Legislative Exchange Council and published in the 1987–88 *Source Book of American State Legislation*. The *New York Times* has repeatedly editorialized in favor of this approach.[4] Several cities, including Pittsburgh, have put it into effect. The results have been impressive.

None of these cities has abolished the tax on buildings. Chiefly they

4. *New York Times,* May 13, July 23, September 26, October 24, November 15, 1983; January 30, July 10, 1984.

have simply raised the taxes on land and lowered those on buildings. In Pittsburgh, city taxes on land were raised to 12.55% while leaving the tax on buildings at 2.475%. Since county and school taxes were not adjusted, the actual relation of the two rates was about three to one. This was sufficient to precipitate a major building program in the city. It also brought additional funds into the city treasury (see *Fortune* 1983). Although no one-to-one correlation is possible between the land tax and other factors in the city's life, it is striking that a recent survey identifies Pittsburgh as the nation's most livable city, and that comparisons of housing prices show them to be the lowest of any major city in the United States.

There is a lesson in this for all local taxation. Land should be taxed at a higher rate than improvements. A similar principle guided our recommendation that agricultural land be taxed on its unimproved value, not on its increased value resulting from regenerative farming practices. Just what difference in rate is required to encourage improvements cannot yet be stated, but the experience of Pittsburgh and other Pennsylvania cities suggests that even a two-to-one ratio gets results.

Henry George believed that a tax on land near its rental value would bring in sufficient revenue to meet the needs of all levels of government. This is no longer true, if indeed it ever was. But even a reduced version of this tax would meet all local needs by capturing much of the gain from rising land values. To put this land tax in local hands, is, therefore, to free localities from depending on state and federal financial help and the accompanying control. To strengthen local community is one of the aims of economics for community.

Local governments could use their new resources in imaginative ways. The rebuilding of decaying cities, encouraged by the land tax itself, could also be furthered with the funds it raises. Cities could give major assistance to workers in moving to worker-ownership of business. Should the social advantages of a high land tax prove themselves on a long-term basis, local governments could take over some state functions and also transmit to the state treasury sufficient funds to avoid a value-added tax and reduce the sales tax. The aim of building larger levels of society from smaller ones could be expressed in such a tax structure.

Concluding Comments

In the above discussion of taxes at the national, state, and local levels, nothing has been said of users fees. These are legitimate and desirable. If certain services are performed by government but benefit only certain segments of society it is proper that they be paid for by the user at their true cost. Current governmental services should be reviewed at all levels with a view to expanding users fees. Where governmental services could be performed equally well by the private sector, government should withdraw from the activity in question.

In the ideal scheme all the means of raising public funds would also function as means of attaining public goals. Income, gift, and inheritance taxes would be retained for their redistributive effects. Taxes designed to internalize costs would become a large element in this ideal system. Tariffs would insure national control of the national economy. The auctioning of rights to mine or severance taxes on the use of scarce resources could set a scale for the economy as a whole. Excise and gasoline taxes would discourage use of harmful substances or make scarce resources available for more primary and production needs. The land tax would end speculation in land, encourage socially beneficial use, and recover for the community unearned profits. Users fees would cover the costs of the services provided.

We believe that a healthy community requires healthy business. We also believe that it requires that the gap between the poor and the wealthy not be too extreme. For those reasons we have devised tax policies that are pro-business and anti-accumulation of great private wealth.

They are pro-business in that tariffs support United States business against international competition. Corporate income taxes and employee taxes are abolished. If the land tax allows the abolition of taxes on buildings, equipment, and inventories, then corporate taxes will be still further simplified. It is true that we introduce new taxes such as pollution taxes and severance taxes and we increase taxes on land, but these should not be an impediment to business. The taxes to internalize externalities would be accompanied by a decrease in government regulations. Severance taxes would increase resource productivity. And the land tax will encourage efficient use of space.

The proposed policies are intended to work against the rapid accumulation of wealth in that they would tax away nearly half of the income from accumulated wealth as well as of its appreciation. This would not necessarily prevent the rich from growing richer, but it would at least slow the pace. Gift and inheritance taxes would reduce the accumulation between generations.

One of us once proposed that there be a limited range of acceptable inequality of income. The suggested ratio was one-to-ten—that the richest not have more than ten times the income of the poorest. That would mean that if the poorest family of four had $9,000, the rich should not be allowed to keep more than $90,000. That would require confiscatory taxation. We think that eventually a healthy community might evolve in which a notion of this sort was politically acceptable. Indeed it seems to us that *unlimited* inequality contradicts the very notion of community. It also seems to us that limits to aggregate growth plus a minimum income will implicitly determine a limited amount left over after all had received the minimum. Even if the total left over went to a single individual, that would still be an implicit maximum. A maximum consistent with more widespread distribution of the surplus would in our view be desirable. We do not propose a maximum income in this book, but we do advocate heavy taxes on large incomes. We hope that over the years a combination of income and inheritance taxes, on the one hand, and social dividends, worker ownership of business, and guaranteed employment on the other, will reduce the spread of incomes from their present exaggerated range. The goal for an economics of community is not equality, but limited inequality. Complete equality is the collectivist's denial of true differences in community. Unlimited inequality is the individualist's denial of interdependence and true solidarity in community. The principle of limited inequality as a condition of community is no modern insight. It is explicit in biblical accounts of the laws of the ancient Hebrews governing landholding, usury, the Sabbath, the jubilee year, and also in the wisdom literature of Proverbs and Psalms. Even the manna that fell from heaven spoiled if accumulated in excess. We get no instruction regarding the proper numerical range of permissible inequality, but on the principle itself the biblical teachings are clear.

18

From World Domination
to National Security

The Meaning of National Security

Neoclassical economics stands in a double relation to national security. First, it aims at maximum economic growth, which involves ever more advanced technology and managerial skills. Success here builds the industrial base that can produce more and more complex armaments in larger numbers. Indeed, the usual measure of economic success, the GNP, largely evolved in World War II to measure the nation's capacity for warfare.

But second, neoclassical economics is inherently nonnational in its outlook. It sees individual persons and firms as the units of economic activity and seeks the largest possible market as the theater of activity. Any structure smaller than the market, including nation-states, is likely to be an impediment or hindrance. Hence this economic theory and practice seek to obliterate national boundaries as much as possible. In this respect they are antithetical to national security interests.

An economics for community works in just the opposite way. It aims at sufficiency of goods for the sake of the community's well-being, and not at the endless growth of production and consumption. The sufficiency sought must take account of the community's need for security, but proponents of this way of thinking are disinclined to identify security with quantity of arms and their technological sophistication.

On the other side, an economics for community is committed to serving the national well-being. It sees that well-being in comprehensive ways, and security is a prominent part thereof. This means that while neoclassical economics will encourage the nation to specialize in what it can produce most efficiently, whatever that proves to be, economics for community is concerned that the nation not depend on others for its necessities, that it be, not autarkic, but self-sufficient in necessities. There can be little doubt that a nation that has not achieved such self-sufficiency is less secure.

There are other dimensions of security important to an economics for community. In *The Twenty-ninth Day*, Lester Brown opened a fresh discussion of the meaning of national security. In common usage the term has become almost synonymous with military capability. But Brown shows how fallacious that identification is. "The contemporary focus of government on military threats to security may not only exclude attention to the newer threats, but may also make the effective address of the latter more difficult" (Brown 1978, p. 295).

What are the greatest threats to the security of the United States? One is environmental: the erosion of its soil, the pollution of its air and water, the extinction of species, the poisoning of the land by chemicals and nuclear waste, and the combined threat of ozone depletion and the greenhouse effect. Of course, most of these are threats to other nations as well, especially Third World nations, but that does not prevent them from being threats to the security of the United States.

A second is the decline of national morale. Nations collapse from a lack of will to do what is needed to survive as often as they do from conquest. The increase of drug abuse and alcoholism, the continuing rise of crime, the decay of the family and community institutions, the decline in the quality of education, lessening participation in political processes, and rampant consumerism bode ill for the future.

A third threat to national security is economic decline. Harold Brown recognized the importance of this factor. "The national security of the United States will in the end depend on whether the industrialized democracies are able to sustain their military, political, and economic strength, postponing present consumption as necessary, even during difficult ecoomic times. Failure to carry through such a program is a sure recipe for deep decline" (Brown 1983, p. xiii). We have pointed out earlier that the United States has moved swiftly from the position of the world's greatest creditor to that of the world's greatest debtor. Its assets are being sold rapidly. Meanwhile it continues to borrow heavily abroad. Increasingly, it will not be able to make its own decisions about its economy. The day may not be far off when creditors will make more overt and visible demands. The annual expenditure of three hundred billion dollars for "defense" contributes to the decline.

There is nothing eccentric in pointing to the importance of these matters for national security. Franklin P. Huddle, who directed the massive congressional study, *Science, Technology, and American Diplomacy*, wrote as follows: "National security requires a stable economy with assured supplies of material for industry. In this sense frugality and conservation of materials are essential to our national security. Security means more than safety from hostile attack: it includes the preservation of a system of civlization" (Huddle 1976, p. 658). Also, President Jimmy Carter stated: "It is likely in the near future that issues of war and peace will be more a function of economic and social problems than of the military-security problems which have dominated international relations since World War II" (Barnet 1981, p. 4).

A fourth threat to security is a nation's loss of control over its borders. This is usually thought of as a nation's inability to defend itself against military invasion. But an inability to enforce immigration law also constitutes a loss of control. A nation may decide to have generous or restrictive immigration laws. In Chapter 12 we advocated rather liberal laws, especially as long as our own policies force people in nearby lands to flee their homes. On the other hand, now that the Cold War has ended, those parts of our immigration policy that were designed to aid those who fled Communist countries could well be changed, reducing legal immigration.

In any case, whatever these laws are, they should be enforced. Turning a blind eye to illegal immigration is unfair not only to citizens who democratically enacted the laws, but also to actual and prospective legal immigrants who go to great trouble and often wait a long time in order to comply with our laws. To reduce immigration requires action on two fronts. First, the incentive to immigrate should be reduced. This means that employment opportunities and social services for illegal immigrants should be reduced. This can be accomplished by strictly enforcing existing laws. Requiring prospective employers to check job applicants with Systematic Alien Verification for Entitlements (SAVE) would help.

Second, the border must be more tightly policed. Although this could be done by other agencies, it would also be an appropriate function for military forces. Part of our military establishment could be redeployed to border patrol. Obviously this does not require nuclear weapons and rockets, but it would require officers and equipment.

One reason a blind eye is turned toward illegal immigration is sympathy for the plight of individuals whose economic or political circumstances are so bad that they are driven to leave their homeland. Another reason is that there are powerful groups in our country who benefit from the availability of cheap labor. It is rather awkward for them to come out in favor of cheap labor in open political debate about what the legal immigration quotas should be; so lax enforcement is a convenient substitute. Illegal immigrants work for lower wages than legal immigrants, often for less than minimum wage.

In arguing against reducing illegal immigration, some people raise the specter of a labor shortage and advocate greater immigration as the cure. A labor shortage with simultaneous unemployment and falling real wages is a bit hard to understand, but, more fundamentally, a real labor shortage would, in our opinion, be a very good thing. It would result in rising wages, which would mean a better income for the vast majority of our citizens. Of course, "international competitiveness" might suffer, but what are we competing for if not a better life for the majority of our citizens? Logically, free immigration, whether *de jure* or *de facto* would lead to the same low wage outcome as free trade with free capital mobility, as discussed in Chapter 11.

Since our whole approach in this book has been "nationalist," in the sense described in the introduction, we have no hesitation in opposing free or easy immigration, or in accepting the military or police action necessary to enforce immigration laws. To some this will appear hard-hearted and exclusionary.[1] We can understand that reaction, and we certainly do not rejoice in the likely prospect of turning away needy people, probably very many of them, until the difficulty of entering the country illegally and of finding work became generally known. But the policies for improvement suggested in this book presuppose a national authority to carry them out, even policies of international cooperation or of devolution of responsibility to a more local level. The whole nationalist approach to economic development (the only viable one, we think) is undercut to the extent that national boundaries become permeable to the free flow of either capital or people.

In general, this nation has a prior duty to help its own citizens, many of whom are in very bad shape, before it tries to solve the problems of other nations. This is true even if Americans feel in some degree historically responsible for other nations' suffering (due often to the failures of

---

1. Although the leadership of the Latino community in the United States usually opposes enforcement efforts, this does not necessarily reflect the interests or the views of most of the Latino population. In the recent Latino National Political survey, "from 66 to 79 percent of the various Hispanic groups agreed or strongly agreed with the statement, 'There are too many immigrants'" (CCN/Clearinghouse Bulletin 2/93, p. 3). This view was shared by noncitizens.

past efforts to solve their problems). The reason is that a nation's capacity to solve other people's problems is generally less than its capacity to solve its own, and even the latter is now seriously overburdened. The United States may elect as a nation to help certain foreigners ahead of its own citizens in certain circumstances. However, such a policy should bear the burden of proof and include the participation of the poor citizens whose needs are being put in second place.

Equally important, opening American doors to large numbers of economic refugees from other countries does not really help in the long run. It does improve the lot of many of those who enter the country illegally. But Virginia D. Abernethy shows that "immigration in a too-crowded world is a zero-sum game" (1993a, p. 296). The gains of some are matched by the losses of others. Furthermore, she argues convincingly that the perceived possibility of some children migrating increases the number of children parents in overpopulated areas choose to have. Thus, opening doors to immigrants increases global population and slows the transition to sustainability in the countries from which the immigrants come. The United States is not helping Third World countries with excessive population growth by admitting their citizens, either legally or illegally. Once the error of the theory of "demographic transition" brought about by modernization, urbanization, and economic growth is acknowledged, the public will recognize that families have, in general, the number of children they believe they can afford and who will constitute an economic benefit. This recognition will lead to radical rethinking of programs of "economic aid" as well as immigration policies (Abernethy 1993b).

Military Expenditures and National Security

Lester Brown states cautiously that the focus on military threats "may" make the response to other threats less effective. There are those, such as John Kenneth Galbraith, who have argued that in the economic realm large government expenditures of this sort actually have beneficial results.[2] They pump funds into the economy and justify large government expenditures in the scientific and technological research that is so important for economic growth.

2. Galbraith did not think these expenditures added much to military security. "I have little faith in the safety or security which derives from a never ending arms race—from a competition to elaborate ever more agonizing weapons to counter those of the enemy" (1958, p. 353).

Galbraith wrote this when American affluence and industrial power seemed assured. Since then, its decline, at least relative to other nations, has been marked. The causes of the decline were studied by the Council on Economic Priorities. Its conclusion was that Galbraith's thesis does not apply, at least not to the recent situation. Military research now has few commercial spinoffs. Also, the huge military requirements draw off from the private sector much of the talent it needs, as Seymour Melman has been persuasively arguing for many years (1965; 1974). According to Melman it should come as no surprise that Japanese and German products are by and large now superior to their American counterparts. Forbidden to make weapons, Japan and Germany have devoted the efforts of their best technical talent to consumer goods, whereas 75% of research in the United States has been military related. The resulting qualitative edge is a big reason for the U.S. trade deficit. And, finally, if the economy is helped by pumping into it large sums of money, it would be helped more if this money went into construction or education (De Grasse 1983).

Lester Brown's cautious statement of concern about the consequences of focusing on military threats was certainly understated for environmental matters. His more recent writings on the subject have been far more forceful (Brown 1986). Huge military expenditures necessarily speed the exhaustion of resources and add to the problems of pollution. If it is now also clear that they cause a decline in the economy, should they be drastically reduced?

There can be no doubt that one function of military expenditure is to respond to domestic pressures and demands. Some observers believe that this is its main function. Confirmation of this comes from the slow pace at which military spending has been reduced since the collapse of the Soviet empire, the demise of the one major military threat to the United States and its allies. Many of the arguments for continuing a high level of expenditures are obviously economic.

Some argue, on the other hand, that during the 1980's the U.S. military buildup *was* required as a realistic response to the danger of Soviet aggression. This nation and others to whose defense it was committed, in this view, were genuinely threatened militarily in such a way that vast armaments were needed for defense. The question whether during the Cold War expenditures were tied chiefly to domestic or to security considerations remains important as we evaluate proposals for the future.

A careful study of this question was carried out by Miroslav Nincic. He showed that American expenditures in arms correlated more often with domestic developments than with acts of the Soviet Union. But he recognized that there were real threats from the Soviet Union intertwined with the arms race itself. "It should . . . be stressed at this point that it would be unwise to slight the role of the mutual hostility that links the superpowers by placing too exclusive an emphasis on internal dynamics. The resulting fear and distrust force each side to be attentive to movements by the other; they proved an authentically perceived need for increased military capacity as well as a convenient justification for indulging domestic interests. In this fashion, moreover, the external and internal context of the arms race is connected by an obvious feedback loop" (Nincic 1982, p. 196).

More recently Hector Correa and Ji Won Kim have undertaken a statistical analysis of the same topic. They conclude that military expenditures by the United States are chiefly affected by inertia and national politics. Spending by the U.S.S.R. also reflected inertia but it was influenced by relations with the U.S. as well (Correa and Kim 1992, pp. 161–175). As late as November 1992, General Gennady Filatov, Chief of the Russian Defense Forces, commented: "I can't say we don't need to prepare for nuclear war . . . Everywhere, I see the power, the might, of America. And when Russia says, 'Let's stop testing nuclear weapons,' you keep going. We say, 'Stop testing SDI,' and you keep going . . . That's why we can't just throw everything away." [The Defense Monitor, vol. 22, no. 1 (1993): 4].

Even if during the Cold War military expenditures were far greater than was needed to defend ourselves and our allies, it can be argued that the policy of massive build-up during the Reagan administration deserves much of the credit for the dismantling of the Soviet threat. It is reasoned that this build-up forced the Soviet Union into an arms race it could not afford and that this contributed to its economic collapse. Hence, military expenditures were justified as an instrument of foreign policy that brought an end to the Cold War and its accompanying dangers.

There may be some truth to this claim, but much less than defenders of the huge U.S. military expenditures imply. Glen Stassen replies to this claim as follows: "According to regular CIA publications on military expenditures, the Soviet Union, which had been increasing its military spending by about *three* percent per year *totally independent of U.S. increases or decreases*, began gradually slowing its spending during the Carter and Reagan years down to two and then one and finally a negative percentage as its economy weakened" (1992, p. 402).

Perhaps the Soviet Union would have reduced its spending much more rapidly had it not faced the massive U.S. build-up of the Reagan years, and perhaps that would have enabled it to deal better with its economic problems. This is mere speculation. The evidence is strong that internal political and economic pressures played a larger role than actual military threats in the military spending of both the U.S. and the U.S.S.R.

Meanwhile, there can be no doubt that the Cold War constituted an enormous threat to the security of all countries. This is not only because of the danger of its turning into a hot war with unprecedented destruction all over the planet. It is also because the confrontation of NATO and Warsaw Pact forces in Europe drained planetary resources. It involved "a total of twelve million men in arms and consume{d} about $600 billion a year, or two-thirds of the world's annual expenditure for armed forces" (Dean and Clausen 1988, p. 1).

Furthermore, the social and economic losses of the United States have been enormous. As early as 1965 Seymour Melman described how the process of deterioration had begun; clearly it has gone much further in subsequent decades.

The United States now is the scene of a drama different from that implicit in her confident ideology. A process of technical, industrial, and human deterioration has been set in motion within American society. The competence of the industrial system is being eroded at its base. Entire industries are falling into technical disrepair, and there is massive loss of productive employment because of inability to hold even domestic markets against foreign competition. Such depletion in economic life produces wide-ranging human deterioration at home. The wealthiest nation on earth has been unable to rally the resources necessary to raise one fifth of its own people from poverty. [Melman 1965, p. 1]

Even if the primary concern about national security is the actual effectiveness of our military forces, other considerations will loom larger than the quantity of expenditures. James Fallows shows that much more careful assessment of what constitutes strength is needed. He sees in-house testing of weapons systems as a major source of insecurity. This is combined with a bias toward complex weapons systems unlikely to be effective except in "narrowly specified conditions" (Fallows 1982, p. 173). He recommends cheaper and simpler weapons.

The most important need, Fallows argues, "is the one most likely to be overlooked, since it lies in the realm of values and character, rather than quantities that can be represented on charts. Before anything else, we must recognize that a functioning military requires bonds of trust, sacrifice, and respect within its ranks, and similar bonds of support between an army and the nation it represents" (pp. 171–72). Military security, too, requires healthy community! The major obstacles to such community within the military are what Fallows sees as "the culture of procurement" and "the careerist ethic" (p. 172). To restore community between the military and the wider society, he recommends reinstating the draft, with the opportunity for conscientious objectors to perform alternate service.

Although we have not studied the situation sufficiently to make independent judgments, we find Fallows's analysis credible, especially in light of recent cases of treason in the U.S. Navy. If our sense of community is so atrophied and the cult of total individualism so hypertrophied that military officers sell secrets to the highest bidder, then our own advances in weaponry threaten us as much as they threaten an "enemy!" If one grows up observing routine 500% cost overruns on military contracts for weapons that are not needed in the first place, then perhaps it is not such a big step to sell directly to the enemy. It is just another way for the individual to line his or her pockets at the expense of the community.

In any case, preoccupation with armed response to massive external challenges has blinded the nation to more probable threats. The United States has developed into a highly centralized society that could be virtually halted in its tracks by a few relatively small acts of sabotage. For example, the electrical grid on which the whole nation depends could be put out of commission by a few well-placed bombs. A blackout would not stop the planes in the air or the tanks in the field, but the backup systems of communication, supply, and management would be disastrously disrupted. Yet defense planning pays little attention to these matters. Decentralized energy production with increasing local dependence on small-scale solar plants would do far more to reduce real national insecurity than additional billions spent on bombs and submarines.

This issue was thoroughly considered by Hunter and Amory B. Lovins, who summarize the dangers as follows.

The United States has reached the point where:
- a few people could probably black out most of the country;
- a small group could shut off three-fourths of the natural gas to the eastern U.S. in one evening without leaving Louisiana;

- a terrorist squad could seriously disrupt much of the oil supply to the nation or even to the world;
- one saboteur could incinerate a city by attacking certain natural gas systems;
- a few people (perhaps just one person) could release enough radioactivity to make much of the U.S. uninhabitable.
- a single hydrogen bomb could probably do *all* these things simultaneously. [Lovins and Lovins 1982, pp. 1–2]

The situation is analogous to that of the Maginot line. Enormous expenditures are made on powerful weapons, yet an enemy could bypass them and incapacitate the nation. A much more careful assessment of real dangers is needed.

Military Needs after the Cold War

The end of any imminent threat from another superpower does not mean that there are no longer any missions for armed services to perform. Complete disarmament is not the appropriate response. Nevertheless, the changed global situation is an occasion for fundamentally rethinking national security needs. We have argued that even during the Cold War our expenditures were excessive so far as military security was concerned and that they reduced the nation's real security. It was the special economic interests within the nation that determined the level of spending more than any real external threat. Now that much of this spending continues without the excuse provided by the Cold War, the importance of domestic considerations has become obvious. In this section we consider the continuing real needs for military power. In the next section we discuss the effects on the domestic economy of the drastic downsizing of military expenditures that would be, militarily speaking, the appropriate response to the changed world situation.

Three military reasons are commonly offered in support of continuing large military expenditures. First, many believe that significant external threats to the United States and its allies still exist. Second, some propose that it is important for the United States to maintain the security of supply lines around the world for the sake of the global economy. Third, some argue that the nation has an important ongoing role in policing the world. We will examine these three arguments.

(1) Although the breakup of the Soviet empire has greatly reduced its threat to our security, there are still powerful armaments under Russian control. The present leadership of Russia shows no signs of aggressive

intent, but the situation is far from stable. A counterrevolution or palace coup could reinstate leaders who would threaten the world again. We must maintain readiness to respond should this happen. Furthermore, some of the weapons of mass destruction are in newly independent parts of the old Soviet Union, whose political situations are even less predictable. There is always the danger that they might use these weapons to hold others hostage.

This is primarily an argument for maintaining an effective nuclear deterrent. It is difficult to imagine a return to large Warsaw Pact land armies that could be viewed as threatening an invasion of Western Europe. Hence, the issue is how many strategic nuclear weapons should be maintained for purposes of deterrence.

At present, Russia seems to be willing, indeed eager, to come to an agreement with the United States that would greatly reduce nuclear weapons on both sides. Russia has learned the hard way that nuclear stockpiles provide no security. Resistance to massive nuclear disarmament comes more from the United States, which wants to take advantage of the situation to become the world's dominant, even exclusive, nuclear superpower.

Even if all the countries of the former Soviet Union were completely disarmed in nuclear terms, a reasonable argument could be made for the United States to retain a nuclear deterrent. There are nuclear weapons in other parts of the world whose use should be deterred. But the quantity of nuclear missiles needed for these purposes is a small fraction of our present store.

The recognition that most of our arsenal is superfluous for deterrence is now widespread. The 1991 START treaty, ratified by the U.S. Senate, reduces strategic warheads held by each side by half to around 6000. START II aims to cut this to the 3000–3500 range and to eliminate MIRV's altogether. But even these figures far exceed what would be necessary for deterrent effect. The Center for Defense Information suggests reducing the number of warheads to 1000, to be deployed only on submarines, as an immediate goal independent of reductions made by others. After this number was reached further reductions could be considered according to what others were doing [*The Defense Monitor*, vol. 22, no. 1 (1993), see especially pages 6–7]. In the September 1988 issue of the *Bulletin of Atomic Scientists* Andrei Kokoshin suggests that 600 would be sufficient.

One may well question whether there is any real need for even that many. Of course, this is a highly technical matter depending in part on the quality of defense available to each side. But in all probability, with reasonable agreements made in other respects, 300 would be sufficient. Jack Mendelssohn reports that "According to former Secretary of Defense Robert McNamara, during the 1962 Cuban missile crisis, when the United States had approximately 5000 strategic warheads to the Soviet Union's 300, 'President Kennedy and I were deterred from even considering a nuclear attack on the USSR by the knowledge that, although such a strike would destroy the Soviet Union, tens of their weapons would survive to be launched against the United States'" (1992, p. 35).

Meanwhile we can celebrate each reduction, recognizing that national security is improved as stocks of nuclear weapons everywhere are reduced, not by the United States maintaining large stocks itself. One very appropriate form of aid to the former Soviet states is to pay for the dismantling of their weapons. This provides them with the hard currency they badly need while directly adding to American security.

(2) Of more apparent importance currently than defending the United States from military attack is protecting supply lines. This need was stated clearly by Caspar Weinberger in his annual report to the Congress in 1984. Among the vital interests that are to be protected by the armed forces of the United States he listed: "To protect access to foreign markets and overseas resources in order to maintain the strength of the United States' industrial, agricultural, and technological base and the nation's well-being" (Dellums 1983, p. 282).

Obviously, the importance to national security of protecting supply lines and trade is a function of national dependence on overseas resources and on trade. The dominant economic policies of the recent past, expressed especially in the Uruguay Round of the GATT and in the NAFTA, have aimed to maximize that dependence. They increase dependence on resources by working for increased throughput as the measure of economic health. They increase dependence on trade by working for specialization of production on a global scale. The more these policies succeed, the less any nation is able to feed and clothe itself out of its own resources. Even a temporary disruption of supply lines will become increasingly disastrous.

The argument of this book has been that these policies are inherently destructive of human well-being. They are also inimical to national security. A nation that cannot survive except in dependence on others can never be entirely secure, no matter how much military power it maintains to protect its supply lines and trade. Meanwhile the cost both in dollars and in resources of maintaining military forces for this purpose must be deducted from any gains thought to derive from this system.

Our proposal is to move in quite the opposite direction. The United States, and other nations as well, should work for relative self-sufficiency, minimizing their dependence on imported resources and international trade. This would also reduce the need for military expenditures designed to protect supply lines.

The centerpiece for this debate is the oil of the Persian Gulf. Concern about control of oil supplies recently involved the United States in a major war in that region. This has been held to demonstrate the need to maintain a large military establishment capable of defending American interests around the world. But does this policy make sense in terms of real national security?

Amory and Hunter Lovins have examined this question:

Earl Ravenal, of the Georgetown University School of Foreign Service, found that in fiscal year 1985 alone, before the *Stark* attack, the United States spent $47 billion projecting power into the Persian Gulf: $468 per barrel imported from the Gulf in that year, or eighteen times the $27 or so that we paid for the oil itself . . . . In fact, if we spent as much to make buildings heat-tight as we spent in *one year* on the military forces meant to protect the Middle Eastern oil fields, we could eliminate the need to import oil from the Middle East. [Lovins and Lovins, pp. 26–27]

National security can, therefore, be projected in either of two ways. One can assume that we must maintain a huge military establishment based on oil in order to secure access to oil around the world and especially in the Persian Gulf. It is needed, in other words, to preserve itself. Or, instead of spending money and using oil to maintain a military establishment of this size, the United States can reduce the size of the military and use the money saved to reduce the civilian economy's dependence on oil. These double savings, in both the military and the civilian sector, will free the nation from the need to import oil from the Persian Gulf and hence from having to maintain the arms necessary to safeguard that source.

It is obvious that the former choice will continue to intensify the greenhouse effect and require additional expenditures to deal with the crises it engenders. It will maintain the dependence on oil while speeding its exhaustion, leading to an eventual crisis of transition. That crisis will render the nation profoundly insecure. The latter choice will slow down the greenhouse effect and contribute to a painless transition without loss of national security. It would enable the armed forces to reduce their use of oil by two-thirds. That reduction, combined with the improved efficiency emphasized by the Lovinses and the reduction of energy use in cities and in agriculture proposed earlier, would make a transition from fossil fuels to solar energy possible without provoking crises or threatening national security.

(3) Actually the quote from Weinberger above neglects the fact that our projection of military power around the world is to protect not only the nation's supply lines and trade but also that of its trading partners. The United States has taken on the role of policing the world. According to the Center for Defense Information, "most of the Pentagon's request for almost $300 Billion in 1993 military spending is to prepare for military action in regional struggles far from U.S. shores" [*The Defense Monitor*, vol. 21, no. 6, (1992): 2].

Calculated simply in terms of national security, United States expenditures on controlling the Persian Gulf were absurd. But some of its allies are genuinely dependent on oil from this source and could not easily become independent. Perhaps it is the role of the United States to police the Gulf for their sake, and perhaps this justifies huge expenditures.

Before concluding that this is the case, we should consider the wider context. The policy of controlling the Gulf led the United States first to arm Iran and then Iraq. In both cases the arms were used against it. If, instead, the United States had worked with its allies to prevent Hussein from building up a great army with modern equipment, the danger he poses to his neighbors—and the need to defend against it—would be much less. Ending the flow of arms to the Middle East might do more to secure access to oil there than building up client states which then turn against the United States. Whether interventionist policies in the Gulf have actually increased the security of the flow of oil to Europe and Japan over time is questionable.

It is also questionable whether the U.S. taxpayer should bear the burden of protecting supply lines for other nations. When the United States was prosperous and Japan and Europe devastated in the aftermath of World War II, it made sense for the United States to assume some global responsibility. But that is not the situation now. The Europeans and the Japanese are quite capable of looking after their own interests. Should international intervention in the Persian Gulf be truly necessary, the strength of the United Nations should be built up so that it could be the intervener. The United States might contribute its share of troops to such an intervention, but it is not in its interest, or in the interests of the world, that it be *the* global policeman.

A clearer and more attractive example of the policeman role now played by the United States is the pacification of Somalia, occurring as we write. Here it seems that military and economic considerations are secondary to humanitarian ones. This is police intervention for the sake of the people of the country that is invaded. Should the United States maintain a large military establishment so as to be able to engage in such intervention as needed around the world?

There may be some short-term justification for such a policy. In the aftermath of the Cold War the United States has military resources matched by no other nation. With no one else in position to act, it may make sense for the United States to do so.

However, there are several reasons not to take Somalia as a precedent on the basis of which to calculate the size of the military establishment the United States should maintain. First, was the intervention necessary? At the time of the intervention, the public did not have sufficient information to form an intelligent judgment. There were those who believed that despite the near anarchy in that country, nonmilitary intervention could have accomplished a better balance of good over evil than the deployment of U.S. troops. It is rare that police actions are permanently effective. Such instances should at best be regarded as exceptions.

Second, a major cause of the chaos in Somalia was the earlier struggle for power in the Horn of Africa between the United States and the Soviet Union. This both introduced large quantities of arms into the region and destabilized traditional patterns of governance with the disastrous results to which we are now responding. Our foreign policy should be geared to avoiding anarchy rather than first creating it and then intervening to end it. Now that the Cold War is over, this policy should be easier to implement.

Third, if police work is necessary, it is far better that it be dispersed. The Organization for African Unity should be in a better position to judge the need in Africa. It should also develop the resources needed for such emergency police work in its member states. This would have its own problems, but it is in the long-term interest of Africa that Africans assume responsibility for decisions of this sort and for implementing them. If a country's problems exceeded its capacities, the United Nations could be called on. Virtually unilateral U.S. intervention is not in the interest of either Africa or the United States. For the U.S. to maintain military power for such purposes is not justified.

A Center for Defense Information study of the role of the United States in twenty-five local wars around the world concludes that

past U.S. involvement in these struggles has not been positive. U.S. weapons, aid, and military intervention have aggravated wars, not solved them. Today the Administration uses foreign wars to justify the continuation of Cold War military spending, the deliberate expansion of weapons sales to other countries, and the indefinite stationing of U.S. forces around the globe. Now it is time to take advantage of growing U.N. readiness to make and keep the peace in the world. Active U.S. support for international political and economic measures to settle and prevent wars is likely to be more successful and less costly than continuing to rely on military action. In a world of declining wars that pose no military threat to the United States, our Cold War global military police force can safely be replaced with smaller forces designed for the defense of the U.S. As an extra benefit, billions of dollars will be freed to deal with other pressing U.S. problems, notably runaway federal spending deficits. [*The Defense Monitor*, vol. 21, no. 6, (1992): 14]

The regional security programs that should take over from U.S. military intervention will meet the needs of much of the world. But it could be argued that in the Western hemisphere it is appropriate for the United States to continue the unilateral policing role that it has recently exercised in Grenada and Panama. It has often been asserted that the United States' security is bound up with its domination of the hemisphere.

In fact, however, this is not truly a matter of security. During the Cold War, scenarios were sometimes proposed of Soviet client states in the Americas threatening the security of the United States. These were never realistic, since these client states would have had no ability to threaten the United States even if U.S. military power had been greatly diminished. Now this whole way of thinking is irrelevant. The issue is whether the United States will allow the people of other countries in this hemisphere to manage their own affairs. If it is argued that the United States needs to control resources and trade in the Western hemisphere, the response is again that its goal should be to minimize that need rather than to heighten it. It can then be secure without imposing its will on others.

The size of military establishment needed by the United States clearly depends on the basic decisions with which this book is concerned throughout. If we are determined to emphasize a global market, then maintenance of security does require that somewhere there be sufficient power to insure minimal disruptions of trade. If we move toward relatively self-sufficient national and regional economies, then the need for a large military declines steeply.

Even apart from this consideration, the end of the Cold War opens the way to massive reductions of military expenditures. These reductions are already beginning, and the debate is only how rapid they should be and how far they should go. William Kaufmann of the Brookings Institute has shown how, without any major change in policy, the military budget can be reduced to 160 billion dollars by the end of this decade, about half of its peak (1990). Budgetary pressures are likely to push politicians in this direction despite the pain suffered by many of their constituents.

If the policies advocated in this book were adopted, $160 billion would still be an absurdly large expenditure for national security. The Center for Defense Information proposes a budget of $104 billion for the defense of the United States in the year 2000 [*The Defense Monitor*, vol 21, no. 4 (1992): 1]. If no significant threat to the nation appears then, still further reductions would be appropriate. No other country now spends this much. A significant, but still small, portion of the money saved should be channeled to regional security systems such as the Organization of American States and especially to the United Nations, whose capacities for policing should be greatly increased.

Problems with Economic Conversion

The evidence is now decisive that military expenditures are more a function of domestic political and economic considerations than military security. The current level of expenditures has no correlation to any present external threat to the nation's security. At the same time it is also clear that the United States has done itself great economic and social damage over the years by diverting so many of its resources into arms and armies. Hence, the initial reaction of many is that the nation should drastically reduce military spending quickly. For example, the Black and Progressive Congressional caucuses have proposed a 50% reduction in just four years.

There are two quite different types of obstacles to following this proposal. The first is the political power of groups that profit from military spending. The second is the extreme difficulty of dealing in a humane way with a rapid shift in the whole economy.

These two factors account for the slow pace of reduction that both Bush and Clinton have proposed. Bush proposed to spend $1.42 trillion over five years. Clinton has proposed $1.36 trillion. Although it seems absurd to continue these vast expenditures for unneeded armaments and overseas bases at a time when urgent national needs cannot be met, we must take seriously the problem of demilitarizing the economy, and especially its human costs.

In 1946 General Eisenhower as Chief of Staff of the United States Army called for the establishment of the military-industrial complex (see appendix A of Melman 1970, pp. 231–234), against whose growing power he later warned us as president. He pointed out that prior to World War II, industry was basically civilian and the nation's capacity for military production was based on the convertibility of plants from civilian to military needs. After World War II, because of the Cold War, the United States moved into a permanent military economy, with a major segment of its resources committed to military preparedness.

Under Kennedy, Seymour Melman argues, Robert McNamara, as Secretary of Defense "made a major institutional change in American society" (1970, p. vii). He installed "an industrial management . . . to control the nation's largest network of industrial enterprises" (Ibid., p. 1). Thus the United States developed alongside its market economy a large command economy geared to military production. This means that much of American industry is just as unaccustomed to market competition as is that of the former Soviet Union! Many of the problems experienced by Eastern Europe in shifting from a bureaucratically managed economy to a competitive one are faced also in the United States as the defense establishment is downsized. Converting this industry to civilian uses not only requires retraining at the technical level but also changing its whole ethos.

The problems posed by a rapid reduction of military expenditures are indicated in another way by Betty G. Lall and Joan Tepper Marlin. They calculate the probable effects on unemployment of reduced military spending:

If defense spending (in FY 1990 dollars) were to be cut from $300 billion to $175 billion within ten years, a $12.5-billion-a-year reduction, it would mean *an average decline of about 6 percent a year and an average reduction of 362,000 defense jobs per year.* Of the layoffs, typically 14 percent, or approximately 51,000 workers would be taken care of by attrition . . . , two thirds of the remaining 312,000 . . . would be re-employed by the end of the fourth month.

The net increase in unemployment after four months would be 104,000 workers. [Lall and Marlin 1992, p. 75]

They go on to calculate that this would involve an $11 billion reduction in GNP each year in a cumulative fashion. There will be both a resultant decline in tax revenue and increased demands for unemployment benefits.

One reason for believing that the effects on labor may be worse than these figures suggest is that many of those who find new work may have to accept lower incomes. The defense industry has been protected from the international market forces that have driven wages down in other sectors and reduced the number of industrial jobs. If the United States continues the policies that are moving much of its industrial production abroad and lowering wages at home at the same time that it reduces the one sector of the economy that has been protected from the effects of these policies, the results may prove much worse than those projected by Lall and Martin.

This becomes clear when we examine the proposals for redeploying our national resources. For example, Seymour Melman and Lloyd J. Dumas propose that the defense industry turn to the production of goods that are now imported, such as machine tools (1992, pp. 509, 522–528, 526). This is an excellent suggestion in terms of the long-term economic health of the nation, but without basic changes in industrial policy it cannot be implemented. The U.S. machine tool industry lost out in international competition. There is no reason to think that an industry that is notoriously undisciplined with regard to costs could succeed where market-oriented industries failed.

The United States has had two drastically different industrial policies. One has been oriented to market competition among individual firms. The other has been committed to bureaucratic management. Meanwhile Japan and continental Europe have developed what Lester Thurow calls "communitarian capitalism" (1992, pp. 24–30). It turns out that Anglo-American individualistic capitalism is not successful in competition with the communitarian form. If the United States demilitarizes its industry without changing its commitment to individualistic capitalism, much of its remaining industry will be lost.

Ann Markusen and Joel Yudken recognize that new policies are required.

Macroeconomic and trade policies should be coordinated with the economic development strategy and its conversion efforts. Trade policies that help to manage transition—instead of letting it expose workers and communities to instant economic death—would be implemented. Trade negotiations with every nation should include safeguards that extend the wages, benefits, and environmental protections of U.S. workers to those in other countries, rather than allowing exploitative conditions there to drive down the domestic quality of life in the name of competitiveness. [1992, p. 251]

Markusen and Yudken recommend that a national commitment be made in three areas to achieve authentic national security.

Environment, health, and community stability—these areas must compete with national security as a major national priority. For fifty years, Americans have devoted the lion's share of their surplus to pursuing national security above all else, with disappointing results for the economy and growing environmental, health, and community crises. Today, it can be argued that resolving environmental, health, and economic crises is an essential dimension of any meaningful definition of national security. Moreover, unlike expenditures on costly MX or Patriot missiles, gains in these three areas would boost productivity in the economy as a whole. [Ibid, p. 249]

Despite the prejudice against governmental involvement in the economy, it may be that the American people will recognize an obligation to the millions of Americans whose livelihood has been bound up with the military industry. If this happens, the nation may be willing to consider helping this industry convert to civilian purposes, recognizing that it cannot immediately be competitive. If the United States makes a clean environment, human health, and community stability its goals, along with a commitment to becoming more self-sufficient economically, the transition from a military economy to a civilian one may be effected without enormous pain.

If military spending is reduced as part of the return to a national economy, the transformation of the armaments industry into a civilian one can play a very positive role. If the industry received sufficient support and protection from foreign competition, some of it could convert to import-substitution production in areas where it might otherwise take time to rebuild an industrial base. Meanwhile the elusive goal of a balanced budget can be attained, and the repayment of accumulated debt can begin. The American economy may regain its health and make its proper contribution to national security.

Security in a Community of Communities

In the post-World War II era, while "internationalists" supported the build-up of a military budget to oppose the Soviet Union, "fiscal conser-

vatives, including members of the National Association of Manufacturers, opposed the big military budgets on the grounds that the country could not afford these massive expenditures. Stalin's secret plan, the
conservatives argued, was to bankrupt the treasury" (Barnet 1981,
p. 55). One may doubt that Stalin had much hope of U.S. bankruptcy,
but four decades later, the fears of those fiscal conservatives are being
realized. We join with them against this form of internationalism.

Indeed, we find that much of the advocacy of internationalism today
is misdirected. We agree with Dudley Seers, who wrote, "To internationalists who claim the world is becoming increasingly 'interdependent,'
and welcome the idea, I would reply that this interdependence is highly
asymmetrical, involving those overseas in accepting not merely cultural
values that the superpowers press on them, but also the arms and other
products, and associated political programmes" (1983, p. 12). Against
this modern internationalism, we, like Seers, support nationalism.

Nevertheless, we would argue that we are internationalists in a truer,
postmodern, sense of that term. Postmodern internationalism does not
relegate national boundaries to unimportance, but focuses instead on a
community of interest among nations, in which nations do together
what they cannot do separately. Today many of the world's problems are
global ones which can only be addressed globally. The greenhouse
effect, acid rain, the depletion of the ozone layer, and the exploitation of
the ocean bed and of Antarctica are examples. Human activity in space
should be another. The protection of the world's biodiversity should be
a global effort. Much research should be internationally cooperative
rather than competitive. The dissemination of some types of information is best done at the global level. The deterrence of military action
across national boundaries is a primary concern of the nation whose
borders are violated, but it is also appropriately the concern of an international body seeking to keep the peace. Hence the international body
needs a peace-keeping force of its own.

Preferably, the international body in question should be, in the first
instance, a multinational region. The European Economic Community
should develop the ability to police its member states as NATO is dis-
banded. It is desirable that the Organization for African Unity gain sufficient strength for this purpose. A similar organization for Latin America
would be desirable to replace the U.S.-dominated Organization of American States.

These functions and others can be carried out and extended only as
nation-states modify their claims to absolute sovereignty. The United

States should accept the rulings of the World Court and the judgments of the United Nations. The current ability of the great powers to thumb their noses at the World Court and to veto majority decisions of the United Nations should be curtailed, although in the latter body a system of weighted votes might be needed. This can happen only as the political and military power of world bodies grows relative to that of nation-states. As this occurs, all will be more secure.

Current trends, however, are leading to the wrong kind of centralization of power. This is especially true of the North American Free Trade Agreement and the General Agreement on Tariffs and Trade. The current GATT proposal, for example, vests enormous power in the Multilateral Trade Organization. This is designed to promote trade and reduce barriers thereto. To that end it is empowered to overrule the laws of the United States government and of individual states, such as those safeguarding the environment, if they are seen as restricting trade. Obviously it will be even freer to set aside the laws of less powerful nations. This is simply not acceptable. Any group with that kind of power must be responsible to the people and not to economic interests alone. That means that it must have the character of a government.

If the world moves further toward an integrated global economy, thereby requiring centralization of power for the adjudication of disputes, then this power should be vested in a political body. A meeting of nongovernmental organizations in Hamburg in November 1992 proposed that in lieu of the MTO an international trade body be set up under the auspices of the General Assembly of the United Nations. If this body had powers comparable to those to be invested in MTO, this would move the United Nations a long way toward becoming a world government.

We consider centralization of power under the United Nations far preferable to the concentration of power in a group that is not responsive to political influence and whose function is purely economic. But we do not favor this much centralization of global power. Our proposal is to give primary emphasis to the national level of the economy. One of the advantages is that this would make the move toward centralized global control—with all its dangers to personal and community freedom—unnecessary. We do not want international control of our national affairs. A global organization should have power only over global matters.

We noted above several threats to national security other than the threat of defeat on the battlefield. Lack of economic self-sufficency is a major one, and much of economics for community is designed to overcome it. The proposed policies would reduce dependence on imported raw materials and foreign markets, as well as insuring adequate agricultural and industrial capability. Our economic proposals are also designed to reduce ecological threats, national demoralization, and economic decline. There is more to economics than the short-run maximization of profit to individuals!

Economics for community can also make a further contribution to security. Although a national economy contributes more to national security than a transnational one, it provides less security than a more decentralized one. If each region within a nation depends on massive imports of essentials from other regions, disruption of transportation can bring the whole nation to its knees. If each region depends on a national electric grid, or on centralized information services, the nation is highly vulnerable. If, on the contrary, each region can continue to function well regardless of damage to transportation, electrical networks, and communications equipment in other regions, the nation as a whole is more secure.

The point can be carried further. If smaller communities within regions are relatively self-sufficient, the life of the nation can continue despite extensive and widely dispersed attacks on its infrastructure. All damage will be local in its effects. Only wholesale destruction can fatally wound a nation's capacity to produce and function.

In this chapter, as in most of the others, we are attending to the United States as a nation-state. We are discussing its security. This is important. But we also envision the decentralization of economic and political power within the nation. If this goes far enough, this country might again become a federation of states, rather than a nation-state. In that case, each state would have some responsibility for its own defense, although it would be protected in part by its federation with the others, and by the reduced, but still significant, military power of the federation as a whole. Could such a federation of independent states be secure?

The idea is so strange that at first glance it seems silly. We are accustomed to thinking of security as the ability to launch a nuclear attack, maintain naval forces on the other side of the planet, and move armies across oceans. None of the fifty states would have such capabilities. The likelihood that any of them would fight a war on another continent is slight. In any case, the federation would discourage such adventures.

But where there is economic self-sufficiency, national security need not involve fighting wars with distant enemies. It does not require the ability to conquer external powers. It requires only the ability to resist aggression against itself. Would a federation of fifty states be a likely victim of conquest? Would these states be in danger from Mexico or Canada?

Even if it made sense to think of either of these countries as becoming aggressive in this way, we doubt that Canada or Mexico would find conquest inviting as long as the fifty states were serious about their own defense and could call on the federation for support. The problems of conquering and controlling fifty independent states would be enormous and the rewards to the conqueror minor.

One argument for maintaining major power at the national level has been the need to surpass the power of the Soviet Union. But decentralization has already occurred there. This is part of what adds to our security. Whereas the intact Soviet empire was regarded by many as a serious threat to the security of the free world, it is much more unlikely that the Ukraine or even Russia would pose a significant threat. Decentralization of the United States would also add to the security of other nations.

This is not proposed as a utopian scheme. Quarrels between states would become more dangerous when they were more independent. Arizona might have reason to fear California if feelings rose too high over the distribution of the Colorado River's water. Of course, there would be a federal court to rule on this question and federal military power to back up the decision. But California might thumb its nose at the federation and use its military power to force its will on Arizona.

We find such a scenario at least as implausible as war between France and Germany within the European Economic Community. Nevertheless, we do recognize that human beings are capable of mutual destruction under almost any system. We believe that the distribution of military power over several levels is the best system that can be devised, but we do not claim that it will put an end to all war.

We do, however, concur with Kirkpatrick Sale, who concludes his discussion of this topic as follows: "The long human record suggests that the problem of defense and warfare is exacerbated, not solved, by the large state, and that smaller societies . . . tend to engage in fighting less and with less violent consequences. Indicating that a world of human scale politics would not be a world without its conflicts and disputations, but would likely be a world of comparative stability" (1986, p. 471).

This is a vision of a shift of power from the nation-state both upward to regional and global agencies and downward to smaller communities. It is a vision that is increasingly gaining acceptance and seems in some ways likely to be realized. Alan Thein Durning rightly notes that the "dominance of the nation-state—thought of as seat of all sovereignty— may be near its zenith. The locus of decision-making seems likely to shift downwards to provinces and indigenous domains even as it shifts upwards to regional bodies, such as the European Community, and global bodies such as the United Nations" (1992, p. 47). We would add only that this redistribution of political power can occur healthily only as economic life is also decentralized.

Civilian Defense

Thus far we have assumed that violence is a mjor element in national defense and that readiness to engage in violence is a necessary part of national security. Our argument has been only that the United States' huge expenditures on arms not only do not add to security but actually detract from it; and we have suggested that the level of violence would decrease if political and military decentalization took place. But there is a further point to be made. A stable peace is the best security, and, as Walter Lippmann stated, "Any real program of peace must rest on the premise that there will be causes of dispute as long as we can foresee, that these disputes have to be decided, and that a way of deciding them must be found which is not war" (1982, p. 182). Gene Sharp, who has devoted his career to studying the role of nonviolent actions in history, concluded that "only the adoption of a substitute type of sanction and struggle as a functional alternative to violence in acute conflicts . . . could possibly lead to a major reduction of political violence in a manner compatible with freedom, justice and human dignity" (1973, p. vi).

Resolving problems without violence is certainly desirable. But most people assume that at some point these efforts fail and that at the national level there must be preparations to use violence to achieve national purposes, at least in self-defense. Sharp, however, dares to propose that "civilian defense" be substituted for military defense. "Civilian defense aims to defeat military aggression by using resistance by the civilian population as a whole to make it impossible for the enemy to establish and maintain political control over the country" (1973, p. 50). He knows that this could not happen without careful preparation. The energies that now go into military training would be directed to preparations for civilian defense:

Police would refuse to locate and arrest patriotic opponents of the invader. Teachers would refuse to introduce his propaganda into the schools—as happened in Norway under the Nazis. Workers and managers would use delays and obstructionism to impede exploitation of their country—as happened in the Ruhr in 1923. Clergymen would preach about the duty to refuse to help the invader—as happened in the Netherlands under the Nazis.

"Politicians, civil servants and judges, by ignoring or defying the enemy's illegal orders, would keep the normal machinery of government and the courts out of his control—as happened in the German resistance to the Kapp Putsch in 1920. Newspapers refusing to submit to censorship would be published illegally in large editions or many small editions—as happened in the Russian 1905 Revolution and in several Nazi-occupied countries. Free radio programs would continue from hidden transmitters—as happened in Czechoslavakia in August, 1968. . . .

In addition . . . civilian defense would set in motion restraining influences both in the invader's own country (stimulating dissension at home, splits in the regime, and in extremes, even resistance) and in the international community (creating diplomatic pressures, political losses, and sometimes economic sanctions) that would be inimical to the invader's interests. [Sharp 1973, pp. 51–52]

Sharp's proposal is a visionary one, and we see no possibility of its being immediately adopted. The kind of community and discipline needed to make it effective is precisely what is now lacking in this country. But in a decentralized federation, some states might adopt this policy rather than devote their limited resources to military defense. Indeed, an Arizona whose people were well prepared for civilian defense might be a less tempting target for conquest than one that relied on an army to defend itself! Eventually, all states, might adopt this posture. A federation of fifty states, each prepared for disciplined civilian defense, would not be an attractive conquest to a foreign power, however easily its troops could gain entrance.

In our present situation this is, of course, fantasy. But in a world that can no longer afford arms and armies, where all use of energy to support them limits the capacity of the next generation to meet its economic needs and adds to the wild facts with which it must deal, we need wild visions of a disarmed world. Sharp has shown us that there is another way, and someday it may be tried. Meanwhile, few would question that a nation ready for civilian defense as a second line of defense would be more secure than one that depended on its armed forces alone.

4

GETTING THERE

19

Possible Steps

This book is about redirecting the economy for the sake of human beings and the whole biosphere. Part Three has described some of the
policies that would move the United States toward healthy community
life. In that sense it was about "getting there." But there is another question. How can the United States get to the point where policies of this
sort can move from theoretical discussion to the political agenda? Part
Four responds to this question in two quite different ways.

The next and final chapter, Chapter 20, treats the most basic theoretical issues of all, the religious and philosophical ones. We believe that
our collective response to the wild facts is above all a matter of religious
conviction and vision. We think we have been suggesting bits and
pieces of this vision throughout this book, but we have not presented or
defended this in any full or coherent way or located it in relation to
other visions. Chapter 20 undertakes this task.

Meanwhile the present chapter moves in a quite different direction,
from hoped-for policies to the question of what types of activities can be
begun in the present context that will lead toward them. It discusses
possible university reforms, building of local communities, steps toward
a relatively self-sufficient national economy as a first move toward further decentralization, bringing the question of scale into public consciousness, and changing the way we measure economic success. In the
Appendix we offer a concrete proposal of a new measure.

The very first step toward redirection must be a widespread recognition that something is wrong, that present policies do not work, that the
wild facts must be taken seriously. This book has taken this step largely
for granted and is addressed chiefly to those who share this awareness.
There is already a large literature that describes the array of problems
we face and shows that pursuing the lines we have followed in the past
only serves to make the problems worse. We particularly commend the
publications of the World Watch Institute to any who are uninformed.

Unfortunately, the first step has not yet been taken by the public at large and their political leaders. Despite deep-seated uneasiness they cling to old patterns of thought. Politicians either do not understand that the situation has changed or fear to address the issue publicly. The press occasionally reports the wild facts but then goes back to its usual news as if nothing had happened.

Perhaps this is inevitable as long as the many problems appear isolated one from another. Then people seek solutions to each separately, and inevitably the perspective from which they seek solutions is the one that has generated the problems. The number and magnitude of the problems troubles people, but this leads more to the psychological need to escape than to deeper reflection about causes. Having no handles on solutions, and even doubting that any are possible, many seek to get what they can now, leaving the future to look out for itself. Others find comfort in technological optimism.

The second step is a widespread recognition that most of the problems faced by humanity today are interconnected and indeed have a common source. This step is one to which this book intends to contribute. To whatever extent this step is taken, the bewilderment and generalized distress felt by so many people who have taken, or resisted, the first step can be mitigated. The sense of being overwhelmed by unnamable powers is overcome. With a new perspective, what is happening becomes intelligible. Its causes can be identified and named. Human responsibility becomes clear.

The third step is the recognition that human beings still have the possibility of choosing a livable future for themselves and their descendants. Humanity is not simply trapped in a dark fate. People can be *attracted* by new ways of ordering their lives, as well as *driven* by the recognition of what will happen if they do not change. This book is very much about this third step. We believe that a glimpse of hopeful possibilities will make it possible for people to take the first and second steps without panic or denial. We also believe that the third step as we have defined it belongs to a family of visions that have grown and spread rapidly in recent years. They come out of feminist and ecological circles as well as out of various strands of religious teaching. They make contact also with Third World liberation thinking. These ideas spread through informal networking and constitute a major cultural movement that is ready to surface and become important in national affairs. It is becoming capable of responding to a half-conscious national hunger for new vision and leadership. "Getting there" in the sense of getting to the point where the policies discussed in Part Three can be seriously debated nationally *could* happen rather quickly.

Nevertheless, the obstacles are enormous. Century-old habits of mind do not give way readily, especially when they are established in all the places of prestige and high leverage.

University Reform

One important institution in which fruitful changes are possible is the university. This is the home of many of the most influential economists as well as opinion-makers in other fields. At present its influence on the discussion is largely negative. It encourages the quest for solutions in the narrowly canalized lines of its departmental structure. This blocks the fresh approaches that are needed and places those who undertake them on the defensive before the authority of the disciplinary mainstream, which in turn undercuts their influence in the university.

Even within the established disciplines there are indications of some reversal of the ever-narrowing focus of research. The computer has made it possible to develop models of complex systems that take numerous factors into consideration. Departments of physics are taking the lead in the use of these new models. Since physics played so large a role in modeling the present disciplinary narrowness, there is reason to hope that its new vision will lead to changes in other disciplines as well.

Furthermore, the study of the complex patterns leads to the discovery that there are unanticipated connections or overlappings of portions of many different disciplines. According to Heinz Pagels, "problems in neuro-science, anthropology, population biology, learning theory, cognitive science, nonlinear dynamics, physics, and cosmology (to name but a few fields) have overlapping components" (Pagels 1988, p. 36). Pagels argues that the divisions among the sciences in the past have been influenced by the available tools for investigation and that the computer will lead to a more complex, less segmented organization.

Although this is a hopeful development, by itself it will not overcome all of the problems built into the disciplinary organization of knowledge discussed in Chapters 1 and 6. Some of these even become more acute as a result of computer use. Modeling itself becomes a new discipline. These continuing limitations on thought imposed by the disciplines are obscurely recognized within the university, so that if the failures of the disciplines can be brought to focused attention, their power over the

academic mind can be broken. This is worth pursuing both for its intrinsic importance and as a possible way of breaking through some of
the obstacles to public discussion of new ways of ordering the economy.
A changed attitude toward the disciplines would help to overcome the
isolation of economic thought from sociology, biology, and physics, to
name only three other fields by which reflection on the economy should
be informed. To this end we propose four specific steps that many universities could take.

1. The university should establish a department, or some other structure, for ongoing study of itself. This would involve the history of universities and of the way they have organized knowledge, and also of how
they have related to the rest of society. It would evaluate the contributions made by the university, study the threats to its freedom of inquiry,
both from without and self-imposed, and it would also ask how responsibly its freedom is exercised. It could go on to a study of the similar and
varied assumptions of the several disciplines and the ways they relate to
one another and to the wider society. The history of science, which now
maintains only a precarious foothold in the university, would be central
here. And this would be a particularly important place to insure diversity of perspectives. Feminists, for example, have recently shown how
different the history of the sciences appears through their eyes.[1]

Such a department should make no pretense of value neutrality. Its
goal would be to increase self-understanding within the university and
to encourage reforms: it should have no political power to enforce
changes. It should make its values as clear as possible and subject them
to the widest criticism and discussion. The generation of such discussion and critical self-evaluation within the disciplines would in itself be
the realization of much of its goal.

2. The university should also establish a department for the study of
cosmology. By cosmology is not meant here a branch of astrophysics,
although information from that discipline should play its role. Instead
the idea is to build up a unified picture of what the world is like, drawing on information generated in all the disciplines in the university. It
should do this in lively interaction with those disciplines. It would address questions and make suggestions as well as passively receive whatever information happens to be generated. The questions it asks will

1. See Sandra Harding's *The Science Question in Feminism* (1986) and Susan R.
Bordo's *The Flight to Objectivity* (1987).

arise out of its own efforts to relate what is learned in humanistic studies to what is learned in the psychological, social, and natural sciences.

3. The university should also establish a department for the study of the social and global crisis. Everyone is aware that social order, and indeed life itself, is now endangered. Bits and pieces of this information show up in the several disciplines. But nowhere in the university is there any effort to gain an overview of what these problems are and how they are related to one another. This department would gather information from all and raise questions to all as it sees relationships that do not appear in the disciplinary approaches. The purpose of this department would be not only to encourage the ordering of research within individual departments to the urgent issues of the time but also to interact with the departments of the university about the possibility that the institution as a whole has some responsibility to order its life in relation to social needs.

4. If sufficient consensus is reached, then the university can also establish interdisciplinary centers to relate its work to urgent issues. Women's studies centers, black studies centers, area studies, and peace studies centers afford models. Although these inevitably begin as interdisciplinary, they should aim to become non-disciplinary.

Actions such as these do not violate any firm commitments of present universities and have varying degrees of support within existing faculties. If they succeed, they would change the ethos of the departments. They would heighten awareness of the historically relative character of the disciplines and of the assumptions on which they are built. They would encourage ordering research to the answering of questions that have practical relevance to urgent human needs. They would heighten awareness that what is studied is in fact permeated by relationships to what others study, so that disciplinary boundaries would soften. In this context, combined with a conscious shift toward the relativization of the deductive approach, economics could free itself from such deep immersion in the fallacy of misplaced concreteness.

Although in the long run, structural changes of this kind are the best bet to redirect the energies of the university into fruitful channels, individuals and groups within the university do not need to wait on top-level decisions. They can expose the atomistic individualism that underlies so many of the academic disciplines and their methods. They can promote holistic and organic ways of thought and display the differences that result. They can press for interdisciplinary discussion and then push these beyond disciplinary boundaries. They can organize research around urgent issues and reject the pressures of the disciplines to set their own agenda. They can help students understand the limitations of the university and its present way of organizing knowledge so that they will not be bound by it.

With all its limitations and the disciplinolatry so prevalent within departments, the university as a whole is still remarkably tolerant of mavericks and critics. Its commitment to free inquiry and radical analysis is often genuine. At least outside of one's own department, one's eccentric view can often gain a hearing. Our criticism of the disciplinary organization of knowledge and its domination of the university is not intended to write off the university as a hopeless case. Far from it. We believe that the university embodies traditions of great value that can be renewed in such a way as to make it again a source of wisdom and guidance to the wider community.

Building Communities

The goal of the changes proposed in this book is a bottom-up society, a community of communities that are local and relatively small. The policies discussed in Part Three would tend to empower such smaller local communities. But it is not necessary to wait for such empowerment from above. Much can be done now at local levels despite the unfavorable ordering of economic and political life. Indeed, if communities do not now exercise such power as they have to sustain and improve their community life, there is danger that they will not effectively employ the improved context we propose be provided for them. Fortunately, there are many instances of community initiative already operative. We will cite three.

The Institute for Local Self-Reliance (ILSR) in New York City decided years ago that "the welfare approach to social justice was not working." They decided that "communities would begin to use their wastes as raw materials, and develop closed-loop systems. That is, goods and services would be produced locally, from local resources, for local consumption. The city, the unit of government closest to most of the people, would expand its political authority, and begin to define itself as . . . a community that took its boundaries seriously and developed a sophisticated planning capacity and economic development responsibility" (Richardson 1982, p. 194).

Among the projects of the ILSR was aid to a South Bronx Group. They organized the Bronx Frontier Development Market. After one year of operation, "it was producing 70 tons of finished compost a week. The compost was used to restore the soil for community gardens in the South Bronx" (Richardson 1982, p. 195). Subsequently the Bronx Frontier Development Market grew to be a larger organization than the ILSR!

Interest in economics for community can be found at the state level as well. The Nebraska Press Association commissioned Stanford Research Institute (SRI) International of Menlo Park, California, to propose directions for Nebraska's future. Based on meetings with citizens throughout the state, SRI published in June 1988 "New Seeds for Nebraska: Moving the Agenda Ahead." What it found was a consensus for moving Nebraska in the direction of a more self-sufficient community. Further, it envisions this statewide community as consisting of a community of many smaller communities.

Participants felt that Nebraska needs to strengthen economic capacity in small communities. Although their economic infra-structure is incomplete in many cases, many of these intermediate-size communities and collections of smaller communities already have important economic building blocks in place. By building additional economic capacity in regional centers, respondents felt that the economies of those areas would grow, providing job opportunities for residents and for people who want to move from the farm but stay in the rural setting or to travel shorter distances to earn off-farm income. Thus, a regional growth center strategy was seen as a way of developing not only mid-size communities, but many of the very smallest communities as well. Further, by focusing on the needs of regions, the unique value of people living in the regions can be better maintained. [SRI, 1988, p. 17]

A particularly interesting program is underway under the auspices of Meadowcreek Project, of Fox, Arkansas. Its goal is in part to demonstrate that even under the current economic system, "buying locally grown agricultural products is more than an appealing idea. It makes sense. The average food item travels 1,300 miles from where it is grown to where it is consumed. Shipping a truckload of produce across the country costs up to $4,500. In addition, a dollar spent on local foods circulates in the local economy, generating $1.81 to $2.78 in other business" (Passmore 1987).

The Meadowcreek Project worked with Hendrix College in Conway, Arkansas, to redirect its purchases toward local produce. Within one year Hendrix increased its purchases of food within the state from 9% to

40%. A similar project is underway with Oberlin College in Ohio. At both schools the examination of buying policies is involving students in a wider examination of economic and ecological issues.

The major obstacles to progress toward shortening supply lines and encouraging the local economy is the convenience of continuing the present pattern. This is first the convenience for a food service manager of buying many types of items from single food distributors, who in turn are tied into national marketing systems. Second, there is the convenience of buying prepared foods. A move toward local purchasing requires some initiative in contacting local suppliers and pushes toward more cooking in local kitchens. However, improved quality more than compensates for the trouble and minimal added costs.

The next step, according to David Orr, Director of Meadowcreek Project, is a more extended program to examine all the food, energy, materials, water, and waste flowing through five campuses, especially with regard to social and environmental costs. The intention is to propose more sustainable alternatives to present patterns. The larger goals of these programs are: "(1) shift the buying power of high visibility, 'leverage' institutions; (2) change the substance and process of education by involving the entire campus community in an ongoing analysis of how they affect the wider world."[2]

Changing Trade Policies

Although much can and should be done to change institutions and to build community wherever possible, there is also urgent need for new policies at the national level. This cannot begin until new ideas about the goal of the American economy are discussed in politically influential circles. The main point of contact in the present discussion for the introduction of these ideas is the debate about trade and protection of American business.

Thus far this has been a very one-sided debate. On the one side have been all those who take the broad view and the long view. These are sure that free trade is the one procedure through which the people as a whole benefit. They recognize that it leads to closing of many factories and the dislocation of millions of people. But they are convinced that this is a price that must be paid. Free trade will lead to greater productivity and economic growth, and from this the people as a whole benefit.

2. These points were made in a letter to the authors, July 29, 1988.

On the other side are those who see their livelihood destroyed or their businesses impoverished. They function as special pleaders who for the sake of their private well-being are asking the government to grant them protection from foreign competition. They offer no theoretical justification for their request, only their particular need. Sometimes they are apologetic, insisting that the protection they seek is only temporary and professing their commitment to free trade as the ideal and norm. This group consists both of workers and factory owners in those industries most vulnerable to competition but not yet destroyed by it.

In this way the public is treated to a classic spectacle of politicians balancing the pressures from special interests with their sense of the general good. The result is a tissue of compromises that reflects more the political power of certain special interests than any objective judgment about the merits of the case for protection of particular commodities. Any protection presents itself as an unfortunate lapse from clearly affirmed ideals.

Our view is that this casting of the discussion reflects erroneous views of the value of free international trade. Such trade has its merits but also its negative effects. It is not justified by the principle of comparative advantage to which appeal is so often made in this connection. We have discussed this at length in Chapter 11. Today the volume and scope of free trade has passed the margin at which it does more harm than good to most of the nations that subject themselves to it. This is now true for the United States.

One promising scenario is that groups aware of how badly they are being hurt by unrestricted imports are becoming aware also of the fact that those who take the high ground against them are in fact lacking in justification. They can begin to shift the debate. Instead of apologizing for begging for an exception from an accepted general rule, they can challenge the general rule. We believe that when the general rule is openly debated, it will collapse. It will then be possible to look empirically at what free trade is in fact doing to our nation. That will lead to consideration of alternatives.

The outcome of such a debate will not be determined by logic alone. The interests of the several segments of society will play a large role. It is important to consider, therefore, who can be enlisted on the side of a national economy.

One group who will be disturbed if they look factually at what is happening are those deeply concerned for national security. Even when this is viewed in the narrowly military sense, no one can be indifferent to the ability of the nation to produce its own arms. Concern at this point has led to the limitation of Pentagon contracts to U.S. businesses. This seems to insure the supply lines, but in fact many crucial components of military hardware are imported from other countries. Breakdown of supply lines to distant parts of the world could bring production to a halt.

Another group of natural allies are all those businessmen who are already seeking protection. This group is growing all the time, or at least until it is wiped out by the competition. It has considerable political power as witnessed by the trade bill passed by the House of Representatives.

But the most important constituency for rethinking national economic policy is labor. Unfortunately labor has already suffered greatly from free trade to the extent that its unions are weakened and its public image has declined. As long as it accepts the ideology that is destroying it, its ability to resist the consequences of that ideology is slight. But when it recognizes that this ideology is invalid, that there are excellent reasons for a different kind of national economy that will protect its relative place in society and give labor a new role in the community, the vigor of the movement can be restored.

There are dangers in each of these alliances. Although we agree that the nation should be able to supply itself with its needed arms, we would not want to encourage continued interest in global domination.

Although we agree that threatened business in general should have protection from imported goods so that the nation can move toward self-sufficiency, we insist that this be accompanied by greatly increased competitiveness among American producers and also with decentralization of production and control.

Although we agree that labor should be protected and the gains of the past century preserved, we do not want to see the renewal of labor militancy directed toward increasing its share of the pie over against capital and the general public. And although we strongly favor moving toward a national economy, we hope this can be done in a gradual and orderly way that will minimize the disruption of the economies of our trading partners. Also we hope that the nationalization of the economy can be accompanied by a strengthened internationalization in dealing with necessarily global issues. Reduced interest in domination and trade should be accompanied by increased interest in cooperative solution of problems.

We count on a fourth group whose support is less tied to economic self interest: a network of persons whose consciousness has been changed by participation in feminist and environmental movements, who have never lost an appreciation for the virtues of thrift and self-reliance, who have all along wanted to keep power closer to the people and to allow people to have a say in the economic as well as the political decisions that shape their lives. Without the leadership of these concerned people, a political coalition of special interest groups cannot succeed.

There is still another group whose support we covet. This is that rather small group of persons who have a deep and knowledgeable concern for the Third World. We are not referring to those who have studied the Third World only from their capital cities and in conversation with Third World elites but rather of those who have dealt with the people and who have observed what has happened to them during the course of development. We need their support not because of their numbers or direct political power but because of their moral authority and their wisdom. We have in mind specifically the kind of people who cooperated in writing the Brundtland Report (*Our Common Future*), which calls attention to the idea of sustainable development, which we discussed in Chapter 3. As the concept of sustainable development is further defined, we believe it will begin to resemble our outline of an economics for community.

We have a practical need for their moral authority because of the charge of immorality that will be directed against the move to a national economy. We will be told that we are shutting the door on the Third World's goods, and condemning their people to poverty just as some of them, by entering the industrial age, are beginning to attain affluence. We will be told that we are protecting the American standard of living only for Americans and at the expense of Third World workers, just when the transfer of technology is beginning to overcome the gap. We will be told that having drawn these people into the world trading pattern we are abandoning it just as they are learning to play the game successfully.

There is enough truth in these harsh charges to cause concern. We agree that the United States has a large responsibility toward these people, and we would be distressed if, as the nation moves toward a national economy, it denies that responsibility. The United States should foster self-sufficiency, at least in agriculture, in all those Third World countries that accept this goal. We need the guidance of those who understand Third World needs from the bottom up in order to act constructively.

Even if the United States turns its back on the rest of the world in a new isolationism, however, that may be a better service to other peoples than the pressures it now exerts upon them in the name of development. Since so little can happen to benefit the majorities in Third World countries apart from fundamental social change, and since in the name of internationalism the United States opposes and often prevents such changes, the end of such internationalism can be a boon. It will lead to the "delinking" for which a number of Third World leaders are calling.[3]

It is important to consider also who will be against the change. First and foremost, it will be opposed by the financial community. Financial institutions have become the most powerful force in the global economy in recent years, superceding industry, as industry has become more of a pawn in the flow of global capital. Those who gain their wealth from the mobility of capital will lose by the change to a national economy. These financiers are today the great cosmopolitans, celebrating the universal interdependence of all parts of the world, and they will complain bitterly about the retreat to "isolationism."

They will be supported by all those economic ideologues who refuse to be persuaded that the structure of their academic discipline is faulty. These will lend great theoretical respectability to the self-interest of the financial community. Often this will be done sincerely. The commitment to free trade among economists has a religious depth that will not easily be uprooted by empirical evidence or rational argument.

There will also be support from special interest groups, first and foremost from importers. They will indeed be hurt by the change, although if it is made gradually and they have plenty of warning, this need not be a major economic issue. Still, their businesses will become less profitable than they now are, and they can be counted on to appreciate this fact. Exporters will also complain as they come to realize that the United States cannot expand exports while cutting imports, since it is our imports that permit other countries to earn the dollars with which to pay for our exports.

A much larger group of retailers will also see restriction of importation of commodities as a loss. For them the loss will be less, since they can shift to U.S.-made products gradually. Nevertheless, compared with the present, they will find it harder to be profitable.

Mass support for the traditional free trade view will come from those

3. See the discussion of these matters in Chapter 15.

who identify themselves primarily as the economist's traditional *Homo economicus,* the rational consumer. Goods manufactured by workers earning U.S. wages will cost more than those that have been imported duty-free from low-wage countries. Also even if reduced international competition is followed by more competition within the nation, the range of choice in many goods will decline, at least for a while. Finally, the quality of many U.S. products is inferior and this situation is likely to continue until more of its best scientists are freed from military research to work on civilian goods and until labor and management become more of a community working together to improve their products.

We have argued in Chapters 11 and 15 that the present cornucopia of imported goods cannot last for the population as a whole. Something will happen to correct the extreme imbalance in trade, and in one way or another this will reduce the ability of most Americans to buy these goods. Labor will in general probably understand that the protection it needs also means that it will be buying American at higher prices. But many workers in low-paid service jobs, the growing segment of our economy, who do not see imports as a threat to their employment, will blame tariffs for the higher cost of living. Their antagonism will be fed by financiers and ideologues.

There is a massive problem here. With the breakdown of community at all levels, human beings have become more like what the traditional model of *Homo economicus* described. Shopping has become the great national pastime. The one place one can be most assured of a welcome is in a store. Status attaches to finding unusual goods and unusual prices. Hence any move that threatens people in their role as consumers, even if it does not deny them what they need in terms of goods, arouses considerable emotional hostility. It may make very difficult any discussion of how to deal with the national problem.

On the basis of massive borrowing and massive sales of national assets, Americans have been squandering their heritage and impoverishing their children. They have done so for the sake of present consumption, the enjoyment of the shopping that accompanies it, and most of all as a way to postpone questioning the efficacy of free trade and continuous growth. Somehow the disproportion between what is thereby gained and lost must be brought effectively to the attention of the public. The willingness to accept restrictions on imports will depend on finding images with mass appeal that show why the current affluence is an illusion and why a national economy is necessary.

The current affluence, however illusory, suggests that this may not be the right time to press for change. It is a good time to expose the theoretical and practical fallacies of the principle of comparative advantage as applied to the situation today. But people will be more willing to consider change when the weakness of the economy is more publicly visible. That time will come again.

Establishing an Optimum Scale

Thus far we have discussed only how to get acceptance for the idea of a relatively self-sufficient national economy. This is for us by no means an end in itself. We believe a national economy can function well for the sake of community in a way that a global one cannot, but there is no guarantee that it will do so. At the same time that we work for a national economy we must encourage the vision of a decentralized one.

More important still is another principle, the principle of right scale. Getting this idea accepted may be harder than that of the right of a nation to protect its producers. It goes against the very deeply held conviction that bigger is better, a virtual axiom of both political parties and of the great majority of the people as well.

There are no obvious constituencies for support of a scale of the economy that is appropriate in relation to the ecosystem. There is the network of those who have learned to think in biospheric ways, but there are no groups whose obvious economic interests lead them to seek ways to restrict the scale of the economy. Yet if this is not accepted, most of what is to be gained from moving to a national economy will be lost. A U.S. economy that dedicates itself to continuing growth will hasten destruction of the planetary environment almost as rapidly as one that is tied into the global economic system. The catastrophes that await humanity down this road are of such magnitude that the preservation of some of labor's gains and the advantages of relative national self-sufficiency will be small consolation.

Therefore, there is no choice but to try to generate a discussion of the proper scale of the economy. This falls outside the modern discipline of economics, which is as committed to endless growth as to free trade. But as in the case of free trade and the principle of comparative advantage, once the topic is seriously discussed the merits of proper scale can be convincingly displayed to those who have not been socialized to believe that the physical world is irrelevant to the economy. Today the wild facts are finding their way effectively into the public consciousness. The problem is to establish their relation to economic growth so that it will not be supposed that all that is needed is a new technology. Environmental degradation must be shown to result from the scale of the economy in general rather than only from allocative mistakes that can be corrected while throughput continues to grow exponentially.

One problem here is that so many have been left with the impression that the "limits to growth" debate and that about the "stationary state economy" are old hat, that somehow they were settled in favor of the orthodox advocates of growth. So many have a vested interest in believing this that it will not be easy to break through. However, we must ask to hear again, in confrontation with the wild facts, the arguments that are supposed to have settled the issue. To those who have not been successfully socialized into a way of seeing the economy as an isolated circular flow, these arguments are not impressive. If the isolation of the discussions of economics from those of physics, chemistry, and biology can be broken, the need to consider scale will prove undeniable. Indeed, even a breakdown of the isolation of micro from macroeconomics may go a long way toward establishing the importance of scale, as was suggested in Chapter 2.

Another way to establish the importance of scale is through the concept of carrying capacity. With present and foreseeable technologies, how many people at an acceptable standard of living can a given area support *indefinitely?* Even the crudest back-of-the-envelope calculation of carrying capacity can serve to inject some reality into economic development plans. Take for example the country of Paraguay. Its population of about four million people is growing at about 2.5% annually. Ninety-eight percent of the Paraguayans live in the eastern half of the country, and only 2% live in the western half, the Chaco. All the land in the east is now owned, and disputes over titles are frequent. Landholdings in the east are now being subdivided by inheritance. It is predictable that rather than face up to either land reform or population control, Paraguay will develop a plan to settle the empty Chaco, just as Brazil did with the "empty" Amazon. If you ask educated Paraguayans how many people can live in the Chaco you will get an answer ranging from five to twenty million. A simple calculation of carrying capacity reveals otherwise. Take the most successful colonists in the Chaco, the Mennonites. Let us generalize their population density to the entire Chaco to see how many people might live there if everyone were as successful as the Mennonites. In 1987 there were 6,650 Mennonites living on 420,000 hectares of land, giving a density of .0158 persons per hectare. Multiply that figure by 100 to get persons per square kilometer (1.58). Multiply that by the number of square kilometers in the Chaco ($247,000 \text{ km}^2$). This gives 390,260, roughly 400,000, or for good measure call it half a million. A half million people will be added to the Paraguayan population in only 5 years, so even under these favorable assumptions colonization of the Chaco would not buy much time. Moreover, the Mennonites' land is better than average Chaco land, and they brought with them the peasant farming traditions of Europe, and a strong community of mutual aid and support, including aid from Mennonites abroad. Paraguayan colonists will have none of these advantages. Furthermore it took the Mennonites 60 years of hard work to reach their present level of prosperity, which is by no means excessive. Nor is it entirely clear that Mennonite agriculture in the region is really sustainable. For these reasons half a million people probably represents an overestimate of carrying capacity in the Chaco. This maximum carrying capacity estimate should be the first datum of any settlement plan in the Chaco. Maybe with some super new technology the Chaco will eventually be able to support ten million people, but for the next decade or two, any estimate above half a million faces a very heavy burden of proof. But it is politically convenient not to know scale limits or carrying capacity, because that would imply a limit to growth. If growth is limited then poverty must be dealt with by either redistribution or population control, which are both taboo. Better not to think about it!

Lest one be tempted to feel superior to the Paraguayans it should be noted that the United States has not recognized scale or carrying capacity in its planning either, and our politicians also blather about the limitless frontiers of *space,* whose carrying capacity for the next generation is certainly less than the Paraguayan Chaco!

But even if scale is considered and thoughtful people acknowledge that it is important, can this muster a political constituency sufficient to affect public policy? If it is to do so, there must be a shift of perception as to what is measured. If the scale is thought of as measuring human well-being and happiness, it will be very difficult to build support for restricting it. Here is where the measures to be proposed in the Appendix can help. The issue of scale refers to the thoughtput of the economy, that is, how much of the planetary resources are used and how much waste is produced. This corresponds closely with what is measured by the GNP. As long as the GNP is thought to measure human well-being, the obstacles to change are enormous. If, however, it becomes clear that increase in GNP may accompany decline in economic welfare, and that improvements in economic welfare may accompany declines in GNP, then the desire to increase the scale of the economy will be reduced. People will be more willing to ask what scale of throughput contributes to sustainable economic welfare. Although we do not think this pushes the question far enough, it will be a good beginning. Public policies can be affected.

Measuring Economic Progress

It is obvious that seeking an optimum scale instead of infinite growth requires a different judgment of economic welfare than the one underlying use of the GNP as the basic measure of progress. It is also the case that a major objection to moving from a global economy to relatively sustainable national and regional ones is that this will reduce gross product. As long as maximum gross product is thought to conduce to economic welfare, it will be difficult to get consideration of alternative forms of economic life. Hence, one step that needs to be taken immediately is to raise the question of whether GNP is a satisfactory guide for those who are genuinely concerned to improve human economic welfare. In Chapter 3 we raised this question and concluded that GNP measures something quite different from economic welfare.

Chapter 7 returned to the discussion of measurements but primarily to show how distorting all measurements of success can be and how inappropriate they are, finally, to an economics for community. They inevitably tend to distort actions that they guide. Nevertheless, this does not justify leaving the GNP as the governing measure of success in today's world! Other measures can be much less seriously distorting than this one.

One response is to leave GNP alone as the proper measure of *economic* success and seek to counterbalance its influence by pointing to social and ecological indicators as of equal or greater importance. The most successful effort in this direction has been the Physical Quality of Life Index (PQLI), composed of three measures: infant mortality, life expectancy at age one, and literacy. Policies geared to improving the conditions measured by PQLI are often quite different from those geared to increasing the GNP. In the environmental area, measures of air pollution, water pollution, soil loss, ozone layer depletion, and global warming are now becoming familiar. We favor the wider dissemination and use of all these measures and many others.

Nevertheless, we are not sanguine that this indirect approach to challenging the hegemony of GNP will suffice. The economy is of such massive and primary importance to most policymakers that their first consideration is likely to be its improvement. They may accept certain social and environmental constraints on economic policies, and these constraints may be influenced by social and environmental indices. But the goal of policymakers will still be, given these constraints, to help the economy succeed.

If so, then the question of what constitutes economic success is of central importance. Today, for practical purposes, economic achievement has come to mean whatever it is that is measured by GNP. But no serious economist will defend this procedure. Hence the issue among economists is not whether GNP is a direct measure of economic well-being but whether it guides policy in ways that are generally for the economic well-being of the nation.

In Chapter 3 we considered two types of alternatives to GNP: Hicksian income and indices of economic welfare. Of the two, Hicksian income is theoretically well defined, whereas economic welfare is not. On the other hand, moving from the formal definition to determining how to calculate Hicksian income in detail is a difficult task that would include many of the same issues faced in a measure of sustainable welfare. It has not yet been attempted, but is at least under discussion in the World Bank and U.N. statistical agencies. Economic welfare has been much more fully discussed, and there have been important, detailed proposals for how to measure it. The latter is the task we have chosen to pursue more thoroughly in the Appendix.

Of available indices the Measure of Economic Welfare developed by Nordhaus and Tobin is the most promising. One step toward changing attitudes and arguments about economic growth would be to bring that measure up to date and to evaluate policies and proposals by it instead of by GNP. If this were done, the proposals made in this book would receive a better hearing than if they are judged by their contribution to increasing GNP. However, there are a number of limitations to MEW, some of them quite important. We believe that what is needed is revision that takes account of proposals involved in the Japanese Net National Welfare measure and Zolotas's Economic Aspects of Welfare. Indeed, what is needed is a new measure.

Because evaluation of policy changes is so heavily dependent on their anticipated effects on economic growth, and because growth is so widely assumed to be the increase in throughput measured by GNP, we believe that a new measure is indispensable to gaining a hearing for proposals that would tend to reduce GNP, as ours would. Accordingly, we have undertaken to propose such a measure. We call it the Index of Sustainable Economic Welfare (ISEW), and we explain it in detail in the Appendix.

The arguments for the ISEW are not based on the discussion of economics for community that constitutes the bulk of this book. They are based on contemporary mainstream economic discussion. Of course, on disputed issues we have taken sides, and the side we take is the one that regards equitable distribution of income as an economic desideratum and pollution and resource exhaustion as economic liabilities. Further, we believe that policies directed to improvement as measured by the ISEW would lead in directions that economics for community calls for. But the arguments for adopting ISEW are formulated without rejecting the individualistic bias of contemporary economic theory. We hope that someday measures of the health of communities could guide policy making rather than the per capita availability of economic goods, but in this chapter we are discussing steps that can be taken *now,* independently of a massive shift in fundamental perspective. We believe that it is urgent to replace the GNP with a measure that does not encourage the growing gap between the rich and the poor and that discourages unsustainable economic practices. The ISEW is far from perfect. All statistical measures are inevitably misleading in many respects. But the difference in policies ordered to the improvement of the ISEW and those ordered to the increase of GNP would be considerable, and they would help to buy time for the deeper changes that are needed.

Attitudinal Changes

The difficulty still remains that although people may recognize that true welfare is increased by reducing throughput, many individuals and businesses will find that this also reduces their immediate profits. Their short-run advantage lies with increasing the throughput. Indeed, this will be true of so many groups considered individually, that the pressure will be hard to resist.

The transition that is needed cannot be effected by appeals to people's political interests alone. It goes too deep. It cuts against patterns of thought and expectation that have been cultivated for generations. It must appeal to long-term interests in unaccustomed ways. The long-term includes the lifetimes of children and grandchildren, and it must assume a deep concern for them. In fact, it goes beyond that. A sustained willingness to change depends on a love of the earth that human beings once felt strongly, but that has been thinned and demeaned as the land was commodified.

Does that mean that the situation is hopeless? Must we assume that people will overuse the earth's resources and sinks despite all warnings as long as they can make an immediate profit, that change will only come when there is nothing left? No! We do not believe that is inevitable. There is always a chance that the right combination of ideas and leadership will strike the right chords at the right time. We, the authors, are not unique. We are like other people, and the same arguments that have convinced us will therefore have similar power over the minds of others, once they are awakened from dogmatic disciplinary slumber.

Love of the earth is not altogether dead within the human heart. There is still concern that children and grandchildren inherit a livable world. There is still a willingness to live a frugal and disciplined life if that can be seen as truly meaningful in relation to the massiveness of the problem. Capacity for sacrifice is not altogether gone. In short there is a religious depth in myriads of people that can find expression in lives lived appropriately to reality. That depth must be touched and tapped, and it must be directed by an honest and encompassing view of reality. If that is done, there is hope.

Our own understanding and commitment is a religious one (explained at greater length in Chapter 20), and we doubt that without that faith we would have either seen what we have seen or persevered in an unwelcoming context in articulating that vision and calling for change. It is our observation that others who share this passion and commitment with us are also deeply religious in varied ways. We have tried to make our case throughout this book in a predominantly secular mode. We think each argument and proposal stands on its own merits in some separation from the wider context that gives it its ultimate meaning for us. But we also think the *real* possibility for change depends on an awakening of the religious depths in a world whose secularity has gone quite stale.

Perhaps the problem is not so much that the religious depths are ineffective in society but that they express themselves so often idolatrously. Explicit religion becomes the sacred canopy that justifies parochial and even selfish interests as well as counterproductive inherited patterns of thought and morality. The same religiousness expresses itself in highly secular contexts in absolutizing secular beliefs, methods, and habits of mind. In some sense it is religiousness that the new vision will have to overcome.

Our point is not that religion is either a good or a bad thing. Our point is only that the changes that are now needed in society are at a level that stirs religious passions. The debate will be a religious one whether that is made explicit or not. The whole understanding of reality and the orientation to it are at stake. We think that to ignore that, to treat the issues as if they could be settled by abstract reason, is misleading. The victory will go to those who can draw forth these deepest energies of the centered self and give them shape and direction. Getting there, if it happens at all, will be a religious event, just as getting to where we are now was a religious event. Idolatry in the guise of misplaced concreteness and disciplinolatry have brought us to the present crisis. Overcoming these is a religious task.

20

The Religious Vision

Alternative Biospheric Visions

In Chapter 10 we discussed briefly what is most essential to the religious understanding that underlies this book, namely, the biospheric vision. However, our efforts to be as inclusive as possible in choosing the premises from which we have argued has led us to underplay this theme, leaving our argumentation, in our own view, not fully grounded. In this chapter we want to develop biospheric thinking in general, but also we want to clarify the form and basis of biospheric thinking that has in fact guided us throughout. We are both Christian theists, and we want to show how our belief supports the biospheric vision.

A second reason for including this chapter is that there are in fact multiple biospheric perspectives. When viewed from a distance against the background of the anthropocentrism and dualism that have dominated the modern world, these various perspectives appear similar. But the theological and philosophical issues that divide them are important not only theoretically but practically. Despite our hope for support from all who share the biospheric perspective, we know that both our own attention to economic issues and the way we have treated them follow from our particular version of the biospheric perspective. Other biospheric perspectives lead to raising different issues and to treating them in different ways. As biospheric thinking becomes more widespread, the importance of these divergences will grow.

There is a third reason for adding this chapter. There are many theists who suppose that belief in God is opposed to biospheric thinking. Like economics, modern Western Christianity has often allied itself to anthropocentrism and the neglect of nature. It has generated suspicion of organismic views of human beings and of their communities, and fear that the distinctiveness of human beings, both their specialness by virtue of having been created *imago dei* and their radical sinfulness, which distinguishes them from the rest of creation, will be obscured. Some modern Christians have been led by their investment in concern for human rights and identification with the oppressed to a suspicion that any major focus on the biosphere is a distraction from social justice issues. We take these suspicions seriously, but we believe that the biospheric perspective can be integrated into and grounded by theocentrism in a way that does not neglect justice, and indeed is required by justice. We want to show this and to channel the energies of our fellow Christian believers in directions that we think are more truly appropriate to our shared heritage.

The biospheric vision is richly inclusive and transformative of human perceptions. Once community with other living things is truly experienced and appreciated, aspects of our thinking and our way of life previously taken for granted become unacceptable. In short it is in itself a religious vision. The rise of this vision, especially through the influence of ecological and feminist sensitivities, has been one of the great advances of this generation. Only as the vision deepens and spreads is there hope for making the changes that are required by the wild facts.

The term "deep ecology" is sometimes used to refer to this vision and the move away from anthropocentrism that it entails. Two of the leaders of this movement, Arne Naess and George Sessions, have proposed eight basic principles for this movement.

1. The well-being and flourishing of human and nonhuman Life on Earth have value in themselves (synonyms: intrinsic value, inherent value). These values are independent of the usefulness of the nonhuman world for human purposes.

2. Richness and diversity of life forms contribute to the realization of these values and are also values in themselves.

3. Humans have no right to reduce this richness and diversity except to satisfy *vital* needs.

4. The flourishing of human life and cultures is compatible with a substantial decrease of the human population. The flourishing of nonhuman life requires such a decrease.

5. Present human interference with the nonhuman world is excessive, and the situation is rapidly worsening.

6. Policies must therefore be changed. These policies affect basic economic, technological, and ideological structures. The resulting state of affairs will be deeply different from the present.

7. The ideological change is mainly that of appreciating *life quality* (dwell-

ing in situations of inherent value) rather than adhering to an increasingly higher standard of living. There will be a profound awareness of the difference between big and great.

8. Those who subscribe to the foregoing points have an obligation directly or indirectly to try to implement the necessary changes. [Devall and Sessions 1985, p. 70]

We find ourselves in basic agreement with the principles of deep ecology as thus formulated. We would reword proposition 4 to refer to a "substantial decrease in the human niche, effected either by a reduction in population or in per capita resource consumption." Still we are in full alliance with those who have defined deep ecology in this way.

But matters are not this simple. For Naess and Sessions our position is in fact excluded from deep ecology despite our acceptance of the eight basic propositions. For them, basic points 1 and 2 are interpreted in terms of "biocentric equality," the intuition "that all things in the biosphere have an equal right to live and blossom and to reach their own individual forms of unfolding and self-realization within the larger self-realization . . . that all organisms and entities in the ecosphere, as parts of the interrelated whole, are equal in intrinsic worth" (Devall and Sessions 1985, p. 67).

We do not share this view. We believe there is more intrinsic value in a human being than in a mosquito or a virus. We also believe that there is more intrinsic value in a chimpanzee or a porpoise than in an earthworm or a bacterium. This judgment of intrinsic value is quite different from the judgment of the importance of a species to the interrelated whole. The interrelated whole would probably survive the extinction of chimpanzees with little damage, but it would be seriously disturbed by the extinction of some species of bacteria. We believe that distinctions of this sort are important as guides to practical life and economic policy and that the insistence that a deep ecologist refuse to make them is an invitation to deep irrelevance.

This dispute may be less substantial than it initially seems. Naess suggests that biocentric equality as an intuition is true in principle, although in the process of living, all species use each other as food, shelter, and so on. This suggests some openness to making judgments about which species it is better to use as food and for shelter and other needs. But the "basic intuition" actually governs the further development of the discussion, turning attention away from these practical issues. We, in contrast, encourage the emergence of a basic vision that will guide practical action by differentiating grades of both instrumental and intrinsic value while affirming the basic intuition that all living things have value independent of their usefulness for human purposes (Birch and Cobb 1981).

Perhaps the most widely influential expression of the biospheric vision has been that of Aldo Leopold (1966). Leopold proposed a land ethics with the fundamental principle: "A thing is right when it tends to preserve the integrity, stability, and beauty of the biotic community; it is wrong when it does otherwise" (Leopold, 1966, p. 240). This gives much clearer guidance to human action than does "biocentric equality." Leopold believed that the feeling expressed in this ethics can arise from the human recognition of kinship and interdependence with all living things.

The strongest objection to Leopold's ethics has come from those who fear that human responsibility to human beings will be drastically subordinated to concern for the health of the land, and that indeed there is no basis for real interest in individual animals. The suffering of individuals seems to count for little if only the integrity, stability, and beauty of the biotic community are in view.

J. Baird Callicott has recently defended Leopold against this charge and has shown that an adequately developed biocentric doctrine can do justice both to the commitment to the whole and to sensitivity to individuals—especially, but not exclusively, human individuals. His formulation is very close to ours in Chapter 9, where we speak of the community of communities as extending to the entire biosphere. In a community of communities there is a special relation to the more immediate community, but there is concern also for the other communities with which it is in relation. Also, the concern for the well-being of the community as a whole cannot be separated from respect for its individual members. Callicott quotes Leopold to show that this is not alien to him: "A land ethic changes the role of *Homo sapiens* from conqueror of the land community to plain member and citizen of it. It implies respect for fellow-members *and also* respect for the community as such" (Callicott 1980, p. 408).

Callicott's vision of the biotic community leads him to project developments in human society in much the way we have: "A human civilization based upon nonpolluting solar energy for domestic use, manufacturing and transportation and small-scale, soil conserving organic agriculture. There would be fewer material *things* and more *services, information,* and an opportunity for aesthetic and recreational activities; fewer people and more bears; fewer parking lots and more wilderness"

(Callicott 1980, p. 415). This indicates that indeed the policies we have advocated in Part Three can flow from the vision of a community of communities including all living things, the vision with which we concluded Part Two. We support Callicott's vision and argument.

Nevertheless, we are not wholly satisfied with it. Although we agree strongly with Callicott's balance of concern for individuals and for the whole, we find some difficulties on both points. Although we agree that it is possible to have respect for all other living creatures, it is not quite clear *why* we should do so. Sometimes the argument seems to be that the awareness of kinship and interdependence by itself generates this respect. We think it may or it may not. When it does not, is there any basis for calling for it, for claiming that one *should* have such respect? In part the argument seems to be that the evolutionary process selects for those who have such wider affections. Again we are not sure that this is true. Callicott's account of evolution puts the emphasis on the greater survival capacity of communities in which there is mutual support. This is indeed one aspect of the process. But evolution seems also to have selected those human communities that had superior technologies and did not hesitate to use them in war against others. It is a mixed process, not altogether benign. We fear that the factors for which evolution has selected may lead human beings to act in ways that will destroy much of the biosphere. This seems to be what is happening, and we doubt that it is safe to await a change of heart brought about by evolutionary selection. Actually we do not see Callicott as doing this. He is presenting us an attractive candidate for an ethic, one that is self-consistent, adequate, and practical. He appeals to people to accept it on the basis of those among their feelings that lead in this direction. We hope his appeal is *widely* successful. But thus far it has not been. We wonder if it is not possible to give stronger grounds for adopting the ethic he supports.

There is some ambiguity also on the side of the "whole" to which he appeals. Occasionally it seems that this might be the cosmos, but generally it seems to be the biotic community or biosphere. We agree that this is as far as it is meaningful to go in seeking to extend a sense of community beyond the human species. But what is the nature of this whole? Where does it exist? Does it exist only in and for the individuals of which it is composed? Callicott's language suggests that this is not what he means. Yet if not, what status does it have? And finally, is the biotic community practically a sufficient and appropriate object of commitment? When biospheric thinking, which we strongly endorse, takes the biosphere as the ultimate object of concern, when it becomes in this sense biocentric, limitations appear.

Biocentrism can fall short of what is needed if it distinguishes too sharply between the animate and the inanimate. Community based on similarity and concern for individuals declines to the vanishing point when inanimate things are included. But something like community based on interconnectedness and interdependence remains. Furthermore, the sense of such community has not been absent to human history. It was common among the pre-European inhabitants of North America. The feeling for the landscape of one's native land is not a strange sentiment even among moderns. The picture of the planet taken from outer space aroused deep feelings of love for the earth as home. A geocentric vision includes the biospheric perspective in its more comprehensive context. We think that the policies we propose are appropriate from a geocentric perspective and indeed can be derived from it. The whole earth should, for its human inhabitants, be like a community of communities.

Systems thinking has led some in this direction. Recently, Lovelock has given moving expression to this sense of the earth in his book on *The Gaia Hypothesis* (1979). It has received surprisingly wide and favorable attention. In much the way biocentric thinking is based on biology, and especially ecology as a branch of biology, Lovelock's geocentric thinking is based on chemistry. He focuses on atmospheric gases and global temperature as affected by them, showing how remarkable their relative constancy of balance is. Whereas it has often been supposed that the composition of the atmosphere was given and happened to make life possible on this planet as it is not possible elsewhere, Lovelock argues that to an extraordinary extent it is the living systems on the planet that produce and maintain the atmosphere. He pictures the earth as a self-regulating system.

From all that has been learned about the interactions of the organic and inorganic parts of the planet "has arisen the hypothesis, the model, in which the Earth's living matter, air, oceans, and land surface form a complex system which can be seen as a single organism and which has the capacity to keep our planet a fit place for life" (Lovelock 1979, p. vii). Earth viewed in this way Lovelock calls Gaia.

Lovelock emphasizes that the processes through which the earth regulates itself are automatic in the sense that they do not involve conscious thought. This is true of homeostatic processes generally. But he argues that "some form of intelligence is required even within an automatic process, to interpret correctly information received from the environment. . . . The body's automatic temperature-regulating system is intelligent to the point of genius" (p. 146). Lovelock sees Gaia as intelligent at least in this limited sense.

If, as Lovelock believes, the earth is properly understood as Gaia, "then we may find ourselves and all other living things to be parts and partners of a vast being who in her entirety has the power to maintain our planet as a fit and comfortable habitat for life" (p. 1). This leads to a quasi-religious vision of human destiny:

The evolution of homo sapiens, with his technological inventiveness and his increasingly subtle communications network, has vastly increased Gaia's range of perception. She is now through us awake and aware of herself. She has seen the reflection of her fair face through the eyes of astronauts and the television cameras of orbiting spacecraft. Our sensations of wonder and pleasure, our capacity for conscious thought and speculation, our restless curiosity and drive are hers to share. This new interrelationship of Gaia with man is by no means fully established; we are not yet a truly collective species, corralled and tamed as an integral part of the biosphere, as we are as individual creatures. It may be that the destiny of mankind is to become tamed so that the fierce, destructive, and greedy forces of tribalism and nationalism are fused into a compulsive urge to belong to the commonwealth of all creatures which constitutes Gaia. It might seem to be a surrender, but I suspect that the rewards, in the form of an increased sense of well-being and fulfillment, in knowing ourselves to be a dynamic part of a far greater entity, would be worth the loss of tribal freedom [Lovelock 1979, p. 148]

Admirable as Lovelock's vision is, and much as we hope to be able to collaborate with those who share it, its limitations should also be noted. Because it focuses on the chemical cycles, those aspects of the earth's living system that are not important for these cycles tend to be slighted. Less important, perhaps, is the obvious fact that the earth is part of a still larger system, so that abstracting it from that larger system as the object of ultimate concern exaggerates its autonomy and continues to encourage devotion to a part rather than to the whole.

We have noted the tendency among biocentric thinkers to focus on the earth's system as a whole in ways that depreciate the importance of the suffering of individual creatures. This tendency is, if anything, stronger in Lovelock's geocentric perspective. We believe there is need for a vision that combines the systemic interests that have been identified by these thinkers with appreciation for the importance of each individual participant in the system quite apart from its contribution to the whole.

The Prophetic Tradition

Our appreciation for the biocentric and geocentric thinkers we have considered, as well as our critique of them, stem from our own immersion in the biblical faith. This leads us to be concerned for individual creatures and their individual suffering and also with the importance of giving our final commitment and loyalty to the whole. To commit oneself finally to anything less than the whole is, in this perspective, idolatry.

Idolatry can be defined formally as treating as ultimate or whole that which is not ultimate or whole. It is very much like the fallacy of misplaced concreteness, which treats as concrete what in fact is abstract. Many instances of that fallacy lead to idolatry. We cannot live without abstractions, and yet there is profound danger when we forget that they are abstractions. Similarly we cannot live without committing ourselves to what is less than ultimate. Yet there is a profound danger when we forget that the object of our commitment is only a part of a larger whole. Everyone commits the fallacy of misplaced concreteness. All of us are idolators. That will always be the human condition. But we must not for that reason cease to distinguish between abstract and concrete in an effort to check our reasoning and correct our errors. Nor can we deny or ignore the difference between the part and the whole, the human and the divine perspective, if we are to submit our thinking to continuous correction. We need a constant reminder that our functional commitments, however worthy, fall short of the ultimate.

The canonical prophets prophesied primarily against their own community, Israel, and it was in this context that there arose the deepest roots of Western individual personhood. The prophet as individual was addressed by God and claimed God's authority for his message. The absolute authority of human community was exposed as idolatrous. No human community can finally control an individual's relation to God.

But for the prophets of Israel this individual autonomy was a minor note in comparison with the importance of community and the assumption that to be a person is to be person-in-community. God's Word is normally addressed to whole communities, and especially to Israel. Israel's chosenness by God was for the highest responsibility. Hence it is criticized most severely for its failings as a community.

In general Christianity derived from the prophetic tradition within Judaism. It accentuated the emphasis on the individual over against natural communities, while elevating itself as a community to a nearly supernatural status. Its history has been filled with prophetic critique of its own life and practice, but it has also often turned prophetic criticism outward against society as a whole and against other religious communities as well. Too often Christian theory and practice, rather than God, have been the norms for this critique and there has been far too little appreciation for the inherent, if penultimate, value of diverse communities.

This one-sided appropriation of the prophetic tradition characterized much of the Protestant Reformation. Among its own believers it established new communities. In the understanding of these communities it continued something of the passion of the Hebrew prophets for the righteousness of Israel as a community. It emphasized the immediacy of each individual to God, modifying that only with respect to the instruments of grace through which God has chosen to express that immediacy. But it failed to emphasize that all human community is an instrument of grace. The Enlightenment took place chiefly on Protestant soil. It swept away the instruments of divine grace and the community that served them. Only the individual and God were left alongside the nation. Individuals might join together in projects that they could not complete alone, but all such associations were contractual. Thus unnurtured, the very idea of community began to atrophy.

As the Enlightenment proceeded even the immediacy of God disappeared. Human beings were immediate to themselves individually, and that was enough. "God" was no longer seen in and through the creatures but was viewed as standing outside them and above them, known to exist only by reason. The creatures functioned quite autonomously without God. Then "God" became redundant and disappeared. The human soul alone was sacred. The rest was atoms in a void. For some, the soul, too, was a part of this meaningless physical world; nothing was sacred.

The children of the Enlightenment spread their gospel everywhere. All the ancient cultures of the world felt the power of the Enlightenment critique. For the enormous accomplishments of their communities rooted in great traditions they heard no support. Then there fell upon them the power of an economic system, rooted in this way of thinking. To succeed in this new system, the ancient cultures required modernization or rationalization, which meant the destruction of the power of tra-

dition and community. Land and labor—that is, the earth and human beings—had to become commodities. The result has been a holocaust, and this process of rationalization and commodification threatens to destroy yet more.

The prophetic tradition as it functioned in Protestant Christianity has failed humankind in one other way. In its biblical origins it appreciated the land not as a commodity but as the creation and gift of God. In the creation story of Genesis it is said that God sees the many creatures as "good" before and quite apart from the creation of human beings. Throughout the Jewish scriptures the land is God's, not a commodity to be owned by human beings. All the creatures are seen as praising God. In Jesus' teaching God cares for the sparrows and for the lilies of the field. Jesus taught that God cares even more for human beings, but the care for the lilies and for the sparrows is not just for the sake of human beings; it is for the lilies and the sparrows themselves.

But this aspect of the prophetic tradition failed to advance and develop in Christianity. On the contrary, the tradition especially in its Protestant form became narrowly focused on God and the human soul. Thus Protestantism paved the way for the anthropocentrism of the Enlightenment and the relegation of the rest of creation to the status of passive matter to be shaped by human beings to human ends.

We, the authors of this book, are heirs through Protestantism of the prophetic tradition and also of the Enlightenment. We understand deeply from within both their purifying and their annihilating power. We do not deny their truth. But we repent of the one-sidedness with which they have functioned. We would combine that truth with another one, the truth powerfully affirmed in the biblical origins of the prophetic tradition that we are persons-in-community, that there is no genuinely human life when community is destroyed. We would affirm that *all* community is to be celebrated, as our Catholic sisters and brothers have long known.

This message, we think, is now the one of greatest urgency for the world. Hence in our book the emphasis lies here. We celebrate all human community as it struggles against the atomization inherent in Enlightenment thought and modern practice, especially economic practice. We rejoice in the extension of community among those of our time who have come to reaffirm community with all peoples, with other animals, with all living things, and with the whole earth. But in this celebration of community we do not want to lose what is valid in the prophetic tradition: the warning against idolatry. This concern forces us to

distinguish ourselves from the biocentric and geocentric forms of biospheric thinking. Penultimately what the biocentric and geocentric thinkers say is what needs to be said. But ultimately their limits, too, must manifest themselves. It is well from the beginning to know that these limits are there and to reserve one's ultimate commitment for God, even though the proper expression of that ultimate commitment in this time and place will be to give ourselves enthusiastically to the penultimate.

The modern prophetic tradition, when it stands alone, can belittle not only human community but all earthly things. The immediacy of God can loom so large that all interest in the world and even in the neighbor appears as a distraction. In this it can unite with some currents in neoplatonic mysticism. Truly to love God sometimes seems to mean that one is totally absorbed in the immediacy of that relationship.

That is not the biblical prophetic view. In the Bible the immediacy of God frees people from absolute worldly loyalties in order to bring about justice and righteousness within the world. The unity of love of God and love of neighbor are affirmed unequivocally. Indeed, the way to serve God truly is to serve the neighbor. What one does to the neighbor, especially the lowly neighbor, one does to God.

It is our strong desire to stand in solidarity with all those who are expanding the horizons of concern. Our interest in this book is certainly not to argue with them but to offer a program of action on which many can agree. Nevertheless, the difference in ultimate perspective can lead to disagreements with respect to how more immediate matters are considered. Where our perspective is distinctive, we need to acknowledge that.

Sometimes there is tension between those who emphasize the appropriateness of concern for individual members of other species and those who focus on the biosphere and its total health, downplaying the importance of individual creatures. The humane society and the ecological movement can be allies in many struggles, but their emphases are different and sometimes clash. One emphasizes fellow feeling for all that suffer. The other emphasizes the interconnectedness of all living things such that the health of one part of the biosphere is important to all. Both points should be made. The task is to integrate them into a larger whole.

Our conviction is that the prophetic theistic point of view provides the best basis for accomplishing this important task. In this perspective each animal is immediate to God. Its suffering is immediate to itself and immediately shared by God. Those who love God will avoid causing unnecessary suffering even to the least of God's creatures.

But whatever else God is, God is also the inclusive whole. The diversity of the innerconnected parts of the biosphere gives richness to the whole that is the divine life. The extinction of species and simplification of the ecosystems impoverishes God even when it does not threaten the capacity of the biosphere to sustain ongoing human life. Hence the danger of collapse of the life-system is by no means the only reason to oppose the decimation of tropical forests!

Some people who do not affirm theism still affirm both the value of individuals and that of the whole system. We are in alliance with them, and we believe that many people intuitively share our conviction that both are important. Our point is that this affirmation can best be grounded in the view that there is a unified whole sensitive to all that transpires within it. We affirm this inclusive unity as the God of the prophetic tradition, and that this prophetic theism can lead beyond some of the costly conflict among those seeking to break out of the anthropocentric heritage which continues to bind the culture.

The Place of Human Beings

Some of those who view the world from a biospheric perspective emphasize that human beings are simply one species among others. They attack the biblical notion of human dominion as a fundamental error and distortion responsible for much of the evil that has been visited on this planet.

On these matters there is a real difference between us and some of those with whom we hope to be allied. Human beings do constitute one species of animals among others. We not only acknowledge that but want to do what we can to reinforce that perception, which struggles against deep-seated habits of denial. The biblical line is not drawn between humanity and the other animals but between God and creatures. The word translated in the English Bible as "all flesh" expresses the commonality.

But human beings are not "simply" one species among others. The human role is unique. It was unique already in hunting and gathering societies even if their relation with their environment was generally less destructive than ours. Even then people experienced a certain dominion. Today that dominion is almost complete. Any improvement of the relations between human and other species will come about by better ways of exercising dominion, not by renouncing it.

The problem has been that the idea of dominion has been misunderstood by the readers of the Bible. It has been forgotten that in God's order the ruler rules for the sake of the ruled. Dominion has been taken to justify exploitation of those over whom it is exercised. There is no doubt that the biblical call for dominion has been responsible for much unjustified cruelty and destruction. But the way forward is to understand it more deeply and more responsibly. The best exercise of dominion now possible would be to make more space for other species to live their lives without human interference. This, in fact, is what many mean by renouncing dominion. But this policy would still come about through human decision and would thereby reflect our dominion.

Some of those who criticize the biblical affirmation of human dominion go much further and much deeper. They see the whole movement of the human spirit toward self-transcendence, the prophetic urge to self-criticism, as part of what is destructive. In *Nature and Madness* (1982), Paul Shepard has given particularly powerful and insightful expression to this line of thought. Rather than seek to understand themselves and change themselves, rather than to relativize their own perspectives in light of a comprehensive one, human beings should, like other animals, be what they are. The cultivation of a distinctive human possibility inevitably leads to anthropocentrism of a dangerous sort. It leads human beings to think that they can manage the course of events rather than allow the natural course to carry through. A naive anthropocentrism is said to be acceptable. Human beings without self-transcendence naturally view the world through human eyes and from their own point of view. But this is harmless. Viewed in that way they function as part of a natural order rather than as standing above it.

The issues posed here are utterly fundamental. If Shepard is correct, then the prophetic-Enlightenment tradition is without any redeeming feature. Its supposed spiritual accomplishments have been simply destructive. The only hope is for those "accomplishments" to wither and die, leaving something more basic in the human soul to express itself again in a healthy way, something that accepts the status of human beings as merely one animal species among others.

The argument has two levels. There is first the question of whether the world would have been better off if the process of "advance" had not occurred—if humanity had continued to live as hunters and gatherers. Even in biblical terms this is a difficult question. It is the question whether humanity would have been better off if there had been no Fall.

The Garden of Eden corresponds to the hunting and gathering society. The Garden in Christian myth differs from the normative condition of humanity as Shepard pictures it in two respects. First, even before the Fall, God gave to human beings dominion over plants and animals. Second, whereas hunting is a part of the normative condition for Shepard, and domestication represents the Fall, in the Garden of Eden dominance is not expressed either in hunting or in domestication. These belong to the fallen condition. There is a less full acceptance of the killing of other animals in the biblical tradition than in Shepard. But we will not pursue that point.

In biblical terms, the state of being before the Fall had a certain perfection. The Fall is a consequence of sin and the cause of suffering for both humanity and other animals. It is certainly not viewed primarily as a gain! Yet there is an ambiguity about the judgment. The knowledge of good and evil remains attractive to human beings and is something they would not cheerfully give up. The salvation for which they hope is not a return to the original innocence of Adam and Eve but something fundamentally better.

We find ourselves continuing this biblical ambivalence. When we observe the hastening march to self-ruin on the part of the world's dominant institutions, and when we see the role played in that by the knowledge of good and evil, we cannot help but see that it might indeed have been better had our ancestors never left the Garden. There is a health about contemporary hunting and gathering societies that our civilizations have taken from us. We think there is an inherent enjoyment of the knowledge of good and evil to which Shepard's formulations are insensitive, but unless some future lies before the planet other than the one that now appears most likely, we have to concede that he is right. In Christian terms, the temptation to eat of the fruit of that tree was indeed a temptation. Human beings, and the biosphere as a whole, would be better off if that fruit had been uneaten.

Even if we concede that point to Shepard, the real issue remains unresolved. Once the Fall has occurred, can humanity return? The Bible says no. An angel blocks the way. Apart from the mythology, the message is clear. That solution is impossible. The knowledge of good and evil that destroyed our innocence must now function to guide us through the fallen world. Shepard, on the other hand, while knowing that there is never any way to duplicate a past situation, holds as the goal whatever approximation is possible—a life in which the knowledge of good and evil is gone.

Shepard's argument against the biblical position is impressive. The force of human transcendence is inherently disruptive. As human society settles into patterns, as community forms, as the immediacy of enjoyment of life becomes possible, criticism disturbs this. In the interest of higher ideals, the good that is real is rejected. Yet the results never embody those ideals. The attainment of a new equilibrium becomes ever more difficult.

The response of the prophetic tradition has often been to become more apocalyptic. Recognizing that human efforts to impose virtue make the course of history more bloody, some believers cry out for a final fulfillment that will reverse all this and yet make some sense of the slaughter bench that is history. Rather than see God as working through human efforts and the transcending perspective that guides those efforts, they appeal to God as one outside the historical process to intervene and put all things right. If that is the best the prophetic tradition can offer, then Shepard is right. Better to abandon the knowledge of good and evil, to accept what is for what it is, than to view it with helpless horror while counting on a supernatural intervention to redeem it in the end.

But we are not convinced that these are the only options. We think that deepening the knowledge of good and evil even now can put our situation into perspective that makes possible choices to reduce if not avoid the catastrophes toward which history hastens. We do not think it would be better if everyone simply went along uncritically in the course of present events.

Of course, in reality, Shepard does not adopt the stance he recommends. There is no more powerful and discerning prophetic voice in our time. It is only by the most radical self-transcendence that he has come to the insight as to the immensely destructive role of self-transcendence in the history of this planet. He is caught in the same dilemma as we, the dilemma of fallen human beings, and his response is the same. It differs in details, but it seeks to deepen the prophetic critique made possible by self-transcendence.

There is, then, really no alternative to the prophetic stance in fallen history. The choice is between calling for the return to the Garden and proposing some end different both from where we began and from where we have been since then. Shepard chooses the Garden; we choose a different end.

Our choice of the latter depends on a somewhat different reading of history. We see, with Shepard, the horrors of history and how often they have been induced by the very efforts to change a situation that the tainted fruit of the tree of knowledge has allowed people to judge as evil. That pattern appears all too clearly in recent times in most of the aid that has been given for development in the Third World. Those who would reform others have done some good and much evil.

Nevertheless here and there are instances in which self-transcendence has led to visions that have inspired actions which, with all their ambiguities, are good. In our lifetime we can cite the work of Gandhi and Martin Luther King as the most influential and widely admired examples. The women's movement has lifted to conscious criticism unrecognized habits of oppression and has begun to deliver on its promise of better modes of human relationship. There are thousands of others. They have not changed the broad sweep of events, but they have shown that good, too, can result from self-transcendence. We have not given up hope, and we continue to appraise hope, not as the final evil but as God's grace to those who persevere.

Biologism and Theism

A more typical exponent of a nontheistic and even antitheistic biocentric point of view is E. O. Wilson. His position is a form of biologism. It is important to him that a scientific biological approach provide the comprehensive framework within which human beings understand themselves. His self-critical defense of this position is refreshingly honest and opens the way for us to explain our preference for a theistic rather than a biologistic form of the biospheric perspective. In his book, *On Human Nature,* Wilson spells out the dilemma of biologism. The first dilemma is that: "The species lacks any goal external to its own biological nature. . . . Traditional religious beliefs have been eroded, not so much by humiliating disproofs of their mythologies as by the growing awareness that beliefs are really enabling mechanisms for survival. Religions, like other human institutions, evolve so as to enhance the persistence and influence of their practitioners" (Wilson 1978, p. 3).

Wilson, to his credit, sees that "the danger implicit in the first dilemma is the rapid dissolution of transcendental goals toward which societies can organize their energies" (p. 3). Of course Wilson is a scientific materialist and does not believe in trancendental goals, but he recognizes their important role in the social order, even if illusory. Rather than base our society on trancendental illusions, Wilson suggests that we "search for a new morality based upon a more truthful definition of man, [that we] dissect the machinery of the mind—and retrace its evolutionary history."

But this only leads us, Wilson points out, to a second dilemma, "which is the choice that must be made among the ethical premises inherent in man's biological nature. . . . We must consciously choose among the alternative emotional guides we have inherited." How are we to decide which emotional guides to follow and which to stifle? "At the center of the second dilemma is found a circularity: we are forced to choose among the elements of human nature by reference to value systems which these same elements created in an evolutionary age now long vanished" (Wilson 1978, p. 196).

Wilson's view is indeed problematic. To the extent that we have inherited value systems genetically, these value systems are a by-product of the earlier environment of the hunter-gatherer, and are not reliable guides for the age of atomic power and genetic engineering. The difficulty is even more general: no moral value (indeed no rational thought at all) can be valid, can have authority, if it is fully explainable as the result of amoral or arational causes. Random mutation and natural selection are amoral and arational events, and although they can certainly explain much, they cannot possibly entirely explain rational and moral thought. Otherwise the theory of evolution would itself be merely a product of genetic chance and natural selection and would in the long run stand or fall not by its legitimate claim to be in large part true, but by its survival value. But Wilson has explicitly admitted this survival value is rather low because in his version the theory must undercut a belief in transcendental value which, right or wrong, does have high survival value in providing a basis for social cohesion. If there is no transcendental source of value that somehow makes contact with nature in the mind, or alternatively, if there is no providential force behind the genetic chance and environmental necessity of evolution, then to what, besides chance or whim, can one appeal in choosing how to remake human nature?

One must admire the hard-headed logical consistency of the scientific materialist at his best. Wilson has followed logic where it has led, and that is to a dilemma. There are two alternatives: affirm transcendental value as a reality to which we can turn for guidance, or affirm the nihilism implicit in scientific materialism and give up all claim to truth or righteousness. Which leap does Wilson make? Neither. He tries to weasel out: "Fortunately, this circularity of the human predicament is not so tight that it cannot be broken through an exercise of will" (Wilson 1978, p. 196).

There are two logical problems with this escape act. First, where does "will" come from for a scientific materialist who expects that "the mind will become more precisely explained as an epiphenomenon of the neuronal machinery of the brain"? (p. 195). Is will a part of the neuronal machinery? If so, it is determined by past evolution and cannot suddenly overthrow its master. Or is will an epiphenomenon? Strange epiphenomenon that can alter the basic phenomena! Or might will be contraband smuggled into the land of scientific materialism from the theistic lands of transcendental value?

The second problem is worse. Even if the general appeal to will were legitimate there remains the question of whether what is specifically asked of will is legitimate. Can will break a logical circularity? Not even the most ardent believers in free will have ever claimed that one could evade a logical conclusion by an exercise of will. One could understand how will might be appealed to as a general urge to action, but not as a criterion for deciding which action to take. The resolution of Wilson's dilemma requires a criterion, not an urge. Not only does Wilson appeal to will while professing not to believe in it (except as an epiphenomenon), but he also requires that will perform the miraculous tasks of breaking a purely logical circularity and serving as a criterion as well as an urge. This just will not do.

As a final irony, Wilson cautions that "Whenever other philosophers let their guard down, deists can, in the manner of process theology, postulate a pervasive transcendental will." Wilson's honest struggle with the insoluble dilemmas of scientific determinism opens the way for us, as process theologians, to fulfill his warning. We are not sure that other philosophers have let down their guard, but we do think his own formulations indicate that there must be something in reality that transcends physical determinism; otherwise thinking and choosing make no sense at all. But when Wilson posits the human will in this capacity, he generates a radical dualism. This runs counter to his whole evolutionary understanding. Also, once something transcendent is affirmed it is arbitrary and ad hoc to restrict it to the human will.

From our point of view as process thinkers it seems better to avoid this apparently metaphysical dualism of blind matter and human will by seeing both as abstractions from the actual events of which the world is made up. We believe that all events, including acts of human willing, are largely the outcome of antecedent events. But we also hold that none are wholly determined by the past. Something happens afresh in each event. There is everywhere some respect in which what happens is decided only as it happens. This is the principle of self-determination that limits the strict predeterminism that scientists so often posit. The human act of choice is the most dramatic, the most vivid instance of a feature of reality that is universal. It is not a metaphysically discontinuous element in an otherwise perfect machine.

If human willing does belong to the same universe as all other events, if it is less free than humans like to think, and if some faint analogue is found in mice and amoeba as well, then there is more to the universe than matter in motion. There are also real options among which to choose. Much as all things are determined by the past, they also transcend the past by virtue of the presence in each event of real possibilities among which only one can be actualized. Usually these "decisions" are trivial, but their cumulative effect in the course of time is not. And in the human case, occasionally, the decision rises to consciousness and has dramatic immediate consequences.

In the human case, at least, these options are experienced as weighted. Some are felt as better than others. Sometimes they appear as right or wrong, true or false. This weighting does not predetermine the outcome. People can resist the claim of righteousness and truth; indeed, they often do. But it is hard to deny that such a claim is present. The direct experience of purpose and choice is as real as anything we experience. It cannot be a sensory illusion since the experience is unmediated by the senses. In this meaning at least we agree with Descartes in believing in a God who, while allowing us to be badly mistaken, does not allow us to be fundamentally and hopelessly deceived.

All of this means that in addition to the past something else is given for each event. It is that which makes of each event a response to its world rather than an inert product. Martin Heidegger once wrote of the "call forward." Whitehead used the term "lure," and emphasized the pull of final causation as well as the push of efficient causation. However it is named, it points to a pervasive feature of the totality within which all events occur and whose neglect leads to perplexities and contradictions. It is that feature by virtue of which possibilities take on weighted relevance to the actual world and become claims upon it. We believe this to be universal throughout the cosmos rather than a peculiar feature of life on this planet. Hence, we connect it to the whole. We call it God. Apart from God, we think, there would be no meaning, no life, no righteousness, no truth, no value. There would be only the mechanistic determination of the present by the past that Wilson envisions. We believe that human life is lived most richly and most rightly when it is lived from God and for God.

Strengths of Theocentrism

We commend this theocentric undergirding of the biospheric perspective on several grounds.

First, it is a check against idolatry. Those who do not consider God at all nevertheless orient themselves around something. In the modern world, in the case of ethicists and economists and many others, this orientation is around the ultimate worth of human beings, whether as individuals (for the economist), or as a collectivity (for some ethicists). But, however valuable, human beings are not of ultimate worth. Treating themselves as if they were has led to the brink of destruction. And such treatment of what is not ultimate as if it were ultimate, of a part as if it were the whole, of what is worthy of relative commitment as if it were worthy of final commitment—that is idolatry.

Of course, speaking of "God" cannot prevent idolatry. Those who think of God are also in grave danger of identifying God with some fragment of the whole, or some figment of the imagination. The use of the word God may heighten the fanaticism that accompanies all idolatries. But the thought of God in the context in which the prophetic tradition has not died at least opens up the subject for critical examination. It can drive the heart and mind beyond idolatry.

This assertion that theism functions as a safeguard against uncriticized idolatry runs counter to deep-seated claims of the Enlightenment in its most fully secularized forms. Atheism and positivism see themselves as destroying the last vestiges of superstition and view theism as idolatrous and superstitious. Whereas humanistic forms of the Enlightenment transfer the sense of the sacred to the human person or the human soul, these more radical approaches undertake to eliminate any ground of religious, and therefore of idolatrous, feeling. By reducing everything to matter and space, or to the immediate data of sense experience, all the mysteries that had tantalized the human mind from time immemorial, tempting it to identify this or that as sacred, were set aside. The only tasks remaining were those of explaining and controlling material processes. People thought that by directing their attention to the practical and answerable questions they could gain control of events and build the society of their dreams.

That expectation has now collapsed. The world constructed by those who refused ultimate questions is not more safe, more just, more loving, or more hopeful than the ones constructed by cultures preoccupied

with ultimate questions. This approach has succeeded in greatly increasing the numbers of people and the quantity of artifacts on the
earth. But even in these accomplishments it is not secure. The growth
economy is faltering. There are massive threats to human life, and now
it appears that the very growth in which such pride has been taken is
the cause of the threat to its continuance. With the abandonment of ultimate questions, horizons shrank to too-limited a range for effective
guidance of human decisions. Even the resources on which the great
expansion of population and goods was built were ignored in planning
for the future. Their limits caught the planners by surprise.

But it may be thought that at least the refusal to spend time with ultimate mysteries has cleared the mind of superstition and error, that
people have understood the limits of what can be known and have appreciated the relativity of beliefs and opinions. Alas, would that it were
so! But we have already seen that built into the very structure of modern
thought are assumptions, false assumptions, that take on the form of
absolutes and that the university has been so organized as to discourage
any question or challenge to these absolutes. We suspect that the modern mind has been more successful than its predecessors in squashing
heresy. It has declared the heretic's teaching meaningless rather than
false, thereby justifying ignoring it rather than attempting to show its
error. Whereas earlier societies have excommunicated publicly, giving
reasons for their actions, modern savants have done so silently. The result is dogmatism. Among economists, for example, no real argument
needs to be given for devoting oneself ultimately to the promotion of
productivity and growth. No recitation of the horrors that this commitment has inflicted upon human beings, not to speak of the other creatures, no explanation that the physical conditions that made growth
possible in the past are rapidly disappearing, no clarification of how human welfare can be met in other ways—none of this has yet sufficed to
shake the conviction so deeply rooted in the discipline that growth is
both the supreme end and the supreme means for achieving the end.
Precisely by limiting the horizons of inquiry one can attain to this state
of mind. The rest, economists often think, is "theology," and hence not
worthy of their time. But if so, then has the application of Enlightenment positivism to thinking about the economy freed it from idolatry?
Or are not the rigid commitments so characteristic of the discipline of
economics an indication that idolatry has reasserted itself, all the more
powerful because its presence is so vehemently denied?

Second, to be theocentric is to recognize a perspective that transcends one's own and embodies the truth about the whole. The world is as God knows it because God's knowledge is God's undistorted inclusion of all things. God knows and values each sparrow and knows and values each human being as well. The sparrow is of value in itself, and human beings are of value in themselves. But it is hard, simply within the world, to compare the value of the sparrow and the value of the human being. It is in God that each value is just what it is and in proper union with all other values.

Ethicists who do not believe in God sometimes say that what we really ought to do in each situation is what an impartial and omniscient spectator would favor. They often deny that this is what religious people mean by "God" because it does not correspond to the idolatrous images of "God" against which they have reacted. But the true God is the omniscient and impartial unifying source of all. What we really should do in each situation is what will correspond to God's purposes and enrich God's life. People can to some extent live "as if." They can make their decisions as if there were such a being while believing that it does not exist. But to believe that God does exist makes the ethical life more authentic. Belief heightens sensitivity to aspects of reality that are otherwise neglected. It gives real importance to what happens in the world, especially to the despised.

Third, belief elicits committedness and directs commitment. Those who strive to avoid idolatry may try to have no commitment at all or else to frame as inclusive a commitment as they can. The former effort is a dangerous and unfruitful one. The latter can lead to results quite similar to theocentrism; for example, a commitment to some relatively encompassing unity such as "Gaia." When it does so, many of the results are quite similar to that of our theism. We rejoice in working together with all who share with us a love of the Earth and a desire to preserve and enhance its living systems. Nevertheless, philosophical and theological positions in their precise details direct commitment in divergent ways. Lovelock's position directs him to those features of the planetary system most crucial for Earth to maintain its chemical balance. Living things have their value only in their contribution to these chemical systems that keep Earth alive. Hence many are unimportant. Their immediacy to themselves makes no claim on human concern. And the rich complexity of the biosphere does not, of itself, have much interest since it is not required by Gaia.

From our theistic point of view maintenance of the Earth's chemical balance is indeed important. If that is lost, the whole biosphere will decay. But the value is located primarily in that entire biosphere. Its rich diversity and complex patterns contribute a rich beauty to the divine life. And each of its individual members is immediate both to itself and to God. From this point of view the commitment of Lovelock to Gaia does not do justice to the intrinsic value of each living thing or of the biosphere as a whole. For all the attractiveness of the Gaia hypothesis, the commitment it elicits to one part of the whole rather than to the whole does lead to distortion. The prophetic critique is relevant.

A fourth reason for recommending theism is that it provides a basis for understanding our relation to the future. Chapter 7 discussed the problem of discounting the future that troubles economic theory. Robert Heilbroner, an economist with unusual breadth of philosophical interest, has written perceptively about this issue with respect to its implications for attitudes toward "the human prospect." Heilbroner is himself committed to the long-term preservation of human life on this planet, and he hopes that others will join him in readiness to make sacrifices to this end. But he does not believe that any argument can be given in favor of this commitment. The voice of rationality, he says, speaks through "a distinguished Professor of political economy" at the University of London: "Suppose that, as a result of using up all the world's resources, human life did come to an end. So what? What is so desirable about an indefinite continuation of the human species, religious convictions apart? It may well be that nearly everybody who is already here on earth would be reluctant to die, and that everybody has an instinctive fear of death. But one must not confuse this with the notion that, in any meaningful sense, generations who are yet unborn can be said to be better off if they are born than if they are not" (Heilbroner 1980, p. 180).

We agree that "religious convictions apart," this may be "rational." But that only points to the importance of religious convictions. Rationality, apart from belief in God, may indeed dictate indifference to the yet unborn. Since they do not now exist, they have no wants to be respected. But rationality that includes a rational belief in God has quite different consequences. God is everlasting, and future lives are as important to God as present lives. To serve God cannot call for sacrifice of future lives for the sake of satisfying the extravagant appetites of the present. Believers in God know that the community to which they belong extends through time. One cannot discount a future that will be immediate to God. Belief in God grounds the ethical course that Heilbroner favors but does not know how to justify.

Concluding Comments

We have not attempted to prove the truth of Christian faith or the existence of God, but we have tried to show that how humans think about themselves and the natural world, and whether we think also of the whole that contains us and enlivens us, does make a difference. We have commended our form of Christian theism as making sense of experience and directing thought and action helpfully. In this exposition we have been critical of various forms of nontheistic biocentrism and geocentrism.

In fact, however, the gulf separating us from some forms of Christianity is as great or greater than what differentiates our form of biospheric perspective from others. Christian theism has done much to bring about the dangerous situation to which the world has come. In varied forms it has supported anthropocentrism, ignored or belittled the natural world, opposed efforts to stop population growth, directed attention away from the urgent needs of this life, treated as of absolute authority for today teachings that were meant to influence a very different world, aroused false hopes, given false assurances, and claimed God's authority for all these sins. Those of us who know the power of Christian faith from within also know how dangerous are its distortions and misdirections of human thought and feeling. To channel the power of faith into life-affirming passion and a sense of belonging to the community of creatures is one of our life purposes.

Our Christian theism has led us to perceive this world in deeply troubling ways. Each passing year we see foreclosed happier possibilities for the future. Today we know the earth will get hotter in the coming decades and that many destructive consequences will follow. We know that the ozone layer will shrink and that much of the protection it has afforded us will be denied to our children and grandchildren. It is too late to avoid the greenhouse effect or the reduction of the ozone shield. The question now is how rapidly and how far the situation will deteriorate. But that question is not unimportant. Our actions now may determine whether the deterioration of the planetary environment can be slowed and stopped at a level that will allow much of the biosphere to survive.

The recognition of possibilities gone forever inspires us with a sense of urgency. Delay is costly to us and even more to our descendants and to the other species with which we share the planet. It is already very late. It is hard to avoid bitterness about what might have been done and about the additional missed opportunities each day. It is hard to avoid resentment toward those who continue so successfully to block the needed changes.

Yet there is hope. On a hotter planet, with lost deltas and shrunken coastlines, under a more dangerous sun, with less arable land, more people, fewer species of living things, a legacy of poisonous wastes, and much beauty irrevocably lost, there will still be the possibility that our children's children will learn at last to live as a community among communities. Perhaps they will learn also to forgive this generation its blind commitment to ever greater consumption. Perhaps they will even appreciate its belated efforts to leave them a planet still capable of supporting life in community.

Afterword: Money, Debt, and Wealth

*That which seems to be wealth may in verity be only the gilded
index of far-reaching ruin.*

—John Ruskin *(Unto this Last,* 1862)

Introduction

For the Common Good is not exhaustive in its coverage of economic
topics. The omission of money in the first edition seemed to us the most
serious one. Ideally we should have had a chapter in Part 1 enitled,
"Misplaced Concreteness: Money," one in Part 2, "From Fetish to Medium of Exchange and Investment," and in Part 3, "Monetary and Financial Reforms." Without fundamental changes in the current thinking
about finance, and in the institutions that embody that thinking, the
other changes we propose may prove insufficient. Nevertheless we were
not ready to give a systematic treatment of these formidable issues. We
are ready now, however, to raise some fundamental questions about the
way money operates in today's economy, and to call attention to some
important proposals for radically different approaches to finance.

Money ranks with the wheel and fire among ancient inventions without which the modern world could not have come into being. But it is
much more mysterious. It is a unit of account that changes size like a
rubber yardstick; a store of value that can swell or shrink over time;
a medium of exchange that often never leaves the bank; an interest-
bearing debt and a non-interest-bearing debt; a commodity (like gold)
and a noncommodity token (paper money). Easily transferable into real
assets by individuals, it is not at all transferable into real assets by the
community. Counterfeiters are sent to jail for making it, but the private

We are grateful for helpful suggestions from D. Batker, S. Carroll, C. Cobb, S. El
Serafy, G. Foy, R. Goodland, and T. Page. They, of course, are not responsible for
any remaining errors.

banking system can create it out of nothing and lend it at interest; it is illegal for citizens to destroy or deface it, but private banks can annihilate it. Some economists think it merely a veil behind which real factors determine economic life, others consider it among the most important of determinants; some think its quantity should be determined by a fixed rule, others that it should be manipulated by public authorities. And, in addition, some people even claim that it inspires a love that is the root of all evil. At least it is a rich source of bewilderment and danger. Probably in today's world more people are "run over and burned" by out-of-control money than by out-of-control wheels and fires.

Money in the Exponential-Growth Culture

Our national institutions governing money and finance are embedded in a culture which has come to accept exponential growth as the norm. Although real wealth cannot grow exponentially for long, our cultural symbol and measure of wealth, money, may indeed grow both exponentially and indefinitely. This lack of symmetry in behavior between the reality measured and the measuring rod has serious consequences.

Exponential growth has the characteristic of a fixed doubling time. The classic example of placing one grain of wheat on the first square of a chessboard, two on the second, four on the third, etc., leads to the last or sixty-fourth square alone containing 2^{63} grains, or about 1000 times the world's annual wheat crop. The board as a whole would contain twice that amount, or 2^{64} grains. As M. King Hubbert put it, the world will not tolerate sixty-four doublings of even a grain of wheat. If the present human population had begun with a single couple, there could not have been more than about thirty-one doublings. At forty-six doublings we would have a population density of one person per square meter over the Earth. Hubbert concluded that the maximum number of doublings of any single biological population or industrial product is on the order of a few tens. And if many biological populations and stocks of industrial goods must double simultaneously, as is the case for an exponentially growing economy, then even a few tens is too many doublings. Clearly Hubbert was right to view "exponential growth as a transient phenomenon in human history" (1993). Nevertheless, as Hubbert also pointed out, "during the last two centuries we have known nothing but exponential growth and in parallel we have evolved what amounts to an exponential-growth culture, a culture so heavily dependent on the continuance of exponential growth for its stability that it is incapable of reckoning with problems of non-growth" (1976, p. 125).

What are the features of this exponential culture? The custom of discounting future values to arrive at an equivalent present value has been discussed earlier in the book, and its anomalies emphasized. Discounting is simply the compound interest calculation run in reverse. But we are more accustomed to running the calculation forward to see how much money we have to set aside to support us in old age. Without exponential growth how can we meet pension fund payments and insurance claims whose actuarial calculation assumed growth? How can the poor get better off, and the rich too, without growth? How can the national deficit be reduced without increasing taxes or reducing government spending, unless we can "grow the economy" as politicians are now putting it? And how can we maintain full employment unless we stimulate investment, and does not investment mean growth? Are we not truly trapped in an exponential-growth culture?

Marx (1867) argued that the exponential-growth culture was a necessary part of capitalism. His historical analysis relates the growth culture to money in the following way. Barter, the exchange of one commodity for a different commodity, symbolized as C—C*, is the simplest and oldest method of exchange. One person has C and prefers C*; another has C* and prefers C. Both are better off after the trade, although no new physical production has occurred. The use value to both individuals has increased, but the exchange value is irrelevant. Barter can be mutually beneficial, but the necessary coincidence of wants severely limits its extent.

The use of money as a medium of exchange overcomes that limit, giving rise to what Marx called simple commodity production, symbolized by C—M—C*. Here money functions to overcome barter's problem of requiring a coincidence of wants. But the focus is still on increasing the use value to each individual. Exchange value, the sum of money M, is entirely instrumental to bringing about the increase in use value by facilitating the exchange of commodities that are exchanged only for the purpose of increasing use values. The process begins and ends with a commodity's use value.

The critical change comes in the next historical step, which Marx called capitalist circulation, symbolized by M—C—M*. The object is no longer the increase of use value, but the expansion of exchange value in money. $M* - M = dM$, and dM must grow. An initial capital M is used to hire labor and buy raw materials, which are then turned into a commodity C, which in turn is sold for a greater amount of money, M*.

The shift of focus from use value to exchange value is crucial. Commodity accumulation and use values, C, are self-limiting. Fifty hammers are not much better than two (one and a spare) as far as use value is concerned. But if we turn our focus to exchange value, then fifty hammers are much better than two, and better yet if available as fifty hammers' worth of fungible money.

The exchange value of commodities in general, abstracted in money, becomes the focus of accumulation. There is nothing to limit how much abstract exchange value one can own. Unlike concrete use values, which spoil or deteriorate when hoarded (due to entropy), abstract exchange value can accumulate indefinitely without spoilage or storage costs. In fact abstract exchange value grows by itself, earning interest, and then interest on the interest. Marx, and Aristotle before him, pointed out the danger in this "money fetishism," which is a particular case of the general fallacy of misplaced concreteness discussed in our first chapter.

In our own time this historical process of abstracting farther away from use value has perhaps been carried to the limit in the so-called "paper economy," which might be symbolized as M—M*, the direct conversion of money into more money without reference to commodities even as an intermediate step. Of course this has long been with us in the form of money in the bank growing at interest. But the scope for money making through tax avoidance, mergers, takeovers, "greenmail," and all forms of insider trading, has increased the apparent ability of money to expand with little reference to use value—indeed, sometimes by the destruction of use values, induced by a tax code that itself confuses wealth with debt—e.g., tax-free interest on junk bonds used to finance leveraged buyouts. This trend reached its zenith in the heyday of Michael Milken, before he went to jail.

The objective of takeovers, as explained by William Greider, is "to extract the capital invested in the underutilized real assets of the corporation so that the money could be redeployed in higher yielding financial instruments. It is another dramatic example of how finance has triumphed over the real economy. Why own a factory when your capital will draw a better real return from paper?" (1989). But as Greider goes on to point out, the fundamental driving force behind the takeovers was the high level of real interest rates in the 1980s. If the real assets embodied in an enterprise could not earn a return that matched the high interest rate, the incentive was to convert the enterprise into cash by disassembling it and selling it off, and investing the money in paper earning the high interest rate.

Of course all investments are in competition with the interest rate, and if they cannot produce a higher yield they should, by the rule of efficiency, be liquidated and the capital invested in something that does beat the interest rate.[1] This supposes that the interest rate itself reflects a kind of marginal real rate of return on capital. But that is only one factor underlying the interest rate, which also reflects monetary policy, balance of payments policy, concern or lack thereof for the future, expectations about the future, both rational and irrational, monopoly power, the pattern of subsidies and penalties in the tax code, etc. When these other factors drive the interest rate up, real assets will be cannibalized and reassembled in faster growing alternatives, just as exploited species will be driven to extinction when their biological growth rate at all population levels falls short of the interest rate, and their place in the sun taken by a faster growing species (as discussed on pp. 156–57). But where are the real investments that will earn more than the old assets, and will they earn enough more to pay for the social cost of displaced laborers, disrupted pensions and medical insurance, and dissolved communities? And if these new investments are so obvious, why would businesspeople not see them and invest in them in the normal course of affairs? Why do we need lawyers, brokers, and accountants to accelerate the process, especially when these people have absolutely no knowledge of either the technological production processes or social community relations that their remote financial activities are disrupting? And when most of them make money on a deal even if it turns out to be a public disaster, we seem to have considerable potential for "moral hazard," the economist's term for a case in which the costs of imprudent risk taking are borne by someone other than the risk taker—a concept we will have further occasion to employ.

Some have tried to save the exponential-growth culture by denying that we live in a finite world. Outer space is infinite, and our destiny is to expand into it, some claim. Earth will be a dandelion gone to seed, sending out spores in all directions. Others (Lewis 1992) do not appeal to outer space but deny that the physical dimension of growth is necessary. What is really growing they say is value, not mass, so economic growth can continue without encountering any physical limit.

However, in the context of economic growth, value does not refer to pixie dust. It means a sum of money equal to price times quantity of commodities. To measure economic growth (growth in real GNP) we hold prices constant so that change in value will come only from change

---

1. This is the allocative efficiency criterion for investments and does not imply sustainability. The latter must be guaranteed by a separate criterion.

in quantity of the commodities. Quantities of goods *and* services have a physical dimension (mass and energy) and are therefore subject to physical laws of conservation and entropy. Even a "service" is always a service of something or somebody for some period of time. Economic value is certainly not reducible to physical laws, but neither is it exempt from them. Real GNP is a value index of quantitative change. The creation of a value index to measure the aggregate quantitative change in output does *not* annihilate the physical dimensions of commodities, thereby allowing the economy to grow forever on a finite planet!

Kenneth Boulding makes a helpful distinction between assets which are "used up" and those which are "worn out." Some things must be used up in order to yield their service—food and fuel, for example. Other things are not necessarily depleted by being used—they wear out over time, but their wearing out is an incidental, even if unavoidable, consequence of the service they render in use. For example, human bodies, capital equipment, and durable consumer goods all eventually wear out but could yield their service even if they did not. But gasoline or food can only yield their services in the act of being used up. These two forms of assets are complementary—the stock of productive machinery needs a flow of energy to animate it, and the flow of energy needs material stocks through which it can be channeled to satisfy human purposes.

Throughout most of history the flow of energy was revenue from the sun, annually captured by plants. Like manna from heaven it was renewed every day, but could not be accumulated for future use except within narrow limits. The world is usually only one harvest away from starvation. With the discovery of fossil fuels, stored sunshine from the distant past has become available. But we cannot directly use it to feed our internal metabolic fire—that still requires sunlight captured by plants, although the plant's ability to capture sunlight can be increased by fertilizers made with fossil fuels. We use fossil fuel to feed the external fires of machines that lighten our labor. But fossil fuels are destined to be used up, and what Frederick Soddy (1926) called the "flamboyant period" based on their use will come to an end.

Although it is possible to accumulate capital for the future, this process is limited by the complementarity of the stock (permanent wealth that gets worn out) with the annual revenue (perishable wealth that gets used up) needed to animate it and maintain it. As the stock grows larger so does its annual depreciation. The maintenance deductions from the future revenue will grow, as will the amount required to run the larger capital stock (human bodies, livestock, machines). The fixed flow of sunlight and the resulting renewable but perishable revenue will prove to be the limiting factor in the accumulation of wealth, since it is the least subject to accumulation and expansion, and its complementarity with the stock of permanent wealth limits the expansion of the latter.

The main point, however, is that the growth of wealth is physically limited while the growth of debt is not. The exact biophysical sequence through which the former limits work themselves out is highly interesting but not the central issue. Whatever the progress of science in discovering new resources and techniques, it could not possibly match the explosive mathematical growth of compound interest.

Aristotle and the Church fathers, as well as the Jewish and Islamic worlds, have all condemned usury as in some sense "unnatural." Aristotle said money is sterile and does not have the physical capacity to reproduce itself like crops and livestock. The problem as we have stated it here is not so much that money is sterile, but that it grows far too rapidly and artificially—mathematically it is hyperfecund, but physically it is barren, as Aristotle said. Therefore, reasoning about wealth in terms of money can become a massive exercise in the fallacy of misplaced concreteness.

The difference between real wealth and money was noted by Nobel Laureate economist James Tobin:

The community's wealth now has two components: the real goods accumulated through past real investment and fiduciary or paper 'goods' manufactured by the government from thin air. Of course, the nonhuman wealth of such a nation 'really' consists only of its tangible capital. But as viewed by the inhabitants of the nation individually, wealth exceeds the tangible capital stock by the size of what we might term the fiduciary issue. This is an illusion, but only one of the many fallacies of composition which are basic to any economy or society. The illusion can be maintained unimpaired as long as society does not actually try to convert all of its paper wealth into goods. [1965, p. 676]

In the following section we will review the well-known process by which commercial banks are able to play a far larger role than government in manufacturing money out of thin air. However, the basic point stands. To maintain the illusion, not only must society not try to convert all its money into real wealth, but it must not try to convert all its "fiduciary issue" into currency—i.e., all its interest-bearing private bank debt (not legal tender) into non-interest-bearing government debt (legal tender).

We conclude that the culture of exponential growth that now dominates Western society, and increasingly the world, is not sustainable. To move away from this culture, toward a culture capable of dealing with problems of nongrowth, would require us to tie money more closely to real wealth. To see how this might be done we need a clear picture of how money is now created and what it really is. We must understand how private banks create money, how they acquired that power historically, and what would be necessary to restore that power entirely to the State.

The Creation of Money

In general we have an adequate common-sense notion of how real wealth is created. It requires work that transforms natural resources into usable goods. The increase of production per worker requires both the organization of labor in specialized roles and the introduction of capital in the form of energy and machines.

The creation of money, on the other hand, is far less well understood by the public. Some think, naively, that this is primarily a matter of the government's printing presses. But this applies only to the legal tender consisting of coins and paper money. This is a small part of the money that actually flows through the economy. Most money is the creation of commercial banks.

Originally, money could be created only by the ruler. As long as the money was a commodity, such as gold, and its value was regulated by the real cost of mining gold, the creation of money was simply the standardization of one commodity as an instrument of exchange. Beginning in the Middle Ages, even when gold circulated as money, there was frequently a difference between the monetary value of the gold coin and the market value of the commodity as gold metal. The one-ounce gold coin with the king's face on it usually had less than an ounce of gold in it, and to that extent was partially token money. The profit to the king of putting less than an ounce of gold in a one-ounce gold coin was called seigniorage. It was justified initially as necessary to defray the expense of coinage, but it was in fact a source of profit to the Crown arising from its prerogative to issue money. Seigniorage is the difference between the monetary value of the token and its commodity value. Today, for paper currency created by the government, the commodity value is nil, so that seigniorage is equal to nearly the full monetary value of the paper currency.

The manufacture of money by governments is thus a source of public income. However, this source is greatly reduced today since most money is now created by private banks. Money creation has become a source of private income. Historically, this shift of the money-creating prerogative began with the goldsmith-bankers, who accepted deposits of gold for safekeeping. Transferring ownership claims to gold in the safe was easier than taking it out and giving it to the other party, who then put it back on deposit for safekeeping with the goldsmith. Hence the practice of payment by check developed. Experience taught the goldsmith-banker that most of the gold just sat in the vault, and that only a small fraction needed to be on hand in the till as reserves against day to day discrepancies between new deposits and withdrawals. Much of the gold could safely be loaned out at interest. Of course there was always the possibility of a panic or run on the goldsmith-banker, so the practice was not without some risk. The goldsmith-bankers in Amsterdam got a law passed making it a hanging offense to start a run on the goldsmith. But one day there was a run, and of course the goldsmith could not pay. The matter was resolved not by hanging the unknown individual who started the run, but by hanging the goldsmith (Barber 1973).

In spite of such setbacks, the practice of keeping fractional reserves against loans grew, and with that practice banks acquired the power to create money, not in the sense of legal tender, but in the sense of customary means of payment, checks, accepted in exchange for goods and services. This growth did not depend on any governmental decision. The fact that this practice linked the public function of supplying money with the private activity of lending at interest is a historical happenstance, not the result of legislative design.[2]

Private creation of money by banks evolved long before it was understood. Joseph Schumpeter (1954, p. 1114) claims that, as late the 1920s, ninety-nine out of one hundred economists believed that banks could not create money any more than cloakrooms could create coats. Part of the confusion may have been the distinction between money (customary means of payment) and legal tender (money that one is legally obliged to accept in payment). Banks do not create legal tender, only governments can do that. But banks do create customary means of payment. The difficulty economists had in recognizing this elicits the following comment from Schumpeter: "This is a most interesting illustra-

---

2. As noted by James Tobin, "It is, after all, historical accident that supplies of transaction media in modern economies came to be byproducts of the banking business and vulnerable to its risks" (1987, p. 275).

tion of the inhibition with which analytic advance has to contend and in particular of the fact that people may be perfectly familiar with a phenomenon for ages and even discuss it frequently without realizing its true significance and without admitting it into their general scheme of thought" (1954, p. 1115).

Although today the fact that commercial banks create much more money than the government is explained in every introductory economics text, we judge that its full significance and effects on the economy have still not been sufficiently considered. As the nature of money is better understood, we believe that it will be possible to develop policies for using it more effectively for the common good.

In an unregulated banking system based on fractional reserves, each bank determines how much in reserves it will keep on hand to meet the net demands of its customers for cash. The smaller the reserves, the more money can be lent, and the greater the bank's profits. Consequently, some banks kept insufficient reserves, leading to their customers' loss of confidence, a run on the bank, and failure. Many depositors lost their money. To reduce this risk, the United States established the Federal Reserve system to regulate the amount of reserves required and provide extra funds in emergencies. The Federal Deposit Insurance Corporation also now insures depositors against losses of up to $100,000, which precludes panicky runs on banks.

Today bank reserves do not consist in gold or any other commodity, but of cash and the bank's own deposits at the Federal Reserve. Banks are legally required to hold reserves against their demand deposits. The fraction of total demand deposits that must be held as reserves is set by law, currently less than 10% on average. Let the legally required fraction of deposits kept as reserves be r. Then actual reserves above the requirement are excess reserves, and their fraction is $1-r$.

To give a numerical example, assume that r is 10%, then $(1-r)$ is 90%. Assume that there is only one bank, a monopoly bank. An additional $100 cash deposit (or creation of new reserves of $100 by the Federal Reserve) results in an additional $100 demand deposit credited to the depositor. So far there is no creation of money, just a change from cash to demand deposit in the books of the depositor. But now the bank has $90 in excess reserves. It can lend out up to $900, creating demand deposits up to that amount in the name of the borrowers. Total additional demand deposits are now $1,000, consisting of the $900 new loans and the $100 demand deposit exchanged for the original cash deposit. Additional reserves are $100 (the original cash deposit). The 10% reserve requirement is met, $900 in new money has been created. The monopoly bank can expand its demand deposits by a factor of $1/r = 1/.1 = 10$ times new reserves, because, being the only bank, it knows that all checks written against these new deposits will be redeposited with it.

If there are many different banks then each bank must assume that checks written on its new demand deposits will be deposited to another bank, and that it will quickly lose that amount of reserves in its account at the Federal Reserve, since that check will be cleared by transferring reserves from its account to the other bank's account at the Federal Reserve. Remember, the bank's deposits with the Federal Reserve count as reserves. Therefore, in the many-bank case, a single bank receiving an additional $100 cash deposit can only safely lend out its excess reserves, namely $90. But as that $90 is spent it is redeposited by the recipient in another bank. The second bank must keep 10% in reserve, so it has excess reserves of $.9 ($90) = 81. The $81 is loaned, spent, and deposited in a third bank, which then can lend $.9 ($81) = 72.90, etc. The result of this process of lending, spending, and redepositing is that the whole banking system, consisting of many different banks, ends up multiplying the new reserves by the same factor of $1/r$ as the monopoly bank does.[3] So the banking system, whether a monopoly bank or many banks, has a reserves-to-deposit multiplier of $1/r$. Of course, if we have a 100% reserve requirement, that would mean that $r = 1$, and consequently the deposit multiplier would be $1/r = 1/1 = 1$, which would mean that banks could not create money.

The above summary of the creation of money by banks is incomplete, since we have not yet drawn attention to the parallel process of demand deposit contraction as reserves are lost. Individual banks lose reserves when checks against it are cleared, and when its customers convert demand deposits into cash. The system as a whole does not lose reserves from check clearing, as this is just a transfer of reserves among banks. The system as a whole loses reserves when the general public decides to hold more cash money and less check money, and when the Federal Reserve reduces total reserves. A reduction in reserves results in a multiple contraction of bank money. As loans are repaid, the receiving bank

3. The chain of redepositing and relending is represented mathematically by the infinite series: $1 + (1-r) + (1-r)^2 + (1-r)^3 + \ldots\ldots + (1-r)^n = 1/r$.

acquires reserves in the amount of the principal plus interest. These are excess reserves to the receiving bank, but lost reserves to the paying banks. Lost reserves require a reduction in loans of ten (or $1/r$) times the lost reserves, so money is destroyed by the repayment of loans. If the receiving bank kept the reserves as excess reserves the reduction in money would be permanent. However, the receiving bank is in business to lend its excess reserves and will make new loans that will soon recreate the money destroyed by repayment of the old loan. There is a continual process of creation and destruction of bank money, with the supply at any instant being the net result of the two processes. If banks keep fully loaned up (no excess reserves) then the money supply is controlled by the government through setting the reserve requirement and controlling the amount of reserves (cash and deposits of commercial banks at the Federal Reserve).

The bank does not increase its assets by the amount of its creation of new money. This creation is offset by the destruction of new money when loans are paid off. But the bank *is* able to charge interest to the borrower on this created money, and that interest is real revenue that does not disappear when the loan is repaid. It can be converted into real assets. If the commercial banking sector is competitive, as it is, it will pay part of that interest to its depositors in order to attract more deposits and be able to create more money and make more loans. The banking system's (or monopoly bank's) gross profit from the original $100 cash deposit is the difference between the interest received on loans of $900 (newly created money) and interest paid on the original $100 cash deposit. Even if the deposit rate of interest were equal to the loan rate of interest there would be considerable margin for profit. Of course, the loan rate is considerably higher than the deposit rate, increasing the margin substantially.

Virtual Wealth

The proposal that money be tied much more closely to real wealth is a radical one. Both to understand it and to develop policies that would implement it require more fundamental thinking about the nature of this elusive entity. But few of those who have reflected profoundly on money and finance have done so with the assumptions we have developed in this book: namely, that economics must be about community and is not reducible to individuals, that it has a real biophysical basis and cannot be dealt with only in categories of idealism, and that the fallacy of misplaced concreteness is the cardinal sin of modern economics.

The one economist who has thought radically about money and finance from this point of view with great insight was Frederick Soddy (1877–1956). He believed that nearly all economic problems would yield to reform of finance, and here we do not agree. We have written this book to propose many other reforms. But we see a congruity between our analyses throughout the book and Soddy's thought and proposals about money.

Frederick Soddy is best known not as an economist, but as the 1921 Nobel Laureate in chemistry, honored for his discovery of the existence of isotopes and general work on radioactive decay with Rutherford.[4] From his own work he was convinced that the atom offered a great potential source of energy for mankind. But he also foresaw its dangers: "If the discovery were made tomorrow, there is not a nation that would not throw itself heart and soul into the task of applying it to war, just as they are now doing in the case of the newly developed chemical weapons of poison-gas warfare . . . If [atomic energy] were to come under existing economic conditions, it would mean the *reductio ad absurdum* of scientific civilization, a swift annihilation" (Soddy 1926, p. 28)

Soddy was convinced that there must be something deeply wrong with "existing economic conditions," with economic thought and institutions, for the gift of scientific knowledge to have become such a threat. Soddy was thus led to a radical critique of economics, which became his central intellectual preoccupation during the latter half of his nearly eighty years. As would be expected of a chemist, he began his economic analysis by explaining the bearing of the first and second laws of thermodynamics on economics, anticipating by fifty years the basic ideas of the magisterial work of Georgescu-Roegen, discussed earlier in this book. The part of the economy that most caught Soddy's attention, however, was money. Precisely because it was the one measurable quantity that did not obey the laws of thermodynamics, he focused on its role in economic life and traced most economic problems to its mysteries.

Soddy was dismissed by economists as a "monetary crank," of the same ilk as Major Douglas or Silvio Gesell. Although he respected

4. Kauffman (1986) provides the best single source on Soddy's work, both as chemist and economist.

these men for having seen the problem, he would have no part in "funny money" solutions. Indeed, he considered the respected canons of sound banking to be themselves little more than funny money schemes to mystify the public for the enrichment of the bankers and their class. But since Soddy is so often dismissed as a crank it is worth recording the contrary opinion of the celebrated Chicago School economist Frank Knight that Soddy's main book, *Wealth, Virtual Wealth and Debt*, was, "brilliantly written and brilliantly suggestive and stimulating" and further that Soddy's practical theses concerning money were "highly significant and theoretically correct" (1927, p. 732).

It is also worth noting that one of Soddy's main proposals, which he called "pound for pound banking," proposed in 1926, is almost identical to the plan for 100% money put forward by the great American economist Irving Fisher in 1935. But by and large Soddy's economics was an embarrassment to everyone but Soddy. Certainly economists paid it little attention, and fellow chemists thought it a shame that such a brilliant scientist wasted his time on something so far afield.

The first step to a proper understanding of money is to return to the fact that money is not wealth; it is no longer even a commodity (like gold or silver). It is a token. A token of what? We are tempted to say a token of wealth, but that is not correct because the value of wealth at any time is much greater than the value of the total stock of money—i.e. there are many more coats in the cloakroom than claim tokens. Money is a token of indebtedness—a debt. Money is a form of community or national debt owned by the individual and owed by the community, exchangeable on demand into wealth by voluntary transference to another individual who is willing to part with the wealth in exchange for the money. The value of the total stock of money is not determined by the stock of wealth in existence (or by the flow of new production), but in a curious way by wealth that individuals think exists but which really does not exist—what Frederick Soddy called virtual wealth.

Virtual wealth is measured by the aggregate value of the real assets that the community voluntarily *abstains* from purchasing in order to hold money instead. To avoid the inconvenience of barter, everyone must hold money, which could be exchanged by the individual for real wealth but is not. In Soddy's words, "This aggregate of exchangeable goods and services which the community continuously and permanently goes without (though individual money owners can instantly demand and obtain it from other individuals) the author terms the Virtual Wealth of the community" (1934, p. 36).

If everyone tried to exchange their money holdings for real assets it could not be done, because all real assets are already owned by someone, and in the final analysis someone has to end up holding the money. So virtual wealth does not really exist over and above the value of all real assets (which is why it is called "virtual"). Yet people as individuals behave as if virtual wealth were real, because they can easily exchange it for real assets.[5] The aggregate of individuals behaves as if it were richer than the community really is by an amount equal to the virtual wealth of the community. The phenomenon of virtual wealth must occur in a monetary economy, unless the money itself is a commodity—a real asset that circulates at its commodity value. The value of each unit of money is simply the virtual wealth divided by the number of units of money in existence. Virtual wealth varies with the size of the population and national income and the business and payment habits of the community. Since virtual wealth is counted as wealth in determining individual behavior but does not really exist, we are justified in considering it more like debt than like wealth.

Virtual wealth cannot be increased simply by issuing more money, because it is determined by the amount of wealth that the community willingly abstains from holding in order to hold money instead. Issuance of more money tokens than the public is willing to hold will result in their exchanging them for real wealth and driving up the price of real assets to the point where the purchasing power of the larger amount of money is reduced to the amount of real wealth that the community is willing to abstain from holding in order to hold money instead. The value of a dollar's worth of debt depends on how many dollars the value of virtual wealth must be divided among.

Who owns the virtual wealth of the community? It is clearly an artifact of community interdependence and interrelationships. It is owned by individuals, yet since it does not really exist no one owns it. But whoever holds money gave up a real asset for it. The only person who can really exchange virtual wealth for real assets is the issuer of money. Whoever is the creator of the token money and is the *first* one to put it in circulation by spending or lending it receives real assets in exchange for tokens. Everyone else has to give up a real asset to get the money that is later given for another real asset. So an amount of real value equal to the virtual wealth is transfered to the issuer of money.

5. Soddy's notion of virtual wealth bears a close resemblance to the "fiduciary issue" described in the earlier quote from James Tobin.

The seigniorage prerogative of the Crown historically has passed, not to the state except marginally, but to the private banking sector, which issues at least nine-tenths of our money. Private bankers are able to lend over 90% of the virtual wealth of the community, which does not really belong to them, and earn interest on it, which does belong to them. Most people would consider that an extraordinarily good deal.

Is it surprising that the institutions that deal in these paper pyramids based on the fallacy of composition should generally try to inspire confidence by giving themselves such names as "Security, Fidelity, Prudential, Guaranty, Trust . . ." corporations? Or that their marble-columned architecture is suggestive of ancient temples, with velvet ropes guiding the faithful to the communion rail where in hushed tones the teller imparts the fiduciary issue? Or that the whole system would have collapsed without the Federal Deposit Insurance Corporation (FDIC)? Indeed, it may now collapse partly because of the FDIC, as banks feel free to play fast and loose with depositors' insured money, and depositors cease being watchdogs since their money is insured. And, to make it much worse, once a bank is "too big to be allowed to fail," because of the cascading collapse of credit and money that results from holding only a small fraction of deposit liabilities in reserve, the bank's stockholders, as well as depositors, are in effect "insured" against loss.

It is important to recognize that money and virtual wealth are social phenomena that arise not from the mere aggregating of atomistic individuals, but from the community consensus and resulting practical general willingness to accept the agreed-upon token as money. Individuals cannot issue their own money. The essence of money is that it be generally accepted as such within a community, and acceptance of the same monetary standard becomes one of the defining bonds of community.[6] The extent to which virtual wealth should be appropriable by private interests rather than for public use by the nation is an issue that is no longer discussed, but should be.[7] We will return to it. But first, we

6. It is possible that money could be issued by states or cities rather than by the nation, which might be a means of promoting localism. If economic decentralization should proceed far enough, local monies should be considered, but in this essay we will treat money only at the national level of community.

7. As Soddy put it, "The old extreme laissez-faire policy of individualistic economics jealously denied to the state the right of competing in any way with individuals in the ownership of productive enterprise, out of which monetary interest or profit can be made, and this was ignorantly extended even to the virtual wealth of the community" (1926, p. 228).

should look carefully at the confusion between debt and wealth, probably the most important example of the fallacy of misplaced concreteness in economics.

Debt versus Wealth

The positive physical quantity two pigs represents wealth that can be seen and touched. But minus two pigs, debt, is an imaginary negative magnitude with no physical dimension. One could as easily have a thousand negative pigs as two. Indeed, according to Soddy, negative numbers were first recognized by Hindu mathematicians for their analogy to debt. Compound interest or exponential growth of negative pigs presents no problem. But exponential growth of positive pigs soon leads to bedlam and ruin.

Given the convenience of owning negative rather than positive pigs, the ruling passion of individuals in a modern economy is to convert wealth into debt in order to derive a permanent future income from it— to convert wealth that perishes into debt that endures, debt that does not rot, costs nothing to maintain, and brings in perennial interest.[8] Individuals cannot amass all the physical supplies that they will require for maintenance during their old age, for like manna it would rot. Therefore they must convert their nonstorable surplus into a lien on future

8. In Soddy's words, "Psychologically the economic aim of the individual is, always has been, and probably always will be, to secure a permanent revenue independent of further effort, proof against the passage of time and the chance of circumstance, to support himself in old age and his family after him in perpetuity. He endeavors to do so by accumulating so much property in the heyday of his youth that he and his heirs may live on the interest on it in perpetuity afterwards. Economic and social history is the conflict of this human aspiration with the laws of physics, which make such a perpetuum mobile impossible, and reduces the problem merely to the method by which one individual may get another individual or the community into his debt and prevent repayment, so that the individual or community must share the produce of their efforts with their creditor" (1926, p. 153).

Many Americans seem to think that the money they contributed to Social Security all their lives exists as capital in a bank somewhere earning interest that will support them in their retirement. But all Social Security does is to give them a lien on future revenue produced by younger cohorts. This intergenerational debt could be repudiated. In fact, when the numerous baby boomers retire and are replaced by smaller cohorts of wage earners, most of whom will not realize the traditional expectation of being richer than their parents, some repudiation of this debt seems likely to occur.

revenue by letting others consume and invest their surplus now in exchange for the right to share in the increased future revenue.

Although debt can follow the law of compound interest, the real energy revenue from future sunshine, the real future income against which the debt is a lien, cannot grow at compound interest for long. When converted into debt, however, wealth discards its corruptible body to take on an incorruptible one. In so doing, debt appears to offer a means of dodging nature, of evading the second law of thermodynamics, the law of randomization, rust, and rot. But the idea that all people can live off the interest of their mutual indebtedness is just another perpetual-motion scheme—a vulgar delusion on a grand scale.

The perpetual-motion delusion of everyone living from interest on debt has arisen, Soddy explains, "Because formerly ownership of land—which, with the sunshine that falls on it, provides a revenue of wealth—secured in the form of rent, a share in the annual harvest without labor or service, upon which a cultured and leisured class could permanently establish itself, the age seems to have conceived the preposterous notion that money, which can buy land, must therefore itself have the same revenue-producing power" (1926, p. 106).

A better example of the fallacy of misplaced concreteness would be hard to find. In a further attempt to elucidate the confusion between wealth and debt, Soddy offers the following: "Still it might have been apparent that a weight, although it is measured by what it will pull up, is nevertheless a pull down. The whole idea of balancing one thing against another in order to measure its quantity involves equating the quantity measured against an equal and opposite quantity. Wealth is the positive quantity to be measured and money as the claim to wealth is a debt" (1926, p. 103).

The fallacy of composition compounds the errors of misplaced concreteness. Because some people can live on interest it does not follow that all people could. Soddy is arguing that what is obviously impossible for the community must be forbidden in some degree to individuals. If it is not forbidden or at least limited in some way, then at some point the exponentially growing liens of debt holders will indent on the slowly growing future revenue to such an extent that the producers of that revenue will no longer be willing to make such a large transfer, and conflict will result. As Soddy put it, "You cannot permanently pit an absurd human convention, such as the spontaneous increment of debt [compound interest], against the natural law of the spontaneous decrement of wealth [entropy]" (1922, p. 30).

The revenue that goes for investment is eventually used up or worn out just as much as the revenue that goes directly to consumption. If the investment is productive it will augment the future flow of revenue, but all that exists in the hands of the lender is a lien on that future revenue.[9] Present surplus accumulation can never be changed into future revenue, but only *ex*changed for it under certain social conventions. In Soddy's words, "Capital merely means unearned income divided by the rate of interest and multiplied by 100" (1922, p. 27).

The logical contradiction between unlimited growth of debt and limited growth of real wealth is translated into a social conflict between the *rentier* (interest recipient) and worker. The conflict will take the form of debt repudiation. Debt grows at compound interest and, as a purely mathematical quantity, encounters no limits to curb its growth. Wealth grows for a while at compound interest, but, having a physical dimension, it sooner or later encounters limits to further growth. The positive feedback of compound interest leads to the explosive growth of debt, which is met by counteracting defensive actions of debt repudiation, i.e., inflation, bankruptcy, confiscatory taxation, fraud, theft—all of which breed violence. Conventional wisdom considers the consequences pathological but accepts compound interest as normal. Logic demands, however, that we constrain compound interest in some way, or accept episodic debt repudiation as a normal and necessary adjustment. Of course inflation, bankruptcy, and fraud also occur as a result of straightforward corruption or incompetence. But the point is that the exponential growth of debt will eventually lead to such occurrences even among ordinarily honest and competent people and institutions.

Soddy paraphrases J. M. Keynes's 1923 discussion of the value of the French franc: the purchasing power of money is settled in the long run by the proportion of his earned income that the worker permits to be taken by the *rentier* (understood here as debt holder). It will continue to fall until the commodity value of money due to the *rentier* falls to that proportion of the national income which, in Keynes's words, "accords

9. As Soddy expressed it: "Capital, by saving to an indefinite extent the expenditure of time in human production, appears to afford a continuous revenue of wealth without further work, but the origin of the wealth produced is in the continued use of capital by human agents, not in the capital itself. There is no ethical principle to which to appeal, in order to equate the time spent in the accumulation against the continuous expenditure necessary to make it productive, or to determine the just division of the wealth produced as between the capitalist and the worker" (1926, p. 326).

with the habits and mentality of the country"—or the habits and mentality of the growing world, in Soddy's paraphrase (1926, p. 198). We understand this to mean that the growth of a *rentier* class living on interest from debt will eventually require the transfer of more income from workers than they will tolerate, resulting in conflict and debt repudiation, usually by inflation, because money debt can grow faster than the production of real wealth.[10]

Money should not bear interest as a condition of its existence, but only when genuinely lent by an owner who gives up its use while it is in the possession of the borrower. When the commercial banking system lends money it gives up nothing, creating the deposits *ex nihilo* up to the limit set by the reserve requirement. There is an opportunity cost to the bank, in that in lending to A it forgoes the opportunity of making the same loan to B. There is an opportunity cost in allocating the virtual wealth among various borrowers, but there is no opportunity cost to the bank in acquiring the virtual wealth in the first place. Unlike an individual, when a bank lends money it does not abstain from spending that money for the duration of the loan. The burden of abstinence is shifted on to the public.

The real lender is the community, which ends up holding more money-debt and fewer real assets. In other words, the community has abstained from the use of real assets, making them available to the bank's borrower in exchange for the money created by the bank and loaned to the borrower. If the community does not want to hold any more money and tries to convert the additional money into real assets, it simply bids up the price of real assets, thus lowering the real value (purchasing power) of its money holdings, the difference going to the banks who created the new money. If the community's demand for virtual wealth has not yet been satisfied, then the community lends voluntarily by holding the extra money and fewer assets. If it does not want to hold the extra money, it lends involuntarily by bidding up prices and reducing the purchasing power of its money holdings to "make room" for the new money that the borrower received. In either case a part of the community's virtual wealth is transferred from the public to the issuer of new money. We know the new money will be spent and increase demand, because the borrower would not pay interest for it if he did not

10. Between 1980 and 1991, the gross federal debt grew at an annual compound rate of 13.3%; consumer debt grew at 9.3% and business debt at 7.8%. Combined total debt grew at an average annual compound rate of about 10%. During the same period GDP grew at less than half that rate (Cavanagh and Clairmonte 1992).

intend to spend it. Prices are eventually bid up, since *ex nihilo* creation of money (demand) is easier and faster than *ex materia* creation of new physical wealth (supply). The very existence of the bulk of our money now depends on this debt never being retired, only continuously rolled over. The existence of money has become a source of private income, and its total supply becomes a "concertina," expanding to fuel a boom (when loans are in demand), and contracting to reinforce a slump (when there is little demand for new loans).

Soddy summarized these issues by pointing out that modern bankers

"have been allowed to regard themselves as the owners of the virtual wealth which the community does *not* posses, and to lend it and charge interest upon the loan as though it really existed and they possessed it. The wealth so acquired by the impecunious borrower is not given up by the lenders, who receive interest on the loan but give up nothing, but is given up by the whole community, who suffer in consequence the loss through a general reduction in the purchasing power of money" [1926, p. 296].

A further contradiction arises from the practice of interest-bearing national debt being used as collateral security by bondholders when they borrow from commercial banks. The bank creates a deposit (new money) for the borrowing bondholder and charges him interest. The public is taxed to enable the government to pay interest on the bond to the bondholder who, in effect, passes the interest on to the bank. Soddy draws the conclusion that "taxes are being paid to the bank for doing what the taxes were imposed to prevent being done, namely, the increase of the currency. Otherwise, there would have been no reason for the State to borrow at interest if it had not wished to prevent the increase of the currency" (1926, p. 298). This is for Soddy the final *reductio ad absurdum* of the monetary system.

Soddy is important because he made a serious effort to reckon with problems of nongrowth. Although he was an enthusiast of scientific progress and a believer in the possibility of abundance for all, thanks to scientific and technical advances, he nevertheless was sure that this could never happen under an economic system that confused debt with wealth and behaved as if growth in the latter would increase the former. His monetary reforms, to be discussed, were aimed at stopping money-debt from behaving in ways that are impossible for wealth to behave. A first step away from a culture of exponential growth, and toward a culture capable of dealing with problems of nongrowth, would be to restrict the ability of money to do some of the things that wealth cannot do. This seems to mean two things: first, limiting the indefinite exponential growth of money values implicit in projections of compound interest growth over long periods; second, limiting the "conjuror's trick" of creating money *ex nihilo* and then destroying it. That power would be taken away from the private banks, and reserved to the government.

Monetary Reform

The comments of Lloyd Mints help us to see why these issues are so vexing:

"If a malignant despot desired to create the utmost confusion among his subjects on questions of public policy, he would surely require that any question of importance invariably be considered jointly with at least one other, unrelated, problem; and if he had a real genius as his advisor, the latter would immediately suggest that joint discussion of private lending operations and monetary policy would serve the purposes of his master very nicely. . . . With a sensible financial structure, these two problems would have nothing in common. It would seem that an evil designer of human affairs had the remarkable prevision to arrange matters so that funds repayable on demand could be made the basis of profitable operations by the depository institutions. It is wholly fortuitous that an income can be earned from the use of such funds, but this being so has resulted in the creation of institutions which have largely taken over the control of the stock of money, an essential governmental function." [1950, p. 4]

Three basic reforms had been suggested by Soddy to make the separation later called for by Mints, and to restore honesty and accuracy to the function of money in the economic system:

1. a 100% reserve requirement for commercial banks;
2. a policy of maintaining a constant price index;
3. freely fluctuating exchange rates internationally.

We believe that these policies remain very sensible even though the world has changed much in the half century since they were suggested.

With a 100% reserve requirement the commercial banking system could no longer create and destroy money. That basic privilege, along with the seigniorage prerogative and the ownership of virtual wealth, would be restored to the State, which would again become the sole "utterer" of money. Banks would have to exist by charging for their "legitimate" services, i.e., those that do not require the creation of money— e.g., safekeeping, checking and clearing of payments, and lending at interest the real money of real depositors (savings or time deposits, not demand deposits). Financial intermediation (lending other people's money) would no longer have any connection with the supply of money, and the wealth lent by the intermediary would be wealth whose use some depositor had forgone for the period of the loan. Every increase in expenditure by borrowers would be matched by an act of saving or abstinence on the part of a depositor, rather than by the private appropriation of part of the virtual wealth of the community.

Frank Knight fully approved of this recommendation, noting in support that "it is absurd and monstrous for society to pay the commercial banking system 'interest' for multiplying several fold the quantity of medium of exchange when (a) a public agency could do it at negligible cost, (b) there is no sense in having it done at all, since the effect is simply to raise the price level, and (c) important evils result, notably the frightful instability of the whole economic system" (1927, p. 732). Knight might have added that the public agency would not only incur the negligible costs of producing the new money, but would also enjoy considerable seigniorage profits.

Three reasons for 100% reserves have been given in the literature. First, the requirement would prevent private banks from creating money, so that the government could exercise more effective control. Through its increased direct control of money, government would be able to exert a stronger indirect effect on employment, national income, and inflation. Everyone recognizes that inflation is mainly a monetary phenomenon, but the monetarist school would go farther and claim that employment and national income are strongly influenced by the money supply as well. Second, 100% reserves would prevent panics and runs on banks—an alternative to the FDIC, which has a "moral hazard" to be considered later. Third, the 100% reserve requirement would recapture the use of virtual wealth and seigniorage for public purposes, thereby reducing the need for government to borrow at interest to finance public works. Following Soddy we have emphasized the third reason, although most discussions emphasize the first and second (Barber 1973).

If the State is then to be the sole issuer of money, what principle will guide it in determining how much money to put into circulation? Money would be created or destroyed by the State as necessary in order to keep the purchasing power of money constant. A price index, similar to but more comprehensive than the present Consumer Price Index, would be devised by a National Statistical Authority. If the index showed a tendency to fall over time, the government would finance its own activities by printing new money. Alternatively it might lower taxes, or use newly minted money to repurchase interest-bearing national debt. In other words, deflation would be corrected by some form of money-creating government deficit. If the index showed a rising tendency, the government would raise taxes, or issue interest-bearing national debt, and *not spend* the revenue so raised. Inflation would be corrected by a money-destroying government surplus. The price index would function analogously to a thermostat, or a governor on a steam engine. It would provide a mechanism for negative or stabilizing feedback. By contrast, the fractional reserve banking system provides destabilizing or positive feedback, since the money supply expands during a boom and contracts during a slump, thereby reinforcing the original tendency. Also, to the extent that banks issue money in an inflationary boom and receive net repayments in a deflationary slump, they tend to be repaid in dollars of greater purchasing power than the dollar lent.

In the language of the "rules versus authority" debate in monetary policy, the constant price index falls in the category of a rule, and was advocated as such by Henry C. Simons (1948), the founder of the Chicago School. Rules have the advantage of being clear and known by all, thus diminishing the uncertainty of business expectations, whereas the actions of authorities are unpredictable and subject to political influence and errors of judgment. Exactly what the rule should be (constant money supply, constant rate of growth in money supply, or constant price index), is of less importance than the adoption of *some* rule. The obvious virtue of the rule of a constant price index is fairness over time, avoiding the well-known problems of inflation and deflation.

We are aware of the technical problems of constructing index numbers: their tendency to "wear out" over time as consumption patterns change, leading to the need to alter weights; the problem of measuring change in terms of beginning weights or ending weights, etc. However, a reasonable consumer price index already exists, and we do routinely measure inflation adequately if not ideally, so this is nothing new. We acknowledge the difficulty of controlling that index by policy, because of lags and changes in the velocity of circulation of money, but again these are problems we already have to face under the present arrangement. Certainly there would be much less slippage in monetary control with 100% reserves.

A more serious difficulty is the existence of "near or quasi-money," e.g. credit cards or highly liquid assets so easily convertible into money that individuals tend to treat them as money in making their plans. The existence of near money blunts the instrument of monetary policy. Financial deregulation has led to the practice of checking deposits being created by unregulated institutions. Clearly, if one is to control the banks' ability to create money, it will not do to allow nonbank private institutions to begin creating money. But that, again, is as much a problem in the existing system as in the alternative we are suggesting.

Since international flows of gold, the monetary base in Soddy's day, would play havoc with any policy of maintaining the internal price level constant, it was necessary to propose insulating internal policy from the vagaries of the international balance of payments. This would be accomplished by a freely fluctuating exchange rate, which would automatically attain equilibrium in the balance of payments at a market rate which, presumably, would reflect a purchasing-power parity between national and foreign currencies. International gold flows and the consequent inflationary and deflationary pressures on the national currency would be eliminated. Since the 1920s, freely fluctuating exchange rates have more or less come into being, but it is important to see their role in the context of Soddy's overall policy, and to remember that Soddy was proposing flexible exchange rates at a time when most economists were firmly wedded to the gold standard.

Unlike Soddy, we do not regard these three policies as a panacea. Nevertheless we believe that tightening the coupling between the real economy and its symbolic monetary control system is very important. If money-debt were not allowed to expand without the simultaneous expansion of credit—i.e., if a lender somewhere actually had to forgo the use of every dollar that a borrower somewhere else spends—then the expansion of debt would be brought more into line with the realistic possibilities for the expansion of wealth. One would expect this identity of one person's credit with another person's abstinence to lead to more conservatism in lending. If someone actually has to give up the money which the borrower receives, many more relevant questions will be asked about the nature of the project and the character and competence of the borrower. This greater demand for information regarding creditworthiness may give the edge to smaller, more locally based financial intermediaries, especially if they are no longer in competition with banks whose money-creating ability confers an advantage on bigness. Borrowing in general would come under greater scrutiny. For example, conservative housing mortgage lending would look better relative to lending to finance leveraged buyouts or foreign currency speculation.

If it is felt that this would be too conservative and that the virtual wealth of the community should be available to finance loans, then the government could set up a lending institution and engage in net lending or net retirement of loans by simply creating and destroying money as changes in the price index dictated. We think, however, that the first claim on virtual wealth (or seigniorage) would be to finance public investment directly without taxing or borrowing. Avoidance of borrowing also avoids future transfers from taxpayers to bondholders. Of course the ability of the government to do this is limited by the tendency of the price index to rise once the value of such public investment exceeds the virual wealth of the community. But at least the virtual wealth of the community would be used by the community (the State) rather than the private banking sector. We see an analogy here with Henry George's proposal (advocated earlier) that land rents should be captured for public purposes. Neither land nor money is the creation of individual labor or initiative. Both are fundamental bases of community, and revenues generated from them, we think, are more appropriately treated as community income than as private income.[11] If public revenues were raised more from these community sources, it would be possible to tax individual labor and initiative at lower rates, thereby reducing the incentive-dampening effects of our present system of taxation.

According to a study by the Federal Reserve Bank of St. Louis (Neumann 1992) seigniorage in the United States has averaged annually over the past forty years about 2% of annual federal expenditures. This concept of seigniorage is the profit yielded from the government's monopoly in issuing base money (i.e., reserves plus currency in circulation). Since seigniorage is by definition profit accruing *to the government*, it is calculated in the literature as profit on the creation only of that part of the money supply which the government itself directly creates, namely,

11. Dr. Arthur Peel of Nunawading, Australia, publishes a short fortnightly paper called "Arthur's Seat," dedicated to economic and monetary matters. In the June 1992 issue he recounts an interesting episode that occurred 175 years ago on the Channel Island of Guernsey. The islanders were in debt as a result of the Napoleonic Wars and in need of infrastructure, especially a public market building. Not wanting to go further in debt the authorities decided to print 4,500 pounds of Guernsey Notes to use to pay for the building. After its completion, some thirty-six shops or stalls in the building were rented out. A portion of the rental payments received each year were burned by the government, until the total burned was 4,500 pounds. The debt was liquidated, or rather vaporized. No interest was ever paid, and rental payments on the shops continue as public revenue to the present day. This seems to us an instructive example of how the virtual wealth of the community can be used for the common good. We do not claim that the massive U.S. debt could be redeemed by reclaiming virtual wealth, but nevertheless think that Mr. Peel's historical parable merits reflection.

"the monetary base rather than the creation of deposits by private depository institutions" (Neumann 1992, p. 30). Yet, as we have seen, the private commercial banks multiply reserves by roughly a factor of ten. So it would seem, as a first approximation, that the "private seigniorage," or if that term is a definitional contradiction, "the private profit from monetary creation analogous to seigniorage," should be about ten times the seigniorage on the monetary base, or about 20% of federal revenues.

As a second approximation, however, we must make two corrections. First, actual reserve requirements are closer to 3% than to our numerical example of 10%. (The latter applies only to accounts above 46.8 million dollars, those below that amount, surely the majority, require only 3%.) Therefore the actual multiplier would be closer to $1/.03 = 33$, than to 10. The other correction takes account of the fact that only part of base money (reserves, not currency in circulation) is multiplied by the factor of 33.[12] The 2% of federal expenditures estimate of seigniorage includes seigniorage on currency in circulation as well as on reserves held by commercial banks. If base money were half reserves and half currency in circulation, then our estimate of private bank seigniorage would be half of 2%, or 1%, times 33, or 33% of public expenditures. Surprisingly, it seems that reserves are currently only about one-sixth of base money, so that private seigniorage would be about $1/6 \times 2\% \times 33 = 11\%$. Reclaiming public ownership of virtual wealth by instituting 100% reserve requirements, while not a financial panacea, yields a significant increase (probably between 11% and 33% of public expenditure) in public revenue. These estimates are crude and serve only to establish that the private seigniorage, while not enormous, is not trivial either.

The "private seigniorage" of commercial banks is such an obvious analog to government seigniorage on reserves that it is quite surprising that we find neither mention nor calculation of it in the literature. Nor do we find "private seigniorage" recognized in the money and banking chapters of the basic textbooks, although they all describe how banks create money. In the case of a single monopoly bank the private seigniorage would all be bank profit. In the case of a purely competitive banking sector the private seigniorage would be competed away in lower fees or higher deposit rates of interest, like excess profit in any purely competetive market with free entry. In either extreme case, or in

12. The effective reserve requirement may be less than 3%, since some deposits have no reserve requirement at all, up to a certain limit. For relevant statistics see the *Federal Reserve Bulletin*, published monthly.

the more realistic in-between case, the government can still convert the private seigniorage into true government seigniorage by moving to a 100% reserve system. Obviously, the 100% mark could be approached gradually over time by raising the reserve requirement a few percent a year.

We argued earlier that money has a tendency to foster the exponential-growth culture because its users become susceptible to the fallacy of misplaced concreteness. This happens for two reasons. First, by virtue of the fact that money can be created out of nothing and can grow forever, we tend to think that wealth, of which it is a symbol, can also do these things. Second, with the historical shift from simple commodity production (C—M—C*) to capitalist circulation (M—C—M*) that money brought about, our attention turned to abstract exchange value, the accumulation of which appears to be unlimited, and away from concrete use value, the increase of which is clearly limited by our capacity to use the items accumulated.

Our proposals do not abolish the exponential-growth culture—they do not directly forbid or even limit the existence of compound interest. But 100% reserve requirements would seem indirectly to slow the exponential-growth culture more than any other financial measure that we can think of. Other policies for physically limiting throughput have been discussed elsewhere in this book, and these are, we think, better measures for combating the consequences of exponential growth than trying indirectly to control throughput by controlling money. Nevertheless, the behavior of money and the real economy should become more congruent. One hundred percent reserves is a step in that direction. In addition, perhaps a general shift in investments from interest-earning assets to dividend-earning equities would be worth promoting. Dividends are variable, *ex post* earnings based on real experience, whereas interest-bearing assets are *ex ante* promises based on expectations which become unrealistic if projected very far into the future.

But what if wealth expands with no expansion in the money supply, would that not make commerce more difficult? Perhaps, but it would soon lead to a fall in prices, which would be the signal for the government to put more money in circulation to maintain the price index constant. The main reason for the constant price index is to maintain fairness between creditors and debtors over time and to avoid the multiple injustices of a rubber yardstick—not a fear that commerce could not be effected with less money relative to goods and services. The amount of virtual wealth held voluntarily by the community will automatically adjust with the population, income level, and payment habits of the community—and that adjusted amount of virtual wealth will be divided up among as many dollars as are in circulation. Current transactions can be conducted in pennies or in dollars and there is no problem (assuming flexible prices). But if debtors have to pay back in dollars that today are worth a hundred times more (or less) than when they borrowed them, problems arise.

Under 100% reserve requirements there would be far less need for the Federal Deposit Insurance Corporation and the perverse incentives that it gives to banks and depositors alike to accept risky loans. The single rule of 100% reserves would make a lot of other banking regulations unnecessary. The feared failure of a few large banks would not cause a succession of failures of other banks as a result of a cascading loss of deposits and monetary contraction. Therefore the "too big to be allowed to fail" doctrine that has governed recent banking regulation would lose most of its rationale. This doctrine in effect extends government "insurance" to stockholders and managers of the banks, as well as to depositors, greatly increasing what economists call "moral hazard"— i.e., the incentive to seek high returns by taking greater risks than are prudent because someone else will have to pay for the loss.

Moral Hazard: Recent Financial Experience

Another way of defining moral hazard is that it is what results from the combination of privatized profit and socialized loss. In the words of Kenneth A. Guenther, executive vice president of the Independent Bankers Association of America, "The combination of interest rate deregulation with 100% deposit insurance is like the invention of gunpowder— sooner or later it was bound to explode" (quoted in Greider, 1989). But deregulation of banking and finance was all the rage under Reagan, and the banking sector wanted "the government off its back." Nowadays the last thing it wants is for the government to leave the scene of the train wreck. Ironically, the degree of government involvement in the financial sector through the Resolution Trust Corporation in its clean-up operations is proving much greater than before. Some S&Ls are making sweetheart deals to buy repossessed S&Ls at bargain prices—and are thereby gaining, at government expense, huge competitive advantages over the S&Ls that were well managed and survived the storm. The latter still have some bad loans on their books, unlike the born-again S&Ls, whose sins were all forgiven by the grace of the government as part of the inducement to the prospective buyer. Those deemed "too big to be allowed to fail" are of course especially favored, further encouraging bigness.

The diminished aversion to risk under the conditions of moral hazard also led U.S. commercial banks to invest heavily in the South (Third World), and thereby contributed to the international debt crisis. One of the reactions to that crisis was for the United States and other Northern creditors to pressure the multilateral development banks to speed up their lending to the South in order to provide them with the foreign currency necessary to pay their debts to Northern commercial banks. Since, under fractional reserve banking, the prevention of Northern commercial bank failure is, to a considerable degree, really in the public interest, this was not an unreasonable thing to do. This was one of the reasons for the increased use of so-called fast disbursing structural adjustment loans by the World Bank to be discussed below.

Moral hazard seems pervasive in the financial world. Does it result from the failure to recognize that wealth cannot grow as fast as debt? Keynes said that whatever is physically possible, ought, with a bit of imagination, to be financially possible. Have we converted this sound dictum into its fallacious inverse, that whatever is financially possible, or even convenient, must be physically possible? The more difficult physical growth becomes as we encounter limits, the harder we try to push the alternatives of financial growth—and growth by merger and global integration. Attempts to encourage increasingly difficult growth with all sorts of guarantees and incentives leads to moral hazard. Moral hazard is one more force pushing us towards debt repudiation as an episodic readjustment of the financial world to the real world. Unfortunately, that repudiation, however logically unavoidable, will likely be both unjust and violent.

To analyze or even recount the recent and unfinished consequences of the financial deregulation disaster in the United States, or the international debt crisis, is far beyond our scope. We are sure that the consequences will eventually have to include a large dose of reregulation in the public interest. Although the world has changed a lot since Soddy's time, we believe that his analysis and suggested policies give us a good starting point for fundamentally rethinking how money can better serve the common good.

The Dangers of International Finance

The common good is under special threat from the international nature of finance. Money flows around the world far more freely than labor, or means of production, or even products. This flow profoundly influences where production will occur and the economic prospects for different parts of the world. It will not be possible to develop stable regional or national economies if regions or nations have no control over the movement of money.

Current trends, unfortunately, are weakening national control. Until now many Third World countries have recognized that their ability to function as independent nations depends on having some financial institutions of their own. They have, therefore, protected these against outside competition. However, a major innovation in the Uruguay Round of the General Agreement on Trade and Tariffs (GATT) is to forbid such practices. Countries failing to subject their institutions to competition with international banks and insurance companies would be penalized by restrictions on their trade in goods. If the new GATT is implemented as now proposed, the great international financial institutions will wipe out local banks and insurance companies in much of the world.

Twenty years ago the greatest power over the global economy may have been that of transnational corporations engaged in production. Today that power has shifted to insitutions dealing with finance. Investment has come increasingly to mean the buying and selling of productive enterprises rather than their establishment or expansion.

Money can also be made on speculation in national currencies. Huge sums can be moved instantaneously around the world to take advantage of even minor fluctuations in exchange rates and interest rates. Our view is that finance should serve productive enterprise and not be siphoned off into speculation. Even a small tax on international financial transactions would inhibit this useless speculative churning.

On the other hand, such a tax would do little to discourage the massive speculative attacks mounted on currencies that are considered overvalued. As long as currencies are artificially valued in international exchange, such attacks will continue, and when they succeed huge profits are reaped by the speculators at the expense of the general public. The best way to end this form of speculation is to adopt freely fluctuating exchange rates.

The chief argument against floating currencies is that the extra risk in international trade resulting from exchange rate fluctuations is a deterrent to trade, specialization, and world economic integration. Flexible exchange rates do not prevent the lending and borrowing associated with unbalanced trade, but they provide faster feedback and a corrective mechanism for overborrowing. When loans must be repaid in a foreign currency, the extra demand for that currency will drive up its price. This will make imports more difficult and exports easier, thus increasing the net amount of foreign currency earned, and reducing the real consumption of the debtor in a visible way. This can lead to less borrowing and reduced dependence on trade.

Whereas most economists and policy makers regard any impediment to integration of the global economy as bad, readers of this book, and especially of Chapter 11, will know that we disagree. We are impressed by the destructive consequences for human community and for the natural environment of policies that aim at replacing national and regional economies with a globally integrated one. Since we think global integration has already gone too far, we welcome the deterrent effects of flexible exchange rates. Unfortunately, we fear that these effects will not be large, given the possibilities that the forward exchange market provides of hedging against exchange rate risks.

In Chapter 11 we urged a policy of balanced trade—i.e., that current exports should pay for current imports, and that capital transfers (debts) between nations should be relatively small. At present, unfortunately, it is the capital account that dominates in the foreign exchange markets, and much of this is short-term debt whose frequent international movement is motivated by speculation rather than real investment. Limits to the degree of acceptable imbalance in the trade account would automatically limit the capital account imbalance, and vice versa. Perhaps a limit on capital transfers would be the best way to enforce a move toward balanced trade.

Long-term international debts contribute even more visibly to the harsh effects of international finance, especially in the Third World. In the 1970s Third World countries borrowed heavily from commercial banks in the United States and other Northern Hemisphere countries. The theory was that this money would be invested in productive development that would produce profits from which it could be repaid. In fact, much of the money was unwisely invested, spent on projects with no economic benefit, or stolen.

When it became clear in the 1980s that earnings from these "investments" would not suffice for repayment, creditors began to pressure multilateral development banks to speed up their lending to the South in order to provide them with the foreign currency necessary to pay their debts to Northern commercial banks. This was one of the reasons for the increased use of so-called fast disbursing structural adjustment loans by the World Bank. Structural adjustment loans were also part of a general shift from project-based to policy-based lending. The rationale was that efficient projects frequently fail because of macroeconomic irrationalities, and that the World Bank was pouring money down the sink to invest in projects that were merely islands of temporary efficiency in a sea of permanent irrationality.

Since the World Bank and IMF are dogmatically certain about what the rational macroeconomic policies are (removal of subsidies, deficit reduction, trade liberalization, and privatization, which together constitute "structural adjustment"), there need be no delays with lengthy study and preparation as in the case of projects, and the loans can move the money quickly. If an efficient policy increases output by more than the interest on the loan, then the country is made better off, at least in conventional terms of more production, just as with any loan. One may, however, ask why is it necessary to borrow money to enact more efficient policies? In part, structural adjustment loans were necessary to induce countries to enact policies that the World Bank and IMF were sure would be good for them, while the countries themselves were not so sure. Even if the borrowing government agreed, the World Bank and IMF needed something to help sell it politically, so the loan took on some aspects of a bribe. Also it can make good sense to borrow for policy reform, if the reform measures cut needed revenues, as for example lowering tariffs would do. So, if one is sure that lowering tariffs is a good policy, then it could make sense to borrow to compensate for lost revenues until new sources could be devised. Of course, it might also make sense to devise the new sources of revenue before reducing tariffs, and thereby avoid borrowing. But not borrowing would mean there would be no inflow of foreign exchange with which to meet payments to the Northern private banks.

The correct decision depends on the interest rate and the productivity of the policy reform. The first is known, but the latter is not. There is in practice not even an attempt to estimate a rate of return for policy loans because it is too intangible. Similarly, no such estimate is made for education and public health loans. In all of these cases it is felt that the theory is solid enough to go ahead without empirical reconfirmation in each case. However, education and public health have a direct and clear connection to welfare, independent of their indirect connection via increased productivity, whereas policy reform has no direct welfare benefits and depends for its justification entirely on the presumed correctness of the indirect effects indicated by neoclassical economic theory. In the background was the awkward need to move foreign exchange South so it could flow back as interest to Northern banks. This was necessary because the failure of a few big banks could cause a cumulative contraction of credit with disastrous consequences. Many banks with heavy Third World loans were too big to be allowed to fail under our fractional reserve banking system.

Part of the willingness to forgo the cost/benefit calculation of rate of return on these loans no doubt derived from the knowledge that such calculations can be, and frequently are, "cooked" to give whatever answer is desired. So the sacrificed empirical test was not such a great change in the *de facto* mode of operation. But is not the World Bank concerned about getting repaid, and would that not lead it to be careful in making loans, at least according to its own best understanding? The fact is that the World Bank will almost always be repaid, even if the project or policy it finances produces only losses. This is because the Bank lends to sovereign governments that have the power to tax and print money. They cannot print foreign exchange, but they can buy it by printing more of their own money and accepting the consequences of inflation and devaluation—or they can tax their people honestly, rather than by inflation. In either case they can pay back the World Bank, and nearly always will do so rather than default and lose their credit rating.

The World Bank will in fact be among the first creditors paid. Add to this the following facts: politicians love to borrow large amounts of money; the World Bank is under pressure to lend more, since repayment flows on past loans are now so large that there is a "negative net flow" of funds to the South from the Bank; its loan officers are evaluated in part by the amount of money they move. It is clear why the quality of the World Bank's portfolio has declined in strictly conventional terms (Wapenhans Report, 1992). The quickest way for a World Bank employee to become unpopular is to slow down the money pump, even if it is by demonstrating irrefutably that a certain loan is stupid. In an institution that stood to lose money from stupid behavior such demonstrations would be rewarded rather than punished. We can also see why the situation has all the earmarks of "moral hazard."

What should the World Bank do? Slow down, devote a larger share of resources to project supervision, make smaller loans, perhaps take an equity position in some projects, or share in the losses to some extent. The latter would help overcome the moral hazard problem and would likely improve project supervision. More vigorous adversarial review of projects internally would help, as would a shift in personnel evaluation criteria from meeting lending targets to actual project performance. More fundamentally, as has been argued elsewhere (Goodland et al. 1992), the World Bank should focus more on investing in natural capital restoration, in resource efficiency, and in domestic production of basic goods and services for local use under local control. This implies a substantial departure from the current export-led model of development, with its celebration of specialization and trade according to comparative advantage. Our reasons for believing that the costs of further globalization outweigh the benefits are detailed in earlier chapters, especially Chapter 11.

A Decentralist Dithyramb

In closing we return to our basic theme of community and relate it to finance in the words of the founder of the Chicago School of Economics, Henry C. Simons. In addition to advocating 100% reserve requirements for commercial banks, Simons thought it would be a good idea to institutionally separate the specifically banking functions of safekeeping, checking, and clearing, from the investment function. He envisaged small investment trusts as complements to the banks:

> But smaller banks, whose executives really know something about local or community enterprises, might be converted into highly useful institutions, mobilizing local funds for local investment, much as building and loan associations once did but on an equity basis....
>
> It is easy to become dithyrambic if, as a libertarian, one contemplates the possibilities of radical decentralization of our capital markets via such localized investment trusts. It might eventually undo, and even reverse, the present artificial economies of inordinate enterprise size, in differential access to capital funds. While giant enterprise aggregations were plagued by a volatile New York Stock Exchange, and supported by only the most inconstant investors, small and moderate-size firms might enjoy the steady loyalty of their communities, acting through local investment trusts, and also a salutary close scrutiny of management by interested local shareholders, indeed by the whole community as a functioning social group.
>
> If local investment trusts really served, as they should, to mobilize mass, small savings in their communities, even our labor problems might be brought

toward good solution. In such circumstances community pressure might inhibit wage demands that would threaten the relative prosperity of local industry, that is, impair its competitive position vis-a-vis other communities. On the other hand, such pressure would also be exerted against needlessly low wage rates that impaired a firm's ability to attract or maintain good quality labor, or impaired the community's ability to hold or recruit good worker-citizens. But this is rhapsody! [Simons 1948, p. 238]

Dithyrambic rhapsody though he may have called it, this vision clearly was what Simons wanted, and it certainly expresses our own idea of the financial requirements of an economics for community. How it was forgotten in the subsequent rise of extreme individualism associated with the current Chicago School is an interesting question for historians of economic thought.

Money and finance are arcane and difficult areas. What we have offered in this afterword is certainly not a technical blueprint for detailed reform, but rather a few basic policy directions, along with a discussion of the first principles from which they are derived, and an attempt to show that at least their initial consequences would seem to be beneficial. We invite the experts to review our proposals and our partial resuscitation of Frederick Soddy. We invite them not only to point out errors, but to come up with something better. We are emboldened in this challenge by the sorry current state of financial affairs just reviewed. We find it hard to imagine how the consequences of following Soddy's three conservative recommendations, especially if "cleaned up" by sympathetic experts, could have possibly been worse than the havoc wreaked by the orthodox monetary mountebanks who continue to confuse debt with wealth.

The Index of Sustainable Economic Welfare

Introduction

Chapters 3 and 19 pointed to the need for a way of measuring the economy that would give better guidance than the GNP to those interested in promoting economic welfare.

One possibility would be to bring up to date one of the welfare measures that has already been proposed. However, on closer examination, none of the available candidates seems adequate today. For example, Zolotas (1981) does not consider sustainability, whereas Nordhaus and Tobin (1972), who do take sustainability into account, do not consider environmental issues that have become increasingly important since their work was published. We find Zolotas more helpful on some points and Nordhaus and Tobin on others. We have learned from the Japanese measure of Net National Welfare. Accordingly, rather than revising and bringing up to date one of the existing measures, we propose to build on their accomplishments and propose a new one, the Index of Sustainable Economic Welfare (ISEW). The ISEW includes some elements not dealt with by any of the three indices that were discussed in Chapter 3, as well as fresh ways of treating topics that were included in them.

The ISEW has undergone a number of revisions since it appeared in the first edition of *For the Common Good*. Some of our revisions are responses to detailed comments on the index we received from Carol Carson and Allan Young of the U.S. Bureau of Economic Analysis, and from E. J. Mishan, Robert Eisner, Robert Gottfried, Thomas Michael Power, Jan Tinbergen, Richard Lamm, and Hans Diefenbacher. Diefenbacher's comments were most interesting because he has constructed a similar index for West

Germany for the years 1950 to 1987. We asked these experts to review the ISEW and to commment on it in return for a small compensation and an agreement to publish their criticisms. In the detailed discussion below, we shall refer to some of their critiques of the original ISEW. Their critiques are available in full in Clifford W. Cobb and John B. Cobb, Jr., *The Green National Product: An Alternative to Gross National Product to Measure Well-Being* (Lanham, Md.: University Press of America, forthcoming).

Two other books of special significance for devising ecologically sensitive economic indicators have also been published since the first edition of *For the Commmon Good.* In *Wasting Assets,* Robert Repetto and the staff of the World Resources Institute have examined the Indonesian national income accounts to determine the effect of subtracting the depletion of natural capital in the form of oil extraction, timber harvesting, and soil loss (Repetto 1989). Although the official Gross Domestic Product of Indonesia grew by 7.1% annually from 1971 to 1984, when resource depletion is taken into account the growth rate was only 4.0%.

The essays in Part 2 of *Ecological Economics,* edited by Robert Costanza, bring together a number of important theoretical insights regarding the appropriate treatment of environmental resources in national income accounting (Costanza 1991). The scholarly journal *Ecological Economics,* also edited by Costanza, promotes an ongoing discussion of these issues.

In the following pages we describe the major theoretical decisions that entered into the formation of the ISEW. We then offer the table of ISEW statistics from 1950 to 1990 and certain other conclusions. The remainder of the appendix explains in detail the columns composing the table.

Personal Consumption

All economic welfare measures with which we are familiar overlap with the GNP by including personal consumption. But from that point on these measures differ from each other as well as from the GNP. We have likewise begun with consumption, but we have been made aware by Power and Mishan that there are some conceptual problems in the relationship between consumption and welfare.

One problem is that the cost of living varies between different regions or cities within the country. A $30,000 income in a high-cost city does not produce the same level of well-being as an equivalent income in a low-cost city. In particular, an equal amount of money spent on housing will yield very different levels of satisfaction. Thus, ideally, one should develop estimates of welfare in each city or region separately and add those adjusted measures instead of lumping all consumption together. However, those statistics are not currently available.

Income Distribution

We have factored in income distribution on the assumption that an additional thousand dollars in income adds more to the welfare of a poor family than it does to a rich family. Though economists generally consider the question of distributional equity to be important, they regard it as a separate issue from the magnitude of economic welfare. Thus one might ask: If the aggregate quantity of benefits (units of welfare) decreases by X percent while the measure of income distribution improves by Y percent, are we better off or worse off? From the perspective of neoclassical economics, there is no way to answer this question. We are aware of the conceptual problems involved in including a distributional component in our Index of Sustainable Economic Welfare. Nevertheless, we believe that continuing to treat distribution as a separate issue has the effect of devaluing its importance in the analysis of economic welfare. We have chosen therefore to make it an integral part of our index.

Net Capital Growth

We have considerably altered what Nordhaus and Tobin did in calculating changes in net capital stock. Specifically, we have included only changes in the stock of fixed reproducible capital and excluded human capital in this calculation.

We have omitted human capital from our calculations of changes in the stock of capital even though we recognize its theoretical importance in sustainable economic welfare. Human capital—the characteristics of the work force, such as health and skillfulness, that make it productive—certainly contributes to economic well-being. Yet having granted that general principle, we question the validity of measuring inputs such as expenditures on medical care or on schooling to derive meaningful estimates of the stock of human capital. We regard the actual sources of human capital formation as yet undefined and thus unmeasurable. To the extent that we include health and education expenditures in our calculations, we treat portions of them as consumption.

The relation between increased medical expenditures and improved health in a well-nourished society is tenuous, and we have not seen evidence that demonstrates any clear contribution of health expenditures to productivity. Intuitively, we might assume that more money spent on medical care will lead to a healthier population, which will in turn lead to lower absenteeism at work and higher productivity. Yet the record on this relationship is ambiguous. According to the U.S. National Center for Health Statistics (as reported in *Statistical Abstract*), the number of "restricted-activity days" per person increased from 16.4 in 1965 to 19.1 in 1980, a period during which real per capita expenditures on health care increased by over 70%. This does not mean that we that we were less healthy in 1980 than in 1965. Other statistics might indicate some degree of health improvement. We cite the "restricted-activity days" statistic merely to demonstrate the ambiguity of any presumed connection between health expenditures and enhanced productivity.

The effect of increased schooling on productivity is also far from definitive. In the work of economists Edward Denison and Theodore Schultz (the latter being a source for Nordhaus and Tobin's human capital calculations), the contribution of education to productivity is assumed to be correlated with inputs such as years of schooling and expenditures per pupil (Denison 1962, 68ff.; Schultz 1961). On its face, that assumption may seem plausible. However, both theoretical and empirical issues raise serious doubts about the validity of using these inputs to estimate "educational capital."

At one stage in the preparation of the ISEW, we included an estimate of human capital based on educational expenditures for members of the labor force. We found that inflation-adjusted per pupil expenditures quadrupled between 1945 and 1985, and our estimate of human capital showed an almost eleven-fold increase during that period. However, since the quality of education does not appear to have improved during that period (and may have declined), the use of school expenditures to measure human capital seems completely inappropriate. Human capital, or at least change in it over time, appears to derive largely from on-the-job training and experience. Until someone devises an ingenious method of measuring the value of the knowledge embodied by workers and managers, a plausible measure of the stock of human capital will remain beyond our reach.

On a theoretical level, the correlation between levels of formal education and earned income differentials may not indicate a causal relation between them, or at least the cause may not fit the human capital model. Lester Thurow suggests that the correlation between education and income may be explained by a model of what he calls "jobs competition" (Thurow 1975, pp. 170–184). In contrast to the usual concept of wage competition, in which workers receive wages according to the skills that they have when they seek employment, the jobs competition model proposes that workers are hired on the basis of their "relative position in the labor queue," which is determined more by their academic degrees than by their actual job-related skills. According to this model, job skills are learned primarily at work rather than through formal education. The higher earnings of college graduates compared to high school graduates is thus based not on their greater stock of knowledge or skills (human capital) but on the fact that employers rely on academic degrees to screen out those they expect it will cost them more to train. Thurow argues that insofar as this model is valid, the function of education is not to confer skill and therefore increased productivity and higher wages on the worker; it is rather to certify his [or her] "trainability" and to confer upon him [or her] a certain status by virtue of this certification. Jobs and higher incomes are then distributed on the basis of this certified status. [1975, p. 172]

The model helps to explain why equalization of the distribution of education since 1950 has not led to a comparable equalization of income distribution and why overall levels of productivity growth have not kept pace with the growth in expenditures on education. It also explains why investment in education continues to provide a relatively high rate of return for an individual, even if it provides only a small return to society. The value of formal education is not that it imparts skills but that it places the individual further up in the labor queue than others: "In effect, education becomes a defensive expenditure necessary to protect one's 'market share.' The larger the class of educated labor and the more rapidly it grows, the more such defensive expenditures become imperative" (ibid., p. 182). In other words, an individual is forced to obtain a college degree to gain access to certain jobs simply because others have the degree. If much of what is spent on education is designed to preserve the relative positions of individuals, the massive increases in educational expenditures since 1950 cannot be counted as a significant factor in productivity gains or as a source of human capital.

Even if Thurow's model of jobs competition is completely invalid, other empirical evidence also casts doubt upon the importance of formal education in the creation of human capital. In particular, the correlation between earned income and education appears to be very weak. Jacob Mincer, one of the leading analysts of investments in human capital, has shown that among white, male, nonfarm workers only 7% of the variation in earned income is accounted for by differences in their levels of education (Mincer 1974, p. 44).[1] (If the whole workforce were included, education would account for an even smaller portion of the variation because of discrimination based on race and gender.) In other words, 93% of the variation is due to other factors, ranging from luck and personal connections to ambition, native ability, and skills learned on the job.

As a consequence of these considerations, we have omitted any estimates of human capital from our calculations of changes in the stock of capital. In principle we agree that human capital should be included, but we believe that medical and educational expenditures vastly overstate actual changes in the stock of human capacities that enhance productivity.

In addition to removing the entire human capital component from

---

1. In the eighth year after the completion of schooling, the level of education accounts for about one-third of the variation in incomes, though this proportion falls rapidly in succeeding years.

the procedure used by Nordhaus and Tobin, we have also redefined the growth requirement as the growth of capital necessary to compensate for depreciation and population growth, without including any consideration of changes in labor productivity. It was not evident, even to Nordhaus and Tobin, why sustainability should mean growth rather than a steady state, i.e., why net capital should grow at the combined rate of population and productivity growth.

The capital stock must be growing at the same rate as population and the labor force. This capital-widening requirement is as truly a cost of staying in the same position as outright capital consumption. This principle is clear enough when growth is simply increase in population and the labor force. Its application to an economy with technological progress is by no means clear. Indeed the concept of national income becomes fuzzy. [Nordhaus and Tobin 1972, p. 6]

When they proposed to include productivity growth as part of the growth requirement, Nordhaus and Tobin may not have foreseen the possibility that productivity would decline, which it has during many of the years since they published their paper. According to their procedure, the growth of sustainable MEW is enhanced by a fall in productivity, which is an absurd result.[2] Instead, declining productivity should expand the growth requirement, because capital must be used to compensate for reduced productivity if the same level of consumption is to be maintained. As a result, one reasonable way of calculating a growth requirement would be to subtract (rather than add) the percentage growth of productivity from the growth of population and the labor force. For our ISEW, we have chosen the more conservative method of leaving productivity changes out of calculations of sustainability altogether.

Foreign vs. Domestic Capital

Besides calculating whether net capital formation is sufficient to keep up with a growing population, we have included a category that takes into account whether the source of capital can be sustained. In the early stages of a nation's economic development, growth may depend on borrowing capital from other countries. However, when an advanced capitalist nation finances its capital accumulation by borrowing from foreign sources, we assume that that reflects a fundamental weakness in the long-term viability of that economy. We therefore add the change in the net U.S. investment position (or subtract it when negative) on the assumption that sustainability requires long-term national self-reliance.

2. Net capital growth, which is added to MEW, is equal to the change in the net capital stock minus the growth requirement, which is composed of changes in the labor force and productivity. If productivity decreases, the growth requirement would grow more slowly, and MEW would grow more rapidly.

Natural Resource Depletion

We have also extended the concern for sustainable production to include the availability of natural resources or "natural capital" rather than merely humanly created capital. Under the category of natural capital we include not only fuels and minerals but wetlands and farmland as well. Zolotas took this issue into account to some extent by correcting for what he regarded as the slight underpricing of fuels and minerals by the market. MEW omits the cost of depleting natural resources altogether. However, this is not an oversight. Instead Nordhaus and Tobin explain why they believe that the exhaustion of resources does not involve any threat to sustainability.

The prevailing standard model of growth assumes that there are no limits on the feasibility of expanding the supplies of nonhuman agents of production . . . Presumably the tacit justification has been that reproducible capital is a near-perfect substitute for land and other exhaustible resources . . . If substitution is not possible in any given technology, or if a particular resource is exhausted, we tacitly assume that "land-augmenting" innovations will overcome the scarcity. These optimistic assumptions about technology stand in contrast to the tacit assumption of environmentalists that no substitutes are available for natural resources. Under this condition, it is easily seen that output will indeed stop growing or will decline. [Nordhaus and Tobin 1972, p. 14]

Thus the question of whether an adjustment for resource depletion needs to be made under the category of sustainability hinges upon this issue of substitution and technological advance. In support of their optimistic view, Nordhaus and Tobin cite a study by Edward Denison that shows a declining proportion of national income being contributed by natural resources from 1909 to 1958 (Denison 1962, p. 13). They also refer to a 1963 study by Barnett and Morse which concluded that, with the exception of forest products, the price of resource-intensive goods had not risen more rapidly than the price of goods in general (Barnett and Morse 1963, Part 3). Thus substitution and technological change had "come to the rescue of scarcity."

The faith in the infinite substitutability of nonrenewable resources is founded on the experience of a peculiar period in history, during which energy was extremely cheap. But now that that era is over, the cost of all resources will increase because of the increasing energy costs of extraction and processing. The falling price of natural resources during the first seventy years of this century was a one-time phenomenon upon which a faulty view of the future has been based.

The path-breaking book *Beyond Oil: The Threat to Food and Fuel in the Coming Decades* by John Gever et al. explains why economists have underestimated the consequences of resource depletion. The problem is that energy is now expensive, not merely in the financial sense of costing more money but also in that it requires increasing amounts of energy to obtain.

The energy output/input ratio—the amount of energy made available as output from a given input of energy for exploration, extraction, and processing—declined for oil from about 100 in the 1940s to 23 in the 1970s (Gever et al. 1986, p. 70).[3] A similar decline occurred for coal. Yet even when the energy cost of energy was rising (because the energy output/input ratio was falling), the cost of energy in dollars could continue to decline. This paradox was possible as long as the dollar price of fossil fuels was low relative to labor costs. Energy-intensive technologies for extracting and refining energy reduced dollar costs as long as they cut labor requirements. Since the price of fossil fuels was falling, the unit price of other resources could be cut as well by the same process of substituting cheap energy inputs for expensive labor. Now that the energy output/input ratio for newly discovered oil has fallen to about 8 and for most other energy sources to less than 5, the days of declining resource costs are permanently at an end.[4]

Thus the money cost of energy rose in the 1970s and will continue to rise in the long run, not simply because of producers' cartels but because of the increasing energy inputs required to discover, extract, and process new sources of energy. According to the authors of *Beyond Oil,* "By 2005 it will be pointless to continue exploring for oil and gas as energy sources in the United States: after that more energy would be used to look for these fuels than the oil and gas we found would contain" (p. 20). Moreover, even when expected new discoveries are included, their analysis shows that "domestic oil and gas stores . . . will be effectively empty by 2020 [while] . . . world oil and gas supplies will last perhaps three decades longer, or more if Third World economies fail to develop" (ibid.).

The point is not that resources are finite. Economists have long recognized that fact, but they have assumed that resources are *effectively* infinite if one is willing to pay a sufficiently high price to get them. Yet energy analysis allows us to see that a resource may be exhausted even when there are vast stocks in the ground, if the energy cost of extraction and processing exceeds the energy content of the unmined resource. Nor is the development of nonpetroleum-based energy sources likely to change the general outlook. Unless unproven technologies such as fusion provide cheap, unlimited energy (which seems doubtful given the track-record of fission compared to its initial promise), no technical changes will substantially alter the basic trend of declining energy resources and higher costs.[5] Even if

3. *Beyond Oil* uses the term "energy profit ratio" to refer to the amount of output energy available relative to the amount of input energy used in a system. We have chosen the term 'energy output/input ratio' instead to avoid the possible confusion that the term profit might refer to financial profit rather than surplus energy.

4. According to Gever and his associates (1986, p. 70), the energy output/input ratio of electricity production is 4 for nuclear power (less if the cost of reactor decommissioning is included) and 2.5 for Western strip-mined coal if the cost of using scrubbers is included.

technological breakthroughs cannot dramatically expand production, economists argue that rising prices will encourage technological improvements in energy efficiency as well as reductions in energy consumption. The idea is that we will be able to maintain our standard of living and even continue to grow by using the dwindling supply of energy more efficiently. The authors of *Beyond Oil* explain why technology offers little hope of achieving this goal. First, they note that advances in the material standard of living have depended on two factors working in combination: knowledge and resources. Growth depended on the embodiment of new ideas in the form of capital, which required the use of energy. As long as energy was declining in cost, the limiting factor in material growth was knowledge. Under those circumstances, a certain degree of optimism that growth could be sustained indefinitely seemed justified. There was no obvious limit to increases in knowledge. However, in recent years, resources have become the limiting factor in growth. By having to spend a larger and larger amount of our resources just to make more resources available, less is left over for improvements in welfare. Thus, Cleveland and his co-authors have calculated that "in the last ten years alone [1974–1984], the fraction of GNP accounted for by natural resource extraction has grown from 4 percent to 10 percent" (Cleveland et al. 1984, pp. 890–897, cited in Gever et al. 1986, p. 101). We can now see that technological advances have traditionally involved a combination of inventiveness and cheap energy. New technology can marginally improve energy efficiency, but, for the most part, material growth is a thing of the past.

Second, the authors of *Beyond Oil* point out that previous estimates of the nation's capacity to conserve energy were overly optimistic because much of what appeared to be conservation actually involved shifts of the kinds of fuels used for particular purposes (fuel efficiency rather than energy efficiency per se). In addition, optimistic estimates of possible improvements in energy efficiency have been based on extrapolations from individual sectors to the entire economy. Yet when the *indirect* energy costs of the technology used to increase energy efficiency are included, the gains in efficiency appear minimal.

If *all* companies substituted labor and capital for fuel, more fuel would be needed somewhere in the economy to increase the amount of labor and capital, and the nation's net savings in energy are reduced. In agriculture, for example, the amount

5. As the authors of *Beyond Oil* note, there are already practical reasons for doubting that fusion will provide a technical fix. "Fusion technology is still decades away from commercial application. Moreover, at least one leading fusion researcher, Lawrence Lidsky of MIT, believes that the particular fusion technology that is being developed most intensively, the deuterium-tritium reaction, will *never* be commercially feasible. According to Lidsky, it produces large quantities of dangerous radiation that would force plants to be even more sophisticated and expensive, per unit of energy produced, than today's fission reactors" (Gever et al. 1986, p. 72).

of fuel used *directly* on a cornfield to grow a kilogram of corn fell 14.6 percent between 1959 and 1970. However, when the calculation includes the fuel used elsewhere in the economy to build the tractors, make the fertilizers and pesticides, and
so on, it turns out that the total energy cost of a kilogram of corn actually rose by
3 percent during that period. [Gever et al. 1986, p. 102–103][6]

Thus, technologically achieved energy conservation does not offer a comprehensive remedy for the declining stock of energy resources. The precise
extent to which energy efficiency gains will be offset by indirect energy
costs is not clear. In some sectors of the energy economy, such as household
heating and automobile fuel consumption, Amory Lovins has calculated
that tremendous energy savings can be achieved by shifting to technologies
that are more energy efficient but require little more capital than current
technologies. In the economy as a whole, however, net energy efficiency
improvements (combining direct and indirect energy costs) are likely to be
minimal.

Nevertheless, some economists have argued that resource depletion
leaves future generations better off than our own if a sufficiently large proportion of those resources are transformed into capital rather than being
consumed in the present.[7] According to this view, depriving ourselves of
present enjoyment of natural resources is inequitable because our present
investments already enable future generations to have a larger economy
than we now have. The implicit assumption behind this view is that capital
constitutes a perfect substitute for (or even an improvement upon) the
natural resource base of a society. At one level this seems plausible. A machine made of steel might reasonably seem like a better gift to the next generation than the deposits of minerals that were used to make it. Yet as E. J.
Mishan notes, "A common belief among economists, that the consumption
of finite resources . . . is offset in value by the formation of other capital, is
erroneous. Under familiar behaviour assumptions, no more than a fraction
of the value of the finite resource is replaced, and this fraction could be
negligible" (Mishan 1984, p. 13, n.5). Even if the entire value of the finite
resource were replaced with capital, this often would not benefit future
generations as much as leaving the resource untapped. First, the production
of the capital would consume resources that future generations might wish
to use for other purposes. Second, capital goods would deteriorate over
time, imposing maintenance costs on future generations that would not occur if the resources were left in their natural state. (An example of this can
be seen in the massive cost of restoring highways in the United States, a

6. Cited from D. Pimentel et al., "Food Production and the Energy Crisis," *Science* 182
(1973): 443.

7. See, for example, Robert Solow, "Intergenerational Equity and Exhaustible Resources,"
Review of Economic Studies, Symposium on the Economics of Exhaustible Resources, 41
(suppl. 1974): 29–45.

cost that would have been imposed by weathering even if they had never been used to carry traffic.) Third, capital cannot ultimately substitute for resources because capital itself is composed of resources. In other words, as discussed in Chapter 10, labor and capital complement the material resources that are transformed into a product. Capital provided for future generations must be accompanied by natural resources to be of any value.

We have already begun to pay the price of profligate use of resources that made possible rapid economic growth in the past. The decline in real wages after 1973 and the slowdown in productivity growth after 1977 are signs of the effect of rising real resource costs, particularly energy resources.

The implications of this prospect of diminishing resources and rising costs for Nordhaus and Tobin's study are clear. The issue of resource exhaustion needed to be included in their measurement of sustainable welfare. Current welfare should have been reduced to the extent that present enjoyment deprives the future of the potential for the same level of economic welfare. Having introduced the idea of sustainability with respect to net capital accumulation, they should have carried over the same logic to the depletion of "natural capital."[8]

Yet even if Nordhaus and Tobin had entertained the notion that the depletion of resources in the present would impoverish future generations, they would likely have minimized the significance of this intergenerational conflict by suggesting that the effects on the future be discounted at the real interest rate. From the perspective of neoclassical economic theory, the damage caused by the exhaustion of resources (either renewable or nonrenewable) should be counted in the present only after it has been discounted (reduced) in proportion to the long-term interest rate. In effect, this theory says that a resource should be exhausted as long as the rate of

---

8. Recent work by William Nordhaus has included resources or natural capital as an element of sustainability. In a paper entitled, "Is Growth Sustainable? Reflections on the Concept of Sustainable Growth," delivered in October 1992 at the International Economic Association, he calculates "Hicksian Income" (the maximum consumption each year that leaves the stock of capital intact) for the years 1950 to 1986. As in the ISEW, he makes a correction for natural resource depletion, but his methodology causes this to be a very small figure. (The same is true of long-term environmental damage from global warming.)

Nordhaus compares his calculation of Hicksian Income with the ISEW as it appeared in the first edition of this book. Hicksian Income grew by 4.41% from 1950 to 1965 and by 2.35% from 1965 to 1986. By contrast, the ISEW grew at annual rates of 3.81% and 1.02% during the same two periods. Thus, the growth slowdown was 2.79% for ISEW and 2.06% for Hicksian Income. (The slowdown on a per capita basis was 2.18% for ISEW and 1.45% for Hicksian Income.) Although Nordhaus emphasizes the difference betwen the "dramatic" slowdown of ISEW and the lesser reduction in the growth rate of Hicksian Income, the latter slowed down three times as much as the decline in the GNP growth rate (which went from 3.75% per year to 3.05%, for a reduction of only .70%.) As in the case of the MEW, a measure that accounts in some way for sustainability indicates that the rate of growth of GNP is based on current consumption of potential future assets. Once again, GNP turns out not to be a good proxy for a measure of sustainable well-being.

increase in its price *in situ* is less than the interest rate. We regard this process of discounting the effects of our present policies on future generations as socially inappropriate, even though the practice is reasonable on an individual level. In other words, the rational procedure for an individual, given the existing set of incentives, is not necessarily a rational policy for a society as a whole. Thus we reject in principle the idea of discounting the effects of resource depletion (and environmental damage) on the future. Instead we propose the view that any reduction in economic welfare in the future below the level currently enjoyed should be counted as if the cost occurred in the present.

The attitude of benign neglect toward the future implicit in the concept of discounting has troubled some leading members of the economics profession. As A. C. Pigou noted in 1924:

There is wide agreement that the state should protect the interests of the future in some degree against the effects of our irrational discounting, and of our preference for ourselves over our descendants. The whole movement for "conservation" in the United States is based upon this conviction. It is the clear duty of government which is the trustee for unborn generations as well as for its present citizens, to watch over and if need be, by legislative enactment, to defend exhaustible natural resources of the country from rash and reckless spoliation. [Pigou 1924, quoted in Batie 1986, p. 10]

Yet in effect, Pigou merely recognized the problem without suggesting an appropriate basis for addressing it. By implying that consideration of the distant future lies outside the bounds of economic theory, he washed his hands of any professional responsibility for thinking about the issue of sustainability.

In our ISEW, we have thus deducted an estimate of the amount that would need to be set aside in a perpetual income stream to compensate future generations for the loss of services from nonrenewable energy resources (as well as other exhaustible mineral resources). In addition, we have deducted for the loss of biological resources such as wetlands and croplands (due to shifts in land use and to erosion and compaction). This may be thought of as an accounting device for depreciating "natural capital" similar to the depreciation of capital subtracted from GNP to arrive at NNP.

Environmental Damage

In the studies by Nordhaus and Tobin and by Zolotas, there is some recognition of the fact that pollution and other environmental damage should be deducted in the calculation of economic welfare. In the area of air and water pollution, we have updated Zolotas's estimates using more recent data and different methodologies for constructing time series. We have also included an estimate for noise pollution. The most important change, however, is the addition of a rather speculative estimate of long-term environmental damage, particularly from climate modification. We have assumed that the damage is cumulative and directly related to consumption of energy and chlorofluorocarbons. As in the case of resource depletion, we have sought to devise methodologies that avoid discounting future costs.

Value of Leisure

We have omitted any imputation of the value of leisure from our Index of Sustainable Economic Welfare because the rather arbitrary assumptions upon which such a calculation are based strike us as being particularly problematic.[9]

To begin with, the meaning of leisure is not entirely clear. Does it simply mean all time spent on activities for which there is no remuneration? In that case, it would include the time of all those who are unemployed, under-employed, or involuntarily retired and who would like to be working. Does it include time spent in such activities as child care and cooking, which may fall into the categories of either work or pleasure within the same household under various circumstances? Finally, how should the value of leisure time be calculated in dollar terms? As Nordhaus and Tobin explain, "In general, time is to be valued at its opportunity cost, the wage rate" (1972,

9. The imputation for leisure also tends to be so large that variations in the assumptions about how to calculate it have an enormous impact on any welfare index that includes it. The rate of growth of the MEW, for example, varies by approximately a factor of 2 according to which assumption one makes about the relation of technological progress to the value of leisure and nonmarket labor. Nevertheless, in each variant, the value of leisure is by far the largest item in the index, constituting from half to three-fifths of total MEW. Excluding leisure raises the growth of per capita sustainable MEW to 0.86% per year during the period 1947 to 1965 compared to 0.40% per year when it is included. Thus the omission of leisure significantly reduces the gap between the growth of MEW and GNP (the latter of which grew annually by 2.2% during this period). We suspect that the inclusion of an imputation for leisure in the ISEW would have similarly widened the gap between its growth rate and that of GNP, thus strengthening our conclusion that an alternative measure of sustainable economic welfare is needed. However, we did not attempt this calculation because we could not find a conceptually sound and empirically well-grounded basis for imputing the value of leisure. In the absence of a solid framework, the massive contribution of leisure to the outcome of welfare measurements is not justified.

As an indication of the absurdities that could result by including leisure, consider the assumption that all nonwork time spent, including time spent sleeping, is leisure. The number of hours of leisure per day for someone working 8 hours would be 16. The total amount of leisure per year would then be approximately 6766 hours per fully employed member of the labor force (and more for part-time employees). If we assume an average real wage rate of $5 per hour (in 1972 dollars) and that the value of the marginal hour of leisure is equal to the wage rate, then the value of leisure to the average worker per year is $33,830, and the total for the work force is in the neighborhood of $3.7 trillion. This would be more than double the value of GNP in 1987 in 1972 dollars.

p. 44). Yet is it appropriate to value the leisure of women and minorities as less than that of white males because the hourly earnings of the former are smaller due to discrimination? These are just a few of the imponderables that make any measurement of the value of leisure conceptually doubtful.

Turning to the empirical evidence on leisure, we find that the growth in the value of leisure, at least since the 1954 survey used by Nordhaus and Tobin, has been due almost exclusively to an increase in the real wage rate, not to any decrease in the number of hours of work being performed. As Zolotas explains:

For the period prior to 1965, leisure data from a sample survey by Robinson and Converse suggest that there has been no change in the amount of free time available to the four major population segments, namely male workers, male non-workers, female workers and female non-workers. This conclusion coincides with the findings of a 1954 survey, which have been used by Tobin and Nordhaus. [Zolotas 1981, p. 95][10]

He later adds that the findings of a 1975 survey show that the number of weekly hours devoted to paid employment had "remained virtually unchanged over the period 1965–1975." He concludes that the reason for the rise in total hours of leisure during that decade (from 34.8 hours per week to 38.5) "is mainly attributable to a decrease in hours devoted to family care from 25.4 a week in 1965 to 20.5 a week in 1975" (p. 97). The extent to which the rise of leisure time is a function of declining fertility rather than a change in child-care patterns is not clear. Nevertheless, since the trade-off here is not between work and leisure, to count this change as a welfare gain is dubious.

In 1987, Louis Harris revealed poll data that there had been a considerable increase in the average number of hours worked per person, from 40.6 hours per week in 1973 to 48.8 hours in 1985 (Harris 1987). There was a corresponding decline in leisure. However, analysis of the questions asked in the surveys indicates that the recorded changes are likely due to different definitions of "work." In 1980 and later years, the term included housework and studying; in 1973, it did not. The National Opinion Research Center and the Census Bureau indicated relatively constant work hours over the same period (Hamilton, pp. 347–356). Therefore, it seems likely that an unchanging work week is the most plausible assumption.

Rather than allowing us to work less and enjoy more leisure, increased market activity has merely intensified status competition. As Zolotas so aptly observes:

It was originally believed that economic growth would eventually shorten working time. This belief has not been confirmed in today's advanced economies. The implication is that mankind is constantly being driven farther away from the point of

10. The survey Zolotas cites comes from Robinson and Converse 1967.

long term equilibrium, where it could sit back and enjoy the fruits of civilization in peace and quiet. The reason is that the growth of the physical product, in the way it takes place in modern economies, is a source of constant stress and compels people to work harder in order to be able to afford the unending stream of "new" goods being supplied by the system. [1981, p. 94]

If this image of perpetual striving is in fact accurate, then the absence of significant growth in leisure should come as no surprise.

Given the difficulties of knowing precisely what is meant by the term *leisure,* as well as the problem of being able to measure changes in it over time, we regard the inclusion of leisure time in a welfare measure as inappropriate. If, in the future, the average work week were to decline significantly (as it apparently did between 1929 and 1954), some imputation for leisure might be called for. Even then conceptual problems of valuing the leisure time of the underemployed and unemployed and of men and women at their various real wage rates would continue to plague the effort. For now, at least, we omit the imputation for leisure because of the dubious calculations involved in it and because it would outweigh all other components in a measure of welfare.

Value of Unpaid Household Labor

The imputation for the value of household services has many of the same problems as the imputation for leisure, yet the warrant is so strong for including nonmarket labor that we could not omit it. The idea that the production of services by members of the household should be included alongside services produced in and for the market is intuitively compelling. In addition, because the figure is much smaller than the imputation for leisure, it does not overwhelm the index. Nevertheless, it, too, has serious problems, and it is a large enough factor that questionable judgments about it have a major effect on the total outcome. After the removal of leisure, the imputation for household services constitutes between a third and a half of the total MEW for Nordhaus and Tobin.

Though we agree in principle that the value of housework should be included in an indicator of economic welfare, the conceptual and empirical difficulties of measuring it are formidable. Conceptually, the main difficulty is in defining housework or household production. Which of the activities within the household should be classified as work as opposed to leisure or an intrinsically satisfying activity? Those who have studied this issue in some detail, particularly the Berks, have discussed some of the rather subtle issues that interfere with any simple calculation of the value of time spent on housework because of these definitional quandaries. For example, when survey respondents are asked to specify whether household activities are work or leisure, some activities (notably cooking and child care) are frequently classified as both (Berk and Berk 1979). Moreover, should those who carry the ultimate responsibility for managing the household (generally women, by virtue of gender expectations) be regarded differently than those who merely carry out specific tasks under supervision?[11] If the distinction between management and labor is important in the market, it should also be considered significant in the home. The time of women, who bear the brunt of this burden, should then be valued not at their wage rate but on the basis of a managerial salary from which the market generally precludes them.

The foregoing comments should clarify why it is enormously difficult to measure empirically either "household production functions" or even time spent doing housework. Yet even though researchers have not known exactly what they were measuring, the few studies that have been done of household time allocation have shown surprisingly similar results for time spent in housework. Despite all of the "labor-saving" household devices introduced in the past eighty years, the decline in the number of hours spent in housework has been negligible. Whereas housewives spent an average of 56 hours per week doing housework in the decade after 1910, they still spent about 53 hours per week in 1965–66. The findings of surveys done in 1924–25 and 1930–31 (Cowan 1983) were similar.[12] For the 1980s, Berk's study showed that the average number of *weekday* hours devoted to housework was 8.5 for housewives and 7 for women who were employed (Berk 1985, p. 64). Since this study required respondents to keep diaries only of *weekday* activities, it is not precisely comparable to previous studies. Nevertheless, it suggests that average weekly hours devoted by women to housework are probably still in the neighborhood of fifty. Berk also notes that the widely touted increase in men's level of housework is largely a mirage, not confirmed by any large-scale studies (ibid., p. 8).

Despite the enormous difficulties in defining the exact boundaries of nonmarket household labor and in measuring its contribution to economic welfare, we could not ignore it. We have chosen to use the rather conservative estimates derived by Robert Eisner, who computes the value of time spent on unpaid household work on the basis of the average wage rate of household domestic workers (Eisner 1985, p. 30). Though this undervalues the managerial aspect of running a household, it avoids the problem of using differential market wage rates for men and women.

11. "The accomplishment of household labor involves thinking about or planning for the task, as well as the actual work demanded by the task itself . . . [O]ur early research . . . revealed a clear distinction between "help" with and "responsibility" for household labor (Berk 1985, p. 69).

12. For the decade after 1910, Cowan cites (on p. 159) an unpublished doctoral dissertation by Leeds from 1917. For the 1920s and 1930s, she refers (on p. 178) to U.S. Department of Agriculture surveys that found a range of hours spent in housework from a high of 61 to a low of 48. For the 1960s, she cites John P. Robinson, *How Americans Use Time: A Social-Psychological Analysis of Everyday Behavior* (New York: Praeger, 1977), pp. 63–64.

Another important issue is whether the productivity of household labor increased during the period covered by our analysis. Since the time required to perform household tasks has not declined, and since the output of household labor has not transparently improved, we have assumed that the aggregate value of household labor has increased only with the size of the population, not with increases in productivity in the market. An alternative model, used by Hans Diefenbacher in his ISEW for Germany, assumes that household labor productivity has increased at the same rate as market productivity. If we applied this model to the ISEW in the United States, the value of services from household labor would have increased from around $300 billion in 1950 to around $1.2 trillion in 1990 (in 1972 dollars). The ISEW would have approximately doubled from its calculated value in 1990. In other words, our final estimate of the ISEW is very sensitive to the assumed level of change of productivity of household labor. As in the case of leisure, this element of the ISEW could easily outweigh all others, according to the assumptions made. Nevertheless, the general movement from a household to a market economy, the movement of more women into market employment, and the increase in the proportion of single-person households, all involve reductions in the reliance on unpaid household labor because there are fewer families with children and fewer households in which someone devotes full time to domestic work. Nevertheless, the amount of time spent in unpaid housework has hardly changed. Perhaps work expands to fill the time available, as Parkinson's Law suggests. At any rate, there is no evidence that the productivity or output per hour of nonmarket housework has risen substantially. We have therefore continued to assume that the real per capita output of nonmarket household services has remained constant (which means that the growth of these services corresponds to the rate of population growth).

Caveats and Limitations

Nothing is better calculated to make one realize the difficulty of estimating economic welfare over time than attempting to devise an index. Consider the limitations of this one.

First, it relies for its base on personal consumption. Although this is certainly a more appropriate measure of welfare than production, it is still questionable. There are many questions one could raise about how much better off human beings become as a result of increased consumption. Above all, it seems likely that marginal increases in consumption bring diminishing returns in satisfaction. In fact, by using distribution of income to weight consumption, we have implicitly assumed that marginal increases in consumption by the poor are of greater value than marginal increases by the rich.

On the other hand, our calculus of economic well-being has failed to take into account the fact that happiness is apparently correlated with relative rather than absolute levels of wealth or consumption. Having more is less important than having more than the "Joneses" (Easterlin 1974). Yet in the absence of any way to quantify this sense of relative well-being, we have ignored this important finding in our index, just as others have.

Second, there are many possible categories of additions and deductions that we have omitted. To the extent that unreported income from the "underground economy" (excluding illegal activities) is not already imputed in national income accounts, we would like to include it in a measure of welfare. Changes in working conditions should also be included, if there were some reasonable way to calculate them.[13] On the deletion side, one might be tempted to subtract expenditures for junk food, tobacco, pornography, and innumerable other items that make questionable contributions to genuine economic welfare. We recognize that this would lead to highly subjective judgments, though we suspect that a consensus might be found about certain items.

Third, we have been forced to make some heroic assumptions in compiling the ISEW. In some cases, we have included estimates of quantities that are inherently unmeasurable, such as the cost imposed upon future generations by the depletion of natural resources. Any estimation of the costs of long-term environmental damage is clouded by a high degree of uncertainty about the precise physical effects of human actions. (How high will temperatures rise as a result of the greenhouse effect and what will the ecological ramifications be? Are there *any* geological structures that can *permanently* hold high-level radioactive wastes and prevent them from contaminating the environment?) We certainly do not presume to have any definitive answers to these and other questions. We have merely made what we regard as moderate conjectures, ones that do not overwhelm the index, but which play a substantial role in its final outcome.

Nevertheless, because the methodologies for estimating the costs of depletion of natural resources and of long-term environmental damage (columns S and T in table A.1) are more speculative than the procedures used for other estimates, we have also calculated the Index of Sustainable Economic Welfare excluding those columns. (In other words, we added the amount in columns S and T to the amount in column X in table A.1 because they were originally subtracted in the calculation of column X.) Although we have not shown this calculation in table A.1, we have included a revised estimate of per capita ISEW, which we label PC-ISEW*, in figure A.1 (following table A.1) and in table A.13. In the latter, we have calculated annual growth rates of three alternative measures of economic welfare: per capita GNP, ISEW, and ISEW*.

---

13. We are indebted to comments by C. O. Matthews on Nordhaus and Tobin's study for this idea. See Nordhaus and Tobin 1972, pp. 88–89.

Explanation of Columns in table A.1

Column A: Year.

Column B: The value of personal consumption expenditures comes from table 1.2 of the *National Income and Product Accounts* (*NIPA*) and July issues of *Survey of Current Business,* both published by the Bureau of Economic Analysis, U.S. Commerce Department. Up to 1984, this was available in 1972 dollars. Since the inflation adjustment for 1985 through 1990 is in 1982 dollars, we estimated GNP for those years in 1972 dollars by calculating the percentage increase in constant 1982 dollars from 1984 onward, then adding the value of that proportional increase in 1972 dollars to each previous year.

Column C: The "index of distributional inequality" was derived from the U.S. Bureau of the Census, *Money Income of Families and Households,* Current Population Reports: Consumer Income, Series P-60, No. 159, table 12, page 39, "Income at Selected Positions and Percentage Share of Aggregate Income in 1947 to 1986 Received by Each Fifth and Top 5 Percent of Families and Unrelated Individuals by Race of Householder" and Series P-60, No. 174, table B-13 for the years 1987 to 1990. These income shares are shown in table A.2–1. We considered five ways to create an index number for each year. (In each case, we set the value in 1951 at 100.)

Harmonic mean. This method emphasizes the variations in the relationship between the highest quintile and other quintiles. The share of the highest quintile is divided by the share of each of the other quintiles. The resulting five ratios are added together and divided by five. In other words, this is the ratio of the highest quintile to the harmonic mean of the five quintiles.

In 1975, for example, the top quintile received about 7.6 times as much income as the lowest quintile, 3.5 times as much as the second quintile, 2.3 times as much as the third quintile, and 1.7 times as much as the fourth quintile. We then added those four numbers (plus 1 to represent the highest quintile's relation to itself) and divided by 5 (that being the number that would be obtained by a perfectly uniform distribution of income). The lowest possible number for a given year is 1 (5 divided by 5), but there is no upper maximum (unlike the Gini coefficient, which varies between 0 and 1).

High quintile option. A second possible index would be the share of the highest income quintile divided by the average of all five quintiles. Since the sum of the shares of the five quintiles is 100%, by defintion, this method amounts to comparing the share of the highest quintile across time. This is perhaps the best index of envy.

Low quintile option. The reverse of the high quintile option involves calculating variations in the share of income by the lowest quintile. The ra-

Table A.1
Index of Sustainable Economic Welfare, 1950–1990

Year A	Personal consumption B	Distributional inequality C	Weighted personal consumption (B/C) D	Services: household labor E(+)	Services: consumer durables F(+)	Services: highways & streets G(+)	Improvement health & education public expenditures H(+)	Expenditures on consumer durables I(−)	Defensive private expenditures/ health & education J(−)	Cost of commuting K(−)	Cost of personal pollution control L(−)	Cost of auto accidents M(−)
1950	337.3	111.1	303.6	311.4	30.2	6.2	4.9	42.6	13.9	9.0	0.0	11.6
1951	341.6	100.0	341.6	315.4	32.9	6.3	4.9	39.1	14.5	8.5	0.0	13.2
1952	350.1	102.0	343.1	319.5	34.9	6.5	5.1	38.0	14.9	8.4	0.0	13.3
1953	363.4	106.4	341.6	323.6	37.3	6.7	5.3	42.1	15.5	9.3	0.0	13.9
1954	370.0	111.1	333.0	327.8	39.3	7.0	5.5	42.5	16.1	9.6	0.0	13.3
1955	394.1	104.2	378.3	332.0	42.2	7.4	5.8	51.1	16.9	10.9	0.0	13.9
1956	405.4	100.0	405.4	336.3	44.2	7.7	6.2	48.8	17.9	10.4	0.0	14.4
1957	413.8	98.0	422.1	340.6	45.7	8.1	6.5	48.6	18.9	10.5	0.0	14.3
1958	418.0	100.0	418.0	345.0	46.3	8.5	6.9	45.3	19.5	9.9	0.1	14.0
1959	440.4	102.0	431.6	349.5	47.6	9.0	7.3	50.7	20.2	10.7	0.1	14.3
1960	452.0	104.2	433.9	354.0	48.8	9.5	7.8	51.4	21.1	11.3	0.1	14.4
1961	461.4	106.4	433.7	358.5	49.4	9.9	8.6	49.3	22.9	10.9	0.1	14.4
1962	482.0	100.0	482.0	363.2	51.0	10.4	9.4	54.7	24.8	11.7	0.1	15.4
1963	500.5	100.0	500.5	367.9	53.0	11.0	10.4	59.7	26.6	12.4	0.2	16.2
1964	528.0	98.0	538.6	372.6	56.2	11.6	11.4	64.8	28.5	12.8	0.2	17.4
1965	557.5	96.2	579.8	377.4	60.4	12.1	12.5	72.6	30.2	14.3	0.3	18.8
1966	585.7	89.3	656.0	382.3	65.2	12.7	15.4	78.4	31.9	14.9	0.3	19.4
1967	602.7	90.9	663.0	387.2	69.6	13.3	17.9	79.5	32.6	15.2	0.4	19.5
1968	634.4	89.3	710.5	392.2	75.2	13.9	19.4	88.3	33.7	16.7	0.5	20.8
1969	657.9	89.3	736.8	397.2	80.3	14.4	20.8	91.8	34.2	17.7	0.7	23.0
1970	672.1	92.6	725.9	402.4	83.9	14.8	22.6	89.1	34.5	17.4	0.8	25.3
1971	696.8	90.9	766.5	407.5	88.5	15.3	23.9	98.2	35.9	19.5	1.0	26.3
1972	737.1	92.6	796.1	412.8	94.7	15.7	25.5	111.1	38.1	21.6	1.3	28.7
1973	767.9	90.9	844.7	418.1	101.9	16.0	27.3	121.3	39.9	23.1	1.4	28.6
1974	762.8	90.9	839.1	423.5	106.2	16.2	29.7	112.3	39.4	22.4	1.6	25.8
1975	779.4	92.6	841.8	429.0	109.7	16.3	30.4	112.7	39.3	22.4	1.7	28.1
1976	823.1	92.6	888.9	434.5	115.0	16.5	32.2	126.6	40.7	25.0	1.9	30.1
1977	864.3	96.2	898.9	440.1	121.7	16.6	32.7	138.0	42.0	27.2	2.1	32.1
1978	903.2	96.2	939.3	445.8	128.9	16.7	34.0	146.8	43.2	28.2	2.4	33.7
1979	927.6	96.2	964.7	451.5	135.0	16.7	35.3	147.2	44.4	29.2	2.6	32.5
1980	931.8	98.0	950.4	457.3	137.9	16.8	37.1	137.5	45.8	28.6	2.9	29.0
1981	950.5	100.0	950.5	463.2	141.1	16.8	38.4	140.9	47.7	29.0	3.2	27.0
1982	963.3	106.4	905.5	469.2	143.4	16.9	37.9	140.5	48.4	27.7	3.6	26.1
1983	1009.2	106.4	948.6	475.3	148.7	16.9	38.2	157.5	49.9	30.2	4.3	26.3
1984	1058.6	106.4	995.0	481.4	156.6	17.1	38.6	177.9	51.9	32.8	4.7	27.8
1985	1108.2	108.7	1019.5	487.6	167.2	17.3	39.9	195.5	53.0	35.3	5.1	29.6
1986	1151.3	108.7	1059.2	493.9	179.4	17.4	40.1	211.7	54.1	33.5	5.5	30.5
1987	1184.0	108.7	1089.3	500.3	190.3	17.5	39.5	215.5	56.8	32.0	4.6	31.3
1988	1226.7	108.7	1128.5	506.7	204.3	17.7	42.4	230.3	60.0	34.3	5.0	31.5
1989	1250.3	108.7	1150.3	513.2	216.2	17.8	43.9	235.7	62.6	34.8	5.0	31.7
1990	1265.6	108.7	1164.4	519.8	224.9	18.0	45.1	234.6	63.2	34.6	5.0	31.9

NOTES:

—All figures are in billions of inflation-adjusted (1972) dollars except column A (year), column C (an index number 1951 = 100), and columns Y and AA (dollars, not billions of dollars).

—The explanation of the columns in table A.1 is given on pages 461–92.

—Figure A.1 on page 464 compares, in graphic form, columns X and AA plus a revised estimate (not shown) of per capita ISEW excluding columns S and T.

—Calculations of columns C, G, H, J, L, M, P, S, U, and V may be found in tables A.2–A.12 on pages 493–504.

—Calculations of the annual changes of per capita GNP and per capita ISEW (columns Y and AA) may be found in table A.13 on page 505.

Costs of water pollution N(−)	Costs of air pollution O(−)	Costs of noise pollution P(−)	Loss of wetlands Q(−)	Loss of farmland R(−)	Depletion of non-renewable resources S(−)	Long-term environmental damage T(−)	Cost of ozone depletion U(−)	Net capital growth V(+)	Change in net international position W(+)	Index of sustainable economic welfare ISEW X(sum)	Per capita ISEW Y	Gross national product Z	Per capita GNP AA
9.0	21.6	2.0	10.0	7.2	46.8	84.0	1.1	−17.2	0.0	380.2	2496.9	534.8	3512.2
9.2	21.8	2.1	10.4	7.8	53.0	86.9	1.3	−1.0	0.2	432.5	2792.6	579.4	3741.0
9.4	22.0	2.2	10.7	8.5	53.4	89.9	1.6	11.1	0.2	448.1	2844.4	600.8	3813.3
9.7	22.2	2.2	11.1	9.1	55.6	92.9	1.9	17.6	0.2	446.8	2789.1	623.6	3893.0
9.9	22.5	2.3	11.4	9.7	54.8	95.8	2.2	23.1	0.2	445.6	2733.4	616.1	3779.2
10.2	22.7	2.4	11.8	10.4	62.5	99.0	2.7	27.3	0.2	478.8	2885.3	657.5	3962.5
10.4	22.9	2.5	12.2	11.0	68.6	102.4	3.2	22.4	2.4	499.9	2959.8	671.6	3976.2
10.7	23.2	2.5	12.5	11.7	71.4	105.7	3.7	21.3	2.3	513.1	2983.4	683.8	3976.0
10.9	23.4	2.6	12.9	12.4	68.2	109.1	4.2	21.5	2.3	516.0	2950.7	680.9	3893.5
11.2	23.6	2.7	13.2	13.0	73.8	112.5	4,8	20.9	2.2	517.0	2907.5	721.7	4058.4
11.5	23.9	2.8	13.6	13.7	77.7	116.2	5.6	21.2	2.2	514.1	2845.6	737.2	4080.3
11.8	24.1	2.9	14.0	14.4	81.0	120.2	6.4	25.4	4.8	518.1	2820.7	756.6	4118.9
12.1	24.7	2.9	14.3	15.1	86.5	124.0	7.5	28.1	4.8	555.1	2975.8	800.3	4290.3
12.4	25.3	3.0	14.7	15.8	94.1	128.0	8.7	28.5	4.7	559.0	2953.7	832.5	4399.1
12.7	25.9	3.1	15.0	16.5	100.9	132.2	10.1	28.7	4.7	583.5	3040.6	876.4	4567.2
13.1	26.6	3.2	15.4	17.2	107.3	136.6	11.6	30.4	4.6	610.1	3140.1	929.3	4782.7
13.4	27.2	3.3	15.8	17.9	117.2	141.2	13.4	31.0	−0.9	667.3	3394.7	984.8	5010.2
13.8	27.9	3.4	16.1	18.7	127.0	146.0	15.4	28.0	−0.8	662.8	3335.6	1011.4	5089.8
14.1	28.6	3.5	16.5	19.4	135.3	151.0	17.7	29.6	−0.7	693.8	3456.9	1058.1	5271.9
14.5	29.3	3.7	16.8	20.1	144.6	156.3	20.2	29.0	−0.7	705.0	3478.5	1087.6	5366.2
14.9	30.0	3.8	17.2	20.9	157.0	161.8	22.7	28.6	−0.7	682.1	3326.6	1085.6	5294.3
15.3	29.1	3.9	17.6	21.6	159.2	167.4	26.1	27.3	3.2	711.3	3425.2	1122.4	5405.0
15.3	28.2	4.0	17.9	22.4	167.1	173.3	29.5	23.2	3.1	712.5	3394.3	1185.9	5649.9
15.3	27.4	4.0	18.3	23.2	171.2	179.5	33.4	19.1	3.0	743.5	3508.6	1254.3	5919.1
15.3	26.6	4.1	18.5	24.0	171.9	185.4	37.4	17.1	2.8	750.0	3506.9	1246.3	5827.8
15.3	25.8	4.1	18.6	24.7	174.2	191.2	40.9	17.9	2.5	748.4	3465.4	1231.6	5702.6
15.3	25.0	4.2	18.8	25.5	180.2	197.4	44.7	14.0	7.1	773.0	3545.5	1298.2	5954.1
15.3	24.2	4.2	19.0	26.3	189.0	203.7	48.2	12.8	−7.8	743.8	3377.2	1369.7	6219.2
15.3	23.6	4.2	19.2	27.1	195.8	210.2	51.6	9.0	2.3	774.7	3480.5	1438.6	6463.1
15.3	23.2	4.3	19.4	27.8	211.2	216.7	54.8	7.8	11.3	793.8	3527.1	1479.4	6573.5
15.3	22.5	4.3	19.5	28.6	221.2	223.0	58.0	3.8	6.4	773.5	3396.3	1475.0	6476.7
15.3	21.5	4.4	19.7	29.4	227.3	229.1	61.2	5.1	17.9	777.4	3379.3	1512.2	6573.6
15.3	19.5	4.4	19.9	30.2	230.5	234.9	64.2	4.8	−2.0	710.5	3058.1	1480.0	6369.8
15.3	19.2	4.5	20.1	31.0	225.8	240.6	67.4	12.5	−16.0	732.3	3122.5	1534.7	6543.5
15.3	19.6	4.5	20.3	31.7	252.2	246.6	70.9	13.1	−50.3	695.3	2933.9	1642.5	6930.4
15.3	18.8	4.6	20.4	32.5	257.1	252.7	74.4	19.0	−20.0	736.3	3077.3	1697.5	7094.3
15.3	18.7	4.6	20.6	33.3	262.3	258.8	76.6	19.8	−21.1	763.1	3158.5	1744.1	7219.0
15.3	18.7	4.6	20.8	34.1	274.8	265.1	78.8	24.4	−23.3	785.4	3220.1	1803.8	7395.4
15.3	18.9	4.7	21.0	34.9	290.1	271.8	81.0	24.9	−43.0	782.8	3178.0	1884.3	7649.7
15.3	18.9	4.7	21.2	35.7	296.9	278.5	83.2	28.5	−44.6	801.2	3220.4	1931.6	7764.4
15.3	18.9	4.8	21.3	36.5	312.6	285.3	85.3	29.4	−34.0	818.2	3253.1	1950.8	7755.9

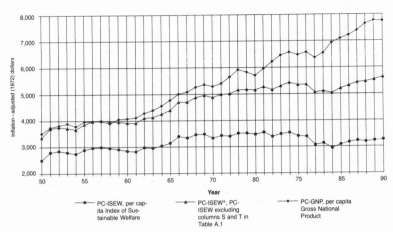

tionale for this method is that improvements in the lot of the poorest segment of society are the most significant because the marginal utility of
added income can be presumed to be greater for them than for others.

Weighted ratios of shares. A fourth possible index would assign arbitrary
weights to the ratio of the quintile shares. The rationale for weighting the
ratios in this way would be based on the concept of the diminishing marginal utility of income: the value of an additional dollar of income is not as
great for the rich as for the poor. Since our index measures inequality rather
than equality, we weighted the highest quintile most heavily and the lowest
quintile the least. We calclulated a normalized index based on the expression $(b + 2c + 3d + 4e + 5f)/b$, where b is the lowest quintile and f the
highest. (In addition to 1,2,3,4,5, we also tested weights of various magnitudes including 1,10,20,30,60. The results were almost completely in
sensitive to these differing weights, so we used the set 1,2,3,4,5 in our
comparison.)

Gini coefficient. The usual measure of distributional equality is the Gini
coefficient, the difference between actual distribution and equal distribution. It gives equal weight to all income levels by calculating the square
root of the sum of the squared differences of each quintile from a 20% share.

The alternative distribution indices are presented in table A.2–2. The
ratio of lowest to highest years is 0.79 for the "harmonic mean" index, 0.91
for the "high quintile" index, 0.80 for the "low quintile" index, 0.79 for the
"weighted" index, and 0.87 for the "Gini coefficient" index. A low number
signifies a large difference between the lowest and highest years and thus
appears as greater variation in the range of calculated values for the ISEW.
The high quintile index flattens the ISEW most, whereas the harmonic
mean index shows the widest variations. The effect of the various indices on
changes in the ISEW is shown in table A.2–B.

We prefer the low quintile index because it gives special weight to the plight of the poorest members of society, which fits well with the theory of justice propounded by John Rawls. He argues that if, living in a socially or economically stratified society, we could not know what our position in that society might be, we would choose social rules that would protect the interests of the poorest or weakest members (Rawls 1971).

The income distribution figures we used do not accurately reflect disposable income differences because they measure pre-tax income and because they do not include all transfer payments. (They do, however, include Social Security payments, unemployment compensation, and certain cash grants to the poor such as AFDC and SSI.) The Census Bureau recently began calculating distribution of after-tax income, net of all transfer payments. (See Bureau of the Census, *Measuring the Effect of Benefits and Taxes on Income and Poverty,* Current Population Reports, Consumer Income, Series P-60, No. 176-RD [for 1989 and 1990], No. 170-RD [for 1987–88], and No. 164-RD [for 1986].) However, since that time series did not go back to 1950, we chose to use the pre-tax series that did. Moreover, the annual changes in the after-tax, after-benefits series closely match the changes in the series we used. Nevertheless, the after-tax, after-benefits series does reveal some valuable information. In 1990, for example, the lowest quintile of households received 3.9% of pre-tax income.[14] After adding capital gains and employer-provided health insurance payments, and subtracting government cash transfers to the poor, the lowest quintile received only 1.1% of income. Subtracting federal and state income taxes, which fall more heavily on the rich than the poor, raises the lowest quintile's share to 1.4%. The graduated income tax has surprisingly little effect on the distribution of disposable income. However, when all forms of transfer payments are added (including the value of Medicare and Medicaid), the lowest quintile's share rises to 5.1%. Thus, cash and noncash transfer payments are much more effective at redistributing income than the income tax. Yet, if we consider that the lowest quintile would receive only 1.1% of income in the absence of transfer payments, it is apparent that efforts to achieve some semblance of equality by means of employment policies, minimum wage laws, and investment incentives have failed.

Column D: Weighted personal consumption is column B (personal consumption) divided by column C (index of distributional inequality) multiplied by 100. (The reason for dividing rather than multiplying is that in column C larger numbers indicate greater *inequality.*)

Column D is the base number from which other modifications are either added or subtracted. We first add four columns (E, F, G, and H) that represent streams of services that are not counted as part of personal consump-

14. The lowest quintile of *families* (as opposed to households) received 4.6% of pre-tax income in 1990. We have used family income in the distributional index. However, the only after-tax data are for households, which are not precisely comparable to families.

tion in the national income accounts. Next, we subtract eight columns (I through P) that represent items intended to compensate for implicit over-estimates of welfare in the measure of personal consumption. We then sub-tract five columns (Q, R, S, T, and U) that represent our estimate of how present activities undermine the sustainability of our natural resource base. Finally, we add two columns (V and W) that represent the degree to which the level of capital accumulation and shifts in control of capital between domestic sources and foreign sources affect the sustainability of the U.S. economy. Thus columns Q through W represent items that reflect the ca-pacity of the economy to continue to provide the same level of welfare over a prolonged period.

Column E: Household services such as cooking, cleaning, and child care contribute to economic welfare even though they are not sold in the market at an observable price. On pages 457–59, we pointed to several theoretical and empirical problems involved in imputing the value of household, non-market labor. We have nevertheless included it because of its tremendous significance as a factor in overall economic welfare.

We have derived this column from figures presented by Robert Eisner in "The Total Incomes System of Accounts," *Survey of Current Business,* Janu-ary 1985. He provides estimates in 1972 dollars for 1946, 1956, 1966, 1971, 1976, and 1981. We have used a regression on the logarithm of those esti-mates to interpolate and extrapolate for other years. Eisner explains the methodology he used: "The value of unpaid household work is taken con-servatively to be the product of annual hours in relevant household activi-ties and the average hourly compensation of household domestic workers. The time estimates were derived from the Michigan Survey Research Cen-ter time use studies of 1965, 1975, and 1981, with the 1975 survey used as the benchmark" (Eisner 1985 p. 30).

Column F: In order to count only the value received each year from capital equipment rather than its initial purchase price, we add the value of the services that flow from consumer durables here and subtract the actual ex-penditures on consumer durables elsewhere (column I). To the extent that household equipment wears out more quickly than it might, it inflates the personal consumption account without contributing to welfare. If washing machines, on average, lasted 100 years rather than 15, fewer would be bought, and personal consumption would not rise as rapidly as it would otherwise, but welfare would not be diminished. By using the estimated value of the service from such equipment rather than its purchase price, we have attempted to overcome this distortion in current measures.

To calculate this column, we used the table entitled "Constant Dollar Net Stock of Consumer Durables," *Survey of Current Business,* March 1979, April 1981, October 1982, August of 1983, 1984, and 1987, and January 1992. For each year we multiplied the total net stock by 22.5%. This accounts for both the imputed value (interest) and depreciation on the stock of capital, a procedure suggested by Robert Eisner. (Actual depreciation averaged around 15% but varied from year to year. Since interest rates also varied from year to year by an unknown amount, we preferred to choose a single value for the combination of depreciation and interest.) The results of using the 22.5% figure also seem intuitively appropriate when we consider the calculated estimate of services. According to our estimate, the services from consumer durables exceeded expenditures in only a few recession years. Why should this be the case? In a no-growth economy, expenditures would equal services (because they would simply replace worn-out goods). In a growing economy, expenditures should slightly exceed services, and in a declining economy services would slightly exceed expenditures.

Column G: With the exception of this column and column H (certain expenditures for health and education), we have not included government expenditures as adding to welfare because they are largely defensive in nature. That is, the growth of government programs does not so much add to net welfare as prevent the deterioration of well-being by maintaining security, environmental health, and the capacity to continue commerce. In addition, some government enterprises, such as transit systems and sewer or water districts, provide services for a fee just as private businesses do. These payments already show up as personal consumption in the national income accounts. However, the government provides some services that could theoretically be offered through the market but which are difficult to meter. The main item in that category is streets and highways. Since the annual value of services from roads is not calculated, we have imputed it from estimates of the value of the stock of streets and highways.

To calculate this column (see table A.3), we used the table entitled "Constant Dollar Gross Stock of Government-Owned Structures, Excluding Military, By Type of Structures," *Survey of Current Business,* March 1980, February 1981, October 1982, August 1983, August 1984, and January 1992. We added together the "highways and streets" columns for federal and state and local governments. (Because estimates of the stock of government-owned structures—for 1984 to 1990—are not disaggregated into highways and streets and other structures, we had to make estimates for those years based on aggregated figures.) We estimated the net stock as being two-thirds of the gross stock, based on the approximate ratio of net to gross for all government-owned nonmilitary structures.

The value of services is much lower than for consumer durables because depreciation accounts for only about 2.5% of net stock of highways, compared to about 15% for consumer durables (see column F). Adding the same average interest rate of 7.5% that we used in calculating the value of services from consumer durables, we arrive at 10% of net stock as the value of services of streets and highways. However, we have assumed that one-fourth of all vehicle miles are for commuting and thus do not represent a service but a defensive expenditure. In other words, only 75% of the services from highways and streets add to welfare. We multiplied 10% by three-fourths, thereby deriving the net value of services as equal to 7.5% of net stock.

Column H: We have excluded most government expenditures from our estimate (but see column G) because they measure inputs or costs rather than outputs or benefits. The correlation between increases in government spending and real increases in welfare is tenuous because of the difficulty of measuring the demand for the kinds of services that government offers. Nevertheless, we have assumed that a portion of the money spent on education and health contributes to welfare and we add it to personal consumption.

With the exception of one-half of public spending on higher education, we regarded most expenditures on education as neither consumption nor investment. Earlier, we explained why we have not considered education as investment: the evidence suggests that it contributes little to productivity. On the other hand, it would be inappropriate to count education as consumption because most schooling appears to be defensive. In other words, people attend school because the failure to attend would mean falling behind in the competition for diplomas or degrees that confer higher incomes on their recipients. (We assume that compulsory attendance laws are not the primary motivation for going to school.) We assume, nevertheless, as Zolotas did in his study, that one-half of post-secondary education is pure consumption, in that it is sought for its own sake rather than to serve another purpose. Thus, we have added one-half of public expenditures (federal, state, and local) for higher education from tables 3.15 and 3.16 of the *National Income and Product Accounts* and various issues of the *Survey of Current Business*. (See table A.4, column c.) We have extrapolated an estimate for 1990 from previous years because the data provided in the January 1992 *Survey of Current Business* for state and local expenditures on higher education is not comparable to the data in the July 1990 *Survey of Current Business*. For example, according to the January 1992 data, state and local governments spent $41.3 billion on higher education in 1987 (current dollars), but according to the July 1990 data, state and local governments spent $55.9 billion. We cannot account for this anomaly. If the lower figures are accurate, then this column would have grown more slowly, reducing the ISEW slightly.

In the case of expenditures on health by the public sector, we have assumed that they are valued as highly as private expenditures for the same purpose. We have added only that portion of public medical expenditures (50%) that are assumed to add to social welfare. (See table A.4, column e.)

We assume the other half are "defensive" expenditures necessary to compensate for the growth of environmental stresses on health (as we do for private health expenditures in column J). Figures up to the year 1989 are derived from the *Statistical Abstract of the United States* (1991, table 136, p. 92). The estimate for 1990 is derived from U.S. Health Care Financing Administration, *Health Care Financing Review,* Fall 1991. Expenditures are adjusted for inflation using the "medical care" component of the Consumer Price Index in the *Statistical Abstract* (1991, table 769, p. 477). (Please note that for this and all later references to the *Statistical Abstract,* we have cited only the 1991 edition. In fact, we often referred to previous editions to fill in gaps in the data.)

Column I: The value of private expenditure on durable goods in constant (1972) dollars comes from the *National Income and Product Accounts,* table 1.2. The estimates for 1985 through 1990 were derived in the same manner as the estimates of personal consumption. The reason for subtracting expenditures on consumer durables is explained in the note on column F.

Column J: This is the inverse of column H. Here we *subtracted* the portions of *private* education and health expenditures that do not contribute to welfare. We subtracted them because they are included in column B, personal consumption, and we classify them as defensive expenditures.

We subtracted all expenditures on private education except one-half of private expenditures on higher education, based on the same rationale given in the explanation of column H. (See table A.5, column d.) The cost of private education, for both total and higher education, was taken from table 2.4 of the *NIPA,* entitled "Personal Consumption Expenditures by Type of Expenditure," and adjusted to 1972 dollars by the implicit price deflator for private education in table 7.12.

Similarly, we subtracted defensive private health expenditures from total welfare. As in the case of public expenditures on health, we assumed that half of the real growth in private health expenditures is purely defensive in nature, i.e., compensating for growing health risks due to urbanization and industrialization. We subtracted one-half of these expenditures. (See table A.5, column f.) Total private health expenditures come from *Statistical Abstract* (1991, table 136, p. 92). Costs are adjusted for 1972 prices by the "medical care" component of the Consumer Price Index in the *Statistical Abstract* (1991, table 769, p. 477).

Column K: The direct (out of pocket) costs of commuting were calculated as follows (see table A.6):

$$C = 0.3 \, (A - 0.3 \, A) + 0.3 \, B$$
$$= 0.3 \, (0.7 \, A) + 0.3 \, B$$
$$= 0.21 \, A + 0.3 \, B$$

where:

C is the direct cost of commuting.

A is the cost of user-operated transport (mainly cars) from the *National Income and Product Accounts*, table 2.4. This figure was adjusted to constant (1972) dollars with the implicit price deflator for personal consumption expenditures on motor vehicles and parts found in the *NIPA*, table 7.12.

0.3 A is the estimated cost of depreciation of private cars (which is excluded here to avoid double counting since it was already included as an element in column F) from the *Statistical Abstract* (1987, table 1040, p. 593).

0.3 is the estimated portion of total noncommercial vehicle miles used in commuting in 1983 (see *Statistical Abstract* 1987, table 1033, p. 591).

B is the price of purchased local transportation (see *National Income and Product Accounts*, table 2.4).

0.3 is the estimated portion of passenger miles on local public transportation used for commuting.

We did not include indirect costs of commuting (the value of the time lost in commuting) in our calculations because we lacked reliable data. In theory, we regard this as a significant cost of the presumably increased congestion that accompanies urban growth, but we could not find a time series showing changes in the amount of time spent commuting to work. Zolotas used an estimate made in 1965–66 of 52 minutes for men and 42 minutes for women. He then assumed an increase of 2 minutes per year, which would mean that by 1980 commuting time should have been 80 minutes for men and 70 minutes for women. In fact, according to the 1980 Census (vol. C 3.223/7:980, *General Social and Economic Characteristics,* p. 70), an average commute in 1980 was 43 minutes long, less than the combined average for men and women in 1965–66. Did commuting time actually decrease over time? Were the methodologies or populations of the two surveys sufficiently different to account for this difference? We simply do not know. Therefore, we have not subtracted the indirect costs of commuting, though doing so would certainly reduce economic welfare each year by tens of billions of dollars.

Column L: One cost imposed on households by pollution is the need to make defensive expenditures on personal pollution control equipment such as air and water filters. The figures in this column from 1972 through 1987 were provided by Carol Carson and Allan Young of the Bureau of Economic Analysis, U.S. Commerce Department. For the years prior to 1972, we assumed that personal expenditures on pollution abatement and control had increased by 20% per year. We assumed that the expenditures in 1988 to 1990 would be equal to the average of the previous four years. These expenditures do not improve welfare, but merely attempt to restore it to some baseline level. Since business and government expenditures are not included in personal consumption expenditures (column B), we have not subtracted their pollution abatement expenditures.

Column M: Damage due to accidents represents a real cost of industrialization and higher traffic densities. Figures are available only for the damage due to motor vehicle accidents. They are derived from *Statistical Abstract* (1991, table 1042, p. 612). They are adjusted for inflation using the Consumer Price Index. The estimates for 1989 and 1990 are based on extrapolations rather than measured values.

Column N: The figures in this column are a composite of two estimates: (1) damage to water quality, primarily from point source discharges (sewage and industrial wastes) and (2) damage due to siltation resulting from erosion from farms, construction sites, and roadways. Although this may involve some double counting (insofar as siltation also damages water quality), we suspect that on the whole we have underestimated the first type of damage because of the lack of data on nonpoint sources of pollution. To include them marginally under erosion costs only partially corrects for a more general underestimation of the total damage.

Damage due to point source discharges. We have estimated the cost of damage from water pollution as $12.0 billion in 1972 and derived estimates for earlier and later years based on subjective estimates and surveys. (We did not include the cost of building sewage treatment facilities because that is a public expenditure and therefore not included in our initial estimate of welfare, i.e., column B, "personal consumption.") The numbers in this column are of limited reliability, though we consider them reasonable and plausible.

A number of factors contribute to the difficulty of making reliable estimates of the dollar value of the damage caused by water pollution:

1. No universally acknowledged measure of "water quality" exists. A number of different elements may contribute to poor water quality, such as biological oxygen demand (or conversely, low dissolved oxygen levels), phosphorus, nitrogen, suspended solids, dissolved solids, turbidity, and temperature. With no means of developing a single composite measure of their joint effects, the term "water quality" has no precise meaning.

2. Even if we had a single composite measure of water quality, the actual measurement of water samples is not very reliable. Infrequent samples, inaccuracy due to the imprecision of measurements, and faulty monitoring and laboratory procedures all contribute to a low level of reliability in measured results.[15]

15. See Gianessi and Peskin 1981, pp. 803–821, and especially pp. 813–817.

3. Precise numerical relations have not been established between the components of water quality (number 1 above) and the capacity of water to support fish or other wildlife or to support swimming and other recreational activities.

4. If a reliable estimate of water pollution could be devised for a particular water basin, the possibility of aggregating data across regions would still elude us. Unlike the problem of air pollution, in which the entire atmosphere serves as a "sink" for airborne wastes and speaking of national air quality has some meaning, an aggregate measure of water quality is complicated by the fact that one river basin or lake may improve while another is becoming more polluted.

5. Even if a reliable baseline estimate could be derived for one year, we would still not know whether water quality were improving or deteriorating without comparable data for other years. Only highly subjective estimates exist.

6. Unlike the relatively direct estimation of air pollution damage (see the note on column O), many of the costs of water pollution must be calculated almost entirely from indirect evidence such as the loss of swimming, fishing, and boating opportunities. Thus, to determine the recreational benefits of improving water quality, economists have had to rely on proxy measures such as changes in the amount of time and money spent on *transportation* to other recreation sites in response to changes in water quality. (In other words, the measure of pollution damage comes from estimating the additional money people are willing to spend to drive to a new recreational site if a closer one has been contaminated.) The outcome of these studies depends heavily on assumptions about the magnitude of the shift in participation rates in water-based recreation that would occur if the 1985 water quality objectives set by Congress were met.

7. Finally, estimates of the cost of water pollution generally attempt to measure only damage resulting from point source discharges (i.e., pollution coming out of municipal and industrial sewers). The cost of damage caused by urban and farmland runoff is not included. Since those nonpoint sources of pollution are often at least as serious as point sources, neglecting their impact considerably underestimates the actual costs or damage from water pollution. As of the late 1970s, when efforts to control point sources had been made for several years but the control of nonpoint sources was minimal, the latter contributed 57% of BOD, 98% of suspended solids, 83% of dissolved solids, 87% of phosphorus, and 88% of nitrogen discharged into U.S. waterways. (These figures are derived from Gianessi and Peskin 1981, p. 804, table 1.)

Keeping those caveats and conditions in mind, we have estimated the total damage from water pollution in 1972 as approximately $12 billion. Three studies cited by Myrick Freeman came to the conclusion that the upper limit of the range of estimated damage to recreation from point source pollution was around $18 billion in 1978 dollars (Freeman 1982, chapter 9). Freeman's own upper estimate of the recreation benefits that would be realized by eliminating point source discharges is $8.7 billion in 1978 dollars (or about $6 billion in 1972 dollars). Adding damage to aesthetics, ecology, property values, and diversionary uses (household and industrial water supplies), his upper estimate of damage is $18.4 billion in 1978 dollars ($12 billion in 1972 dollars). Though Freeman's best estimate for damage from point source pollution is only $9.4 billion ($6 billion in 1972 dollars), we have used the less conservative figures on the assumption that the inclusion of nonpoint source pollution would at least double the *total* pollutant load in many river basins and increase it several-fold in others. Thus, a $12 billion estimate of water pollution damage in 1972 may even be conservative.

In the absence of any reliable time series data about water pollution, our estimates of changes in pollution damage over time are not very reliable. According to the Conservation Foundation's *State of the Environment: An Assessment at Mid-Decade,* "the years 1974 to 1981 saw little change in water quality with respect to the conventional pollution indicators." This finding is based on the U.S. Geological Survey's National Ambient Stream Quality Accounting Network. It is confirmed by a 1984 survey of the Association of State and Interstate Water Pollution Control Administrators and the 1982–83 National Fisheries Survey. (See page 109 of the Conservation Foundation report.) We assume that this overall lack of improvement means that the improvements that did take place as a result of more stringent pollution controls were offset by the growth of population and polluting activities. By contrast with the unvarying levels of the 1970s and 1980s, we have assumed that water quality declined during the 1950s and 1960s at 3% per year before a concerted national effort was undertaken to address the issue.

Damage due to siltation. In addition to the estimates of damage to water quality, we have included data on the effects of erosion from farmland as well as streambanks, roadbanks, and construction sites. We assume here that the deterioration of water quality due to these nonpoint sources has already been included in a general way in the calculations in Part 1. In Part 2, our estimate is of the costs of dredging navigable rivers and the damage siltation poses to dams and other water impoundments, as well as the costs of sediment-related flooding and other off-stream effects. The Conservation Foundation estimated that this damage was in the range of $3.2 to $13.0 billion in 1980, with a best estimate of around $6.0 billion. That would be about $3.3 billion in 1972 dollars (using the implicit GNP deflator).

Estimating changes in these costs over time is difficult. Two point estimates of the amount of total erosion exist for 1977 and 1982, derived from the National Resources Inventory, which was undertaken in both of those years by the Soil Conservation Service in conjunction with Iowa State University. In both 1977 and 1982, total erosion was estimated at 6.5 billion tons. We have assumed that that five-year trend has been constant since 1972 when the massive growth of grain exports led to shifts in land use, particularly the plowing of marginal, erosion-prone soils, in an attempt to profit from the high levels of world demand. We have assumed that during the previous twenty-two years erosion increased by an average of 1% per year. We recognize that estimates for these previous years are essentially speculative and would prefer reliable data. We also realize that farmland erosion may have remained approximately constant during that period in the absence of data to the contrary. Nevertheless, we believe that the overall problem of sedimentation from erosion probably increased during this period as a function of general economic growth, particularly from urban construction and the development of the interstate highway system.

Column O: Following Myrick Freeman's analysis, as we did with water pollution, we have divided estimates of the costs of air pollution into six categories: (1) damage to agricultural vegetation, (2) materials damage, (3) costs of cleaning soiled goods, (4) acid rain damage, (5) urban disamenities, and (6) aesthetics.

1. We have estimated damage to agricultural vegetation at $4 billion. According to a study by Heintz, Herschaft, and Horak in 1976, entitled "National Damages of Air and Water Pollution," the damage to agricultural vegetation due to oxidants in 1973 was $2.8 billion. Freeman suggests this estimate is too low because it fails to reflect the fact that farmers have not only sustained crop damage from air pollution but have also shifted to less profitable crops. We have assumed this added cost would raise the total cost of air pollution damage to crops to approximately $4 billion in 1970 (in 1972 dollars).

2. We have estimated materials damage due to corrosion of paint, metals, rubber, and so on at $6 billion. Zolotas uses an estimate from Liu and Yu of $38.4 billion in 1970, and since that amount is only about 3% of the net stock of fixed reproducible wealth owned by households for that year (including all residential structures and durable equipment), that rate of deterioration due to air pollution may in fact be plausible. We have chosen $6 billion as our estimate to bring it more into line with Freeman's middle estimate of $3.2 billion.

3. We are using the same figure as Zolotas for our estimate of the cost of cleaning soiled materials as a result of air pollution—$5 billion. That figure is derived from Liu and Yu and is confirmed by Freeman's estimate that a 20% reduction in airborne particulates would reduce cleaning costs by $0.6 to $3.8 billion. Though additional reductions in particulates would not have correspondingly dramatic results, this nevertheless suggests that an estimate of $5 billion for total damage in this category is reasonable and perhaps conservative.

4. Based on Freeman, we have conservatively estimated total damage to forests and aquatic ecosystems due to acid rain as $1.5 billion in 1972 dollars. (See Freeman 1982, p. 107.)

5. We have estimated the total reduction in the quality of urban life as a result of air pollution to be approximately $9 billion. This involves two components: (1) a reduction in property values in proportion to the level of pollution in an area and (2) the necessity of paying higher wages to attract people to work in areas with high levels of pollution. Freeman estimates reduced property values to be $4 billion as a result of stationary sources and $1.5 billion as a result of mobile sources (both in 1972 dollars). For wage differentials, he cites a study by Meyer and Leone that concluded that wage differentials necessary to attract workers to pollution prone areas were $6.1 billion for particulates, $2.1 billion for sulfur dioxide, and $5.1 billion for nitrogen oxides. If all of these factors (reduction in property values and wage differentials) were simply additive, the total reduction in quality of life would be $18.8 billion. Since there is overlap among their effects and with other damage estimates (such as that between cleaning costs and property values), we have included only $9 billion, or approximately one-half of the total from this category.

6. We have assumed a total of $4.5 billion in damage to aesthetic values due to loss of visibility and enjoyment in national parks and other scenic areas. This is based on a study in the region surrounding the Four Corners Power Plant, where residents said that they would be willing to pay $85 per year to improve the aesthetic conditions of the area considerably. Since our estimate of $4.5 billion amounts to about $20 per person per year to pay for visibility improvements, we believe that it is a plausible figure.

Adding these figures (vegetative damage, $4 billion; corrosion and materials damage, $6 billion; cleaning and soiling, $5 billion; acid rain, $1.5 billion; reduction in urban quality of life, $9 billion; and aesthetic costs, $4.5 billion), we arrive at a total of $30.0 billion in costs associated with air pollution for 1970 (in 1972 dollars).

If this $30 billion estimate seems excessive, we would like to point out that we consider it conservative, since we excluded from our calculations all estimates of air pollution's damage to health. That damage may be included indirectly in the estimate of wage differentials, but we have deliberately avoided including health costs as a separate category. We have also excluded health costs because we have put in two other columns (H and J) that specifically eliminate "defensive" health expenditures from the estimation of health benefits. Despite this, we suspect that some portion of health damage due to air pollution *could* be included here without double counting because many respiratory ailments (such as colds, flu, and bronchitis) do not require medical attention, yet they are exacerbated and prolonged by exposure to air pollution. Other chronic conditions that cause discomfort and reduce productivity but which do not require medical attention—from shortness of breath to headaches to burning eyes—would all constitute damage to health from air pollution that would not show up as "defensive" health expenditures. We suspect that these costs would amount to several billion dollars per year.

Furthermore, we have not included any estimate of the cost of increased mortality in our calculation of the costs of air pollution, in part because this might involve some double counting. We are also not satisfied with the idea of setting a dollar value on human life. On the other hand, neglecting this category altogether, as we have done, implicitly places zero value on human life (or more precisely on the value of living a longer life). We are not happy with that result either. Nevertheless, if we were to include some measure of the costs of increased mortality, we would base it on the value of life revealed in the willingness of people to pay to reduce the overall death rate in a large population. Since all of us make trade-offs between activities involving a higher probability of death and measurable benefits, this procedure reflects the value we implicitly place upon the probability of remaining alive. If the value per death avoided (in this probabilistic sense) is approximately $1 million in our society as some studies suggest, we can determine the dollar cost of air pollution on mortality rates at least within an order of magnitude. With that dollar value as a baseline figure, it is possible to estimate the damage of air pollution once the physical relation between air pollution and mortality is known. Freeman cites a number of studies that derive estimates of the elasticity of mortality with respect to air pollution of between 0.01 and 0.09 (meaning a 1% increase in air pollution causes an increase in mortality of between 0.01% and 0.09%). Using those figures and Freeman's calculations, we arrived at a best estimate of the cost of increased mortality due to air pollution of about $13 billion (in 1972 dollars). This is based on estimates of mortality benefits of about $10.5 and $12 billion for 20% and 60% reductions in air pollution, respectively. We assume that eliminating the remaining 40% of air pollution would add only $1 billion in benefits. In any case, we assume that the addition of the costs of higher mortality associated with air pollution would add another $10 to $15 billion in 1970 to the $30 billion estimate we are in fact using.

Our estimate of time series for air pollution damage is based on the EPA's estimates of ambient air pollution, as summarized in the *Statistical Abstract* (1991, table 359, p. 209). However, data are available only from 1977 to 1988. We assume that ambient air conditions deteriorated by 1% per year in the 1950s, by 2.4% per year in the 1960s, improved by 3.0% per year from 1971 to 1977 (as a result of the Clean Air Act of 1970), and that the conditions in 1989 and 1990 were the same as in 1988. We combined the index of ambient levels of particulates, sulfur dioxide, and nitrogen dioxide for each year and created an index number to show changes over time. (See table A.7.) A better model would calculate the damage from each type of pollutant each year and add the sum of those dollar figures together, but we do not have the sophistication to develop such a model. In addition, since ambient air levels vary considerably by location, damage estimates should be calculated in each county or region and then added together for a national estimate.

Column P: The damage caused by noise pollution in the United States in 1972 was estimated to be $4 billion by the World Health Organization (according to an article on noise pollution in the 1972 *Congressional Quarterly Almanac,* p. 980). We have assumed that from 1950 to 1972 the growth of industrialization, the expansion of the highway system, and the increase in the number of airports caused noise pollution to get worse at 3% per year. We have assumed that, since 1972, noise abatement regulations have slowed the rate to 1% per year.

Column Q: To calculate the value of the loss of wetlands, we first estimated the value per acre of the flow of services from an acre of wetland at $600 (1972 dollars). This is approximately one-third more than the median value of $448 per acre per year estimated for flood protection, water purification, provision of wildlife habitat, and aesthetics by T.R. Gupta and J.H. Foster in "Economic Criteria for Freshwater Wetland Policy in Massachusetts."[16] Our estimate was higher than Gupta and Foster's because they did not account for what economists call "consumers' surplus" in their valuations. (Consumers' surplus means the amount that purchasers or beneficiaries of an item or service would have been willing to pay above and beyond the actual price. We do not know how much this would actually be in the case of wetland services, so we have made a reasonable estimate.) In addition, $600 is a relatively conservative figure, since calculations of the value of salt water wetlands have arrived at figures three to twenty times as high. (See Lugo and Brinson, "Calculations of the Value of Saltwater Wetlands," in Greeson, Clark, and Clark 1979, p. 124.) The estimated loss of 600,000 acres per year through 1973 comes from the *Environmental Quality 1981: 12th Annual Report of the Council on Environmental Quality* (July 1982), and the estimated loss of 300,000 acres per year in subsequent years comes from the testimony of Robert A. Jantzen, Director of the U.S. Interior Department's Fish and Wildlife Service before the Senate Environment and Public Works Committee on 20 November 1981.

The loss of the stream of benefits from wetlands is a cumulative process. In other words, if 600,000 acres of wetlands were filled or drained in two successive years, at the end of the second year the loss would equal the

16. From *The American Journal of Agricultural Economics,* 57 (1): 40–45; cited in Greeson, Clark, and Clark 1979, p. 88.

stream of benefits flowing from 1.2 million acres of wetlands. Thus we have added the loss of benefits from wetlands each year to the total from the previous year.

Our base figure of $10 billion for 1950 is largely arbitrary. We estimated that a total of approximately 100 million acres of wetlands were filled in North America to make way for farming and other activities from the colonial period to 1950. (This is based on a decline from approximately 215 million original acres to about 110 million in 1950, according to *Wetlands of the U.S.: Current Status and Recent Trends,* Fish and Wildlife Service, March 1984, p. 29.) We reasoned that the value of each of the initial tens of millions of acres of lost wetlands was lower than the marginal value of the remaining acres that were filled in recent decades. (Likewise, the value of the last million acres on the continent will obviously be greater than $600 per acre because of the greater scarcity of the resource then.) Thus we multiplied an average value of $100 an acre of services from wetlands by 100 million acres to arrive at $10 billion as a plausible estimate of the cumulative loss to that time.

Column R: This column reflects two logically distinct ways in which the biologically productive capacity of farmland has been reduced. On the one hand, urban expansion (including the construction of highways) permanently removes land from production by paving it over. On the other hand, poor land management that destroys the soil through erosion, compaction, and decomposition of organic matter removes land gradually from production by lowering its productivity. Measuring either of these losses in dollar terms is both complicated and somewhat arbitrary, but because of the importance of food production in the long-run sustainability of the economy, we feel that it is imperative to make an attempt at measuring this loss.

As a result of the industrialization of agriculture, particularly since World War II, the productivity of labor and other nonenergy inputs (including farmland) increased steadily over time as those inputs were replaced by increasing amounts of energy (including embodied energy such as fertilizers or machines that themselves required energy to produce). This led to the assumption that crop yields would continue to increase indefinitely as new genetic strains were developed and new techniques were applied. From that perspective, the loss of a fraction of a percent of the cropland base to nonagricultural uses each year, or a slight annual decline in productivity of the underlying soil base, is insignificant if technological progress grows faster than those sources of decline.

In a world of continuously declining real energy costs, that perspective would be partially valid (though with some reservations because chemical inputs cannot entirely substitute for the organic content of the soil beyond a certain point). However, as we noted in the introduction, the real cost of energy is rising and will continue to rise because of the increasing energy cost required to discover, extract, and process new sources of energy. The implications of the rapid depletion of low-cost energy resources available for agriculture are staggering. For over forty years, the use of energy-intensive inputs to agriculture has masked the declining size and quality of the soil base upon which farming ultimately depends. Fertilizer has increased crop yields dramatically, but at the cost of breaking down the humus in the soil, oxidizing the soil carbon, and allowing farmers to ignore the effects of erosion. As long as fertilizer is relatively cheap, the effects of this degradation can be temporarily overcome by adding more fertilizer, though that merely exacerbates the problem in the long run. Likewise, irrigation can boost yields considerably as long as water can be pumped from rivers or aquifers at low cost. However, as energy (including embodied energy) costs rise and as aquifers are depleted, this source of growth in agriculture will be shown to be unsustainable. Moreover, the process of irrigation can itself lead to soil degradation if it increases either the erosion or salinity of the soil.

Economists also tend to downplay the loss and deterioration of cropland by pointing out that there are over 100 million acres of land that are currently either not being used or being used as rangelands or pasture that could be brought into crop production. Undoubtedly some of this land will in fact be brought into production in the future as energy inputs to agriculture become more expensive and as some of the land currently being used for crops becomes exhausted from overuse. Nevertheless, this land is not already being used as cropland for economic reasons and because it has high erosion potential. Robert Healy has reported that "Most of the land with high or medium potential for conversion is in soil classes IIe, IIIe, or IVe, and 'e' stands for erodible. According to the 1980 RCA draft (pp. 3–4), even the better of those soils are dangerously erodible when in crop production" (1982, p. 115). In other words, the sanguine view that the loss of valuable cropland can be compensated for by converting other land to more intensive use is not supported by the facts.

Another pernicious practice in economics that downplays the significance of soil loss is to discount future costs and benefits. Thus the present value of farmland is based on the productivity of the land, but only after the value of future yields has been reduced by a compound interest formula. The damage caused by erosion or urbanization to future productivity thus appears to be insignificant in conventional economic analyses. In effect, this theory says that a "rational" farmer *should* deplete the soil as long as the discounted stream of net revenues from unsustainable farming is greater than the discounted stream of net revenues from a farm managed on a sustained-yield basis. If farming unsustainably yields a higher stream of revenues, the surplus can be invested elsewhere, making the next generation better off (in theory) than if the farmer transfers the land in its undepleted state.

Our purpose is to calculate the *sustainable* economic welfare of our activities. We have therefore subtracted the cumulative damage to the long-term productivity of land that results from urbanization and poor land management. We would like to have estimated the undiscounted costs our current practices impose on our descendants, who will no longer be able make up for the loss of land area and declining soil quality with fossil fuels. However, we were forced to settle for estimates that are undoubtedly based only on the discounted value of lost productivity (especially in the discussion below of losses due to deteriorating soil). Thus we believe that our estimates understate the magnitude of the cost being imposed on the future as a result of unsustainable practices.

Losses due to urbanization. The amount of farmland that has been lost to urbanization is the subject of a great deal of controversy. The 1981 National Agricultural Lands Study (NALS) created a furor by arguing that the rate of farmland loss had grown from about one million acres per year in the period 1958–1967 to about three million acres per year in the period 1967–1975. Recognizing certain methodological and definitional problems in the study, we have chosen to assume that the one million acres per year figure has probably been constant throughout the period of our study (1950–1990) and that the proportion of cropland being converted to urban uses has remained at about 30% of that. In other words, we have adopted a conservative estimate for cropland loss due to urbanization of 300,000 acres per year. (This compares to the estimate in the NALS of 600,000 acres per year of cropland or 800,000 acres per year of cropland plus potential cropland.)

We then estimated that the value of an average acre of converted cropland, based on its productivity in the absence of high applications of fertilizers and other energy-intensive inputs, would be $100 per acre per year, or a capitalized value of $1,000 per acre (in 1972 dollars). We are assuming that the underlying value of farmland exceeds the market value today. Since our aim is to calculate *sustainable* economic welfare, we have chosen a figure that represents the value of land *as if* cheap energy sources had already been depleted. Without nitrogen fertilizer (derived from natural gas), for example, farm output would be lower, and food prices would be higher. The demand by farmers for high quality agricultural land would increase, raising its price. We regard that (unknown) price as the appropriate one to use when calculating the value of land lost to urbanization. We believe $1,000 per acre to be conservative, even if it seems high in terms of current market prices. It should be remembered that the best land for urban uses is generally the highest quality farmland in terms of slope, drainage, and other soil characteristics. Thus with urbanization it is generally the most valuable croplands that have been converted.

We began this calculation with an estimated accumulated loss of $1 billion to represent the value of services from farmland that had already been lost through urbanization by 1950. Since 15 million acres were in urban areas by that date, and another 24 million had been transformed into highways and rights-of-way by then,[17] our estimate of $1 billion implies that the average value of the loss to agriculture was about $25 per acre per year. As in the case of wetlands, we have assumed that the marginal utility or value of the first acres removed from agriculture was lower than the value of the land most recently urbanized.

In summary, we have calculated that urbanization annually removes from the cropland base a stream of agricultural services worth $30 million (300,000 acres times $100 per acre) and that the total cost is an accumulation of these losses, beginning with a loss of $1 billion in 1950. (See table A.8, column d.)

Losses due to deteriorating soil. The visible loss of land to urbanization is probably not as serious a problem as the less evident harm to the quality of land resulting from poor management practices. Economists tend to downplay productivity losses resulting from mismanagement because tangible productivity (in terms of yield per acre, though not in terms of yield per unit of energy input) has increased rapidly over the past forty years. In addition, productivity losses due to soil depletion are probably not linear, which means that the effects of erosion and compaction and loss of organic matter from the soil may not show up in yield reductions until the soil is irreversibly damaged. This is especially true, as noted above, when chemical fertilizers mask the effects of soil depletion temporarily, even as they contribute to it in the longer run.

As a result, calculating the loss of soil productivity is difficult. We expect that our estimates of this cost do not represent the true cost of current practices, because the impact on the future has presumably been discounted and because loss of productivity is measured only against yields inflated by energy-intensive inputs.

In 1980, economists at the Soil Conservation Service of the U.S. Department of Agriculture estimated that agricultural productivity losses resulting from erosion were approximately $1.3 billion (or about $0.7 billion in 1972 dollars).[18] Since we do not know the methodology for arriving at that result, we checked it using an alternative method of calculation and a different data source. The NALS estimated in 1977 that 1.7 million acre-equivalents of land were lost each year due to erosion. If we assume that about one-half of the serious erosion takes place on cropland, then a per acre cost of about

17. *Statistical Abstract* 1982, table 1154, p. 658, from U.S. Department of Agriculture, *Major Uses of Land in the United States: 1978.*

18. From "Background for 1985 Farm Legislation," Agricultural Information Bulletin Number 486, January 1985; also cited in *Environmental Quality 1984: Fifteenth Annual Report of the Council on Environmental Quality.*

$800 for this eroded land would yield the same result as the SCS estimate. (Thus, 1.7 million acre-equivalents divided by 2, times $800 per acre = $680 million or $0.68 billion).

We have assumed, as we did in the discussion of the impact of erosion on watercourses (see explanation of column N), that the rate of erosion has remained fairly constant since 1972 and that it increased by 1% per year from 1950 up to that point. We have also assumed that some damage had already occurred before 1950. Thus we have begun our calculation with a cumulative loss of $5 billion in 1949, with further costs added to that. (See table A.8, column b.)

The damage to soil from compaction by heavy machinery was estimated at $3.0 billion in 1980 ($1.67 billion in 1972 dollars) by R. Neil Sampson in *Farmland or Wasteland* (1981). We assume that that figure increased by 3% per year both before and after 1980. (See table A.8, column c.)

The amount in column R represents the total from the two types of soil loss: urbanization and deterioration, of which the latter is divided into two components. (See table A.8, column e.)

Column S: We consider the depletion of nonrenewable resources as a cost borne by future generations that should be subtracted from (debited to) the capital account of the present generation.

In order to estimate the proper amount to subtract for depletion of "natural capital," we began by considering a procedure developed by Salah El Serafy of the World Bank in an article entitled, "The Proper Calculation of Income from Depletable Natural Resources" (El Serafy 1988). El Serafy's approach is to estimate the amount of money that would need to be set aside from the proceeds of the liquidation of an asset (such as a mineral deposit) to generate a permanent income stream that would be as great in the future as the portion of receipts from the nonrenewable assets that are consumed in the present.

An owner of a wasting asset, if he is to consume no more than his income, must relend some part of his receipts in order for the interest on it to make up for the expected failure of receipts from his wasting asset in the future. This proposition, which can be found in J.R. Hicks's *Value and Capital,* led me to convert the mineral asset concerned into a perpetual income stream. The finite series of earnings from the resource, say a 10-year series of annual extraction leading to the extinction of the resource, has to be converted to an infinite series of true income such that the capitalized value of the two series be equal. From the annual earnings from sale, an income portion has to be identified, capable of being spent on consumption, the remainder, the capital element, being set aside year after year to be invested in order to create a perpetual stream of income that would sustain the same level of "*true*" income, both during the life of the resource as well as after the resource had been exhausted. I set out to find the two constituent portions of current receipts: the capital portion and the income portion. Under certain assumptions which are neither too restricting nor unrealistic, I arrived at the ratio of true income to total receipts, viz:

$$X/R = 1 - \frac{1}{(1 + r)^{n + 1}}$$

where X is true income; R total receipts (net of extraction cost); r the rate of discount; and n the number of periods over which the resource is to be liquidated. $R - X$ would be the "user cost" or "depletion factor" that should be set aside as a capital investment and totally excluded from GDP [or in this case from ISEW]. [El Serafy 1988]

We applaud this model as the best attempt we have seen to come to grips with the proper method of accounting for depletion of nonrenewable resources or "natural capital." As a general principle, we agree with the capitalization of current income to yield a permanent income, but we are not entirely satisfied with the details of El Serafy's model.

First, the calculation of n, the number of years until a resource is exhausted, poses some conceptual problems. The longevity of a mineral deposit at a specified rate of extraction is not a simple physical fact. The availability of the resource is a function not only of how much is "out there" but also of the intensity of the effort (in labor, capital, and energy) used to extract it. In other words, in El Serafy's equation, n (years to exhaustion of resource) is dependent on an exogenous variable, extraction costs. The equation is thus unspecified or indeterminate.[19]

Second, we doubt the appropriateness of the simplifying assumption in El Serafy's model that the price of nonrenewable resources in relation to the general price level will remain constant in the future. As a result of increasing extraction costs, we expect energy prices to rise relative to other prices over time. From before 1900 to 1972, the declining cost of energy permitted resource prices to remain stable. During that period the proportion of GNP devoted to mineral resources fluctuated between 3% and 4%. However, that trend has shifted, presumably irreversibly. As noted above on page 451, the proportion of GNP devoted to mineral resources jumped from 4% to 10% from 1972 to 1982. Although this drastic increase has been somewhat reversed as a result of temporary declines in demand for oil and thus of oil prices, the analysis by Gever et al. in *Beyond Oil* suggests that the real price of oil and other energy sources can be expected to begin climbing again in the 1990s, pushing up the price of all energy-intensive mineral exploration and mining as well.

19. El Serafy suggests taking the conceptual problem of rising extraction costs into account by proposing that "reserves . . . be adjusted *downward* by a factor that would reflect the rising future costs of extraction" (El Serafy 1988, p. 22). This adjustment would reflect the closure of mines and wells when market prices are below extraction (and processing) costs. This is clearly an ad hoc adjustment that is exogenous to the basic model. Nevertheless, this is the most satisfactory treatment of it we have found.

As a result of rising resource prices, the amount set aside to maintain a permanent income stream in El Serafy's model should be some portion of the future price of extracted minerals, not of the current price. Otherwise the income stream would pay for less in the future than in the present, thus violating the avowed principle of creating equal real incomes in each time period. Consequently, using the R calculated on the simplifying assumption of constant prices would provide an insufficient amount to cover future claims against the income stream. However, since we cannot predict the future price of resources any more than El Serafy could, we cannot offer a specific way to replace R in the equation. Nevertheless, we are more inclined than El Serafy to say that future resource prices relative to general price levels will be higher than today's.

Third, on a very practical level, it is not clear to us how one would estimate the value of R from existing sources, at least in the United States. The *Census of Minerals* provides data on the value of shipments, capital expenditures, cost of supplies, and value added in mining, and it defines value added as the sum of the first two values minus the third. Presumably, in El Serafy's equation, R is supposed to indicate rent, the return or "profit" to the enterprise holding the mineral rights. In principle, this could be calculated as a residual after subtracting wages, interest, and other production costs from value added, but in practice the data are not presented in a way that makes that possible.

Summarizing these criticisms of El Serafy's model, we can see that there is a great deal of arbitrariness in any effort to account for depletion of "natural capital." Our arguments suggest that the appropriate value of R might be several times as large as current market prices (to account for future price increases). The value of n cannot be specified in the equation without taking into account some estimate of extraction costs. In addition, since the real cost of a resource is a function of the cost of extracting it, as well as the limitation of its total quantity, R (receipts minus extraction costs) is not the proper figure for a welfare index. We have therefore used R plus extraction costs. Because extraction costs are "regrettable necessities," they should not be eliminated from this column, which will be subtracted to arrive at a welfare measure.

To avoid some of the conceptual and data-gathering problems in El Serafy's model, we have chosen to develop an alternative method of evaluating the value of depleted resources. We are seeking, as did he, to determine the amount of income from the sale of a resource that would have to be reinvested to sustain the income at the same level. Rather than trying to estimate the longevity of resource deposits, we have used a method based on physical quantities. For each unit of nonrenewable resource depleted, we have estimated the amount of money that would have to be invested in a process to create a perpetual stream of output of a renewable substitute for it. Calculating the expected cost of reproducing an equivalent physical product reduces somewhat the need to speculate about the changes in the relative prices of nonrenewable resources and the discount rate at which those prices should be evaluated. Thus one way to deal with the problem of estimating the long-run value of the oil that is extracted would be to consider the marginal cost of producing close substitutes such as "gasohol" from sugar cane or other organic material. This procedure obviates the need to use a zero discount rate because it assumes that depletable resources can be used in the present to create the capital necessary to provide a permanent stream of substitutes.

We have estimated the amount of money that would have had to be spent each year to replace the amount of resources extracted (produced) in that year. We have focused on energy resources because they account for 75% to 80% of the value of raw materials produced in the United States and because we have used a physical measure of energy to aggregate various sources (coal, oil, natural gas, and nuclear power) into a single number, which is not possible for other minerals. Moreover, cheap energy can compensate for the costs of extracting minerals from low-grade ores, but high-grade zinc or copper ores can do little to provide more energy.

We derived the total amount of nonrenewable energy (measured in quadrillions of BTUs) produced each year from table 2 of the *Annual Energy Review* of the Energy Information Administration of the U.S. Department of Energy. We divided that number by 5.8 million (the approximate number of BTUs per barrel of oil) to estimate the barrel equivalent of energy produced. We then multiplied that number by the constant dollar replacement cost per barrel, which, by assumption, increased at 3% per year from 1950 to 1990. In 1988, we assumed that the cost of replacement was $75 per barrel in nominal dollars, or approximately $26.50 in 1972 constant dollars. (See table A.9.)

The estimate of $75 per barrel as the nominal replacement cost in 1988 might seem rather high at first glance, particularly since the world price of oil that year was around $12. However, that lower figure has little to do with the cost of providing replacement fuel from a renewable source. (If the replacement is not from a renewable source, then this methodology does not overcome the problem of how to compare the claims of present and future consumers of a nonrenewable resource. In that case, the appropriate price to use in the accounting is indeterminate.) Yet even renewable energy from biomass could be produced for less than $75 per barrel in 1988. Why have we used such a high figure?

According to a study entitled *Ethanol: Economic and Policy Tradeoffs,* published by the Economic Research Service of the U.S. Department of Agriculture in 1988, ethanol would have been cost-competitive with oil selling at $40 per barrel if biomass conversion were not receiving a subsidy and if corn were selling at $2.00 per bushel. If the price of corn were $4.00 per bushel, the break-even price of ethanol would rise to $50 per barrel. This is not the full story, however. The authors of the study note that ethanol now accounts for about one-half of 1% of the energy content of gasoline in the United States and that doubling or tripling production "would begin to place strong upward pressure on corn and other grain prices, thereby increasing the production cost of ethanol and reducing its competitiveness with alternative energy sources" (p. vi). In other words, devoting millions of acres to growing crops for alcohol would drive up the price of land, of food, and of the crops grown for fuel as well. Using tens or hundreds of millions acres of cropland to increase the production of ethanol by a factor of one hundred (to one-half of the energy content of gasoline used in the United States) would presumably drive agricultural prices up much further than current agricultural price supports. The price of corn might reach $15 or $20 per bushel, which would drive the cost of producing ethanol up to over $100 per barrel. This does not even consider the cost of increased erosion if the organic residue of corn and other crops were removed from the land. According to a 1984 report, *Energy Use and Production in Agriculture,* by the Council for Agriculture Science and Technology in Ames, Iowa, the removal of crop residues could increase erosion by up to nine times. The energy cost of conservation measures to counteract those effects could be high enough to eliminate any net energy derived from ethanol production. According to Hopkinson and Day (1980), the net energy derived from sugar cane that is transformed into alcohol ranges from 0.8 to 1.7, according to whether the processing plant uses petroleum or bagasse (the sugar cane stalk) as its source of energy. The 0.8 figure signifies that 8 units of energy are produced for every 10 units consumed. In other words, the net energy is negative. Even the 1.7 figure is low, and it does not include the cost of transporting the ethanol to its end use. Since the energy cost of ethanol production is so high, the high monetary cost is not surprising.

Consequently, $75 would appear a conservative estimate in 1988 of the cost per barrel of replacing the energy produced in the United States. As another basis of comparison, we might also consider that the United States was already spending the equivalent of over $468 per barrel of oil from the Persian Gulf before the Gulf War if the cost of military expenditures to guarantee supplies are factored into the cost (Lovins and Lovins, pp. 26–27).

The estimated 3% annual growth of the real replacement cost of energy is based on several factors. First, the increase in the amount of energy produced would require more farmland to be devoted to the purpose of providing biomass as a feedstock for ethanol production. Also, as world population grows, the demand for alternative uses of the land (for growing food) has grown as well. Second, since a large part of the cost of producing ethanol (planting, harvesting, processing) is the cost of energy, higher energy costs form a positive feedback or self-reinforcing loop. Third, the energy cost of extracting all of the resources needed to produce the capital equipment used in ethanol production is rising as well.

The choice of the 3% estimated growth rate is partly arbitrary. However, a comparison with the rate of growth of the cost per foot of oil drilling will show that it is not unreasonable. Drilling costs per well rose by 5.7% from 1970 to 1975, 7.4% from 1975 to 1980, and by 12.4% in 1981 and 6.5% in 1982. After that, the world price of oil fell, exploration was cut back, and drilling was presumably limited to wells with lower cost. Nevertheless, during the period of rising oil prices, the rising drilling cost illustrates the basic principle that when the limits of a resource are being reached, the cost of extracting the next unit is higher than it was for the previous unit. This principle presumably applies also to renewable fuels, though not as dramatically as to oil and gas. Thus we used a growth rate of cost per barrel approximately half the one revealed for fossil fuels extraction in the 1970s.

Another way to derive the cost of resource depletion might have been to estimate the size of a tax on nonrenewable resources that would be high enough to prevent them from increasing in price faster than prices in general. The tax would achieve what Talbot Page calls the "conservation criterion" for equitable resource depletion (Page 1977, chapter 8). Nevertheless, we are not sure how to estimate the appropriate size of the hypothetical tax or how to incorporate it into the ISEW, so we have not followed this procedure.

Column T: In addition to using up mineral and fuel resources, our collective behavior also burdens the future by dumping waste products into the environment that will have long-term consequences. For example, the value of protecting health and security by keeping radioactive elements with long half-lives out of the environment for thousands of years is enormous but never calculated. Nevertheless, it would appear that the benefits (costs avoided) of permanent disposal far outweigh the costs of temporary storage and final disposal, assuming a method of long-term disposal can ever be devised. The cost of disposing wastes from the Hanford weapons development center amounts to several billion dollars per year, wastes that comprise only a portion of the total that have been generated in the United States. The costs of maintaining and protecting these facilities will continue indefinitely. There are still no reliable estimates of the costs of decommissioning atomic power reactors and disposing of their high-level wastes. Thus, the costs imposed on future generations by atomic power generation each year may amount to several tens of billions of dollars.

As large as the costs of radioactive waste management may be, they pale by comparison with the potential costs of climate change. The costs to the future imposed by industrial and agricultural activities that add carbon dioxide, nitrous oxide, and methane to the atmosphere (thereby contributing to the "greenhouse effect" and global climate change) have only recently begun to be assessed. Although there is scientific controversy over the expected magnitude of the greenhouse effect, due to the limited capacity of computer models to simulate all of the key interactions in global climate, the most likely effect of a doubling of carbon dioxide (and other heat-trapping compounds) would be an increase in temperature of 1.5 to 4.5 degrees Centigrade, with the greatest warming occuring at high latitudes. Although some elements of the models may overstate the effect of greenhouse gases, other elements that could accelerate global warming are understated. As an example of acceleration, warmer average temperatures increase the release of carbon dioxide and methane due to higher levels of biological decomposition, which in turn contributes to further warming (Abrahamson, p. 12). If the temperature in the northern polar region rises sufficiently to thaw land containing large peat deposits, the decay of that peat could add considerable amounts of carbon dioxide to the atmosphere. Thus, human releases of greenhouse gases could set in motion irreversible processes that would alter climate even more than current models predict. In addition, since the models presume a gradual increase in temperature over a period of decades, a climate shift resulting from changes in ocean currents could cause unforeseen problems to arise rapidly (Broecker, "Greenhouse Surprises," in Abrahamson 1989, chapter 13).

Because the weather patterns of the earth are determined largely by temperature differences between the poles and the equator, warmer poles will mean that ocean currents and continental weather systems will become less vigorous.

Global warming since around 1950 has generally not been as bad as computer models predict should be caused by the increased level of carbon dioxide in the atmosphere. One plausible explanation of this anomaly is that the increased levels of humanly generated sulfates in the atmosphere have counteracted warming trends in the Northern Hemisphere. However, since sulfates remain in the atmosphere for months, whereas greenhouse gases remain for years, the warming trend is likely to be dominant in the long run (Cline 1992).

The full extent of the physical damage likely to ensue from the cumulative effects of climate change is difficult to predict. The flooding of cities and erosion of beaches that will result from higher sea levels are only the first level of the threat. Even the disruption of established agricultural patterns as a result of drought and increasingly variable and unpredictable weather will not be the most serious consequence of these changes. The greatest threat is ecological. The almost instantaneous change (on a geological scale) of the global climate could have harmful effects on all but the most resilient species of plants and animals in those regions of the planet most drastically affected by climate change. A 3 degree Centigrade increase in temperature in the United States, for example, would force vegetation belts around 200 miles northward, causing the extinction of thousands of species that cannot disperse at the required speed (Peters in Abrahamson 1989, chapter 6).

A recent economic study by William R. Cline, who relies on the views of the majority of scientists on the Intergovernmental Panel on Climate Change (IPCC), indicates that a 2.5 degree Centigrade warming by 2025 would generate around $60 billion (1990 dollars) in annual tangible losses and perhaps another $60 billion annually in intangible losses, particularly species loss.[20] Cline points out that the IPCC's "best guess" probably underestimates the amount of warming by ignoring the short-term "masking" of potential warming by sulfates from urban pollution. There are various other positive feedback mechanisms that may have been underestimated by the IPCC, such as the release of methane from peat deposits and increased trapping of heat by clouds in the upper atmosphere as warming causes a redistribution of clouds from the lower to the upper atmosphere.

In bending over backwards to take account of criticism of the global warming hypothesis, Cline may have bent too far. Thus, his $120 billion per year damage figure in 2025 is probably conservative. In addition to accepting temperature change estimates that he acknowledges are probably underestimates, he also assigns too much weight to conservative damage estimates. For example, when he examines the effects of warming on agriculture, he focuses on the carbon fertilization effects of increased carbon dioxide, even after noting that the laboratory results which demonstrate this effect are biased by the presence of adequate water and fertilizer. In addition, these studies ignore the fact that weeds will have access to increased carbon dioxide as well and that increased biomass production may lead to a higher ratio of carbohydrate to protein, hardly a nutritional gain.

Although we recognize that greenhouse gases vary in the extent to which they trap heat, we have assumed for simplicity that the amount of long-term damage to the climate and the environment is directly proportional to the consumption of fossil fuels and nuclear energy—in effect to nonrenewable energy consumption. We have therefore begun by adding the total quantity of nonrenewable energy consumed each year in quadrillions of BTUs, starting in 1900. (These figures are derived from table 1 of the *Annual Energy Review* of the Energy Information Administration of the U.S. Department of Energy.) Assuming that a barrel of crude oil contains approximately 5.8 million BTUs, we calculated the total barrel equivalents of energy consumed each year from 1900 to 1990. We then imagined that a tax or rent of $0.50 per barrel-equivalent had been levied on all nonrenewable energy consumed during that period and set aside to accumulate in a non-interest-bearing account. (See table A.10.) That account might be thought of as a fund available to compensate future generations for the long-term damage caused by the use of fossil fuels and atomic energy. We are implicitly assum-

---

20. William R. Cline, *Global Warming: The Economic Stakes* (Washington, D.C.: Institute for International Economics, 1992). A more comprehensive book by Cline, entitled *The Economics of Global Warming*, was not available at the time of this writing.

ing that the cumulative undiscounted future damage caused by consuming a barrel of oil or its equivalent in the present are equal to $.50 in 1972 dollars. If Cline's estimate of $120 billion in annual damage is approximately right, that would mean the accumulated "stock" of damage in 2025 would be around $1.2 trillion. That serves as an indirect confirmation of the reasonableness of our estimate of $285 billion (1972 dollars) as the stock of damage in 1990.

Column U: The discovery of holes in the ozone layer over the North and South Poles in recent years has convinced most scientists that releases of chlorofluorocarbons (CFCs) have caused severe damage to a crucial shield against the sun's ultraviolet light.

In the eight years between November 1978 and October 1986, the amount of ozone in the stratosphere above the mid-northern hemisphere declined by somewhere between 4.4% to 7.4%.[21] One likely effect of the increase in ultraviolet radiation reaching the earth's surface will be a higher incidence of skin cancer, particularly among fair-skinned people. The risk of contracting malignant melanoma has already risen from a lifetime risk factor of 1 in 600 in 1950 to 1 in 135 in 1987.[22] In fact, the direct consequence to humans—the rising incidence of skin cancer—is only the least significant of the consequences of allowing increased ultraviolet radiation to reach the earth's surface. In theory, humans could protect themselves from the harmful effects of increased radiation (though even this behavior change would constitute a cost imposed on the future). However, plants and animals cannot protect themselves from changes brought about by reduced ozone in the upper atmosphere. Thus the ecological effects of greater UV radiation are likely to be much greater than the health effects, though no one knows precisely what they will be.

The calculations in table A.11 for this column involve multiplying the cumulative world production of CFC-11 and CFC-12 by $5 per kilogram.[23](Since about one-third of CFC production has taken place in the United States, the $5 per kilogram estimate actually amounts to $15 per kilogram of U.S. production.) The lifetimes of CFC-11 and CFC-12 are 75 and 110 years, respectively. (Other CFCs and halogenated compounds also contribute to ozone depletion, but the only time series data we found were for CFC-11 and CFC-12, so we have restricted our estimates to those compounds.)

21. Donald Heath of NASA's Goddard Space Flight Center, testimony in hearings before Subcommittee on Health and Environment, Committee on Energy and Commerce, U.S. House of Representatives, *Ozone Layer Depletion,* Serial 100–7, March 9, 1987, p. 32.

22. Darrel Rigel, testimony in *Ozone Layer Depletion* hearings, pp. 70–80.

23. Data on cumulative production (from major producers in reporting countries) comes from testimony in *Ozone Layer Depletion* hearings, pp. 435–436. The estimates that we have used for 1986 through 1990 are extrapolations based on regression analysis.

In the absence of data for 1986 to 1990, we have extrapolated the sum of cumulative production of CFC-11 and CFC-12 for those years by means of regression analysis. Although the regression on the logarithm provides a better fit (R-squared = .97) than the linear model (R-squared = .91), we used the latter, more conservative, growth estimate. Using the logarithmic extrapolation (i.e., assuming a constant percentage increase in CFC production) would have produced a 1990 damage estimate of $133.4 billion instead of $85.3 billion. In that case, per capita ISEW would have been around $3,060, indicating a decline rather than improvement in the last years of the 1980s.

Our assumption that the damage from ozone depletion due to cumulative CFC production and release in the United States is equal to $15 per kilogram amounts to the same as assuming that each individual in the United States would demand about $960 (1972 dollars) in 1985 to compensate for the risks involved in producing and having produced CFCs. Or it may be thought of as the amount that would need to be set aside to compensate future generations for having made their planet less habitable.

Column V: For economic welfare to be sustained over time, the supply of capital must grow to meet the demands of an increasing population. More specifically, we have assumed that one element of economic sustainability is constant or increasing quantities of capital available for each worker. We have followed the general procedure used by Nordhaus and Tobin. However, unlike them, we have excluded human capital from our estimates for reasons explained earlier. We have thus calculated net capital growth by adding the amount of new capital stock (increases in fixed reproducible capital) minus the capital requirement, the amount necessary to maintain the same level of capital per worker. We estimated the capital requirement by multiplying the percent change in the labor force by the stock of capital from the previous year. (See table A.12, column h.) Actually, we used a five-year rolling average of changes in labor force and capital to smooth out year to year fluctuations. (See table A.12, columns d and f.)

Figures for fixed reproducible capital are derived from *Survey of Current Business,* August 1982, August 1987, and January 1992. The estimate of the size of the labor force comes from the *Economic Report of the President,* table B-29, which uses the estimates of the U.S. Bureau of Labor Statistics, *Employment and Earnings.*

Column W: The U.S. net international position measures the amount that Americans invest overseas minus the amount invested by foreigners in the United States. The annual change in the net international position indicates whether the United States is moving in the direction of net lending (if positive) or net borrowing (if negative). If the change is positive, the United States has in effect increased its capital assets. If it is negative, part of U.S.

capital formation is in fact based on the borrowed wealth of foreign interests that must eventually be repaid with interest. We have thus included annual changes in the net international position as a measure of the sustainability of the welfare of our economy.

As the United States became heavily indebted in the 1980s and its net international investment position deteriorated, Robert Eisner and other economists criticized the method of calculating this value. They pointed out that by valuing American assets held abroad at their historic purchase price rather than current market value, the methodology underestimated the net U.S. position. (American assets overseas are older and thus more likely to be undervalued than foreign-owned assets in the United States that have been acquired more recently.)

The values in this column are derived from *Statistical Abstract* (1988, table 1330, p. 758) for 1950 to 1981, with some years from 1950 to 1975 being interpolated. From 1950 to 1981, the difference between historic costs and market value would not have altered the net international position substantially. For the period from 1982 to 1990, however, the Bureau of Economic Analysis has developed estimates of net international position with assets valued at market value, which provides a more useful estimate of net investment than historic cost estimates. (See *Survey of Current Business,* June 1991. Or see *Economic Report of the President, 1992,* table B-99, p. 411.) The figures each year have been adjusted for inflation using the implicit GNP deflator in the *National Income and Product Accounts,* table 7.4.

Column X: The column marked ISEW, or Index of Sustainable Economic Welfare, starts with "Weighted personal consumption" (column D), adds four columns (E through H), subtracts thirteen columns (I through U), and adds two columns (V and W).

Column Y: Per capita ISEW is calculated by dividing ISEW by the population (from *Statistical Abstract,* 1991, table 2, p. 7).

Column Z: The value of GNP comes from the *National Income and Product Accounts,* table 1.2. We made the same adjustment for 1985 through 1990 as we did for personal consumption in Column B.

Column AA: Per capita GNP is GNP divided by the population.

Table A.2-A
Alternative Income Distribution Indexes

Year	Harmonic mean index	Top quintile index	Low quintile index	Weighted ratios index	Gini coefficient index
a	b	c	d	e	f
50	109.0	102.6	111.1	112.2	104.4
51	100.0	100.0	100.0	100.0	100.0
52	102.0	100.7	102.0	102.2	101.4
53	100.8	98.3	106.4	106.3	98.9
54	106.2	100.5	111.1	111.7	102.2
55	101.2	99.3	104.2	104.1	100.0
56	98.1	98.6	100.0	99.8	98.6
57	95.3	97.1	98.0	97.5	96.7
58	97.1	97.6	100.0	99.6	97.5
59	99.6	98.8	102.0	102.0	99.4
60	101.3	99.3	104.2	104.4	100.3
61	105.3	101.4	106.4	107.2	103.0
62	99.6	99.3	100.0	100.1	99.7
63	99.2	99.0	100.0	100.0	99.7
64	98.5	99.0	98.0	98.0	99.4
65	96.5	98.3	96.2	95.9	98.1
66	92.0	97.4	89.3	88.7	96.1
67	92.5	97.1	90.9	90.3	95.9
68	92.0	97.4	89.3	88.6	95.9
69	92.4	97.6	89.3	88.6	96.1
70	95.0	98.3	92.6	92.1	97.5
71	94.9	98.8	90.9	90.6	98.1
72	96.6	99.5	92.6	92.6	99.2
73	95.1	98.8	90.9	90.7	98.1
74	94.7	98.6	90.9	90.6	98.1
75	95.9	98.8	92.6	92.5	98.6
76	95.9	98.8	92.6	92.5	98.9
77	99.0	99.8	96.2	96.4	100.3
78	99.0	99.8	96.2	96.3	100.3
79	99.5	100.2	96.2	96.6	100.6
80	100.1	100.0	98.0	98.5	100.6
81	102.4	100.7	100.0	100.7	101.9
82	107.9	102.6	106.4	107.7	105.0
83	108.1	102.6	106.4	107.8	105.2
84	108.9	103.1	106.4	107.9	105.5
85	110.8	104.6	108.7	108.2	107.2
86	112.8	105.0	108.7	110.6	108.0
87	113.0	105.3	108.7	110.8	108.3
88	113.9	105.8	108.7	110.9	108.8
89	115.9	107.2	108.7	111.2	110.5
90	114.5	106.5	108.7	111.1	109.1

Lowest year of each index divided by highest year:
(low numbers signify a more dispersed index)

0.7938	0.9058	0.8038	0.7897	0.8678

Table A.2-B
Effects of Alternative Income Distribution
Indexes on Per Capita ISEW

Year	Harmonic mean index PC-ISEW	Top quintile index PC-ISEW	Low quintile index PC-ISEW	Weighted ratios index PC-ISEW	Gini coefficient index PC-ISEW
a	b	c	d	e	f
50	2536.0	2661.4	2496.9	2478.4	2624.9
51	2792.6	2792.6	2792.6	2792.6	2792.6
52	2844.8	2872.9	2844.4	2841.0	2858.6
53	2906.3	2964.0	2789.1	2791.3	2950.5
54	2828.4	2949.5	2733.4	2721.8	2911.4
55	2951.3	2997.6	2885.3	2885.9	2980.3
56	3005.8	2995.0	2959.8	2964.2	2993.4
57	3052.9	3006.7	2983.4	2997.5	3017.5
58	3023.0	3009.6	2950.7	2960.7	3011.5
59	2966.5	2987.2	2907.5	2909.4	2970.8
60	2914.2	2963.9	2845.6	2840.0	2938.8
61	2844.7	2935.7	2820.7	2802.4	2897.5
62	2987.5	2994.6	2975.8	2973.8	2983.0
63	2973.8	2979.4	2953.7	2953.0	2961.0
64	3028.8	3012.3	3040.6	3040.6	3000.8
65	3129.6	3074.9	3140.1	3148.7	3081.8
66	3295.3	3118.0	3394.7	3418.3	3156.6
67	3279.1	3122.4	3335.6	3358.3	3163.0
68	3352.7	3163.4	3456.9	3482.9	3213.8
69	3357.5	3168.9	3478.5	3506.1	3219.2
70	3238.3	3120.5	3326.6	3344.2	3147.7
71	3269.7	3130.4	3425.2	3436.7	3155.6
72	3237.2	3130.4	3394.3	3393.3	3142.7
73	3334.1	3190.4	3508.6	3518.0	3217.5
74	3350.4	3202.4	3506.9	3519.2	3220.3
75	3329.1	3220.6	3465.4	3470.5	3227.1
76	3402.9	3289.4	3545.5	3550.8	3285.5
77	3260.7	3229.7	3377.2	3366.6	3209.4
78	3358.3	3328.0	3480.5	3473.9	3307.0
79	3384.2	3352.3	3527.1	3509.3	3339.6
80	3310.6	3314.5	3396.3	3376.8	3292.0
81	3284.0	3349.7	3379.3	3350.4	3301.1
82	3001.8	3200.1	3058.1	3009.1	3111.0
83	3058.1	3269.8	3122.5	3069.5	3166.7
84	2837.7	3066.6	2933.9	2873.6	2968.7
85	2994.6	3245.5	3077.3	3096.4	3138.3
86	2999.1	3310.8	3158.5	3081.2	3187.2
87	3048.4	3364.7	3220.1	3135.8	3237.9
88	2970.6	3304.8	3178.0	3085.7	3173.0
89	2933.4	3284.4	3220.4	3115.7	3146.2
90	3016.6	3348.9	3253.1	3152.8	3236.3

Table A.3
Value of the Services of Highways and Streets

Year	Net stock of federal, state & local highways	Imputed services of highways
a	b	c
50	82.8	6.2
51	84.3	6.3
52	86.5	6.5
53	89.5	6.7
54	93.4	7.0
55	98.2	7.4
56	102.5	7.7
57	107.7	8.1
58	113.8	8.5
59	119.9	9.0
60	126.0	9.5
61	132.6	9.9
62	139.1	10.4
63	147.0	11.0
64	154.4	11.6
65	161.8	12.1
66	169.8	12.7
67	177.3	13.3
68	185.1	13.9
69	191.7	14.4
70	197.8	14.8
71	203.9	15.3
72	208.8	15.7
73	213.2	16.0
74	216.2	16.2
75	218.0	16.3
76	220.2	16.5
77	221.2	16.6
78	222.5	16.7
79	223.1	16.7
80	223.5	16.8
81	224.1	16.8
82	225.1	16.9
83	226.0	16.9
84	227.7	17.1
85	230.3	17.3
86	231.7	17.4
87	233.9	17.5
88	235.8	17.7
89	237.7	17.8
90	240.1	18.0

Table A.4
Public Expenditures on Health and Education Counted as Personal Consumption

Year	Public expenditures on higher education	Public expenditures on higher education for consumption (b/2)	Public expenditures on health	Public expenditures on improving health (d/2)	Public expenditures on health and education for consumption (c + e)
a	b	c	d	e	f
50	2.2	1.1	7.6	3.8	4.9
51	2.0	1.0	7.9	3.9	4.9
52	2.2	1.1	8.1	4.0	5.1
53	2.2	1.1	8.4	4.2	5.3
54	2.4	1.2	8.7	4.3	5.5
55	2.6	1.3	9.0	4.5	5.8
56	2.9	1.4	9.5	4.7	6.2
57	3.2	1.6	9.9	4.9	6.5
58	3.6	1.8	10.1	5.1	6.9
59	4.1	2.1	10.4	5.2	7.3
60	4.8	2.4	10.7	5.4	7.8
61	5.4	2.7	11.8	5.9	8.6
62	6.0	3.0	12.9	6.4	9.4
63	7.0	3.5	13.9	7.0	10.4
64	7.8	3.9	14.9	7.5	11.4
65	9.2	4.6	15.9	7.9	12.5
66	10.8	5.4	20.0	10.0	15.4
67	12.5	6.3	23.2	11.6	17.9
68	12.6	6.3	26.2	13.1	19.4
69	13.2	6.6	28.5	14.2	20.8
70	14.8	7.4	30.5	15.3	22.6
71	15.4	7.7	32.4	16.2	23.9
72	16.1	8.0	35.0	17.5	25.5
73	17.2	8.6	37.3	18.7	27.3
74	17.8	8.9	41.5	20.7	29.7
75	18.9	9.5	41.9	21.0	30.4
76	19.3	9.7	45.1	22.6	32.2
77	19.6	9.8	45.9	22.9	32.7
78	19.9	10.0	48.1	24.0	34.0
79	20.6	10.3	50.0	25.0	35.3
80	21.7	10.9	52.4	26.2	37.1
81	22.2	11.1	54.5	27.3	38.4
82	21.3	10.6	54.5	27.3	37.9
83	21.6	10.8	54.7	27.4	38.2
84	21.5	10.8	55.7	27.8	38.6
85	22.0	11.0	57.8	28.9	39.9
86	22.1	11.1	58.0	29.0	40.1
87	22.7	11.3	60.1	30.0	41.4
88	23.6	11.8	61.3	30.6	42.4
89	24.5	12.2	63.4	31.7	43.9
90	25.4	12.7	64.8	32.4	45.1

Table A.5
Defensive Private Expenditures on Health and Education

Year	Private expenditures on education	Private expenditures on higher education	Defensive expenditures on private education $b - (c/2)$	Private expenditures on health	Defensive expenditures on private health $(e/2)$	Defensive expenditures on private health and education $(d + f)$
a	b	c	d	e	f	g
50	3.6	1.6	2.9	22.1	11.1	13.9
51	3.8	1.6	3.0	22.9	11.5	14.5
52	4.0	1.6	3.2	23.6	11.8	14.9
53	4.1	1.7	3.3	24.5	12.2	15.5
54	4.3	1.7	3.4	25.3	12.7	16.1
55	4.6	1.8	3.7	26.4	13.2	16.9
56	4.8	1.9	3.9	28.0	14.0	17.9
57	5.2	2.1	4.1	29.4	14.7	18.9
58	5.4	2.2	4.3	30.5	15.2	19.5
59	5.6	2.3	4.5	31.5	15.7	20.2
60	6.0	2.4	4.8	32.6	16.3	21.1
61	6.2	2.5	5.0	35.9	17.9	22.9
62	6.6	2.6	5.3	39.0	19.5	24.8
63	7.0	2.7	5.6	42.0	21.0	26.6
64	7.4	2.9	5.9	45.1	22.6	28.5
65	7.9	3.3	6.3	47.8	23.9	30.2
66	8.7	3.5	6.9	50.1	25.0	31.9
67	9.0	3.6	7.2	50.7	25.4	32.6
68	9.8	3.8	7.9	51.5	25.8	33.7
69	10.3	4.0	8.4	51.7	25.8	34.2
70	10.7	4.1	8.6	51.9	25.9	34.5
71	10.9	4.3	8.8	54.1	27.1	35.9
72	11.4	4.4	9.2	57.7	28.9	38.1
73	11.5	4.5	9.3	61.2	30.6	39.9
74	11.1	4.4	9.0	61.0	30.5	39.4
75	11.5	4.4	9.3	60.0	30.0	39.3
76	11.8	4.4	9.6	62.2	31.1	40.7
77	11.7	4.4	9.5	64.9	32.5	42.0
78	12.2	4.5	9.9	66.5	33.2	43.2
79	12.4	4.6	10.1	68.6	34.3	44.4
80	12.6	4.7	10.2	71.2	35.6	45.8
81	12.8	4.9	10.4	74.6	37.3	47.7
82	12.9	4.8	10.5	75.9	38.0	48.4
83	13.5	5.0	11.1	77.7	38.9	49.9
84	14.1	5.1	11.6	80.5	40.3	51.9
85	15.1	5.3	12.5	81.1	40.5	53.0
86	15.8	5.4	13.1	82.1	41.0	54.1
87	16.6	5.5	13.9	85.8	42.9	56.8
88	17.9	5.7	15.1	89.8	44.9	60.0
89	19.1	5.8	16.2	92.8	46.4	62.6
90	19.6	5.9	16.7	93.0	46.5	63.2

Table A.6
Cost of Commuting

Year	User-operated transportation	Purchased local transportation	Cost of commuting (.21b + .3c)
a	b	c	d
50	34.2	6.1	9.0
51	32.4	5.6	8.5
52	32.3	5.4	8.4
53	37.1	5.1	9.3
54	39.2	4.7	9.6
55	45.7	4.4	10.9
56	43.3	4.3	10.4
57	43.8	4.2	10.5
58	41.8	3.9	9.9
59	45.6	3.9	10.7
60	48.4	3.9	11.3
61	46.6	3.6	10.9
62	50.5	3.6	11.7
63	53.9	3.5	12.4
64	56.2	3.4	12.8
65	63.2	3.3	14.3
66	66.5	3.3	14.9
67	67.5	3.2	15.2
68	74.7	3.3	16.7
69	79.2	3.5	17.7
70	78.3	3.4	17.4
71	87.8	3.4	19.5
72	97.8	3.4	21.6
73	105.3	3.4	23.1
74	101.5	3.5	22.4
75	101.8	3.5	22.4
76	113.8	3.6	25.0
77	124.4	3.6	27.2
78	129.0	3.7	28.2
79	133.4	3.8	29.2
80	131.2	3.5	28.6
81	133.6	3.2	29.0
82	127.8	3.0	27.7
83	139.4	3.0	30.2
84	152.1	3.0	32.8
85	163.6	3.0	35.3
86	155.3	2.9	33.5
87	148.0	3.1	32.0
88	159.2	3.0	34.3
89	161.7	2.9	34.8
90	160.5	2.9	34.6

Table A.7
Cost of Air Pollution

Year	NO_2	SO_2	Particulate matter	Ambient air pollution index	Cost of air pollution
a	b	c	d	e	f
50	Assumed ambient air			89.0	21.6
51	pollution increase of			89.9	21.8
52	1.0% per year from			90.8	22.0
53	1950 to 1960			91.7	22.2
54				92.7	22.5
55				93.6	22.7
56				94.5	22.9
57				95.5	23.2
58				96.5	23.4
59				97.4	23.6
60	Assumed increase of			98.4	23.9
61	2.4% per year from			99.4	24.1
62	1961 to 1970			101.9	24.7
63				104.4	25.3
64				106.9	25.9
65				109.6	26.6
66				112.2	27.2
67				115.0	27.9
68				117.8	28.6
69				120.7	29.3
70	Assumed decrease of			123.7	30.0
71	3.0% per year from			120.0	29.1
72	1971 to 1977			116.4	28.2
73				112.9	27.4
74				109.5	26.6
75				106.2	25.8
76				103.0	25.0
77	100.0	100.0	100.0	100.0	24.3
78	100.0	93.0	99.0	97.3	23.6
79	100.0	86.0	101.0	95.7	23.2
80	97.3	78.1	102.7	92.7	22.5
81	95.0	74.6	96.6	88.7	21.5
82	92.2	68.8	80.2	80.4	19.5
83	91.5	66.0	79.6	79.0	19.2
84	92.6	67.3	81.9	80.6	19.6
85	91.5	63.0	78.1	77.5	18.8
86	92.6	60.9	77.8	77.1	18.7
87	92.2	59.5	79.6	77.1	18.7
88	92.6	60.2	80.8	77.9	18.9
89				77.9	18.9
90				77.9	18.9

NOTE:
Index number 1977=100.

Table A.8
Loss of Agricultural Land
(Erosion, Compaction, Urbanization)

Year	Erosion productivity loss	Compaction productivity loss	Agricultural land lost by urbanization	Total loss of agricultural land (b + c + d)
a	b	c	d	e
50	5.6	0.7	1.0	7.2
51	6.1	0.7	1.0	7.8
52	6.7	0.7	1.1	8.5
53	7.3	0.7	1.1	9.1
54	7.9	0.8	1.1	9.7
55	8.5	0.8	1.2	10.4
56	9.0	0.8	1.2	11.0
57	9.7	0.8	1.2	11.7
58	10.3	0.9	1.2	12.4
59	10.9	0.9	1.3	13.0
60	11.5	0.9	1.3	13.7
61	12.1	0.9	1.3	14.4
62	12.8	1.0	1.4	15.1
63	13.4	1.0	1.4	15.8
64	14.0	1.0	1.4	16.5
65	14.7	1.1	1.5	17.2
66	15.4	1.1	1.5	17.9
67	16.0	1.1	1.5	18.7
68	16.7	1.2	1.5	19.4
69	17.4	1.2	1.6	20.1
70	18.1	1.2	1.6	20.9
71	18.7	1.3	1.6	21.6
72	19.4	1.3	1.7	22.4
73	20.1	1.3	1.7	23.2
74	20.8	1.4	1.7	24.0
75	21.5	1.4	1.8	24.7
76	22.2	1.5	1.8	25.5
77	22.9	1.5	1.8	26.3
78	23.6	1.6	1.8	27.1
79	24.3	1.6	1.9	27.8
80	25.0	1.7	1.9	28.6
81	25.7	1.7	1.9	29.4
82	26.4	1.8	2.0	30.2
83	27.1	1.8	2.0	31.0
84	27.8	1.9	2.0	31.7
85	28.5	1.9	2.1	32.5
86	29.2	2.0	2.1	33.3
87	29.9	2.1	2.1	34.1
88	30.6	2.1	2.1	34.9
89	31.3	2.2	2.2	35.7
90	32.0	2.2	2.2	36.5

Table A.9
Depreciation of Nonrenewable Resources
(Using Replacement Cost of Energy as Proxy)

Year	Nonrenewable energy production (quadrillions of BTUs)	Barrel equivalents (b/5.8) (billions of barrels)	Replacement cost/barrels @ 3%/year increase	Total replacement cost
a	b	c	d	e
50	32.6	5.6	8.3	46.8
51	35.8	6.2	8.6	53.0
52	35.0	6.0	8.9	53.4
53	35.4	6.1	9.1	55.6
54	33.8	5.8	9.4	54.8
55	37.4	6.4	9.7	62.5
56	39.8	6.9	10.0	68.6
57	40.1	6.9	10.3	71.4
58	37.2	6.4	10.6	68.2
59	39.1	6.7	11.0	73.8
60	39.9	6.9	11.3	77.7
61	40.3	7.0	11.6	81.0
62	41.8	7.2	12.0	86.5
63	44.1	7.6	12.4	94.1
64	45.8	7.9	12.8	100.9
65	47.3	8.2	13.2	107.3
66	50.1	8.6	13.6	117.2
67	52.7	9.1	14.0	127.0
68	54.5	9.4	14.4	135.3
69	56.4	9.7	14.9	144.6
70	59.4	10.2	15.3	157.0
71	58.5	10.1	15.8	159.2
72	59.5	10.3	16.3	167.1
73	59.2	10.2	16.8	171.2
74	57.6	9.9	17.3	171.9
75	56.6	9.8	17.8	174.2
76	56.8	9.8	18.4	180.2
77	57.8	10.0	19.0	189.0
78	58.1	10.0	19.6	195.8
79	60.8	10.5	20.2	211.2
80	61.8	10.6	20.8	221.2
81	61.5	10.6	21.4	227.3
82	60.5	10.4	22.1	230.5
83	57.5	9.9	22.8	225.8
84	62.3	10.7	23.5	252.2
85	61.6	10.6	24.2	257.1
86	61.0	10.5	24.9	262.3
87	62.0	10.7	25.7	274.8
88	63.5	10.9	26.5	290.1
89	63.1	10.9	27.3	296.9
90	64.5	11.1	28.1	312.6

Table A.10
Energy Consumption as a Measure of Long-Term Environmental Damage

Year	Total energy consumption, quadrillions of BTUs	Barrel equivalents of energy consumed (b/5.8) (billions of barrels)	Cumulative $.50 tax per barrel (billions $)	Year	Total energy consumption, quadrillions of BTUs	Barrel equivalents of energy consumed (f/5.8) (billions of barrels)	Cumulative $.50 tax per barrel (billions $)
a	b	c	d	e	f	g	h
1900	7.3	1.3	0.6	1945	30.1	5.2	70.7
1901	8.0	1.4	1.3	1946	29.0	5.0	73.2
1902	8.4	1.5	2.0	1947	31.4	5.4	75.9
1903	9.9	1.7	2.9	1948	32.5	5.6	78.7
1904	9.8	1.7	3.7	1949	30.0	5.2	81.3
1905	11.0	1.9	4.7	1950	31.7	5.5	84.0
1906	11.5	2.0	5.7	1951	34.1	5.9	86.9
1907	13.4	2.3	6.8	1952	33.8	5.8	89.9
1908	11.8	2.0	7.9	1953	34.9	6.0	92.9
1909	13.0	2.2	9.0	1954	33.9	5.8	95.8
1910	14.3	2.5	10.2	1955	37.4	6.4	99.0
1911	14.0	2.4	11.4	1956	38.9	6.7	102.4
1912	15.1	2.6	12.7	1957	38.9	6.7	105.7
1913	16.1	2.8	14.1	1958	38.8	6.7	109.1
1914	14.9	2.6	15.4	1959	40.5	7.0	112.5
1915	15.4	2.7	16.7	1960	42.1	7.3	116.2
1916	17.1	2.9	18.2	1961	46.2	8.0	120.2
1917	18.8	3.2	19.8	1962	44.7	7.7	124.0
1918	19.7	3.4	21.5	1963	46.5	8.0	128.0
1919	16.8	2.9	22.9	1964	48.6	8.4	132.2
1920	19.0	3.3	24.6	1965	50.6	8.7	136.6
1921	15.8	2.7	25.9	1966	53.6	9.2	141.2
1922	16.5	2.9	27.4	1967	55.3	9.5	146.0
1923	21.0	3.6	29.2	1968	58.7	10.1	151.0
1924	19.8	3.4	30.9	1969	61.5	10.6	156.3
1925	20.2	3.5	32.6	1970	63.7	11.0	161.8
1926	21.7	3.7	34.5	1971	65.0	11.2	167.4
1927	21.0	3.6	36.3	1972	68.4	11.8	173.3
1928	21.5	3.7	38.2	1973	71.3	12.3	179.5
1929	22.9	4.0	40.1	1974	69.1	11.9	185.4
1930	21.5	3.7	42.0	1975	67.2	11.6	191.2
1931	18.1	3.1	43.6	1976	71.2	12.3	197.4
1932	15.7	2.7	44.9	1977	73.7	12.7	203.7
1933	16.2	2.8	46.3	1978	74.9	12.9	210.2
1934	17.2	3.0	47.8	1979	75.7	13.1	216.7
1935	18.3	3.2	49.4	1980	72.8	12.6	223.0
1936	20.6	3.6	51.1	1981	70.8	12.2	229.1
1937	21.9	3.8	53.0	1982	67.1	11.6	234.9
1938	19.0	3.3	54.7	1983	66.5	11.5	240.6
1939	20.8	3.6	56.4	1984	70.1	12.1	246.6
1940	23.0	4.0	58.4	1985	70.4	12.1	252.7
1941	25.7	4.4	60.6	1986	70.6	12.2	258.8
1942	26.7	4.6	62.9	1987	73.4	12.7	265.1
1943	29.1	5.0	65.5	1988	77.3	13.3	271.8
1944	30.4	5.2	68.1	1989	78.2	13.5	278.5
				1990	78.3	13.5	285.3

Table A.11
Cumulative Damage from Ozone Production

Year	Cumulative production CFC-11 (000s metric tons)	Cumulative production CFC-12 (000s metric tons)	Sum (b + c)	Damage 1 kg=$5 annual damage (.005 × d)
a	b	c	d	e
50	18.6	198.3	216.9	1.1
51	27.6	234.5	262.1	1.3
52	41.2	271.7	312.9	1.6
53	58.5	318.2	376.7	1.9
54	79.4	367.1	446.5	2.2
55	105.6	425.0	530.6	2.7
56	138.1	493.6	631.7	3.2
57	172.0	567.8	739.8	3.7
58	201.6	641.2	842.8	4.2
59	237.1	728.8	965.9	4.8
60	286.9	828.3	1115.2	5.6
61	347.3	936.8	1284.1	6.4
62	425.4	1064.9	1490.3	7.5
63	518.7	1211.3	1730.0	8.7
64	629.8	1381.4	2011.2	10.1
65	752.6	1571.4	2324.0	11.6
66	893.7	1787.6	2681.3	13.4
67	1053.4	2030.4	3083.8	15.4
68	1236.5	2297.9	3534.4	17.7
69	1453.8	2595.1	4048.9	20.2
70	1619.9	2916.2	4536.1	22.7
71	1955.1	3257.8	5212.9	26.1
72	2262.0	3637.7	5899.7	29.5
73	2611.1	4061.0	6672.1	33.4
74	2980.8	4503.8	7484.6	37.4
75	3294.8	4884.8	8179.6	40.9
76	3634.7	5295.5	8930.2	44.7
77	3955.1	5678.3	9633.4	48.2
78	4264.0	6050.4	10314.4	51.6
79	4553.5	6407.6	10961.1	54.8
80	4843.1	6757.8	11600.9	58.0
81	5130.0	7109.1	12239.1	61.2
82	5401.5	7437.1	12838.6	64.2
83	5693.2	7792.5	13485.7	67.4
84	6005.6	8174.6	14180.2	70.9
85	6332.4	8550.9	14883.3	74.4
86			15320.6	76.6
87			15757.9	78.8
88			16195.2	81.0
89			16632.4	83.2
90			17069.7	85.3

NOTE: In the absence of data for 1986 to 1990, we have extrapolated the sum of cumulative production for those years by means of regression analysis. Although the regression on the logarithm provides a better fit ($R = .97$) than the linear model ($R = .91$), we used the latter, more conservative growth estimate. Using the log would have produced a 1990 damage estimate of 133.4, not 85.3.

Table A.12

Net Capital Growth

Year	Labor force	% change in labor force	Rolling average % change in labor force	Net stock of fixed capital	Rolling average of net stock of fixed capital	Change in rolling average of capital stock f − f(t−1)	Capital requirement for labor d × f(t−1)	Net capital growth (g − h)
a	b	c	d	e	f	g	h	i
45	53060			735.8				
46	56720	6.90%		743.1				
47	59350	4.64%		750.3				
48	60621	2.14%		757.5				
49	61286	1.10%	3.69%	764.8	750.3			
50	62208	1.50%	3.26%	772.0	757.5	7.2	24.4	−17.2
51	62017	−0.31%	1.81%	806.8	770.3	12.7	13.7	−1.0
52	62138	0.20%	0.93%	841.6	788.5	18.3	7.1	11.1
53	63015	1.41%	0.78%	876.4	812.3	23.8	6.2	17.6
54	63643	1.00%	0.76%	911.2	841.6	29.3	6.2	23.1
55	65023	2.17%	0.89%	946.0	876.4	34.8	7.5	27.3
56	66552	2.35%	1.42%	981.2	911.3	34.9	12.5	22.4
57	66929	0.57%	1.50%	1016.4	946.2	35.0	13.7	21.3
58	67639	1.06%	1.43%	1051.6	981.3	35.0	13.5	21.5
59	68369	1.08%	1.45%	1086.8	1016.4	35.1	14.2	20.9
60	69628	1.84%	1.38%	1122.0	1051.6	35.2	14.0	21.2
61	70459	1.19%	1.15%	1168.8	1089.1	37.5	12.1	25.4
62	70614	0.22%	1.08%	1215.6	1129.0	39.8	11.8	28.1
63	71833	1.73%	1.21%	1262.4	1171.1	42.2	13.7	28.5
64	73091	1.75%	1.35%	1309.2	1215.6	44.5	15.8	28.7
65	74455	1.87%	1.35%	1356.0	1262.4	46.8	16.4	30.4
66	75770	1.77%	1.47%	1416.2	1311.9	49.5	18.5	31.0
67	77347	2.08%	1.84%	1476.4	1364.0	52.2	24.1	28.0
68	78737	1.80%	1.85%	1536.6	1418.9	54.8	25.3	29.6
69	80734	2.54%	2.01%	1596.8	1476.4	57.5	28.5	29.0
70	82771	2.52%	2.14%	1657.0	1536.6	60.2	31.6	28.6
71	84382	1.95%	2.18%	1720.0	1597.4	60.8	33.4	27.3
72	87034	3.14%	2.39%	1783.0	1658.7	61.3	38.2	23.2
73	89429	2.75%	2.58%	1846.0	1720.6	61.9	42.8	19.1
74	91949	2.82%	2.64%	1909.0	1783.0	62.4	45.4	17.1
75	93775	1.99%	2.53%	1972.0	1846.0	63.0	45.1	17.9
76	96158	2.54%	2.65%	2034.3	1908.9	62.8	48.9	14.0
77	99009	2.96%	2.61%	2096.5	1971.6	62.7	49.9	12.8
78	102251	3.27%	2.72%	2158.8	2034.1	62.5	53.6	9.0
79	104962	2.65%	2.68%	2221.0	2096.5	62.4	54.6	7.8
80	106940	1.88%	2.66%	2270.0	2156.1	59.6	55.8	3.8
81	108670	1.62%	2.48%	2327.1	2214.7	58.6	53.4	5.1
82	110204	1.41%	2.17%	2360.3	2267.4	52.8	48.0	4.8
83	110550	0.31%	1.58%	2400.0	2315.7	48.3	35.7	12.5
84	113544	2.71%	1.59%	2470.3	2365.6	49.9	36.8	13.1
85	115461	1.69%	1.55%	2548.2	2421.2	55.6	36.6	19.0
86	117834	2.06%	1.64%	2623.8	2480.6	59.3	39.6	19.8
87	119865	1.72%	1.70%	2692.8	2547.0	66.5	42.1	24.4
88	121669	1.51%	1.94%	2771.0	2621.2	74.2	49.3	24.9
89	123869	1.81%	1.76%	2843.0	2695.8	74.5	46.0	28.5
90	124787	0.74%	1.57%	2906.2	2767.3	71.6	42.2	29.4

Conclusion

To the extent that the Index of Sustainable Economic Welfare measures the true health of our economy from 1950 to 1990, the results are rather discouraging. Per capita ISEW was only about 16.5% higher in 1990 than it was at the beginning of the period—approximately $3,253 per person, compared to $2,793 in 1951. (See the note to table A.13 about the choice of 1951 as the base year.) According to Table A.13, the average annual increase from 1951 to 1990 was 0.39% per year.

The overall increase in ISEW masks a more important pattern of changes decade by decade. From 1951 to 1960, per capita ISEW increased by an average of 0.21% per year. From 1960 to 1970, however, it increased by about 1.57% per year, about one percentage point slower than per capita GNP (which grew at a rate of 2.64% per year that decade). During the period from 1970 to 1980, per capita ISEW grew by 0.21% per year, as it had during the 1950s. Finally, during the 1980s per capita ISEW actually declined by 0.43% per year. Thus an overall increase during the period from 1951 to 1990 masks the variations among the four decades and the decline of the 1980s.

When we exclude resource depletion and long-term environmental damage (columns S and T from table A.1) from the calculation of per capita ISEW, the results still show a somewhat similar pattern. This variant of per capita ISEW grew more slowly during the 1970s and 1980s than during the 1960s, although it did not actually decline. This can be seen in table A.13 in the column marked "PC-ISEW*" and in figure A.1. Thus the dramatic difference between output (GNP) and welfare (ISEW) is based in large part on

Table A.13
Annual Per Capita Growth of ISEW and GNP

Years	PC-GNP	PC-ISEW	PC-ISEW*	Years	PC-GNP	PC-ISEW	PC-ISEW*
50–60	1.51%	1.31%	1.56%	51–60	0.97%	0.21%	0.65%
51–60	0.97%	0.21%	0.65%	60–70	2.64%	1.57%	2.22%
50–65	2.08%	1.54%	1.82%	70–80	2.04%	0.21%	0.91%
51–65	1.77%	0.84%	1.25%	80–90	1.82%	−0.43%	0.52%
50–77	2.14%	1.12%	1.61%				
51–77	1.97%	0.73%	1.29%				
50–90	2.00%	0.66%	1.30%				
51–90	1.89%	0.39%	1.08%				

NOTES: PC-ISEW* means PC-ISEW excluding column S (resource depletion) and column T (long-term environmental damage). We have given 1950 and 1951 as alternative base years for calculations of annual changes because the change in per capita ISEW between those years was greater than at any other time from 1950 to 1990. (See table A.1, column Y.) Due to this anomaly, we consider 1951 to be the appropriate year from which to make comparisons.

the components (including column U, ozone depletion) that focus on the effects of current consumption patterns on sustainable well-being.

Another major factor in the variation of per capital ISEW was the change in income distribution. For example, whereas personal consumption increased by about 37.5% from 1961 to 1968, weighting personal consumption by changes in income distribution led to an increase of almost 64%. (This weighting factor—along with the jump in net capital growth from negative to positive—is also largely responsible for the anomalous increase in ISEW from 1950 to 1951.) By contrast, in the 1980s the growing gap in income inequality had a tremendous effect on the decline in economic welfare as measured by the ISEW. The almost 11% deepening of inequality caused weighted personal consumption to grow by only about 22%, while measured consumption grew by 33%.

Changes in net capital growth also had a strong influence on the shifts in ISEW. From the mid-1950s to the mid-1970s, net capital growth advanced steadily. It grew slowly for about a decade, but resumed solid growth after 1984. However, part of the apparent improvement in investments during that latter period was offset by the decline in the net international position from 1984 to 1990. The growth of net capital investment in recent years seems therefore to be largely based on borrowing capital from abroad and therefore not sustainable.

Efforts to control air pollution and to reduce accidents have paid off by improving economic welfare during the 1970s and 1980s. The cost of air pollution peaked in 1970, and the economic damages caused by car accidents peaked in 1978. Improvements in both areas since those dates have had the effect of countering the generally downward trend in ISEW. They offer evidence that the government's choice of policies can indeed have a positive effect on economic welfare even if they do not increase physical output.

In order to compare the ISEW with the MEW by Nordhaus and Tobin, as well as the EAW by Zolotas, we have calculated the annual growth of per capita ISEW from 1951 to 1965 and from 1951 to 1977. (We used 1951 rather than 1950 because the latter was so radically different from the results for the rest of that decade.) From 1951 to 1965, per capita ISEW increased by 0.84% per year, while per capita MEW grew at a rate of 0.40% per year from 1947 to 1965. Similarly, from 1951 to 1977 per capita ISEW grew at 0.73% per year while per capita EAW showed an increase of only 0.63% from 1950 to 1977. Thus ISEW suggests more improvement than either EAW or MEW during comparable periods.

Despite the year to year variations in ISEW, it indicates a long-term trend from the late 1970s to the present that is indeed bleak. Economic welfare has been deteriorating for a decade, largely as a result of growing income inequality, the exhaustion of resources, and unsustainable reliance on capital from overseas to pay for domestic consumption and investment. Although these three factors might be addressed through separate policy initiatives, they are in fact intertwined. The most fundamental problem in terms of sustainable economic welfare is the decline in the quality of energy resources as measured by the ratio of energy output to energy input. As a result of this entropic process, the discovery and extraction of domestic oil will soon take more energy than is made available, thereby bringing to a close the era of cheap energy. This also means that the domestic production of capital equipment (which embodies energy) will become increasingly costly, and the United States will remain a net borrower. The reliance on foreign capital will perpetuate the decline in the value of the dollar and of the American standard of living. In addition, reductions in the amount of energy available per worker will lead to a long-term decline in worker productivity, though improved management may be able to counter that trend for short periods. As increasing competition lowers the returns to labor, and as returns to scarce capital increase, the income gap is likely to worsen if actions are not taken to improve equality.

The purpose of an index that strives to measure economic well-being is not simply to show us how we are presently faring or are likely to fare. It should also reveal the kinds of policies that would enable a nation to improve its welfare. As we have seen, improvements in car safety and reductions in air pollution have made small but important contributions to raising the level of economic welfare. Social policies during the 1960s seem to have improved economic welfare by reducing income inequality. Economic welfare can thus be improved by enacting appropriate policies.

Clearly the important question then becomes whether our nation is going to continue in its efforts to increase total output or whether we are going to redirect our focus towards the enhancement of sustainable economic welfare. Are the policies of our government going to be guided by GNP, or by ISEW or some other measure of sustainable welfare?

References

Abernethy, Virginia D. 1993a. *Population Politics: The Choices that Shape Our Future.* New York: Insights Books.

Abernethy, Virginia D. 1993b. "The Demographic Transition Revisited: Lessons for Foreign Aid and U.S. Immigration Policy." *Ecological Economics* (in press).

Abraham, Dean E., ed. 1989. *The Challenge of Global Warming.* Washington, D.C.: Island Press.

Abramovitz, Moses. 1979. "Economic Growth and Its Discontents." In *Economics and Human Welfare,* edited by M. Boskin. New York: Academic Press.

Adams, Walter, and James Brock. 1987. *The Bigness Complex.* New York: Pantheon.

Ariyaratne, A. T. 1985. *Collected Works.* Vol. 3, edited by Nandansena Ratnapala. Sri Lanka: Vishna Lekha.

Arrow, Kenneth. 1966. *Social Choice and Individual Values.* 2d ed. New York: Wiley.

Babbage, Charles. [1832] 1963. *On the Economy of Machinery and Manufactures.* London. Reprint. New York: Kelley.

Bagehot, Walter. 1953. *Economic Studies.* Stanford, Calif.: Academic Reprints.

Barber, Benjamin R. 1986. "Against Economics: Capitalism, Socialism, but Whatever Happened to Democracy?" In *Democratic Capitalism?* edited by Fred E. Bauman. Charlottesville: University of Virginia Press.

Barber, G. Russell, Jr. 1973. "The One Hundred Percent Reserve System." *American Economist* 17, no. 1: 115–127.

Barnet, Richard J. 1981. *Real Security: Restoring American Power in a Dangerous Decade.* New York: Simon & Schuster.

Barnett, Harold, and Chandler Morse. 1963. *Scarcity and Growth.* Baltimore: Johns Hopkins University Press.

Batie, Sandra S. 1986. "Why Soil Erosion: A Social Science Perspective." In *Conserving Soil: Insights from Socioeconomic Research,* edited by Stephen B. Lovejoy and Ted L. Napier. Ankeny, Iowa: Soil Conservation Society of America.

Becker, Gary, and Nigel Tomes. 1979. "An Equilibrium Theory of the Distribution of Income and Intergenerational Mobility." *Journal of Political Economy* 87, no. 61.

Belloc, Hilaire. 1913. *The Servile State.* London: T. N. Foulis.

Bentham, Jeremy. [1879] 1970. *An Introduction to the Principles of Morals and Legislation.* Reprint. London: University of London.

Berk, Richard A., and Sarah Fenstermaker Berk. 1979. *Labor and Leisure at Home: Content and Organization of the Household Day.* Beverly Hills, Calif.: Sage.

Berk, Sarah Fenstermaker. 1985. *The Gender Factory.* New York: Plenum.

Bernstein, Richard J. 1976. *The Restructuring of Economic and Political Theory.* New York: Harcourt Brace Jovanovitch.

Berry, Wendell. 1977. *The Unsettling of America.* San Francisco: Sierra Club.

———. 1981. *The Gift of Good Land: Further Essays Cultural and Agricultural.* San Francisco: North Point.

———. 1987. "A Defense of the Family Farm." In *Home Economics.* San Francisco: North Point.

Birch, Charles, and John B. Cobb, Jr. 1981. *The Liberation of Life.* Cambridge: Cambridge University Press.

Bloom, Alan. 1987. *The Closing of the American Mind.* New York: Simon & Schuster.

Bluestone, Barry, and Bennett Harrison. 1982. *The Deindustrialization of America.* New York: Basic.

Bordo, Susan R., 1987. *The Flight to Objectivity.* Albany: SUNY Press.

Boulding, Kenneth E. 1964. *The Meaning of the Twentieth Century.* New York: Harper & Row.

———. 1968. *Beyond Economics.* Ann Arbor: University of Michigan Press.

Bowles, Samuel, and Herbert Gintis. 1986. *Democracy and Capitalism: Property, Community and the Contradictions of Modern Social Thought.* New York: Basic.

Braverman, Harry. 1974. *Labor and Monopoly Capital.* New York: Monthly Review Press.

Brewer, Anthony. 1985. "Trade with Fixed Real Wages and Mobile Capital." *Journal of International Economics* 18:177–86.

Brown, Harold. 1983. *Thinking about National Security.* Boulder, Colo.: Westview.

Brown, Lester R. 1978. *The Twenty-ninth Day.* New York: Norton.

———. 1986. "Redefining National Security." Chap. 11 in *State of the World, 1986.* New York: Norton.

Brown, Lester R., William Chandler, Christopher Flavin, Sandra Postel, Linda Starke, and Edward Wolf. 1984. *State of the World, 1984.* New York: Norton.

Brown, Lester R., William Chandler, Christopher Flavin, Jodi Jacobson, Cynthia Pollock, Sandra Postel, Linda Starke, and Edward Wolf. 1987. *State of the World, 1987.* New York: Norton.

Brownell, Baker. 1950. *The Human Community: Its Philosophy and Practice for a Time of Crisis.* New York: Harper.

Brueggemann, Walter. 1977. *The Land: Place as Gift, Promise and Challenge in Biblical Faith.* Philadelphia: Fortress.

Buber, Martin. 1949. *Paths in Utopia.* Translated by R. F. C. Hull. London: Routledge & Kegan Paul.

Bunch, Roland. 1982. *Two Ears of Corn: A Guide to People-Centered Agricultural Improvement.* Oklahoma City: World Neighbors.

Bunker, Stephen G. 1984. "Modes of Extraction, Unequal Exchange, and the Progressive Underdevelopment of an Extreme Periphery: The Brazilian Amazon." *American Journal of Sociology* 89, no. 5: 1017–64.

———. 1985. *Underdeveloping the Amazon.* Urbana: University of Illinois Press.

Burkitt, Brian. 1984. *Radical Political Economy: An Introduction to the Alternative Economics.* New York: New York University Press.

Cairnes, J. E. 1875. *The Character and Logical Method of Political Economy.* 2d ed. London: Macmillan.

Callicott, J. Baird. 1980. "The Search for an Environmental Ethic." In *Matters of Life and Death,* 2d ed., edited by Tom Regan. New York: Random House.

Carey, Henry C. 1965. *Principles of Political Economy.* Reprint. New York: A. M. Kelly.

Cavanagh, John H., and Frederick F. Clairmonte. 1992. "US Finance Capitalism: The Tottering Empire." *Third World Economics* 16–31 October, no. 51: 17–20.

Christensen, Paul P. 1989. "Historical Roots for Ecological Economics: Biophysical versus Allocative Approaches." *Ecological Economics* 1, no. 1:17–36.

Clark, Colin. 1976. *Mathematical Bioeconomics.* New York: Wiley.

Cleveland, C. J., R. Costanza, C.A.S. Hall, and R. Kaufmann. 1984. "Energy and the U.S. Economy: A Biophysical Perspective." *Science* 225: 890–897.

Cline, William R. 1992. *Global Warming: The Economic Stakes.* Washington, D.C.: Institute for International Economics.

A more comprehensive book by Cline, entitled *The Economics of Global Warming,* was not available at the time of this writing.

Coase, R. H. 1937. "The Nature of the Firm." *Economica,* November, pp. 386–405.

Colander, D., and A. Klamer. 1987. "The Making of an Economist." *Economic Perspectives* 1:95–111.

Correa, Hector, and Ji Won Kim. 1992. "A Casual Analysis of the Defense Expenditures of the USA and the USSR." *Journal of Peace Research* 29, no. 2 (May): 161–175.

Costanza, Robert, ed. 1991. *Ecological Economics: The Science and Management of Sustainability.* New York: Columbia University Press. (Proceedings of a 1990 conference of the International Society for Ecological Economics, held at the World Bank in Washington, D.C.)

Cowan, Ruth Schwartz. 1983. *More Work for Mother.* New York: Basic.

Culbertson, John M. 1984. *International Trade and the Future of the West.* Madison, Wis.: Twenty-First Century Press.

———. 1986. "A Realistic View of International Trade and National Trade Policy." *Journal of International Law and Politics* 18, no. 4: 1119–1135.

Daly, Herman E. 1974. "The Economics of the Steady State." *American Economic Review.*

———. 1980. "The Economic Thought of Frederick Soddy." *History of Political Economy* 12, no. 4.

———. 1982. "Chicago School Individualism Versus Sexual Reproduction: A Critique of Becker and Tomes." *Journal of Economic Issues.*

———. 1985. "The Circular Flow of Exchange Value and the Linear Throughput of Matter-Energy: A Case of Misplaced Concreteness." *Review of Social Economy.*

Davies, David G. 1986. *United States Taxes and Tax Policies.* Cambridge, Mass.: Cambridge University Press.

Davis, W. Jackson. 1979. *The Seventh Year: Industrial Civilization in Transition.* New York: Norton.

Dean, Jonathan, and Peter Clausen. 1988. *The INF Treaty and the Future of Western Security.* Cambridge, Mass.: Union of Concerned Scientists.

De Grasse, Robert, Jr. 1983. *Military Expansion, Economic Decline.* New York: Council on Economic Priorities.

Dellums, Ronald V. 1983. *Defense Sense: The Search for a Rational Military Policy.* Cambridge, Mass.: Ballinger.

Dempsey, Bernard W. 1958. *The Functional Economy.* Englewood Cliffs, N.J.: Prentice-Hall.

Denison, Edward W. 1962. *The Sources of Economic Growth in the United States and the Alternatives before Us.* New York: Committee for Economic Development.

Devall, Bill, and George Sessions. 1985. *Deep Ecology: Living As If Nature Mattered.* Salt Lake City, Utah: Gibbs M. Smith.

Drewnowski, Jan. 1961. "The Economic Theory of Socialism: A Suggestion for Reconsideration." *Journal of Political Economy* 69, no. 4.

Drucker, Peter. 1954. *The Practice of Management.* New York: Harper.

———. 1987. "The Rise and Fall of the Blue-Collar Worker." *Wall Street Journal,* April 22, 32.

Duchrow, Ulrich. 1987. *Global Economy: A Confessional Issue for the Churches.* Translated by David Lewis. Geneva: WCC Publications.

Dumbald, Edward, ed. 1955. *The Political Writings of Thomas Jefferson.* Indianapolis: Bobbs Merrill.

Durning, Alan Thein. 1992. *Guardians of the Land: Indigenous Peoples and the Health of the Planet.* Washington, D.C.: Worldwatch Institute.

Easterlin, Richard. 1974. "Does Economic Growth Improve the Human Lot? Some Empirical Evidence." In *Nations and Households in Economic Growth.* New York: Academic Press.

Eckstein, Otto. 1983. "The NIPA Accounts: A User's View." In *The U.S. National Income and Public Accounts,* edited by Murray F. Foss. Chicago: University of Chicago Press.

Edgeworth, F. Y. 1881. *Mathematical Psychics.* London: C. K. Paul.

Eggers, Melvin A., and A. Dale Tussing. 1965. *The Composition of Economic Activity.* New York: Holt, Rinehart, & Winston.

Eisner, Robert. 1985. "The Total Incomes System of Accounts." *Survey of Current Business,* January.

El Serafy, Salah. 1988. "The Proper Calculation of Income from Depletable Natural Resources." In *Environmental and Resource Accounting and Their Relevance to the Measurement of Sustainable Income,* edited by Ernst Lutz and Salah El Serafy. Washington, D.C.: World Bank.

Ely, Richard T., Mary S. Shine, and George S. Wehrwein. 1922. *Outlines of Land Economics.* Vol. 1, *Classification of Land.* Ann Arbor, Mich.: Edwards.

Ely, Richard T., and George S. Wehrwein. 1984. *Land Economics.* Madison: University of Wisconsin.

Etzioni, Amitai. 1983. *An Immodest Agenda.* New York: McGraw Hill.

Fallows, James. 1982. *National Defense.* New York: Random House.

Fearnside, Phillip M. 1986. *Human Carrying Capacity of the Brazilian Rainforest.* New York: Columbia University Press.

Feldstein, Martin. 1981. "Reviewing Business Investment." *Wall Street Journal.* June 19, 24.

Fisher, Irving. 1906. *The Nature of Capital and Income.* London: Macmillan.

Fornos, Werner. 1987. *Gaining People, Losing Ground.* Washington, D.C.: Population Institute.

Fortune. 1983. "Higher Taxes that Promote Development." August 8.

Foy, George. 1987. "The Extension of Economic Principles to Provide a Conceptual Framework for Environmental Accounting." Ph.D. diss., Louisiana State University, Baton Rouge.

Freeman, A. Myrick. 1982. *Air and Water Pollution Control: A Benefit-Cost Assessment*. New York: Wiley.

Friedman, Milton. 1949. "The Marshallian Demand Curve." *Journal of Political Economy* 57: 489.

———. 1962. *Capitalism and Freedom*. Chicago: University of Chicago Press.

Furkiss, Victor. 1974. *The Future of Technological Civilization*. New York: Braziller.

Galbraith, John Kenneth. 1958. *The Affluent Society*. New York: Mentor.

George, Henry. 1879. *Progress and Poverty*. New York: Random House.

George, Susan. 1976. *How the Other Half Dies*. New York: Penguin.

———. 1988. *A Fate Worse than Debt*. New York: Grove.

Georgescu-Roegen, Nicholas. 1950. "Economic Theory and Agrarian Economics." *Oxford Economic Papers* 12.

———. 1971. *The Entropy Law and the Economic Process*. Cambridge, Mass.: Harvard University Press.

Gever, John, Robert Kaufmann, David Skole, and Charles Vorosmarty. 1987. *Beyond Oil*. Cambridge, Mass.: Ballinger.

Gevetz, Harry, ed. 1967. *Democracy and Elitism*. New York: Scribners.

Gianessi, Leonard P., and Henry M. Peskin. 1981. "Analysis of National Water Pollution Control Policies: 2. Agricultural Sediment Control." *Water Resources Research* 17, no. 2: 803–21.

Gilder, George. 1981. *Wealth and Poverty*. New York: Basic.

Goldschmidt, Walter R. 1978. *As You Sow: Three Studies in the Social Consequences of Agribusiness*. Montclair, N.J.: Allanheld, Osmun.

Goodland, R. J. A. 1987. "How to Save the Jungle: Opportunities for Personal Action." November 7. Mimeograph.

Goodland, R. J. A., and Howard S. Irwin. 1975. *Amazon Jungle: Green Hell to Red Desert?* Amsterdam: Elsevier.

Goodland, R. J. A., Herman Daly, and Salah El Serafy, eds. 1992. *Population, Technology, and Lifestyles: The Transition to Sustainability*. Washington, D.C.: Island Press.

Gossen, Herrmann Heinrich. [1854] 1983. *The Laws of Human Relations*. Reprint. Cambridge, Mass.: MIT Press.

Gottwald, N. K., ed. 1986. *Social Scientific Criticism of the Hebrew Bible and Its Social World*. Volume 7 of *Semeia*.

Gould, Carol C. 1978. *Marx's Social Ontology: Individuality and Community in Marx's Theory of Social Reality*. Cambridge, Mass.: MIT Press.

Goulet, Denis. 1983. *Mexico: Development Strategies for the Future*. Notre Dame, Ill.: University of Notre Dame Press.

Greeson, Phillip, John Clark, and Judith Clark, eds. 1979. *Wetland Functions and Values: The State of Our Understanding*. Minneapolis: American Water Works Association.

Greider, William. 1989. *The Trouble with Money*. Knoxville, Tenn.: Whittle Direct Books.

Gupta, T. R., and J. H. Foster. 1975. "Economic Criteria for Freshwater Wetland Policy in Massachusetts." *American Journal of Agricultural Economics* 57, no. 1:40–45.

Hamilton, Richard F. 1991. "Work and Leisure: On the Reporting of Poll Results." *Public Opinion Quarterly* 55, no. 3 (Fall): 347–356.

Haney, Lewis H. 1949. *History of Economic Thought.* 4th ed. New York: Macmillan.

Harding, Sandra. 1986. *The Science Question in Feminism.* Ithaca, N.Y.: Cornell University Press.

Harrington, Michael. 1986. *The Next Left.* New York: Henry Holt.

Harris, Louis. 1987. *Inside America.* New York: Vintage.

Hayek, F. A. 1945. "The Use of Knowledge in Society." *American Economic Review* 35, no. 4: 519–530.

Healey, Robert G. 1982. Note to Michael Brewer and Robert Boxley, "The Potential Supply of Cropland." In *The Cropland Crisis: Myth or Reality?* edited by Pierre R. Crosson. Baltimore: Johns Hopkins University Press.

Heer, David M. 1975. "Marketable Licenses for Babies: Boulding's Proposal Revisited." *Social Biology,* Spring.

Heilbroner, Robert. 1980. *An Inquiry into the Human Prospect: Updated and Reconsidered for the 1980's.* New York: Norton.

Henderson, Hazel. 1978. *Creating Alternative Futures.* New York: Berkley.

Henry, James. 1986. "Where the Money Went." *New Republic.* April 14.

Hicks, J. R. 1948. *Value and Capital.* 2d ed. Oxford: Clarendon.

Hinkelammert, Franz. J. 1986. *The Ideological Weapons of Death: A Theological Critique of Capitalism.* Translated by Phillip Berryman. Maryknoll, N.Y.: Orbis.

Hirsh, Fred. 1976. *The Social Limits to Growth.* Cambridge, Mass.: Harvard University Press.

Hopkinson, C. S. Jr., and J. W. Day, Jr. 1980. "Net Energy Analysis of Alcohol Production from Sugarcane." *Science* 207 (January).

Hubbert, M. King. 1993. "Exponential Growth as a Transient Phenomenon in Human History." In Daly, H., and K. Townsend, eds. *Valuing the Earth: Economics, Ecology, Ethics.* Cambridge, Mass.: M.I.T. Press.

Huddle, Franklin P. 1976. "The Evolving National Policy for Materials." *Science.* February 20.

Jackson, Wes. 1987. *Altars of Unhewn Stone: Science and the Earth.* San Francisco: North Point.

Jacobs, Jane. 1960. *The Economy of Cities.* New York: Random House.

Jaszi, George. 1973. "Comment." In *The Measurement of Economic and Social Performance,* edited by Milton Moss. New York: National Bureau of Economic Research, Columbia University Press.

Jevons, William Stanley. 1924. *The Theory of Political Economy.* 4th ed. London: Macmillan.

Jonas, Hans. 1966. *The Phenomenon of Life.* New York: Harper & Row.

Kapp, K. W. 1972. "Environmental Disruption and Social Costs." In *Political Economy of the Environment.* Hawthorne, N.Y.: Mouton.

Kauffman, George B., ed. 1986. *Frederick Soddy (1877–1956).* Boston: D. Reidel Publishing Company.

Kaufmann, William. 1990. *Glasnost, Perestroika, and U.S. Defense Spending.* Washington, D.C.: The Brookings Institute.

Kelso, Louis O., and Patricia Hetter. 1967. *Two Factor Theory: How to Turn Eighty Million Workers into Capitalists on Borrowed Money.* New York: Random House.

Keynes, John Maynard. 1933. "National Self-Sufficiency." In *The Collected Writings of John Maynard Keynes,* vol. 21. Edited by Donald Moggeridge. London: Macmillan Cambridge University Press, for the Royal Economic Society.

———. [1936] 1973. *The General Theory of Employment, Interest, and Money.* Reprint. London: Macmillan.

Knight, Frank. 1927. "Review of Wealth, Virtual Wealth, and Debt." *Saturday Review of Literature,* p. 732.

Koenig, René. 1968. *The Community.* Translated by Edward Fitzgerald. New York: Schocken.

Kohr, Leopold. 1957. *The Breakdown of Nations.* New York: Rinehart.

Kristol, Irving. 1980. "Of Economics and Eco-Mania." *Wall Street Journal.* September 19, 28.

Krugman, Paul. 1987. "Is Free Trade Passé?" *Economic Perspectives* 1, no. 2.

Kurien, C. T. 1978. *Poverty, Planning and Social Transformation.* Bombay: Allied Publishers.

Lall, Betty G., and Joan Tepper Marlin. 1992. *Building a Peace Economy.* Boulder: Westview Press.

Laslet, Peter. 1965. *The World We Have Lost.* New York: Scribner.

Lauderdale, James Maitland. 1819. *An Inquiry into the Nature and Origin of Public Wealth and into the Means and Causes of Its Increase.* 2d ed. Edinburgh: Constable.

Lea, Stephen E. G., Roger M. Tarpy, and Paul Webley. 1987. *The Individual in the Economy: A Survey of Economic Psychology.* Cambridge: Cambridge University Press.

Leontief, Wassily. 1982. *Science* 217 (July 9): 104–105.

Leopold, Aldo. 1966. *Sand County Almanac.* New York: Ballantine.

Lewis, Martin W. 1992. *Green Delusions: An Environmentalist Critique of Radical Environmentalism.* Durham, N.C.: Duke University Press.

Lippmann, Walter. 1982. "The Political Equivalent of War." *Atlantic Monthly.* August, 182.

Lipsey, Richard, Peter Steiner, and Douglas Purvis. 1987. *Economics.* 8th ed. New York: Harper & Row.

Lipton, Michael. 1976. *Why Poor People Stay Poor: Urban Bias in World Development.* Cambridge, Mass.: Harvard University Press.

Love, Sam. 1977. "Redividing North America." *Ecologist* 7, no. 7: 318–319.

Lovelock, J. E. 1979. *Gaia: A New Look at Life on Earth.* Oxford: Oxford University Press.

Lovins, Amory B. 1977. *Soft Energy Paths: Toward a Durable Peace.* Cambridge, Mass.: Ballinger.

Lovins, Amory B., and L. Hunter Lovins. 1982. *Brittle Power: Energy Strategy for National Security.* Andover, Mass.: Brick House.

———. 1985. *Visitor's Guide.* 2d ed. Old Snowmass, Colo.: Rocky Mountain Institute.

———. 1987. "Energy: The Avoidable Oil Crisis." *The Atlantic.* December: 22–30.

McDonald, Glenn M., and James R. Markusen. 1985. "A Rehabilitation of Absolute Advantage." *Journal of Political Economy* 93, no. 2: 227–97.

Macey, Samuel L. 1980. *Clocks and Cosmos: Time in Western Life and Thought.* Hamden, Conn.: Anchor.

McGaughey, William J., Jr. 1981. *A Shorter Work Week in the 1980's.* White Bear Lake, Minn.: Thistlerose.

Maital, Shlomo. 1982. *Minds, Markets, and Money.* New York: Basic.

Markusen, Ann, and Joel Yudken. 1992. *Dismantling the War Economy.* New York: Basic Books.

Marshall, Alfred. 1925. *Principles of Economics.* 8th ed. London: Macmillan.

Marx, Karl. 1867. *Capital,* vol. 1, chapters 2 and 3.

Melman, Seymour. 1965. *Our Depleted Society.* New York: Dell.

———. 1970. *Pentagon Capitalism.* New York: McGraw Hill.

———. 1974. *The Permanent War Economy.* New York: Simon & Schuster.

Melman, Seymour, and Lloyd J. Dumas. 1992. "Planning for Economic Conversion." *The Nation* (April 16, 1992): 509, 522–528.

Mendelssohn, Jack. 1992. "Dismantling the Arsenals." *The Brookings Review* (Spring): 34–39.

Menger, Karl. 1950. *Principles of Economics.* Translated by James Dingwall and Bert F. Hoselitz. Glencoe, Ill.: Harper & Row.

Mill, John Stuart. [1859] 1952. *On Liberty.* Reprint. Chicago: Encyclopedia Britannica Great Books.

———. 1973. *Principles of Political Economy,* edited by William Ashby. Clifton, N.J.: Kelly.

Millikan, R. A. 1930. "The Alleged Sins of Science." *Scribner's Magazine* 872: 119–130.

Mincer, Jacob. 1974. *Schooling, Experience, and Earnings.* New York: National Bureau of Economic Research.

Mints, Lloyd. 1950. *Monetary Policy for a Competitive Society.* New York: McGraw-Hill.

Mishan, E. J. 1984. "GNP—Measurement or Mirage." *National Westminster Bank Quarterly Review.*

Morton, Nelle. 1983. *The Journey Is Home.* Boston: Beacon.

Moss, Milton, ed. 1973. *The Measurement of Economic and Social Performance.* New York: Columbia University Press, for the National Bureau of Economic Research.

Mulcahey, Richard E. 1952. *The Economics of Heinrich Pesch.* New York: Holt.

Munson, Richard. 1987. *The Energy Switch: Alternatives to Nuclear Power.* Cambridge, Mass.: Union of Concerned Scientists.

Neumann, Manfred J. M. 1992. "Seigniorage in the United States: How Much Does the U.S. Government Make from Money Production?" *Review,* Federal Reserve Bank of St. Louis, 74, no. 2 (March/April): 29–40.

Nincic, Miroslav. 1982. *The Arms Race: The Political Economy of Military Growth.* New York: Praeger.

Nisbett, Robert. 1966. *The Sociological Imagination.* New York: Basic.

Nordhaus, William. 1977. "Metering Economic Growth." In *Prospects for Growth: Changing Expectations for the Future,* edited by Kenneth D. Wilson. New York: Basic.

Nordhaus, William, and James Tobin. 1972. "Is Growth Obsolete?" In *Economic Growth,* National Bureau of Economic Research General Series, no. 96E. New York: Columbia University Press.

O'Boyle, Edward J. 1985. Science, Technology, and Economic Systems. Workshop of the Institute for Theological Encounter with Science and Technology.

Ohlin, Bertil. 1933. *Interregional and International Trade.* Cambridge, Mass.: Harvard University Press.

Orr, David W. 1979. "Modernization and the Ecological Perspective." In *The Global Predicament,* edited by David W. Orr and Marvin S. Soroos. Chapel Hill: University of North Carolina Press.

Ozawa, Martha N. 1982. *Income Maintenance and Work Incentives.* New York: Prange.

Page, Talbot. 1977. *Conservation and Economic Efficiency.* Baltimore: Johns Hopkins University Press.

Pagels, Heinz. 1988. *The Dreams of Reason: The Computer and the Rise of the Sciences of Complexity.* New York: Simon & Schuster.

Parmar, Samuel L. 1974. "Ethical Guidelines and Social Options." *Anticipation* no. 18 (August).

Passmore, Sam. 1987. "Hendrix Turns to Arkansas Produce." *Arkansas Gazette.* June 10.

Perrings, Charles. 1987. *Economy and Environment.* Cambridge: Cambridge University Press.

Petty, William. *The Economic Writings of Sir William Petty,* edited by C. H. Hull. Vol. 1. London: Cambridge University Press.

Pigou, A. C. 1920. *The Economics of Welfare.* London: Macmillan.

Pitt, David C. 1976. *The Social Dynamics of Development.* Oxford: Pergamon.

Pius XI. 1931. *Quadragesimo Anno.*

Polanyi, Karl. [1944] 1957. *The Great Transformation.* Reprint. Boston: Beacon.

Power, Thomas Michael. 1988. *The Economic Pursuit of Quality.* Armonk, N.Y.: Sharp.

Quarry, Michael, Joseph Blasi, and Corey Rosen. 1986. *Taking Stock: Employee Ownership at Work.* Cambridge, Mass.: Ballinger.

Rabushka, Alvin. 1985. *From Adam Smith to the Wealth of America.* New Brunswick, N.J.: Transaction.

Raines, John C. 1982. "Economics and the Justification of Sorrows." In *Community and Capital in Conflict: Plant Closings and Job Loss,* edited by John C. Raines, Lenora E. Benson, and David Mac I. Gracie. Philadelphia: Temple University Press.

Ramsay, William, and Milton Russell. 1978. "Time—Adjusted Health Impacts from Electricity Generation." *Public Policy* 26, no. 3.

Rawls, John. 1971. *A Theory of Justice.* Cambridge: Harvard University Press.

Repetto, Robert. 1987. "Creating Incentives for Sustainable Forest Development." *Ambio* 16, no. 2–3:94–99.

Repetto, Robert, William Magrath, Michael Wells, Christine Beer, and Fabrizio Rossini. 1989. *Wasting Assets: Natural Resources in the National Income Accounts.* Washington, D.C.: World Resources Institute.

Rhoads, Steven E. 1985. *The Economist's View of the World.* Cambridge: Cambridge University Press.

Ricardo, David. 1951. *Principles of Political Economy and Taxation.* Sraffa Edition, Cambridge.

Richardson, John M., Jr. 1982. *Making It Happen: A Positive Guide to the Future.* Washington, D.C.: U.S. Association for the Club of Rome.

Robertson, D. H. 1956. *Economic Commentaries.* London: Staples.

Robins, Philip K., Robert G. Speilgelman, Samuel Wiener, and Joseph G. Bell. 1980. *A Guaranteed Annual Income*. New York: Academic Press.

Robinson, J. P., and P. E. Converse. 1967. *Seventy-six Basic Tables of Time Budget Research Data for the United States*. Ann Arbor: University of Michigan Survey Research Center.

Rosen, Cory M., Katherine J. Klein, and Karen M. Young. 1986. *Employees Ownership in America*. Lexington, Mass.: Heath.

Ruggles, Richard. 1983. "The United States National Income Accounts, 1947–1977: Their Conceptual Basis and Evolution." In *The U.S. National Income and Product Accounts,* edited by Murray F. Foss. Chicago: University of Chicago Press.

Rybeck, Walter, and Ronald D. Pasguariello. 1987. "Combating Modern-Day Feudalism: Land as God's Gift." *Christian Century.* May 13.

Sagoff, Mark. 1988. "Some Problems with Environmental Economics." *Environmental Ethics,* Spring.

Sale, Kirkpatrick. 1986. *Human Scale*. New York: Cowan, McCown, & Gesgheyon.

Sampson, R. Neil. 1981. *Farmland or Wasteland*. Emmaus, Penna.: Rodale.

Samuelson, Paul. 1962. "Economists and the History of Ideas." *American Economic Review* 52.

Sauvy, Alfred. 1948. *Théorie Générale de la Population*. 2 vols. Paris: Presses Universitaires.

Schultz, Theodore W. 1961. "Education and Economic Growth." In *Social Forces Influencing American Education,* edited by Nelson B. Henry. Chicago: University of Chicago Press.

Schumacher, E. F. 1979. *Good Work*. New York: Harper & Row.

Schumpeter, Joseph. 1954. *History of Economic Analysis*. New York: Oxford University Press.

———. 1975. "The Future of Private Enterprise in the Face of Modern Socialistic Tendencies." *History of Political Economy* 7, no. 3: 294–298.

Schurr, Sam, et al. 1979. *Energy in America's Future: The Choices before Us*. Baltimore: Johns Hopkins University Press.

Schwartz, Barry. 1987. *The Battle for Human Nature*. New York: Norton.

Schwarz, Edward. 1982. "Economic Development as If Neighborhoods Mattered." In *Community and Capital in Conflict: Plant Closing and Job Loss,* edited by John C. Raines, Lenora E. Benson, and David Mc I. Gracie. Philadelphia: Temple University Press.

Seabrook, Jeremy. 1978. *What Went Wrong?* New York: Pantheon.

Seers, Dudley. 1983. *The Political Economy of Nationalism*. Oxford: Oxford University Press.

Sharp, Gene. 1973. *The Politics of Nonviolent Action*. Boston: Porter Sargent.

———. 1980. *Social Power and Political Freedom*. Boston: Porter Sargent.

Shepard, Paul. 1982. *Nature and Madness*. San Francisco: Sierra Club.

Sherman, Howard J. 1966. *Elementary Aggregate Economics*. New York: Appleton-Century-Crofts, Meredith.

Sik, Ota. 1985. *For a Humane Economic Democracy*. Translated by Fred Eidlin and William Graf. New York: Praeger.

Simon, Julian. 1981. *The Ultimate Resource*. Princeton, N.J.: Princeton University Press.

————. 1982. Interview with William F. Buckley, Jr. Reprinted in *Population and Development Review* (March): 205–218.

Simons, Henry C. 1948. *Economic Policy for a Free Society.* Chicago: University of Chicago Press.

————. 1950. *Federal Income Tax Reform.* Chicago: University of Chicago Press.

Sinsheimer, R. L. 1978. "The Presumptions of Science." *Daedalus,* pp. 23–25.

Sismondi, J. C. L. Simonde de. 1827. *Nouveaux Principes d'Economie Politique ou de la Richesse dans ses Rapports avec la Population.* Paris.

Smith, Adam. [1759] 1971. *The Theory of Moral Sentiments.* New York: Garland. 1971.

————. 1776. *Wealth of Nations.* New York: Random House.

Soddy, Frederick. 1922. *Cartesian Economics: The Bearing of Physical Science upon State Stewardship.* London: Hendersons.

————. 1926. *Wealth, Virtual Wealth, and Debt: The Solution of the Economic Paradox.* Hawthorne, Calif.: Omni Publications, 3rd ed. 1961 (1st ed., London, 1926).

————. 1934. *The Role of Money,* London.

————. 1943. *The Arch Enemy of Economic Freedom.* London.

Soleri, Paolo. 1969. *Arcology: The City in the Image of Man.* Cambridge, Mass.: MIT Press.

Stackhouse, Max L. 1985. "Jesus and Economics." In *The Bible in American Law, Politics, and Political Rhetoric,* edited by James Turner Johner. Philadelphia: Fortress.

Stanford Research Institute. 1988. *New Seeds for Nebraska: Moving the Agenda Ahead.* Menlo Park, Calif.: SRI International.

Stassen, Glen. 1992. "The 'Freeze Crowd' and the Peace Challenge." *Christianity and Crisis* (December 14): 402–403.

Stewart, Frances. 1977. *Technology and Underdevelopment.* Boulder, Colo.: Westview.

Stigler, George. 1946. "The Economics of Minimum Wage Legislation." *American Economic Review* 36.

Stiglitz, J. E. 1979. "A Neoclassical Analysis of the Economics of Natural Resources." In *Scarcity and Growth Reconsidered,* edited by V. Kerry Smith. Baltimore: Johns Hopkins University Press.

Thimm, Alfred L. 1980. *The False Promise of Codetermination.* Lexington, Mass.: Heath.

Thurow, Lester C. 1975. "Education and Economic Equality." In *The "Inequality" Controversy: Schooling and Distributive Justice,* edited by Donald M. Levine and Mary Jo Bane. New York: Basic.

————. 1976. "Implications of Zero Economic Growth." In *The Steady-State Economy.* Vol. 5 of *US Economic Growth from 1976 to 1986: Prospects, Problems, and Patterns.* Joint Economic Committee. Washington, D.C.: U.S. Government Printing Office.

————. 1981. *Zero-Sum Society.* New York: Penguin.

————. 1983. *Dangerous Currents.* New York: Random House.

————. 1985. *The Zero-Sum Solution: Building a World-Class American Economy.* New York: Simon & Schuster.

————. 1992. "Communitarian vs. Individualistic Capitalism." *The Responsive Community* 2, no. 4 (Fall): 24–30.

Tobin, James. 1965. "Money and Economic Growth." *Econometrica* October: 676.

———. 1987. "Financial Intermediaries." In Eatwell, John, et al., eds. *The World of Economics: The New Palgrave.* New York: W. W. Norton, 1991, pp. 261–278.

Tocqueville, Alexis de. 1945. *Democracy in America.* New York: Vintage.

Toennies, Ferdinand. 1965. *Community and Society.* Translated by Charles P. Loomis. New York: Harper & Row.

Torrey, Archer. 1985. *The Land and Biblical Economics.* New York: Henry George Institute.

Trenn, Thaddeus J. 1979. "The Central Role of Energy in Soddy's Holistic and Critical Approach to Nuclear Science, Economics, and Social Responsibility." *The British Journal for the History of Science* 12: 42.

Ture, Norman. 1981. Cited by S. Jackson and N. Jonas, "Whittling Away at the Corporate Tax Burden." *Business Week.* April 20.

Turner, Frederick. 1986. "Design for New Academy: An End to Division by Department." *Harper Magazine.* September, pp. 47–53.

Ure, Andrew. [1835] 1967. *The Philosophy of Manufacturers.* London: Knight. Reprint. London: Cass.

U.S. Department of Agriculture. 1980. Report and Recommendations on Organic Farming.

Vaizey, John. 1962. *The Economics of Education.* London: Faber & Faber.

Vitousek, Peter M. et al. 1986. "Human Appropriation of the Products of Photosynthesis." *BioScience* 34, No. 6: 368–73.

Wachtel, Paul L. 1983. *The Poverty of Affluence: A Psychological Portrait of the American Way of Life.* New York: Free Press.

Walras, Leon. 1954. *Elements of Pure Economics.* Homewood, Ill.: Irwin.

Walzer, Michael. 1983. *Spheres of Justice: A Defense of Pluralism and Equality.* New York: Basic Books.

Wapenhans Report. 1992. *Effective Implementation: Key to Development Impact* (R92-125). Washington, D.C.: World Bank.

Ward, Barbara, and René Dubos. 1972. *Only One Earth.* New York: Norton.

Warman, Arturo. 1980. *We Come to Object.* Baltimore: Johns Hopkins University Press.

Wasserman, Louis. 1979. "The Essential Henry George." In *Critics of Henry George,* edited by Robert V. Andelson. London: Associated University Presses.

Wattenberg, Ben, and Hans Zinsmeister. 1986. "The Birth Dearth: The Geopolitical Consequences." *Public Opinion,* December/January.

Weber, Susan, ed. 1987. *USA by Numbers.* Washington, D.C.: Zero Population Growth.

Weiner, Norbert. 1964. *God and Golem, Inc.* Cambridge, Mass.: MIT Press.

Weisskopf, Walter. 1971. *Alienation and Economics.* New York: Dutton.

Welt, Leo G. B. 1984. *Trade Without Money: Barter and Countertrade.* New York: Harcourt Brace Jovanovich.

Whitehead, A. N. 1925. *Science and the Modern World.* New York: Macmillan.

———. 1929a. *The Function of Reason.* Boston: Beacon.

———. 1929b. *Process and Reality.* New York: Harper.

Wilson, E. O. 1978. *On Human Nature.* Cambridge, Mass.: Harvard University Press.

Wogaman, Phillip. 1968. *Guaranteed Annual Income: The Moral Issues*. Nashville: Abingdon.

Wood, Nancy, ed. 1972. *Hollering Sun*. New York: Simon & Schuster.

World Commission on Employment and Development Staff. 1987. *Our Common Future*. Oxford: Oxford University Press.

Zagen, Robert, and Michael P. Rosow. 1982. *The Innovative Organization: Productivity Programs in Action*. New York: Pergamon.

Zolotas, Xenophon. 1981. *Economic Growth and Declining Social Welfare*. New York: New York University Press.

Zwerdling, Daniel. 1980. *Workplace Democracy: A Guide to Workplace Participation and Self-Management Experiments in the United States*. New York: Harper & Row, Colophon Edition.

Index

521